Macroeconomics

Fourteenth Canadian Edition

Campbell R. McConnell
University of Nebraska–Emeritus

Stanley L. Brue
Pacific Lutheran University

Sean M. Flynn
Scripps College

Thomas P. Barbiero
Ryerson University

Macroeconomics
Fourteenth Canadian Edition

The Internet addresses listed in the text were accurate at the time of publication. The inclusion of a Web site does not indicate an endorsement by the authors or McGraw-Hill Ryerson, and McGraw-Hill Ryerson does not guarantee the accuracy of the information presented at these sites.

ISBN-13: 978-1-25-908911-4
ISBN-10: 1-25-908911-8

1 2 3 4 5 6 7 8 9 10   TCP   1 9 8 7 6 5

Printed and bound in Canada.

Care has been taken to trace ownership of copyright material contained in this text; however, the publisher will welcome any information that enables them to rectify any reference or credit for subsequent editions.

DIRECTOR OF PRODUCT MANAGEMENT: Rhondda McNabb
SENIOR PRODUCT MANAGER: James Booty
PRODUCT MANAGER: Kevin O'Hearn
SENIOR MARKETING MANAGER: Joy Armitage Taylor
PRODUCT DEVELOPER: Sarah Fulton
SENIOR PRODUCT TEAM ASSOCIATE: Stephanie Giles
SUPERVISING EDITOR: Cathy Biribauer
PHOTO/PERMISSIONS RESEARCH: Alison Lloyd Baker
COPY EDITOR: Judy Sturrup
PLANT PRODUCTION COORDINATOR: Scott Morrison
MANUFACTURING PRODUCTION COORDINATOR: Emily Hickey
COVER AND INTERIOR DESIGN: Lightbox Visuals Communications Inc.
COVER IMAGE: © Kelly Redinger/Design Pics/Corbis/Royalty Free
PAGE LAYOUT: Aptara®, Inc.
PRINTER: Transcontinental Printing Group

Dedication

To my grandson, Simone, and past instructors.

About the Authors

Campbell R. McConnell earned his Ph.D. from the University of Iowa after receiving degrees from Cornell College and the University of Illinois. He taught at the University of Nebraska–Lincoln from 1953 until his retirement in 1990. He is also coauthor of *Contemporary Labor Economics,* ninth edition; *Essentials of Economics,* second edition; *Macroeconomics: Brief Edition;* and *Microeconomics: Brief Edition* (all The McGraw-Hill Companies), and has edited readers for the principles and labour economics courses. He is a recipient of both the University of Nebraska Distinguished Teaching Award and the James A. Lake Academic Freedom Award and is past president of the Midwest Economics Association. Professor McConnell was awarded an honorary Doctor of Laws degree from Cornell College in 1973 and received its Distinguished Achievement Award in 1994. His primary areas of interest are labour economics and economic education. He has an extensive collection of jazz recordings and enjoys reading jazz history.

Stanley L. Brue carried out his undergraduate work at Augustana College (South Dakota) and received its Distinguished Achievement Award in 1991. He received his Ph.D. from the University of Nebraska–Lincoln. He is retired from a long career at Pacific Lutheran University, where he was honoured as a recipient of the Burlington Northern Faculty Achievement Award. Professor Brue has also received the national Leavey Award for excellence in economic education. He has served as national president and chair of the Board of Trustees of Omicron Delta Epsilon International Economics Honorary. He is coauthor of *Economic Scenes,* fifth edition (Prentice-Hall); *Contemporary Labor Economics,* ninth edition; *Essentials of Economics,* second edition; *Macroeconomics: Brief Edition; Microeconomics: Brief Edition* (all The McGraw-Hill Companies); and *The Evolution of Economic Thought,* seventh edition (South-Western). For relaxation, he enjoys international travel, attending sporting events, and skiing with family and friends.

Sean M. Flynn did his undergraduate work at the University of Southern California before completing his Ph.D. at U.C. Berkeley, where he served as the Head Graduate Student Instructor for the Department of Economics after receiving the Outstanding Graduate Student Instructor Award. He teaches at Scripps College (of the Claremont Colleges) and is the author of *Economics for Dummies* (Wiley) and coauthor of *Essentials of Economics,* second edition; *Macroeconomics: Brief Edition;* and *Microeconomics: Brief Edition* (all The McGraw-Hill Companies). His research interests include finance, behavioural economics, and health economics. An accomplished martial artist, he has represented the United States in international aikido tournaments and is the author of *Understanding Shodokan Aikido* (Shodokan Press). Other hobbies include running, travelling, and enjoying ethnic food.

Thomas P. Barbiero received his Ph.D. from the University of Toronto after completing undergraduate studies at the same university. He is a professor in the Department of Economics at Ryerson University in Toronto. His research interests include the economic history of Canada and modern Italy, and international institutions. He spends his summers in Fontanarosa, a small town in his native region of Campania in southern Italy. It is situated in the vineyards of the Taurasi wine growing area. There he indulges in his favourite pastime: consuming good food and wine.

Brief Contents

Website Bonus Chapters available on Connect

CHAPTER 15B: Financial Economics

CHAPTER 16B: Current Issues in Macro Theory and Policy

CHAPTER 18B: The Economics of Developing Countries

Contents

WEBSITE BONUS CHAPTERS AVAILABLE ON CONNECT

CHAPTER 15B: Financial Economics

CHAPTER 16B: Current Issues in Macro
Theory and Policy

CHAPTER 18B: The Economics of Developing
Countries

Preface

Welcome to the Fourteenth Canadian Edition of *Macroeconomics*. Thousands of Canadian students have studied economics from the Canadian editions of *Macroeconomics* and *Microeconomics*. An estimated 15 million students worldwide have now used a version of the McConnell textbooks, making them the world's best-selling economic principles textbooks.

A Note About the Cover

We chose the cover for the Fourteenth Canadian Edition to reference global climate change, which many scientists believe has been due to human activity, particularly since the dawn of the Industrial Revolution.

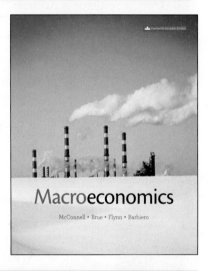

Fundamental Objectives

We have three main goals for *Macroeconomics*:

- Help the beginning student master the principles essential for understanding economic problems, specific economic issues, and the policy alternatives.

- Help the student understand and apply the economic perspective, and reason accurately and objectively about economic matters.

- Promote a lasting student interest in economics and the economy.

What's New and Improved?

One of the benefits of writing a successful text is the opportunity to revise—to delete the outdated and insert the new, to rewrite misleading or ambiguous statements, to introduce more relevant illustrations, to improve the organizational structure, and to enhance the learning aids.

We trust you will agree that we have used this opportunity wisely and fully. Some of the more significant changes include the following.

Restructured Introductory Chapters

We have divided the five introductory chapters common to *Macroeconomics*, and *Microeconomics* into two parts. Part 1 contains Chapter 1 (Limits, Alternatives, and Choices) and Chapter 2 (The Market System and the Circular Flow). The content in Part 2 has changed and now consists of the following three chapters: Chapter 3 (Demand, Supply, and Market Equilibrium), Chapter 4 (Market Failures: Public Goods and Externalities), and Chapter 5 (Government's Role and Government Failure).

As restructured, the three chapters that now form Part 2 give students an overview of

- The efficiency and allocation benefits of competitive markets

- How and why governments can help when there are cases of market failure

- Issues of government failure so that students do not assume that government intervention is an easy or guaranteed panacea for the misallocations and inefficiencies caused by market failure

Our new approach responds to suggestions by reviewers to boost the analysis of government failure so that students may better understand many of the problems currently besetting the Canadian economy.

For macroeconomics instructors, the new sequence provides a theoretical grounding that can help students better understand issues such as excessive government deficit spending and why there may be insufficient regulation of the financial sector. And because Chapters 4 and 5 are both optional and modular, instructors can skip them if they wish to move directly from Chapter 3's discussion of supply and demand to the core macroeconomics chapters.

New "Consider This" and "Last Word" Boxes

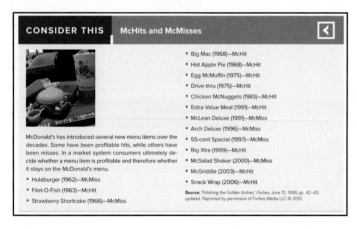

CONSIDER THIS   **McHits and McMisses**

McDonald's has introduced several new menu items over the decades. Some have been profitable hits, while others have been misses. In a market system consumers ultimately decide whether a menu item is profitable and therefore whether it stays on the McDonald's menu.

- Hulaburger (1962)—McMiss
- Filet-O-Fish (1963)—McHit
- Strawberry Shortcake (1966)—McMiss
- Big Mac (1968)—McHit
- Hot Apple Pie (1968)—McHit
- Egg McMuffin (1975)—McHit
- Drive-thru (1975)—McHit
- Chicken McNuggets (1983)—McHit
- Extra Value Meal (1991)—McHit
- McLean Deluxe (1991)—McMiss
- Arch Deluxe (1996)—McMiss
- 55-cent Special (1997)—McMiss
- Big Xtra (1999)—McHit
- McSalad Shaker (2000)—McMiss
- McGriddle (2003)—McHit
- Snack Wrap (2006)—McHit

Source: "Polishing the Golden Arches," *Forbes*, June 15, 1998, pp. 42–43, updated. Reprinted by permission of Forbes Media LLC © 2010.

The Consider This boxes are used to provide analogies, examples, or stories that help drive home central economic ideas in a student-oriented, real-world manner. For instance, a Consider This box titled "McHits and McMisses" illustrates consumer sovereignty through a listing of successful and unsuccessful products. Another Consider This box looks at how street entertainers overcome the problem of being unable to exclude non-paying clients from enjoying the entertainment they provide. These brief vignettes illustrate key points in a lively, colourful, and easy-to-remember way. We have added fourteen new Consider This boxes in this edition.

The Last Word pieces are lengthier applications or case studies that are placed near the end of each chapter. For example, the Last Word section for Chapter 1 (Limits, Alternatives, and Choices) examines pitfalls to sound economic reasoning, while the Last Word section for Chapter 4 (Market Failures: Public Goods and Externalities) examines cap-and-trade versus carbon taxes as policy responses to excessive carbon dioxide emissions. There are eight new Last Word sections in this edition.

If you are unfamiliar with *Macroeconomics*, we encourage you to thumb through the chapters to take a quick look at these highly visible features.

New Chapter on Government's Role and Government Failure

We have responded to instructor suggestions by placing this new chapter on Government's Role and Government Failure in the introductory section of the book. Its early placement gives students a taste of political economy and the practical difficulties with government regulation and intervention. Topics covered include the special-interest effect, rent seeking, regulatory capture, political corruption, and unintended consequences.

ZIRP, QE, and Operation Twist provided massive economic stimulus during and after the Great Recession. But there remain many worries about unintended consequences.

When the U.S. financial crisis reached its peak in 2008, the Fed acted aggressively to prevent bank runs and stabilize the financial system by acting as a lender of last resort. It also did its best to get the economy moving again by lowering short-term interest rates to nearly zero—a strategy that came to be known as the zero interest rate policy, or ZIRP.

When ZIRP by itself didn't seem to be causing enough stimulus, the Fed also began engaging in trillions of dollars' worth of bond purchases. Those purchases went by the name of quantitative easing, or QE, because the Fed printed up electronic money to pay for the purchases, thereby massively increasing (easing) the total quantity of money in circulation. The Fed's hope was that the additional money would lead to additional spending and lending that would boost aggregate demand by increasing consumption and investment. Later, the policy known as Operation Twist lowered longer-term interest rates.

One important effect of ZIRP and Operation Twist was to help the U.S. federal government engage in aggressive deficit-financed fiscal stimulus. Thanks to ZIRP and Operation Twist, the federal government was able to fund large deficits by issuing 10-year bonds at nominal interest rates of about 2 percent—substantially lower than the historical average of about 6 percent.

But the Federal Reserve didn't just help the U.S. federal government with low interest rates. It also served as the federal government's primary lender. In 2012, for instance, the Federal Reserve purchased over 70 percent of all U.S. government debt. Thus, 70 percent of the federal government's new borrowing came from the Federal Reserve in the form of newly printed money that the Fed created in order to fund its open-market purchases of U.S. government bonds.

The consensus among economists was that the Fed's aggressive use of ZIRP and QE were warranted by the severity of the financial crisis and the historically slow pace with which the economy recovered after the 2007–2009 recession. However, concerns were also raised about possible unintended consequences.

One worry had to do with the large annual budget deficits that the U.S. federal government was running. While many economists felt that the large deficits were appropriate given the sluggish economy, others believed that the U.S. federal government was overspending and taking resources away from the private sector. As a result, they felt that the Fed's use of ZIRP and QE was making it too easy for the U.S. Congress to overspend and run large budget deficits because the Fed would always provide a ready buyer for the bonds that had to be issued to finance those large deficits.

A longer-term worry was that when ZIRP ended and interest rates began to rise again toward normal levels, the U.S. federal government would be suddenly confronted with huge interest costs. Consider the $16 trillion of debt that had accumulated by 2013: $16 trillion borrowed at 2 percent interest generates annual interest payments of $320 billion per year. But if the interest rate on U.S. government debt were to rise back to its historical average of 6 percent, the annual interest payments on $16 trillion would come to $960 billion per year. Such a huge increase in annual interest payments would likely require either massive budget cuts or even more borrowing, unless the economy began to grow so quickly that increased tax revenues were enough to compensate for the increased interest payments.

Another problem with extremely low interest rates is that they punish savers. A senior citizen who has saved for retirement will find that her investments yield very low rates of return when the Fed is keeping interest rates low. Instead of being able to live off of the interest generated by her investments, she may find herself spending down her accumulated wealth because the interest payments amount to nearly nothing.

The chapter begins, however, by reminding students of government's great power to improve equity and efficiency. When read along with Chapter 4 on market failure, this new chapter on government failure should provide students with a balanced perspective. After learning why government intervention is needed to counter market failures, they will also learn that governments often have difficulty in fulfilling their full potential for improving economic outcomes.

An optional appendix incorporates the material on public choice theory and voting paradoxes that was formerly located in Chapter 17 of the thirteenth edition. Instructors wishing to give their students an even deeper appreciation of government failure may wish to assign this appendix.

Meanwhile, the material on asymmetric information that was located in Chapter 17 of the thirteenth edition has been moved into an appendix attached to the current edition's Chapter 4 on market failure. That way, instructors wishing to give their students a deeper look at market failure will have the material on asymmetric information located immediately after that chapter's discussion of public goods and externalities.

New Discussions of the Financial Crisis and the Recession

Our modernization of the macroeconomics in the previous edition has met with great success, measured by reviews, instructor feedback, and market response. We recast the entire macro analysis in terms of the modern, dominant paradigm of macroeconomics, using economic growth as the central backdrop and viewing business fluctuations as significant and costly variations in the rate of growth. In this paradigm, business cycles result from demand shocks (or, less often, supply shocks) in conjunction with inflexible short-run product prices and wages. The degree of price and wage stickiness decreases with time. In our models, the *immediate short run* is a period in which both the price level and wages are not only sticky, but stuck; the *short run* is a period in which product prices are flexible but wages are not; and the *long run* is a period in which both product prices and wages are fully flexible. Each of these three periods–and thus each of the models based on them–is relevant to understanding the actual macro economy and its occasional difficulties.

In this edition, we have mainly focused on incorporating into our new macroeconomic schema an analysis of the financial crisis, the recession, and the recovery. Given that the Great Recession started in the United States, we contrast Canada's policy response to that of the U.S. We first introduce the debate over the policy response to the 2008-2009 recession (the recession started in 2007 in the U.S. and ended in 2009) in Chapter 6 (An Introduction to Macroeconomics) via a new Last Word that briefly lays out the major opposing viewpoints about the nature and size of the stimulus that was applied during and after the crisis.

In Chapter 7 (Measuring the Economy's Output), we note that output usually expands over time, but not always, as demonstrated by the recession. In Chapter 8 (Economic Growth), we discuss how the recession relates to the growth/production possibilities dynamics of Figure 8.2. In Chapter 9 (Business Cycles, Unemployment, and Inflation), we have a new Last Word that contrasts the recovery in Canada with the very slow U.S. recovery in employment after the Great Recession.

In Chapter 10 (Basic Macroeconomic Relationships), we include two Consider This boxes, one on how the paradox of thrift applied to consumer behaviour during the recession and the other on the riddle of plunging investment spending at the same time the interest rate dropped to near zero during the recession. In Chapter 11 (The Aggregate Expenditures Model), we use the recession as a timely application of how a decline in aggregate expenditures can produce a recessionary expenditure gap and a highly negative GDP gap.

Chapter 12 (Aggregate Demand and Aggregate Supply) features a new Last Word on the debate among economists as to why the recovery from the 2008–2009 recession was so slow in the U.S. compared to Canada, despite the historically unprecedented amounts of monetary and fiscal stimulus that were applied by U.S. policymakers. In Chapter 14 (Money, Banking, and Money Creation), we updated the section on the financial crisis and added a new Last Word on the potential dangers of excessive leverage in the financial system and whether banking regulators should be more vigilant. Chapter 15 (Interest Rates and Monetary Policy) features a new Last Word on monetary policies in the U.S. during the recession and recovery, which includes a discussion of new policy initiatives, including quantitative easing, the zero interest rate policy, and Operation Twist.

The new inclusions will help students see the relevance of the models to what they are seeing in the news and perhaps experiencing in their own lives. The overall tone of *Macroeconomics* continues to be optimistic with respect to the long-term growth prospects of market economies.

Reorganized and Extended End-of-Chapter Questions and Problems

The thirteenth edition featured separate sections for end-of-chapter Questions and Problems. Due to demand on the part of instructors for an increase in the number of problems that are both autogradable and algorithmic, we have for the fourteenth edition added about ten new questions per chapter and have, in addition, revised our organizational scheme for questions and problems.

The questions and problems are now divided into three categories: Discussion Questions, Review Questions, and Problems.

- The Discussion Questions are analytic and often allow for free responses.

- The Review Questions focus on the apprehension of key concepts but are worded so as to always require specific answers, thereby allowing for autograding.

- The Problems are quantitative and require specific answers so that they, too, are both autogradable and, where appropriate, algorithmic.

All of the questions and problems are assignable through McGraw-Hill Ryerson's Connect and we have additionally aligned all of the questions and problems with the learning objectives presented at the beginning of chapters.

Current Discussions and Examples

The fourteenth edition of *Macroeconomics* refers to and discusses many current topics. Examples include surpluses and shortages of tickets at the Olympics; creative destruction; oil and gasoline prices; cap-and-trade systems and carbon taxes; the value-added tax; lotteries; the increase in long-term unemployment; the difficulty of targeting fiscal stimulus; the slow recovery from the Great Recession; the rise of the federal budget deficits and public debt; the effect of rising dependency ratios on economic growth; innovative Bank of Canada policies, including the response to quantitative easing by the U.S. central bank, the low interest rate policy, and explicit inflation targets; the effect of the low interest rate policy on savers; trade adjustment assistance; the European Union and the eurozone; changes in exchange rates; and many other current topics.

Chapter-by-Chapter Changes

Each chapter of *Macroeconomics*, Fourteenth Canadian Edition, contains updated data reflecting the current economy, revised Learning Objectives, and reorganized and expanded end-of-chapter content. Several chapters also contain one or more additional Quick Review boxes to help students review and solidify content as they are reading along. In addition to these changes, each chapter contains the following updates:

Chapter 1: Limits Alternatives, and Choices features three refreshed Consider This pieces, a more concise definition of macroeconomics, and wording improvements that clarify the main concepts.

Chapter 2: The Market System and the Circular Flow contains a heavily revised introductory section on the different types of economic systems found in the world today as well as a new section on how the market system deals with risk and uncertainty. There is more material on risk and its effects on economic behaviour. This short section provides a brief, non-technical framework for students to understand how the market economy deals with risk and uncertainty. There is also a new Consider This box on how insurance encourages investment by transferring risk from those who do not wish to bear it to those who are willing to bear it as a business proposition.

Chapter 3: Demand, Supply, and Market Equilibrium contains a short new section in the appendix that introduces students to markets with vertical supply curves so that the concept of perfectly inelastic supply will come more easily to microeconomics students and the concept of vertical long-run aggregate supply will come more easily to macroeconomics students.

Chapter 4: Market Failures: Public Goods and Externalities includes a new Consider This piece on how musicians have reacted to the reality that Internet file sharing has transformed recorded music from a private good into a public good. There is also a new appendix that explains market failures caused by asymmetric information. The appendix gives instructors the option of extending and deepening this chapter's study of market failure. Its content previously appeared in Chapter 17 of the thirteenth edition.

Chapter 5: Government's Role and Government Failure is a new chapter that offers a balanced treatment of both the great benefits as well as the possible drawbacks of government economic intervention and regulation. The chapter includes topics of interest for both microeconomics and macroeconomics students, such as regulatory capture, the collective-action problem, bureaucratic inertia, the tendency for politicians to run budget deficits to please voters, and the special-interest effect. So, while Chapter 4 makes the case for government regulation to compensate for market failures, this new chapter introduces students to the fact that government interventions are themselves susceptible to both allocative and productive inefficiency. As noted previously, the chapter also includes an appendix that incorporates the voting and public choice material that appeared in Chapter 17 of the thirteenth edition for instructors who wish to present their students with the most prominent theoretical models dealing with government failure.

Chapter 6: An Introduction to Macroeconomics benefits from extensive revisions to the chapter's header structure, several new Quick Reviews and a new Last Word that covers, in a brief and accessible form, the major opposing policy viewpoints about the effectiveness and ideal size of government stimulus during and after the 2008–2009 recession.

Chapter 7: Measuring the Economy's Output features two clarifications driven directly by student input. First, the table giving Canadian GDP by both the expenditure method and the income method is more clearly referenced in all instances so as to reduce any possible confusion as to which part of the table is being referred to. Second, there is now a more detailed explanation of the statistical discrepancy that appears when the income method is used to calculate GDP.

Chapter 8: Economic Growth benefits from extensive data updates, a new Quick Review to help solidify comprehension, and a new Last Word that discusses the challenges to economic growth posed by falling birth rates and a greying population.

Chapter 9: Business Cycles, Unemployment, and Inflation features a new Last Word on the slow recovery of employment after the Great Recession. There are also two new Consider This vignettes that discuss, respectively, the relationship between downwardly sticky wages and unemployment and the idea that moderate inflation rates may help to lower unemployment by allowing firms to cut real wages without cutting nominal wages.

Chapter 10: Basic Macroeconomic Relationships features a revised header structure to better guide students through the material, a new Quick Review to help solidify retention, and substantial revisions to several graphs and their captions to further refine and clarify the fundamental concepts introduced in this chapter.

Chapter 11: The Aggregate Expenditures Model has substantial changes to a key figure in order to improve clarity as well as a heavily revised list of Learning Objectives.

Chapter 12: Aggregate Demand and Aggregate Supply features a new Last Word on the discussion economists have been having as to why the recovery from the Great Recession has been so slow despite monetary and fiscal stimulus.

Chapter 13: Fiscal Policy, Deficits, Surpluses, and Debt features extensive data updates to help students understand the recent federal budget deficits.

Chapter 14 Money, Banking, and Money Creation features a new Last Word on the dangers of leverage in the banking system and compares the Canadian and U.S. systems. The chapter also contains four new Quick Reviews to help students better retain the chapter's material.

Chapter 15: Interest Rates and Monetary Policy features a new section on the Bank of Canada's monetary policy initiatives after the Great Recession, and looks at the U.S. central bank's (the Federal Reserve) use of quantitative easing (QE), forward guidance, the zero interest rate policy (ZIRP), and Operation Twist. There is also a new Last Word discussing the potential unintended consequences of QE and ZIRP.

Chapter 15 Bonus: Financial Economics is now a Bonus chapter. It features extensive data updates, five new Quick Reviews, and revised section headers to increase clarity.

Chapter 16: Long-Run Macroeconomic Adjustments features data updates, an extended discussion of the Laffer Curve, and a new Quick Review.

Chapter 16 Bonus: Current Issues in Macro Theory and Policy has a new Quick Review plus a brief discussion of the Bank of Canada's decisions to (1) use an explicit inflation target and (2) pre-announce the likely duration of open-market operations. There is also a discussion of quantitative easing, although this was not implemented in Canada.

Chapter 17 International Trade features extensive data updates, several revised figure captions, and three new Quick Reviews.

Chapter 18 Exchange Rates and the Balance of Payments features revised problems, extensive data updates, four new Quick Reviews, and a new set of Learning Objectives.

Chapter 18 Bonus: The Economics of Developing Countries features extensive data revisions and an all-new set of Discussion Questions.

Integrated Text and Website

We continue to integrate the eBook with our extensive supplementary learning offerings.

WORKED PROBLEM 2.1   Least Cost Production

Worked Problems are hyperlinked within the eBook and provide students with a step-by-step illustration of how to solve a problem. These pieces consist of side-by-side computational questions and the computational procedures used to derive the answers. In essence, they extend the textbook's explanations involving computations–for example, of real GDP, real GDP per capita, the unemployment rate, the inflation rate, per-unit production costs, and more. At relevant points in the text, the **Worked Problem** hyperlink directs the student to Connect for this additional support.

MATH 4.1   The Optimal Amount of a Public Good

For those students who want to explore the mathematical details of the theoretical concepts covered in the text, **Math** indicators direct the students to **See the Math** exercises on Connect.

ORIGIN OF THE IDEA 3.1   Demand and Supply

Also included in the eBook are links to **Origin of the Idea** articles. These brief histories examine the origins of 70 major ideas identified in the book. Students will find it interesting to learn about economists who first developed such ideas as opportunity cost, equilibrium price, the multiplier, and comparative advantage and elasticity. Clicking on the Origin of the Idea title hyperlinks students to Connect for this extension material.

To help students understand graphing concepts used in the text, Connect offers a Graphing Tool Introduction and assignable graphing exercises called Graphing Extras.

Bonus Chapters

Bonus chapters are available in the eBook. They are 15B, Financial Economics; 16B, Current Issues in Macro Theory and Policy; and 18B, The Economics of Developing Countries.

Distinguishing Features

- **Comprehensive Explanations at an Appropriate Level** *Macroeconomics* is comprehensive, analytical, and challenging, yet fully accessible to a wide range of students. Its thoroughness and accessibility enable instructors to select topics for special classroom emphasis with confidence that students can independently read and comprehend other assigned material in the book. Where needed, an extra sentence of explanation is provided. Brevity at the expense of clarity is false economy.

- **Fundamentals of the Market System** Many economies throughout the world are making difficult transitions from planning systems to market systems. Our detailed description of the institutions and operation of the market system in Chapter 2 (The Market System and the Circular Flow) is even more relevant than before. We pay particular attention to property rights, entrepreneurship, freedom of enterprise and choice, competition, and the role of profits, because these concepts are often misunderstood by beginning students.

- **Extensive Treatment of International Economics** We give the principles and institutions of the global economy extensive treatment. The appendix to Chapter 3 (Demand, Supply, and Market Equilibrium) has an application on exchange rates. Chapter 17 (International Trade) examines key facts of international trade, specialization and comparative advantage, arguments for protectionism, impacts of tariffs and subsidies, and various trade agreements. Chapter 18 (Exchange Rates and the Balance of Payments) discusses the balance of payments and fixed and floating exchange rates. Bonus Chapter 18B (The Economics of Developing Countries) takes a look at the special problems faced by developing countries and how the advanced industrial countries try to help them.

  As noted previously in this preface, Chapter 17 (International Trade) is constructed such that instructors who want to cover international trade early in the course can assign it immediately after Chapter 3. Comprehending Chapter 17 requires only a good understanding of production possibilities analysis, and supply and demand analysis. International competition, trade flows, and financial flows are integrated throughout the micro and macro sections. Global Perspective boxes add to the international flavour of the book.

- **Early and Extensive Treatment of Government** The public sector is an integral component of modern capitalism. This book introduces the role of government early. Chapter 4 (Market Failures: Public Goods and Externalities) systematically discusses public goods and government policies toward externalities. Chapter 5 (Government's Role and Government Failure) details the factors that cause government failure.

- **Step-by-Step, Two-Path Macro** As in the previous edition, our text continues to be distinguished by a systematic step-by-step approach in developing ideas and building models. Explicit assumptions about price and wage stickiness are posited and then systematically peeled away, yielding new models and extensions, all in the broader context of growth, expectations, shocks, and degrees of price and wage stickiness over time.

  In crafting this step-by-step macro approach, we took care to preserve the two-path macro that many instructors appreciated. Instructors who so choose can bypass the immediate short-run model (Chapter 11) and can proceed without loss of continuity directly to the short-run AD–AS model (Chapter 12), fiscal policy, money and banking, monetary policy, and the long-run AD–AS analysis.

- **Emphasis on Technological Change and Economic Growth** This edition continues to emphasize economic growth. Chapter 1 (Limits, Alternatives, and Choices) uses the production possibilities curve to show the basic ingredients of growth. Chapter 8 (Economic Growth) discusses the causes of growth, looks at productivity growth, and addresses some controversies surrounding economic growth. The Last Word in that chapter examines the rapid economic growth in China. Bonus Chapter 18B focuses on developing countries and the growth obstacles they confront.

- **Integrated Text and Website** Selected interactive graphs are available on Connect.

Organizational Alternatives

Although instructors generally agree as to the content of principles of economics courses, they sometimes differ as to how to arrange the material. *Macroeconomics* includes seven parts, and that provides considerable organizational flexibility. For example, the two-path macro enables covering the full aggregate expenditures model or advancing directly from the basic macro relationships chapter to the AD-AS model. Also, the section of Chapter 16 that discusses the intricacies of the relationship between short-run and long-run aggregate supply can easily be appended to Chapter 12 on AD and AS.

Finally, Chapter 17 on international trade can easily be covered immediately after Chapter 3 on supply and demand for instructors who want an early discussion of international trade.

Pedagogical Aids

Macroeconomics is highly student oriented. The Fourteenth Canadian Edition is accompanied by a variety of high-quality supplements that help students master the subject and help instructors implement customized courses.

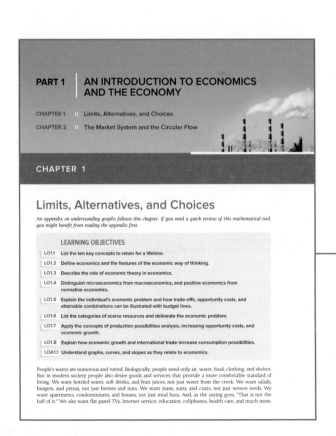

- **Learning Objectives** The Learning Objectives have been expanded in the fourteenth edition. We set out the Learning Objectives at the start of each chapter so the chapter's main concepts can be easily recognized. We have also tied the Learning Objectives to each of the numbered sections in each chapter and the Questions and Problems at the end of each chapter. In addition, the chapter summaries are organized by Learning Objective.

- **Terminology** A significant portion of any introductory course is terminology. Key terms are highlighted in bold type the first time they appear in the text. A glossary of definitions can be found at the end of the book. Users of the eBook can hover their cursor over each bolded term to see its definition.

- **Ten Key Concepts** Ten Key Concepts have been identified to help students organize the main principles. The Ten Key Concepts are introduced in Chapter 1 and each one is reinforced throughout the textbook by an icon.

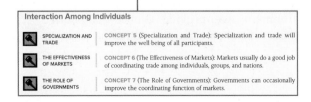

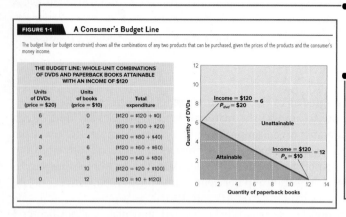

FIGURE 1-1   A Consumer's Budget Line

The budget line (or budget constraint) shows all the combinations of any two products that can be purchased, given the prices of the products and the consumer's money income.

- **Graphics with Supporting Data** Where possible we have tried to provide data to support our graphs. In such cases a data table now appears in the same figure with the graph.

- **Key Graphs** We have labelled graphs having special relevance as Key Graphs. There is a quick quiz of four questions related to each Key Graph, with answers provided at the bottom of the graph.

- **Reviewing the Chapter** Important things should be said more than once. You will find a Chapter Summary at the conclusion of every chapter as well as two or three Quick Reviews within each chapter. The summary at the end of each chapter is presented by Learning Objective. These review statements will help the student to focus on the essential ideas of each chapter and also to study for exams.

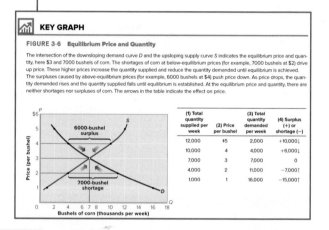

KEY GRAPH

FIGURE 3-6   Equilibrium Price and Quantity

The intersection of the downsloping demand curve *D* and the upsloping supply curve *S* indicates the equilibrium price and quantity, here $3 and 7000 bushels of corn. The shortages of corn at below-equilibrium prices (for example, 7000 bushels at $2) drive up price. These higher prices increase the quantity supplied and reduce the quantity demanded until equilibrium is achieved. The surpluses caused by above-equilibrium prices (for example, 6000 bushels at $4) push price down. As price drops, the quantity demanded rises and the quantity supplied falls until equilibrium is established. At the equilibrium price and quantity, there are neither shortages nor surpluses of corn. The arrows in the table indicate the effect on price.

- **Global Perspective Boxes** Each nation increasingly functions in a global economy. To help the student gain an appreciation of this wider economic environment, we provide Global Perspective features that compare Canada to other nations.

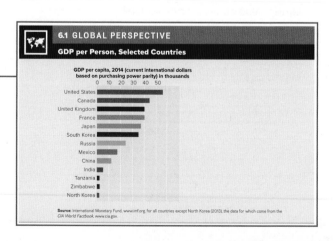

6.1 GLOBAL PERSPECTIVE

GDP per Person, Selected Countries

Appendix on Graphs Being comfortable with graphical analysis and a few related quantitative concepts will be a big advantage to students in understanding the principles of economics. The appendix to Chapter 1, which reviews graphing, line slopes, and linear equations, should not be skipped.

Appendix to Chapter 1

A1.1 / Graphs and Their Meanings

LOA1.1 Understand graphs, curves, and slopes as they relate to economics.

If you glance quickly through this text, you will find many graphs. Some seem simple, while others are more complicated. All are included to help you visualize and understand economic relationships. Physicists and chemists sometimes illustrate their theories by building arrangements of multicoloured wooden balls, representing protons, neutrons, and electrons, which are held in proper relation to one another by wires or sticks. Economists use graphs to illustrate their models. By understanding these illustrations you can more readily make sense of economic relationships.

Construction of a Graph

A *graph* is a visual representation of the relationship between two economic quantities or variables. Figure A1-1 is a hypothetical illustration showing the relationship between income and consumption for the economy as a whole. Without even studying economics, we would logically expect that people would buy more goods and services when their incomes go up. Thus, it is not surprising to find in

Figure A1-1 that total consumption in the economy increases as total income increases.

The information in Figure A1-1 is expressed both graphically and in table form. Here is how it is done: We want to show graphically how consumption changes as income changes. We therefore represent income on the **horizontal axis** of the graph and consumption on the **vertical axis**.

Now we arrange the vertical and horizontal scales of the graph to reflect the ranges of values of consumption and income, and mark the scales in convenient increments. As you can see in Figure A1-1, the values marked on the scales cover all the values in the table. The values on both axes are indicated in $100 increments.

Because the graph has two dimensions, each point within it represents an income value and its associated consumption value. To find a point that represents one of the five income-consumption combinations in the table, we draw straight lines from the appropriate values on the vertical and horizontal axes. For example, to plot point *c* ($200 income, $150 consumption), draw straight lines up from the horizontal (income) axis at $200 and across from the vertical (consumption) axis at $150. These straight

Discussion Questions

1. Explain the law of demand. Why does a demand curve slope downward? How is a market demand curve derived from individual demand curves? [LO3.2]

2. What are the determinants of demand? What happens to the demand curve when any of these determinants changes? Distinguish between a change in demand and a change in the quantity demanded, noting the cause(s) of each. [LO3.2]

3. Explain the law of supply. Why does the supply curve slope upward? How is the market supply curve derived from the supply curves of individual producers? [LO3.2]

4. What are the determinants of supply? What happens to the supply curve when any of these determinants changes? Distinguish between a change in supply and a change in the quantity supplied, noting the cause(s) of each. [LO3.3]

5. In 2001, an outbreak of foot-and-mouth disease in Europe led to the burning of millions of cattle carcasses. What impact do you think this had on the supply of leather goods, the supply of leather, and the price of leather goods? [LO3.5]

6. For each stock in the stock market, the number of shares sold daily equals the number of shares purchased. That is, the quantity of each firm's shares demanded equals the quantity supplied. So, if this equality always occurs, why do the prices of stock shares ever change? [LO3.5]

7. What do economists mean when they say "price floors and ceilings stifle the rationing function of prices and distort resource allocation"? [LO3.6]

Discussion Questions, Review Questions, and Problems The Study Questions have been split into Review Questions, Discussion Questions, and Problems, better aligning them with Learning Objectives and adding new autogradable (through Connect) quantitative questions.

Review Questions

1. What effect will each of the following have on the demand for small automobiles such as the Mini-Cooper and Fiat 500? [LO3.2]

   a. Small automobiles become more fashionable.

   b. The price of large automobiles rises (with the price of small autos remaining the same).

   c. Income declines and small autos are an inferior good.

   d. Consumers anticipate that the price of small autos will greatly come down in the near future.

   e. The price of gasoline substantially drops.

2. True or False? A change in quantity demanded is a shift of the entire demand curve to the right or to the left. [LO3.2]

3. What effect will each of the following have on the supply of auto tires? [LO3.3]

   a. A technological advance in the methods of producing tires.

   b. A decline in the number of firms in the tire industry.

   c. An increase in the prices of rubber used in the production of tires.

   d. The expectation that the equilibrium price of auto tires will be lower in the future than currently

   e. A decline in the price of the large tires used for semitrucks and earth-hauling rigs (with no change in the price of auto tires)

   f. The levying of a per-unit tax on each auto tire sold

   g. The granting of a 50-cent-per-unit subsidy for each auto tire produced

4. "In the corn market, demand often exceeds supply and supply sometimes exceeds demand." "The price of corn rises and falls

in response to changes in supply and demand." In which of these two statements are the terms "supply" and "demand" used correctly? Explain. [LO3.3]

5. Suppose that in the market for computer memory chips, the equilibrium price is $50 per chip. If the current price is $55 per chip, then there will be _____ of memory chips. [LO3.4]

   a. A shortage

   b. A surplus

   c. An equilibrium quantity

   d. None of the above

6. Critically evaluate the following statement: "In comparing the two equilibrium positions in Figure 3.7b, I note that a smaller amount is actually demanded at a lower price. This refutes the law of demand." [LO3.5]

7. Label each of the following scenarios with the set of symbols that best indicates the price change and quantity change that occur in the scenario. In some scenarios, it may not be possible from the information given to determine the direction of a particular price change or a particular quantity change. We will symbolize those cases as, respectively, P? and Q? The four possible combinations of price and quantity changes are [LO3.5]

   P↑ Q?   P? Q↑

   P↑Q?   P? Q↓

   a. On a hot day, both the demand for lemonade and the supply of lemonade increase.

   b. On a cold day, both the demand for ice cream and the supply of ice cream decrease.

Problems

1. Suppose there are three buyers of candy in a market: Tex, Dex, and Rex. The market demand and the individual demands of Tex, Dex, and Rex for candy are given in the table below. [LO3.2]

   a. Fill in the missing values in the table below.

   b. Which buyer demands the least at a price of $5? The most at a price of $7?

   c. Which buyer's quantity demanded increases the most when the price is lowered from $7 to $6?

   d. In which direction would the market demand curve shift if Tex withdrew from the market? What if Dex doubled his purchases at each possible price?

   e. Suppose that, at a price of $6, the total quantity demanded increases from 19 to 38. Is this a change in the quantity demanded or a change in demand?

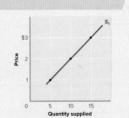

a. Use the figure to fill in the quantity supplied on supply curve S_1 for each price in the table below.

Price	S_1 Quantity supplied	S_2 Quantity supplied	Change in quantity supplied
$3	_____	4	_____
2	_____	2	_____
1	_____	0	_____

b. If production costs were to increase, the quantities supplied at each price would be as shown by the third column of the table (S_2 Quantity supplied). Use that data to draw supply curve S_2 on the same graph as supply curve S_1.

Price per candy	Individual quantities demanded								Total quantity demanded
	Tex		Dex		Rex			
$8	3	+	1	+	0	=		—
7	8	+	2	+	—	=		12
6	—	+	3	+	4	=		19
5	17	+	—	+	6	=		27
4	23	+	5	+	8	=		—

2. The figure that follows shows the supply curve for tennis balls, S_1. Use the figure and the table to give your answers to the following questions. [LO3.3]

Comprehensive Learning and Teaching Package

The Fourteenth Canadian Edition is also accompanied by a variety of high-quality supplements that help students master the subject and help instructors implement customized courses.

MARKET LEADING TECHNOLOGY

Learn Without Limits

connect McGraw-Hill Connect® is an award-winning digital teaching and learning platform that gives students the means to better connect with their coursework, with their instructors, and with the important concepts that they will need to know for success now and in the future. With Connect, instructors can take advantage of McGraw-Hill's trusted content to seamlessly deliver assignments, quizzes and tests online. McGraw-Hill Connect is the only learning platform that continually adapts to each student, delivering precisely what they need, when they need it, so class time is more engaging and effective. Connect makes teaching and learning personal, easy, and proven.

Connect Key Features

SMARTBOOK As the first and only adaptive reading experience, SmartBook is changing the way students read and learn. SmartBook creates a personalized reading experience by highlighting the most important concepts a student needs to learn at that moment in time. As a student engages with SmartBook, the reading experience continuously adapts by highlighting content based on what each student knows and doesn't know. This ensures that he or she is focused on the content needed to close specific knowledge gaps, while it simultaneously promotes long-term learning.

connectINSIGHT Connect Insight is Connect's new one-of-a-kind visual analytics dashboard–now available for both instructors and students–that provides at-a-glance information regarding student performance, which is immediately actionable. By presenting assignment, assessment, and topical performance results together with a time metric that is easily visible for aggregate or individual results, Connect Insight gives the user the ability to take a just-in-time approach to teaching and learning that was never before available. Connect Insight presents data that empowers students and helps instructors improve class performance in a way that is efficient and effective.

Simple Assignment Management

With Connect, creating assignments is easier than ever, so instructors can spend more time teaching and less time managing. Instructors can

- Assign SmartBook learning modules
- Edit existing questions and create their own questions
- Draw from a variety of text specific questions, resources, and test bank material to assign online
- Streamline lesson planning, student progress reporting, and assignment grading to make classroom management more efficient than ever

Smart Grading

When it comes to studying, time is precious. Connect helps students learn more efficiently by providing feedback and practice material when they need it, where they need it.

- Automatically score assignments, giving students immediate feedback on their work and comparisons with correct answers.

- Access and review each response; manually change grades or leave comments for students to review.

- Track individual student performance—by question, assignment, or in relation to the class overall—with detailed grade reports.

- Reinforce classroom concepts with practice tests and instant quizzes.

- Integrate grade reports easily with Learning Management Systems including Blackboard, D2L, and Moodle.

Instructor Library

The Connect Instructor Library is a repository for additional resources to improve student engagement in and out of the class. It provides all the critical resources instructors need to build their course.

- Access Instructor resources.

- View assignments and resources created for past sections.

- Post your own resources for students to use.

Instructor Resources

- ***Instructor's Manual*** The Instructor's Manual is prepared by text author Thomas Barbiero of Ryerson University and Shawn D. Knabb of Western Washington University. Available again in this edition as a Microsoft® Office Word document, the manual includes a Chapter Overview, What's New, Instructional Objectives, Comments and Teaching Suggestions, Student Stumbling Blocks, Lecture Notes, Last Words, and quiz questions.

- ***Solutions Manual*** Prepared by the text author and checked for accuracy by Amy Peng of Ryerson University, the Solutions Manual includes the answers to all end-of-chapter questions and problems.

- ***Microsoft® PowerPoint® Presentation Software*** Prepared by Mehdi Arzandeh, University of Manitoba, this presentation system is found on the Instructor's Site of Connect. It offers visual presentations that may be edited and manipulated to fit a particular course format.

- ***Computerized Test Banks*** Prepared by David Kaun of Ryerson University, the Computerized Test Bank contains about 6000 multiple-choice and true/false questions, and hundreds of short-answer questions with suggested answers.

Image Gallery

The complete set of figures from the text can be downloaded from the image gallery on Connect and easily embedded into instructors' PowerPoint slides.

Superior Learning Solutions and Support

The McGraw-Hill Education team is ready to help instructors assess and integrate any of our products, technology, and services into your course for optimal teaching and learning performance. Whether it's helping your students improve their grades, or putting your entire course online, the McGraw-Hill Education team is here to help you do it. Contact your Learning Solutions Consultant today to learn how to maximize all of McGraw-Hill Education's resources.

For more information, please visit us online: http://www.mheducation.ca/highereducation/educators/digital-solutions

Acknowledgements

The Fourteenth Canadian Edition of *Macroeconomics* has benefited from a number of perceptive reviewers, who were a rich source of suggestions for this revision. To each of you, and others we may have inadvertently overlooked, thank you for your considerable help in improving *Macroeconomics*. Reviewers include:

Bruno Fullone, George Brown College
Sandra Hadersbeck, Okanagan College
Derek Heatherington, Champlain College
Nargess Kayhani, Mount Saint Vincent University
John Saba, Champlain College
Xuda Song, York University
Carl Weston, Mohawk College
Andrew Wong, University of Alberta

We are greatly indebted to an all-star group of professionals at McGraw-Hill Ryerson—in particular James Booty, Senior Product Manager; Cathy Biribauer, Supervising Editor; Sarah Fulton, Product Developer; Stephanie Giles, Senior Product Team Associate; and Joy Armitage Taylor, Executive Marketing Manager—for their publishing and marketing expertise. We thank Judy Sturrup for her thorough and sensitive editing, Keri Johnson for her selection of the Consider This and Last Word photos, Lightbox Visuals for the cover and interior design, and Gianluigi Pelloni of the University of Bologna (Rimini Campus) and Jose Luis Alvarez Arce of the University of Navarra in Pamplona, Spain, for their helpful suggestions and insights.

Campbell R. McConnell
Stanley L. Brue
Sean M. Flynn
Thomas P. Barbiero

CHAPTER 1

Limits, Alternatives, and Choices

An appendix on understanding graphs follows this chapter. If you need a quick review of this mathematical tool, you might benefit from reading the appendix first.

LEARNING OBJECTIVES

LO1.1 List the ten key concepts to retain for a lifetime.

LO1.2 Define economics and the features of the economic way of thinking.

LO1.3 Describe the role of economic theory in economics.

LO1.4 Distinguish microeconomics from macroeconomics, and positive economics from normative economics.

LO1.5 Explain the individual's economic problem and how trade-offs, opportunity costs, and attainable combinations can be illustrated with budget lines.

LO1.6 List the categories of scarce resources and delineate the economic problem.

LO1.7 Apply the concepts of production possibilities analysis, increasing opportunity costs, and economic growth.

LO1.8 Explain how economic growth and international trade increase consumption possibilities.

LOA1.1 Understand graphs, curves, and slopes as they relate to economics.

People's wants are numerous and varied. Biologically, people need only air, water, food, clothing, and shelter. But in modern society people also desire goods and services that provide a more comfortable standard of living. We want bottled water, soft drinks, and fruit juices, not just water from the creek. We want salads, burgers, and pizzas, not just berries and nuts. We want jeans, suits, and coats, not just woven reeds. We want apartments, condominiums, and houses, not just mud huts. And, as the saying goes, "That is not the half of it." We also want flat-panel TVs, Internet service, education, cellphones, health care, and much more.

Fortunately, society possesses productive resources, such as labour and managerial talent, tools and machinery, and land and mineral deposits. These resources, employed in the economic system (or simply the economy), help us produce goods and services that satisfy many of our economic wants. But the blunt reality is that our economic wants far exceed the productive capacity of our scarce (limited) resources. We are forced to make choices. This unchanging truth underlies the definition of **economics**, which is the social science concerned with how individuals, institutions, and society make optimal (best) choices under conditions of scarcity.

Numerous problems and issues arise from the challenge of making optimal choices under conditions of scarcity. Although it is tempting to plunge into them, that sort of analysis must wait until we discuss some important preliminaries.

ORIGIN OF THE IDEA 1.1   Economics

1.1 / Ten Key Concepts to Retain for a Lifetime

LO1.1   List the 10 key concepts to retain for a lifetime.

Suppose you unexpectedly meet your Introductory Economics professor on the street five or ten years after you complete this course. What will you be able to tell her you retained from the course? More than likely you will not be able to remember very much. To help you retain the main ideas that economics has to offer, we have come up with *10 key concepts* that we believe are essential to understanding the world around you and will help you in your chosen career. These key concepts will be reinforced throughout the textbook so that you will, we hope, retain them long after the course is over. When a key concept is about to be discussed, you will be alerted with an icon and the concept description.

The 10 key concepts are simply listed here; you will find elaboration of each key concept as we progress through the textbook. At the end of the course you should review these 10 key concepts. They will help you to organize and better understand the materials you have studied. We have divided the 10 key concepts into three categories: (a) concepts that pertain to the individual, (b) concepts that explain the interaction among individuals, and (c) concepts that deal with the economy as a whole and the standard of living.

Economics is concerned with the efficient use of scarce resources to obtain the maximum satisfaction of society's unlimited wants.

The Individual

 FACING TRADE-OFFS | **CONCEPT 1** (Facing Trade-offs): Scarcity in relation to wants means you face trade-offs; therefore, you have to make choices.

 OPPORTUNITY COSTS | **CONCEPT 2** (Opportunity Costs): The cost of the choice you make is what you give up for it, or the opportunity cost.

CHOOSING A LITTLE MORE OR LESS | **CONCEPT 3** (Choosing a Little More or Less): Choices are usually made at the margin; we choose a little more or a little less of something.

 THE INFLUENCE OF INCENTIVES | **CONCEPT 4** (The Influence of Incentives): The choices you make are influenced by incentives.

Interaction Among Individuals

 SPECIALIZATION AND TRADE | **CONCEPT 5** (Specialization and Trade): Specialization and trade will improve the well-being of all participants.

 THE EFFECTIVENESS OF MARKETS | **CONCEPT 6** (The Effectiveness of Markets): Markets usually do a good job of coordinating trade among individuals, groups, and nations.

 THE ROLE OF GOVERNMENTS | **CONCEPT 7** (The Role of Governments): Governments can occasionally improve the coordinating function of markets.

The Economy as a Whole and the Standard of Living

 PRODUCTION AND THE STANDARD OF LIVING | **CONCEPT 8** (Production and the Standard of Living): The standard of living of the average person in a particular country is dependent on its production of goods and services. A rise in the standard of living requires a rise in the output of goods and services.

 MONEY AND INFLATION | **CONCEPT 9** (Money and Inflation): If the monetary authorities of a country annually print money in excess of the growth of output of goods and services, this practice will eventually lead to inflation.

 INFLATION–UNEMPLOYMENT TRADE-OFF | **CONCEPT 10** (Inflation-Unemployment Trade-off): In the short run, society faces a short-run trade-off between inflation and its level of unemployment.

As you read the text, be on the lookout for the icon that alerts you that one of these concepts is being discussed. We now turn to our first topic, the economic way of thinking.

1.2 / The Economic Way of Thinking

LO1.2 Define economics and the features of the economic way of thinking.

Close your eyes for a minute and pretend you are in paradise, a place where you can have anything you want whenever you desire it. On a particular day, you might decide you want a new pair of jeans, a new notebook computer, a cellular phone, tickets to see Justin Bieber, and a new red Ferrari sports car to cruise around in. Your friends might have a completely different list of wants, but in paradise all of their desires also will be satisfied. Indeed, everyone's desires are satisfied. The following day you can start all over and have any request fulfilled. And so it will continue, forever. Your body will never get old or sick, you will have all the friends and love you want, etc., etc.

Of course, paradise may be waiting for us in the afterlife, but in this world our wants greatly outstrip our ability to satisfy them. Whenever our wants are greater than the resources to meet those desires, we have an economic problem. It is this reality that gives economists their unique perspective. This **economic perspective** or *economic way of thinking* has several crucial and closely interrelated features.

Scarcity and Choice

The economic resources needed to make goods and services are in limited supply. This **scarcity** restricts options and requires choices. Because we can't have it all, we must decide what we will have and what we must forgo.

At the core of economics is the idea that "there is no free lunch." You may get treated to lunch, making it free to you, but there is a cost to someone—ultimately society. Scarce inputs of land, equipment, farm labour, the labour of cooks and waiters, and managerial talent are required. Because these resources could be used in other production activities, they and the other goods and services that could have been produced are sacrificed in making the lunch available. Economists call these sacrifices **opportunity costs**. To get more of one thing, you forgo the opportunity to get something else. That sacrifice is the opportunity cost of the choice. For example, you have $100 that you can spend on a pair of jeans or shoes. The opportunity cost of buying the shoes is the jeans you could have purchased, and vice versa.

  OPPORTUNITY COSTS

ORIGIN OF THE IDEA 1.2   Utility

Purposeful Behaviour

Economics assumes that human behaviour reflects rational self-interest. Individuals look for and pursue opportunities to increase their **utility**—the pleasure, happiness, or satisfaction obtained from consuming a good or service. They allocate their time, energy, and money to maximize their satisfaction. Because they weigh costs and benefits, their decisions are purposeful or rational, not random or chaotic.

Consumers are purposeful in deciding what goods and services to buy. Business firms are purposeful in deciding what products to produce and how to produce them. Government entities are purposeful in deciding what public services to provide and how to finance them.

CONSIDER THIS   **Free for All?**

Free products are seemingly everywhere. Sellers from time to time offer free apps, free cellphones, and no-fee chequing accounts. Dentists give out free toothbrushes. At provincial visitor centres there are free brochures and maps.

Does the presence of so many free products contradict the economist's assertion that there is no free lunch? No! Scarce resources are used to produce each of these products, and because those resources have alternative uses, society gives up something else to get the "free" good. Because alternatives must be forsaken, there is no such thing as a free lunch.

So why are these goods offered for free? In a word: marketing. Firms sometimes offer free products to entice people to try them and perhaps subsequently purchase them. Getting to try out the free version of an app may eventually entice you to buy a payed version that has more features. In other cases, a product is free only in conjunction with a purchase. To get the soft drink, you must buy the large pizza. To get the free cellphone, you need to sign up for a year (or more) of cellphone service.

But while "free" products may come at no cost to the individuals receiving them, they are never free to society because their manufacture requires the use of resources that could have been put to alternative uses.

This does not imply that people and institutions are immune to faulty logic and therefore are perfect decision makers. They sometimes make mistakes. Nor does it mean that people's decisions are unaffected by emotion or the decisions of those around them. Indeed, economists acknowledge that people are sometimes impulsive or emulate what others do. "Purposeful behaviour" simply means that people make decisions with some desired outcome in mind.

Rational self-interest is not the same as selfishness. In the economy, increasing one's own wage, rent, interest, or profit normally requires identifying and satisfying *somebody else's* wants! Also, people make personal sacrifices for others. They contribute time and money to charities because they derive pleasure from doing so. Parents help pay for their children's education for the same reason. These self-interested but unselfish acts help maximize the giver's satisfaction as much as any purchase of goods or services. Self-interested behaviour is simply behaviour designed to increase personal satisfaction, however it may be derived.

ORIGIN OF THE IDEA 1.3   Marginal Analysis

Marginal Analysis: Comparing Benefits and Costs

The economic perspective focuses largely on **marginal analysis**—comparisons of *marginal benefits* and *marginal costs*. To economists, marginal means *extra, additional,* or *a change in.* Most choices or decisions involve changes in the status quo (the existing state of affairs). Should you attend school for another year or not? Should you study an extra hour for an exam? Should you add fries to your fast-food order? Similarly, should a business expand or reduce its output? Should government increase or decrease health care funding?

 CHOOSING A LITTLE MORE OR LESS

CONSIDER THIS   **Fast Food Lines**

The economic perspective is useful in analyzing all sorts of behaviours. Consider an everyday example: the behaviour of customers at a fast-food restaurant. When customers enter the restaurant, they go to the shortest line, believing that line will minimize their time cost of obtaining food. They are acting purposefully; time is limited, and people prefer using it in some way other than standing in line.

If one fast-food line is temporarily shorter than other lines, some people will move to that line. These movers apparently view the time saving from the shorter line (marginal benefit) as exceeding the cost of moving from their present line (marginal cost). The line switching tends to equalize line lengths. No further movement of customers between lines occurs once all lines are about equal.

Fast-food customers face another cost–benefit decision when a clerk opens a new station at the counter. Should they move to the new station or stay put? Those who shift to the new line decide that the time saving from the move exceeds the extra cost of physically moving. In so deciding, customers must also consider just how quickly they can get to the new station compared with others who may be contemplating the same move. (Those who hesitate in this situation are lost!)

Customers at the fast-food establishment do not have perfect information when they select lines. Thus, not all decisions turn out as expected. For example, you might enter a short line only to find that the person in front of you is ordering hamburgers and fries for forty people in the Greyhound bus parked out back (and also that the employee taking orders is a trainee!). Nevertheless, at the time you made your decision, you thought it to be optimal.

Finally, customers must decide what food to order when they arrive at the counter. In making their choices, they again compare marginal costs and marginal benefits in attempting to obtain the greatest personal satisfaction for their expenditure.

Economists believe that what is true for the behaviour of customers at fast-food restaurants is true for economic behaviour in general. Faced with an array of choices, consumers, workers, and businesses rationally compare marginal costs and marginal benefits when making decisions.

Each option will have marginal benefits and marginal costs. In making choices, the decision maker will compare those two amounts. For example, you and your fiancée are shopping for an engagement ring. Should you buy a ¼-carat diamond, a ½-carat diamond, a ¾-carat diamond, or a larger one? The marginal cost of the larger diamond is the added expense beyond the smaller diamond. The marginal benefit is the greater lifetime pleasure (utility) from the larger stone. If the marginal benefit of the larger diamond exceeds its marginal cost, you buy the larger stone. But if the marginal cost is more than the marginal benefit, buy the smaller diamond instead, even if you can afford the larger stone.

In a world of scarcity, the marginal benefit associated with some specific option always includes the marginal cost of doing without something else. Spending money on the larger diamond may mean forgoing a honeymoon to an exotic location. Opportunity costs, the value of the next best thing forgone, are always present whenever a choice is made.

1.3 / Theories, Principles, and Models

LO1.3 Describe the role of economic theory in economics.

Like the physical and life sciences, as well as other social sciences, economics relies on the **scientific method**. That procedure consists of several elements:

- Observing real-world behaviour and outcomes.

- Formulating a possible explanation of cause and effect (hypothesis) based on those observations.

- Testing this explanation by comparing the outcomes of specific events to the outcome predicted by the hypothesis.

- Accepting, rejecting, or modifying the hypothesis based on these comparisons.

- Continuing to test the hypothesis against the facts. As favourable results accumulate, the hypothesis evolves into a theory. A very well tested and widely accepted theory is referred to as an economic law or an **economic principle**–a statement about economic behaviour or the economy that enables prediction of the probable effects of certain actions. Combinations of such laws or principles are incorporated into models, which are simplified representations of how parts of the economy work, such as a market or segment of the economy.

Economists develop theories of the behaviour of individuals (consumers, workers) and institutions (businesses, governments) engaged in the production, exchange, and consumption of goods and services. Theories, principles, and models are *purposeful simplifications*. The full scope of economic reality itself is too complex and bewildering to be understood as a whole. In developing theories, principles, and models, economists remove the clutter and simplify.

Economic principles and models are highly useful in analyzing economic behaviour and understanding how the economy operates. They are the tools for ascertaining cause and effect (or action and outcome) within the economic system. Good theories do a good job of explaining and predicting. They are supported by facts concerning how individuals and institutions actually behave in producing, exchanging, and consuming goods and services.

There are some other things you should know about economic principles.

- *Generalizations* Economic principles are generalizations relating to economic behaviour or to the economy itself. Economic principles are expressed as the tendencies of typical or average consumers, workers, or business firms. For example, economists say that consumers buy more of a particular product when its price falls. Economists recognize that some consumers may increase their purchases by a large amount, others by a small amount, and a few not at all. This *price-quantity principle* holds both for the typical consumer and for consumers as a group.

ORIGIN OF THE IDEA 1.4   Ceteris Paribus

- ***Other-Things-Equal Assumption*** In constructing their theories, economists use the *ceteris paribus* or **other-things-equal assumption**–the assumption that factors other than those being considered do not change. They assume that all variables except those under immediate consideration are held constant for a particular analysis. For example, consider the relationship between the price of Pepsi and the amount of it purchased. Assume that of all the factors that might influence the amount of Pepsi purchased (for example, the price of Pepsi, the price of Coca-Cola, and consumer incomes and preferences), only the price of Pepsi varies. This is helpful because the economist can then focus on the relationship between the price of Pepsi and purchases of Pepsi in isolation without being confused by changes in other variables.

MATH 1.1 Ceteris Paribus

- ***Graphical Expression*** Many economic models are expressed graphically. Be sure to read the appendix at the end of this chapter as a review of graphs.

1.4 / Microeconomics and Macroeconomics

LO1.4 **Distinguish microeconomics from macroeconomics, and positive economics from normative economics.**

Economists develop economic principles and models at two levels, microeconomics and macroeconomics.

Microeconomics

Microeconomics is the part of economics concerned with decision making by individual customers, workers, households, and business firms. At this level of analysis, we observe the details of their behaviour under a figurative microscope. We measure the price of a specific product, the number of workers employed by a single firm, the revenue or income of a particular firm or household, or the expenditures of a specific firm, government entity, or family. In microeconomics, we examine the grains of sand, the rocks, and the shells, not the beach.

Macroeconomics

Macroeconomics examines the performance and behaviour of the economy as a whole. It focuses its attention on economic growth, the business cycle, interest rates, inflation, and the behaviour of major economic aggregates such as the government, household, and business sectors. An **aggregate** is a collection of specific economic units treated as if they were one unit. Therefore, we might lump together the millions of consumers in the Canadian economy and treat them as if they were one huge unit called *consumers*.

In using aggregates, macroeconomics seeks to obtain an overview, or general outline, of the structure of the economy and the relationships of its major aggregates. Macroeconomics speaks of such economic measures as total output, total employment, total income, aggregate expenditures, and the general level of prices in analyzing various economic problems. Very little attention is given to the specific units that make up the various aggregates. Figuratively, macroeconomics looks at the beach, not the grains of sand, the rocks, and the shells.

The last few years have been an exciting time to study macroeconomics. The global financial crisis that spread to Canada in late 2008 resulted in a deep recession, which has been dubbed the Great Recession. You will have a much better understanding of what causes recessions, unemployment, inflation, and changes in the standard of living of the average Canadian once you have finished your course in introductory macroeconomics.

The micro–macro distinction does not mean that economics is so highly compartmentalized that every topic can be readily labelled as either macro or micro; many topics and subdivisions of economics are rooted in both. For example, while the problem of unemployment is usually treated as a macroeconomic topic (because unemployment relates to aggregate production), economists recognize that the decisions made by *individual* workers on how long to search for jobs and the ways in which *specific* labour markets encourage or impede hiring are also crucial in determining the unemployment rate.

Positive and Normative Economics

Both microeconomics and macroeconomics contain elements of positive economics and normative economics. **Positive economics** focuses on facts and cause-and-effect relationships. It includes description, theory development, and theory testing. Positive economics avoids value judgments. It tries to establish scientific statements about economic behaviour and deals with what the economy is actually like. Such scientifically based analysis is essential to good policy analysis.

Economic policy, on the other hand, involves **normative economics**, which incorporates value judgments about what the economy *should* be like or what particular policy actions *should* be recommended to achieve a desirable goal. Normative economics looks at the desirability of certain aspects of the economy. It underlies expressions of support for particular economic policies.

Positive economics concerns *what is*, while normative economics embodies subjective feelings about *what ought to be*. For example, a positive statement would be, "The unemployment rate in France is higher than that in Canada." A normative statement would be, "France ought to undertake policies to make its labour market more flexible to reduce unemployment rates." When you see words such as "ought" or "should" in a sentence, you are likely encountering a normative statement.

Most of the disagreement among economists involves normative, value-based policy questions. Of course, there is often some disagreement about which theories or models best represent the economy and its parts. But economists agree on a full range of economic principles. Most economic controversy thus reflects differing opinions or value judgments about what society should be like.

- Economics examines how individuals, institutions, and society make choices under conditions of scarcity.
- The economic way of thinking stresses (a) resource scarcity and the necessity of making choices, (b) the assumption of purposeful (or rational) behaviour, and (c) comparisons of marginal benefit and marginal cost.
- In choosing among alternatives, people incur opportunity costs—the value of the next-best option.

- Economists use the scientific method to establish economic theories, which are cause–effect generalizations about the economic behaviour of individuals and institutions.
- Microeconomics focuses on specific decision-making within an economy; macroeconomics examines the economy as a whole.
- Positive economics deals with factual statements (what is); normative economics involves value judgments (what ought to be).

1.5 | The Individual's Economic Problem

LO1.5 Explain the individual's economic problem and how trade-offs, opportunity costs, and attainable combinations can be illustrated with budget lines.

Both individuals and society face the **economic problem**, which is the need to make choices because economic wants are virtually unlimited but the means (income, time, resources) for satisfying those wants are limited. We will construct a simple microeconomic model to look at the general economic problem faced by an individual.

Limited Income

We all have a finite amount of income, even the wealthiest among us. Even members of the Thomson and Weston families–Canada's richest–have to decide how to spend their money, and the majority of us have much

1.1 GLOBAL PERSPECTIVE

Average Income, Selected Nations

Average income (total income/population), and therefore typical individual budget constraints, vary greatly among nations.

Country	Per capita income, 2013 (U.S. dollars, based on exchange rates)
Norway	$100,818
Switzerland	84,815
United States	53,042
Canada	51,958
France	42,503
Japan	38,634
South Korea	25,977
Brazil	11,208
Mexico	10,307
China	6,807
Pakistan	1,275
Mali	715
Rwanda	639
Congo	484

Source: World Bank, www.worldbank.org.

more limited means. Our income comes to us in the form of wages, interest, rent, and profit, although we may also receive money from government programs or from family members. As Global Perspective 1.1 shows, the average income of Canadians in 2013 was US$51,958. In the poorest nations, it was less than $500.

Unlimited Wants

For better or worse, most people have virtually unlimited wants. We desire various goods and services that provide utility. Our wants extend over a wide range of products, from *necessities* (food, shelter, and clothing) to *luxuries* (perfumes, yachts, and sports cars). Some wants, such as basic food, shelter, and clothing, have biological roots. Other wants—for example, specific kinds of food, shelter, and clothing—arise from the conventions and customs of society.

Over time, as new and improved products are introduced, economic wants tend to change and multiply, fuelled by new products. Only recently have people wanted iPods, Internet service, digital cameras, or camera phones, because those products did not exist a few decades ago. Also, the satisfaction of certain wants may trigger others: the acquisition of a Ford Focus or a Honda Civic has been known to whet the appetite for a Lexus or a Mercedes.

Services, as well as goods, satisfy our wants. Car repair work, the removal of an inflamed appendix, legal and accounting advice, and haircuts all satisfy human wants. Actually, we buy many goods, such as automobiles and washing machines, for the services they render. The differences between goods and services are often smaller than they appear to be.

For most people, the desires for goods and services cannot be fully satisfied. Bill Gates may have all that he wants for himself, but it is clear from his massive charitable giving that he keenly wants better health care for the world's poor. Our desires for a particular good or service can be satisfied; over a short period of

CONSIDER THIS   Countries Living Beyond Their Means

In late 2009, financial markets turned their attention to Greece, a country whose government had gone on a spending spree, and did not like what they saw: an accumulated debt that was about 130 percent of the country's income (referred to as Gross Domestic Product, or GDP). Moreover, in 2010 Greece's annual budget shortfall was more than 10 percent of GDP, one of the highest in the world and unsustainable given its poor prospects for economic growth. The Greek government was forced to institute strict austerity measures that led to the contraction of the economy in both 2010 and 2011. In early 2012, a deal was struck between the Greek government and those who had loaned it money (bond holders). Unfortunately for the bond holders, they had to take a "haircut": they will not receive all of their money back and some may lose as much as 75 percent of their investment. By 2013, the debt of the Greek government had risen to 175 percent of its GDP. Other nations in Europe also have high debt loads compared to GDP; these include Ireland, Portugal, and Italy. Greece and other nations were able to consume beyond their means by borrowing, but inevitably in a world of scarcity this practice cannot be sustained.

time we can surely get enough toothpaste or pasta. And one appendectomy is plenty. But our broader desire for more goods and services and higher-quality goods and services seems to be another story.

Because we have limited income (usually through our work) but seemingly insatiable wants, it is in our self-interest to pick and choose goods and services that maximize our satisfaction, given the limitations we face. It should be noted that while we are stressing limited income, there is rarely enough of all the other things people desire, such as health, time, physical/mental abilities, and much, much more.

The Budget Line

We can depict the economic problem facing individuals using a **budget line** (or, more technically, *budget constraint*), a schedule or curve that shows various combinations of two products a consumer can purchase with a specific money income. Although we assume two products, the analysis generalizes to the full range of products available to consumers.

To understand this idea, suppose that you received a bookstore gift card as a birthday present. The $120 card is soon to expire. You take the card to the store and confine your purchase decisions to two alternatives: DVDs and paperback books. DVDs are $20 each and paperback books are $10 each. Your purchase options are shown in the table in Figure 1-1.

At one extreme, you might spend the entire $120 on 6 DVDs at $20 each and have nothing left to spend on books. Or, by giving up 2 DVDs and thereby gaining $40, you can have 4 DVDs at $20 each and 4 books at $10 each. And so on to the other extreme, at which you could buy 12 books at $10 each, spending your entire gift card on books with nothing left to spend on DVDs.

The graph in Figure 1-1 shows the budget line. Note that, unlike the table, the graph is not restricted to whole units of DVDs and books. Every point on the graph represents a possible combination of DVDs and books, including fractional quantities. The slope of the graphed budget line measures the ratio of the price of books (P_b) to the price of DVDs (P_{dvd}); more precisely, the slope is $P_b/P_{dvd} = \$(-10)/\$(+20) = -\frac{1}{2}$. So you must forgo 1 DVD (measured on the vertical axis) to buy 2 books (measured on the horizontal axis). This yields a slope of $-\frac{1}{2}$ or -0.5.

The budget line illustrates several ideas.

ATTAINABLE AND UNATTAINABLE COMBINATIONS

All of the combinations of DVDs and books on or inside the budget line are *attainable* from the $120 of money income. You can afford to buy, for example, 3 DVDs at $20 each and 6 books at $10 each. You obviously can also afford to buy 2 DVDs and 5 books, thereby using up only $90 of the $120 available on your gift card. But to achieve maximum utility you will want to spend the full $120. The budget line shows all combinations that cost exactly the full $120.

| FIGURE 1-1 | A Consumer's Budget Line |

The budget line (or budget constraint) shows all the combinations of any two products that can be purchased, given the prices of the products and the consumer's money income.

THE BUDGET LINE: WHOLE-UNIT COMBINATIONS OF DVDS AND PAPERBACK BOOKS ATTAINABLE WITH AN INCOME OF $120		
Units of DVDs (price = $20)	Units of books (price = $10)	Total expenditure
6	0	($120 = $120 + $0)
5	2	($120 = $100 + $20)
4	4	($120 = $80 + $40)
3	6	($120 = $60 + $60)
2	8	($120 = $40 + $80)
1	10	($120 = $20 + $100)
0	12	($120 = $0 + $120)

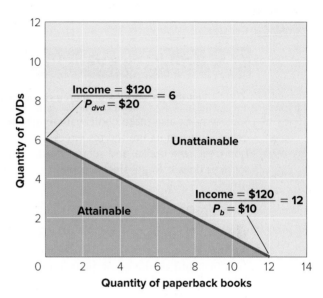

In contrast, all combinations beyond the budget line are *unattainable*. For example, the $120 limit does not allow you to purchase 5 DVDs at $20 each and 5 books at $10 each. That $150 expenditure would clearly exceed the $120 limit. In Figure 1-1 the attainable combinations are on and within the budget line; the unattainable combinations are beyond the budget line.

ORIGIN OF THE IDEA 1.5 Opportunity Costs

TRADE-OFFS AND OPPORTUNITY COSTS

The budget line in Figure 1-1 illustrates the idea of trade-offs arising from limited income. To obtain more DVDs, you have to give up some books. For example, to obtain the first DVD you trade off 2 books. So the opportunity cost of the first DVD is 2 books. To obtain the second DVD, the opportunity cost is also 2 books. The straight-line budget constraint, with its constant slope, indicates constant opportunity cost. That is, the opportunity cost of 1 extra DVD remains the same (= 2 books) as more DVDs are purchased. And the opportunity cost of 1 extra book does not change (= ½ DVD) as more books are bought.

CHOICE

Limited income forces people to choose what to buy and what to forgo to fulfill wants. You will select the combination of DVDs and paperback books that you think is best. That is, you will evaluate your marginal benefits and marginal costs (here, product price) to make choices that maximize your satisfaction. Other people with the same $120 gift card would undoubtedly make different choices.

INCOME CHANGES

The location of the budget line varies with money income. An increase in money income shifts the budget line to the right; a decrease in money income shifts it to the left. To verify this, recalculate the table in Figure 1-1, assuming the card value (income) is (a) $240 and (b) $60, and then plot the new budget lines in the graph. No wonder people like to have more income: having more money shifts their budget line outward and enables them to buy more goods and services. But even with more income, people will still face spending trade-offs, choices, and opportunity costs.

WORKED PROBLEM 1.1   Budget Line

1.6 / Society's Economic Problem

LO1.6 **List the categories of scarce resources and delineate the nature of society's economic problem.**

Society must also make choices under conditions of scarcity. It, too, faces the economic problem. Should it devote more of its limited resources to the criminal justice system (police, courts, and prisons) or to education (teachers, books, and schools)? If it decides to devote more resources to both, what other goods and services does it forgo? Health care? Energy development?

Scarce Resources

Society has limited or scarce **economic resources**, meaning all natural, human, and manufactured resources that go into the production of goods and services. That includes the entire set of factory and farm buildings and all the equipment, tools, and machinery used to produce manufactured goods and agricultural products; all transportation and communication facilities; all types of labour; and land and mineral resources.

Resource Categories

Economists classify economic resources into four general categories.

LAND

Land means much more to the economist than it does to most people. To the economist, **land** includes all natural resources ("gifts of nature") used in the production process. These include forests, mineral and oil deposits, water resources, wind power, sunlight, and arable land.

LABOUR

The resource **labour** consists of the physical actions and mental activities that people contribute to the production of goods and services. The work-related activities of a logger, retail clerk, machinist, teacher, professional hockey player, and nuclear physicist all fall under the general heading of labour.

CAPITAL

For economists, **capital** (or capital goods) includes all manufactured aids used in producing consumer goods and services: tools and machinery, as well as all factory, storage, transportation, and distribution facilities. Note that the term *capital* does not refer to money. Because money produces nothing, economists do not include it as an economic resource. Money (or money capital or financial capital) is simply a means of purchasing capital goods.

Capital goods differ from consumer goods because consumer goods satisfy wants directly, while capital goods do so indirectly by aiding the production of consumer goods. For example, large commercial baking ovens (capital goods) help make loaves of bread (consumer goods).

Economists refer to the purchase of capital goods as **investment**. The amount of training and education that a person acquires through his or her lifetime is referred to as *human capital,* since it is similar to an investment in capital goods in that it can enhance output. But you should note that human capital is normally categorized under labour resources.

ENTREPRENEURIAL ABILITY

Finally, there is the special human resource, distinct from labour, called **entrepreneurial ability**. It is supplied by **entrepreneurs**, who perform several crucial economic functions:

- The entrepreneur takes the initiative in combining the resources of land, labour, and capital to produce a good or a service. Both a sparkplug and a catalyst, the entrepreneur is the driving force behind production and the agent who combines the other resources in what is hoped will be a successful business venture.

- The entrepreneur makes the strategic business decisions that set the course of an enterprise.

- The entrepreneur innovates. He or she commercializes new products, new production techniques, or even new forms of business organization.

- The entrepreneur bears risk. Innovation is risky, as nearly all new products and ideas are subject to the possibility of failure as well as success. Progress would cease without entrepreneurs who are willing to take on risk by devoting their time, effort, and ability–as well as their own money and the money of others–to commercializing new products and ideas that may enhance society's standard of living.

Because land, labour, capital, and entrepreneurial ability are combined to produce goods and services, they are called the **factors of production**, or simply *inputs*.

QUICK REVIEW 1.2

- Because wants exceed incomes, individuals face an economic problem: they must decide what to buy and what to forgo.

- A budget line (budget constraint) shows the various combinations of two goods that a consumer can purchase with a specific money income.

- Straight-line budget constraints imply constant opportunity costs associated with obtaining more of either of the two goods.

- Economists categorize economic resources as land, labour, capital, and entrepreneurial ability.

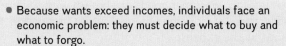

1.7 / Production Possibilities Model

LO1.7 Apply the concepts of production possibilities analysis, increasing opportunity costs, and economic growth.

Society uses its **scarce resources** to produce goods and services. The alternatives and choices it faces can best be understood through a macroeconomic model of production possibilities. To keep things simple, let's initially assume:

- *Full Employment* The economy is employing all its available resources.

- *Fixed Resources* The quantity and quality of the factors of production are fixed.

- *Fixed Technology* The state of technology (the methods used to produce output) is constant.

- *Two Goods* The economy is producing only two goods: pizzas and industrial robots. Pizzas symbolize **consumer goods**, products that satisfy our wants directly; industrial robots (for example, the kind used to weld automobile frames) symbolize **capital goods**, products that satisfy our wants indirectly by making possible more efficient production of consumer goods.

| TABLE 1-1 | Production Possibilities of Pizzas and Robots with Full Employment and Productive Efficiency | | | | |

	PRODUCTION ALTERNATIVES				
Type of product	A	B	C	D	E
Pizzas (in hundred thousands)	0	1	2	3	4
Robots (in thousands)	10	9	7	4	0

Production Possibilities Table

A production possibilities table lists the different combinations of two products that can be potentially produced with a specific set of resources, assuming full employment. Table 1-1 contains such a simple economy that is producing pizzas and industrial robots; the data are, of course, hypothetical. At alternative A, this economy would be devoting all its available resources to the production of industrial robots (capital goods); at alternative E, all resources would go to pizza production (consumer goods). Those alternatives are unrealistic extremes; an economy typically produces both capital goods and consumer goods, as in B, C, and D. As we move from alternative A to E, we increase the production of pizzas at the expense of the production of industrial robots.

Because consumer goods satisfy our wants directly, any movement toward E looks tempting. In producing more pizzas, society increases the satisfaction of its current wants. But there is a cost: More pizzas means fewer industrial robots. This shift of resources to consumer goods catches up with society over time because the stock of capital expands more slowly, thereby reducing potential future production. By moving toward alternative E, society chooses "more now" at the expense of "much later."

By moving toward A, society chooses to forgo current consumption, thereby freeing up resources that can be used to increase the production of capital goods. By building up its stock of capital this way, society will have greater future production and, therefore, greater future consumption. By moving toward A, society is choosing "more later" at the cost of "less now."

It is generally true that, at any point in time, a fully employed economy must sacrifice some of one good to obtain more of another good. Scarce resources prohibit such an economy from having more of both goods. Society must choose among alternatives. There is no such thing as a free pizza or a free industrial robot. Having more of one thing means having less of something else. For example, if Canadians want more spending on health care, they may have to be satisfied with less spending on education.

Production Possibilities Curve

The data presented in a production possibilities table are shown graphically as a **production possibilities curve**. Such a curve displays the different combinations of goods and services that society can potentially produce in a fully employed economy, assuming a fixed availability of supplies of resources and fixed technology. We arbitrarily represent the economy's output of capital goods (here, industrial robots) on the vertical axis and the output of consumer goods (here, pizzas) on the horizontal axis, as shown in **Figure 1-2 (Key Graph).**

Each point on the production possibilities curve represents some maximum output of the two products. The curve is a *constraint* because it shows the limit of attainable outputs. Points on the curve are attainable as long as the economy uses all of its available resources. Points lying inside the curve are also attainable, but they reflect less total output and therefore are not as desirable as points on the curve. Points inside the curve imply that the economy could have more of both industrial robots and pizzas if it achieved full employment. As you will see in Chapter 8, economic fluctuations are inherent in any economy, and when economic downturns occur, unemployment rises, characterized by points inside the production possibilities curve. One of the main goals of macroeconomics is to understand why an economy can settle inside the production possibilities curve and what policy measures should be undertaken to get the economy back to the

KEY GRAPH

FIGURE 1-2 The Production Possibilities Curve

Each point on the production possibilities curve represents some maximum combination of two products that can be produced if full employment and full production are achieved. When operating on the curve, more robots means fewer pizzas, and vice versa. Limited resources and a fixed technology make any combination of robots and pizzas lying outside the curve (such as at *W*) unattainable. Points inside the curve are attainable, but they indicate that full employment and productive efficiency are not being realized.

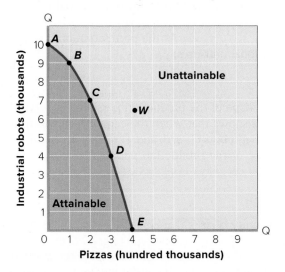

PRODUCTION ALTERNATIVES					
Type of product	A	B	C	D	E
Pizzas (in hundred thousands)	0	1	2	3	4
Robots (in thousands)	10	9	7	4	0

Quick Quiz

1. Production possibilities curve *ABCDE* is bowed out from the origin because
   a. The marginal benefit of pizzas declines as more pizzas are consumed.
   b. The curve gets steeper as we move from *E* to *A*.
   c. It reflects the law of increasing opportunity costs.
   d. Resources are scarce.

2. The marginal opportunity cost of the second unit of pizzas is
   a. 2 units of robots
   b. 3 units of robots
   c. 7 units of robots
   d. 9 units of robots

3. The total opportunity cost of 7 units of robots is
   a. 1 unit of pizzas
   b. 2 units of pizzas
   c. 3 units of pizzas
   d. 4 units of pizzas

4. All points on this production possibilities curve necessarily represent
   a. Society's optimal choice
   b. Less than full use of resources
   c. Unattainable levels of output
   d. Full employment

Answers 1.c 2.a 3.b 4.d

full employment of all its resources, particularly labour. Points lying beyond the production possibilities curve, like *W*, would represent a greater output than the output at any point on the curve. Such points are, however, unattainable with the current availability of resources and technology. In Chapter 8, we will investigate how economic growth allows productive capacity that is now unattainable to occur over time.

Law of Increasing Opportunity Costs

Figure 1-2 clearly shows that more pizzas means fewer industrial robots. The number of units of industrial robots that must be given up to obtain another unit of pizzas is, of course, the opportunity cost of that unit of pizzas.

In moving from alternative A to alternative B in Table 1-1, the cost of 1 additional unit of pizzas is 1 less unit of industrial robots. But when additional units are considered–B to C, C to D, and D to E–an important economic principle is revealed: For society, the opportunity cost of each additional unit of pizzas is greater than the opportunity cost of the preceding one. When we move from A to B, just 1 unit of industrial robots is sacrificed for 1 more unit of pizzas; but in going from B to C we sacrifice 2 additional units of industrial robots for 1 more unit of pizzas; then 3 more of industrial robots for 1 more of pizzas; and finally 4 for 1. Conversely, confirm that as we move from E to A, the cost of an additional unit of industrial robots (on average) is ¼, ⅓, ½, and 1 unit of pizzas, respectively, for the four successive moves.

Our example illustrates the **law of increasing opportunity costs**. As the production of a particular good increases, the opportunity cost of producing an additional unit rises.

SHAPE OF THE CURVE

The law of increasing opportunity costs is reflected in the shape of the production possibilities curve: The curve is bowed out from the origin of the graph. Figure 1-2 shows that when the economy moves from A to E, it must give up successively larger amounts of industrial robots (1, 2, 3, and 4) to acquire equal increments of pizzas (1, 1, 1, and 1). This is shown in the slope of the production possibilities curve, which becomes steeper as we move from A to E.

ECONOMIC EXPLANATION

The economic explanation for the law of increasing opportunity costs is that *economic resources are not completely adaptable to alternative uses.* Many resources are better at producing one type of good than at producing others. Consider land. Some land is highly suited to growing the ingredients necessary for pizza production. But, as pizza production expands, society has to start using land that is less bountiful for farming. Other land is rich in mineral deposits and therefore well suited to producing the materials needed to make industrial robots. That land will be the first land devoted to the production of industrial robots. But as society steps up the production of robots, it must use land that is less and less suited to making their components.

If we start at A and move to B in Figure 1-2, we can shift resources whose productivity is relatively high in pizza production and low in industrial robots. But as we move from B to C, C to D, and so on, resources highly productive in making pizzas become increasingly scarce. To get more pizzas, resources will be needed whose productivity in making industrial robots is relatively great. It will take increasingly more of such resources, hence greater sacrifices of industrial robots, to achieve each 1-unit increase in pizzas. This lack of perfect flexibility, or interchangeability, on the part of resources is the cause of increasing opportunity costs for society.

WORKED PROBLEM 1.2   Production Possibilities

Optimal Allocation

Of all the attainable combinations of pizzas and industrial robots on the curve in Figure 1-2, which is optimal (best)? That is, what specific quantities of resources should be allocated to pizzas and what specific quantities to industrial robots in order to maximize satisfaction?

Recall that economic decisions centre on comparisons of marginal benefit (MB) and marginal cost (MC). Any economic activity should be expanded as long as marginal benefit exceeds marginal cost and should be reduced if marginal cost exceeds marginal benefit. The optimal amount of the activity occurs where MB = MC. Society needs to make a similar assessment about its production decision.

Consider pizzas. We already know from the law of increasing opportunity costs that the marginal cost of additional units of pizzas will rise as more units are produced. At the same time, we need to recognize that the extra or marginal benefits that come from producing and consuming pizza decline with each successive

FIGURE 1-3	Optimal Allocation: MB = MC

Optimal allocation requires the expansion of a good's output until its marginal benefit (MB) and marginal cost (MC) are equal. No resources beyond that point should get allocated to the product. Here, allocative efficiency occurs when 200,000 pizzas are produced.

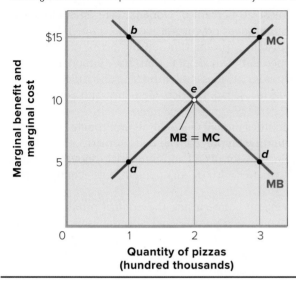

**Quantity of pizzas
(hundred thousands)**

unit of pizza. Consequently, each successive unit of pizza brings with it both increasing marginal costs and decreasing marginal benefits.

The optimal quantity of pizza production is indicated by point *e* at the intersection of the MB and MC curves: 200,000 units in Figure 1-3. Why is this amount the optimal quantity? If only 100,000 units of pizzas were produced, the marginal benefit of an extra unit of them (point *a*) would exceed its marginal cost (point *b*). In money terms, MB is $15, while MC is only $5. When society gains something worth $15 at a marginal cost of only $5, it is better off. In Figure 1-3, net gains can continue to be realized until pizza production has been increased to 200,000.

In contrast, the production of 300,000 units of pizzas is excessive. There the MC of an added unit is $15 (point *c*) and its MB is only $5 (point *d*). This means that 1 unit of pizzas is worth only $5 to society but costs society $15 to obtain. This is a losing proposition for society!

So resources are being efficiently allocated to any product when the marginal benefit and marginal cost of its output are equal (MB = MC). Suppose that by applying the above analysis to industrial robots, we find that their optimal (MB = MC) quantity is 7000. This would mean that alternative *C* (200,000 units of pizzas and 7000 units of industrial robots) on the production possibilities curve in Figure 1-2 would be optimal for this economy.

QUICK REVIEW 1.3

- The production possibilities curve illustrates (a) scarcity of resources, implied by the area of unattainable combinations of output lying outside the production possibilities curve; (b) choice among outputs, reflected in the variety of attainable combinations of goods lying along the curve; (c) opportunity cost, illustrated by the downward slope of the curve; and (d) the law of increasing opportunity costs, reflected in the bowed-outward shape of the curve.

- A comparison of marginal benefits and marginal costs is needed to determine the best or optimal output mix on a production possibilities curve.

1.8 / Unemployment, Growth, and the Future

LO1.8 Explain how economic growth and international trade increase consumption possibilities.

In the depths of the Great Depression of the 1930s, almost 20 percent of workers were unemployed and one quarter of Canadian production capacity was idle. Subsequent downturns have been much less severe. During the relatively deep 2008–2009 recession, for instance, production fell by a comparably smaller 2.8 percent and the unemployment rate peaked at 8.7 percent. Almost all nations have experienced widespread unemployment and unused production capacity from business downturns at one time or another. Since 2000, for example, many nations–including Argentina, Japan, Mexico, Germany, and South Korea–have had economic downturns and unemployment.

How do these realities relate to the production possibilities model? Our analysis and conclusions change if we relax the assumption that all available resources are fully employed. The five alternatives in Table 1-1 represent maximum outputs; they illustrate the combinations of pizzas and industrial robots that can be produced when the economy is operating at full employment. With unemployment, this economy would produce less than each alternative shown in the table.

Graphically, we represent situations of unemployment by points inside the original production possibilities curve (reproduced here in Figure 1-4). Point *U* is one such point. Here the economy is falling short of the various maximum combinations of pizzas and industrial robots represented by the points on the production possibilities curve. The arrows in Figure 1-4 indicate three possible paths back to full employment. A move toward full employment would yield a greater output of one or both products.

A Growing Economy

When we drop the assumptions that the quantity and quality of resources and technology are fixed, the production possibilities curve shifts position and the potential maximum output of the economy changes.

FIGURE 1-4   **Unemployment, Productive Inefficiency, and the Production Possibilities Curve**

Any point inside the production possibilities curve, such as *U*, represents unemployment or a failure to achieve productive efficiency. The arrows indicate that, by realizing full employment and productive efficiency, the economy could operate on the curve. This means it could produce more of one or both products than it is producing at point *U*.

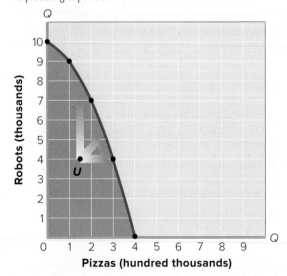

FIGURE 1-5	Economic Growth and the Production Possibilities Curve

The increase in supplies of resources, the improvements in resource quality, and the technological advances that occur in a dynamic economy move the production possibilities curve outward and to the right, allowing the economy to have larger quantities of both types of goods.

PRODUCTION ALTERNATIVES					
Type of product	A′	B′	C′	D′	E′
Pizzas (in hundred thousands)	0	2	4	6	8
Robots (in thousands)	14	12	9	5	0

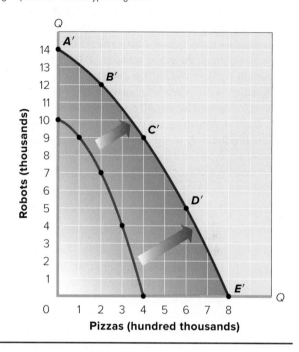

INCREASES IN FACTOR SUPPLIES

Although factor supplies are fixed at any specific moment, they change over time via more education and training. Historically, the economy's stock of capital has increased at a significant, though unsteady, rate. And although some of our energy and mineral resources are being depleted, new sources are also being discovered. The development of irrigation systems, for example, adds to the supply of arable land.

The net result of these increased supplies of the factors of production is the ability to produce more of both consumer goods and capital goods. Thus, twenty years from now the production possibilities may supersede those shown in Table 1-1. The new production possibilities might look like those in the table in Figure 1-5. The greater abundance of resources will result in a greater potential output of one or both products at each alternative. The economy will have achieved economic growth in the form of expanded potential output. Thus, when an increase in the quantity or quality of resources occurs, the production possibilities curve shifts outward and to the right, as illustrated by the move from the inner curve to curve A′B′C′D′E′ in Figure 1-5. This sort of shift represents growth of economic capacity that, when used, means **economic growth**: a larger total output.

ADVANCES IN TECHNOLOGY

An advancing technology brings both new and better goods and improved ways of producing them. For now, let's think of technological advance as being only improvements in the methods of production–for example, the introduction of computerized systems to manage inventories and schedule production. These advances alter our previous discussion of the economic problem by allowing society to produce more goods with available resources. As with increases in resource supplies, technological advances make possible the production of more industrial robots *and* more pizzas.

A real-world example of improved technology is the recent surge of new innovations relating to computers, communications, and biotechnology. Technological advances have dropped the prices of computers

CONSIDER THIS   Women, the Workforce, and Production Possibilities

We have seen that more and better-quality factors of production and improved technology shift a nation's production possibilities curve outward. An example of more resources is the large increase in the number of employed women in Canada within the past five decades: 62 percent of adult Canadian women work full-time or part-time in paid jobs today, compared to only 40 percent in 1965.

Over recent decades, women have greatly increased their productivity in the workplace, mostly by becoming better educated and professionally trained. As a result, they can earn higher wages. Because those higher wages have increased the opportunity cost—the forgone wage earnings—of staying at home, women have substituted employment in the labour market for the now more "expensive" traditional home activities. This substitution has been particularly pronounced among married women. Along with other factors, such as changing attitudes and expanded job access, the rising earnings of women have produced a substantial increase in the number of women workers in Canada. This increase in the quantity of available resources has helped push the Canadian production possibilities curve outward.

and greatly increased their speed. Improved software has greatly increased the everyday usefulness of computers. Cellphones and the Internet have increased communications capacity, enhancing production and improving the efficiency of markets. Advances in biotechnology have resulted in important agricultural and medical discoveries. These and other new and improved technologies have contributed to both global and Canadian economic growth (outward shifts of the nation's production possibilities curve).

Conclusion: Economic growth is the result of (1) increases in supplies of factors of production, (2) improvements in factor quality, and (3) technological advances. The consequence of growth is that a full-employment economy can enjoy a greater output of both consumption goods and capital goods. While static, no-growth economies must sacrifice some of one good to obtain more of another, dynamic, growing economies can have larger quantities of both goods. In Chapter 8 we will go into much more detail about the causes of economic growth and Canada's growth record.

Present Choices and Future Possibilities

An economy's current chosen position on its production possibilities curve helps determine the future location of that curve. Let's designate the two axes of the production possibilities curve as *goods for the future* and *goods for the present*, as in Figure 1-6. Goods for the future are such things as capital goods, research and education, and preventive medicine. They increase the quantity and quality of property resources, enlarge the stock of technological information, and improve the quality of human resources. As we have already seen, goods for the future, such as capital goods, are the ingredients of economic growth. Goods for the present are consumer goods, such as food, clothing, and entertainment.

Now consider two hypothetical economies, Presentville and Futureville, which are initially identical in every respect except one: Presentville's current chosen position on its production possibilities curve strongly favours present goods over future goods. Point *P* in Figure 1-6a indicates that choice. It is located quite far down the curve to the right, indicating a high priority for goods for the present, at the expense of fewer goods for the future. Futureville, in contrast, makes a current choice that stresses larger amounts of future goods and smaller amounts of present goods, as shown by point *F* in Figure 1-6b.

Now, other things equal, we can expect Futureville's future production possibilities curve to be farther to the right than Presentville's future production possibilities curve. By currently choosing an output more favourable to technological advances and to increases in the quantity and quality of resources, Futureville will achieve greater economic growth than Presentville. In terms of capital goods, Futureville is choosing to make larger current additions to its "national factory" by devoting more of its current output to capital than Presentville. The payoff from this choice for Futureville is greater future production capacity and economic growth. The opportunity cost is fewer consumer goods in the present for Futureville to enjoy.

KEY GRAPH

FIGURE 1-6   **Present Choices and Future Locations of a Production Possibilities Curve**

(a) Presentville's current choice to produce more present goods and fewer future goods, as represented by point *P*, will result in a modest outward shift of the production possibilities curve in the future. (b) Futureville's current choice of producing fewer present goods and more future goods, as depicted by point *F*, will lead to a greater outward shift of the production possibilities curve in the future

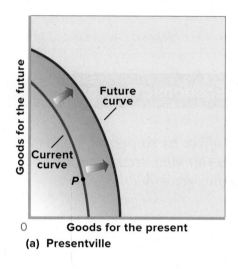

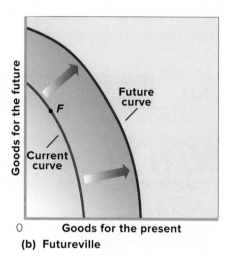

Is Futureville's choice "better" than Presentville's? That we cannot say. The different outcomes simply reflect different preferences and priorities in the two countries. But each country will have to live with the economic consequences of its choice.

A Qualification: International Trade

Production possibilities analysis implies that an individual nation is limited to the combinations of output indicated by its production possibilities curve. But we must modify this principle when international specialization and trade exist.

You will see in later chapters that an economy can circumvent, through international specialization and trade, the output limits imposed by its domestic production possibilities curve. Under international specialization and trade, each nation first specializes in the production of those items for which it has the lowest opportunity costs (due to an abundance of the necessary resources). Countries then engage in international trade, with each country exchanging the items that it can produce at the lowest opportunity costs for the items that other countries can produce at the lowest opportunity costs.

International specialization and trade allow a nation to get more of a desired good at less sacrifice of some other good. Rather than sacrifice three units of domestically produced robots to get a third unit of domestically produced pizza, as in Table 1-1, a nation that engages in international specialization and trade might be able to do much better. If it specializes in robots while another country specializes in pizza, then it may be able to obtain the third unit of pizza by trading only two units of domestically produced robots for one unit of foreign-produced pizza. Specialization and trade have the same effect as having more and better resources or discovering improved production techniques; both increase the quantities of capital and consumer goods available to society. Expansion of domestic production possibilities and international trade are two separate routes for obtaining greater output. Much more will be said about international trade in Chapter 17.

- Unemployment causes an economy to operate at a point inside its production possibilities curve.
- Increases in resource supplies, improvements in resource quality, and technological advances cause economic growth, which is depicted as an outward shift of the production possibilities curve.

- An economy's present choice of capital and consumer goods helps determine the future location of its production possibilities curve.
- International specialization and trade enable a nation to obtain more goods than its production possibilities curve would indicate.

The **LAST** WORD   Pitfalls to Sound Economic Reasoning

Because they affect us so personally, we often have difficulty thinking accurately and objectively about economic issues.

Here are some common pitfalls to avoid in successfully applying the economic perspective.

Biases Most people bring a bundle of biases and preconceptions to the field of economics. For example, some might think that corporate profits are excessive or that lending money is always superior to borrowing money. Others might believe that government is necessarily less efficient than businesses, or that more government regulation is always better than less. Biases cloud thinking and interfere with objective analysis. All of us must be willing to shed biases and preconceptions that are not supported by facts.

Loaded Terminology The economic terminology used in newspapers and broadcast media is sometimes emotionally biased, or loaded. The writer or spokesperson may have a cause to promote or an axe to grind and may slant comments accordingly. High profits may be labelled "obscene," low wages may be called "exploitive," or self-interested behaviour may be identified as "greed." Government workers may be referred to as "mindless bureaucrats" and those favouring stronger government regulations may be called "socialists." To analyze economic issues objectively, you must be prepared to reject or discount such terminology.

Fallacy of Composition Another pitfall in economic thinking is the assumption that what is true for one individual or part of a whole is necessarily true for a group of individuals or the whole. This is a logical fallacy called the *fallacy of composition;* the assumption is not correct. A statement that is valid for an individual or part is not necessarily valid for the larger group or whole. A noneconomic analogy might be that you can see the action better if you leap to your feet to see an outstanding play at a football game. But if everyone leaps to their feet at the same time, nobody—including you—will have a better view than when all remained seated.

Here are two economic examples: An individual shareholder can sell shares of, say, BlackBerry Limited stock without affecting the price of the stock. The individual's sale will not noticeably reduce the share price because the sale is a negligible fraction of the total shares of BlackBerry being bought and sold. But if all the BlackBerry shareholders decide to sell their shares on the same day, the market will be flooded with shares and the stock price will fall precipitously. Similarly, a single cattle ranch can increase its revenue by expanding the size of its livestock herd. The extra cattle will not affect the price of cattle when they are brought to market. But if all ranchers as a group expand their herds, the total output of cattle will increase so much that the price of cattle will decline when the cattle are sold. If the price reduction is relatively large, ranchers as a group might find that their income has fallen despite their having sold a greater number of cattle because the fall in price overwhelms the increase in quantity.

Post Hoc Fallacy You must think very carefully before concluding that because event A precedes event B, A is the cause of B. This kind of faulty reasoning is known as the *post hoc, ergo propter hoc,* or "after this, therefore because of this" fallacy. To give another noneconomic example: The Calgary Flames hire a new coach and the team's record improves. Is the new coach the cause? Maybe. Perhaps the presence of more experienced and talented players or an easier schedule is the true cause. Another example is that the rooster crows before dawn, but does not cause the sunrise.

Correlation and Causation Do not confuse correlation, or connection, with causation. Correlation between two events or two sets of data indicates only that they are associated in some systematic and dependable way. For example, we may find that when variable X increases, Y also increases. But this correlation does not necessarily mean that there is causation—that increases in X cause increases in Y. The relationship could be purely coincidental or dependent on some other factor, Z, not included in the analysis.

Here is an example: Economists have found a positive correlation between education and income. In general, people with more education earn higher incomes than those with less education. Common sense suggests that education is the cause and higher incomes are the effect; more education implies a more knowledgeable and productive worker, and such workers receive larger salaries.

But causation could also partly run the other way. People with higher incomes could buy more education, just as they buy more furniture and steaks. Or is part of the relationship explainable in still other ways? Are education and income correlated because the characteristics required for succeeding in education—ability and motivation—are the same ones required to be a productive and highly paid worker? If so, then people with those traits will probably both obtain more education and earn higher incomes. But greater education will not be the sole cause of the higher income.

Question

Studies indicate that married men on average earn more income than unmarried men of the same age and education level. Why must we be cautious in concluding that marriage is the cause and higher income is the effect?

Chapter Summary

LO1.1 LIST THE TEN KEY CONCEPTS TO RETAIN FOR A LIFETIME.

- The 10 key concepts can be divided into three categories: (a) concepts that pertain to the individual (Facing Trade-offs, Opportunity Costs, Choosing a Little More or Less, and The Influence of Incentives); (b) concepts that explain the interaction among individuals (Specialization and Trade, The Effectiveness of Markets, and The Role of Governments); and (c) concepts that deal with the economy as a whole and the standard of living (Production and the Standard of Living, Money and Inflation, and Inflation–Unemployment Trade-off).

LO1.2 DEFINE ECONOMICS AND THE FEATURES OF THE ECONOMIC WAY OF THINKING.

- Economics is the social science that examines how individuals, institutions, and society make choices under conditions of scarcity. Central to economics is the idea of opportunity cost: the value of the good, service, or time forgone to obtain something else.

- The economic perspective includes three elements: scarcity and choice, purposeful behaviour, and marginal analysis. It sees individuals and institutions making rational decisions based on comparisons of marginal benefits and marginal costs.

LO1.3 DESCRIBE THE ROLE OF ECONOMIC THEORY IN ECONOMICS.

- Economists employ the scientific method, in which they form and test hypotheses of cause-and-effect relationships to generate theories, principles, and laws. Economists often combine principles and laws into representations called models.

LO1.4 DISTINGUISH MICROECONOMICS FROM MACROECONOMICS, AND POSITIVE ECONOMICS FROM NORMATIVE ECONOMICS.

- Microeconomics examines specific economic units or institutions. Macroeconomics looks at the economy as a whole or its major aggregates.

- Positive economics deals with facts; normative economics reflects value judgments.

LO1.5   EXPLAIN THE INDIVIDUAL'S ECONOMIC PROBLEM AND HOW TRADE-OFFS, OPPORTUNITY COSTS, AND ATTAINABLE COMBINATIONS CAN BE ILLUSTRATED WITH BUDGET LINES.

- Individuals face an economic problem. Because their wants exceed their incomes, they must decide what to purchase and what to forgo. Society also faces the economic problem. Societal wants exceed the available resources necessary to fulfill them. Society, therefore, must decide what to produce and what to forgo.

- Graphically, a budget line (or budget constraint) illustrates the economic problem for individuals. The line shows the various combinations of two products that a consumer can purchase with a specific money income, given the prices of the two products.

LO1.6   LIST THE CATEGORIES OF SCARCE RESOURCES AND DELINEATE THE ECONOMIC PROBLEM.

- Economic resources are inputs into the production process and can be classified as land, labour, capital, and entrepreneurial ability. Economic resources are also known as factors of production or inputs.

- Economists illustrate society's economic problem through production possibilities analysis. Production possibilities tables and curves show the different combinations of goods and services that can be produced in a fully employed economy assuming that resource quantity, resource quality, and technology are fixed.

LO1.7   APPLY THE CONCEPTS OF PRODUCTION POSSIBILITIES ANALYSIS, INCREASING OPPORTUNITY COSTS, AND ECONOMIC GROWTH.

- An economy that is fully employed and thus operating on its production possibilities curve must sacrifice the output of some types of goods and services to increase the production of others. The gain in one type of good or service is always accompanied by an opportunity cost in the form of the loss in some other type of good or service.

- Because resources are not equally productive in all possible uses, shifting resources from one use to another creates increasing opportunity costs. The production of additional units of one product requires the sacrifice of increasing amounts of the other product.

- The optimal (best) point on the production possibilities curve represents the most desirable mix of goods and is determined by expanding the production of each good until its marginal benefit (MB) equals its marginal cost (MC).

LO1.8   EXPLAIN HOW ECONOMIC GROWTH AND INTERNATIONAL TRADE INCREASE CONSUMPTION POSSIBILITIES.

- Over time, technological advances and increases in the quantity and quality of resources enable the economy to produce more of all goods and services—that is, to experience economic growth.

- Society's choice as to the mix of consumer goods and capital goods in current output is a major determinant of the future location of the production possibilities curve and thus of the extent of economic growth.

- International trade enables a nation to obtain more goods from its limited resources than its production possibilities curve would indicate.

Terms and Concepts

economics	macroeconomics	investment
economic perspective	aggregate	entrepreneurial ability
scarcity	positive economics	entrepreneurs
opportunity cost	normative economics	factors of production
utility	economic problem	scarce resources
marginal analysis	budget line	consumer goods
scientific method	economic resources	capital goods
economic principle	land	production possibilities curve
other-things-equal assumption	labour	law of increasing opportunity costs
microeconomics	capital	economic growth

Discussion Questions

1. What is an opportunity cost? How does the idea relate to the definition of economics? Which of the following decisions would entail the greater opportunity cost: allocating a square block in the heart of Toronto for a surface parking lot or allocating a square block at the edge of a typical suburb for such a lot? Explain.   [LO1.2]

2. Cite three examples of recent decisions that you made in which you (at least implicitly) weighed marginal cost and marginal benefit. [LO1.2]

3. What is meant by the term *utility* and how does the idea relate to purposeful behaviour? [LO1.2]

4. What are the key elements of the scientific method and how does this method relate to economic principles and laws? [LO1.3]

5. State (a) a positive economic statement of your choice, and then (b) a normative economic statement relating to your first statement. [LO1.4]

6. How does the slope of a budget line illustrate opportunity costs and trade-offs? How does a budget line illustrate scarcity and the effect of limited incomes? [LO1.4]

7. What are economic resources? What categories do economists use to classify them? Why are resources also called factors of production? Why are they called inputs? [LO1.6]

8. Why is money not considered to be a capital resource in economics? Why is entrepreneurial ability considered a category of economic resource, distinct from labour? What are the major functions of the entrepreneur? [LO1.6]

9. Specify and explain the typical shapes of marginal benefit and marginal cost curves. How are these curves used to determine the optimal allocation of resources to a particular product? If current output is such that marginal cost exceeds marginal benefit, should more or fewer resources be allocated to this product? Explain. [LO1.7]

10. Suppose that, on the basis of a nation's production possibilities curve, an economy must sacrifice 10,000 pizzas domestically to get the one additional industrial robot it desires, but that it can get the robot from another country in exchange for 9000 pizzas. Relate this information to the following statement: *Through international specialization and trade, a nation can reduce its opportunity cost of obtaining goods and thus move outside its production possibilities curve.* [LO1.8]

Review Questions

1. Match each term with the correct definition. [LO1.2]

economics

opportunity cost

marginal analysis

utility

a. The next-best thing that must be forgone in order to produce one more unit of a given product.

b. The pleasure, happiness, or satisfaction obtained from consuming a good or service.

c. The social science concerned with how individuals, institutions, and society make optimal (best) choices under conditions of scarcity.

d. Making choices based on comparing marginal benefits with marginal costs.

2. Indicate whether each of the following statements applies to microeconomics or macroeconomics: [LO1.3]

a. The unemployment rate in Canada was 6.8 percent in September 2014.

b. A software firm discharged fifteen workers last month and transferred the work to India.

c. An unexpected freeze in central Florida reduced the citrus crop and caused the price of oranges to rise.

d. Canadian output, adjusted for inflation, increased by 1.9 percent in 2013.

e. Last week ScotiaBank lowered its interest rate on business loans by one-half of one percentage point.

f. The consumer price index rose by 0.9 percent from January 2013 to December 2013.

3. Suppose that you initially have $100 to spend on books or movie tickets. The books start off costing $25 each and the movie tickets start off costing $10 each. For each of the following situations, would the attainable set of combinations that you can afford increase or decrease? [LO1.5]

a. Your budget increases from $100 to $150 while the prices stay the same.

b. Your budget remains $100, the price of books remains $25, but the price of movie tickets rises to $20.

c. Your budget remains $100, the price of movie tickets remains $10, but the price of a book falls to $15.

4. Suppose that you are given a $100 budget at work that can be spent only on two items: staplers and pens. If staplers cost $10 each and pens cost $2.50 each, then the opportunity cost of purchasing one stapler is [LO1.5]

a. 10 pens

b. 5 pens

c. No pens

d. 4 pens

5. For each of the following situations involving marginal cost (MC) and marginal benefit (MB), indicate whether it would be best to produce more, fewer, or the current number of units. [LO1.5]

a. 3000 units at which MC = $10 and MB = $13

b. 11 units at which MC = $4 and MB = $3

c. 43,277 units at which MC = $99 and MB = $99

d. 82 units at which MC < MB

e. 5 units at which MB < MC

6. Explain how (if at all) each of the following events affects the location of a country's production possibilities curve: [LO1.7]

a. The quality of education increases.

b. The number of unemployed workers increases.

c. A new technique improves the efficiency of extracting copper from ore.

d. A devastating earthquake destroys numerous production facilities.

7. What are the two major ways in which an economy can grow and push out its production possibilities curve?   [LO1.8]

a. Better weather and nicer cars

b. Higher taxes and lower spending

c. Increases in resource supplies and advances in technology

d. Decreases in scarcity and advances in auditing

Problems

1. Potatoes cost Janice $1 per kilogram, and she has $5.00 that she could possibly spend on potatoes or other items. If she feels that the first kilogram of potatoes is worth $1.50, the second kilogram is worth $1.14, the third kilogram is worth $1.05, and all subsequent kilograms are worth $0.30, how many kilograms of potatoes will she purchase? What if she only had $2 to spend?   [LO1.2]

2. Pham can work as many or as few hours as she wants at the university bookstore for $9 per hour. But due to her hectic schedule, she has just 15 hours per week that she can spend working either at the bookstore or at other potential jobs. One potential job, at a café, will pay her $12 per hour for up to 6 hours per week. She has another job offer at a garage that will pay her $10 an hour for up to 5 hours per week. And she has a potential job at a daycare centre that will pay her $8.50 per hour for as many hours as she can work. If her goal is to maximize the amount of money she can make each week, how many hours will she work at the bookstore?   [LO1.2]

3. Suppose you won $15 on a lottery ticket at the local 7-Eleven and decided to spend all the winnings on candy bars and bags of peanuts. Candy bars cost $0.75 each while bags of peanuts cost $1.50 each.   [LO1.6]

a. Construct a table showing the alternative combinations of the two products that are available.

b. Plot the data in your table as a budget line in a graph. What is the slope of the budget line? What is the opportunity cost of one more candy bar? Of one more bag of peanuts? Do these opportunity costs rise, fall, or remain constant as each additional unit of the product is purchased?

c. Does the budget line tell you which of the available combinations of candy bars and bags of peanuts to buy?

d. Suppose that you had won $30 on your ticket, not $15. Show the $30 budget line in your diagram. Has the number of available combinations increased or decreased?

4. Suppose that you are on a desert island and possess exactly 20 coconuts. Your neighbour, Friday, is a fisherman, and he is willing to trade 2 fish for every 1 coconut that you are willing to give him. Another neighbour, Kwame, is also a fisherman, and he is willing to trade 3 fish for every 1 coconut.   [LO1.6]

a. On a single figure, draw budget lines for trading with Friday and for trading with Kwame. (Put coconuts on the vertical axis.)

b. What is the slope of the budget line from trading with Friday?

c. What is the slope of the budget line from trading with Kwame?

d. Which budget line features a larger set of attainable combinations of coconuts and fish?

e. If you are going to trade coconuts for fish, would you rather trade with Friday or with Kwame?

5. Below is a production possibilities table for consumer goods (automobiles) and capital goods (forklifts).   [LO1.7]

a. Show these data graphically. Upon what specific assumptions is this production possibilities curve based?

b. If the economy is at point C, what is the cost of one more automobile? Of one more forklift? Which characteristic of the production possibilities curve reflects the law of increasing opportunity costs, its shape or its length?

c. If the economy characterized by this production possibilities table and curve were producing 3 automobiles and 20 forklifts, what could you conclude about its use of its available resources?

d. Is production at a point outside the production possibilities curve currently possible? Could a future advance in technology allow production beyond the current production possibilities curve? Could international trade allow a country to consume beyond its current production possibilities curve?

PRODUCTION ALTERNATIVES

Type of production	A	B	C	D	E
Automobiles	0	2	4	6	8
Forklifts	30	27	21	12	0

6. Look at Figure 1-3. Suppose that the cost of cheese falls, so that the marginal cost of producing pizza decreases. Will the MC curve shift up or down? Will the optimal amount of pizza increase or decrease? [LO1.7]

7. Referring to the table in Problem 5, suppose that improvement occurs in the technology of producing forklifts but not in the technology of producing automobiles. Draw the new production possibilities curve. Now assume that a technological advance occurs in producing automobiles but not in producing forklifts. Draw the new production possibilities curve. Now draw a production possibilities curve that reflects technological improvement in the production of both goods. [LO1.8]

8. On average, households in China save 40 percent of their annual income each year, whereas households in Canada save less than 5 percent. Production possibilities are growing at roughly 9 percent annually in China and 3.5 percent in Canada. Use graphical analysis of *present goods* versus *future goods* to explain the differences in growth rates. [LO1.8]

Appendix to Chapter 1

LOA1.1 Understand graphs, curves, and slopes as they relate to economics.

If you glance quickly through this text, you will find many graphs. Some seem simple, while others are more complicated. All are included to help you visualize and understand economic relationships. Physicists and chemists sometimes illustrate their theories by building arrangements of multicoloured wooden balls, representing protons, neutrons, and electrons, which are held in proper relation to one another by wires or sticks. Economists use graphs to illustrate their models. By understanding these illustrations you can more readily make sense of economic relationships.

Construction of a Graph

A *graph* is a visual representation of the relationship between two economic quantities or variables. Figure A1-1 is a hypothetical illustration showing the relationship between income and consumption for the economy as a whole. Without even studying economics, we would logically expect that people would buy more goods and services when their incomes go up. Thus, it is not surprising to find in Figure A1-1 that total consumption in the economy increases as total income increases.

The information in Figure A1-1 is expressed both graphically and in table form. Here is how it is done: We want to show graphically how consumption changes as income changes. We therefore represent income on the **horizontal axis** of the graph and consumption on the **vertical axis**.

Now we arrange the vertical and horizontal scales of the graph to reflect the ranges of values of consumption and income, and mark the scales in convenient increments. As you can see in Figure A1-1, the values marked on the scales cover all the values in the table. The values on both axes are indicated in $100 increments.

Because the graph has two dimensions, each point within it represents an income value and its associated consumption value. To find a point that represents one of the five income–consumption combinations in the table, we draw straight lines from the appropriate values on the vertical and horizontal axes. For example, to plot point c ($200 income, $150 consumption), draw straight lines up from the horizontal (income) axis at $200 and across from the vertical (consumption) axis at $150. These straight

FIGURE A1-1   The Relationship Between Income and Consumption

Two sets of data that are positively or directly related, such as consumption and income, graph as an upsloping line.

Income per week	Consumption per week	Point
$ 0	$ 50	a
100	100	b
200	150	c
300	200	d
400	250	e

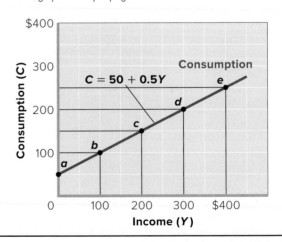

lines intersect at point *c*, which represents this particular income-consumption combination. You should verify that the other income-consumption combinations shown in the table are properly located on the graph. Finally, by assuming that the same general relationship between income and consumption prevails for all other incomes, we draw a line or smooth curve to connect these points. That line or curve represents the income-consumption relationship.

If the curve is a straight line, as in Figure A1-1, we say that the relationship is *linear*. (It is permissible, and even customary, to refer to straight lines in graphs as "curves.")

Direct and Inverse Relationships

The line in Figure A1-1 slopes upward to the right, depicting a direct relationship between income and consumption. By a **direct relationship** (or **positive relationship**) we mean that two variables–in this case, consumption and income–change in the *same* direction. An increase in consumption is associated with an increase in income; a decrease in consumption accompanies a decrease in income. When two sets of data are positively or directly related, they always graph as an *upsloping* line, as in Figure A1-1.

In contrast, two sets of data may be inversely related. Consider Figure A1-2, which shows the relationship between the price of basketball tickets and game attendance at Informed University (IU). Here we have an **inverse relationship** (or negative relationship) because the two variables change in *opposite* directions. When ticket prices decrease, attendance increases. When ticket prices increase, attendance decreases. The six data points in the table are plotted in the graph. Observe that an inverse relationship always graphs as a *downsloping* line.

Dependent and Independent Variables

Although it is not always easy, economists seek to determine which variable is the *cause* and which is the *effect*. Or, more formally, they seek the independent variable and the dependent variable. The **independent variable** is the cause or source; it is the variable that changes first. The **dependent variable** is the effect or outcome; it is the variable that changes because of the change in the independent variable. As in our income-consumption example, income generally is the independent variable and consumption the dependent variable. Income causes consumption to be what it is rather than the other way around. Similarly, ticket prices (set in advance of the season and printed on the ticket) determine attendance at Informed University basketball games; attendance at games does not determine the printed ticket prices for those games. Ticket price is the independent variable, and the quantity of tickets purchased is the dependent variable.

You may recall from your high school courses that mathematicians put the independent variable (cause) on the horizontal axis and the dependent variable (effect) on the vertical axis. Economists are less tidy; their graphing of independent and dependent variables is more arbitrary. Their conventional graphing of the income-consumption relationship is consistent with mathematical convention but economists put price and cost data on the vertical axis. Hence, economists' graphing of IU's ticket price-attendance data differs from the normal mathematical procedure. This does not present a problem, but we want you to be aware of this fact to avoid any possible confusion.

Other Things Equal

Our simple two-variable graphs purposely ignore many other factors that might affect the amount of consumption occurring at each income level or the number of people who attend IU basketball games at each possible ticket price. When economists plot the relationship between any two variables, they employ the *ceteris paribus* (other things equal) assumption. Thus, in Figure A1-1, all factors other than income that might affect the amount of consumption are held constant. Similarly, in Figure A1-2, all factors other than ticket price that might influence attendance at IU basketball games are assumed constant. In reality, other things are not equal; they often change and when they do, the relationship represented in our two tables and graphs will change. Specifically, the lines we have plotted will *shift* to new locations.

Consider a stock market "crash." The dramatic drop in the value of stocks might cause people to feel less wealthy and therefore less willing to consume at each level of income. The result might be a downward shift of the consumption line. To see this, you should plot a new consumption line in Figure A1-1, assuming that consumption is, say, $20 less at each income level. Note that the relationship remains direct; the line merely shifts downward to reflect less consumption spending at each income level.

Similarly, factors other than ticket prices might affect IU game attendance. If IU loses most of its games, attendance at IU games might fall at each ticket price. To see this, redraw the graph in Figure A1-2, assuming that 2000 fewer fans attend IU games at each ticket price.

Slope of a Line

Lines can be described in terms of their slopes and their intercepts. The **slope of a straight line** is the ratio of

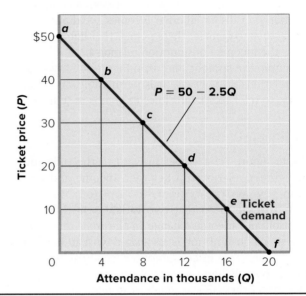

FIGURE A1-2   **The Relationship Between Ticket Prices and Attendance**

Two sets of data that are negatively or inversely related, such as ticket price and the attendance at basketball games, graph as a downsloping line.

Ticket price	Attendance, thousands	Point
$50	0	a
40	4	b
30	8	c
20	12	d
10	16	e
0	20	f

the vertical change (the rise or drop) to the horizontal change (the run) between any two points of the line—or rise over run.

POSITIVE SLOPE

Between point c and point d in Figure A1-1 the rise or vertical change (the change in consumption) is +$50 and the run or horizontal change (the change in income) is +$100. Therefore

$$\text{Slope} = \frac{\text{vertical change}}{\text{horizontal change}} = \frac{+50}{+100} = \frac{1}{2} = 0.5$$

Note that our slope of ½ or 0.5 is positive because consumption and income change in the same direction; that is, consumption and income are directly or positively related.

The slope of 0.5 tells us that there will be $0.50 increase in consumption for every $1 increase in income. Similarly, there will be a $0.50 decrease in consumption for every $1 decrease in income.

NEGATIVE SLOPE

Between any two of the identified points in Figure A1-2—say, point c and point d—the vertical change is −10 (the drop) and the horizontal change is +4 (the run). Therefore

$$\text{Slope} = \frac{\text{vertical change}}{\text{horizontal change}} = \frac{-10}{+4} = -2\frac{1}{2} = -2.5$$

This slope is negative because ticket price and attendance have an inverse or negative relationship.

Note that on the horizontal axis attendance is stated in thousands of people. So the slope of −10/+4 or −2.5 means that lowering the price by $10 will increase attendance by 4000 people. That ratio also implies that a $2.50 price reduction will increase attendance by 1000 people.

SLOPES AND MEASUREMENT UNITS

The slope of a line will be affected by the choice of units for either variable. If, in our ticket-price illustration, we had chosen to measure attendance in individual people, our horizontal change would have been 4000 and the slope would have been

$$\text{Slope} = \frac{-10}{+4000} = \frac{-1}{+400} = -0.0025$$

The slope depends on the units by which variables are measured.

SLOPES AND MARGINAL ANALYSIS

Recall that economics largely deals with changes from the status quo. The concept of slope is important in economics because it reflects marginal changes—those involving one more (or one less) unit. For example, in Figure A1-1 the 0.5 slope shows that $0.50 of extra or marginal consumption is associated with each $1 change in income. In this example, people collectively will consume $0.50 of any $1

| **FIGURE A1-3** | **Infinite and Zero Slopes** |

(a) A line parallel to the vertical axis has an infinite slope. Here, purchases of digital cameras remain the same no matter what happens to the price of bananas.

(b) A line parallel to the horizontal axis has a slope of zero. In this case, consumption remains the same no matter what happens to the divorce rate. In both parts (a) and (b), the two variables are totally unrelated to each other.

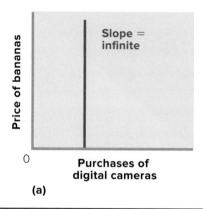

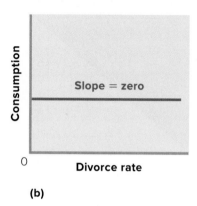

(a)

(b)

increase in their incomes and reduce their consumption by $0.50 for each $1 decline in income.

INFINITE AND ZERO SLOPES

Many variables are unrelated, or independent of one another. For example, the quantity of digital cameras purchased is not related to the price of bananas. In Figure A1-3a we represent the price of bananas on the vertical axis and the quantity of digital cameras demanded on the horizontal axis. The graph of their relationship is the line parallel to the vertical axis. The line's vertical slope indicates that the same quantity of cameras is purchased no matter what the price of bananas. The slope of the vertical line is *infinite*.

Similarly, aggregate consumption is completely unrelated to the nation's divorce rate. In Figure A1-3b we put consumption on the vertical axis and the divorce rate on the horizontal axis. The line parallel to the horizontal axis represents this lack of relatedness. This line has a slope of *zero*.

Vertical Intercept

A line can be positioned on a graph (without plotting points) if we know its slope and its vertical intercept. We have already discussed the slope. The **vertical intercept** of a line is the point where the line meets the vertical axis. In Figure A1-1 the intercept is $50. This intercept means that if current income were zero, consumers would still spend $50. They might do this through borrowing or by selling some of their assets. Similarly, the $50 vertical intercept in Figure A1-2 shows that at a $50 ticket price, IU's basketball team would be playing in an empty arena.

Equation of a Linear Relationship

If we know the vertical intercept and slope, we can describe a line succinctly in equation form. In its general form, the equation of a straight line is

$$y = a + bx$$

where y = dependent variable

a = vertical intercept

b = slope of line

x = independent variable

For our income-consumption example, if C represents consumption (the dependent variable) and Y represents income (the independent variable), we can write $C = a + bY$. By substituting the known values of the intercept and the slope, we get

$$C = 50 + 0.5Y$$

This equation also allows us to determine the amount of consumption C at any specific level of income. You should use it to confirm that at the $250 income level, consumption is $175.

When economists reverse mathematical convention by putting the independent variable on the vertical axis and the dependent variable on the horizontal axis, then y stands for the independent variable, rather than the dependent variable, in the general form. We noted previously that this case is relevant for our IU ticket price–attendance data. If P represents the ticket price

KEY GRAPH

FIGURE A1-4   Determining the Slopes of Curves

The slope of a non-linear curve changes from point to point on the curve. The slope at any point (say, *B*) can be determined by drawing a straight line that is tangent to that point (line *bb'*) and calculating the slope of that line.

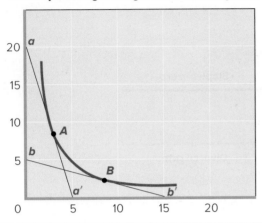

(independent variable) and *Q* represents attendance (dependent variable), their relationship is given by

$$P = 50 - 2.5Q$$

where the vertical intercept is 50 and the negative slope is −2½ or −2.5. Knowing the value of *P* lets us solve for *Q*, our dependent variable. You should use this equation to predict IU ticket sales when the ticket price is $15.

Slope of a Non-linear Curve

We now move from the simple world of linear relationships (straight lines) to the more complex world of non-linear relationships (curvy line). The slope of a straight line is the same at all its points. The slope of a line representing a non-linear relationship changes from one point to another. Such lines are always referred to as *curves*.

Consider the downsloping curve in Figure A1-4. Its slope is negative throughout, but the curve flattens as we move down along it. Thus, its slope constantly changes; the curve has a different slope at each point.

To measure the slope at a specific point, we draw a straight line tangent to the curve at that point. A straight line is *tangent* at a point if it touches, but does not intersect, the curve at that point. Thus line *aa'* is tangent to the curve in Figure A1-4 at point *A*. The slope of the curve at that point is equal to the slope of the tangent line. Specifically, the total vertical change (drop) in the tangent line *aa'* is −20 and the total horizontal change (run) is +5. Because the slope of the tangent line *aa'* is −20/+5, or −4, the slope of the curve at point *A* is also −4.

Line *bb'* in Figure A1-4 is tangent to the curve at point *B*. Following the same procedure, we find the slope at *B* to be −5/+15, or −⅓. Thus, in this flatter part of the curve, the slope is less negative.

APPENDIX / Summary

LOA1.1 Understand graphs, curves, and slopes as they relate to economics.

- Graphs are a convenient and revealing means of representing economic relationships.

- Two variables are positively or directly related when their values change in the same direction. The line (curve) representing two directly related variables slopes upward.

- Two variables are negatively or inversely related when their values change in opposite directions. The line (curve) representing two inversely related variables slopes downward.

- The value of the dependent variable (the effect) is determined by the value of the independent variable (the cause).

- When the other factors that might affect a two-variable relationship are allowed to change, the graph of the relationship will likely shift to a new location.

- The slope of a straight line is the ratio of the vertical change to the horizontal change between any two points. The slope of an upsloping line is positive; the slope of a downsloping line is negative.

- The slope of a line or curve depends on the units used in measuring the variables. It is especially relevant for economics because it measures marginal changes.

- The slope of a horizontal line is zero; the slope of a vertical line is infinite.

- The vertical intercept and slope of a line determine its location; they are used in expressing the line—and the relationship between the two variables—as an equation.

- The slope of a curve at any point is determined by calculating the slope of a straight line tangent to the curve at that point.

APPENDIX / Terms and Concepts

horizontal axis
vertical axis
direct relationship
positive relationship
inverse relationship

independent variable
dependent variable
slope of a straight line
vertical intercept

APPENDIX / Discussion Questions

LOA1.1 Understand graphs, curves, and slopes as they relate to economics.

1. Briefly explain the use of graphs as a means of representing economic relationships.   [LOA1.1]

2. Describe the graphical relationship between ticket prices and the number of people choosing to visit amusement parks. Is that relationship consistent with the fact that, historically, park attendance and ticket prices have both risen? Explain.   [LOA1.1]

3. Look back at Figure A1-2, which shows the inverse relationship between ticket prices and game attendance at Informed University.   [LOA1.1]

   a. Interpret the meaning of both the slope and the intercept.

   b. If the slope of the line were steeper, what would that say about how ticket sales respond to increases in ticket prices?

   c. If the slope of the line stayed the same but the intercept increased, what could you say about how ticket sales respond to increases in ticket prices?

APPENDIX / Review Questions

1. Indicate whether each of the following relationships is usually a direct relationship or an inverse relationship. [LOA1.1]

   a. A sports team's winning percentage and attendance at its home games.

   b. Higher temperatures and sweater sales.

   c. A person's income and how often he or she shops at discount stores.

   d. Higher gasoline prices and kilometers driven in automobiles.

2. Erin grows pecans. The number of bushels (B) that she can produce depends on the number of centimeters of rainfall (R) that her orchards get. The relationship is given algebraically as follows: $B = 3000 + 800R$. Match each part of this equation with the correct term. [LOA1.1]

B	slope
3000	dependent variable
800	vertical intercept
R	independent variable

APPENDIX / Problems

1. Graph and explain the relationships you would expect to find between the following: [LOA1.1]

   a. The number of centimetres of rainfall per month and the sale of umbrellas

   b. The amount of tuition and the level of enrolment at a college or university

   c. The popularity of a music artist and the price of her concert tickets

2. Indicate how each of the following might affect the data shown in Figure A1-2 of this appendix: [LOA1.1]

   a. IU's athletic director schedules higher-quality opponents.

   b. A National Basketball Association (NBA) team locates in the city where IU also plays.

   c. IU signs a contract to have all of its home games televised.

3. The following table contains data on the relationship between saving and income. Rearrange these data into a meaningful order and graph them on the accompanying grid. What is the slope of the line? What is the vertical intercept? Write the equation that represents this line. What would you predict saving to be at the $12,500 level of income?   [LOA1.1]

Income (per year)	Saving (per year)
$15,000	$1,000
0	−500
10,000	500
5,000	0
20,000	1,500

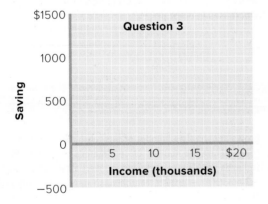

4. Construct a table from the data shown in the accompanying graph. Which is the dependent variable and which the independent variable? Summarize the data in equation form.   [LOA1.1]

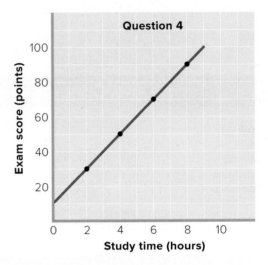

5. Suppose that when the interest rate on loans is 16 percent, businesses find it unprofitable to invest in machinery and equipment. However, when the interest rate is 14 percent, $5 billion worth of investment is profitable. At 12 percent interest, a total of $10 billion of investment is profitable. Similarly, total investment increases by $5 billion for each successive 2-percentage-point decline in the interest rate.   [LOA1.1]

   Describe the relevant relationship between the interest rate and investment, in a table, graphically, and as an equation. Put the interest rate on the vertical axis and investment on the horizontal axis. In your equation, use the form $i = a - bI$, where i is the interest rate, a is the vertical intercept, $-b$ is the slope of the line (which is negative), and I is the level of investment.

6. Suppose that $C = a + bY$, where C = consumption, a = consumption at zero income, b = slope, and Y = income.   [LOA1.1]

   a. Are C and Y positively related or negatively related?

   b. If graphed, would the curve for this equation slope upward or downward?

   c. Are the variables C and Y inversely or directly related?

   d. What is the value of C if $a = 10$, $b = 0.50$, and $Y = 200$?

   e. What is the value of Y if $C = 100$, $a = 10$, and $b = 0.25$?

7. The accompanying graph shows curve *XX′* and tangents at points *A, B,* and *C*. Calculate the slope of the curve at these three points.   [LOA1.1]

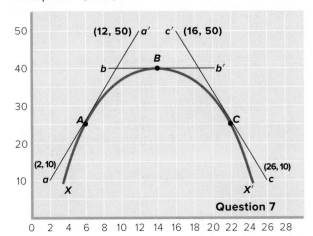

Question 7

8. In the accompanying graph, is the slope of curve *AA′* positive or negative? Does the slope increase or decrease as we move along the curve from *A* to *A′*? Answer the same two questions for curve *BB′*.   [LOA1.1]

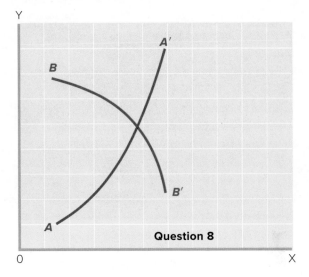

Question 8

CHAPTER 2

The Market System and the Circular Flow

Suppose you are at a mall in Edmonton and are assigned to compile a list of all the individual goods and services there, including the different brands and variations of each type of product. That task would be daunting and the list would be long! And even though a single shopping mall in Edmonton contains a remarkable quantity and variety of goods, it is only a tiny part of the Canadian economy.

Who decided that the particular goods and services available at the mall and in the broader Canadian economy should be produced? How did the producers determine which technology and types of factors to use in producing these particular goods? Who will obtain these products? What accounts for the new and improved products among these goods? This chapter will answer these and related questions.

2.1 / Economic Systems

LO2.1 Differentiate between laissez-faire capitalism, the command system, and the market system.

Every society needs to develop an **economic system**–a particular set of institutional arrangements and a coordinating mechanism–to respond to the economic problem. The economic system determines what goods are produced, how they are produced, who gets them, how to accommodate change, and how to promote technological progress.

Economic systems differ as to (1) who owns the factors of production and (2) the method used to motivate, coordinate, and direct economic activity.

Economic systems can be classified by the degree to which they rely on decentralized decision making based on markets and prices or centralized government control based on orders and mandates. At one extreme lies *laissez-faire capitalism,* in which government intervention is at a very minimum, and markets and prices are allowed to direct nearly all economic activity. At the other extreme lie *command systems* in which governments have total control over all economic activity. The vast majority of national economies lie somewhere in the middle, using some mixture of centralized government regulation and decentralized markets and prices. These economies are said to have *market systems* or *mixed economies.*

Laissez-Faire Capitalism

In **laissez-faire capitalism**–or pure capitalism–the government's role is limited to protecting private property from theft and aggression, and establishing a legal environment in which contracts can be enforced and people can interact in markets to buy and sell goods, services, and resources.

The term *laissez-faire* is French for "let it be"; that is, keep the government from interfering with the economy. Proponents of laissez-faire believe that such interference reduces human welfare. They maintain that any government that intervenes widely in the economy will end up being corrupted by special interests who will use the government's economic influence to benefit themselves rather than society at large.

To prevent that from happening, the proponents of laissez-faire argue that government should restrict itself to preventing individuals and firms from coercing each other. By doing so, it will ensure that only mutually beneficial economic transactions are negotiated and completed. That should lead to the highest possible level of human satisfaction because, after all, who knows better what people want than the people themselves?

It is important to note, however, that no society has ever employed a laissez-faire system. In fact, no government has *ever* limited its economic actions to the short list of functions that would be allowed under laissez-faire. Instead, every government known to history has undertaken a wider range of economic activities, many of which are widely popular, including industrial safety regulations, various taxes and subsidies, occupational licensing requirements, and income redistribution.

Thus, you should think of laissez-faire capitalism as a hypothetical system that is viewed by proponents as the ideal to which all economic systems should strive–but which is opposed by those who welcome greater government intervention in the economy.

ORIGIN OF THE IDEA 2.1 Laissez-faire

The Command System

The polar opposite of laissez-faire capitalism is the **command system** in which government owns most property resources and in which economic decisions are made according to a central economic plan created and enforced by the government. The command system is also known as *socialism* or *communism.*

Under the command system, a central planning board appointed by the government makes all major decisions concerning the use of resources, the composition and distribution of output, and the organization of production. The government owns most of the business firms, which produce according to government directives. The central planning board determines production goals for each enterprise and specifies the amount of resources to be allocated to each enterprise so that it can reach its production goals. The division of output between capital and consumer goods is centrally decided, and capital goods are allocated among industries on the basis of the central planning board's long-term priorities.

A pure command economy would rely exclusively on a central plan to allocate the government-owned property resources. But, in reality, even the preeminent command economy–the Soviet Union–tolerated some private ownership and incorporated some markets before its collapse in 1992. Recent reforms in Russia and most of the eastern European nations have, to one degree or another, transformed their command economies to capitalistic, market-oriented systems. China's reforms have not gone as far, but they have greatly reduced the reliance on central planning. Although government ownership of resources and capital in China is still extensive, the nation has increasingly relied on free markets to organize and coordinate its economy. North Korea and Cuba are the last prominent remaining examples of largely centrally planned economies. Other countries using mainly the command system include Turkmenistan, Laos, Belarus, Myanmar, and Iran. Later in this chapter we will explore the main reasons for the general demise of command systems.

The Market System

The vast majority of the world's economies use the **market system**, which is also known as *capitalism* or a *mixed economy*.

The market system is characterized by a mixture of centralized government economic initiatives, and decentralized actions taken by individuals and firms. The precise mixture varies from country to country, but in each case the system features the private ownership of resources, and the use of markets and prices to coordinate and direct economic activity.

In the market system, individuals and businesses seek to achieve their economic goals through their own decisions regarding work, consumption, and production. The system allows for the private ownership of capital, communicates through prices, and coordinates economic activity through markets–places where buyers and sellers come together to buy and sell goods, services, and resources.

Participants act in their own self-interest, and goods and services are produced and resources are supplied by whoever is willing and able to do so. The result is competition among independently acting buyers and sellers of each product and resource, and an economic system in which decision making is widely dispersed.

The market system also offers high potential monetary rewards that create powerful incentives for existing firms to innovate and for entrepreneurs to pioneer new products and processes despite the financial risks involved and despite most innovations failing to catch on with consumers.

In the capitalism practiced in Canada and most other countries, the government plays a substantial role in the economy. It not only provides the rules for economic activity but also promotes economic stability and growth, provides certain goods and services that would otherwise be underproduced or not produced at all, and modifies the distribution of income. The government, however, is not the dominant economic force in deciding what to produce, how to produce it, and who will get it. That force is the market.

2.2 / Characteristics of the Market System

LO2.2 List the main characteristics of the market system.

An examination of some of the key features of the market system in detail will be instructive.

Private Property

In a market system, private individuals and firms, not the government, own most of the property resources (land and capital). It is this extensive private ownership of capital that gives capitalism its name. This right of **private property**, coupled with the freedom to negotiate binding legal contracts, enables individuals and businesses to obtain, use, and dispose of property resources as they see fit. The right of property owners to designate who will receive their property when they die sustains the institution of private property.

Property rights encourage investment, innovation, exchange, maintenance of property, and economic growth. No one would stock a store, build a factory, or clear land for farming if someone else, or the government itself, could take that property for his or her own benefit.

The most important consequence of property rights is that they encourage people to cooperate by helping to ensure that only *mutually agreeable* economic transactions take place. To consider why this is true, imagine a world without legally enforceable property rights. In such a world, the strong could simply take whatever they wanted from the weak without giving them any compensation. But in a world of legally enforceable property rights, any person wanting something from you has to get you to agree to give it to them. And you can say no. The result is that if they really want what you have, they must offer you something that you value more highly in return. That is, they must offer you a mutually agreeable economic transaction–one that benefits you as well as them.

Property rights also extend to intellectual property through patents, copyrights, and trademarks. Such long-term protection encourages people to write books, music, and computer programs, and to invent new products and production processes without fear that others will steal them and the rewards they may bring.

Moreover, property rights facilitate exchange. The title to an automobile or the deed to a cattle ranch assures the buyer that the seller is the legitimate owner. Also, property rights encourage owners to maintain or improve their property so as to preserve or increase its value. Finally, property rights enable people to use their time and resources to produce more goods and services, rather than using them to protect and retain the property they have already produced or acquired.

Freedom of Enterprise and Choice

Closely related to private ownership of property is freedom of enterprise and choice. The market system requires that various economic units make certain choices, which are expressed and implemented in the economy's markets:

- **Freedom of enterprise** ensures that entrepreneurs and private businesses are free to obtain and use economic resources to produce their choice of goods and services and to sell them in their chosen markets.

- **Freedom of choice** enables owners to employ or dispose of their property and money as they see fit. It also allows workers to enter any line of work for which they are qualified. Finally, it ensures that consumers are free to buy the goods and services that best satisfy their wants.

These choices are free only within broad legal limitations, of course. Illegal choices–such as selling human organs or buying illicit drugs–are punished through fines and imprisonment. Global Perspective 2.1 reveals that the degree of economic freedom varies greatly from economy to economy.

Self-Interest

In the market system, **self-interest** is the motivating force of the various economic units as they express their free choices. Self-interest simply means that each economic unit tries to achieve its own particular goal, which usually requires delivering something of value to others. Entrepreneurs try to maximize profit and minimize loss. Property owners try to get the highest price for selling or renting their resources. Workers try to maximize their utility (satisfaction) by finding jobs that offer the best combination of wages, hours, fringe benefits, and working conditions. Consumers try to obtain the products they want at the lowest possible price and apportion their expenditures to maximize their utility. The motive of self-interest gives direction and consistency to what might otherwise be a chaotic economy.

ORIGIN OF THE IDEA 2.2 Self-Interest

2.1 GLOBAL PERSPECTIVE

Index of Economic Freedom, Selected Nations

The Index of Economic Freedom measures economic freedom using 10 broad categories, such as trade policy, property rights, and government intervention, with each category containing more than 50 specific criteria. The Index then ranks 184 nations according to the degree of economic freedom. A few selected rankings for 2015 are listed here.

FREE
| 1 Hong Kong |
| 2 Singapore |
| 5 Switzerland |

MOSTLY FREE
| 6 Canada |
| 12 United States |
| 13 United Kingdom |
| 20 Japan |

MODERATELY FREE
| 42 Poland |
| 40 Belgium |
| 73 France |

MOSTLY UNFREE
| 100 Zambia |
| 139 China |
| 143 Russia |

REPRESSED
| 169 Argentina |
| 176 Venezuela |
| 177 Cuba |
| 178 North Korea |

Source: © 2015 by The Heritage Foundation. All Rights Reserved.

Competition

The market system depends on **competition** among economic units. The basis of this competition is freedom of choice exercised in pursuit of a monetary return. Very broadly defined, competition requires the following:

- Independently acting sellers and buyers operating in a particular product or factor market

- Freedom of sellers and buyers to enter or leave markets, on the basis of their economic self-interest

Competition among buyers and sellers diffuses economic power within the businesses and households that make up the economy. When there are independently acting sellers and buyers in a market, no single buyer or seller is able to dictate the price of the product or factor because others can undercut that price.

Competition also implies that producers can enter or leave an industry; there are no insurmountable barriers to an industry's expanding or contracting. This freedom of an industry to expand or contract provides the economy with the flexibility needed to remain efficient over time. Freedom of entry and exit enables the economy to adjust to changes in consumer tastes, technology, and factor availability.

The diffusion of economic power inherent in competition limits the potential abuse of that power. A producer that charges more than the competitive market price will lose sales to other producers. An employer who pays less than the competitive market wage rate will lose workers to other employers. A firm that fails to exploit new technology will lose profits to firms that do. And a firm that produces shoddy products will be punished as customers switch to higher-quality items made by rival firms. Competition is the basic regulatory force in the market system.

Markets and Prices

We may wonder why an economy based on self-interest does not collapse in chaos. If consumers want breakfast cereal but businesses choose to produce running shoes and resource suppliers decide to make computer software, production would seem to be deadlocked by the apparent inconsistencies of free choices.

In reality, the millions of decisions made by households and businesses are highly coordinated with one another. Markets and prices are key components of the market system. They give the system its ability to coordinate millions of daily economic decisions. A **market** is an institution or mechanism that brings buyers (demanders) and sellers (suppliers) into contact. A market system conveys the decisions made by buyers and sellers of products and factors. The decisions made on each side of the market determine a set of product and factor prices that guide resource owners, entrepreneurs, and consumers as they make and revise their choices and pursue their self-interest.

Just as competition is the regulatory mechanism of the market system, the market system itself is the organizing and coordinating mechanism. It is an elaborate communication network through which innumerable individual free choices on the part of consumers and producers are recorded, summarized, and balanced. Those who respond to market signals and heed market dictates are rewarded with greater profit and income; those who do not respond to those signals and choose to ignore market dictates are penalized. Through this mechanism society decides what the economy should produce, how production can be organized efficiently, and how the fruits of production are to be distributed among the various units that make up the economy.

QUICK REVIEW 2.1

- The market system rests on the private ownership of property, freedom of enterprise, and freedom of choice.

- Property rights encourage people to cooperate and make mutually agreeable economic transactions.

- The market system permits consumers, resource suppliers, and businesses to pursue and further their self-interest.

- Competition diffuses economic power and limits the actions of any single seller or buyer.

- The coordinating mechanism of capitalism is a system of markets and prices.

Technology and Capital Goods

In the market system, competition, freedom of choice, self-interest, and personal reward provide the opportunity and motivation for technological advance. The monetary rewards for new products or production techniques accrue directly to the innovator. The market system, therefore, encourages extensive use and rapid development of complex capital goods: tools, machinery, large-scale factories, and facilities for storage, communication, transportation, and marketing.

Advanced technology and capital goods are important because the most direct methods of production are often the least efficient. The only way to avoid that inefficiency is to rely on capital goods. It would be ridiculous for a modern farmer to go at production with bare hands. There are huge benefits to be derived from creating and using such capital equipment as plows, tractors, storage bins, and so on. More efficient production means much more abundant output.

Specialization

The extent to which market economies rely on **specialization** is astonishing. Specialization is the use of resources of an individual, region, or nation to produce one or a few goods or services rather than the entire range of goods and services. Those goods and services are then exchanged for a full range of desired products. The majority of consumers produce virtually none of the goods and services they consume, and they consume little or nothing of the items they produce. The person working nine to five installing windows in commercial aircraft may rarely fly. Many farmers sell their milk to the local dairy and then buy butter at the local grocery store. Society learned long ago that self-sufficiency breeds inefficiency. The jack-of-all-trades may be a very colourful individual but is certainly not an efficient producer.

DIVISION OF LABOUR

Human specialization–called the **division of labour**–contributes to a society's output in several ways:

- *Specialization Makes Use of Differences in Ability* Specialization enables individuals to take advantage of existing differences in their abilities and skills. If Peyton is strong, athletic, and good at throwing a football, and Beyoncé is beautiful, agile, and can sing, their distribution of talents can be most efficiently used if Peyton plays professional football and Beyoncé records songs and gives concerts.

> **ORIGIN OF THE IDEA 2.3**   Specialization: Division of Labour

- *Specialization Fosters Learning by Doing* Even if the abilities of two people are identical, specialization may still be advantageous. By devoting time to a single task, a person is more likely to develop the skills required and to improve techniques than they are if they work at a number of different tasks. You learn to be a good lawyer by studying and practising law.

- *Specialization Saves Time* By devoting time to a single task, a person avoids the loss of time incurred in shifting from one job to another. Also, time is saved when people don't fumble around with tasks they are not trained to do.

  For all these reasons, specialization increases the total output society derives from limited resources.

GEOGRAPHIC SPECIALIZATION

Specialization also works on a regional and international basis. It is conceivable that apples could be grown in Saskatchewan, but because of the unsuitability of the land, rainfall, and temperature, the costs would be very high. And it is conceivable that wheat could be grown in British Columbia, but such production would be costly for similar geographical reasons. So Saskatchewan farmers produce products–wheat in particular–for which their resources are best suited, and British Columbians (especially in the Okanagan Valley) do the same, producing apples and other fruits. By specializing, both regional economies produce more than is needed locally. Then, very sensibly, Saskatchewan and British Columbia exchange some of their surpluses–wheat for apples, apples for wheat.

Similarly, on an international scale, Canada specializes in producing such items as commercial aircraft (Bombardier) and communication equipment (BlackBerry Limited), which it sells abroad in exchange for digital video cameras from Japan, bananas from Honduras, and woven baskets from Thailand. Both human specialization and geographic specialization are needed to achieve efficiency in the use of limited resources.

Use of Money

A rather obvious characteristic of any economic system is the extensive use of money. Money performs several functions, but first and foremost it is a **medium of exchange**. It makes trade easier.

Specialization requires exchange. Exchange can, and sometimes does, occur through **barter**–swapping goods for goods (say, exchanging wheat for apples). But barter poses serious problems because it requires a *coincidence of wants* between the buyer and the seller. In our example, we assumed that Saskatchewan had excess wheat to trade and wanted apples. And we assumed that British Columbia had excess apples to trade and wanted wheat. So an exchange occurred. But if such a coincidence of wants is missing, trade will not occur.

Suppose that Saskatchewan has no interest in British Columbia's apples but wants potatoes from Prince Edward Island. And suppose that Prince Edward Island wants British Columbia's apples but not Saskatchewan's wheat. And, to complicate matters, suppose that British Columbia wants some of Saskatchewan's wheat but none of Prince Edward Island's potatoes. We summarize the situation in Figure 2-1.

In none of the cases shown in the figure is there a coincidence of wants. Trade by barter would obviously be difficult. Instead, people in each province use **money**, which is simply a convenient social invention to facilitate exchanges of goods and services. Historically, people have used cattle, cigarettes, shells, stones, pieces of metal, and many other commodities as money with varying degrees of success. To serve as money, an item needs to pass only one test. It must be generally acceptable to sellers in exchange for their goods and services. Money is socially defined: Whatever society accepts as a medium of exchange *is* money.

Today, most economies use pieces of paper as money. The use of paper dollars (currency) as a medium of exchange is what enables Saskatchewan, British Columbia, and Prince Edward Island to overcome their trade stalemate, as demonstrated in Figure 2-1.

On a global basis, specialization and exchange are complicated by the fact that different nations have different currencies. But swapping dollars, yen, euros, pounds, and pesos for one another in markets in

---

FIGURE 2-1   **Money Facilitates Trade when Wants Do Not Coincide**

The use of money as a medium of exchange permits trade to be accomplished despite a non–coincidence of wants. (1) Saskatchewan trades the wheat that British Columbia wants for money; (2) Saskatchewan trades the money it receives from British Columbia for the potatoes it wants from Prince Edward Island; (3) Prince Edward Island trades the money it receives from Saskatchewan for the apples it wants from British Columbia.

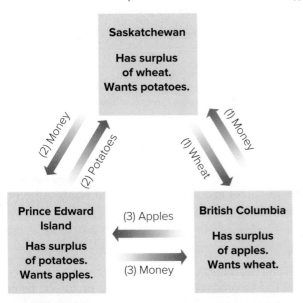

which currencies are bought and sold makes it possible for people living in different countries to exchange goods and services without resorting to barter. Chapter 17 goes into much more detail about the workings of the foreign exchange markets.

Active but Limited Government

An active but limited government is the final characteristic of market systems in modern advanced industrial economies. Although a market system promotes a high degree of efficiency in the use of its resources, it has certain inherent shortcomings called *market failures*. We will discover in subsequent chapters that governments can often increase the overall efficiency of the economic system in several ways. However, governments have their own set of shortcomings that can themselves cause substantial misallocations of resources. Consequently, we will also investigate several types of so-called government failures. As we will discover in Chapters 13 and 15, there are times when the central government, along with the central bank, needs to take action if a market economy is experiencing recession or inflation.

QUICK REVIEW 2.2

- The market systems of modern industrial economies are characterized by extensive use of technologically advanced capital goods. Such goods help these economies achieve greater efficiency in production.
- Specialization is extensive in market systems; it enhances efficiency and output by enabling individuals,

regions, and nations to produce the goods and services for which their resources are best suited.
- The use of money in market systems facilitates the exchange of goods and services that specialization requires.

2.3 / Five Fundamental Questions

LO2.3 Explain how the market system answers the five fundamental questions of what to produce, how to produce, who obtains the output, how to adjust to change, and how to promote progress.

The key features of the market system help explain how market economies respond to five fundamental questions:

1. What goods and services will be produced?
2. How will the goods and services be produced?
3. Who will get the goods and services?
4. How will the system accommodate change?
5. How will the system promote progress?

These five questions highlight the economic choices underlying the production possibilities curve discussed in Chapter 1. They reflect the reality of scarce resources in a world of unlimited wants. All economies, whether market or command, must address these five questions.

What Will Be Produced?

How will a market system decide on the specific types and quantities of goods and services to be produced? The simple answer is this: The goods and services that can be produced at a continuing profit will be produced, while those whose production generates a continuing loss will be discontinued. Profits and losses are the difference between the total revenue (TR) a firm receives from the sale of its products and the total cost (TC) of producing those products. (For economists, the total cost includes not only wage and salary payments to labour, and interest and rental payments for capital and land, but also payments to the entrepreneur for organizing and combining the other resources to produce a product.)

Continuing economic profit (TR > TC) in an industry results in expanded production and the movement of resources toward that industry. Existing firms grow and new firms enter. The industry expands. Continuing losses (TC > TR) in an industry lead to reduced production and the departure of resources from that industry. Some existing firms shrink in size; others go out of business. The industry contracts.

In the market system, consumers are sovereign (in command). **Consumer sovereignty** is crucial in determining the types and quantities of goods produced. Consumers spend their income on the goods they are most willing and able to buy. Through these **dollar votes** they register their wants in the market. If the dollar votes for a certain product are large enough to create a profit, businesses will produce that product and offer it for sale. In contrast, if the dollar votes do not create sufficient revenues to cover costs, businesses will not produce the product. Through their dollar votes consumers collectively direct resources to industries that are meeting their wants and away from industries that are not.

The dollar votes of consumers determine not only which industries will continue to exist but also which products will survive or fail. Only profitable industries, firms, and products survive, so firms are not really free to produce whatever products they want. Consumers' buying decisions make the production of some products profitable and the production of other products unprofitable, thus restricting the choice of businesses in deciding what to produce. Businesses must match their production choices with consumer choices or else face losses and eventual bankruptcy.

The same holds true for resource (factor) suppliers. The employment of resources derives from the sale of the goods and services that the resources help produce. Autoworkers are employed because automobiles are sold. There are few remaining professors of early Latin because there are few people who want to learn the Latin language. Resource suppliers that want to earn income are not truly free to allocate their resources to the production of goods or services that consumers do not value highly. Consumers register their preferences in the market; producers and resource suppliers, prompted by their own self-interest, try to satisfy those preferences.

CONSIDER THIS   McHits and McMisses

McDonald's has introduced several new menu items over the decades. Some have been profitable hits, while others have been misses. In a market system consumers ultimately decide whether a menu item is profitable and therefore whether it stays on the McDonald's menu.

- Hulaburger (1962)—McMiss
- Filet-O-Fish (1963)—McHit
- Strawberry Shortcake (1966)—McMiss

- Big Mac (1968)—McHit
- Hot Apple Pie (1968)—McHit
- Egg McMuffin (1975)—McHit
- Drive-thru (1975)—McHit
- Chicken McNuggets (1983)—McHit
- Extra Value Meal (1991)—McHit
- McLean Deluxe (1991)—McMiss
- Arch Deluxe (1996)—McMiss
- 55-cent Special (1997)—McMiss
- Big Xtra (1999)—McHit
- McSalad Shaker (2000)—McMiss
- McGriddle (2003)—McHit
- Snack Wrap (2006)—McHit

Source: "Polishing the Golden Arches," *Forbes*, June 15, 1998, pp. 42–43, updated. Reprinted by permission of Forbes Media LLC © 2010.

How Will the Goods and Services Be Produced?

What combinations of resources and technologies will be used to produce goods and services? How will the production be organized? The answer is that it will be done in ways that minimize the cost per unit of output, because inefficiency drives up costs and lowers profits. As a result, any firm wishing to maximize its profits will make great efforts to minimize production costs. These efforts will include using the right mix of labour and capital, given the prices and productivity of those resources. They also mean locating production facilities optimally to minimize production and transportation expenses.

Those efforts will be intensified if the firm faces competition, as consumers strongly prefer low prices and will shift their purchases over to the firms that can produce a quality product at the lowest possible price. Any firm foolish enough to use higher-cost production methods will go bankrupt as it is undersold by its more efficient competitors who can still make a profit when selling at a lower price, because competition eliminates high-cost producers.

WORKED PROBLEM 2.1   Least Cost Production

Least-cost production means that firms must employ the most economically efficient technique of production in producing their output. The most efficient production technique depends on the following:

- The available technology; that is, the available body of knowledge and techniques that can be used to combine economic resources to produce the desired results

- The prices of the needed resources

A technique that requires just a few inputs of resources to produce a specific output may be highly inefficient economically if those resources are valued very highly in the market. Economic efficiency requires obtaining a particular output of product with the least input of scarce resources, when both output and resource inputs are measured in dollars and cents.

Who Will Get the Output?

The market system enters the picture in two ways when determining the distribution of total output. Generally, any product will be distributed to consumers on the basis of their ability and willingness to pay its existing market price. If the price of some product—say, a small sailboat—is $3000, then buyers who are willing and able to pay that price will get it; those unwilling or unable to pay the price will not.

The ability to pay the prices for sailboats and other products depends on the amount of income that consumers have, along with the prices of, and preferences for, various goods. If consumers have sufficient income and want to spend their money on a particular good, they can have it. And the amount of income they have depends on (1) the quantities of the property and human resources they supply and (2) the prices those resources command in the factor market. Factor prices (wages, interest, rent, profit) are crucial in determining the size of each person's income and therefore each person's ability to buy part of the economy's output. If a lawyer earning $300 an hour and a janitor earning $10 an hour both work the same number of hours each year, then each year the lawyer will be able to purchase thirty times more of society's output than the janitor.

How Will the System Accommodate Change?

Market systems are dynamic: consumer preferences, technology, and supplies of resources can all change at the same time. This means that the particular allocation of resources that is now the most efficient for a specific pattern of consumer tastes, range of technological alternatives, and amount of available resources will become obsolete and inefficient as consumer preferences change, new techniques of production are discovered, and resource supplies change over time. Can the market economy adjust to such changes?

Suppose consumer tastes change. For instance, assume that consumers decide they want more fruit juice and less milk than the economy currently provides. Those changes in consumer tastes will be communicated to producers through an increase in spending on fruit juice and a decline in spending on milk.

Other things equal, prices and profits in the fruit juice industry will rise and those in the milk industry will fall. Self-interest will induce existing competitors to expand output and entice new competitors to enter the prosperous fruit juice industry and will, in time, force firms to scale down–or even exit–the depressed milk industry.

The higher prices and greater economic profit in the fruit juice industry will not only induce that industry to expand but will give it the revenue needed to obtain the resources necessary to its growth. Higher prices and profits will permit fruit juice producers to draw more resources from less urgent alternative employment. The reverse occurs in the milk industry, where fewer workers and other resources are employed. These adjustments in the economy are automatic responses to the changes in consumer tastes. This is consumer sovereignty at work.

The market system is a gigantic communications network. Through changes in prices and profits it communicates changes in consumer demand and elicits appropriate responses from businesses and resource suppliers. By affecting price and profits, changes in consumer demand direct the expansion of some industries and the contraction of others. Those adjustments are conveyed to the factor market. As expanding industries employ more factors of production and contracting industries employ fewer, the resulting changes in factor prices (wages and salaries, for example) and the flow of income steer resources from the contracting industries to the expanding industries.

This *directing* or *guiding function of prices and profits* is a core element of the market system. Without such a system, a government planning board or some other administrative agency would have to direct businesses and resources into the appropriate industries. A similar analysis shows that the system can and does adjust to other fundamental changes–for example, to changes in technology and in the prices of various resources.

How Will the System Promote Progress?

Society desires economic growth (greater output) and higher standards of living (greater output *per person*). How does the market system promote technological improvements and capital accumulation, both of which contribute to a higher standard of living for society?

TECHNOLOGICAL ADVANCE

The market system provides a strong incentive for technological advance and enables better products and processes to supplant inferior ones. An entrepreneur or firm that introduces a popular new product will gain revenue and economic profit at the expense of rivals.

Technological advance also includes new and improved methods that reduce production or distribution costs. By passing on part of its cost reduction to the consumer through a lower product price, the firm can increase sales and obtain economic profit at the expense of rival firms.

Moreover, the market system promotes the rapid spread of technological advance throughout an industry. Rival firms must follow the lead of the most innovative firm or else suffer immediate losses and eventual failure. In some cases, the result is **creative destruction**: the creation of new products and production methods completely destroys the market positions of firms that are wedded to existing products and older ways of doing business. For example, the advent of compact discs largely demolished long-play vinyl records, and iPods and other digital technologies subsequently supplanted CDs.

CAPITAL ACCUMULATION

Most technological advances require additional capital goods. The market system provides the resources necessary to produce additional capital goods through increased dollar votes for those goods.

But who will count the dollar votes for capital goods? Entrepreneurs and business owners. As receivers of profit income, they often use part of that income to purchase capital goods. Doing so yields even greater profit income in the future if the technological innovation that required the additional capital good is successful. Also, by paying interest or selling ownership shares, the entrepreneur and firm can attract some of the income of households to cast dollar votes for the production of more capital goods. In Chapter 8, the importance of capital goods to economic growth will be discussed further.

- The output mix of the market system is determined by profits, which in turn depend heavily on consumer preferences. Economic profits cause industries to expand; losses cause industries to contract.

- Competition forces industries to use the least costly production methods.

- In a market economy, consumer income and product prices determine how output will be distributed.

- Competitive markets reallocate resources in response to changes in consumer tastes, technological advances, and changes in availability of resources.

- Competitive markets create incentives for technological advance and capital accumulation, both of which contribute to increases in standards of living.

2.4 / The Invisible Hand

LO2.4 Explain the operation of the Invisible Hand and why market economies usually do a better job than command economies at transforming economic resources into desirable output.

In his 1776 book, *The Wealth of Nations,* Adam Smith first noted that the operation of a market system creates a curious unity between private interests and social interests. Firms and resource suppliers, seeking to further their own self-interest and operating within the framework of a highly competitive market system, will simultaneously, as though guided by an **invisible hand**, promote the public or social interest. For example, we have seen that in a competitive environment, businesses seek to build new and improved products to increase profits. Those enhanced products increase society's well-being. Businesses also use the least costly combination of resources to produce a specific output because it is in their self-interest to do so. To act otherwise would be to forgo profit or even to risk business failure. But, at the same time, to use scarce resources in the least costly way is clearly in the social interest as well. It frees up resources to produce something else that society desires.

Self-interest, awakened and guided by the competitive market system, is what induces responses appropriate to the changes in society's wants. Businesses seeking to make higher profits and to avoid losses, and resource suppliers pursuing greater monetary rewards, negotiate changes in the allocation of resources and end up with the output that society wants. Competition guides self-interest such that self-interest automatically and quite unintentionally furthers the best interest of society. The invisible hand ensures that when firms maximize their profits and resource suppliers maximize their incomes, these groups also help maximize society's output and income.

Of the various virtues of the market system, three merit re-emphasis:

- *Efficiency* The market system promotes the efficient use of resources, by guiding them into the production of the goods and services most wanted by society. It forces the use of the most efficient techniques in organizing resources for production, and it encourages the development and adoption of new and more efficient production techniques.

- *Incentives* The market system encourages skill acquisition, hard work, and innovation. Greater work skills and effort mean greater production and higher incomes, which usually translate into a higher standard of living. Similarly, the assumption of risks by entrepreneurs can result in substantial profit incomes. Successful innovations generate economic rewards.

- *Freedom* The major noneconomic argument for the market system is its emphasis on personal freedom. In contrast to central planning, the market system coordinates economic activity without coercion. The market system permits—indeed, it thrives on—freedom of enterprise and choice. Entrepreneurs and workers are free to further their own self-interest, subject to the rewards and penalties imposed by the market system itself.

Of course, no economic system, including the market system, is flawless. The global financial crisis that gripped most economies in 2008–2009 highlighted some of the shortcomings of unfettered financial markets.

The Demise of the Command System

Our discussion of how a market system answers the five fundamental questions provides insights into why the command systems of the Soviet Union, Eastern Europe, and China (prior to its market reforms) failed. Those systems encountered two insurmountable problems: the coordination problem and the incentive problem.

THE COORDINATION PROBLEM

The first difficulty was the coordination problem. The central planners had to coordinate millions of individual decisions by consumers, resource suppliers, and businesses. Consider what it takes to set up a factory to produce tractors. The central planners had to establish a realistic annual production target: for example, 1000 tractors. They then had to make available all the necessary inputs–labour, machinery, electric power, steel, tires, glass, paint, and transportation–for the production and delivery of those 1000 tractors.

Because the outputs of many industries serve as inputs to other industries, the failure of any single industry to achieve its output target caused a chain reaction of repercussions. For example, if iron mines, for want of machinery or labour or transportation, did not supply the steel industry with the required inputs of iron ore, the steel mills were unable to fulfill the input needs of the many industries that depended on steel. Steel-using industries that produced capital goods (such as factory equipment and modes of transportation) were unable to fulfill their planned production goals. Eventually the chain reaction spread to all firms that used steel as an input and from there to other input buyers or final consumers.

The coordination problem became more difficult as the economies expanded. Products and production processes grew more complex, and the number of industries requiring planning increased. Planning techniques that worked for the simpler economy proved highly inadequate and inefficient for the larger economy. Bottlenecks and production stoppages became the norm, not the exception. In trying to cope, planners further suppressed product variety, focusing on one or two products in each product category.

A lack of a reliable success indicator added to the coordination problem in the Soviet Union and China (prior to its market reforms). We have seen that market economies rely on profit as a success indicator. Profit depends on consumer demand, production efficiency, and product quality. In contrast, the major success indicator for the command economies usually was a quantitative production target that the central planners assigned. Production costs, product quality, and product mix were secondary considerations. Managers and workers often sacrificed product quality because they were being awarded bonuses

CONSIDER THIS   The Two Koreas

North Korea is one of the few command economies still standing. After the Second World War, Korea was divided into North Korea and South Korea. North Korea, under the influence of the Soviet Union, established a command economy that emphasized government ownership and central government planning. South Korea established a market economy based upon private ownership and the profit motive. Today, the differences in the economic outcomes of the two systems are striking.

	North Korea	South Korea
GDP	$40 billion*	$1.8 trillion*
GDP per capita	$1,800*	$34,400*
Exports	$3.8 billion	$617 billion
Imports	$4.0 billion	$537 billion
Agriculture as % of GDP	24.6%	2.4%

*Based on purchasing power equivalencies to the U.S. dollar in 2013.

Source: *CIA World Fact Book*, 2015, www.cia.gov.

for meeting quantitative, not qualitative, targets. If meeting production goals meant sloppy assembly work, so be it.

It was difficult, at best, for planners to assign quantitative production targets without unintentionally producing distortions in output. If the plan specified a production target for producing nails in terms of *weight* (tons of nails), the enterprise made only large nails. But if it specified the target as a *quantity* (thousands of nails), the firm made small nails and lots of them! That is precisely what happens in centrally planned economies.

THE INCENTIVE PROBLEM

The command economies also faced an incentive problem. Central planners determined the output mix. When they misjudged how many automobiles, shoes, shirts, and chickens were wanted at the government-determined prices, persistent shortages and surpluses of those products often arose. But as long as the managers who oversaw the production of those goods were rewarded for meeting their assigned production goals, they had no incentive to adjust production in response to the shortages and surpluses. And there were no fluctuations in prices and profitability to signal that more or less of certain products was desired. Thus, many products were unavailable or in short supply, while other products were overproduced and sat for months or years in warehouses.

The command systems of the former Soviet Union and China before its market reforms also lacked entrepreneurship. Central planning did not trigger the profit motive, nor did it reward innovation and enterprise. The route for getting ahead was through participation in the political hierarchy of the Communist Party. Moving up the hierarchy meant better housing, better access to health care, and the right to shop in special stores. Meeting production targets and manoeuvring through the minefields of party politics were measures of success in "business." But a definition of business success based solely on political savvy is not conducive to technological advance, and is often disruptive to existing products, production methods, and organizational structures.

2.5　The Circular Flow Model

LO2.5 Describe the mechanics of the circular flow model.

The dynamic market economy creates continuous, repetitive flows of goods and services, resources, and money. The **circular flow diagram**, shown in **Figure 2-2 (Key Graph)**, illustrates those flows for a simplified economy in which there is no government. Observe that in the diagram we group this economy's decision makers into *businesses* and *households*. Additionally, we divide this economy's markets into the *factor market* and the *product market*.

ORIGIN OF THE IDEA 2.4　Circular Flow Diagram

Households

The cream coloured rectangle on the right side of the circular flow diagram in Figure 2-2 represents **households**, which are defined as one or more persons occupying a housing unit. There are currently about nine million households in the Canadian economy. Households buy the goods and services that businesses make available in the product market. Households obtain the income needed to buy those products by selling resources in the factor market.

All the resources in our no-government economy are ultimately owned or provided by households. For instance, the members of one household or another directly provide all of the labour and entrepreneurial ability in the economy. Households also own all of the land and all of the capital in the economy either directly, as personal property, or indirectly, as a consequence of owning all of the businesses in the economy (and thereby controlling all of the land and capital owned by businesses). Thus, all of the income in the economy—all wages, rents, interest, and profits—flows to households because they provide the economy's labour, land, capital, and entrepreneurial ability.

KEY GRAPH

FIGURE 2-2 The Circular Flow Diagram

Factors of production flow from households to businesses through the factor market, and products flow from businesses to households through the product market. Opposite these real flows are monetary flows. Households receive income from businesses (their costs) through the factor market, and businesses receive revenue from households (their expenditures) through the product market.

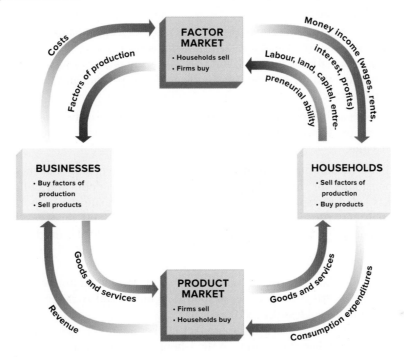

Quick Quiz

1. **The factor market is where**
   a. Households sell products and businesses buy products.
   b. Businesses sell factors of production and households sell products.
   c. Households sell factors of production and businesses buy factors of production (or the services of factors).
   d. Businesses sell factors of production and households buy factors of production (or the services of factors).

2. **Which of the following would be determined in the product market?**
   a. A manager's salary
   b. The price of equipment used in a bottling plant

   c. The price of 80 hectares of farm land
   d. The price of a new pair of athletic shoes

3. **In this circular flow diagram**
   a. Money flows counterclockwise.
   b. Resources flow counterclockwise.
   c. Goods and services flow clockwise.
   d. Households are on the selling side of the product market.

4. **In this circular flow diagram**
   a. Households spend income in the product market.
   b. Firms sell resources to households.
   c. Households receive income through the product market.
   d. Households produce goods.

Answers: 1. c; 2. d; 3. b; 4. a

Businesses

The cream coloured rectangle on the left side of the circular flow diagram represents **businesses**, which are economic entities (firms) that purchase factors of production and provide goods and services to the economy. These commercial establishments attempt to earn profits for their owners by offering goods and services for sale. Businesses fall into three main categories.

- A **sole proprietorship** is an unincorporated business owned and operated by a single person. The proprietor (the owner) provides all of the labour and produces all of the output. Examples include an arborist who runs her own tree-cutting business and an independent accountant who helps his clients with their taxes.

- A **partnership** is a natural outgrowth of the sole proprietorship. In a partnership, two or more individuals (the partners) agree to own and operate a business together. They pool their financial resources and business skills to operate the business, and they share any profits or losses that the business may generate. Many law firms and dental practices are organized as partnerships, as are a wide variety of firms in many other industries.

- A **corporation** is an independent legal entity that can–on its own behalf–acquire resources, own assets, produce and sell products, incur debts, extend credit, sue and be sued, and otherwise engage in any legal business activities.

The fact that a corporation is an independent legal entity means that its owners bear no personal financial responsibility for the fulfillment of the corporation's debts and obligations. For instance, if a corporation has failed to repay a loan to a bank, the bank can sue the corporation but not its owners. Professional managers run most corporations. They are hired and supervised by a board of directors that is elected annually by the corporation's owners. BlackBerry Limited, Bombardier, Ford, and Air Canada are examples of large corporations, but corporations come in all sizes and operate in every type of industry.

There are currently about 1.1 million businesses in Canada, ranging from enormous corporations like the Royal Bank of Canada, with 2014 revenues of about $34 billion and 78,000 employees, to single-person sole proprietorships with sales of less than $100 per day.

Businesses sell goods and services in the product market in order to obtain revenue, and they incur costs in the resource market when they purchase the labour, land, capital, and entrepreneurial ability that they need to produce their respective goods and services.

Product Market

The purple rectangle at the bottom of Figure 2-2 represents the **product market**, where the goods and services produced by businesses are bought and sold. Households use the income they receive from the sale of resources to buy goods and services. The money that they spend on goods and services flows to businesses as revenue.

Factor Market

Finally, the purple rectangle at the top of the circular flow diagram in Figure 2-2 represents the **factor market**, or resource market, in which households sell resources to businesses. The households sell resources to generate income, and the businesses buy resources to produce goods and services. Productive resources flow from households to businesses while money flows from businesses to households in the form of wages, rents, interest, and profits.

To summarize, the circular flow model depicts a complex web of economic activity in which businesses and households are both buyers and sellers. Businesses buy resources and sell products. Households buy products and sell resources. The counterclockwise flow of economic resources and finished products in Figure 2-2 is paid for by the clockwise flow of money income and consumption expenditures.

2.6 / How the Market System Deals with Risk

LO2.6 Explain how the market system deals with risk.

Producing goods and services is risky. Input shortages can suddenly arise. Consumer preferences can quickly change. Natural disasters can destroy factories and cripple supply chains. For an economic system to maximize its potential, it must develop methods for assessing and managing risk. The market system does so by confronting business owners with the financial consequences of their decisions. If they manage risks well, they may prosper. If they manage risks poorly, they may lose everything.

The Profit System

As explained in Chapter 1, entrepreneurial ability is the economic resource that organizes and directs the other three resources of land, labour, and capital toward productive uses. The owners of a firm may attempt to supply the entrepreneurial ability themselves. Or they can hire professional managers to supply the necessary leadership and decision making. Either way, it falls to those acting as the firm's entrepreneurs to deal with risk.

They are guided toward sensible decisions by the so-called profit system. This system is actually a profit-and-loss system because the entrepreneurs who must deal with risk and uncertainty gain profits if they choose wisely, but suffer losses if they choose poorly. That provides them with a large financial incentive to avoid unnecessary risks and make prudent decisions.

By contrast, risk management tends to be done very poorly in command economies because the central planners who must allocate resources and deal with risk do not themselves face the possibility of losing money if they make bad decisions. As government employees, they tend to receive the same salaries whether things go well or poorly.

Shielding Employees and Suppliers from Business Risk

Under the market system, only a firm's owners are subject to business risk and the possibility of losing money. By contrast, the firm's employees and suppliers are shielded from business risk because they are legally entitled to receive their contracted wages and payments on time and in full regardless of whether the firm is earning a profit or generating a loss.

To see how this works, consider a pizza parlour that is being started in a small town. Its investors put up $50,000 to get it going. They rent a storefront, lease ovens, purchase computers, and set some money aside as a reserve. The firm then has to attract employees. To do so, it will offer wage contracts that promise to pay employees every two weeks, whether or not the firm is making a profit or generating a loss. This guarantee shields the firm's employees from the risks of owning and operating the business. They will get paid even if the pizza parlour is losing money.

CONSIDER THIS   Insurance

Insurance promotes economic growth and investment by transferring risk from those who have a low tolerance for risk to those who have a high tolerance for risk. Consider fire insurance. Homeowners pay a monthly premium in exchange for which their insurance company guarantees to reimburse them if their house burns down. That guarantee transfers the risk of fire damage from the homeowners (who do not want to bear the risk) to the insurance company's owners (who are happy to bear the risk as a business proposition).

The insurance company will save the premiums that it receives from homeowners to help cover the rebuilding costs of any homes that do end up burning down. It is quite possible that there will be so many fires that the insurance company will spend more money repairing fire damage than it received in premiums. If that happens, the insurance company will suffer a loss that will fall on the insurance company's owners. Their personal wealth will decline in order to make up for the unexpectedly high number of fires. Thus, the insurance company's owners ultimately bear the fire risk; it is to them that the insurance contract transfers risk.

But if the number of fires is unexpectedly small, the insurance company will turn a nice profit and the insurance company's owners will benefit from having been willing to bear the fire risk that the homeowners did not wish to bear. More importantly, the economy's overall level of investment rises because the availability of insurance means those who dislike risk are much more willing to invest their savings in the construction and purchase of capital goods like houses, cars, and factories.

In the same way, the contracts that the firm signs with its suppliers and with anyone who loans the firm money (for instance, the local bank) will also specify that they will be paid on time and in full no matter how the firm is doing in terms of profitability.

DEALING WITH LOSSES

So what happens if the firm starts losing money? In that case, the owners will take the financial hit. To be specific, suppose that the pizza parlour loses $1500 during the month of October because it runs up $11,500 in costs but generates only $10,000 in revenue. In that situation, the investors' wealth will shrink by $1500 as the firm is forced to dip into its reserve to cover the loss. If the firm continues to lose money in subsequent months and exhausts the reserve, the owners will then have to decide whether they want to close the shop or put in additional money in the hope that things will turn around.

But throughout all those months of losses, the suppliers and employees are safeguarded. Because they are paid on time and in full, they are shielded from the firm's business risks and whether it is generating a profit or a loss. As a result, however, they are not legally entitled to share in the profits if the firm does end up being profitable. That privilege is reserved under the market system for the firm's owners as their reward for bearing business risk. In exchange for making sure that everyone else is shielded if things go badly, the owners are legally entitled to take all of the profits if things go well.

Benefits of Restricting Business Risk to Owners

There are two major benefits that arise from the market system's restriction of business risk to owners and investors.

ATTRACTING INPUTS

Many people deeply dislike risk and would not be willing to participate in a business venture if they were exposed to the possibility of losing money. That is the case with many workers, who just want to do their jobs and get paid twice a month without having to worry about whether their employer is doing well or not. The same is true for most suppliers, who just want to get paid on time and in full for the inputs they supply to the firm.

For both groups, the concentration of business risk on owners and investors is very welcome because they can supply their resources to a firm without having to worry about the firm's profitability. That sense of security makes it much easier for firms to attract labour and other inputs, which in turn helps the economy innovate and grow.

FOCUSING ATTENTION

The profit system helps to achieve prudent risk management by focusing both the responsibility and the rewards for successfully managing risk onto a firm's owners. They can provide the risk-managing input of entrepreneurial ability themselves or hire it by paying a skilled manager. But either way, some individual's full-time job includes the specialized task of managing risk and making prudent decisions about the allocation of resources. By contrast, in a command system, the responsibility for managing risk tends to be spread out over several layers of government and many different committees so that nobody is personally responsible for bad outcomes.

QUICK REVIEW 2.5

- The market system incentivizes the prudent management of business risk by concentrating any profit or loss upon a firm's owners and investors.

- The market system shields employees, suppliers, and lenders from business risks but in exchange for that protection, they are excluded from any profit that may be earned.

- By focusing risk on owners and investors, the market system (a) creates an incentive for owners and investors to hire managerial and entrepreneurial specialists to prudently mange business risks and (b) encourages the participation of workers, suppliers, and lenders who dislike risk.

The **LAST WORD** | Shuffling the Deck

Economist Donald Boudreaux marvels at the way the market system systematically and purposefully arranges the world's tens of billions of individual resources.

In *The Future and Its Enemies,* Virginia Postrel notes the astonishing fact that if you thoroughly shuffle an ordinary deck of 52 playing cards, chances are practically 100 percent that the resulting arrangement of cards has never before existed. Never. Every time you shuffle a deck, you produce an arrangement of cards that exists for the first time in history.

The arithmetic works out that way. For a very small number of items, the number of possible arrangements is small. Three items, for example, can be arranged only six different ways. But the number of possible arrangements grows very quickly. The number of different ways to arrange five items is 120 . . . for ten items it's 3,628,800 . . . for fifteen items it's 1,307,674,368,000.

The number of different ways to arrange 52 items is 8.066 × 10^{67}. This is a big number. No human can comprehend its enormousness. By way of comparison, the number of possible ways to arrange a mere 20 items is 2,432,902,008,176,640,000—a number larger than the total number of seconds that have elapsed since the beginning of time ten billion years ago—and this number is Lilliputian compared to 8.066 × 10^{67}.

What's the significance of these facts about numbers? Consider the number of different resources available in the world—my labour, your labour, your land, oil, tungsten, cedar, coffee beans, chickens, rivers, the Empire State Building, [Microsoft] Windows, the wharves at Houston, the classrooms at Oxford, the airport at Miami, and on and on and on. No one can possibly count all of the different, productive resources available for our use. But we can be sure that this number is at least in the tens of billions.

When you reflect on how incomprehensibly large is the number of ways to arrange a deck containing a mere 52 cards, the mind boggles at the number of different ways to arrange all the world's resources.

If our world were random—if resources combined together haphazardly, as if a giant took them all into his hands and tossed them down like so many [cards]—it's a virtual certainty that the resulting combination of resources would be useless. Unless this chance arrangement were quickly rearranged according to some productive logic, nothing worthwhile would be produced. We would all starve to death. Because only a tiny fraction of possible arrangements serves human ends, any arrangement will be useless if it is chosen randomly or with inadequate knowledge of how each and every resource might be productively combined with each other.

And yet, we witness all around us an arrangement of resources that's productive and serves human goals. Today's arrangement of resources might not be perfect, but it is vastly superior to most of the trillions upon trillions of other possible arrangements.

How have we managed to get one of the minuscule number of arrangements that works? The answer is private property—a social institution that encourages mutual accommodation.

Private property eliminates the possibility that resource arrangements will be random, for each resource owner chooses a course of action only if it promises rewards to the owner that exceed the rewards promised by all other available courses.

[The result] is a breathtakingly complex and productive arrangement of countless resources. This arrangement emerged over time (and is still emerging) as the result of billions upon billions of individual, daily, small decisions made by people seeking to better employ their resources and labour in ways that other people find helpful.

Source: Abridged from Donald J. Boudreaux, "Mutual Accommodation," *Ideas on Liberty*, May 2000, pp. 4–5. Reprinted with permission.

Question

What explains why millions of economic resources tend to get arranged logically and productively rather than haphazardly and unproductively?

Chapter Summary

LO2.1 DIFFERENTIATE BETWEEN LAISSEZ-FAIRE CAPITALISM, THE COMMAND SYSTEM, AND THE MARKET SYSTEM.

- Laissez-faire capitalism is a hypothetical economic system in which government's role would be restricted to protecting private property and enforcing contracts. All real-world economic systems have featured a more extensive role for government. Governments in command systems own nearly all property and resources and make nearly all decisions about what to produce, how to produce it, and who gets the output. Most countries today, including Canada, have market systems in which the government does play a large role, but in which most property and resources are privately owned and markets are the major force in determining what to produce, how to produce it, and who gets it.

LO2.2 LIST THE MAIN CHARACTERISTICS OF THE MARKET SYSTEM.

- The market system is characterized by the private ownership of resources, including capital, and the freedom of individuals to engage in economic activities of their choice to advance their material well-being. Self-interest is the driving force of such an economy, and competition functions as a regulatory or control mechanism.

- In the market system, markets, prices, and profits organize and make effective the many millions of individual economic decisions that occur daily.

- Specialization, the use of advanced technology, and the extensive use of capital goods are common features of market systems. Functioning as a medium of exchange, money eliminates the problems of bartering and permits easy trade and greater specialization, both domestically and internationally.

LO2.3   EXPLAIN HOW THE MARKET SYSTEM ANSWERS THE FIVE FUNDAMENTAL QUESTIONS OF WHAT TO PRODUCE, HOW TO PRODUCE, WHO OBTAINS THE OUTPUT, HOW TO ADJUST TO CHANGE, AND HOW TO PROMOTE PROGRESS.

- Every economy faces five fundamental questions: (1) What goods and services will be produced? (2) How will the goods and services be produced? (3) Who will get the goods and services? (4) How will the system accommodate change? (5) How will the system promote progress?

- The market system produces products whose production and sale yield total revenue sufficient to cover total cost. It does not produce products for which total revenue continually falls short of total cost. Competition forces firms to use the lowest-cost production techniques.

- Positive economic profit (total revenue minus total cost) indicates that an industry is prosperous and promotes its expansion. Losses signify that an industry is not prosperous and hasten its contraction.

- Consumer sovereignty means that both businesses and resource suppliers are subject to the wants of consumers. Through their dollar votes, consumers decide on the composition of output.

- The prices that a household receives for the resources it supplies to the economy determine that household's income. This income determines the household's claim on the economy's output. Those who have income to spend get the products produced in the market system.

- By communicating changes in consumer tastes to entrepreneurs and resource suppliers, the market system prompts appropriate adjustments in the allocation of the economy's resources. The market system also encourages technological advance and capital accumulation, both of which raise a nation's standard of living.

LO2.4   EXPLAIN THE OPERATION OF THE INVISIBLE HAND AND WHY MARKET ECONOMIES USUALLY DO A BETTER JOB THAN COMMAND ECONOMIES AT TRANSFORMING ECONOMIC RESOURCES INTO DESIRABLE OUTPUT.

- Competition, the primary mechanism of control in the market economy, promotes a unity of self-interest and social interests. As if directed by an invisible hand, competition harnesses the self-interest motives of businesses and resource suppliers to further the social interest.

- The command systems of the former Soviet Union and pre-reform China met their demise because of coordination difficulties caused by central planning and the lack of profit incentives that encourage product improvement, produce new products, and give rise to entrepreneurship.

LO2.5   DESCRIBE THE MECHANICS OF THE CIRCULAR FLOW MODEL.

- The circular flow model illustrates the flow of resources and products from households to businesses and from businesses to households, along with the corresponding monetary flows. Businesses are on the buying side of the resource market and the selling side of the product market. Households are on the selling side of the resource market and the buying side of the product market.

LO2.6   EXPLAIN HOW THE MARKET SYSTEM DEALS WITH RISK.

- By focusing business risks onto owners, the market system encourages the participation of workers and suppliers who dislike risk, while at the same time creating a strong incentive for owners to manage business risks prudently.

Terms and Concepts

economic system	market	invisible hand
laissez-faire capitalism	specialization	circular flow diagram
command system	division of labour	household
market system	medium of exchange	businesses
private property	barter	sole proprietorship
freedom of enterprise	money	partnership
freedom of choice	consumer sovereignty	corporation
self-interest	dollar votes	product market
competition	creative destruction	factor market

Discussion Questions

1. Contrast how a market system and a command economy try to cope with economic scarcity. [LO2.1]

2. How does self-interest help achieve society's economic goals? Why is there such a wide variety of desired goods and services in a market system? In what way are entrepreneurs and businesses at the helm of the economy but commanded by consumers? [LO2.2]

3. Why is private property, and the protection of property rights, essential to the success of the market system? How do property rights encourage cooperation? [LO2.2]

4. What are the advantages of using capital goods in the production process? What is meant by the term *division of labour*? What are the advantages of specialization in the use of human and material resources? Explain why exchange is the necessary consequence of specialization. [LO2.2]

5. What problem does barter entail? Indicate the economic significance of money as a medium of exchange. What is meant by the statement "We want money only to part with it"? [LO2.2]

6. Evaluate and explain each of the following hypothetical statements: [LO2.2]

   a. The market system is a profit-and-loss system.

   b. Competition is the disciplinarian of the market economy.

7. Some large hardware stores such as Canadian Tire boast of carrying as many as 20,000 different products in each store. What motivated the producers of those individual products to make them and offer them for sale? How did the producers decide on the best combinations of factors to use? Who made those factors available, and why? Who decides whether these particular hardware products should continue to be produced and offered for sale? [LO2.3]

8. What is meant by the term *creative destruction*? How does the emergence of MP3 (or iPod) technology relate to this idea? [LO2.3]

9. In a sentence, define the phrase *Invisible Hand*. [LO2.3]

10. In market economies firms rarely worry about the availability of inputs to produce their products, whereas in command economies input availability is a constant concern. Why is there a difference? [LO2.4]

11. Distinguish between the factor market and the product market in the circular flow model. In what way are businesses and households both sellers and buyers in this model? What are the flows in the circular flow model? [LO2.5]

12. How does shielding employees and suppliers from business risk help to improve economic outcomes? Who is responsible for managing business risks in the market system? [LO 2.6]

Review Questions

1. Decide whether each of the following describes a command system, a market system, or a laissez-faire system. [LO2.1]

   a. A woman cannot open a flower shop unless the central government decides to allow it.

   b. Shops stock and sell the goods their customers want but the government levies a sales tax on each transaction in order to fund elementary schools, public libraries, and welfare programs for the poor.

   c. The only taxes levied by the government are to pay for national defense, law enforcement, and a legal system designed to enforce contracts between private citizens.

2. Match each term with the correct definition. [LO2.2]

   private property   self-interest
   freedom of enterprise   competition
   mutually agreeable   market
   freedom of choice

   a. An institution that brings buyers and sellers together.

   b. The right of private persons and firms to obtain, control, employ, dispose of, and bequeath land, capital, and other property.

   c. The presence in a market of independent buyers and sellers who compete with one another and who are free to enter and exit the market as they each see fit.

   d. The freedom of firms to obtain economic resources, decide what products to produce with those resources, and sell those products in markets of their choice.

   e. What each individual or firm believes is best for itself and seeks to obtain.

   f. Economic transactions willingly undertaken by both the buyer and the seller because each feels that the transaction will make him or her better off.

   g. The freedom of resource owners to dispose of their resources as they think best, of workers to enter any line of work for which they are qualified, and of consumers to spend their incomes in whatever way they feel is most appropriate.

3. True or False? Money must be issued by a government for people to accept it. [LO2.2]

4. Assume that a business firm finds that its profit is greatest when it produces $40 worth of product A. Suppose also that

each of the three techniques shown in the table (Resource Units Required) will produce the desired output.   [LO2.3]

a. With the factor prices shown, which technique will the firm choose? Why? Will production using that technique entail profit or loss? What will be the amount of that profit or loss? Will the industry expand or contract? When will that expansion or contraction end?

b. Assume now that a new technique, Technique 4, is developed. It combines 2 units of labour, 2 of land, 6 of capital, and 3 of entrepreneurial ability. In view of the resource prices in the table, will the firm adopt the new technique? Explain your answer.

c. Suppose that an increase in the labour supply causes the price of labour to fall to $1.50 per unit, all other resource prices remaining unchanged. Which technique will the producer now choose? Explain.

d. "The market system causes the economy to conserve most in the use of resources that are particularly scarce in supply. Resources that are scarcest relative to the demand for them have the highest prices. As a result, producers use these resources as sparingly as is possible." Evaluate this statement. Does your answer to part c, above, bear out this contention? Explain.

RESOURCE UNITS REQUIRED

Resource	Price per unit of resource	Technique 1	Technique 2	Technique 3
Labour	$3	5	2	3
Land	4	2	4	2
Capital	2	2	4	5
Entrepreneurial ability	2	4	2	4

5. Identify each of the following quotes as being an example of either the coordination problem, the invisible hand, creative destruction, or the incentive problem.   [LO2.4]

a. "If you compare a list of today's most powerful and profitable companies with a similar list from 30 years ago, you will see lots of new entries."

b. "Managers in the old Soviet Union often sacrificed product quality and variety because they were being awarded bonuses for quantitative, not qualitative, targets."

c. "Each day, central planners in the old Soviet Union were tasked with setting 27 million prices—correctly."

d. "It is not from the benevolence of the butcher, the brewer, or the baker that we expect our dinner, but from their regard to their own interest."

6. True or False? Households sell finished products to businesses. [LO2.6]

7. Franklin, John, Henry, and Harry have decided to pool their financial resources and business skills in order to open up and run a coffee shop. They will share any profits or losses that the business generates and will be personally responsible for making good on any debt that their business undertakes. Their business should be classified as a   [LO2.6]

a. Corporation

b. Sole proprietorship

c. Partnership

d. None of the above

8. Ted and Fred are the owners of a gas station. They invested $150,000 each and pay an employee named Lawrence $35,000 per year. This year revenues are $900,000, while costs are $940,000. Who is legally responsible for bearing the $40,000 loss?   [LO2.6]

a. Lawrence

b. Ted

c. Fred

d. Ted and Fred

c. Lawrence, Ted, and Fred

Problems

1. Suppose Natasha currently makes $50,000 per year working as a manager at a cable TV company. She develops two possible entrepreneurial business opportunities. In one, she will quit her job to start a hand-made soap company. In the other, she will try to develop an Internet-based competitor to the cable company. For the soap-making opportunity, she anticipates annual revenue of $465,000 and costs for the necessary land, labour, and capital of $395,000 per year. For the Internet opportunity, she anticipates costs for land, labour, and capital of $3,250,000 per year as compared to revenues of $3,275,000 per year.   [LO2.3]

a. Should she quit her current job to become an entrepreneur?

b. If she does quit her current job, which opportunity should she pursue?

2. With current technology, suppose a firm is producing 400 loaves of banana bread daily. Also assume that the least-cost combination of resources in producing those loaves is 5 units of labour, 7 units of land, 2 units of capital, and 1 unit of entrepreneurial ability, selling at per-unit prices of $40, $60, $60, and $20, respectively.   [LO2.3]

   a. If the firm can sell these 400 loaves at $2 per unit, what is its total revenue? Its total cost? Its profit or loss? Will it continue to produce banana bread?

   b. If this firm's situation is typical for the other makers of banana bread, will resources flow toward or away from this bread?

3. Let us put dollar amounts on the flows in the circular flow diagram of Figure 2-2.   [LO2.5]

   a. Suppose that businesses buy a total of $100 billion of the four resources (labour, land, capital, and entrepreneurial ability) from households. If households receive $60 billion in wages, $10 billion in rent, and $20 billion in interest, how much are households paid for providing entrepreneurial ability?

   b. If households spend $55 billion on goods and $45 billion on services, how much in revenues do businesses receive in the product market?

PART 2 | PRICE, QUANTITY, AND EFFICIENCY

CHAPTER 3 :: Demand, Supply, and Market Equilibrium

CHAPTER 4 :: Market Failures: Public Goods and Externalities

CHAPTER 5 :: Government's Role and Government Failure

CHAPTER 3

Demand, Supply, and Market Equilibrium

LEARNING OBJECTIVES

LO3.1 Characterize and give example of markets.

LO3.2 Describe *demand* and explain how it can change.

LO3.3 Describe *supply* and explain how it can change.

LO3.4 Relate how supply and demand interact to determine market equilibrium.

LO3.5 Explain how changes in supply and demand affect equilibrium prices and quantities.

LO3.6 Identify what government-set prices are and how they can cause surpluses and shortages.

LOA3.1 (Appendix) Illustrate how supply and demand analysis can provide insights into actual-economy situations.

The model of supply and demand is the economics profession's greatest contribution to human understanding, because it explains the operation of the markets on which we depend for nearly everything that we eat, drink, or consume. The model is so powerful and so widely used that, to many people, it *is* economics.

This chapter explains how the model works and how it can explain both the *quantities* that are bought and sold in markets and the *prices* at which they trade.

3.1 / Markets

LO3.1 Characterize and give example of markets.

Markets bring together buyers (demanders) and sellers (suppliers). The corner gas station, an e-commerce website, the local music store, a farmer's roadside stand–all are familiar markets. The Toronto Stock Exchange and the Winnipeg Commodity Exchange are markets where buyers and sellers of stocks, bonds, and farm commodities from all over the world communicate with one another to buy and sell. Auctioneers bring together potential buyers and sellers of art, livestock, used farm equipment, and sometimes real estate. In labour markets, new college or university graduates sell and employers buy specific labour services.

Some markets are local, while others are national or international. Some are highly personal, involving face-to-face contact between demander and supplier; others are faceless, with buyer and seller never seeing or knowing each other.

To keep things simple, in this chapter we will focus on markets in which large numbers of independently acting buyers and sellers come together to buy and sell standardized products. Markets with these characteristics are the economy's most highly competitive, and include the wheat market, the stock market, and the market for foreign currencies. All such markets involve demand, supply, price, and quantity. As you will soon see, the price is discovered through the interacting decisions of buyers and sellers.

In Chapter 12, we will study *aggregate demand* and *aggregate supply*, which consist of the combined demand and combined supply in all markets of an economy, including markets external to a national economy. We will see that aggregate markets don't always come to an equilibrium where all the resources in an economy are fully employed, and thus sometimes require policy action by governments.

ORIGIN OF THE IDEA 3.1   Demand and Supply

3.2 / Demand

LO3.2 Describe *demand* and explain how it can change.

Demand is a schedule or a curve that shows the various amounts of a product that consumers are willing and able to purchase at each of a series of possible prices during a specified period of time.[1] Demand shows the quantities of a product that will be purchased at various possible prices, *other things equal*. Demand can easily be shown in table form. Figure 3-1 shows a hypothetical demand schedule for a single consumer purchasing bushels of corn.

The table in Figure 3-1 reveals the relationship between the various prices of corn and the quantity of corn a particular consumer would be willing *and able* to purchase at each of these prices. We say willing *and able* because willingness alone is not effective in the market. You may be willing to buy a plasma television set, but if that willingness is not backed by the necessary dollars, it will not be effective and, therefore,

As price falls, the quantity demanded rises, and as price rises, the quantity demanded falls.

---

[1] This definition is obviously worded to apply to product markets. To adjust it to apply to factor markets, substitute the word *factor* for *product* and the word *businesses* for *consumers*.

FIGURE 3-1 **An Individual Buyer's Demand for Corn**

Because price and quantity demanded are inversely related, an individual's demand schedule graphs as a downsloping curve such as *D*. Specifically, the law of demand says that, other things equal, consumers will buy more of a product as its price declines. Here and in later figures, *P* stands for price, and *Q* stands for quantity (either demanded or supplied).

Price per bushel	Quantity demanded (bushels per week)
$5	10
4	20
3	35
2	55
1	80

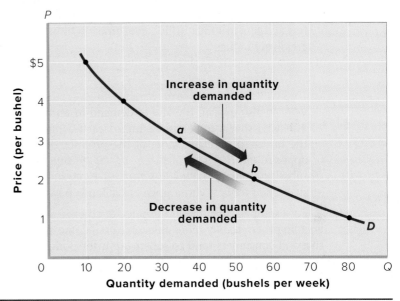

---

will not be reflected in the market. If the price of corn were $5 per bushel, our consumer would be willing and able to buy 10 bushels per week; if it were $4, the consumer would be willing and able to buy 20 bushels per week, and so forth.

The table in Figure 3-1 does not tell us which of the five possible prices will actually exist in the corn market. That depends on the interaction between demand and supply. Demand is simply a statement of a buyer's plans, or intentions, with respect to the purchase of a product.

To be meaningful, the quantities demanded at each price must relate to a specific period—a day, a week, a month, etc. Saying, "A consumer will buy 10 bushels of corn at $5 per bushel" is meaningless. Saying, "A consumer will buy 10 bushels of corn per week at $5 per bushel" is meaningful. Unless a specific time period is stated, we do not know whether the demand for a product is large or small.

ORIGIN OF THE IDEA 3.2   Law of Demand

Law of Demand

A fundamental characteristic of demand is this: *Other things equal, as price falls the quantity demanded rises, and as price rises the quantity demanded falls.* There is a negative or *inverse* relationship between price and quantity demanded. This inverse relationship is called the **law of demand**.

The *other-things-equal* assumption is crucial here (see Chapter 1). Many factors other than the price of the product being considered affect the amount purchased. The quantity of Nike shoes purchased will depend not only on the price of Nike shoes but also on the prices of substitutes such as Reebok, Adidas, and New Balance. The law of demand in this case says that fewer Nikes will be purchased if the price of Nikes rises *and if the prices of Reebok, Adidas, and New Balance shoes all remain constant.* In other words, if the *relative price* of Nikes rises, fewer Nikes will be bought.

ORIGIN OF THE IDEA 3.3   Diminishing Marginal Utility

Why is there an inverse relationship between price and quantity demanded? Let's look at two explanations:

- In any specific time period, each buyer of a product will derive less satisfaction (or benefit, or utility) from each successive unit of the product consumed. The second Big Mac will yield less additional satisfaction to the consumer than the first, and the third still less than the second. That is, consumption is subject to **diminishing marginal utility**. And because successive units of a particular product yield less and less marginal utility, consumers will buy additional units only if the price of those units is progressively reduced.

ORIGIN OF THE IDEA 3.4   Income and Substitution Effects

- We can also explain the law of demand in terms of *income* and *substitution* effects. The **income effect** indicates that a lower price increases the purchasing power of a buyer's money income, enabling the buyer to purchase more of the product than she or he could buy before. A higher price has the opposite effect. The **substitution effect** suggests that at a lower price buyers have the incentive to substitute what is now a less expensive product for other products that are now *relatively* more expensive. The product whose price has fallen is now a better deal relative to the other products.

For example, a decline in the price of chicken will increase the purchasing power of consumer incomes, enabling them to buy more chicken (the income effect). At a lower price, chicken is relatively more attractive and consumers tend to substitute it for pork, beef, and fish (the substitution effect). The income and substitution effects combine to make consumers able and willing to buy more of a product at a low price than at a high price.

The Demand Curve

The inverse relationship between price and quantity demanded for any product can be represented on a simple graph, in which, by convention, we measure *quantity demanded* on the horizontal axis and *price* on the vertical axis. In Figure 3-1 we plotted the five price-quantity data points listed in the table and connected the points with a smooth curve, labelled *D*. Such a curve is called a **demand curve**. Its downward slope reflects the law of demand–people buy more of a product, service, or factor as its price falls. The relationship between price and quantity demanded is inverse (or negative). We also refer to the demand curve as the *marginal benefit curve*, a concept introduced in Chapter 1. The demand curve tells us the extra benefit the consumer derives from one more unit of a good or service.

MATH 3.1   The Demand Function

The table and the graph in Figure 3-1 contain exactly the same data and reflect the same relationship between price and quantity demanded. But the graph shows that relationship more simply and clearly than a table or a description in words.

Market Demand

So far, we have concentrated on just one consumer. By adding the quantities demanded by all consumers at each of the various possible prices, we can get from *individual* demand to *market* demand. If there are just three buyers in the market, as represented in Figure 3-2, it is relatively easy to determine the total quantity demanded at each price. Figure 3-2 shows the graphical summing procedure: At each price we sum horizontally the individual quantities demanded to obtain the total quantity demanded at that price; we then plot the price and the total quantity demanded as one point of the market demand curve. At the price of $3, for example, the three individual curves yield a total quantity demanded of 100 bushels (= 35 + 39 + 26).

FIGURE 3-2 | **Market Demand for Corn, Three Buyers**

The market demand curve D is the horizontal summation of the individual demand curves (D_1, D_2, and D_3) of all the consumers in the market. At the price of $3, for example, the three individual curves yield a total quantity demanded of 100 bushels.

Price per bushel	Quantity Demanded							Total quantity demanded per week
	Joe		Jen		Jay			
$5	10	+	12	+	8	=		30
4	20	+	23	+	17	=		60
3	35	+	39	+	26	=		100
2	55	+	60	+	39	=		154
1	80	+	87	+	54	=		221

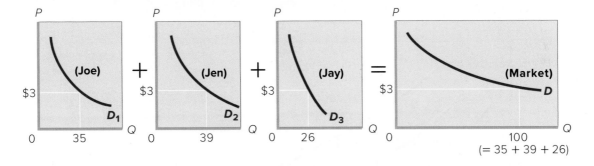

Competition, of course, ordinarily entails many more than three buyers of a product. To avoid hundreds or thousands or millions of additions, we suppose that all the buyers in a market are willing and able to buy the same amounts at each of the possible prices. Then we just multiply those amounts by the number of buyers to obtain the market demand. This is how we arrived at the demand schedule and demand curve D_1, in Figure 3-3, for a market with 200 corn buyers. The table in Figure 3-3 shows the calculations for 200 corn buyers.

Determinants of Demand

In constructing a demand curve such as D_1 in Figure 3-3, we assume that price is the most important influence on the amount of any product purchased, even though other factors can and do affect purchases. These factors, called **determinants of demand**, are assumed to be constant when a demand curve like D_1 is drawn. They are the *other things equal* in the relationship between price and quantity demanded. When any of these determinants changes, the demand curve will shift to the right or left.

The basic determinants of demand are (1) consumers' tastes (preferences), (2) the number of consumers in the market, (3) consumers' incomes, (4) the prices of related goods, and (5) consumers' expectations.

Changes in Demand

A change in one or more of the determinants of demand will change the demand data (the demand schedule) in the table accompanying Figure 3-3, and therefore the location of the demand curve there. A change in the demand schedule—or, graphically, a shift in the demand curve—is called a *change in demand.*

If consumers desire to buy more corn at each possible price than is reflected in column 2 of the table in Figure 3-3, that *increase in demand* is shown as a shift of the demand curve to the right—say, from D_1 to D_2.

FIGURE 3-3   Changes in the Demand for Corn

A change in one or more of the determinants of demand causes a change in demand. An increase in demand is shown as a shift of the demand curve to the right, as from D_1 to D_2. A decrease in demand is shown as a shift of the demand curve to the left, as from D_1 to D_3. These changes in demand are to be distinguished from a change in quantity demanded, which is caused by a change in the price of the product, as shown by a movement from, say, point a to point b on fixed demand curve D_1.

MARKET DEMAND FOR CORN, 200 BUYERS, D_1	
(1) **Price per bushel**	**(2) Total quantity** **demanded per week**
$5	2,000
4	4,000
3	7,000
2	11,000
1	16,000

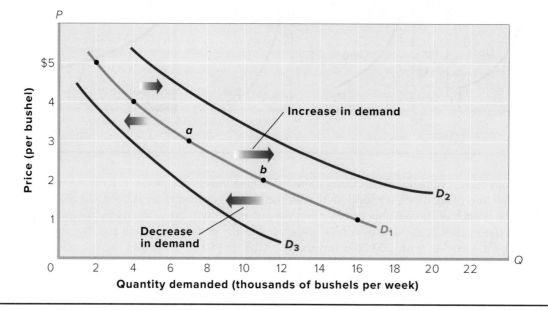

Conversely, a *decrease in demand* occurs when consumers buy less corn at each possible price than is indicated in column 2 of the table in Figure 3-3. The leftward shift of the demand curve from D_1 to D_3 in Figure 3-3 shows that situation.

Now let's see how changes in each determinant affect demand.

TASTES

A favourable change in consumer tastes (preferences) for a product—a change that makes the product more desirable—means that more of it will be demanded at each price. Demand will increase; the demand curve will shift rightward. An unfavourable change in consumer preferences will decrease demand, shifting the demand curve to the left.

New products may affect consumer tastes; for example, the introduction of digital cameras has greatly decreased demand for film cameras. Consumers' concern over the health hazards of cholesterol and obesity have increased the demand for broccoli, low-calorie sweeteners, and fresh fruit, while decreasing the demand for beef, veal, eggs, and whole milk. Over the past several years, the demand for coffee drinks and table wine has greatly increased, driven by changes in tastes. So, too, has the demand for touch-screen mobile phones and fuel-efficient hybrid vehicles.

NUMBER OF BUYERS

An increase in the number of buyers in a market increases demand; a decrease in the number of buyers decreases demand. For example, the rising number of older persons in Canada in recent years has increased the demand for motor homes, medical care, and retirement communities.

Immigration to Canada from many parts of the world has greatly increased the demand for a whole range of ethnic goods and services, particularly in southern Ontario and British Columbia. Improvements in communications have given financial markets international range and have thus increased the demand for stocks and bonds. International trade agreements have reduced foreign trade barriers to Canadian farm commodities, increasing the number of buyers and the demand for those products.

In contrast, the emigration (out-migration) from many small rural communities has reduced the population and thus the demand for housing, home appliances, and auto repair in those towns.

INCOME

How changes in income affect demand is more complex. For most products, a rise in income causes an increase in demand. Consumers typically buy more steaks, furniture, and electronic equipment as their incomes increase. Conversely, the demand for such products declines as income falls. A product for which demand varies directly with money income is called a **normal good**.

Although most products are normal goods, there are some exceptions. As incomes increase beyond some point, the demand for used clothing, retread tires, and third-hand automobiles may decrease, because the higher incomes enable consumers to buy new versions of those products. Similarly, rising incomes may cause the demand for charcoal grills to decline as wealthier consumers switch to gas grills. Goods for which demand varies *inversely* with money income are called **inferior goods**.

PRICES OF RELATED GOODS

A change in the price of a related good may either increase or decrease the demand for a product, depending on whether the related good is a substitute or a complement. A **substitute good** is one that can be used in place of another good. A **complementary good** is one that is used together with another good.

- **Substitutes** Häagen-Dazs ice cream and Baskin-Robbins ice cream are substitute goods (or, simply, *substitutes*). When two products are substitutes, an increase in the price of one will increase the demand for the other. Conversely, a decrease in the price of one will decrease the demand for the other. For example, when the price of Häagen-Dazs ice cream rises, consumers will demand less of it and increase their demand for Baskin-Robbins ice cream. When the price of Colgate toothpaste declines, the demand for Crest declines. So it is with other product pairs such as Nike and Reebok shoes, Molson and Labatt beer, or Chevrolet and Ford pickup trucks. They are *substitutes in consumption*.

- **Complements** Because complementary goods (or, simply, *complements*) are used together, they are typically demanded jointly. Examples include computers and software, cellphones and cellular service, and snowboards and lift tickets. If the price of a complement (for example, lettuce) goes up, the demand for the related good (salad dressing) will decline. Conversely, if the price of a complement (for example, tuition) falls, the demand for a related good (textbooks) will increase.

- **Unrelated Goods** The vast majority of goods that are not related to one another are called *independent goods*. Examples are butter and golf balls, potatoes and automobiles, and bananas and wristwatches. A change in the price of one does not affect the demand for the other.

CONSUMER EXPECTATIONS

Changes in consumer expectations may shift demand. A newly formed expectation of higher future prices may cause consumers to buy now in order to beat the anticipated price rises, thus increasing current demand. That is often what happens in so-called hot real estate markets. Buyers rush in because they think the price of new homes will continue to escalate rapidly. Some buyers fear being priced out of the market and therefore not obtaining the home they desire. Other buyers–speculators–believe they will be able to sell the houses later at a higher price. Whichever their motivation, these buyers increase the demand for houses.

Similarly, a change in expectations concerning future income may prompt consumers to change their current spending. For example, first-round NHL draft choices may splurge on new luxury cars in anticipation of lucrative professional hockey contracts. Or workers who become fearful of losing their jobs may reduce their demand for, say, vacation travel.

In summary, an *increase* in demand–the decision by consumers to buy larger quantities of a product at each possible price–may be caused by

- A favourable change in consumer tastes
- An increase in the number of buyers
- An increase in incomes if the product is a normal good
- A decrease in incomes if the product is an inferior good
- An increase in the price of a substitute good
- A decrease in the price of a complementary good
- A new consumer expectation that prices and incomes will be higher in the future

Reverse these generalizations to explain a *decrease* in demand. Table 3-1 provides additional illustrations of the determinants of demand.

Changes in Quantity Demanded

A *change in demand* must not be confused with a *change in quantity demanded*. A **change in demand** is a shift of the entire demand curve to the right (an increase in demand) or to the left (a decrease in demand). It occurs because the consumer's state of mind about purchasing the product has been altered in response to a change in one or more of the determinants of demand. Recall that *demand* is a schedule or a curve; therefore, a *change in demand* means a change in the schedule and a shift of the curve.

In contrast, a **change in quantity demanded** is a movement from one point to another point–from one price-quantity combination to another–on a fixed demand curve. The cause of such a change is an increase or decrease in the price of the product under consideration. In Figure 3-3, for example,

TABLE 3-1	Determinants of Demand Curve Shifts
Determinant	**Examples**
Change in buyer tastes	Physical fitness rises in popularity, increasing the demand for jogging shoes and bicycles; cellphone popularity rises, reducing the demand for land-line phones.
Change in number of buyers	A decline in the birth rate reduces the demand for children's toys.
Change in income	A rise in incomes increases the demand for such normal goods as restaurant meals, sports tickets, and tablet computers, while reducing the demand for such inferior goods as cabbage, turnips, and inexpensive wine.
Change in the prices of related goods	A reduction in airfares reduces the demand for bus transportation (substitute goods); a decline in the price of Blu-ray DVD players increases the demand for Blu-ray DVD movies (complementary goods).
Change in consumer expectation	Political instability in South America creates an expectation of higher future coffee bean prices, thereby increasing today's demand for coffee beans.

a decline in the price of corn from $5 to $4 will increase the quantity of corn demanded from 2000 to 4000 bushels.

In Figure 3-3, the shift of the demand curve D_1 to either D_2 or D_3 is a change in demand. But the movement from point a to point b on curve D_1 represents a change in quantity demanded: Demand has not changed; it is the entire curve, and it remains fixed in place.

QUICK REVIEW 3.1

- A market is any arrangement that facilitates the purchase and sale of goods, services, or resources.
- Demand is a schedule or a curve showing the amount of a product that buyers are willing and able to purchase at each possible price in a series of prices, in a particular time period.
- The law of demand states that, other things equal, the quantity of a good purchased varies inversely with its price.

- The demand curve shifts because of changes in (a) consumer tastes, (b) the number of buyers in the market, (c) consumer income, (d) the prices of substitute or complementary goods, and (e) consumer expectations.
- A change in demand is a shift of the demand curve; a change in quantity demanded is a movement from one point to another on a fixed demand curve.

3.3 / Supply

LO3.3 Describe *supply* and explain how it can change.

Supply is a schedule or curve that shows the amounts of a product that producers are willing and able to make available for sale at each of a series of possible prices during a specific period.[2] Figure 3-4 is a hypothetical supply schedule for a single producer of corn. It shows the quantities of corn that will be supplied at various prices, other things equal.

Law of Supply

The table in Figure 3-4 shows a direct relationship between price and quantity supplied. As price rises, the quantity supplied rises; as price falls, the quantity supplied falls. This relationship is called the **law of supply**. A supply schedule tells us that, other things equal, firms will produce and offer for sale more of their product at a high price than at a low price. The higher the price, the greater the incentive and the greater the quantity supplied.

Price is an obstacle from the standpoint of the consumer, who is on the paying end. The higher the price, the less the consumer will buy. But the supplier is on the receiving end of the product's price. To the supplier, price represents *revenue*, which serves as an incentive to produce and sell a product. The higher the price, the greater the incentive and the greater the quantity supplied.

Consider a farmer in Ontario who is deciding how much corn to plant. As corn prices rise, as shown in the table in Figure 3-4, the farmer finds it profitable to plant more. And the higher corn prices enable the Ontario farmer to cover the increased costs associated with more intensive cultivation and the use of more seed, fertilizer, and pesticide. The overall result is more corn.

Now consider a manufacturer. Beyond some quantity of production, manufacturers usually encounter increasing *marginal cost*–the added cost of producing one more unit of output. Certain productive resources–in particular, the firm's plant and machinery–cannot be expanded quickly, so the firm uses

---

[2] This definition is worded to apply to product markets. To adjust it to apply to factor markets, substitute the word *factor* for *product* and the word *owner* for *producer*.

| FIGURE 3-4 | An Individual Producer's Supply of Corn |

Because price and quantity supplied are positively related, a firm's supply schedule is an upsloping curve such as S. Specifically, the law of supply says that, other things equal, firms will supply more of a product as its price rises.

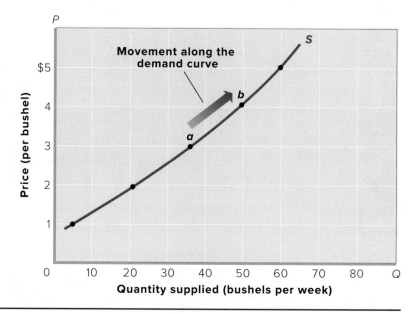

Price per bushel	Quantity supplied (bushels per week)
$5	60
4	50
3	35
2	20
1	5

more of other resources, such as labour, to produce more output. But as labour becomes more abundant relative to the fixed plant and equipment, the additional workers have relatively less space and access to equipment. For example, the added workers may have to wait to gain access to machines. As a result, each added worker produces less added output, and the marginal cost of successive units of output rises accordingly. The firm will not produce the more costly units unless it receives a higher price for them. Again, price and quantity supplied are directly related.

The Supply Curve

As with demand, it is convenient to represent individual supply graphically. In Figure 3-4, curve S is the **supply curve** that corresponds to the price–quantity data in the accompanying table. The upward slope of the curve reflects the law of supply–a producer will offer more of a good, service, or factor for sale as its price rises. The relationship between price and quantity supplied is positive or direct.

MATH 3.2 The Supply Function

Market Supply

Market supply is derived from individual supply in exactly the same way that market demand is derived from individual demand. We sum the quantities supplied by each producer at each price. That is, we obtain the market supply curve by horizontally adding the supply curves of the individual producers. The price–quantity supplied data in the table in Figure 3-5 are for an assumed 200 identical producers in the market, each willing to supply corn according to the supply schedule shown in Figure 3-4. Curve S_1 in Figure 3-5 is a graph of the market supply data. Note that the axes in Figure 3-5 are the same as those used in our graph of market demand (Figure 3-2). The only difference is that we change the label on the horizontal axis from *quantity demanded* to *quantity supplied*.

| FIGURE 3-5 | Changes in the Supply of Corn |

A change in one or more of the determinants of supply causes a shift in supply. An increase in supply is shown as a rightward shift of the supply curve, as from S_1 to S_2. A decrease in supply is depicted as a leftward shift of the curve, as from S_1 to S_3. In contrast, a change in the quantity supplied is caused by a change in the product's price and is shown by a movement from one point to another, as from point a to point b, on a fixed supply curve.

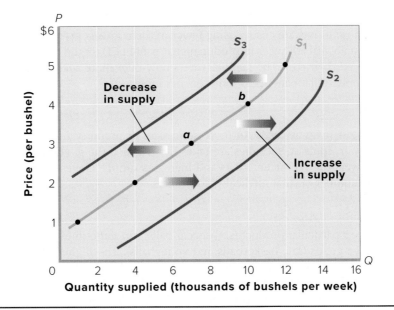

MARKET SUPPLY OF CORN, 200 PRODUCERS, S_1	
(1) Price per bushel	(2) Total quantity supplied per week
$5	12,000
4	10,000
3	7,000
2	4,000
1	1,000

Determinants of Supply

In constructing a supply curve, we assume that price is the most significant influence on the quantity supplied of any product. But other factors (the "other things equal") can and do affect supply. The supply curve is drawn on the assumption that these other things are fixed and do not change. If one of them does change, a *change in supply* will occur, meaning that the entire supply curve will shift.

The basic **determinants of supply** are (1) factor prices, (2) technology, (3) taxes and subsidies, (4) prices of other goods, (5) price expectations, and (6) the number of sellers in the market. A change in any one or more of these determinants of supply will move the supply curve for a product either to the right or to the left. A shift to the *right*, as from S_1 to S_2 in Figure 3-5, signifies an *increase* in supply: Producers supply larger quantities of the product at each possible price. A shift to the *left*, as from S_1 to S_3, indicates a *decrease* in supply.

Changes in Supply

Let's consider how changes in each of the determinants affect supply. The key idea is that costs are a major factor underlying supply curves; anything that affects costs (other than changes in output itself) usually shifts the supply curve.

FACTOR PRICES

The prices of the factors used as inputs in the production process determine the costs of production. Higher *factor* prices raise production costs and, assuming a particular *product* price, squeeze profits. That reduction in profits reduces the incentive for firms to supply output at each product price. For example, an increase in the prices of iron ore and coke will increase the cost of producing steel for Dofasco and reduce its supply.

In contrast, lower *factor* prices reduce production costs and increase profits. So, when input prices fall, firms supply greater output at each product price. For example, a decrease in the price of iron ore will decrease the price of steel.

TECHNOLOGY

Improvements in technology (techniques of production) enable firms to produce units of output with fewer inputs. Because inputs are costly, using fewer of them lowers production costs and increases supply. For example, technological advances in producing flat-panel LCD (liquid crystal display) computer monitors have greatly reduced their cost. The manufacturers now offer more such monitors than previously at various prices; the supply of flat-panel LCD monitors has increased.

TAXES AND SUBSIDIES

Businesses treat most taxes as costs. An increase in sales or property taxes will increase production costs and reduce supply. In contrast, subsidies are taxes in reverse. If the government subsidizes the production of a good, that lowers the producers' costs and increases supply. Government subsidies will, for example, help increase the number of rural medical practitioners.

PRICES OF OTHER GOODS

Firms that produce a particular product (say, soccer balls) can sometimes use their plants and equipment to produce alternative goods (say, basketballs and volleyballs). The higher prices of these other goods may entice soccer ball producers to switch production to those other goods to increase profits. This substitution in production results in a decline in the supply of soccer balls. Alternatively, when the prices of basketballs and volleyballs decline relative to the price of soccer balls, producers of those goods may decide to produce more soccer balls instead, increasing their supply.

PRODUCER EXPECTATIONS

Changes in expectations about the future price of a product may affect the producer's current willingness to supply that product. Ontario farmers anticipating a higher corn price in the future might withhold some of their current corn harvest from the market, thereby causing a decrease in the current supply of corn. In contrast, in many types of manufacturing industries, expectations that price will increase may induce firms to add another shift of workers or to expand their production facilities, causing current supply to increase.

NUMBER OF SELLERS

Other things equal, the larger the number of suppliers, the greater the market supply. As more firms enter an industry, the supply curve shifts to the right. Conversely, the smaller the number of firms in the industry, the less the market supply. This means that as firms leave an industry, the supply curve shifts to the left. Canada and the United States, for example, have imposed restrictions on haddock fishing to replenish dwindling stocks. As part of that policy, the federal government has bought the boats of some of the

TABLE 3-2	Determinants of Supply Curve Shifts
Determinant	**Examples**
Change in factor prices	A decrease in the price of microchips increases the supply of computers; an increase in the price of crude oil reduces the supply of gasoline.
Change in technology	The development of more effective wireless technology increases the supply of cellphones.
Change in taxes and subsidies	An increase in the excise tax on cigarettes reduces the supply of cigarettes; a decline in subsidies to universities reduces the supply of higher education.
Change in prices of other goods	An increase in the price of cucumbers decreases the supply of watermelons.
Change in producer expectations	An expectation of a substantial rise in future log prices decreases the supply of logs today.
Change in number of suppliers	An increase in the number of tattoo parlours increases the supply of tattoos; the formation of women's professional basketball leagues increases the supply of women's professional basketball games.

haddock fishers as a way of putting them out of business and decreasing the catch. The result has been a decline in the market supply of haddock.

Table 3-2 is a checklist of the determinants of supply, along with further illustrations.

Changes in Quantity Supplied

The distinction between a *change in supply* and a *change in quantity supplied* mirrors the distinction between a change in demand and a change in quantity demanded. Because supply is a schedule or curve, a **change in supply** means a change in the entire schedule and a shift of the entire curve. An increase in supply shifts the curve to the right; a decrease in supply shifts it to the left. The cause of a change in supply is a change in one or more of the determinants of supply.

In contrast, a **change in quantity supplied** is a movement from one point to another on a fixed supply curve. The cause of such a movement is a change in the price of the specific product being considered. Consider supply curve S_1 in Figure 3-5. A decline in the price of corn from $4 to $3 decreases the quantity of corn supplied per week from 10,000 to 7000 bushels. This movement from point *b* to point *a* along S_1 is a change in quantity supplied, not a change in supply. Supply is the full schedule of prices and quantities shown, and this schedule does not change when the price of corn changes.

QUICK REVIEW 3.2

- A supply schedule or curve shows that, other things equal, the quantity of a good supplied varies directly with its price.

- The supply curve shifts because of changes in (a) factor prices, (b) technology, (c) taxes and subsidies, (d) prices of other goods, (e) producer expectations, and (f) the number of sellers.

- A change in supply is a shift of the supply curve; a change in quantity supplied is a movement from one point to another on a fixed supply curve.

<table>
<tr><td>**3.4**</td><td># Market Equilibrium</td></tr>
</table>

LO3.4 Relate how supply and demand interact to determine market equilibrium.

With our understanding of demand and supply, we can now show how the decisions of buyers of corn interact with the decisions of the sellers to determine the price and quantity of corn. In the table in **Figure 3-6 (Key Graph)**, columns 1 and 2 repeat the market supply of corn (from Figure 3-5), and columns 2 and 3 repeat the market demand for corn (from the table in Figure 3-3). We assume this is a competitive market, so that neither buyers nor sellers can set the price.

Equilibrium Price and Quantity

We are looking for the equilibrium price and equilibrium quantity. The **equilibrium price** (or market-clearing price) is the price at which the intentions of buyers and sellers match. It is the price at which quantity demanded equals quantity supplied. The table in Figure 3-6 reveals that at $3, *and only at that price*, the number of bushels of corn that sellers wish to sell (7000) is identical to the number consumers want to buy (also 7000). At $3 and 7000 bushels of corn, there is neither a shortage nor a surplus of corn. So 7000 bushels of corn is the **equilibrium quantity**: the quantity at which the intentions of buyers and sellers match so that the quantity demanded and the quantity supplied are equal.

Graphically, the equilibrium price is indicated by the intersection of the supply curve and the demand curve in Figure 3-6. (The horizontal axis now measures both quantity demanded and quantity supplied.) With neither a shortage nor a surplus at $3, the market is *in equilibrium*, meaning "in balance" or "at rest."

MATH 3.3 Equilibrium Price and Quantity

Competition among buyers and among sellers drives the price to the equilibrium price, where it will remain unless it is subsequently disturbed by changes in demand or supply (shifts of the curves). To better understand the uniqueness of the equilibrium price, let's consider other prices. At any above-equilibrium price, quantity supplied exceeds quantity demanded. For example, at the $4 price, sellers will offer 10,000 bushels of corn, but buyers will purchase only 4000. The $4 price encourages sellers to offer lots of corn but discourages many consumers from buying it. The result is a **surplus** (or excess supply) of 6000 bushels. If corn sellers produced them all, they would find themselves with 6000 un-sold bushels of corn.

Surpluses drive prices down. Even if the $4 price existed temporarily, it could not persist. The large surplus would prompt competing sellers to lower the price to encourage buyers to take the surplus off their hands. As the price fell, the incentive to produce corn would decline and the incentive for consumers to buy corn would increase. As shown in Figure 3-6, the market would move to its equilibrium at $3.

Any price below the $3 equilibrium price would create a shortage; quantity demanded would exceed quantity supplied. Consider a $2 price, for example. We see both from column 2 of the table and from the demand curve in Figure 3-6 that quantity demanded exceeds quantity supplied at that price. The result is a **shortage** (or excess demand) of 7000 bushels of corn. The $2 price discourages sellers from devoting re-sources to corn and encourages consumers to desire more bushels than are available. The $2 price cannot persist as the equilibrium price. Many consumers who want to buy corn at this price will not obtain it. They will express a willingness to pay more than $2 to get corn. Competition among these buyers will drive up the price, eventually to the $3 equilibrium level. Unless disrupted by supply or demand changes, the $3 price of corn will continue to prevail.

Rationing Function of Prices

The ability of the competitive forces of supply and demand to establish a price at which selling and buying decisions are consistent is called the *rationing function of prices*. In our case, the equilibrium price of

KEY GRAPH

FIGURE 3-6 Equilibrium Price and Quantity

The intersection of the downsloping demand curve *D* and the upsloping supply curve *S* indicates the equilibrium price and quantity, here $3 and 7000 bushels of corn. The shortages of corn at below-equilibrium prices (for example, 7000 bushels at $2) drive up price. These higher prices increase the quantity supplied and reduce the quantity demanded until equilibrium is achieved. The surpluses caused by above-equilibrium prices (for example, 6000 bushels at $4) push price down. As price drops, the quantity demanded rises and the quantity supplied falls until equilibrium is established. At the equilibrium price and quantity, there are neither shortages nor surpluses of corn. The arrows in the table indicate the effect on price.

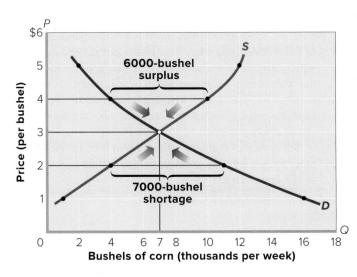

(1) Total quantity supplied per week	(2) Price per bushel	(3) Total quantity demanded per week	(4) Surplus (+) or shortage (−)
12,000	$5	2,000	+10,000↓
10,000	4	4,000	+6,000↓
7,000	3	7,000	0
4,000	2	11,000	−7,000↑
1,000	1	16,000	−15,000↑

Quick Quiz

1. **Demand curve *D* in Figure 3-6 is downsloping because**
   a. Producers offer less product for sale as the price of the product falls.
   b. Lower prices of a product create income and substitution effects, which lead consumers to purchase more of it.
   c. The larger the number of buyers in a market, the lower the product price.
   d. Price and quantity demanded are directly (positively) related.

2. **Supply curve *S***
   a. Reflects an inverse (negative) relationship between price and quantity supplied
   b. Reflects a direct (positive) relationship between price and quantity supplied

   c. Depicts the collective behaviour of buyers in this market
   d. Shows that producers will offer more of a product for sale at a low product price than at a high product price

3. **At the $3 price**
   a. Quantity supplied exceeds quantity demanded.
   b. Quantity demanded exceeds quantity supplied.
   c. The product is abundant and a surplus exists.
   d. There is no pressure on price to rise or fall.

4. **At price $5 in this market**
   a. There will be a shortage of 10,000 units.
   b. There will be a surplus of 10,000 units.
   c. Quantity demanded will be 12,000 units.
   d. Quantity demanded will equal quantity supplied.

Answers: 1.b; 2. b; 3. d; 4. b

CONSIDER THIS   Ticket Scalping: Unfair Criticism!

Ticket prices for athletic events and musical concerts are usually set far in advance of the events. Sometimes the original ticket price is too low to be the equilibrium price. Lines form at the ticket window, and a severe shortage of tickets occurs at the printed price. What happens next? Buyers who are willing to pay more than the original price bid up the ticket price in resale ticket markets.

Tickets sometimes get resold for much greater amounts than the original price—in a market transaction known as *scalping*. For example, the original buyer of an NHL ticket to a Vancouver Canucks game may resell a $75 ticket to an important game for $200, $250, or more. The media sometimes denounce scalpers for "ripping off" buyers by charging "exorbitant" prices.

But is scalping really a rip-off? We must first recognize that such ticket resales are voluntary transactions. If both buyer and seller did not expect to gain from the exchange, it would not occur! The seller must value the $200 more than seeing the sporting event, and the buyer must value seeing the sporting event at $200. So there are no losers or victims

here: Both buyer and seller benefit from the transaction. The scalping market simply redistributes assets (game or concert tickets) from those who would rather have the money (and the other things money can buy) to those who would rather have the tickets.

Does scalping impose losses or injury on the sponsors of the event? If the sponsors are injured, it is because they initially priced tickets below the equilibrium level. Perhaps they did this to create a long waiting line and the attendant media publicity. Alternatively, they may have had a genuine desire to keep tickets affordable for lower-income, ardent fans. In either case, the event sponsors suffer an opportunity cost in the form of less ticket revenue than they might have otherwise received. But such losses are self-inflicted and quite separate and distinct from the fact that some tickets are later resold at a higher price.

So, is ticket scalping undesirable? Not on economic grounds! It is an entirely voluntary activity that benefits both sellers and buyers.

$3 clears the market, leaving no burdensome surplus for sellers and no inconvenient shortage for potential buyers. It is the combination of freely made individual decisions that sets this market-clearing price. In effect, the market outcome says that all buyers who are willing and able to pay $3 for a bushel of corn will obtain it; all buyers who cannot or will not pay $3 will go without corn. Similarly, all producers who are willing and able to offer corn for sale at $3 a bushel will sell it; all producers who cannot or will not sell for $3 per bushel will not sell their product.

Efficient Allocation

A competitive market such as we have described not only rations goods to consumers but also allocates society's resources efficiently to the particular product. Competition among corn producers forces them to use the best technology and right mix of productive resources. If they didn't, their costs would be too high relative to the market price, and they would be unprofitable. The result is **productive efficiency**: the production of any particular good in the least costly way. When society produces corn at the lowest achievable per-unit cost, it is expending the smallest amount of resources to produce that product and therefore is making available the largest amount of resources to produce other desired goods. Suppose society has only $100 worth of resources available. If it can produce a bushel of corn using $3 of those resources, then it will have available $97 of resources remaining to produce other goods. This is clearly better than producing the corn for $5 and having only $95 of resources available for the alternative uses.

Competitive markets also produce **allocative efficiency**: the *particular mix* of goods and services most highly valued by society (minimum-cost production assumed). For example, society wants land suitable for growing corn to be used for that purpose, not to grow dandelions. It wants diamonds to be used for jewellery, not to be crushed up and used as an additive to give concrete more sparkle. It wants iPods and MP4 players, not cassette players and tapes. Moreover, society does not want to devote all its resources to corn, diamonds, and portable digital music players. It wants to assign some resources to wheat, gasoline, and cell-phones. Competitive markets make those proper assignments.

MATH 3.4 Allocative Efficiency

The equilibrium price and quantity in competitive markets usually produce an assignment of resources that is "right" from an economic perspective. Demand essentially reflects the marginal benefit (MB) of the good (the extra benefit received from consuming one more unit of a good or service) and supply reflects the marginal cost (MC) of the good (the extra cost associated with producing one more unit of a good or service). The market ensures that firms produce all units of goods for which MB exceeds MC, and no units for which MC exceeds MB. At the intersection of the demand and supply curves, MB equals MC and allocative efficiency results. As economists say, there is neither an underallocation of resources nor an overallocation of resources to the product.

3.5 / Changes in Supply, Demand, and Equilibrium

LO3.5 Explain how changes in supply and demand affect equilibrium prices and quantities.

We know that demand might change because of fluctuations in consumer tastes or incomes, changes in consumer expectations, or variations in the prices of related goods. Supply might change in response to changes in resource prices, technology, or taxes. What effects will such changes in supply and demand have on equilibrium price and quantity?

Changes in Demand

Suppose that the supply for some good (for example, potatoes) is constant and demand increases, as shown in Figure 3-7a. As a result, the new intersection of the supply and demand curves is at higher values on both the price and quantity axes. An increase in demand raises both equilibrium price and equilibrium quantity. Conversely, a decrease in demand, such as that shown in Figure 3-7b, reduces both equilibrium price and equilibrium quantity. (The value of graphical analysis is now apparent: We need not fumble with columns of figures to determine the outcomes; we need only compare the new and the old points of intersection on the graph.)

Changes in Supply

What happens if demand for some good (for example, flash drives) is constant but supply increases, as in Figure 3-7c? The new intersection of supply and demand is located at a lower equilibrium price but at a higher equilibrium quantity. An increase in supply reduces equilibrium price but increases equilibrium quantity. In contrast, if supply decreases, as in Figure 3-7d, equilibrium price rises while equilibrium quantity declines.

Complex Cases

When both supply and demand change, the effect is a combination of the individual effects. As you study the following cases, keep in mind that each effect on the demand and supply curves has to be considered independently.

1. ***Supply Increase, Demand Decrease*** What effect will a supply increase and a demand decrease for some good (for example, apples) have on equilibrium price? Both changes decrease price, so the net result is a price drop greater than that resulting from either change alone.

   What about equilibrium quantity? Here the effects of the changes in supply and demand are opposed: The increase in supply increases equilibrium quantity, but the decrease in demand reduces it. The direction of the change in equilibrium quantity depends on the relative sizes of the changes in supply and demand. If the increase in supply is larger than the decrease in demand, the equilibrium quantity will increase. But if the decrease in demand is greater than the increase in supply, the equilibrium quantity will decrease.

FIGURE 3-7   Changes in Demand and Supply, and the Effects on Price and Quantity

The increase in demand from D_1 to D_2 in panel (a) increases both equilibrium price and quantity. The decrease in demand from D_1 to D_2 in panel (b) decreases both equilibrium price and quantity. The increase in supply from S_1 to S_2 in panel (c) decreases equilibrium price and increases equilibrium quantity. The decline in supply from S_1 to S_2 in panel (d) increases equilibrium price and decreases equilibrium quantity. The boxes in the top right corners summarize the respective changes and outcomes. The upward arrows in those boxes signify increases in demand (D), supply (S), equilibrium price (P), and equilibrium quantity (Q); the downward arrows signify decreases in these items.

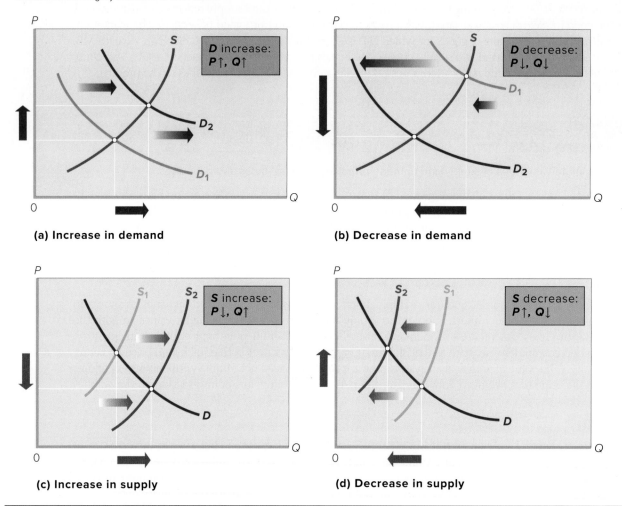

(a) Increase in demand

(b) Decrease in demand

(c) Increase in supply

(d) Decrease in supply

2. **Supply Decrease, Demand Increase** A decrease in supply and an increase in demand for some good (for example, gasoline) both increase price. Their combined effect is an increase in equilibrium price greater than that caused by either change separately. But their effect on the equilibrium quantity is again indeterminate, depending on the relative sizes of the changes in supply and demand. If the decrease in supply is larger than the increase in demand, the equilibrium quantity will decrease. In contrast, if the increase in demand is greater than the decrease in supply, the equilibrium quantity will increase.

3. **Supply Increase, Demand Increase** What if supply and demand both increase for some good (for example, cellphones)? A supply increase drops equilibrium price, while a demand increase boosts it. If the increase in supply is greater than the increase in demand, the equilibrium price will fall. If the opposite holds, the equilibrium price will rise.

CONSIDER THIS | Salsa and Coffee Beans

If you forget the other-things-equal assumption, you can encounter situations that seem to be in conflict with the laws of demand and supply. For example, suppose salsa manufacturers sell 1 million bottles of salsa at $4 a bottle in one year, 2 million bottles at $5 in the next year, and 3 million at $6 in the year thereafter. Price and quantity purchased vary directly, and these data seem to be at odds with the law of demand.

But there is no conflict here; the data do not refute the law of demand. The catch is that the law of demand's other-things-equal assumption has been violated over the three years in the example. Specifically, because of changing tastes and rising incomes, the demand for salsa has increased sharply, as in Figure 3-7a. The result is higher prices and larger quantities purchased.

Another example is the fact that the price of coffee beans occasionally has shot upward at the same time that the quantity of coffee beans harvested has declined. These events seemingly contradict the direct relationship between price and quantity denoted by supply. The other-things-equal assumption underlying the upsloping supply curve was violated. Poor coffee harvests decreased supply, as in Figure 3-7d, increasing the equilibrium price of coffee and reducing the equilibrium quantity.

The laws of demand and supply are not refuted by observations of price and quantity made over periods of time in which either demand or supply changes.

The effect on equilibrium quantity is certain: The increases in supply and demand both raise the equilibrium quantity. Therefore, the equilibrium quantity will increase by an amount greater than that caused by either change alone.

MATH 3.5 Changes in Supply, Demand, and Equilibrium

4. ***Supply Decrease, Demand Decrease*** What about decreases in both supply and demand? If the decrease in supply is greater than the decrease in demand, equilibrium price will rise. If the reverse is true, equilibrium price will fall. Because the decreases in supply and demand each reduce equilibrium quantity, we can be sure that equilibrium quantity will fall.

Table 3-3 summarizes these four cases. To understand them fully you should draw supply and demand diagrams for each case to confirm the effects listed in Table 3-3.

Special cases arise when a decrease in demand and a decrease in supply, or an increase in demand and an increase in supply, exactly cancel each other out. In both cases, the net effect on equilibrium price will be zero; price will not change.

The optional appendix accompanying this chapter provides additional examples of situations in which both supply and demand change at the same time.

TABLE 3-3   Effects of Changes in Both Supply and Demand

	Change in supply	Change in demand	Effect on equilibrium price	Effect on equilibrium quantity
1	Increase	Decrease	Decrease	Indeterminate
2	Decrease	Increase	Increase	Indeterminate
3	Increase	Increase	Indeterminate	Increase
4	Decrease	Decrease	Indeterminate	Decrease

3.6 / Application: Government-Set Prices

LO3.6 Identify what government-set prices are and how they can cause surpluses and shortages.

Prices in most markets are free to rise or fall to their equilibrium levels, no matter how high or low that might be. However, government sometimes concludes that supply and demand will produce prices that are unfairly high for buyers or unfairly low for sellers. So government may place legal limits on how high or low a price or prices may go. Is that a good idea?

Price Ceilings

A **price ceiling** is the maximum legal price a seller may charge for a product or service. A price at or below the ceiling is legal; a price above it is not. The rationale for establishing price ceilings (or ceiling prices) on specific products is that they purportedly enable consumers to obtain some essential good or service that they could not afford at the equilibrium price. Examples are rent controls and usury laws, which specify maximum prices in the forms of rent and the interest that can be charged to borrowers.

GRAPHICAL ANALYSIS

We can easily demonstrate the effects of price ceilings graphically using the example of gasoline. Let's suppose that rapidly rising world income boosts the purchase of automobiles and shifts the demand for gasoline to the right so that the equilibrium or market price reaches $1.25 per litre, shown as P_0 in Figure 3-8. The rapidly rising price of gasoline greatly burdens low-income and moderate-income households, who pressure the federal government to "do something." To keep gasoline prices down, the government imposes a ceiling price, P_c, of $0.75 per litre. To be effective, a price ceiling must be below the equilibrium price. A ceiling price of $1.50, for example, would have no effect on the price of gasoline in the current situation.

To be effective, a price ceiling on gasoline must be below the equilibrium price.

| FIGURE 3-8 | A Price Ceiling Results in a Shortage |

A price ceiling is a maximum legal price, such as P_c. When the ceiling price is below the equilibrium price, a persistent product shortage results. Here, that shortage is shown by the horizontal distance between Q_d and Q_s.

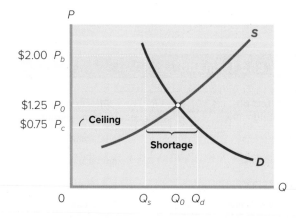

What are the effects of this $0.75 ceiling price? The rationing ability of the free market is rendered ineffective. Because the ceiling price, P_c, is below the market-clearing price, P_0, there is a shortage of gasoline. The quantity of gasoline demanded at P_c is Q_d and the quantity supplied is only Q_s; an excess demand or shortage of amount $Q_d - Q_s$ occurs.

The price ceiling, P_c, prevents the usual market adjustment in which competition among buyers bids up price, inducing more production and rationing some buyers out of the market. That process would normally continue until the shortage disappeared at the equilibrium price and quantity, P_0 and Q_0.

RATIONING PROBLEM

How will the government apportion the available supply, Q_s, among buyers who want the greater amount, Q_d? Should gasoline be distributed on a first-come, first-served basis–that is, to those willing and able to get in line the soonest or stay in line the longest? Or should gas stations distribute it on the basis of favouritism? Since an unregulated shortage does not lead to an equitable distribution of gasoline, the federal government must establish some formal system for rationing it to consumers. One option is to issue ration coupons, which allow coupon-holders to purchase a fixed amount of gasoline per month. The rationing system might require the printing of coupons for Q_s litres of gasoline and then the equal distribution of the coupons among consumers so that the wealthy family of four and the poor family of four both receive the same number of coupons.

CREDIT CARD INTEREST CEILINGS

Over the years there have been many calls in Canada for interest-rate ceilings on credit card accounts. The usual rationale for interest-rate ceilings is that the chartered banks and retail stores issuing such cards are presumably taking unfair advantage of users–and, in particular, lower-income users–by charging interest rates that average about 20 percent per year.

What might be the response if the Canadian government imposed a below-equilibrium interest rate on credit cards? The lower interest income associated with a legal interest ceiling would require the issuers of cards to reduce their costs or enhance their revenues:

- Card issuers might tighten credit standards to reduce losses due to nonpayment and collection costs. Then, low-income and young Canadians who have not yet established their creditworthiness would find it more difficult to obtain credit cards.

- The annual fee charged to cardholders might be increased, as might the fee charged to merchants for processing credit card sales. Similarly, card users might be charged a fee for every transaction.

- Card users now have a post-purchase grace period during which the credit provided is interest-free. That period might be shortened or eliminated.

- Certain enhancements that accompany some credit cards (for example, extended warranties on products bought with a card) might be eliminated.

- Oil companies such as Petro-Canada, that issue their own cards to consumers who buy from their gasoline stations, might increase their prices to help offset the decline of interest income; customers who pay cash would in effect be subsidizing customers who use credit cards.

Price Floors

A **price floor** is a minimum price fixed by the government. A price at or above the price floor is legal; a price below it is not. Price floors above equilibrium prices are usually invoked when society believes that the free functioning of the market system has not provided a sufficient income for certain groups of resource suppliers or producers. Supported prices for some agricultural products and current minimum wages are two examples of price (or wage) floors. Let's analyze the results of imposing a price floor on wheat.

Suppose that many farmers have extremely low incomes when the price of wheat is at its equilibrium value of $3 per bushel. The federal government decides to help by establishing a legal price floor or price support of $4 per bushel.

What will be the effects? At any price above the equilibrium price, quantity supplied will exceed quantity demanded–that is, there will be an excess supply or surplus of the product. Prairie farmers will be willing to produce and offer for sale more than private buyers are willing to purchase at the price floor. As we saw with a price ceiling, an imposed legal price disrupts the rationing ability of the free market.

Supported prices for some agricultural products are an example of price floors.

GRAPHICAL ANALYSIS

Figure 3-9 illustrates the effect of a price floor on wheat. Suppose that S and D are the supply and demand curves for wheat. Equilibrium price and quantity are P_0 and Q_0, respectively. If the federal government imposes a price floor of P_f, farmers will produce Q_s, but private buyers will purchase only Q_d. The surplus is the excess of Q_s over Q_d. The government can cope with the surplus resulting from a price floor in only two ways:

1. It can restrict supply (for example, by asking farmers in Alberta, Saskatchewan, and Manitoba to agree to take a certain amount of land out of production) or increase demand (for example, by researching new uses for the product involved). These actions may reduce the difference between the equilibrium price and the price floor and thereby reduce the size of the resulting surplus.

2. It can purchase the surplus output at the $4 price (thereby subsidizing Prairie farmers) and store or otherwise dispose of it.

FIGURE 3-9   **A Price Floor Results in a Surplus**

A price floor is a minimum legal price, such as P_f. When the price floor is above the equilibrium price, a persistent product surplus results. Here that surplus is shown by the horizontal distance between Q_s and Q_d.

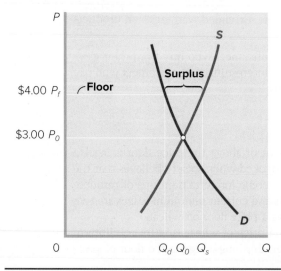

ADDITIONAL CONSEQUENCES

Price floors such as P_f in Figure 3-9, not only disrupt the rationing ability of prices but also distort resource allocation. Without the price floor, the $3 equilibrium price of wheat would cause financial losses and force high-cost wheat producers to plant other crops or abandon farming altogether. But the $4 price floor allows them to continue to grow wheat and remain farmers. So society devotes too many of its scarce resources to wheat production and too few to producing other, more valuable, goods and services. It fails to achieve allocative efficiency.

That's not all. Consumers of wheat-based products pay higher prices because of the price floor. Taxpayers pay higher taxes to finance the government's purchase of the surplus. Also, the price floor causes potential environmental damage by encouraging wheat farmers to bring marginal land into production. The higher price also prompts imports of wheat. But, since such imports would increase the quantity of wheat supplied and thus undermine the price floor, the government needs to erect tariffs (taxes on imports) to keep the foreign wheat out. Such tariffs usually prompt other countries to retaliate with their own tariffs against Canadian agricultural or manufacturing exports.

As you will see in Chapter 12, the *minimum wage*, which imposes a legal floor under the wage of the least skilled worker, is one of the reasons that the price level does not fall during recessions.

It is easy to see why economists sound the alarm when politicians advocate imposing price ceilings or price floors such as price controls, interest-rate caps, or agricultural price supports. In all these cases, good intentions lead to bad economic outcomes. Government-controlled prices cause shortages or surpluses, distort resource allocation, and produce negative side effects.

QUICK REVIEW 3.3

- In competitive markets, prices adjust to the equilibrium level at which quantity demanded equals quantity supplied.

- The equilibrium price and quantity are those indicated by the intersection of the supply and demand curves for any product or resource.

- An increase in demand increases equilibrium price and quantity; a decrease in demand decreases equilibrium price and quantity.

- An increase in supply reduces equilibrium price but increases equilibrium quantity; a decrease in supply increases equilibrium price but reduces equilibrium quantity.

- Over time, equilibrium price and quantity may change in directions that seem at odds with the laws of demand and supply because the other-things-equal assumption is violated.

- Government-controlled prices in the form of ceilings and floors stifle the rationing functions of prices, distort resource allocations, and cause negative side effects.

The LAST WORD | A Legal Market for Human Organs?

A legal market might eliminate the present shortage of human organs for transplant. But many serious objections exist to turning human body parts into commodities for purchase and sale.

It has become increasingly commonplace in medicine to transplant kidneys, lungs, livers, eye corneas, pancreases, and hearts from deceased individuals to those whose organs have failed or are failing. But surgeons and many of their patients face a growing problem: Too few donated organs are available for transplant. Not everyone who needs a transplant can get one. It is estimated that over 4500 patients are waiting for an organ transplant in Canada. Indeed, an inadequate supply of donated organs causes an estimated 250 Canadian deaths per year.

Why Shortages? Seldom do we hear of shortages of desired goods in market economies. What is different about organs for transplant? One difference is that no legal market exists for human organs. To understand this situation, observe the demand curve D_1 and supply curve S_1 in the accompanying figure. The downward slope of the demand curve tells us that if there were a market for human organs, the quantity of organs demanded would be greater at lower prices than at higher prices. Vertical supply curve S_1 represents the fixed quantity of human organs now donated via consent before death. Because the price of these donated organs is in effect zero, quantity demanded, Q_3, exceeds quantity supplied, Q_1. The shortage of $Q_3 - Q_1$ is rationed through a waiting list of those in medical need of transplants. Many people die while still on the waiting list.

Use of a Market A market for human organs would increase the incentive to donate organs. Such a market might work like this: An individual might specify in a legal document a willingness to sell one or more usable human organs on death or brain death. The person could specify where the money from the sale would go, for example, to family, a church, an educational institution, or a charity. Firms would then emerge to purchase organs and resell them where needed for profit. Under such a system, the supply curve of usable organs would take on the normal upward slope of typical supply curves. The higher the expected price of an organ, the greater the number of people willing to have their organs sold at death. Suppose that the supply curve is S_2 in the figure. At the equilibrium price P_1, the number of organs made available for transplant (Q_2) would equal the number purchased for transplant (also Q_2). In this generalized case, the shortage of organs would be eliminated and, of particular importance, the number of organs available for transplanting would rise from Q_1 to Q_2. More lives would be saved and enhanced than under the present donor system.

Objections In view of this positive outcome, why is there no such market for human organs? Critics of market-based solutions have two main objections. The first is a moral objection: Critics feel that turning human organs into commodities commercializes human beings and diminishes the special nature of human life. They say

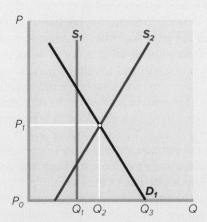

there is something unseemly about selling and buying body organs as if they were bushels of wheat or ounces of gold. Moreover, critics note that the market would ration the available organs (as represented by Q_2 in the figure) to people who either can afford them (at P_1) or have health insurance for transplants. Second, a health cost objection suggests that a market for body organs would greatly increase the cost of health care. Rather than obtaining freely donated (although too few) body organs, patients would have to pay market prices for them, increasing the cost of medical care.

Rebuttal Supporters of market-based solutions to organ shortages point out that the market is simply being driven underground. Worldwide, an illegal market in human organs worth an estimated $1 billion annually has emerged. As in other illegal markets, the unscrupulous tend to thrive.

Question

In some countries, such as France, every corpse is available for doctors to "harvest" the organs unless the deceased, while still alive, signed a form forbidding the organs to be harvested. In Canada and the USA, it is the opposite: No harvesting is allowed unless the deceased signed, while still alive, an organ donor form authorizing doctors to harvest any needed organs. Use supply and demand figures to show in which country organ shortages are likely to be less severe.

Chapter Summary

LO3.1   CHARACTERIZE AND GIVE EXAMPLES OF MARKETS.

- Markets bring buyers and sellers together. Some markets are local, others international. Some have physical locations while others are online. For simplicity, this chapter focuses on highly competitive markets in which large numbers of buyers and sellers come together to buy and sell standardized products. All such markets involve demand, supply, price, and quantity, with price being discovered through the interacting decisions of buyers and sellers.

LO3.2   DESCRIBE *DEMAND* AND EXPLAIN HOW IT CAN CHANGE.

- Demand is a schedule or curve representing the willingness of buyers in a specific period to purchase a particular product at each of various prices. The law of demand implies that consumers will buy more of a product at a low price than at a high price. Therefore, other things equal, the relationship between price and quantity demanded is negative or inverse and is graphed as a downsloping curve.

- Market demand curves are found by adding horizontally the demand curves of the many individual consumers in the market.

- Changes in one or more of the determinants of demand (consumer tastes, the number of buyers in the market, the money incomes of consumers, the prices of related goods, and consumer expectations) shift the market demand curve. A shift to the right is an increase in demand; a shift to the left is a decrease in demand. A change in demand is different from a change in the quantity demanded, the latter being a movement from one point to another point on a fixed demand curve because of a change in the product's price.

LO3.3   DESCRIBE *SUPPLY* AND EXPLAIN HOW IT CAN CHANGE.

- Supply is a schedule or curve showing the amounts of a product that producers are willing to offer in the market at each possible price during a specific period. The law of supply states that, other things equal, producers will offer more of a product at a high price than at a low price. Thus, the relationship between price and quantity supplied is positive or direct, and supply is graphed as an upsloping curve.

- The market supply curve is the horizontal summation of the supply curves of the individual producers of the product.

- Changes in one or more of the determinants of supply (factor prices, technology, taxes and subsidies, price expectations, or the number of sellers in the market) shift the supply curve of a product. A shift to the right is an increase in supply; a shift to the left is a decrease in supply. In contrast, a change in the price of the product being considered causes a change in the quantity supplied, which is shown as a movement from one point to another point on a fixed supply curve.

LO3.4   RELATE HOW SUPPLY AND DEMAND INTERACT TO DETERMINE MARKET EQUILIBRIUM.

- The equilibrium price and quantity are established at the intersection of the supply and demand curves. The interaction of market demand and market supply adjusts the price to the point at which the quantity demanded and quantity supplied are equal. This is the equilibrium price. The corresponding quantity is the equilibrium quantity.

- The ability of market forces to synchronize selling and buying decisions to eliminate potential surpluses and shortages is known as the *rationing function of prices*.

LO3.5   EXPLAIN HOW CHANGES IN SUPPLY AND DEMAND AFFECT EQUILIBRIUM PRICES AND QUANTITIES.

- A change in either demand or supply changes the equilibrium price and quantity. Increases in demand raise both equilibrium price and equilibrium quantity; decreases in demand lower both equilibrium price and equilibrium quantity. Increases in supply lower equilibrium price and raise equilibrium quantity; decreases in supply raise equilibrium price and lower equilibrium quantity.

- Simultaneous changes in demand and supply affect equilibrium price and quantity in various ways, depending on their direction and relative magnitudes.

LO3.6   IDENTIFY WHAT GOVERNMENT-SET PRICES ARE AND HOW THEY CAN CAUSE SURPLUSES AND SHORTAGES.

- A price ceiling is a maximum price set by government and is designed to help consumers. Effective price ceilings produce persistent product shortages, and if an equitable distribution of the product is sought, government must ration the product to consumers

- A price floor is a minimum price set by government and is designed to aid producers. Effective price floors lead to persistent product surpluses; the government must either purchase the product or eliminate the surplus by imposing restrictions on production or increasing private demand.

- Government-set prices stifle the rationing function of prices and distort the allocation of resources.

Terms and Concepts

demand	substitute goods	change in quantity supplied
law of demand	complementary goods	equilibrium price
diminishing marginal utility	change in demand	equilibrium quantity
income effect	change in quantity demanded	surplus
substitution effect	supply	shortage
demand curve	law of supply	productive efficiency
determinants of demand	supply curve	allocative efficiency
normal good	determinants of supply	price ceiling
inferior goods	change in supply	price floor

Discussion Questions

1. Explain the law of demand. Why does a demand curve slope downward? How is a market demand curve derived from individual demand curves?   [LO3.2]

2. What are the determinants of demand? What happens to the demand curve when any of these determinants changes? Distinguish between a change in demand and a change in the quantity demanded, noting the cause(s) of each.   [LO3.2]

3. Explain the law of supply. Why does the supply curve slope upward? How is the market supply curve derived from the supply curves of individual producers?   [LO3.2]

4. What are the determinants of supply? What happens to the supply curve when any of these determinants changes? Distinguish between a change in supply and a change in the quantity supplied, noting the cause(s) of each.   [LO3.3]

5. In 2001, an outbreak of foot-and-mouth disease in Europe led to the burning of millions of cattle carcasses. What impact do you think this had on the supply of cattle hides, hide prices, the supply of leather goods, and the price of leather goods?   [LO3.5]

6. For each stock in the stock market, the number of shares sold daily equals the number of shares purchased. That is, the quantity of each firm's shares demanded equals the quantity supplied. So, if this equality always occurs, why do the prices of stock shares ever change?   [LO3.5]

7. What do economists mean when they say "price floors and ceilings stifle the rationing function of prices and distort re-source allocation"?   [LO3.6]

Review Questions

1. What effect will each of the following have on the demand for small automobiles such as the Mini-Cooper and Fiat 500?   [LO3.2]

   a. Small automobiles become more fashionable.

   b. The price of large automobiles rises (with the price of small autos remaining the same).

   c. Income declines and small autos are an inferior good.

   d. Consumers anticipate that the price of small autos will greatly come down in the near future.

   e. The price of gasoline substantially drops.

2. True or False? A change in quantity demanded is a shift of the entire demand curve to the right or to the left.   [LO3.2]

3. What effect will each of the following have on the supply of auto tires?   [LO3.3]

   a. A technological advance in the methods of producing tires

   b. A decline in the number of firms in the tire industry

   c. An increase in the prices of rubber used in the production of tires

   d. The expectation that the equilibrium price of auto tires will be lower in the future than currently

   e. A decline in the price of the large tires used for semi-trucks and earth-hauling rigs (with no change in the price of auto tires)

   f. The levying of a per-unit tax on each auto tire sold

   g. The granting of a 50-cent-per-unit subsidy for each auto tire produced

4. "In the corn market, demand often exceeds supply and supply sometimes exceeds demand." "The price of corn rises and falls in response to changes in supply and demand." In which of these two statements are the terms "supply" and "demand" used correctly? Explain.   [LO3.3]

5. Suppose that in the market for computer memory chips, the equilibrium price is $50 per chip. If the current price is $55 per chip, then there will be _____ of memory chips.   [LO3.4]

   a. A shortage

   b. A surplus

   c. An equilibrium quantity

   d. None of the above

6. Critically evaluate the following statement: "In comparing the two equilibrium positions in Figure 3.7b, I note that a smaller amount is actually demanded at a lower price. This refutes the law of demand."   [LO3.5]

7. Label each of the following scenarios with the set of symbols that best indicates the price change and quantity change that occur in the scenario. In some scenarios, it may not be possible from the information given to determine the direction of a particular price change or a particular quantity change. We will symbolize those cases as, respectively, P? and Q? The four possible combinations of price and quantity changes are   [LO3.5]

   P↑ Q?   P? Q↑

   P↑Q?   P? Q↓

   a. On a hot day, both the demand for lemonade and the supply of lemonade increase.

   b. On a cold day, both the demand for ice cream and the supply of ice cream decrease.

c. When Hawaii's Mt. Kilauea erupts violently, the demand on the part of tourists for sightseeing flights increases but the supply of pilots willing to provide these dangerous flights decreases.

d. In a hot area of Arizona where they generate a lot of their electricity with wind turbines, the demand for electricity falls on windy days as people switch off their air conditioners and enjoy the breeze. But at the same time, the amount of electricity supplied increases as the wind turbines spin faster.

8. Suppose the total demand for wheat and the total supply of wheat per month in the Winnipeg grain market are as shown in the table to the right. Suppose that the government establishes a price ceiling of $3.70 for wheat. What might prompt the government to establish this price ceiling? Explain carefully the main effects. Demonstrate your answer graphically. Next, suppose that the government establishes a price floor of $4.60 for wheat. What will be the main effects of this price floor? Demonstrate your answer graphically.   [LO3.6]

Thousands of bushels demanded	Price per bushel	Thousands of bushels supplied
85	$3.40	72
80	3.70	73
75	4.00	75
70	4.30	77
65	4.60	79
60	4.90	81

9. A price ceiling will result in a shortage only if the ceiling price is _____ the equilibrium price.   [LO3.6]

a. Less than

b. Equal to

c. Greater than

d. Louder than

Problems

1. Suppose there are three buyers of candy in a market: Tex, Dex, and Rex. The market demand and the individual demands of Tex, Dex, and Rex for candy are given in the table below.   [LO3.2]

a. Fill in the missing values in the table below.

b. Which buyer demands the least at a price of $5? The most at a price of $7?

c. Which buyer's quantity demanded increases the most when the price is lowered from $7 to $6?

d. In which direction would the market demand curve shift if Tex withdrew from the market? What if Dex doubled his purchases at each possible price?

e. Suppose that, at a price of $6, the total quantity demanded increases from 19 to 38. Is this a change in the quantity demanded or a change in demand?

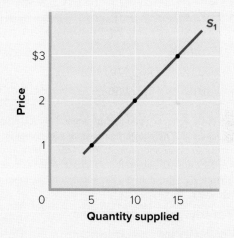

	Individual quantities demanded			
Price per candy	Tex	Dex	Rex	Total quantity demanded
$8	3 +	1 +	0 =	—
7	8 +	2 +	_ =	12
6	_ +	3 +	4 =	19
5	17 +	_ +	6 =	27
4	23 +	5 +	8 =	—

2. The figure that follows shows the supply curve for tennis balls, S_1. Use the figure and the table to give your answers to the following questions.   [LO3.3]

a. Use the figure to fill in the quantity supplied on supply curve S_1 for each price in the table below.

Price	S_1 Quantity supplied	S_2 Quantity supplied	Change in quantity supplied
$3	_____	4	_____
2	_____	2	_____
1	_____	0	_____

b. If production costs were to increase, the quantities supplied at each price would be as shown by the third column of the table (S_2 Quantity supplied). Use that data to draw supply curve S_2 on the same graph as supply curve S_1.

c. In the fourth column of the table, enter the amount by which the quantity supplied at each price changes due to the increase in product costs. (Use positive numbers for increases and negative numbers for decreases.)

d. Did the increase in production costs cause a decrease in supply or a decrease in quantity supplied?

3. Refer to the expanded table below from Review Question 8.   [LO3.4]

a. What is the equilibrium price? At what price is there neither a shortage nor a surplus? Fill in the surplus–shortage column and use it to confirm your answers.

b. Graph the demand for wheat and the supply of wheat. Be sure to label the axes of your graph correctly. Label equilibrium price P and equilibrium quantity Q.

c. How big is the surplus or shortage at $3.40? At $4.90? How big a surplus or shortage results if the price is 60 cents higher than the equilibrium price? If it is 30 cents lower than the equilibrium price?

Thousands of bushels demanded	Price per bushel	Thousands of bushels supplied	Surplus (+) or shortage (−)
85	$3.40	72	_____
80	3.70	73	_____
75	4.00	75	_____
70	4.30	77	_____
65	4.60	79	_____
60	4.90	81	_____

4. How will each of the following changes in demand and/or supply affect equilibrium price and equilibrium quantity in a competitive market? That is, do price and quantity rise, fall, or remain unchanged, or are the answers indeterminate because they depend on the magnitudes of the shifts? Use supply and demand to verify your answers.   [LO3.5]

a. Supply decreases and demand is constant.

b. Demand decreases and supply is constant.

c. Supply increases and demand is constant.

d. Demand increases and supply increases.

e. Demand increases and supply is constant.

f. Supply increases and demand decreases.

g. Demand increases and supply decreases.

h. Demand decreases and supply decreases.

5. **Advanced analysis** Assume that demand for a commodity is represented by the equation $P = 10 - 0.2Q_d$ and supply by the equation $P = 2 + 0.2Q_s$, where Q_d and Q_s are quantity demanded and quantity supplied, respectively, and P is price. Using the equilibrium condition $Q_s = Q_d$, solve the equations to determine equilibrium price. Now determine equilibrium quantity. Graph the two equations to substantiate your answers.   [LO3.5]

6. Suppose that the demand and supply schedules for rental apartments in the city of Gotham are as given in the table below.   [LO3.6]

Monthly rent	Apartments demanded	Apartments supplied
$2,500	10,000	15,000
2,000	12,500	12,500
1,500	15,000	10,000
1,000	17,500	7,500
500	20,000	5,000

a. What are the market equilibrium rental price per month and the market equilibrium number of apartments demanded and supplied?

b. If the municipal government can enforce a rent-control law that sets the maximum monthly rent at $1500, will there be a surplus or a shortage? Of how many units? How many units will actually be rented each month?

c. Suppose that a new government wants to keep out the poor. It declares that the minimum allowable rent is $2500 per month. If the government can enforce that price floor, will there be a surplus or a shortage? Of how many units? How many units will actually be rented each month?

d. Suppose that the government wishes to decrease the market equilibrium monthly rent by increasing the supply of housing. Assuming that demand remains unchanged, by how many units of housing would the government have to increase the supply of housing in order to get the market equilibrium rental price to fall to $1500 per month? To $1000 per month? To $500 per month?

Appendix to Chapter 3

A3.1 / Additional Examples of Supply and Demand

LOA3.1 Illustrate how supply and demand analysis can provide insights into actual-economy situations.

Our discussion has clearly demonstrated that supply and demand analysis is a powerful tool for understanding equilibrium prices and quantities. The information provided in the main body of this chapter is fully sufficient for moving forward in the book, but you may find that additional examples of supply and demand are helpful. This optional appendix provides several concrete illustrations of changes in supply and demand. It also applies supply and demand analysis to non-priced goods (goods owned in common and not bought and sold in markets).

Your instructor may assign all, some, or none of this appendix, depending on time availability and personal preference.

Changes in Supply and Demand

As Figure 3-6 demonstrates, changes in supply and demand cause changes in price, quantity, or both. The following applications illustrate this fact in several real-world markets. The simplest situations are those in which either supply changes while demand remains constant, or demand

changes while supply remains constant. Let's consider two such simple cases first, before looking at more complex applications.

LETTUCE

Every now and then, the media report that extreme weather has severely reduced the size of some crop. Suppose, for example, that a severe freeze destroys a sizable portion of the lettuce crop. This unfortunate situation implies a significant decline in supply, which we represent in Figure A3-1 as a leftward shift of the supply curve from S_1 to S_2. At each price, consumers desire as much lettuce as before, so the freeze does not affect the demand for lettuce. That is, demand curve D_1 does not shift.

What are the consequences of the reduced supply of lettuce for equilibrium price and quantity? As shown in Figure A3-1, the leftward shift of the supply curve disrupts the previous equilibrium in the market for lettuce and drives the equilibrium price up from P_1 to P_2.

Consumers respond to that price hike by reducing the quantity of lettuce demanded from Q_1 to Q_2. Equilibrium in the market is restored at P_2 and Q_2. Consumers who are willing and able to pay price P_2 obtain lettuce; consumers unwilling or unable to pay that price do not. Some

---

FIGURE A3-1 **The Market for Lettuce**

The decrease in the supply of lettuce, shown here by the shift from S_1 to S_2, increases the equilibrium price of lettuce from P_1 to P_2 and reduces the equilibrium quantity from Q_1 to Q_2.

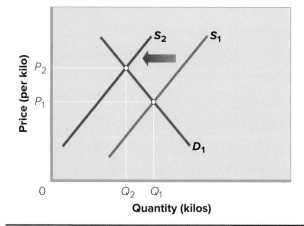

consumers continue to buy as much lettuce as before, even at the higher price. Others buy some lettuce but not as much as before, and still others forgo lettuce altogether. The latter two groups use the money they would have spent on lettuce to obtain other products, say, carrots. (Because of our other-things-equal assumption, the prices of other products have not changed.)

EXCHANGE RATES

Exchange rates are the prices at which one currency can be traded (exchanged) for another. Exchange rates are normally determined in foreign exchange markets. One exchange market is the euro–Canadian dollar market, in which the currency used in most of Europe, the euro, is exchanged for Canadian dollars. In Canada, this market is set up so that euros are priced in dollars–that is, the "product" being traded is the euro and the "price" to buy that product is quoted in dollars. Thus, the market equilibrium price one day might be $1.25 to buy one euro, while on another day it might be $1.50 to buy one euro.

Foreign exchange markets are used by individuals and companies that need to make purchases or payments in a different currency. Canadian companies exporting goods to Germany, for instance, wish to be paid in Canadian dollars. Thus, their German customers will need to convert euros into dollars. The euros that they bring to the euro–dollar market will become part of the overall market supply of euros. Conversely, a Canadian mutual fund may wish to purchase some real estate in France, but will need to pay in euros since the current French owners will accept only euros as payment. Thus, the Canadian mutual fund has a demand to purchase euros that will form part of the overall market demand for euros. The mutual fund will bring dollars to the euro-dollar foreign exchange market in order to purchase the euros it desires.

Sometimes the demand for euros increases. This might be because a European product surges in popularity in foreign countries. For example, if a new German-made automobile is a big hit in Canada, car dealers here will demand more euros with which to pay for more units of that new model. This will shift the demand curve for euros to the right, as from D_1 to D_2 in Figure A3-2. Given the fixed euro supply curve S_1, the increase in demand raises the equilibrium exchange rate (the equilibrium number of dollars needed to purchase one euro) from $1.25 to $1.50. The equilibrium quantity of euros purchased increases from Q_1 to Q_2. Because a higher dollar amount is now needed to purchase one euro, economists say that the dollar has *depreciated*–gone down in value–relative to the euro. Alternatively, the euro has *appreciated*–gone up in value–relative to the Canadian dollar because one euro now buys $1.50 rather than $1.25.

PINK SALMON

Now let's see what happens when both supply and demand change at the same time. Several decades ago, people who caught salmon earned as much as $2 for each kilogram of pink salmon–the type used mainly for canning–brought to the buyer. In Figure A3-3 that price is represented as P_1, at the intersection of supply curve S_1 and demand curve D_1. The corresponding quantity of pink salmon is shown as Q_1 kilograms. As time passed, supply and demand changed in the market for pink salmon.

FIGURE A3-2   **The Market for Euros**

The increase in the demand for euros, shown here by the shift from D_1 to D_2, increases the equilibrium price of a euro from $1.25 to $1.50 and increases the equilibrium quantity of euros from Q_1 to Q_2. The Canadian dollar has depreciated.

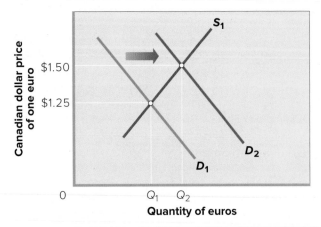

FIGURE A3-3   The Market for Pink Salmon

In the last two decades, the supply of pink salmon has increased and the demand for pink salmon has decreased. As a result, the price of pink salmon has declined, as from P_1 to P_2. Because supply has increased more than demand has decreased, the equilibrium quantity of pink salmon has increased, as from Q_1 to Q_2.

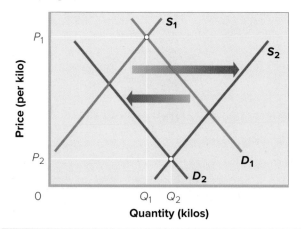

On the supply side, improved technology in the form of larger, more efficient fishing boats greatly increased the catch and lowered the cost of obtaining it. Also, high profits at price P_1 encouraged many new fishers to enter the industry. As a result of these changes, the supply of pink salmon greatly increased and the supply curve shifted to the right, as from S_1 to S_2 in Figure A3-3.

Over the same years, the demand for pink salmon declined, as represented by the leftward shift from D_1 to D_2 in Figure A3-3. That decrease resulted from increases in consumer income and reductions of the price of substitute products. As buyers' incomes rose, consumers shifted demand away from canned fish and toward higher-quality fresh or frozen fish, including more-valued Atlantic, Chinook, Sockeye, and Coho salmon. Moreover, the emergence of fish farming, in which salmon are raised in ocean net pens, lowered the prices of these substitute species. That, too, reduced the demand for pink salmon.

The altered supply and demand reduced the price of pink salmon to as low as $0.20 per kilogram, as represented by the drop in price from P_1 to P_2 in Figure A3-3. Both the supply increase and the demand decrease helped reduce the equilibrium price. However, in this particular case the equilibrium quantity of pink salmon increased, as represented by the move from Q_1 to Q_2. Both shifts of the curves reduced the equilibrium price, but equilibrium quantity increased because the increase in supply exceeded the decrease in demand.

GASOLINE

The price of gasoline has increased rapidly in Canada over the past several years. For example, the average price of a litre of gasoline rose from around $0.60 in 2004 to about $1.40 in 2011. What caused the price of gasoline to more than double? How would we diagram this increase?

We begin in Figure A3-4 with the price of a litre of gasoline at P_1, representing the $0.60 price. Simultaneous supply and demand factors disturbed this equilibrium. On the supply side, supply uncertainties relating to Middle East politics and warfare, and expanded demand for oil by fast-growing countries such as China, pushed up the price of a barrel of oil from $37 in 2004 to over $100 in 2011. Oil is the main input for producing gasoline, so any sustained rise in its price boosts the per-unit cost of producing gasoline. Such cost rises decrease the supply of gasoline, as represented by the leftward shift of the supply curve from S_1 to S_2 in Figure A3-4. At times, refinery breakdowns in North America also contributed to this reduced supply.

While the supply of gasoline declined between 2004 and 2011, the demand for gasoline increased, as depicted by the rightward shift of the demand curve from D_1 to D_2. Incomes in general were rising over these years because the Canadian economy was rapidly expanding. Rising incomes raise demand for all normal goods, including gasoline. An increased number of more fuel-efficient SUVs and light trucks on the road also contributed to growing gas demand.

The combined decrease in gasoline supply and increase in gasoline demand boosted the price of gasoline from $0.60 to $1.40, as represented by the rise from P_1 to P_2 in Figure A3-4. Because the demand increase outweighed the supply decrease, the equilibrium quantity expanded here, from Q_1 to Q_2.

| FIGURE A3-4 | The Market for Gasoline |

An increase in the demand for gasoline, as shown by the shift from D_1 to D_2, coupled with a decrease in supply, as shown by the shift from S_1 to S_2, boosts equilibrium price (here, from P_1 to P_2). In this case, equilibrium quantity increases from Q_1 to Q_2 because the increase in demand outweighs the decrease in supply.

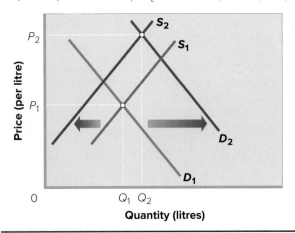

In other periods the price of gasoline has *declined* as the demand for gasoline has increased. Test your understanding of the analysis by explaining how such a price decrease could occur.

SUSHI

Consumption of sushi has soared in Canada in recent years. Nevertheless, the price of sushi has remained relatively constant.

Supply and demand analysis helps explain this circumstance of increased quantity and constant price. A change in tastes has increased the Canadian demand for sushi. Many first-time consumers of sushi find it highly tasty. And, as implied by the growing number of sushi bars in Canada, the supply of sushi has also expanded.

We represent these supply and demand changes in Figure A3-5 as the rightward shift of the demand curve from D_1 to D_2 and the rightward shift of the supply curve from S_1 to S_2. Observe that the equilibrium quantity of sushi increases from Q_1 to Q_2 and the equilibrium price remains constant at P_1. The increase in supply, which taken alone would reduce the price, has perfectly offset the increase in demand, which taken alone would

| FIGURE A3-5 | The Market for Sushi |

Equal increase in the demand for sushi, as from D_1 to D_2, and in the supply of sushi, as from S_1 to S_2, expand the equilibrium quantity of sushi (here from Q_1 to Q_2), while leaving the price of sushi unchanged at P_1.

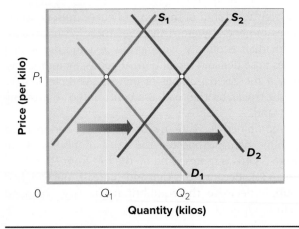

raise the price. The price of sushi does not change but the equilibrium quantity greatly increases, because both the increase in demand and the increase in supply act to expand purchases and sales.

Simultaneous increases in demand and supply can cause the price to rise, fall, or remain constant, depending on the relative magnitudes of the supply and demand increases. In this case, the price remained constant.

A3.2 / Upsloping versus Vertical Supply Curves

As you already know, the typical good or service possesses an upsloping supply curve because a higher market price will cause producers to increase the quantity supplied. There are, however, some goods and services whose quantities supplied are fixed and totally unresponsive to changes in price. Examples include the amount of land in a given area, the number of seats in a stadium, and the limited part of the electromagnetic spectrum that is reserved for cellular telephone transmissions. These sorts of goods and services have vertical supply curves because the same fixed amount is available no matter what price is offered to suppliers.

Reactions to Demand Shifts

Markets react very differently to a shift in demand depending upon whether they have upsloping or vertical supply curves.

UPSLOPING SUPPLY CURVES

When a market has an upsloping supply curve, any shift in demand will cause both the equilibrium price and the equilibrium quantity to adjust. Consider Figure A3-2. When the demand for euros increases, the movement from the initial equilibrium to the final equilibrium involves the equilibrium

price rising from \$1.25 to \$1.50 while the equilibrium quantity increases from Q_1 to Q_2. Price and quantity both change.

VERTICAL SUPPLY CURVES

When a market has a vertical supply curve, any shift in demand will cause only the equilibrium price to change; the equilibrium quantity remains the same because the quantity supplied is fixed and cannot adjust.

Consider Figure A3-6, in which the supply of land in Toronto is fixed at quantity Q_0. If demand increases from D_1 to D_2, the movement from the initial equilibrium at point a to the final equilibrium at point b is accomplished solely by a rise in the equilibrium price from P_1 to P_2. Because the quantity of land is fixed, the increase in demand cannot cause any change in the equilibrium quantity supplied. The entire adjustment from the initial equilibrium to the final equilibrium has to come in the form of a higher equilibrium price.

This fact explains why real estate prices are so high in Toronto and other major cities. Any increase in demand cannot be met by a combination of increases in price and increases in quantity. With the quantity of land in fixed supply, any increase in demand results solely in higher equilibrium land prices.

FIGURE A3-6 The Market for Land in Toronto

Because the quantity of land in Toronto is fixed at Q_0, the supply curve is vertical above Q_0 in order to indicate that the same quantity of land will be supplied no matter what the price is. As demand increases from D_1 to D_2, the equilibrium price rises from P_1 to P_2. Because the quantity of land is fixed at Q_0, the movement from equilibrium a to equilibrium b involves only a change in the equilibrium price; the equilibrium quantity remains at Q_0 because land is in fixed supply.

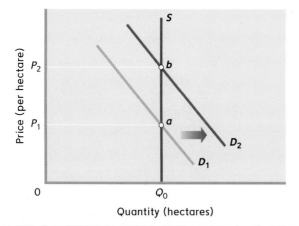

Preset Prices

In the body of this chapter we saw that an effective government-imposed price ceiling (legal maximum price) causes quantity demanded to exceed quantity supplied–a shortage. An effective government-imposed price floor (legal minimum price) causes quantity supplied to exceed quantity demanded–a surplus. Put simply, shortages result when prices are set below equilibrium prices, and surpluses result when prices are set above equilibrium prices. We now want to establish that shortages and surpluses can occur in markets other than those in which government imposes price floors and ceilings. Such market imbalances happen when the seller or sellers set prices in advance of sales and the prices selected turn out to be below or above equilibrium prices. Consider the following two examples.

OLYMPIC FIGURE SKATING FINALS

Tickets for the women's figure skating championship at the Olympics are among the world's hottest tickets. The popularity of this event and the high incomes of buyers translate into tremendous ticket demand. Olympic officials set the price for the tickets in advance. Invariably, the price, although high, is considerably below the equilibrium price that would equate quantity demanded and quantity supplied. A severe shortage of tickets therefore occurs in this *primary market*–the market involving the official ticket office. The shortage, in turn, creates a *secondary market* in which buyers bid for tickets held by initial purchasers rather than the original seller.

Scalping tickets–selling them above the original ticket price–may be legal or illegal, depending on local laws.

Figure A3-7 shows how the shortage in the primary ticket market looks in terms of supply and demand analysis. Demand curve D represents the strong demand for tickets, and supply curve S represents the supply of tickets. The supply curve is vertical because a fixed number of tickets are printed to match the capacity of the arena. At the printed ticket price of P_1, the quantity of tickets demanded, Q_2, exceeds the quantity supplied, Q_1. The result is a shortage of ab–the horizontal distance between Q_2 and Q_1 in the primary market.

If the printed ticket price had been the higher equilibrium price, P_2, no shortage of tickets would have occurred. But at the lower price P_1, a shortage and secondary ticket market will emerge among those buyers willing to pay more than the original price and those sellers willing to sell their purchased tickets for more than the printed price. Wherever there are shortages and secondary markets, we can safely assume that the original price was set below the equilibrium price.

OLYMPIC CURLING PRELIMINARIES

Contrast the shortage of tickets for the women's figure skating finals at the Olympics to the surplus of tickets for one of the preliminary curling matches. Curling is a popular spectator sport in Canada and a few other nations, but it does not draw many fans in most countries, so the demand for tickets to most of the preliminary curling events is not very strong. We demonstrate this weak demand as D in Figure A3-8. As in our previous example, the supply of tickets is fixed by the size of the arena and is shown as vertical line S.

FIGURE A3-7   **The Market for Tickets to Olympic Women's Figure Skating Finals**

The demand curve D and the supply curve S produce an equilibrium price above the P_1 price printed on the ticket. At price P_1 the quantity of tickets demanded, Q_2, greatly exceeds the quantity of tickets available (Q_1). The resulting shortage of ab ($= Q_2 - Q_1$) gives rise to a legal or illegal secondary market.

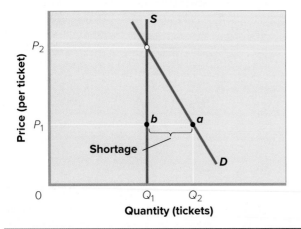

FIGURE A3·8 The Market for Tickets to the Olympic Curling Preliminaries

The demand curve D and the supply curve S produce an equilibrium price below the P_1 price printed on the ticket. At price P_1 the quantity of tickets demanded is less than the quantity of tickets available. The resulting surplus of ba ($= Q_1 - Q_2$) means the event is not sold out.

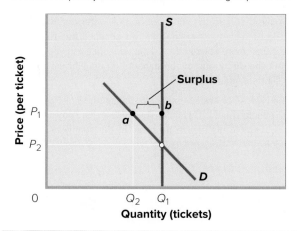

We represent the printed ticket price as P_1 in Figure A3-8. In this case the printed price is much higher than the equilibrium price of P_2. At the printed ticket price, quantity supplied is Q_1 and quantity demanded is Q_2. So a surplus of tickets of ba ($= Q_1 - Q_2$) occurs. No ticket scalping occurs and there are numerous empty seats. Only if Olympic officials had priced the tickets at the lower price, P_2, would the event have sold out. (Actually, Olympic officials try to adjust to demand realities for curling contests by holding them in smaller arenas and by charging less for tickets. Nevertheless, the stands are rarely full for the preliminary contests, which compete against final events in other winter Olympic sports.)

APPENDIX / Summary

LOA3.1 Illustrate how supply and demand analysis can provide insights into actual-economy situations.

• A decrease in the supply of a product increases its equilibrium price and reduces its equilibrium quantity. In contrast, an increase in the demand for a product boosts both its equilibrium price and its equilibrium quantity.

• Simultaneous changes in supply and demand affect equilibrium price and quantity in various ways, depending on the relative magnitudes of the changes in supply and demand. Equal increases in supply and demand, for example, leave equilibrium price unchanged.

• Products (such as land) whose quantities supplied do not vary with price have vertical supply curves. For these products, any shift in demand will lead to a change in the equilibrium price but no change in the equilibrium quantity.

• Sellers set prices of some items, such as tickets, in advance of the event. These items are sold in the primary market that involves the original seller and buyers. If preset prices turn out to be below the equilibrium prices, shortages occur and scalping in legal or illegal secondary markets arises. The prices in the secondary market then rise above the preset prices. In contrast, surpluses occur when the preset prices happen to exceed the equilibrium prices.

APPENDIX / Discussion Questions

1. Why are shortages or surpluses more likely with preset prices, such as for tickets, than with flexible prices, such as for gasoline? [**LOA3.1**]

2. Most scalping laws make it illegal to sell—but not to buy—tickets at prices above those printed on the tickets. Assuming that is the case, use supply and demand analysis to explain why the equilibrium ticket price in an illegal secondary market tends to be higher than in a legal secondary market. [LOA3.1]

3. How high (or how low) are gasoline prices now? Go to **gasbuddy.com** and follow the links to find the current retail price of gasoline in your area. How does the current price of regular gasoline compare with the price a year ago? What must have happened to either supply, demand, or both to explain the observed price change? [LOA3.1]

4. Suppose the supply of apples sharply increases because of perfect weather conditions throughout the growing season. Assuming no change in demand, explain the effect on the equilibrium price and quantity of apples. Explain why quantity demanded increases even though demand does not change. [LOA3.1]

5. Assume the demand for lumber suddenly rises because of a rapid growth of demand for new housing. Assume no change in supply. Why does the equilibrium price of lumber rise? What would happen if the price did not rise under the demand and supply circumstances described? [LOA3.1]

6. Assume that both the supply of bottled water and the demand for bottled water rise during the summer but that supply increases more rapidly than demand. What can you conclude about the directions of the impacts on equilibrium price and equilibrium quantity? [LOA3.1]

7. When asked for investment advice, humourist Will Rogers joked that people should, "Buy land. They ain't making any more of the stuff." Explain his advice in terms of the supply and demand model. [LOA3.1]

APPENDIX / Review Questions

1. Will the equilibrium price of orange juice increase or decrease in each of the following situations? [LOA3.1]

   a. A medical study reporting that orange juice reduces cancer is released at the same time that a freak storm destroys half of the orange crop in Florida.

   b. The prices of all beverages except orange juice fall by half while unexpectedly perfect weather in Florida results in an orange crop that is 20 percent larger than normal.

2. Consider the market for coffee beans. Suppose that the prices of all other caffeinated beverages go up 30 percent while at the same time a new fertilizer boosts production at coffee plantations dramatically. Which of the following best describes what is likely to happen to the equilibrium price and quantity of coffee beans? [LOA3.1]

   a. Both the equilibrium price and the quantity will rise.

   b. The equilibrium price will rise but the equilibrium quantity will fall.

   c. The equilibrium price may rise or fall but the equilibrium quantity will rise for certain.

   d. Neither the price change nor the quantity change can be determined for certain.

   e. None of the above.

3. A price ceiling will result in a shortage only if the ceiling price is _____ the equilibrium price. [LOA3.1]

   a. Less than

   b. Equal to

   c. Greater than

   d. Faster than

4. Suppose that you are the economic advisor to a municipal government that has to deal with a politically embarrassing surplus caused by a price floor that the government recently imposed. Your first suggestion is to get rid of the price floor, but the politicians don't want to do that. Instead, they present you with the following list of options that they hope will get rid of the surplus while keeping the price floor. Identify each one as either *could work* or *can't work*. [LOA3.1]

   a. Restricting supply

   b. Decreasing demand

   c. Purchasing the surplus at the floor price

5. Suppose both the demand for olives and the supply of olives decline by equal amounts over some time period. Use graphical analysis to show the effect on equilibrium price and quantity. [LOA3.1]

6. Governments can use subsidies to increase demand. For instance, a government can pay farmers to use organic fertilizers rather than traditional fertilizers. That subsidy increases the demand for organic fertilizer. Consider two industries, one in which supply is nearly vertical and the other in which supply is nearly horizontal. Assume that firms in both industries would prefer a higher market equilibrium price because a higher market equilibrium price would mean higher profits. Assuming that both industries have similarly sloped demand curves, which industry would probably spend more resources lobbying the government to increase the demand for its output? [LOA3.1]

   a. The industry with a nearly flat supply curve

   b. The industry with a nearly vertical supply curve

1. Demand and supply often shift in the retail market for gasoline. Here are two demand curves and two supply curves for litres of gasoline in the month of May in a small town in New Brunswick. Some of the data are missing. [LOA3.1]

| Price | Quantities demanded | | Quantities supplied | |
	D_1	D_2	S_1	S_2
$4.00	5000	7500	9000	9500
____	6000	8000	8000	9000
2.00	____	8500	____	8500
____	____	9000	5000	____

a. Use the following facts to fill in the missing data in the table. If demand is D_1 and supply is S_1, the equilibrium quantity is 7000 litres per month. When demand is D_2 and supply is S_1, the equilibrium price is $3.00 per litre. When demand is D_2 and supply is S_1, there is an excess demand of 4000 litres per month at a price of $1.00 per litre. If demand is D_1 and supply is S_2, the equilibrium quantity is 8000 litres per month.

b. Compare two equilibriums. In the first, demand is D_1 and supply is S_1. In the second, demand is D_1 and supply is S_2. By how much does the equilibrium quantity change? By how much does the equilibrium price change?

c. If supply falls from S_2 to S_1 while demand declines from D_2 to D_1, does the equilibrium price rise, fall, or stay the same? What if only supply falls? What if only demand falls?

d. Suppose that supply is fixed at S_1 and that demand starts at D_1. By how many litres per month would demand have to increase at each price level such that the equilibrium price per litre would be $3.00? $4.00?

2. The table below shows two demand schedules for a given style of men's shoes—that is, how many pairs per month will be demanded at various prices at a men's clothing store in Winnipeg called Stromnord. [LOA3.1]

Price	D_1 Quantity demanded	D_2 Quantity demanded
$75	53	13
70	60	15
65	68	18
60	77	22
55	87	27

Suppose that Stromnord has exactly 65 pairs of this style of shoe in inventory at the start of the month of July and will not receive any more pairs of this style until at least August 1.

a. If demand is D_1, what is the lowest price that Stromnord can charge so that it will not run out of this model of shoe in the month of July? What if demand is D_2?

b. If the price of shoes is set at $75 for both July and August and demand will be D_2 in July and D_1 in August, how many pairs of shoes should Stromnord order for August if it wants to end the month of August with exactly zero pairs of shoes in its inventory? What if the price is set at $55 for both months and demand is D_1 in July and D_2 in August?

3. Answer the following questions using the table below. [LOA3.1]

a. If this table reflects the supply of and demand for tickets to a particular World Cup soccer game, what is the stadium capacity?

b. If the preset ticket price is $45, would we expect to see a secondary market for tickets? Explain why or why not. Would the price of a ticket in the secondary market be higher than, the same as, or lower than the price in the primary (original) market?

c. Suppose for some other World Cup game that the quantities of tickets demanded are 20,000 lower at each ticket price than shown in the table. If the ticket price remains $45, would the event be a sell-out? Explain why or why not.

Quantity demanded, thousands	Price	Quantity supplied, thousands
80	$25	60
75	35	60
70	45	60
65	55	60
60	65	60
55	75	60
50	85	60

Math Appendix to Chapter 3

A3.1 / The Mathematics of Market Equilibrium

A market equilibrium is the price and the quantity, denoted as the pair (Q^*, P^*), of a commodity bought or sold at price P^*. The following mathematical note provides an introduction to how a market equilibrium (Q^*, P^*) is derived.

The market equilibrium is found by using the market demand (buyers' behaviour), the market supply (sellers' behaviour), and the negotiating process (to find the agreed-upon price and quantity, namely P^* and Q^*, on which to transact). The market equilibrium is identified by the condition reached at the end of the negotiating process, that at the price they negotiated, P^*, the quantity of the commodity that buyers are willing to buy, denoted as Q_d, and the quantity sellers are willing to sell, denoted as Q_s, match exactly.

The Demand Curve

The equation describing the downsloping demand when the demand curve is a straight line, in which Q_d represents the quantity demanded by buyers and P the price, is

$$P = a - bQ_d$$

The demand equation and curve below tell us that if the price is higher than a, the buyers will not buy; thus, for a transaction to occur the price must be lower. The demand equation and curve also tell us that at a price lower than a the quantity demanded by the buyers increases. Buyers' behaviour, as described by the demand equation, is that at lower prices buyers buy more quantity.

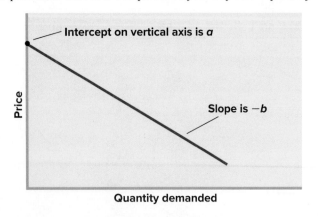

Intercept on vertical axis is a

Slope is $-b$

Price

Quantity demanded

The Supply Curve

The equation describing the upsloping market supply function when the supply curve is a straight line, in which Q_s represents the quantity supplied by sellers and P the price, is

$$P = c + dQ_s$$

If the price is lower than c, the sellers will sell nothing, as the figure below shows. If the price is c or higher, then the supply equation states that sellers facing higher prices sell more quantity. Sellers' behaviour, as described by the supply curve and equation, is that at higher prices sellers make more quantity available.

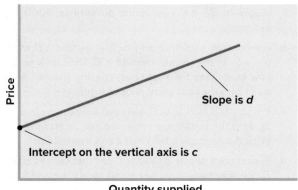

Price

Slope is d

Intercept on the vertical axis is c

Quantity supplied

The Market Equilibrium

The negotiating process (in which price or quantity or both adjust) provides the mechanism by which, eventually, buyers and sellers agree upon a price, P^*, and a quantity, Q^*, at which they can buy and sell and thus complete the transaction. At the end of the negotiating process, the quantity demanded by the buyers, Q_d, is equal to the quantity supplied by the sellers, Q_s (at the agreed-upon price), and thus the market is in equilibrium. The mathematical representation of such a negotiating process is described as follows.

At the agreed price, P^*, the equilibrium condition of the negotiating process—the equality in the quantity demanded and supplied—is

$$Q_d = Q_s$$

Having denoted Q^* as the equilibrium quantity, then it must be that $Q^* = Q_d = Q_s$. To solve for the equilibrium quantity Q^* and the equilibrium price P^*, the demand and supply functions are used. With Q^* the equilibrium quantity, for the buyers is

$$P^* = a - bQ^*$$

and for the sellers is

$$P^* = c + dQ^*$$

Now, since P^* is the same agreed-upon price by both buyer and seller, then

$$a - bQ^* = c + dQ^*$$

giving the equilibrium quantity, Q^*, as

$$Q^* = \frac{(a - c)}{(b + d)}$$

To find P^*, substitute $\dfrac{(a - c)}{(b + d)}$ in the supply (or demand) function.

$$P^* = c + d = \frac{(a - c)}{(b + d)}, \text{ thus}$$

$$P^* = \frac{(ad - bc)}{(b + d)}$$

The equilibrium is $(Q^*, P^*) = \left[\dfrac{(a - c)}{(b + d)}, \dfrac{(ad - bc)}{(b + d)} \right]$

The market equilibrium may also be represented diagrammatically, as shown below.

Example

Assume the demand for a pair of jeans is represented by the equation

$$P = 100 - 0.2Q_d$$

Assume the supply of a pair of jeans is represented by the equation

$$P = 20 + 0.2Q_s$$

Assume quantities are expressed in pairs of jeans per day, and the price in dollars.

To find the equilibrium price, P^*, and equilibrium quantity, Q^*, substitute Q^* for Q_d and Q_s and P^* for P in the demand and supply equations. To solve for Q^*

$$100 - 0.2Q^* = 20 + 0.2Q^*$$

$$0.4Q^* = 80$$

$$Q^* = 200$$

To solve for P^*

$$P^* = 100 - 0.2(200)$$

$$= 60$$

The equilibrium quantity of pairs of jeans is 200 per day, and the equilibrium price is $60 per pair of jeans.

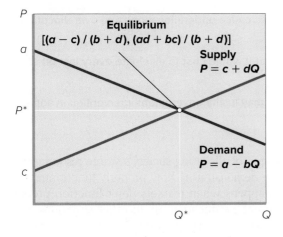

CHAPTER 4

Market Failures: Public Goods and Externalities

LEARNING OBJECTIVES

LO4.1 Differentiate between demand-side market failures and supply-side market failures.

LO4.2 Explain the origin of both consumer surplus and producer surplus, and explain how properly functioning markets maximize their sum, economic surplus, while optimally allocating resources.

LO4.3 Describe free riding and public goods, and illustrate why private firms cannot normally produce public goods.

LO4.4 Explain how positive and negative externalities cause underallocations and overallocations of resources.

LO4.5 Show why we normally won't want to pay what it would cost to eliminate every last bit of a negative externality such as air pollution.

LOA4.1 (Appendix) Describe how information failures may justify government intervention in some markets.

Competitive markets usually do a remarkably effective job of allocating society's scarce resources to their most highly valued uses. Thus, we begin this chapter by demonstrating how properly functioning markets efficiently allocate resources. We then explore what happens when markets don't function properly. In some circumstances, economically desirable goods are not produced at all. In other situations, they are either overproduced or underproduced. This chapter focuses on these situations, which economists refer to as **market failures**.

In such situations, an economic role for government may arise. We will examine that role as it relates to public goods and so-called externalities–situations where market failures lead to sub-optimal outcomes that the government may be able to improve upon by using its powers to tax, spend, and regulate. The government may, for instance, pay for the production of goods that the private sector fails to produce. It may also act to reduce the production of goods and services that the private sector overproduces. Implementing such policies can, however, be both costly and complicated. We will conclude the chapter by noting the government inefficiencies that can potentially hinder government's efforts to improve economic outcomes.

4.1 / Market Failures in Competitive Markets[1]

LO4.1 Differentiate between demand-side market failures and supply-side market failures.

In Chapter 3 we asserted that ". . . competitive markets usually produce an assignment of resources that is 'right' from an economic perspective." We now want to focus on the word "usually" and discuss exceptions. We must do this because unfortunately the presence of robust competition involving many buyers and many sellers may not, by itself, be enough to guarantee that a market will allocate resources correctly. Market failures sometimes happen in competitive markets. The focus of this chapter is to explain how and why such market failures can arise.

Fortunately, the broad picture is simple. Market failures in competitive markets fall into just two categories:

- A **demand-side market failure** happens when demand curves do not reflect consumers' full willingness to pay for a good or service.

- A **supply-side market failure** occurs when supply curves do not reflect the full cost of producing a good or service.

Demand-Side Market Failures

Demand-side market failures arise because it is impossible in certain cases to charge consumers what they are willing to pay for a product. Consider outdoor fireworks displays. People enjoy fireworks and would therefore be *willing* to pay to see them if the only way to see them was to have to pay for the right to do so. But because such displays are outdoors and in public, people don't actually *have* to pay to see them because there is no way to exclude those who haven't paid from also enjoying the show. Private firms will therefore be unwilling to produce outdoor fireworks displays, as it will be nearly impossible for them to raise enough revenue to cover production costs.

Supply-Side Market Failures

Supply-side market failures arise in situations in which a firm does not have to pay the full cost of producing its output. Consider a coal-burning power plant. The firm running the plant will have to pay for all of the land, labour, capital, and entrepreneurship that it uses to generate electricity by burning coal. But if the firm is not charged for the smoke that it releases into the atmosphere, it will fail to pay another set of costs–the costs that its pollution imposes on other people. These include future harm from global warming, toxins that affect wildlife, and possible damage to agricultural crops downwind.

A market failure arises because it is not possible for the market to correctly weigh costs and benefits in a situation in which some of the costs are completely unaccounted for. The coal-burning power plant produces more electricity and generates more pollution than it would if it had to pay for each tonne of smoke that it released into the atmosphere. The extra units that are produced are units of output for which the costs are *greater than* the benefits. Obviously, these units should not be produced.

[1] Other market failures arise when there are not enough buyers or sellers to ensure competition. In those situations, the lack of competition allows either buyers or sellers to restrict purchases or sales below optimal levels for their own benefit. As an example, a monopoly–a firm that is the only producer in its industry–can restrict the amount of output that it supplies to drive up the market price and increase its own profit.

4.2 / Efficiently Functioning Markets

LO4.2 Explain the origin of both consumer surplus and producer surplus, and explain how properly functioning markets maximize their sum, economic surplus, while optimally allocating resources.

The best way to understand market failure is to understand how properly functioning competitive markets achieve economic efficiency. We touched on this subject in Chapter 3, but we now want to expand and deepen that analysis, both for its own sake and to set up our discussion of public goods and externalities. Two conditions must hold if a competitive market is to produce efficient outcomes: (1) the demand curve in the market must reflect consumers' full willingness to pay, and (2) the supply curve in the market must reflect all the costs of production. If these conditions hold, then the market will produce only units for which benefits are at least equal to costs. It will also maximize the amount of benefits surpluses that are shared between consumers and producers.

ORIGIN OF THE IDEA 4.1 Consumer Surplus

Consumer Surplus

The benefit surplus received by a consumer or consumers in a market is called **consumer surplus**. It is defined as the difference between the maximum price a consumer is (or consumers are) willing to pay for a product and the actual price that they do pay.

The maximum price that a person is willing to pay for a unit of a product depends on the opportunity cost of his consumption alternatives. Suppose that Ted is offered the chance to purchase an apple. He would of course like to have it for free, but the maximum amount he would be willing to pay depends on the alternative uses to which he can put his money. If his maximum willingness to pay for that particular apple is $1.25, then we know that he is willing to forgo up to–but not more than–$1.25 of other goods and services. Paying even one cent more would entail having to give up too much of other goods and services.

It also means that if Ted is charged any market price less than $1.25, he will receive a consumer surplus equal to the difference between the $1.25 maximum price that he would have been willing to pay and the lower market price. For instance, if the market price is $0.50 per apple, Ted will receive a consumer surplus of $0.75 per apple (= $1.25 − $0.50). In nearly all markets, consumers individually and collectively gain greater total utility or satisfaction in dollar terms from their purchases than the amount of their expenditures (= product price × quantity). This utility surplus arises because each consumer who buys the product only has to pay the market equilibrium price even though many of them would have been willing to pay more than the equilibrium price to obtain the product.

The concept of maximum willingness to pay also gives us another way to understand demand curves. Consider Table 4-1, where the first two columns show the maximum amounts that six consumers would

TABLE 4-1	**Consumer Surplus**		
(1) Person	(2) Maximum price willing to pay	(3) Actual price (equilibrium price)	(4) Consumer surplus
Bob	$13	$8	$5 (= $13 − $8)
Beata	12	8	4 (= $12 − $8)
Bill	11	8	3 (= $11 − $8)
Bella	10	8	2 (= $10 − $8)
Brent	9	8	1 (= $9 − $8)
Betty	8	8	0 (= $8 − $8)

each be willing to pay for a bag of oranges. Bob, for instance, would be willing to pay a maximum of $13 for a bag of oranges. Betty, by contrast, would only be willing to pay a maximum of $8 for a bag of oranges.

Notice that the maximum prices these individuals are willing to pay represent points on a demand curve because the lower the market price, the more bags of oranges will be demanded. At a price of $12.50, for instance, Bob will be the only person listed in the table who will purchase a bag. But at a price of $11.50, both Bob and Beata will want to purchase a bag. And at a price of $10.50, Bob, Beata, and Bill will each purchase a bag. The lower the price, the greater the total quantity demanded as the market price falls below the maximum prices of more and more consumers.

Lower prices also imply larger consumer surpluses. When the price is $12.50, Bob only gets $0.50 in consumer surplus because his maximum willingness to pay of $13 is only $0.50 higher than the market price of $12.50. But if the market price were to fall to $8, then his consumer surplus would be $5 (= $13 − $8). The third and fourth columns of Table 5-1 show how much consumer surplus each of our six consumers will receive if the market price of a bag of oranges is $8. Only Betty receives no consumer surplus because her maximum willingness to pay exactly matches the $8 equilibrium price.

It is easy to show on a graph both the individual consumer surplus received by each particular buyer in a market and the collective consumer surplus received by all buyers. Consider Figure 4-1, which shows the market equilibrium price P_1 = $8 as well as the downsloping demand curve D for bags of oranges. Demand curve D includes not only the six consumers named in Table 4-1 but also every other consumer of oranges in the market. The individual consumer surplus of each particular person who is willing to buy at the $8 market price is simply the vertical distance from the horizontal line that marks the $8 market price up to that particular buyer's maximum willingness to pay. The collective consumer surplus obtained by all of our named and unnamed buyers is found by adding together each of their individual consumer surpluses.

To obtain the Q_1 bags of oranges represented, consumers collectively are willing to pay the total amount shown by the sum of the green triangle and blue rectangle under the demand curve and to the left of Q_1. But consumers need to pay only the amount represented by the blue rectangle (= $P_1 \times Q_1$). So the green triangle is the consumer surplus in this market. It is the sum of the vertical distances between the demand curve and the $8 equilibrium price at each quantity up to Q_1. Alternatively, it is the sum of the gaps

---

| **FIGURE 4-1** | **Consumer Surplus** |

Consumer surplus—shown as the green triangle—is the difference between the maximum price consumers are willing to pay for a product and the lower equilibrium price, here assumed to be $8. For quantity Q_1, consumers are willing to pay the sum of the amounts represented by the green triangle and the blue rectangle. Because they need to pay only the amount shown as the blue rectangle, the green triangle shows consumer surplus.

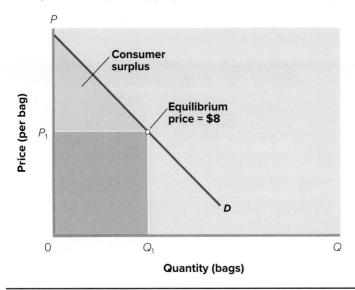

between maximum willingness to pay and actual price, such as those we calculated in Table 4-1. Thus, consumer surplus can also be defined as the area that lies below the demand curve and above the price line that extends horizontally from P_1.

Consumer surplus and price are inversely (negatively) related. Given the demand curve, higher prices reduce consumer surplus; lower prices increase it. To test this generalization, draw in an equilibrium price above $8 in Figure 4-1 and observe the reduced size of the triangle representing consumer surplus. When price goes up, the gap narrows between the maximum willingness to pay and the actual price. Next, draw in an equilibrium price below $8 and see that consumer surplus increases. When the price declines, the gap widens between maximum willingness to pay and actual price.

Producer Surplus

Like consumers, producers also receive a benefit surplus in markets. This **producer surplus** is the difference between the actual price a producer receives (or producers receive) and the minimum acceptable price that a consumer would have to pay the producer to make a particular unit of his or her product.

A producer's minimum acceptable price for a particular unit will equal the producer's marginal cost of producing that particular unit. That marginal cost will be the sum of the rent, wages, interest, and profit that the producer will need to pay in order to obtain the land, labour, capital, and entrepreneurship required to produce that particular unit. In this section, we are assuming that the marginal cost of producing a unit will include *all* of the costs of production. Unlike the coal-burning power plant mentioned above, the producer must pay for all of the costs, including the cost of pollution. In later sections, we will explore the market failures that arise in situations where firms do not have to pay all of their costs.

In addition to equalling marginal cost, a producer's minimum acceptable price can also be interpreted as the opportunity cost of bidding resources away from the production of other products. To see why this is true, suppose that Leah is an apple grower. The resources necessary for her to produce one apple could be used to produce other things. To get them directed toward producing an apple, it is necessary to pay Leah what it will cost her to bid the necessary resources away from other entrepreneurs who would like to use them to produce other products. Leah would, naturally, like to get paid as much as possible to produce the apple for you. But her minimum acceptable price is the lowest price you could pay her such that she can just break even after bidding away from other uses the land, labour, capital, and entrepreneurship necessary to produce the apple.

WORKED PROBLEM 4.1   Consumer and Producer Surplus

The size of the producer surplus earned on any particular unit will be the difference between the market price that the producer actually receives and the producer's minimum acceptable price. Consider Table 4-2, which shows the minimum acceptable prices of six different orange growers. With a market

TABLE 4-2	Producer Surplus		
(1) **Person**	**(2)** **Minimum** **acceptable price**	**(3)** **Actual price** **(equilibrium price)**	**(4)** **Producer surplus**
Carlos	$3	$8	$5 (= $8 − $3)
Courtney	4	8	4 (= $8 − $4)
Carla	5	8	3 (= $8 − $5)
Cindy	6	8	2 (= $8 − $6)
Carmela	7	8	2 (= $8 − $7)
Chad	8	8	0 (= $8 − $8)

price of $8, Carlos–for instance–has a producer surplus of $5, which is equal to the market price of $8 minus his minimum acceptable price of $3. Chad, by contrast, receives no producer surplus because his minimum acceptable price of $8 just equals the market equilibrium price of $8.

Carlos's minimum acceptable price is lower than Chad's minimum acceptable price because Carlos is a more efficient producer than Chad, by which we mean that Carlos produces oranges using a less-costly combination of resources than Chad uses. The differences in efficiency between Carlos and Chad are likely due to differences in the type and quality of resources available to them. Carlos, for instance, may own land perfectly suited to growing oranges, while Chad has land in the desert that requires costly irrigation if it is to be used to grow oranges. Thus, Chad has a higher marginal cost of producing oranges.

The minimum acceptable prices that producers are willing to accept form points on a supply curve because the higher the price, the more bags of oranges will be supplied. At a price of $3.50, for instance, only Carlos would be willing to supply a bag of oranges. But at a price of $5.50, Carlos, Courtney, and Carla would all be willing to supply a bag of oranges. The higher the market price, the more oranges will be supplied as the market price surpasses the marginal costs and minimum acceptable prices of more and more producers. Thus, supply curves shown in this competitive market are both marginal-cost curves and minimum-acceptable-price curves.

The supply curve in Figure 4-2 includes not only the six producers named in Table 4-2 but also every other producer of oranges in the market. At the market price of $8 per bag, Q_1 bags are produced because only those producers whose minimum acceptable prices are less than $8 per bag will choose to produce oranges with their resources. Those lower acceptable prices for each of the units up to Q_1 are shown by the portion of the supply curve lying to the left of and below the assumed $8 market price.

The individual producer surplus of each of these sellers is thus the vertical distance from each seller's respective minimum acceptable price on the supply curve up to the $8 market price. Their collective producer surplus is shown by the blue triangle in Figure 4-2. In that figure, producers collect revenues of $P_1 \times Q_1$, which is the sum of the blue and green triangles. As shown by the supply curve, however, revenues of only those illustrated by the green triangle would be required to entice producers to offer Q_1 bags of oranges for sale. The sellers therefore receive a producer surplus shown by the blue triangle. That surplus is

FIGURE 4-2 **Producer Surplus**

Producer surplus—shown as the blue triangle—reflects the difference between the equilibrium price producers receive for a product (here, $8) and the lower minimum payments they are willing to accept. For quantity Q_1, producers receive the sum of the amounts represented by the blue triangle plus the green triangle. Because they need to receive only the amount shown by the green triangle to produce Q_1, the blue triangle represents producer surplus.

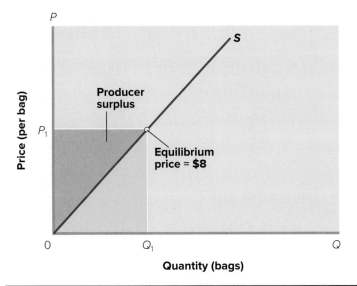

the sum of the vertical distances between the supply curve and the $8 equilibrium price at each of the quantities to the left of Q_1.

There is a direct (positive) relationship between equilibrium price and the amount of producer surplus. Given the supply curve, lower prices reduce producer surplus; higher prices increase it. If you pencil in a lower equilibrium price than $8, you will see that the producer surplus triangle gets smaller. The gaps between the minimum acceptable payments and the actual prices narrow when the price falls. If you pencil in an equilibrium price above $8, the size of the producer surplus triangle increases. The gaps between minimum acceptable payments and actual prices widen when the price increases.

Efficiency Revisited

In Figure 4-3 we bring together the demand and supply curves of Figures 4-1 and 4-2 to show the equilibrium price and quantity and the previously described regions of consumer and producer surplus. All markets that have downsloping demand curves and upsloping supply curves yield consumer and producer surplus.

Because we are assuming in Figure 4-3 that the demand curve reflects buyers' full willingness to pay and the supply curve reflects all the costs facing sellers, the equilibrium quantity in Figure 4-3 reflects economic efficiency, which consists of productive efficiency and allocative efficiency.

- **Productive efficiency** is achieved because competition forces orange growers to use the best technologies and combinations of resources available. Doing so minimizes the per-unit cost of the output produced.

- **Allocative efficiency** is achieved because the correct quantity of oranges—Q_1—is produced relative to other goods and services.

There are two ways to understand why Q_1 is the correct quantity of oranges. Both involve realizing that any resources directed toward the production of oranges are resources that could have been used to produce other products. Thus, the only way to justify taking any amount of any resource (land, labour, capital, entrepreneurship, etc.) away from the production of other products is if it brings more utility or satisfaction when devoted to the production of oranges than it would if it were used to produce other products.

| **FIGURE 4-3** | **Efficiency: Maximum Combined Consumer and Producer Goods** |

At quantity Q_1 the combined amount of consumer surplus, shown as the blue triangle, and producer surplus, shown as the green triangle, is maximized. Efficiency occurs because, at Q_1, maximum willingness to pay, indicated by the points on the demand curve, equals minimum acceptable price, shown by the points on the supply curve.

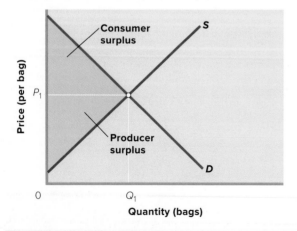

The first way to see why Q_1 is the allocatively efficient quantity of oranges is to note that demand and supply curves can be interpreted as measuring marginal benefit (MB) and marginal cost (MC). Recall from the discussion relating to Figure 1-3 that optimal allocation is achieved at the output level where MB = MC. We have already seen that supply curves are marginal cost curves. As it turns out, demand curves are marginal benefit curves. This is true because the maximum price that a consumer would be willing to pay for any particular unit is equal to the benefit of consuming that unit. Thus, each point on a demand curve represents both some consumer's maximum willingness to pay and the marginal benefit gained from consuming the particular unit in question.

Thus, combining the fact that supply curves are MC curves with the fact that demand curves are MB curves, we see that points on the demand curve in Figure 4-3 measure the marginal benefit of oranges at each level of output, while points on the supply curve measure the marginal cost of oranges at each level of output. As a result, MB = MC where the demand and supply curves intersect–which means that the equilibrium quantity Q_1 must be allocatively efficient.

To gain a deeper understanding of why Q_1 is allocatively efficient, notice that for every unit up to Q_1 marginal benefit exceeds marginal cost (MB > MC). And because marginal cost includes the opportunity cost of not making other things with the resources needed to make these units, we know that people are better off when the resources necessary to make these units are allocated to producing oranges rather than to producing anything else.

The second way to see why Q_1 is the correct quantity of oranges is based on our analysis of consumer and producer surplus and the fact that we can interpret demand and supply curves in terms of maximum willingness to pay and minimum acceptable price. In Figure 4-3, the maximum willingness to pay on the demand curve for each bag of oranges up to Q_1 exceeds the corresponding minimum acceptable price on the supply curve. Thus, each of these bags adds a positive amount (= maximum willingness to pay *minus* minimum acceptable price) to the *total* of consumer and producer surplus.

The fact that maximum willingness to pay exceeds minimum acceptable price for every unit up to Q_1 means that people gain more utility from producing and consuming those units than they would if they produced and consumed anything else that could be made with the resources that went into making those units. This is true because both the maximum willingness to pay and the minimum acceptable price take opportunity costs into account. As long as the maximum willingness to pay exceeds the minimum acceptable price, people are willing to pay more to consume a unit of the good in question (here, bags of oranges) than they would pay to consume anything else that could be made with the same resources. Only at the equilibrium quantity Q_1–where the maximum willingness to pay exactly equals the minimum acceptable price–does society exhaust all opportunities to produce units for which benefits exceed costs (including opportunity costs). Producing Q_1 units therefore achieves allocative efficiency because the market is producing and distributing only those units that make people happier with bags of oranges than they would be with anything else that could be produced with the same resources.

Geometrically, producing Q_1 units maximizes the combined area of consumer and producer surplus in Figure 4-3. In this context, the combined area is referred to as *total surplus.* Thus, when Q_1 units are produced, total surplus is equal to the large triangle formed by the green consumer surplus triangle and the blue producer surplus triangle.

When demand curves reflect buyers' full willingness to pay and when supply curves reflect all the costs facing sellers, competitive markets produce equilibrium quantities that maximize the sum of consumer and producer surplus. Allocative efficiency occurs at the market equilibrium quantity, where three conditions exist simultaneously:

1. MB = MC (Figure 1-3).

2. Maximum willingness to pay = minimum acceptable price.

3. Total surplus (= sum of consumer and producer surplus) is at a maximum.

Economists are enamoured of markets because properly functioning markets automatically achieve allocative efficiency. Other methods of allocating resources–such as government central planning–do exist.

But since they cannot do any better than properly functioning markets–and may in many cases do much worse–economists usually prefer that resources be allocated through markets whenever properly functioning markets are available.

Efficiency Losses (or Deadweight Losses)

Figures 4-4a and 4-4b demonstrate that **efficiency losses (or deadweight losses)**–reductions of combined consumer and producer surplus–result from both underproduction and overproduction. First, consider Figure 4-4a, which analyzes the case of underproduction by considering what happens if output falls from the efficient level Q_1 to the smaller amount Q_2. When that happens, the sum of consumer and producer surplus, previously *abc*, falls to *adec*. So the combined consumer and producer surplus declines by the amount of the blue triangle to the left of Q_1. That triangle represents an efficiency loss to buyers and sellers. And because buyers and sellers are members of society, it represents an efficiency loss to society.

For output levels from Q_2 to Q_1, the maximum willingness to pay by consumers (as reflected by points on the demand curve) exceeds the minimum acceptable price of sellers (as reflected by points on the supply curve). By failing to produce units of this product for which a consumer is willing to pay more than a producer is willing to accept, society suffers a loss of net benefits. As a concrete example, consider a particular unit for which a consumer is willing to pay $10 and a producer is willing to accept $6. The $4 difference between those values is a net benefit that will not be realized if this unit is not produced. In addition, the resources that should have gone to producing this unit will go instead to producing other products that will not generate as much utility as if those resources had been used here to produce this unit of this product. The triangle *dbe* in Figure 4-4a shows the total loss of net benefits that results from failing to produce the units from Q_2 to Q_1.

In contrast, consider the case of overproduction shown in Figure 4-4b, in which the number of oranges produced is Q_3 rather than the efficient level Q_1. In Figure 4-4b the combined consumer and producer surplus therefore declines by *bfg*–the blue triangle to the right of Q_1. This triangle subtracts from the total consumer and producer surplus of *abc* that would occur if the quantity had been Q_1. That is, for all units from zero to Q_1, benefits exceed costs, so that those units generate the economic surplus shown by triangle *abc*. But the units from Q_1 to Q_3 are such that costs exceed benefits. Thus, they generate an economic loss shown by triangle *bfg*. The total economic surplus for all units from zero to Q_3 is therefore the economic surplus given by *abc* for the units from 0 to Q_1 *minus* the economic loss given by *bfg* for the units from Q_1 to Q_3.

FIGURE 4-4   **Efficiency Losses (or Deadweight Losses)**

Quantity levels less than or greater than the efficient quantity Q_1 create efficiency losses. Triangle *dbe* shows the efficiency loss associated with underproduction at output Q_2. Triangle *bfg* in panel (b) illustrates the efficiency loss associated with overproduction at output level Q_3.

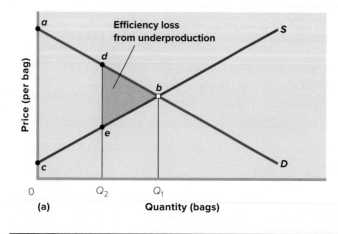

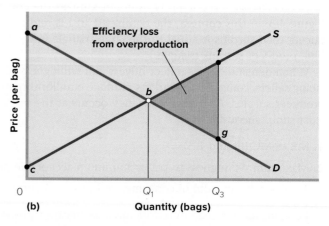

Producing any unit beyond Q_1 generates an economic loss because the willingness to pay for such units on the part of consumers is less than the minimum acceptable price to produce such units on the part of producers. As a concrete example, note that producing an item for which the maximum willingness to pay is, say, $7 and the minimum acceptable price is, say, $10 subtracts $3 from society's net benefits. Such production is uneconomical and creates an efficiency loss (or deadweight loss) for society. Because the net benefit of each bag of oranges from Q_1 to Q_3 is negative, we know that the benefits from these units are smaller than the opportunity costs of the other products that could have been produced with the resources that were used to produce these bags of oranges. The resources used to produce the bags from Q_1 to Q_3 could have generated net benefits instead of net losses if they had been directed toward producing other products. The brown triangle *bfg* to the right of Q_1 in Figure 4-4b shows the total efficiency loss from over-production at Q_3.

The magic of markets is that when demand reflects consumers' full willingness to pay and when supply reflects all costs, the market equilibrium quantity will automatically equal the allocatively efficient output level. Under these conditions, the market equilibrium quantity will ensure that there are neither efficiency losses from underproduction nor efficiency losses from overproduction. As we are about to see, however, such losses do happen when either demand does not reflect consumers' full willingness to pay or supply does not reflect all costs.

QUICK REVIEW 4.1

- Market failures in competitive markets have two possible causes: demand curves that do not reflect consumers' full willingness to pay and supply curves that do not reflect producers' full cost of production.

- Consumer surplus is the difference between the maximum price a consumer is willing to pay for a product and the lower price actually paid.

- Producer surplus is the difference between the minimum price a producer is willing to accept for a product and the higher price actually received.

- At the equilibrium price and quantity in competitive markets, marginal benefit equals marginal cost, maximum willingness to pay equals minimum acceptable price, and the total of consumer surplus and producer surplus is maximized. These individual conditions each define allocative efficiency.

- Quantities less than or greater than the allocatively efficient level of output create efficiency losses, also called deadweight losses.

4.3 / Public Goods

LO4.3 Describe free riding and public goods, and illustrate why private firms cannot normally produce public goods.

As you have learned, demand-side market failures arise in competitive markets when demand curves fail to reflect consumers' full willingness to pay for a good or service. In such situations, markets fail to produce all of the units for which there are net benefits because demand curves under-report how much consumers are willing and able to pay. This underreporting problem reaches its most extreme form in the case of a public good: markets may fail to produce *any* of the public good because its demand curve may reflect *none* of its consumers' willingness to pay.

Private Goods Characteristics

We have seen that a full range of **private goods** are produced through the competitive market system. These are the goods offered for sale in stores, in shops, and on the Internet. Examples include automobiles, clothing, personal computers, household appliances, and sporting goods. Private goods have two characteristics: rivalry and excludability.

- **Rivalry** (in consumption) means that when one person buys and consumes a product, it is not available for another person to buy and consume. When Adams purchases and drinks a bottle of mineral water, it is not available for Benson to purchase and consume.

- **Excludability** means that sellers can keep people who do not pay for a product from obtaining its benefits. Only people who are willing and able to pay the market price for bottles of water can obtain these drinks and the benefits they confer.

Consumers fully express their personal demands for private goods in the market. If Adams likes bottled mineral water, that fact will be known by her desire to purchase the product. Other things equal, the higher the price of bottled water, the fewer bottles she will buy. So Adams's demand for bottled water will reflect an inverse relationship between the price of bottled water and the quantity of it demanded. This is simply *individual* demand, as described in Chapter 3.

The *market* demand for a private good is the horizontal summation of the individual demand schedules (review Figure 3-2). Suppose there are just two consumers in the market for bottled water and the price is $1 per bottle. If Adams will purchase 3 bottles and Benson will buy 2, the market demand will reflect that consumers demand 5 bottles at the $1 price. Similar summations of quantities demanded at other prices will generate the market demand schedule and curve.

Suppose the equilibrium price of bottled water is $1. Adams and Benson will buy a total of 5 bottles, and the sellers will obtain total revenue of $5 (= $1 × 5). If the sellers' cost per bottle is $0.80, their total cost will be $4 (= $0.80 × 5). So sellers charging $1 per bottle will obtain $5 of total revenue, incur $4 of total cost, and earn $1 of profit for the 5 bottles sold.

Because firms can profitably tap market demand for private goods, they will produce and offer them for sale. Consumers demand private goods, and profit-seeking suppliers produce goods that satisfy the demand. Consumers willing to pay the market price obtain the goods; nonpayers go without.

A competitive market not only makes private goods available to consumers but also allocates society's resources efficiently to the particular product. There is neither underproduction nor overproduction of the product.

Public Goods Characteristics

Goods that have the opposite characteristics of private goods are called **public goods**. Public goods are distinguished by nonrivalry and nonexcludability.

- **Nonrivalry** (in consumption) means that one person's consumption of a good does not preclude consumption of the good by others. Everyone can simultaneously obtain the benefit from a public good such as national defense, street lighting, a global positioning system, or environmental protection.

CONSIDER THIS   **Street Entertainers**

Street entertainers are often found in tourist areas of major cities. These entertainers illuminate the concepts of free riders and public goods. Most street entertainers have a hard time earning a living from their activities (unless event organizers pay them) because they have no way of excluding nonpayers from the benefits of their entertainment. They essentially are providing public, not private, goods and must rely on voluntary payments. The result is a significant free-rider problem. Only a few in the audience put money in the container or instrument case, and many who do so contribute only token amounts. The rest are free riders who obtain the benefits of the street entertainment and retain their money for purchases that *they* initiate.

Street entertainers are acutely aware of the free-rider problem, and some have found creative ways to lessen it. For example, some entertainers involve the audience directly in the act. This usually creates a greater sense of audience willingness (or obligation) to contribute money at the end of the performance. "Pay for performance" is another creative approach to lessening the free-rider problem. A good example is the street entertainer painted up to look like a statue. When people drop coins into the container, the "statue" makes a slight movement. The greater the contributions, the greater the movement. But these human statues still face a free-rider problem: Nonpayers also get to enjoy the acts.

- **Nonexcludability** means there is no effective way of excluding individuals from the benefit of the good once it comes into existence. Once in place, you cannot exclude someone from benefiting from national defense, street lighting, a global positioning system, or environmental protection.

These two characteristics create a **free-rider problem**. Once a producer has provided a public good, everyone–including nonpayers–can obtain the benefit. Because most people do not voluntarily pay for something that they can obtain for free, most people become free riders. These free riders like the public good and would be willing to pay for it if producers could somehow force them to pay–but nonexcludability means that there is no way for producers to withhold the good from the free riders without also denying it to the few who do pay. As a result, free riding means that the free riders' willingness to pay is not expressed in the market. From the viewpoint of producers, free riding reduces demand. The more free riding, the less demand. And if all consumers free ride, demand will collapse all the way to zero.

The low or even zero demand caused by free riding makes it virtually impossible for private firms to profitably provide public goods. With little or no demand, firms have no potential to tap market demand for revenues and profits. As a result, they will not produce public goods. Society will therefore suffer efficiency losses because goods for which marginal benefits exceed marginal costs are not produced. Thus, if society wants a public good to be produced, it will have to direct government to provide it. Because the public good will still feature nonexcludability, the government won't have any better luck preventing free riding or charging people for it. But because the government can finance the provision of the public good through the taxation of other things, the government does not have to worry about profitability. It can therefore provide the public good even when private firms can't.

Examples of public goods include national defence, outdoor fireworks displays, the light beams thrown out by lighthouses, public art displays, public music concerts, MP3 music files posted to file-sharing websites, and ideas and inventions that are not protected by patents or copyrights. Each of these goods or services shows both nonrivalry and nonexcludability.

In a few special cases, private firms can provide public goods because the production costs of these public goods can be covered by the profits generated by closely related private goods. For instance, private companies can make a profit providing broadcast TV–which is a nonrival, nonexcludable public good–because they control who gets to air TV commercials, which are rival and excludable private goods. The money that broadcasters make from selling airtime for ads allows them to turn a profit despite having to give their main product, broadcast TV, away for free.

Unfortunately, only a few public goods can be subsidized in this way by closely related private goods. For the large majority of public goods, private provision is unprofitable. As a result, there are only two remaining ways for a public good to be supplied: private philanthropy or government provision. For many less expensive or less important public goods, like fireworks displays or public art, society may feel comfortable relying on private philanthropy. But when it comes to public goods like national defence, people normally look to the government.

This leads to an important question: Once a government decides to produce a particular public good, how can it determine the optimal amount that it should produce? How can it avoid either underallocating or overallocating society's scarce resources to the production of the public good?

One person's consumption of a public good does not preclude consumption of the same good by others.

Optimal Quantity of a Public Good

If consumers need not reveal their true demand for a public good in the marketplace, how can society determine the optimal amount of that good? The answer is that the government has to try to estimate the demand for a public good through surveys or public votes. It can then compare the marginal benefit (MB) of an added unit of the good against the government's marginal cost (MC) of providing it. Adhering to the MB = MC rule, government can provide the right—meaning efficient—amount of the public good.

Demand for Public Goods

The demand for a public good is somewhat unusual. Suppose Adams and Benson are the only two people in the society, and their marginal willingness to pay for a public good–this time, national defence–is as shown in columns 1, 2, and 3 in Table 4-3.

Notice that the schedules in Table 4-3 are demand schedules. Rather than depicting demand in the usual way–the quantity of a product someone is willing to buy at each possible price–these schedules show the price someone is willing to pay for an extra unit of each possible quantity. That is, Adams is willing to pay $4 for the first unit of the public good, $3 for the second, $2 for the third, and so on.

Suppose the government produces one unit of this public good. Because of the nonexcludability characteristic of a public good, Adams's consumption of the good does not preclude Benson from also consuming it, and vice versa. So both consume the good, and neither volunteers to pay for it. But from Table 4-3, column 4, we can find the amount these two people would be willing to pay, together. Columns 1 and 2 show that Adams would be willing to pay $4 for the first unit of the public good; columns 1 and 3 show that Benson would be willing to pay $5 for it. So the two people are jointly willing to pay $9 (= $4 + $5) for this unit.

For the second unit of the public good, the collective price they are willing to pay is $7 (= $3 from Adams plus $4 from Benson), for the third unit they will pay $5 (= $2 plus $3), and so on. By finding the collective willingness to pay for each additional unit (column 4), we can construct a collective demand schedule (a willingness-to-pay schedule) for the public good. Here, we are not adding the quantities demanded at each possible price as when we determine the market demand for a private good. Instead, we are adding *the prices that people are willing to pay for the last unit of the public good at each possible quantity demanded.*

Figure 4-5 shows the same adding procedure graphically, using the data from Table 4-3. Note that we sum Adams's and Benson's willingness-to-pay curves *vertically* to derive the collective willingness-to-pay curve (demand curve). The summing procedure is upward from the lower graph to the middle graph to the top (total) graph. For example, the height of the collective demand curve D_c at two units of output in the top graph is $7, the sum of the amounts that Adams and Benson are each willing to pay for the

TABLE 4-3	**Demand for a Public Good, Two Individuals**					
(1) Quantity of public good	**(2)** Adams's willingness to pay (price)		**(3)** Benson's willingness to pay (price)		**(4)** Collective willingness to pay (price)	
1	$4	+	$5	=	$9	
2	3	+	4	=	7	
3	2	+	3	=	5	
4	1	+	2	=	3	
5	0	+	1	=	1	

FIGURE 4-5	The Optimal Amount of a Public Good

Two people—Adams and Benson—are the only members of a hypothetical economy. (a) D_1 shows Adams's willingness to pay for various quantities of a particular public good. (b) D_2 shows Benson's willingness to pay for these same quantities of this public good. (c) The collective demand for this public good is shown by D_c and is found by summing vertically Adam's and Benson's individual willingness-to-pay curves. The supply (S) of the public good is upsloping, reflecting rising marginal costs. The optimal amount of the public good is 3 units, determined by the intersection of D_c and S. At that output, marginal benefit (reflected in the collective demand curve D_c) equals marginal cost (reflected in the supply curve S).

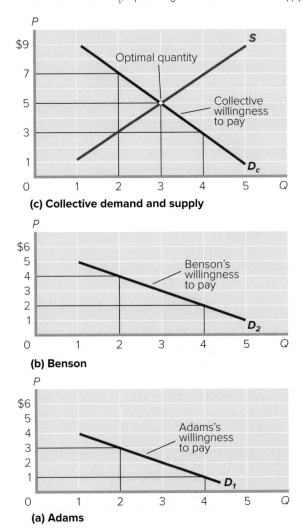

(c) Collective demand and supply

(b) Benson

(a) Adams

second unit (= $3 + $4). Likewise, the height of the collective demand curve at four units of the public good is $3 (= $1 + $2).

What does it mean in Figure 4-5a that, for example, Adams is willing to pay $3 for the second unit of the public good? It means that Adams expects to receive $3 of extra benefit or utility from that unit. And we know from the law of diminishing marginal utility that successive units of any good yield less and less added benefit. This is also true for public goods, explaining the downward slope of the willingness-to-pay curves of both Adams and Benson, and of the collective demand curve. These curves, in essence, are marginal benefit curves.

WORKED PROBLEM 4.2 Optimal Amount of a Public Good

Comparing MB and MC

We can now determine the optimal quantity of the public good. The collective demand curve D_c in Figure 4-5c measures society's marginal benefit of each unit of this particular good. The supply curve S in that figure measures society's marginal cost of each unit. The optimal quantity of this public good occurs where marginal benefit equals marginal cost, or where the two curves intersect. In Figure 4-5c that point is three units of the public good, where the collective willingness to pay for the last (third) unit—the marginal benefit—just matches that unit's marginal cost ($5 = $5). As we saw in Chapter 1, equating marginal benefit and marginal cost efficiently allocates society's scarce resources.

Cost–Benefit Analysis

The above example suggests a practical means, called **cost-benefit analysis**, for deciding whether to provide a particular public good and how much of it to provide. Like our example, cost-benefit analysis (or marginal benefit–marginal cost analysis) involves a comparison of marginal costs and marginal benefits.

CONCEPT

Suppose the federal government is contemplating a highway construction plan. Because the economy's resources are limited, any decision to use more resources in the public sector will mean fewer resources for the private sector. There will be both a cost and a benefit. The cost is the loss of satisfaction resulting from the accompanying decline in the production of private goods; the benefit is the extra satisfaction resulting from the output of more public goods. Should the needed resources be shifted from the private to the public sector? The answer is yes if the benefit from the extra public goods exceeds the cost that results from having fewer private goods. The answer is no if the cost of the forgone private goods is greater than the benefit associated with the extra public goods.

ILLUSTRATION

Roads and highways can be run privately, as excludability is possible by using toll gates. However, the federal highway system is almost entirely nonexclusive because anyone with a car can get on and off most federal highways without restriction anytime they want. Federal highways therefore satisfy one characteristic of a public good, non-excludability. The other characteristic, nonrivalry, is also satisfied by the fact that unless a highway is already extremely crowded, one person's driving on the highway does not preclude another person's driving on the highway. Thus, the federal highway system is effectively a public good. This leads us to ask the following: Should the federal government expand the national highway system? If so, what is the proper size or scope for the overall project?

Table 4-4 lists a series of increasingly costly highway projects: widening existing two-lane highways, building new two-lane highways, building new four-lane highways, and building new six-lane highways. The extent to which government should undertake highway construction depends on the costs and benefits. The costs are largely the costs of constructing and maintaining the highways; the benefit is an improved flow of people and goods throughout the country.[2]

The table shows that total benefit (column 4) exceeds total cost (column 2) for plans A, B, and C, indicating that some highway construction is economically justifiable. We see this directly in column 6, where total costs (column 2) are subtracted from total annual benefits (column 4). Net benefits are positive for plans A, B, and C. Plan D is not justifiable because net benefits are negative.

But the question of optimal size or scope for this project remains. Comparing the marginal cost (the change in total cost) and the marginal benefit (the change in total benefit) relating to each plan determines the answer. In this case, plan C (building new four-lane highways) is the best plan. For plans A and B, the marginal benefits exceed the marginal costs. Plan D's marginal cost ($10 billion) exceeds the marginal benefit ($3 billion) and therefore cannot be justified; it overallocates resources to the project. Plan C is closest

---

[2] Because the costs of public goods typically are immediate while the benefits often accrue over longer time periods, economists convert both costs and benefits to present values for comparison. Using present value properly accounts for the time value of money.

TABLE 4-4		Cost–Benefit Analysis for a National Highway Construction Project (billions of dollars)			
(1) Plan	(2) Total cost of project	(3) Marginal cost	(4) Total benefit	(5) Marginal benefit	(6) Net benefit (4) – (2)
No new construction	$ 0	$ 4	$ 0	$ 5	$0
A: Widen existing highways	4	6	5	8	1
B: Two-lane highways	10	8	13	10	3
C: Four-lane highways	**18**	10	**23**	**10**	**5**
D: Six-lane highways	28		26		–2

to the optimum because its marginal benefit ($10 billion) still exceeds marginal cost ($8 billion) but approaches the MB = MC (or MC = MB) ideal.

This **marginal cost = marginal benefit rule** actually tells us which plan provides society with the maximum net benefit. You can confirm directly in column 6 that the maximum net benefit (= $5 billion) is associated with plan C.

Cost-benefit analysis shatters the myth that *economy in government* and *reduced government spending* are synonymous. "Economy" is concerned with using scarce resources efficiently. If the costs of a proposed government program exceed its benefits, then the proposed public program should not be undertaken, but if the benefits exceed the costs, then it would be uneconomical or wasteful not to spend on that government program. Economy in government does not mean minimization of public spending; it means allocating resources between the private and public sectors and among public goods to achieve maximum net benefit.

QUASI-PUBLIC GOODS

The government provides many goods that fit the economist's definition of a public good. However, it also provides other goods and services that could be produced and delivered in such a way that exclusion would be possible. Such goods, called **quasi-public goods**, include education, streets and highways, police and fire protection, libraries and museums, preventive medicine, and sewage disposal. They could all be priced and provided by private firms through the market system. But, as we noted earlier, because they all have substantial positive externalities, they would be underproduced by the market system. Therefore, government often provides them to avoid the underallocation of resources that would otherwise occur.

CONSIDER THIS | Responding to Digital Free Riding

Four teenage friends start a rock band. They practice hard, master their instruments, write their own songs, and do gig after gig for nearly nothing at local bars to gain experience and perfect their music. After nearly five years of effort, they get signed to a major record label. But the year is 2005 and record sales are collapsing due to digital piracy. The rise of Internet file sharing has turned music into a public good and sales of recorded music are shrinking as hundreds of millions of music lovers have become digital free riders.

At first, the band struggles with the new reality. If they can't make a living selling music, they might have to quit music and get regular jobs. But then they realize that while recorded music is now free for anyone who wants it to be free, live music isn't. And neither are T-shirts or memorabilia.

So the band promotes itself online and allows free downloads to help propel its popularity. Then it charges steep prices at live concerts and makes sure that its T-shirts and memorabilia also generate substantial revenues. By doing so, the band adjusts to the new reality in which music has become a public good but live concerts and T-shirts have not. They charge for the items that are still private goods.

THE REALLOCATION PROCESS

How are resources reallocated from the production of private goods to the production of public and quasi-public goods? If the resources of the economy are fully employed, government must free up resources from the production of private goods and make them available for producing public and quasi-public goods. It does so by reducing private demand for them. And it does that by levying taxes on households and businesses, taking some of their income out of the circular flow. With lower incomes and hence less purchasing power, households and businesses must curtail their consumption and investment spending. As a result, the private demand for goods and services declines, as does the private demand for resources. So by diverting purchasing power from private spenders to government, taxes remove resources from private use.

Government then spends the tax proceeds to provide public and quasi-public goods and services. Taxation releases resources from the production of private consumer goods (food, clothing, television sets) and private investment goods (printing presses, boxcars, warehouses). Government shifts those resources to the production of public and quasi-public goods (post offices, submarines, parks), changing the composition of the economy's total output.

QUICK REVIEW 4.2

- Public goods are characterized by nonrivalry and non-excludability.

- The demand (marginal benefit) curve for a public good is found by vertically adding the prices all the members of society are willing to pay for the last unit of output at various output levels.

- The socially optimal amount of a public good is the amount at which the marginal cost and marginal benefit of the good are equal.

- Cost–benefit analysis is the method of evaluating alternative projects by comparing the marginal cost and marginal benefit and applying the MC = MB rule.

- The government uses taxes to allocate resources from the production of private goods to the production of public and quasi-public goods.

4.4 / Externalities

LO4.4 Explain how positive and negative externalities cause underallocations and overallocations of resources.

In addition to providing public goods, governments can also improve the allocation of resources in the economy by correcting for market failures caused by externalities. An **externality** occurs when some of the costs or the benefits of a good or service are passed on to or spill over to someone other than the immediate buyer or seller. Such spillovers are called externalities because they are benefits or costs that accrue to some third party that is external to the market transaction.

There are both positive and negative externalities. An example of a spillover cost or a *negative externality* is the cost of breathing polluted air; an example of a spillover benefit or a *positive externality* is the benefit of having everyone else inoculated against some communicable disease. When there are negative externalities, there is an overproduction of the product and an overallocation of resources to this product. Conversely, positive externalities result in underproduction of the product and an underallocation of resources. We can demonstrate both graphically.

ORIGIN OF THE IDEA 4.2   Externalities

Negative Externalities

Negative externalities cause supply-side market failures. These failures happen because producers do not take into account the costs that their negative externalities impose on others. This failure to account for all production costs causes firms' supply curves to shift to the right of (or below) where they would be if firms properly accounted for all costs. Consider the costs of breathing polluted air that are imposed on third parties living downwind of smoke-spewing factories. Because polluting firms do not take account of such costs, they oversupply the products they make, producing units for which total costs (including those that fall on third parties) exceed total benefits. The same is true when airlines fail to account for the costs that noisy jet engines impose on people living near airports and when biodiesel factories that convert dead animal parts into fuel release foul-smelling gases that disgust those living nearby.

An example of a negative externality is the cost of breathing polluted air.

Figure 4-6a illustrates how negative externalities affect the allocation of resources. When producers shift some of their costs onto the community as externality costs, producers' marginal costs are lower than they would be if they had to pay for these costs. So their supply curves do not include or capture all the costs associated with the production of their goods. A polluting producer's supply curve, such as S in Figure 4-6a, therefore understates the total cost of production. The firm's supply curve lies to the right of the full-cost supply curve S_t, which would include the spillover cost. Through polluting and thus transferring cost to others in society, the firm enjoys lower production costs and has the supply curve S.

The outcome is shown in Figure 4-6a, where equilibrium output Q_e is larger than the optimal output Q_o. This means that resources are overallocated to the production of this commodity; too many units of it are produced. In fact, there is a net loss to society for every unit from Q_o to Q_e because, for those units, the supply curve that accounts for all costs, S_t, lies above the demand curve. Therefore, MC exceeds MB for those units. The resources that went into producing those units should have been used elsewhere in the economy to produce other things.

In terms of our previous analysis, the negative externality results in an efficiency loss represented by triangle abc.

FIGURE 4-6   ## Negative Externalities and Positive Externalities

(a) With negative externalities borne by society, the producers' supply curve S is to the right of (below) the full-cost curve S_t. Consequently, the equilibrium output Q_e is greater than the optimal output Q_o and the efficiency loss is abc. (b) When positive externalities accrue to society, the market demand curve D is to the left of (below) the full-benefit demand curve D_t. As a result, the equilibrium output Q_e is less than the optimal output Q_o and the efficiency loss is xyz.

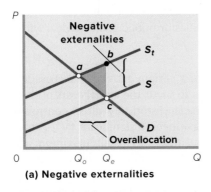

(a) Negative externalities

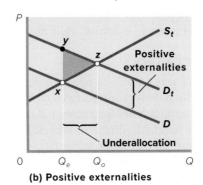

(b) Positive externalities

Positive Externalities

Positive externalities cause demand-side market failures. These failures happen because market demand curves in such cases fail to include the willingness to pay of the third parties who receive the external benefits caused by the positive externality. This failure to account for all benefits shifts market demand curves to the left of (or below) where they would be if they included all benefits and the willingness to pay of both the third parties and the primary beneficiaries. Because demand curves fail to take into account all benefits when there are positive externalities, markets in such cases fail to produce all units for which benefits (including those that are received by third parties) exceed costs. As a result, products featuring positive externalities are underproduced.

Vaccinations are a good example of how positive externalities reduce demand and shift demand curves down and to the left. When John gets vaccinated against a disease, he benefits not only himself (because he can no longer contract the disease) but also everyone else around him (because they know that in the future he will never be able to infect them). These other people would presumably be willing to pay some positive amount of money for the benefits they receive when John is vaccinated. But because his vaccination is a public good, there is no way to make them pay.

To see why his vaccination is a public good, note that the vaccination benefits that John provides to others feature nonrivalry and nonexcludability. There is nonrivalry because the protection his vaccination provides to one person does not lessen the protection that it provides to other people. There is nonexcludability because once he is vaccinated, there is no way to exclude anyone in particular from benefiting from his vaccination. Thus, the market demand for vaccinations will only include John's personal willingness to pay for the benefits that he personally receives from the vaccination. The market demand will fail to include the benefits that others receive. As a result, demand will be too low and vaccinations will be underproduced.

Figure 4-6b shows the impact of positive externalities on resource allocation. When external benefits occur, the market demand curve D lies to the left of the full-benefits demand curve, D_t. That is, D does not include the external benefits of the product, whereas D_t does. The outcome is that the equilibrium output, Q_e, is less than the optimal output, Q_o. The market fails to produce enough vaccinations and resources are underallocated to this product. The underproduction implies that society is missing out on a significant amount of potential net benefits. For every unit from Q_e to Q_o, the demand curve that accounts for all benefits, D_t, lies above the supply curve that accounts for all costs—including the opportunity cost of producing other items with the resources that would be needed to produce these units. Therefore, MB exceeds MC for each of these units and we know that society should redeploy some of its resources away from the production of other things in order to produce these units that generate net benefits.

In terms of our previous analysis, the positive externality results in an efficiency loss represented by triangle xyz.

Government Intervention

Government intervention may be called upon to achieve economic efficiency when externalities affect large numbers of people or when community interests are at stake. Government can use direct controls and taxes to counter negative externalities; it may provide subsidies or public goods to deal with positive externalities.

DIRECT CONTROLS

The direct way to reduce negative externalities from a certain activity is to pass legislation limiting that activity. Such direct controls force the offending firms to incur the actual costs of the offending activity. To date, this approach has dominated public policy in Canada. Historically, direct controls in the form of uniform emissions standards—limits on allowable pollution—have been a significant factor in Canadian air pollution policy. Clean-air legislation forces factories, cars, and businesses to install "maximum achievable control technology" to reduce emissions. Clean-water legislation limits the amount of heavy metals, detergents, and other pollutants firms can discharge into rivers and bays. Toxic-waste laws mandate special procedures and dump sites for disposing of contaminated soil and solvents. Violating these laws means fines and, in some cases, imprisonment.

CONSIDER THIS | The Fable of the Bees

Economist Ronald Coase received the Nobel Prize for his **Coase theorem**, which pointed out that, under the right conditions, private individuals can often negotiate their own mutually agreeable solutions to externality problems through *individual bargaining* without the need for government interventions like pollution taxes.

This is a very important insight because it means that we shouldn't automatically call for government intervention every time we see a potential externality problem. Consider the positive externalities that bees provide by pollinating farmers' crops. Should we assume that beekeeping will be underprovided unless the government intervenes with, for instance, subsidies to encourage more hives and hence more pollination?

As it turns out, no. Research has shown that farmers and beekeepers long ago used individual bargaining to develop customs and payment systems that avoid free riding by farmers and that encourage beekeepers to keep the optimal number of hives. Free riding is avoided by the custom that all farmers in an area simultaneously hire beekeepers to provide bees to pollinate their crops. And farmers always pay the beekeepers for their pollination services because if they didn't, no beekeeper would ever work with them in the future—a situation that would lead to massively reduced crop yields due to a lack of pollination.

The Fable of the Bees is a good reminder that it is a fallacy to assume that the government must always get involved to remedy externalities. In many cases, the private sector can solve both positive and negative externality problems on its own.

ORIGIN OF THE IDEA 4.3 Coase Theorem

Direct controls raise the marginal cost of production because the firms must operate and maintain pollution-control equipment. The supply curve S in Figure 4-7b, which does not reflect the external costs, shifts leftward (upward) to the full-cost supply curve, S_t. Product price increases, equilibrium output falls from Q_e to Q_o, and the initial overallocation of resources shown in Figure 4-7a is corrected. Observe that the efficiency loss shown by triangle abc in Figure 4-7a disappears after the overallocation is corrected in Figure 4-7b.

FIGURE 4-7 | Correcting for Negative Externalities

(a) Negative externalities result in an overallocation of resources. (b) Government can correct this overallocation in two ways: (1) using direct controls, which would shift the supply curve from S to S_t and reduce output from Q_e to Q_o, or (2) imposing a specific tax, T, that would also shift the supply curve from S to S_t, eliminating the overallocation of resources and thus the efficiency loss.

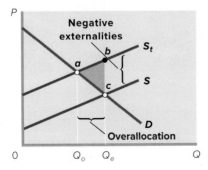

(a) Negative externalities

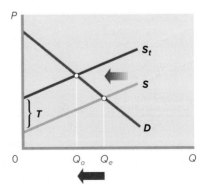

(b) Correcting the overallocation of resources via direct controls or via a tax

SPECIFIC TAXES

A second policy approach to negative externalities is for government to levy taxes or charges specifically on the related good. For example, the government has placed a manufacturing tax on CFCs, which deplete the stratospheric ozone layer protecting Earth from excessive solar ultraviolet radiation. Facing such a tax, manufacturers must decide whether to pay the tax or expend additional funds to purchase or develop substitute products. In either case, the tax raises the marginal cost of producing CFCs, shifting the private supply curve for this product leftward.

In Figure 4-7b, a tax equal to T per unit increases the firm's marginal cost, shifting the supply curve from S to S_t. The equilibrium price rises and the equilibrium output declines from Q_e to the economically efficient level Q_o. The tax eliminates the initial overallocation of resources and therefore the efficiency loss.

SUBSIDIES AND GOVERNMENT PROVISION

Where positive externalities are large and diffuse, as in our earlier example of vaccinations, government has three options for correcting the underallocation of resources:

1. **Subsidies to Buyers** Figure 4-8a shows the supply-demand situation for positive externalities. Government could correct the underallocation of resources–for example, to inoculations–by subsidizing consumers of the product; it could give each new mother a discount coupon to be used to obtain a series of vaccinations for her child. The coupon would reduce the price to the mother by, say, 50 percent. As shown in Figure 4-8b, this program would shift the demand curve for inoculations from too-low D to the appropriate D_t. The number of vaccinations would rise from Q_e to the optimal Q_o, eliminating the underallocation of resources and efficiency loss shown in Figure 4-8a.

2. **Subsidies to Producers** A subsidy to producers is a specific tax in reverse. Taxes impose an extra cost on producers, while subsidies reduce producers' costs. As shown in Figure 4-8c, a subsidy of U per inoculation to physicians and medical clinics would reduce their marginal costs and shift their supply curve rightward from S_t to S'_t. The output of inoculations would increase from Q_e to the optimal level Q_o, correcting the underallocation of resources and efficiency loss shown in (a).

FIGURE 4-8   **Correcting for Positive Externalities**

(a) Positive externalities result in an underallocation of resources. (b) This underallocation can be corrected by a subsidy to consumers, which shifts market demand from D to D_t and increases output from Q_e to Q_o. (c) Alternatively, the underallocation can be eliminated by providing producers with a subsidy of U, which shifts their supply curve from S_t to S'_t, increasing output from Q_e to Q_o and eliminating the underallocation and thus the efficiency loss shown in (a).

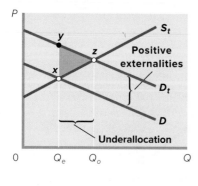

(a) Positive externalities

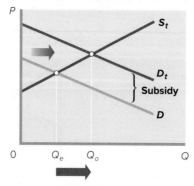

(b) Correcting the underallocation of resources via a subsidy to consumers

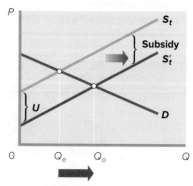

(c) Correcting the underallocation of resources via a subsidy to producers

TABLE 4-5	Methods for Dealing with Externalities	
Problem	**Resource allocation outcome**	**Ways to correct**
Negative externalities (spillover costs)	Overproduction of output and therefore overallocation of resources	1. Private bargaining 2. Liability rules and lawsuits 3. Tax on producers 4. Direct controls 5. Market for externality rights
Positive externalities (spillover benefits)	Underproduction of output and therefore underallocation of resources	1. Private bargaining 2. Subsidy to consumers 3. Subsidy to producers 4. Government provision

3. Government Provision Finally, where positive externalities are large, the government may decide to provide the product for free to everyone. The Canadian government largely eradicated the crippling disease polio by administering free vaccines to all children. India ended smallpox by paying people in rural areas to come to public clinics to have their children vaccinated.

Table 4.5 lists several methods for correcting externalities, including those we have discussed thus far.

4.5 / Society's Optimal Amount of Externality Reduction

LO4.5 Show why we normally won't want to pay what it would cost to eliminate every last bit of a negative externality such as air pollution.

Negative externalities such as pollution reduce the utility of those affected. These spillovers are not economic goods but economic "bads." If something is bad, shouldn't society eliminate it? Why should society allow firms or municipalities to discharge *any* impure waste into public waterways or to emit *any* pollution into the air?

 CHOOSING A LITTLE MORE OR LESS

Economists answer these questions by pointing out that reducing pollution and negative externalities is not free. There are costs as well as benefits to reducing pollution. As a result, the correct question to ask when it comes to cleaning up negative externalities is not, "Do we pollute a lot or pollute zero?" That is an all-or-nothing question that ignores marginal costs and marginal benefits. Instead, the correct question is, "What is the optimal amount to clean up–the amount that equalizes the marginal cost of cleaning up with the marginal benefit of a cleaner environment?"

If we ask that question, we see that reducing a negative externality has a price. Society must decide how much of a reduction it wants to buy. High costs may mean that totally eliminating pollution entirely might not be desirable, even if it is technologically feasible. Because of the law of diminishing returns, cleaning up the last 10 percent of pollutants from an industrial smokestack is normally far more costly than cleaning up the prior 10 percent.

The marginal cost (MC) to the firm and hence to society–the opportunity cost of the extra resources used–rises as pollution is reduced further. At some point MC may rise so high that it exceeds society's marginal benefit (MB) of further pollution abatement (reduction). Additional actions to reduce pollution will therefore lower society's well-being; total cost will rise more than total benefit, as the more pollution reduction society accomplishes, the lower the utility (and benefit) of the next unit of pollution reduction.

MC, MB, and Equilibrium Quantity

Figure 4.9 shows both the rising marginal-cost curve, MC, for pollution reduction and the downsloping marginal-benefit curve, MB, for pollution reduction. MB slopes downward because of the law of diminishing marginal utility: the more pollution reduction society accomplishes, the lower the utility (and benefit) of the next unit of pollution reduction.

The **optimal reduction of an externality** occurs when society's marginal cost and marginal benefit of reducing that externality are equal (MC = MB). In Figure 4-9 this optimal amount of pollution abatement is Q_1 units. When MB exceeds MC, additional abatement moves society toward economic efficiency; the added benefit of cleaner air or water exceeds the benefit of any alternative use of the required resources. When MC exceeds MB, additional abatement reduces economic efficiency; there would be greater benefits from using resources in some other way than to further reduce pollution.

In reality, it is difficult to measure the marginal costs and benefits of pollution control. Nevertheless, Figure 4-9 demonstrates that some pollution may be economically efficient. This is so not because pollution is desirable but because, beyond some level of control, further abatement may reduce society's net well-being. As an example, it would cost the government billions of dollars to clean up every last piece of litter in Canada. Thus, it would be better to tolerate some trash blowing around if the money saved by picking up less trash would yield larger net benefits when spent on other things.

Shifts in Locations of the Curves

The locations of the marginal-cost and marginal-benefit curves in Figure 4.9 are not forever fixed. They can, and probably do, shift over time. For example, suppose that the technology of pollution-control equipment improved noticeably. We would expect the cost of pollution abatement to fall, society's MC curve to shift rightward and the optimal level of abatement to rise. Or suppose that society were to decide that it wanted cleaner air and water because of new information about the adverse health effects of pollution. The MB curve in Figure 4.9 would shift rightward, and the optimal level of pollution control would increase beyond Q_1. Test your understanding of these statements by drawing the new MC and MB curves in Figure 4.9.

FIGURE 4-9   **Society's Optimal Amount of Pollution Abatement**

The optimal amount of externality reduction—in this case, pollution abatement—occurs at Q_1, where society's marginal cost (MC) and marginal benefit (MB) of reducing the spillover are equal.

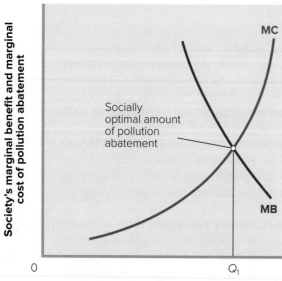

Government's Role in the Economy

Market failures can be used to justify government interventions in the economy. The inability of private-sector firms to break even when attempting to provide public goods and the overproduction and underproduction problems caused by positive and negative externalities mean that government can have an important role to play if society's resources are to be efficiently allocated to the goods and services that people most highly desire.

Correcting for market failures is not, however, an easy task. To begin with, government officials must correctly identify the existence and the cause of any given market failure. That, by itself, may be difficult, time consuming, and costly. But even if a market failure is correctly identified and diagnosed, government may still fail to take appropriate corrective action due to the context of politics. To serve the public, politicians need to get elected. To stay elected, officials (prime ministers, Members of Parliament, mayors, council members, or school board members) need to satisfy their particular constituencies. At best, the political realities complicate government's role in the economy; at worst, they produce undesirable economic outcomes.

In the political context, over-regulation can occur in some cases, under-regulation in others. Some public goods and quasi-public goods can be produced not because their benefits exceed their costs but because their benefits accrue to firms located in regions served by powerful elected officials. Inefficiency can easily creep into government activities because of the lack of a profit incentive to hold down costs. Policies to correct negative externalities can be politically blocked by the very parties that are producing the spillovers. In short, the economic role of government, although critical to a well-functioning economy, is not always perfectly carried out.

Economists use the term *government failure* to describe economically inefficient outcomes caused by shortcomings in the public sector.

QUICK REVIEW 4.3

- Policies for coping with the overallocation of resources caused by negative externalities are (1) private bargaining, (2) liability rules and lawsuits, (3) direct controls, (4) specific taxes, and (5) markets for externality rights.

- Policies for correcting the underallocation of resources associated with positive externalities are (1) private bargaining, (2) subsidies to producers, (3) subsidies to consumers, and (4) government provision.

- The optimal amount of negative-externality reduction occurs where society's marginal cost and marginal benefit of reducing the externality are equal.

- Political pressures often lead governments to respond inefficiently when attempting to correct for market failures.

The **LAST WORD** | Carbon Dioxide Emissions, Cap-and-Trade, and Carbon Taxes

Cap-and-trade systems and carbon taxes are two approaches to reducing carbon dioxide (CO_2) emissions.

Externality problems are property rights problems. Consider a trash dump. Because the owner of the landfill has full rights to his land, people wishing to dump their trash into the landfill have to pay him. This payment implies that there is no externality: he happily accepts their trash in exchange for a dumping fee.

By contrast, because nobody owns the atmosphere, all air pollution is an externality since there is no way for those doing the polluting to work out a payment to compensate those affected by the pollution, or for those threatened with pollution to simply refuse to be polluted upon.

Conventional property rights therefore cannot fix the externalities associated with air pollution. But that does not mean property rights can't help fight pollution. The trick to making them work is to assign property rights not to the atmosphere itself, but to *polluting* the atmosphere. This is done in cap-and-trade systems, under which the government sets an annual limit, or cap, on the number of tonnes of a pollutant that firms can emit into the atmosphere.

Consider carbon dioxide, or CO_2. It is a colourless, odourless gas that many scientists consider to be a contributing cause of climate change, specifically global warming. To reduce CO_2 emissions, the Canadian government might set a cap of 5 billion tonnes of CO_2 emissions per year (which would be about 10 percent below 2009 emissions levels). The government then prints out emissions permits that sum to the limit set in the cap and distributes them to polluting firms. Once they are distributed, the only way a firm can legally emit a tonne of CO_2 is if it owns a permit to do so.

Under this policy, the government can obviously adjust the total amount of air pollution by adjusting the cap. This by itself improves efficiency because the cap imposes scarcity. Because each firm has only a limited number of permits, each firm has a strong incentive to maximize the net benefits that it produces from every tonne of pollution that it emits. But the cap-and-trade scheme leads to even greater improvements in efficiency because firms are free to trade (sell) them to each other.

For instance, suppose Smokestack Toys owns permits for 100 tonnes of CO_2 emissions and could use them to produce toy cars that would generate profits of $100,000. There is a power plant, however, that could make up to $1 million of profits by using those 100 tonnes of emissions permits to generate electricity. Because firms can trade their permits, Smokestack Toys will sell its permits to the power plant for more than the $100,000 in profits that it could make if it kept them and produced toy cars. And the power plant will gladly pay more than $100,000 for those permits because it can turn around and use them to make up to $1 million of profits by using them to generate electricity.

Society will benefit hugely from this transaction because while 100 tonnes of CO_2 will be emitted no matter which firm uses the permits, society will receive much greater net benefits when they are used by the power plant, as indicated by the fact that the power plant can produce much larger profits than the toy company when using the same amount of this scarce resource.

Several words of caution are in order, however. Cap-and-trade systems have proven very difficult to implement in cases where it is difficult for regulators to effectively check whether firms are obeying the system. This has been a major problem with the European Union's cap-and-trade system for CO_2 emissions. Because nearly every type of industrial activity releases CO_2 into the atmosphere, enforcement involves monitoring many thousands of factories of all sizes. That is very difficult and cheating has resulted. In addition, politically connected industries got politicians to give them exemptions or free permits.

By contrast, a cap-and-trade system on sulfur dioxide emissions from coal burning public utilities has worked very well in Canada since the 1980s. But in that case, there were only a few polluting utilities and they were already being monitored for emissions. So there was very little ability to cheat. In addition, all of the firms were treated equally, with no firms allowed exemptions or free permits.

Due to the mixed results, many economists have concluded that a cap-and-trade system would not be the best way to curb CO_2 emissions. They believe that there are simply too many sources of pollution to make monitoring either possible or cost-effective. And it seems likely that politically connected industries will be granted exemptions. So, instead, many economists favour a carbon tax, which would involve taxing each tonne of coal, each litre of gasoline, and each barrel of oil on the basis of how much carbon it contains (and thus how much CO_2 will eventually be released into the atmosphere when it is used). By raising the cost of polluting, the tax would reduce consumption and lessen the externalities associated with CO_2 emissions. It would also be nearly impossible to evade so that we would not have to worry about cheating.

Question

Distinguish between a carbon tax and a cap-and-trade strategy for reducing carbon dioxide and other so-called greenhouse gases (that are believed by many scientists to be causing global warming). Which of the two strategies do you think would have the most political support in an election in your home province? Explain your thinking.

Chapter Summary

LO4.1 DIFFERENTIATE BETWEEN DEMAND-SIDE MARKET FAILURES AND SUPPLY-SIDE MARKET FAILURES.

- A market failure happens in a particular market when the market produces an equilibrium level of output that either overallocates or underallocates resources to the product being traded in the market.

- In competitive markets that feature many buyers and many sellers, market failures can be divided into two types. Demand-side market failures occur when demand curves do not reflect consumers' full willingness to pay. Supply-side market failures occur when supply curves do not reflect all production costs, including those that may be borne by third parties.

LO4.2 EXPLAIN THE ORIGIN OF BOTH CONSUMER SURPLUS AND PRODUCER SURPLUS, AND EXPLAIN HOW PROPERLY FUNCTIONING MARKETS MAXIMIZE THEIR SUM, ECONOMIC SURPLUS, WHILE OPTIMALLY ALLOCATING RESOURCES.

- Consumer surplus is the difference between the maximum price that a consumer is willing to pay for a product and the lower price actually paid. Producer surplus is the difference between the minimum price that a producer is willing to accept for a product and the higher price actually received. Collectively, consumer surplus is represented by the triangle under the demand curve and above the actual price, whereas producer surplus is shown by the triangle above the supply curve and below the actual price.

- Graphically, the combined amount of producer and consumer surplus is represented by the triangle to the left of the intersection of the supply and demand curves that is below the demand curve and above the supply curve. At the equilibrium price and quantity in competitive markets, marginal benefit equals marginal cost, maximum willingness to pay equals minimum acceptable price, and the combined amount of consumer surplus and producer surplus is maximized.

- Output levels less than or greater than the equilibrium output create efficiency losses—reductions in the combined amount of consumer surplus and producer surplus. Underproduction creates efficiency losses because output is not being produced for which maximum willingness to pay exceeds minimum acceptable price. Overproduction creates efficiency losses because output is being produced for which minimum acceptable price exceeds maximum willingness to pay.

LO4.3 DESCRIBE FREE RIDING AND PUBLIC GOODS, AND ILLUSTRATE WHY PRIVATE FIRMS CANNOT NORMALLY PRODUCE PUBLIC GOODS.

- Public goods are distinguished from private goods. Private goods are characterized by rivalry (in consumption) and excludability. One person's purchase and consumption of a private good precludes others from also buying and consuming it. Producers can exclude nonpayers (free riders) from receiving the benefits. In contrast, public goods are characterized by nonrivalry (in consumption) and nonexcludability. Public goods are not profitable to private firms because nonpayers (free riders) can obtain and consume those goods. Only government is willing to provide desirable public goods, financing them through taxation.

- The collective demand schedule for a particular public good is found by summing the prices each individual is willing to pay for an additional unit. Graphically, that demand curve is therefore found by summing vertically the individual demand curves for that good. The resulting total demand curve indicates the collective willingness to pay for (or marginal benefit of) the last unit of any given amount of the public good.

- The optimal quantity of a public good occurs where the society's willingness to pay for the last unit—the marginal benefit of the good—equals the marginal cost of the good.

LO4.4 EXPLAIN HOW POSITIVE AND NEGATIVE EXTERNALITIES CAUSE UNDERALLOCATIONS AND OVERALLOCATIONS OF RESOURCES.

- Externalities or spillovers are costs or benefits that accrue to someone other than the immediate buyer or seller. Such costs or benefits are not captured in market demand or supply curves and therefore cause the output of certain goods to vary from society's optimal output. Negative externalities (or spillover costs or external costs) result in an overallocation of resources to a particular product. Positive externalities (or spillover benefits or external benefits) are accompanied by an underallocation of resources to a particular product.

- Direct controls and specific taxes can improve resource allocation in situations where negative externalities affect many people and community resources. Both direct controls (such as smokestack emission standards) and specific taxes (such as taxes on firms producing toxic chemicals) increase production costs and hence product price. As product price rises, the externality and overallocation of resources are reduced, because less of the output is produced.

- Government can correct the underallocation of resources that results from positive externalities in a particular market either by subsidizing consumers (which increases market demand) or subsidizing producers (which increases market supply). Such subsidies increase the equilibrium output, reducing or eliminating the positive externality and consequent underallocation of resources.

- The Coase theorem suggests that under the right circumstances private bargaining can solve externality problems. Thus, government intervention is not always needed to deal with externality problems.

LO4.5   SHOW WHY WE NORMALLY WON'T WANT TO PAY WHAT IT WOULD COST TO ELIMINATE EVERY LAST BIT OF A NEGATIVE EXTERNALITY SUCH AS AIR POLLUTION.

- The socially optimal amount of externality abatement occurs where society's marginal cost and marginal benefit of reducing the externality are equal. This optimal amount of pollution abatement is likely to be less than a 100 percent reduction. Changes in technology or changes in society's attitudes toward pollution can affect the optimal amount of pollution abatement.

- Market failures present government with opportunities to improve the allocation of society's resources and thereby enhance society's total well-being. But even when government correctly identifies the existence and cause of a market failure, political pressures may make it difficult or impossible for government officials to implement a proper solution.

Terms and Concepts

market failures

demand-side market failure

supply-side market failure

consumer surplus

producer surplus

efficiency losses (or deadweight losses)

private goods

rivalry

excludability

public goods

nonrivalry

nonexcludability

free-rider problem

cost–benefit analysis

marginal cost = marginal benefit rule

quasi-public goods

externality

Coase theorem

optimal reduction of an externality

Discussion Questions

1. Explain the two causes of market failures. Given their definitions, could a market be affected by both types of market failures simultaneously?   [LO4.1]

2. Use the ideas of consumer surplus and producer surplus to explain why economists say competitive markets are efficient. Why are below- or above-equilibrium levels of output inefficient, according to these two sets of ideas?   [LO4.2]

3. What are the two characteristics of public goods? Explain the significance of each for public provision as opposed to private provision. What is the free-rider problem as it relates to public goods? Is Canadian border patrol a public good or a private good? Why? How about satellite TV? Explain.   [LO4.3]

4. What divergences arise between equilibrium output and efficient output when (a) negative externalities and (b) positive externalities are present? How might government correct these divergences? Cite an example (other than the text examples) of an external cost and an external benefit.   [LO4.4]

5. Why are spillover costs and spillover benefits also called negative and positive externalities? Show graphically how a tax can correct for a negative externality and how a subsidy to producers can correct for a positive externality. How does a subsidy to consumers differ from a subsidy to producers in correcting for a positive externality?   [LO4.4]

6. An apple grower's orchard provides nectar to a neighbour's bees, while the beekeeper's bees help the apple grower by pollinating his apple blossoms. Use Figure 4-6b to explain why this situation of dual positive externalities might lead to an underallocation of resources to both apple growing and beekeeping. How might this underallocation get resolved via the means suggested by the Coase theorem?   [LO4.4]

7. The Lojack car recovery system allows the police to track stolen cars. As a result, they not only recover 90 percent of Lojack-equipped stolen cars but also arrest many auto thieves and shut down many chop shops that dismantle stolen vehicles to get at their used parts. Thus, Lojack provides both private benefits and positive externalities. Should the government consider subsidizing Lojack purchases?   [LO4.4]

8. Explain why zoning laws, which allow certain land uses only in specific locations, might be justified in dealing with a problem of negative externalities. Explain why in areas where buildings sit close together tax breaks to property owners for installing extra fire prevention equipment might be justified in view of positive externalities. Explain why excise taxes on beer might be justified in dealing with a problem of external costs.   [LO4.5]

Review Questions

1. Draw a supply-and-demand graph and identify the areas of consumer surplus and producer surplus. Given the demand curve, what impact will an increase in supply have on the amount of consumer surplus shown in your diagram? Explain why.   [LO4.2]

2. Assume that candle wax is traded in a perfectly competitive market in which the demand curve captures buyers' full willingness to pay while the supply curve reflects all production costs. For each of the following situations, indicate whether the total

output should be increased, decreased, or kept the same in order to achieve allocative and productive efficiency. [LO4.2]

a. Maximum willingness to pay exceeds minimum acceptable price.

b. MC > MB.

c. Total surplus is at a maximum.

d. The current quantity produced exceeds the market equilibrium quantity.

3. Efficiency losses _____. [LO4.2]

a. Are not possible if suppliers are willing to produce and sell a product

b. Can only result from underproduction

c. Can only result from overproduction

d. None of the above

4. Draw a production possibilities curve with public goods on the vertical axis and private goods on the horizontal axis. Assuming the economy is initially operating on the curve, indicate how the production of public goods might be increased. How might the output of public goods be increased if the economy is initially operating at a point inside the curve? [LO4.3]

5. Use the distinction between the characteristics of private and public goods to determine whether the following should be produced through the market system or provided by government: (a) French fries, (b) airport screening, (c) court systems, (d) mail delivery, and (e) medical care. State why you answered as you did in each case. [LO4.3]

6. Match each of the following characteristics or scenarios with either the term *negative externality* or the term *positive externality*. [LO4.4]

a. Overallocation of resources

b. Tammy installs a very nice front garden, raising the property values of all the other houses on her block.

c. Market demand curves are too far to the left (too low).

d. Underallocation of resources

e. Water pollution from a factory forces neighbors to buy water purifiers.

7. Use marginal cost/marginal benefit analysis to determine if the following statement is true or false: "The optimal amount of pollution abatement for some substances, say, dirty water from storm drains, is very low; the optimal amount of abatement for other substances, say, cyanide poison, is close to 100 percent." [LO4.5]

Problems

1. Refer to Table 4-1. If the six people listed in the table are the only consumers in the market and the equilibrium price is $11 (not the $8 shown), how much consumer surplus will the market generate? [LO4.2]

2. Refer to Table 4-2. If the six people listed in the table are the only producers in the market and the equilibrium price is $6 (not the $8 shown), how much producer surplus will the market generate? [LO4.2]

3. Look at Tables 4-1 and 4-2 together. What is the total surplus if Bob buys a unit from Carlos? If Beata buys a unit from Courtney? If Bob buys a unit from Chad? If you match up pairs of buyers and sellers so as to maximize the total surplus of all transactions, what is the largest total surplus that can be achieved? [LO4.2]

4. **ADVANCED ANALYSIS** Assume the following values for Figures 4-4a and 4-4b: $Q_1 = 20$ bags, $Q_2 = 15$ bags, $Q_3 = 27$ bags. The market equilibrium price is $45 per bag. The price at point a is $85 per bag. The price at point c is $5 per bag. The price at point f is $59 per bag. The price at point g is $31 per bag. Apply the formula for the area of a triangle (area = ½ × base × height) to answer the following questions. [LO4.2]

a. What is the dollar value of the total surplus (producer surplus plus consumer surplus) when the allocatively efficient output level is being produced? How large is the dollar value of the consumer surplus at that output level?

b. What is the dollar value of the deadweight loss when output level Q_2 is being produced? What is the total surplus when output level Q_2 is being produced?

c. What is the dollar value of the deadweight loss when output level Q_3 is produced? What is the dollar value of the total surplus when output level Q_3 is produced?

5. On the basis of the following three individual demand schedules for a particular good, and assuming these three people are the only ones in the society, determine (a) the market demand schedule on the assumption that the good is a private good and (b) the collective demand schedule on the assumption that the good is a public good. [LO4.3]

P	$Q_d(D_1)$	$Q_d(D_2)$	$Q_d(D_3)$
$8	0	1	0
7	0	2	0
6	0	3	1
5	1	4	2
4	2	5	3
3	3	6	4
2	4	7	5
1	5	8	6

6. Use your demand schedule for a public good, determined in problem 5, and the following supply schedule to ascertain the optimal quantity of this public good.   [LO4.3]

P	Q$_s$
$19	10
16	8
13	6
10	4
7	2
4	1

7. Look at Tables 4-1 and 4-2, which show, respectively, the willingness to pay and willingness to accept of buyers and seller of bags of oranges. For the following questions, assume that the equilibrium price and quantity will depend on the indicated changes in supply and demand. Assume that the only market participants are those listed by name in the two tables.   [LO4.4]

a. What is the equilibrium price and quantity for the data displayed in the two tables?

b. What if, instead of bags of oranges, the data in the two tables dealt with a public good like fireworks displays. If all the buyers free ride, what will be the quantity supplied by private sellers?

c. Assume that we are back to talking about bags of oranges (a private good), but that the government has decided that tossed orange peels impose a negative externality on the public that must be rectified by imposing a $2-per-bag tax on sellers. What is the new equilibrium price and quantity? If the new equilibrium quantity is the optimal quantity, by how many bags were oranges being overproduced before?

Appendix to Chapter 4

A4.1 / Information Failures

LOA4.1 Describe how information failures may justify government intervention in some markets.

This chapter discussed the two most common types of market failure: public goods and externalities. But there is also another, subtler, type of market failure. This one results when either buyers or sellers have incomplete or inaccurate information and their cost of obtaining better information is prohibitive. Technically stated, this market failure is the result of **asymmetric information**–information unequally available to buyers and sellers about price, quality, or some other aspect of the good or service.

Sufficient market information is normally available to ensure that goods and services are produced and purchased efficiently. But in some cases, inadequate information makes it difficult to distinguish trustworthy from untrustworthy sellers or buyers. In these markets, society's scarce resources may not be used efficiently, implying that the government should intervene by increasing the information available to the market participants. Under rare circumstances the government may itself supply a good for which information problems have prohibited efficient production.

 THE ROLE OF GOVERNMENTS

ORIGIN OF THE IDEA A4.1 Information Failures

Inadequate Buyer Information About Sellers

Inadequate information among buyers about sellers and their products can cause market failure in the form of underallocation of resources. Two examples will help you understand this point.

EXAMPLE: GASOLINE MARKET

Assume an absurd situation: Suppose there is no system of weights and measures established by law, no government inspection of gasoline pumps, and no law against false advertising. Each gas station can use whatever measure it chooses; it can define a gallon of gas as it pleases. A station can advertise that its gas is 87 octane when, in fact, it is only 75. It can rig its pumps to indicate that it is providing more gas than the amount being delivered.

Obviously, the consumer's cost of obtaining reliable information under such chaotic conditions is exceptionally high, if not prohibitive. Customers or their representatives would have to buy samples of gas from various gas stations, have them tested for octane level, and test the accuracy of calibrations at the pump. And these activities would have to be repeated regularly, since a station owner could alter the product quality and the accuracy of the pump at will.

Because of the high cost of obtaining information about the seller, many consumers would opt out of this chaotic market. One tankful of a 50 percent mixture of gasoline and water would be enough to discourage most motorists from further driving. More realistically, the conditions in this market would encourage consumers to vote for political candidates who promise to provide a government solution. The oil companies and honest gasoline stations would most likely welcome government intervention. They would realize that accurate information, by enabling this market to work, would expand their total sales and profits.

The government has in fact intervened in the market for gasoline and other markets with similar potential information difficulties. It has established a system of weights and measures, employed inspectors to check the accuracy of gasoline pumps, and passed laws against fraudulent claims and misleading advertising. Clearly, these government activities have produced net benefits for society.

EXAMPLE: LICENSING OF SURGEONS

Suppose that anyone could hang out a shingle and claim to be a surgeon, much as anyone can become a house painter. The market would eventually sort out the true surgeons from those who were learning by doing or were fly-by-night operators. As people died from unsuccessful surgery, lawsuits for malpractice eventually would identify and eliminate most of the medical impostors. People needing surgery for themselves or their loved ones could obtain information from newspaper reports or from people who had undergone similar operations. But this process of obtaining information for those needing surgery would take considerable time and would impose unacceptably high human and economic costs. There is a fundamental difference between getting an amateurish paint job on one's house and being on the receiving end of heart surgery by a bogus physician! The marginal cost of obtaining information about surgeons would be excessively high. The risk of proceeding without good information would result in much less surgery than is desirable—an underallocation of resources to surgery.

The government has remedied this market failure through a system of qualifying tests and licensing. The licensing provides consumers with inexpensive information about a service they buy infrequently. The government has taken a similar role in several other areas of the economy. For example, it approves new medicines, regulates the securities industry, and requires warnings on containers of potentially hazardous substances. It also requires warning labels on cigarette packages and disseminates information about communicable diseases. And it issues warnings about unsafe toys and inspects restaurants for health-related violations.

Inadequate Seller Information About Buyers

Just as inadequate information about sellers can keep markets from achieving economic efficiency, so can inadequate information about buyers. The buyers may be consumers who buy products, or firms that buy resources.

MORAL HAZARD PROBLEM

Private markets may underallocate resources to a particular good or service for which there is a severe **moral hazard problem**. The moral hazard problem is the tendency of one party to a contract to alter her or his behaviour after the contract is signed in ways that could be costly to the other party.

Suppose a firm offers an insurance policy that pays a set amount of money per month to couples that divorce. The attractiveness of such insurance is that it would pool the economic risk of divorce among thousands of people and, in particular, would protect spouses and children from the economic hardship that divorce often brings. Unfortunately, the moral hazard problem reduces the likelihood that insurance companies can profitably provide this type of insurance. After taking out such insurance, married couples would have less incentive to get along and to iron out marital difficulties. Some couples might be motivated to obtain a divorce, collect the insurance, and then continue to live together. Such insurance could even promote more divorces, the very outcome it is intended to protect against. The moral hazard problem would force the insurer to charge such high premiums for this insurance that few policies

would be bought. If the insurer could identify in advance those people most prone to altering their behaviour, the firm could exclude them from buying it. But the firm's marginal cost of getting such information is too high compared with the marginal benefit. Thus, this market would fail. Although divorce insurance is not available in the marketplace, society recognizes the benefits of insuring against the hardships of divorce. It has corrected for this underallocation of hardship insurance through child-support laws that dictate payments to the spouse who retains the children, when the economic circumstances warrant such payments. Alimony laws also play a role.

The moral hazard problem is also illustrated in the following statements:

- Drivers may be less cautious because they have car insurance.

- Medical malpractice insurance may increase the amount of malpractice.

- Guaranteed contracts for professional athletes may reduce the quality of their performance.

- Employment compensation insurance may lead some workers to shirk.

- Government insurance on bank deposits may encourage banks to make risky loans.

ADVERSE SELECTION PROBLEM

Another problem resulting from inadequate information about buyers is the **adverse selection problem**. This problem arises when information known by the first party to a contract is not known by the second and, as a result, the second party incurs major costs. Unlike the moral hazard problem, which arises after a person signs a contract, the adverse selection problem arises at the time a person signs a contract.

In insurance, the adverse selection problem is that people who are most likely to need insurance payouts are those who buy insurance. For example, those in poorest health are more likely to buy the most generous health insurance policies. Or, at the extreme, a person planning to hire an arsonist to torch his failing business has an incentive to buy fire insurance.

The adverse selection problem thus tends to eliminate the pooling of low and high risks, which is the basis of profitable insurance. Insurance rates then must be so high that few people would want to (or be able to) buy such insurance.

Where private firms underprovide insurance because of information problems, the government often establishes some type of social insurance. It can require everyone in a particular group to take the insurance and thereby can overcome the adverse selection problem. For example, in Canada every citizen is covered by publicly funded health care insurance. The national health care program requires universal participation: people who are most likely to need the health care benefits are automatically participants in the program. So, too, are those not likely to need the benefits. Consequently, no adverse selection problem emerges.

Advocates of our publicly funded health care system point out that we need such a system because private markets would make it impossible for many Canadians who are seriously ill, or are at high risk of serious diseases, to get adequate health insurance. Private insurers would be unwilling to take on clients at high risk for developing serious diseases because of the very high costs this would entail for the insurer. Thus, advocates of our present health care system claim that private markets would underallocate resources to health care. Such underallocation of resources in private markets is a powerful argument for a fully publicly funded health care system.

Qualification

Households and businesses have found ingenious ways to overcome information difficulties without government intervention. For example, many firms offer product warranties to overcome the lack of information about themselves and their products. Franchising also helps overcome this problem. When you visit a McDonald's or a Holiday Inn, you know precisely what you are going to get, unlike when you stop at Slim's Hamburger Shop or the Ghost Buster Motel.

Also, some private firms and organizations specialize in providing information to buyers and sellers. Credit reports provide information about credit histories and past bankruptcies to lending institutions and insurance companies. Brokers, bonding agencies, and intermediaries also provide information to clients.

Economists agree, however, that the private sector cannot remedy all information problems. In some situations, government intervention is desirable to promote an efficient allocation of society's scarce resources.

APPENDIX / Summary

A4.1 Describe how information failures may justify government intervention in some markets.

- Asymmetric information occurs when buyers and sellers do not have the same information about a product. It is a source of potential market failure, causing society's scarce resources to be allocated inefficiently.

- Asymmetric information can cause a market to fail if the party that has less information decides to withdraw from the market because it fears that that its lack of knowledge may be exploited the party that has more information.

- If the party that has less information reduces its participation in a market, the reduction in the size of the market may cause an underallocation of resources to the product produced for the market.

- The moral hazard problem is the tendency of one party to a contract to alter its behaviour in ways that are costly to the other party; for example, a person who buys insurance may willingly incur added risk.

- The adverse selection problem arises when one party to a contract has less information than the other party and incurs a cost because of that asymmetrical information. For example, an insurance company offering no-medical-exam-required life insurance policies may attract customers who have life-threatening diseases.

APPENDIX / Terms and Concepts

asymmetric information
moral hazard problem

adverse selection problem

APPENDIX / Discussion Questions

1. Because medical records are private, an individual applying for private health insurance in Canada will know more about his own health conditions than will the insurance companies to which he is applying for medical services not covered by our national health care system. Is this likely to increase or decrease the insurance premium that he will be offered? Why?   [LOA4.1]

2. Why is it in the interest of new homebuyers as well as builders of new homes to have government building codes and building inspectors?   [LOA4.1]

3. Place an M beside the items in the following list that describe a moral hazard problem and an A beside those that describe an adverse selection problem: [LOA4.1]

a. A person with a terminal illness buys several life insurance policies through the mail.

b. A person drives carelessly because he or she has automobile insurance.

c. A person who intends to torch his warehouse takes out a large fire insurance policy.

d. A professional athlete who has a guaranteed contract fails to stay in shape during the off-season.

e. A woman who anticipates having a large family takes a job with a firm that offers exceptional child care benefits.

APPENDIX / Review Questions

1. People drive faster when they have auto insurance. This is an example of   [LOA4.1]

a. Adverse selection

b. Asymmetric information

c. Moral hazard

2. Government inspectors who check on the quality of services provided by retailers as well as government requirements for licensing in various professions are both attempts to resolve   [LOA4.1]

a. The moral hazard problem

b. The asymmetric information problem

3. True or False? A market may collapse and have relatively few transactions between buyers and sellers if buyers have more information than sellers.   [LOA4.1]

APPENDIX / Problems

1. Consider a used car market with asymmetric information. Owners of used cars know what their vehicles are worth but have no way of credibly demonstrating those values to potential buyers. Thus, potential buyers must always worry that the used car they are being offered may be a low-quality "lemon."   [LOA4.1]

a. Suppose that there are equal numbers of good and bad used cars in the market and that good used cars are worth $13,000 while bad used cars are worth $5000. What is the average value of a used car?

b. By how much does the average value exceed the value of a bad used car? By how much does the value of a good used car exceed the average value?

c. Would a potential seller of a good used car be willing to accept the average value as payment for her vehicle?

d. If a buyer negotiates with a seller to purchase the seller's used car for a price equal to the average value, is the car more likely to be good or bad?

e. Will the used car market come to feature mostly—if not exclusively—lemons? How much will used cars end up costing if all the good cars are withdrawn?

CHAPTER 5

Government's Role and Government Failure

LEARNING OBJECTIVES

LO5.1 Describe how government's power to coerce can be economically beneficial and list some of the difficulties associated with managing and directing the government.

LO5.2 Discuss *government failure* and explain why it happens.

LOA5.1 (Appendix) Explain the difficulties of conveying economic preferences through majority voting.

Governments in market economies perform several economic tasks. As discussed in various places in the book, these include promoting production and trade by defining property rights, enforcing contracts, and settling disputes; enforcing laws designed to maintain competition; redistributing income via taxes and transfers; reallocating resources by producing public goods and intervening to correct negative and positive externalities; and promoting economic growth and full employment.

In this chapter, we deepen our understanding of government's role in the market economy by examining some of the difficulties that democratic governments face when making specific laws related to the economy.

We will find that governments sometimes pursue policies for which costs outweigh benefits. These inefficient outcomes happen often enough that we need to be just as vigilant in looking for instances of *government failure* as we are in looking for instances of *market failure*.

5.1 / Government's Economic Role

LO5.1 Describe how government's power to coerce can be economically beneficial and list some of the difficulties associated with managing and directing the government.

As discussed in Chapter 2, the Canadian economy is a *market system* that uses mostly markets and prices to coordinate and direct economic activity. But the government also has a prominent role in how the economy functions. Among other things, the government sets the laws governing economic activity, provides goods and services that would otherwise be underproduced by private firms, and modifies the distribution of income. The government also promotes both economic stability and economic growth.

Government's Right to Coerce

One key difference between the economic activities of government and those of private firms and individuals is that government possesses the legal right to force people to do things. Whereas private-sector economic activities consist primarily of voluntary transactions, government has the legal right to enforce involuntary transactions. Among other things, the government can put you in jail if you do not pay your taxes, fine you if you violate pollution laws, jail you if you commit fraud, and remove your business license if you violate health and safety regulations.

FORCE AND ECONOMIC EFFICIENCY

From an economic perspective, the government's ability to force people to do things can be quite beneficial because it can be used to increase economic efficiency.

Correcting for Market Failures Consider public goods and externalities. As discussed in Chapter 4, these market failures cause resource misallocations. When it comes to both public goods and products offering positive externalities, private producers fail to produce enough output because it is impossible to charge many of the beneficiaries for the benefits that they receive from the producers' products. In such cases, the government can improve economic efficiency by using involuntarily collected tax money to subsidize production.

By contrast, products that generate negative externalities are overproduced by the private sector because many of their costs are borne by third parties rather than by their producers. The government can reduce that overproduction and improve economic efficiency by using involuntary policies such as direct controls, pollution taxes, and cap-and-trade schemes to force producers to bear higher costs.

Reducing Private-Sector Economic Risks Government's ability to force people to do things is also crucial in reducing private-sector economic risks. To begin with, the government helps to ensure that only mutually agreeable transactions take place by making blackmail, extortion, and other forms of private coercion illegal.

CONSIDER THIS | Market Failure and the Need for Government

Suppose a municipality—say, Saskatoon, Saskatchewan—requires a new road. In the absence of a government request that a private firm build it, it is unlikely that a private firm will build the required road on its own initiative. Or, to express it another way, private markets will not make available public goods. The citizens of Saskatoon have to elect a government to either direct a private firm to build the road, or hire the people and buy the capital equipment needed to construct the road on its own.

Why would a private firm not undertake to build a road on its own? The obstacle is common property rights. The land on which the road is to be built must be owned by the firm before it would consider building the road. Lands used by all citizens are most often held publicly. The firm would thus need to get the consent of all the citizens affected. Such unanimity would be difficult to achieve. Indeed, it is the difficulty of making collective decisions that makes government action essential in the creation of an infrastructure—such as roads and airports—necessary to facilitate the functioning of markets. Not only must a decision be made to build the road, but then the decision must be made as to who should bear the cost. The free-rider problem arises here. Every individual hopes someone else will pay for the needed road. In this way, he or she can have the benefits without contributing to the cost. The free-rider problem can potentially arise in all situations where collective action must be taken. Unless we have a central authority—government—with the monopoly power to impose costs on all members of a society, many socially useful projects will not be undertaken.

In a pathbreaking book, *The Logic of Collective Action*,[1] Mancur Olson pointed out 40 years ago that, contrary to popular belief, groups of individuals with common interests do not necessarily attempt to further those common interests. In many instances, group members attempt to further their own personal interests. A few years later, the political scientist Garrett Hardin popularized the term "the tragedy of the commons"[2] to describe the problems that arise when there are common property rights. For example, where there are common property rights to a natural resource, it is typically overexploited. The cod stocks on Canada's east coast have suffered just that fate.

[1] Mancur Olson, *The Logic of Collective Action* (Cambridge: Cambridge University Press, 1965).

[2] Garrett Hardin, "The Tragedy of the Commons," *Science* 162 (1968); 1243–48.

The government also uses its legal powers to outlaw various forms of theft, deception, and discrimination as well as restraints on trade, price-fixing, and refusal to honour a contract.

These limitations encourage economic activity by giving greater security to both individuals and firms. Because they know that the government will use its massive resources to arrest and punish those who break the law, they know that other individuals and firms are less likely to try to take advantage of them. That reduction in risk encourages higher levels of investment, the formation of more new businesses, and the introduction of more new goods and services. In economic terminology, both allocative and productive efficiency increase.

The Problem of Directing and Managing Government

As just discussed, the government can substantially improve allocative and productive efficiency if it directs its awesome coercive powers toward rectifying market failures and providing a low-risk economic environment for the private sector. However, it has only been in recent centuries that democratic political institutions have been able to tame government and direct it toward those goals. Until that happened, most governments were tyrannical, with their powers almost always directed toward enriching the small minority that controlled each government.

Because modern democratic governments serve much broader constituencies, they are much more likely to pursue economic policies with widespread social benefits. Their ability to deliver economically optimal outcomes is hindered, however, by the wide variety of government failures that this chapter will discuss in detail

But before discussing them, it will be useful to first point out that governing a nation is not easy. In particular, governments face the daunting challenge of organizing hundreds of thousands of employees to carry out thousands of tasks–everything from cleaning sewers to researching cures for cancer to delivering the mail. An understanding of those challenges and complexities will give you a better sense of how well most governments manage to do despite all of the problems associated with government failure.

NO INVISIBLE HAND

Government economic policies are not self-correcting. Unlike the private sector–where competitive forces and Adam Smith's *invisible hand* help to automatically direct resources to their best uses–poorly designed government policies can misallocate resources indefinitely unless active steps are taken by legislators or administrators.

MASSIVE SIZE AND SCOPE

Identifying and correcting inefficient government policies is hampered by government's massive size and scope. Consider the Canadian federal government. In 2014, it had about 263,000 employees spread over

CONSIDER THIS   Does Big Government Equal Bad Government?

You will sometimes hear politicians (and maybe your grumpy uncle) complaining about Big Government. Their implication is that large government initiatives are inherently inefficient or incompetent.

Since economics is focused on efficiency, you might wonder where economists stand on the subject.

The answer is that economists focus not on bigness or smallness, per se, but on marginal benefits (MB) and marginal costs (MC). Spending should be increased up to the point where MB = MC. For some programs that will be a small dollar amount. For other programs that will be a large dollar amount.

Thus, economists don't see much point in having an abstract debate over Big Government versus Little Government. What matters is allocative and productive efficiency and directing government's limited resources toward the programs that generate the largest net benefits for society.

From that vantage point, we should not condemn large government programs just for being large. We must first compare MB with MC. Only if MB < MC should large programs be reduced or eliminated.

225 agencies that were collectively charged with enforcing hundreds of thousands of pages of laws and regulations while attempting to wisely spend about $250 billion.

THE NEED FOR BUREAUCRACY

By law, those 263,000 federal employees are ultimately supervised and directed by just 338 elected officials. Since 338 elected officials could never hope to directly supervise 263,000 people, governments rely on many layers of supervisors and supervisors-of-supervisors to manage the government's affairs. They collectively form a massive, hierarchical, many-layered bureaucracy.

THE NEED FOR PAPERWORK AND INFLEXIBILITY

To make sure that laws are uniformly enforced and do not vary at the whim of individual bureaucrats, the bureaucracy is regulated by detailed rules and regulations governing nearly every possible action that any individual bureaucrat might be called upon to make. These rules and regulations ensure that laws and regulations are uniformly applied. But they do so at the cost of massive amounts of paperwork and an inability to expeditiously process nonroutine situations and requests.

THE INFORMATION AGGREGATION PROBLEM

Because of their massive size and scope, bureaucracies have difficulty with effectively aggregating and conveying information from their bottom layers to their top layers. As a result, top officials will tend to make many inefficient choices because they do not have enough information to sensibly compare the marginal benefit and marginal cost of individual programs and because they are unable to comprehensively assess opportunity costs and where to best spend funds across the wide variety of programs run by the government.

LACK OF ACCOUNTABILITY

Governments also struggle with accountability. Democratic elections do take place for the elected officials at the top, but because the government undertakes so many activities simultaneously, it is difficult for the electorate to know the details of even a small fraction of what the government is up to at any particular time. As a result, hundreds of individual programs may be poorly run without affecting the re-election chances of the incumbent politicians who are supposed to be supervising everything.

Within the bureaucracy itself, individual accountability is also hard to enforce because most bureaucrats have civil service protections that effectively guarantee them a job for life. Those protections reduce corruption by shielding bureaucrats from political pressures. But they also severely constrain the ability of elected officials to hold individual bureaucrats personally responsible for bad decisions.

- Government's ability to enforce nonvoluntary transactions can improve economic outcomes by compensating for resource misallocations and by providing a low-risk economic environment for individuals and firms.
- Government economic actions are not automatically self-correcting (as with the invisible hand in competitive markets).

- Democratic governments face several challenges in directing and supervising government's actions, including inflexibility, information aggregation, comparing of marginal costs with marginal benefits, assessment of opportunity costs, and accountability.

5.2 / Government Failure

LO5.2 Discuss *government failure* and explain why it happens.

The term **government failure** refers to economically inefficient outcomes caused by shortcomings in the public sector. One cause of government failure is the voting issue that we discuss at length in this chapter's Appendix. But government failures caused by voting problems are somewhat unique in that they are driven by a lack of information about voter preferences. By contrast, most instances of government failure happen *despite* government officials knowing what voters prefer.

In these situations, government failures occur because the incentive structures facing government officials lead them either to put their own interests ahead of voter interests or to put the interests of a minority of voters ahead of those of a majority of voters. Let's examine what public interest theory has to say about these situations.

Representative Democracy and the Principal–Agent Problem

Our system of representative democracy has the advantage of allowing us to elect full-time representatives who can specialize in understanding the pros and cons of different potential laws and who have more time to digest their details than the average citizen. But the system also suffers from principal-agent problems.

Conflicts known as **principal–agent problems** arise when tasks are delegated by one group of people (principals) to another group of people (agents). The conflicts arise because the interests of the agents may not be the same as the interests of the principals, so that the agents may end up taking actions that are opposed by the principals whom they are supposed to be representing.

In the business world, principal-agent problems often arise when the managers of a company (the agents) take actions that are not in the best interests of the company's shareholders (the principals). Examples include the managers spending huge amounts of company money on executive jets and lavish offices or holding meetings at expensive resorts. These luxuries are obviously very enjoyable to managers but are, of course, not in the best interests of shareholders because the money spent on them could either be reinvested back into the firm to increase future profits or be paid out to shareholders immediately as dividends. But to the extent that managers are free to follow their own interests rather than those of their shareholders, they may indeed take these and other actions that are not in the better interests of their shareholders. Hence the conflicts.

In a representative democracy, principal-agent problems often arise because politicians have goals such as re-election that may be inconsistent with pursuing the best interests of their constituents. Indeed, casual reflection suggests that *sound economics* and *good politics* often differ. Sound economics calls for the public sector to pursue various programs as long as marginal benefits exceed marginal costs. Good politics, however, suggests that politicians support programs and policies that will maximize their chances of getting re-elected and staying in office. The result may be that the government will promote the goals of groups of voters that have special interests to the detriment of the larger public.

SPECIAL-INTEREST EFFECT

Efficient public decision-making is often impaired by the **special-interest effect**. This is any outcome of the political process where a small number of people obtain a government program or policy that gives them large gains at the expense of a much greater number of persons who individually suffer small losses.

The small group of potential beneficiaries is well informed and highly vocal on the issue in question, and they press politicians for approval. The large number of people facing very small individual losses, however, are generally uninformed on the issue. Politicians feel they will lose the campaign contributions and votes of the small special-interest group that backs the issue if they legislate against it but will not lose the support of the large group of uninformed voters, who are likely to evaluate the politicians on other issues of greater importance to them.

The special-interest effect is also evident in so-called *pork-barrel politics*, a means of securing a government project that yields benefits mainly to a single political district and its political representative. In this case, the special-interest group comprises local constituents, while the larger group consists of relatively uninformed taxpayers scattered across a much larger geographic area. Politicians clearly have a strong incentive to secure government projects ("pork") for their local constituents.

Finally, a politician's inclination to support the smaller group of special beneficiaries is enhanced because special-interest groups are often quite willing to help finance the campaigns of right-minded politicians and politicians who "bring home the bacon." The result is that politicians may support special-interest programs and projects that cannot be justified on economic grounds.

RENT-SEEKING BEHAVIOUR

The appeal to government for special benefits at taxpayers' or someone else's expense is called **rent seeking**. The term *rent* in rent seeking is used loosely to refer to any payment in excess of the minimum amount that would be needed to keep a resource employed in its current use. Those engaged in rent seeking are attempting to use government influence to get themselves into a situation in which they will get paid more for providing a good or service than the minimum amount you would actually have to pay them to provide that good or service. (These excess, or surplus, payments are akin to *land rent*, which is also a surplus payment.)

Rent seeking goes beyond the usual profit seeking through which firms try to increase their profits by adjusting their output levels, improving their products, and incorporating cost-saving technologies. Rent seeking looks to obtain extra profit or income by influencing government policies. Corporations, trade associations, labour unions, and professional organizations employ vast resources to secure favourable government policies that result in rent—higher profit or income than would otherwise occur. The government is able to dispense such rent directly or indirectly through laws, rules, hiring, and purchases. Elected officials are willing to provide such rent because they want to be responsive to key constituents, who in turn help them remain in office.

Here are some examples of rent-providing legislation or policies: tariffs on foreign products that limit competition and raise prices to consumers, tax breaks that benefit specific corporations, government construction projects that create union jobs but cost more than the benefits they yield, occupational licensing that goes beyond what is needed to protect consumers, and large subsidies to farmers by taxpayers. None of these is justified by economic efficiency.

Clear Benefits, Hidden Costs

Some critics say that vote-seeking politicians will ignore economic rationality by failing to weigh costs and benefits objectively when deciding which programs to support. Because political officeholders must seek voter support every few years, they favour programs that have immediate and clear-cut benefits and vague or deferred costs.

Such biases may lead politicians to reject economically justifiable programs and to accept programs that are economically irrational. For example, a proposal to construct or expand mass-transit systems in large metropolitan areas may be economically rational on the basis of benefit–cost analysis, but if (1) the program is to be financed by immediate increases in highly visible income or sales taxes and (2) benefits will occur only years from now when the project is completed, then the vote-seeking politician may oppose the program.

Another example of possible political bias is the distribution of health care expenditures by both the federal and provincial governments in Canada. Certain government health care expenditures on a relatively small number of Canadians may lead to much media attention, but may not be the most efficient expenditures of health care resources from society's standpoint. But it is this kind of positive and visible front-page coverage that politicians desire in their attempts to get re-elected.

Unfunded Liabilities

The political tendency to favour spending priorities that have immediate payouts but deferred costs also leads to many government programs having unfunded liabilities. A government creates an **unfunded liability** when it commits to making a series of future expenditures without simultaneously committing to collect enough tax revenues to pay for those expenditures.

Chronic Budget Deficits

A government runs an annual **budget deficit** whenever its tax revenues are less than its spending during a particular year. To make up for the shortfall, the government must borrow money, usually by issuing bonds. Whatever it borrows in a given year gets added to its overall pile of debt, which is the accumulation of all past budget deficits and budget surpluses.

Many governments run budget deficits year after year. These chronic deficits can be attributed to a pair of conflicting incentives that confront politicians. On the one hand, many government programs are highly popular with voters, so that there is almost always political pressure to either maintain or increase spending. On the other hand, hardly anyone likes paying taxes, so there is almost always political pressure to reduce taxes. Faced with those two conflicting pressures, politicians tend to opt for spending levels that exceed tax revenues. That may be problematic because chronic deficits can pose several economic challenges, including:

- *Economic Inefficiency* Deficits may allow the government to control and direct an inefficiently large fraction of the economy's resources. To the extent that deficit spending facilitates an underallocation of resources to the private sector and an overallocation of resources to the government sector, there will be a tendency to underproduce private goods and overproduce public goods. If that occurs, the economy will experience a decrease in both allocative and productive efficiency.

- *Debt Crises* A government's accumulated debt level may rise so high that investors lose faith in the government's ability or willingness to repay its debts. If that happens, the government will find itself in the middle of a **debt crisis**, unable to borrow any more money. Cut off from borrowing, the government will be forced to undertake some combination of drastic spending cuts or massive tax increases. Either of those actions will tend to plunge the economy into a recessionary period in which unemployment rises and output falls.

Misdirection of Stabilization Policy

Economies go through alternating periods of expansion and recession. These are multiyear periods during which output expands, employment increases, and living standards rise alternating with shorter periods during which output contracts, employment decreases, and living standards fall.

Governments often attempt to smooth out these so-called *business cycles* by using two types of macroeconomic stabilization policies:

- **Fiscal policy** attempts to use changes in tax rates and spending levels to offset the business cycle. For example, if the economy is going into a recessionary period with falling output and rising unemployment, the government may attempt to stimulate the economy by lowering tax rates or increasing government spending. Either action should increase spending on goods and services and consequently induce business to produce more output and hire more workers.

- **Monetary policy** attempts to use changes in interest rates to regulate the economy. In particular, the government can use its control over the money supply to lower interest rates during a recession. The lower interest rates stimulate spending by making it cheaper for individuals and businesses to borrow money to pay for capital goods such as houses, cars, and machinery. As spending on those items increases, firms are induced to produce more output and hire more workers.

POLITICIZATION OF FISCAL AND MONETARY POLICY

Fiscal and monetary policy are both subject to politicization. In the case of fiscal policy, if the economy goes into recession and there are calls to stimulate the economy through lower taxes or increased spending, politicians often spend more time attempting to target any tax cuts or spending increases toward special interests than they do making sure that their fiscal policy actions will actually stimulate the overall economy. The recession also provides political cover for increasing the size of the deficit.

Monetary policy can be similarly politicized, with the biggest problem being that incumbent politicians will want to cut interest rates to boost the economy right before they are up for re-election. That is problematic because monetary stimulus is only helpful if the economy is in recession. If the economy is doing well, monetary stimulus can actually make things worse because it can raise the rate of inflation and drive up prices all over the economy.

To prevent that, most countries have put politically independent central banks in charge of monetary policy. In Canada, the Bank of Canada serves this function. Other top central banks include the Federal Reserve (U.S.), the Bank of Japan, the Bank of England, and the European Central Bank. Each is run by professional economists who are insulated from political pressures so that they may use their independent expertise and judgment to decide if and when monetary stimulus should be used.

Limited and Bundled Choice

Public choice theorists point out that the political process forces citizens and their elected representatives to be less selective in choosing public goods and services than they are in choosing private goods and services.

In the marketplace, the citizen as a consumer can exactly satisfy personal preferences by buying certain goods and not buying others. However, in the public sector the citizen as a voter is confronted with, say, only two or three candidates for an office, each representing a different bundle of programs (public goods and services). None of these bundles of public goods is likely to fit exactly the preferences of any particular voter, yet the voter must choose one of them. The candidate who comes closest to voter Smith's preference may endorse national health insurance, increases in Old Age Security benefits, subsidies to tobacco farmers, and tariffs on imported goods. Smith is likely to vote for that candidate even though Smith strongly opposes tobacco subsidies.

Parliament is confronted with a similar limited-choice, bundled-goods problem. Appropriations legislation combines hundreds, even thousands, of spending items into a single bill. Many of these spending items may be completely unrelated to the main purpose of the legislation, yet Members of Parliament must vote the entire package–yea or nay. Unlike consumers in the marketplace, they cannot be selective.

Bureaucracy and Inefficiency

Some economists contend that public agencies are generally less efficient than private businesses. The reason is that the market system creates incentives and pressures for internal efficiency that are absent from the public sector. The market system imposes a very obvious test of performance on private firms: the test of profit and loss. An efficient firm is profitable and therefore successful; it survives, prospers, and grows. An inefficient firm is unprofitable and unsuccessful; it declines and in time goes bankrupt and ceases to exist. But no similar, clear-cut test exists with which to assess the efficiency or inefficiency of public agencies.

Furthermore, economists assert that government employees, together with the special-interest groups they serve, often gain sufficient political clout to block attempts to pare down or eliminate their agencies. Politicians who attempt to reduce the size of huge federal bureaucracies such as those relating to agriculture, education, and health and welfare incur sizable political risk because bureaucrats and special-interest groups will team up to defeat them.

Finally, critics point out that there is a tendency for government bureaucrats to justify their continued employment by looking for and eventually finding new "problems" to solve. It is not surprising that social problems, as defined by government, tend to persist or even expand.

INEFFICIENT REGULATION AND INTERVENTION

Governments regulate many aspects of the market economy. Examples include health and safety regulations, environmental laws, banking supervision, restrictions on monopoly power, and the imposition of wage and price controls. These interventions are designed to improve economic outcomes, but several forms of regulation and intervention have been known to generate outcomes that are less beneficial than intended.

Regulatory Capture A government agency that is supposed to supervise a particular industry is said to have suffered from **regulatory capture** if its regulations and enforcement activities come to be heavily influenced by the industry that it is supposed to be regulating. Regulatory capture is often facilitated by the fact that nearly everyone who knows anything about the details of a regulated industry works in the industry. So when it comes time for the regulatory agency to find qualified people to help write intelligent regulations, it ends up hiring a lot of people from regulated firms. Those individuals bring their old opinions and sympathies with them when they become bureaucrats. As a result, many regulations end up favouring the interests of the regulated firms.

Deregulation as an Alternative Economists are divided about the intensity and inefficiency of regulatory capture as well as what to do about it. One potential solution is for the government to engage in **deregulation** and intentionally remove most or even all of the regulations governing an industry. Deregulation solves the problem of regulatory capture because there is no regulatory agency left to capture. But it only works well in terms of economic efficiency if the deregulated industry becomes competitive and is automatically guided toward allocative and productive efficiency by competitive forces and the invisible hand. If the deregulated industry instead tends toward monopoly or ends up generating substantial negative externalities, continued regulation might be the better option.

Proponents of deregulation often cite the deregulation of interstate trucking, railroads, and airlines in the 1970s and 1980s as examples of competition successfully replacing regulation. They do so because after regulation was removed, robust competition led to lower prices, increased output, and higher levels of productivity and efficiency. But for government agencies tasked with environmental protection, human safety, and financial regulation, there is less confidence as to whether competitive pressures might be able to replace regulation. For those industries, regulation may always be necessary. If so, then some amount of regulatory capture may always be likely due to the fact that regulated firms will always want to capture their regulators.

Government's Poor Investment Track Record Governments are often asked to use taxpayer money to directly invest in private businesses that have been unable to secure funding from private sources such as banks. Unfortunately, researchers have found that low and negative rates of return are the norm for government investments. In addition, government funding often allows inefficient firms to persist in operation long after competitive forces would have put them out of operation and freed up their resources for higher-valued projects elsewhere in the economy.

Critics also note that many government investments look like prime examples of rent seeking and the special-interest effect, especially when the firms receiving government investments are found to have made substantial financial contributions to influential politicians. In too many cases, the government's investment decisions appear to be based on political connections rather than on whether specific investments can produce substantial net benefits for society.

Loan Guarantees   The government also tends to earn low or negative returns when it subsidizes private-sector investments with **loan guarantees**.

Socializing Losses, Privatizing Gains   Government loan guarantees can be socially beneficial if they help to increase the production of beneficial products that are being underproduced by the private sector—as would be the case for products that generated positive externalities. But the loan guarantees also provide an inducement toward reckless investing because they remove from private investors any consideration of losses. Indeed, loan guarantees are often criticized for "socializing losses and privatizing gains" because if things go wrong, any losses go to the taxpayer, while if things go well, any profits go to private investors.

In addition, the process by which loan guarantees are awarded is often criticized for being highly politicized and likely to award loan guarantees not to the firms whose projects are the most likely to increase economic efficiency but to those with the best political connections. On the other hand, there may be legitimate cases where a new technology that would generate net benefits cannot be developed without government loan guarantees, so proponents of loan-guarantee programs argue that the programs should remain in place, but with tight controls against rent seeking and the special-interest effect.

Corruption

Political corruption is the unlawful misdirection of governmental resources or actions that occurs when government officials abuse their entrusted powers for personal gain. For instance, a police supervisor engages in political corruption if she accepts a bribe in exchange for illegally freeing a thief who had been lawfully arrested by another officer. Similarly, a government bureaucrat engages in political corruption if he refuses to issue a building permit to a homebuilder who is in full compliance with the law unless the homebuilder makes a "voluntary contribution" to the bureaucrat's favourite charity.

While relatively uncommon in Canada, political corruption is a daily reality in many parts of the world, as can be seen in Global Perspective 5.1, which gives the percentages of survey respondents in fifteen countries who reported that they or someone else in their household had paid a bribe during the previous twelve months.

Political corruption comes in two basic forms. In the first, a government official must be bribed to do what he should be doing for free as part of his job—as with the bureaucrat in our earlier example who demands a bribe to issue a permit to a homebuilder who is in full compliance with the law. In the second, a government official demands a bribe to do something that she is not legally entitled to do—as with the police supervisor in our earlier example who illegally freed a thief.

If a candidate accepts campaign contributions from a special interest group and then shows subsequent support for that group's legislative goals, has a subtle form of political corruption taken place? While there are strong opinions on both sides of the issue, it is often hard to tell in any particular case whether a special interest's campaign contribution amounts to a bribe. On the one hand, the special interest may indeed be trying to influence the politician's vote. On the other hand, the special interest may simply be trying to support and get elected a person who already sees things their way and who would vote the way they wanted no matter what anyone did.

That being said, the impression of impropriety lingers and so laws have been passed in Canada limiting the amount of money that individuals can donate to specific candidates and making it illegal for certain

5.1 GLOBAL PERSPECTIVE

Percentage of Households Paying a Bribe in the Past Year

The Global Corruption Barometer is an international survey that asks individuals about their personal experiences with government corruption. The 2010–2011 survey of 105,507 people in 100 countries included a question that asked participants whether they or anyone in their respective households had paid a bribe in any form during the previous 12 months. Here are the results for 10 selected countries.

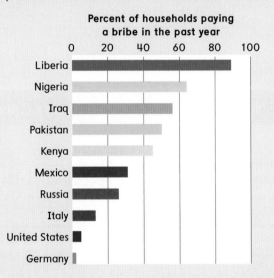

Percent of households paying a bribe in the past year

groups such as companies to donate money directly to individual politicians (as distinct from directing funds toward supporting specific issues or advocacy groups–which is both legal and unrestricted). Proponents of these laws hope that the limitations strike a good balance–allowing contributions to be large enough that individuals and groups can meaningfully support candidates they agree with but keeping contributions small enough that no one individual or group can singlehandedly donate enough money to sway a politician's vote.

Imperfect Institutions

Such criticisms of public-sector inefficiency shatter the concept of a benevolent government that responds with precision and efficiency to the wants of its citizens. The market system of the private sector is far from perfectly efficient, and government's economic function is mainly to correct that system's shortcomings. But the public sector, too, is subject to deficiencies in fulfilling its economic function.

Because the market system and public agencies are both imperfect, it is sometimes difficult to determine whether a particular activity can be performed with greater success in the private sector or the public sector. It is easy to reach agreement on opposite extremes: national defence must lie with the public sector, while automobile production can best be accomplished by the private sector. But what about health insurance? Parks and recreation areas? Fire protection? Garbage collection? Housing? Education? It is hard to say absolutely that it should be assigned to either the public sector or the private sector. After all, the goods and services just mentioned are provided in part by *both* private enterprises and public agencies.

- Unlike the private sector—where the profit motive helps to ensure efficiency and variety—government lacks a strong incentive to be efficient and typically offers only limited and bundled choices.

- Regulatory capture occurs when a regulated industry can control its government regulator and get it to implement policies that favour the industry.

- Political corruption occurs when government officials abuse their powers for personal gain.

The LAST WORD | Singapore's Efficient and Effective Health Care System

How does Singapore deliver some of the best health care in the world while spending less per person than Canada?

In every health-quality category monitored by the World Health Organization, the small island nation of Singapore is either number one in the world or near the top of the list. Among other achievements, Singapore has the world's lowest rate of infant mortality and the world's fourth highest life expectancy.

One might expect that achieving these exceptional outcomes would be extremely expensive. But Singapore is also number one in another category: it spends less per person on health care than any other developed nation. In 2010 Canada spent about 10 percent of its GDP on health care. Singapore spent just 3.8 percent.

How does Singapore deliver world-class health care while spending less than any other developed nation? The answer is a unique combination of government mandates to encourage competition, high out-of-pocket costs for consumers, and laws requiring people to save for future health expenditures.

Competition is encouraged by forcing hospitals to post prices for each of their services. Armed with this information, patients can shop around for the best deal. The government also publishes the track record of each hospital on each

service so that consumers can make informed decisions about quality as well as price. With consumers choosing on the basis of cost and quality, local hospitals compete to reduce costs and improve quality.

Singapore also insists upon high out-of-pocket costs in order to avoid the overconsumption and high prices that result when insurance policies pick up most of the price for medical procedures. Indeed, out-of-pocket spending represents about 92 percent of all non-government health-care spending in Singapore compared to just less than 10 percent in Canada.

Having to pay for most medical spending out of pocket, however, means that Singapore's citizens are faced with having to pay for most of their health care themselves. How can this be done without bankrupting the average citizen? The answer is mandatory health savings accounts.

Singapore's citizens are required to save about 6 percent of their incomes into MediSave accounts. MediSave deposits are private property so that people have an incentive to spend the money in their accounts wisely. In addition, the citizens of Singapore also know that they won't be left helpless if the money in their MediSave accounts runs out. The government subsidizes the health care of those who have exhausted their MediSave accounts as well as the health care of the poor and others who have not been able to accumulate much money in their MediSave accounts.

Given the present universal health care system in Canada, which according to most Canadians functions quite well, it is unlikely that they would opt for a Singapore-style MediSave system.

Question

What are the three major cost-reducing features of the Singapore health care system? Which one do you think has the largest effect on holding down the price of medical care in Singapore? How

difficult do you think it would be to implement the missing elements in Canada? Explain.

Chapter Summary

LO5.1 DESCRIBE HOW GOVERNMENT'S POWER TO COERCE CAN BE ECONOMICALLY BENEFICIAL AND LIST SOME OF THE DIFFICULTIES ASSOCIATED WITH MANAGING AND DIRECTING THE GOVERNMENT.

- Government's legal right to use coercion and force can help to improve economic efficiency by correcting for market failures and by enforcing laws and regulations that reduce the risk that individuals and firms will be taken advantage of.

LO5.2 DISCUSS *GOVERNMENT FAILURE* AND EXPLAIN WHY IT HAPPENS.

- Special interests can succeed in perpetuating policies that are opposed by the majority of voters because the costs of organizing and motivating groups to take political action increase with group size. This collective action problem implies that special interests can perpetuate unpopular policies as long as the costs of organizing an opposition exceed the costs that the general public is currently suffering as a result of those policies.

- There are powerful incentives for politicians to accommodate rent seeking and support special-interest legislation.

- Because voters like receiving the benefits of government programs but do not like having to pay the taxes necessary to finance them, politicians tend to favour programs that offer easily identified immediate benefits but vague or deferred costs.

- When the economy goes into recession, politicians often use the need for fiscal policy stimulus as political cover to direct lower taxes or increased spending towards politically powerful special-interest groups. To prevent politicians from using lower interest

rates and monetary stimulus as a way of increasing their re-election chances, most governments have put politically independent central banks in charge of monetary policy.

- Economic theorists cite several reasons why government might be inefficient in providing public goods and services: (a) citizens as voters as well as governmental representatives face limited and bundled choices of public goods and services, whereas consumers in the private sector can be highly selective in their choices; (b) government bureaucracies have less incentive to operate efficiently than do private businesses; (c) regulated industries may sometimes capture their government regulatory agencies and mould government policies that are in their own best interests.

- Government's track record as an investor in private-sector firms is very poor, with most government investments into private sector businesses generating low or negative returns for taxpayers.

- Government attempts to increase private investment by offering loan guarantees often cause resources to be misdirected towards high-risk projects that have an extremely low likelihood of success. These arrangements "socialize losses and privatize gains" because if the businesses go bankrupt, the government bears the losses, but if they do well, private individuals receive the profits.

- Political corruption may cause governmental resources or actions to be misdirected.

- Neither governments nor markets are perfect economic institutions. Each has its own set of shortcomings and citizens should be aware of where each is likely to fail and where each is likely to succeed.

Terms and Concepts

government failure
principal–agent problems
special-interest effect
rent seeking
unfunded liability

budget deficit
debt crisis
fiscal policy
monetary policy
unintended consequences

regulatory capture
deregulation
loan guarantees
political corruption

Discussion Questions

1. Why might citizens interested in maximizing economic efficiency be happy to invest their government with the right to coerce them in at least some situations?   [LO5.1]

2. Jean Baptiste Colbert was the minister of finance under King Louis XIV of France. He famously observed that "The art of taxation consists in so plucking the goose as to obtain the largest possible amount of feathers with the smallest possible amount of hissing." How does his comment relate to special interests and the collective action problem?   [LO5.2]

3. What is rent seeking and how does it differ from the kinds of profit maximization and profit seeking that we discussed in previous chapters? Provide an actual or a hypothetical example of rent seeking by a firm in an industry, a union, and a professional association (for example, physicians or lawyers). Why do elected officials often accommodate rent-seeking behaviour, particularly by firms, unions, and professional groups located in their home ridings?   [LO5.2]

4. How does the problem of limited and bundled choice in the public sector relate to economic efficiency? Why are public bureaucracies possibly less efficient than business firms?   [LO5.2]

5. Explain the reasoning behind the following statement: "Politicians would make more rational economic decisions if they weren't running for re-election every few years."   [LO5.2]

6. Critique the following statement: "Thank goodness we have so many government regulatory agencies. They keep Big Business in check."   [LO5.2]

Review Questions

1. Select all of the following that are true. To an economist, a coercive government can be useful in order to   [LO5.1]

   a. Reallocate resources in order to improve efficiency

   b. Fight negative externalities

   c. Ensure low gasoline prices

   d. Provide a low-risk economic environment for individuals and firms

2. To an economist, a government program is too big if an analysis of that program finds that MB _____ MC.   [LO5.1]

   a. Is greater than

   b. Is less than

   c. Is equal to

   d. Is less than twice as large as

   e. Is more than twice as large as

3. Tammy Hall is the mayor of a large Canadian city. She has just established the Office of Window Safety. Because windows sometimes break and spray glass shards, every window in the city will now have to pass an annual safety inspection. Property owners must pay the $5-per-window cost—and, by the way, Tammy has made her nephew the new head of the Office of Window Safety. This new policy is an example of   [LO5.2]

   a. Political corruption

   b. Earmarks

   c. Rent seeking

   d. Adverse selection

4. _____ occur when politicians commit to making a series of future expenditures without simultaneously committing to collect enough tax revenues to pay for those expenditures.   [LO5.2]

   a. Budget deficits

   b. Debt crises

   c. Loan guarantees

   d. Unfunded liabilities

Problems

1. Suppose that there are 1 million federal workers at the lowest level of the federal bureaucracy and that above them are multiple layers of supervisors and supervisors of supervisors. Assume that each higher level is one-tenth the size of the one below it because the government is using a 10:1 ratio of supervisees to supervisors. That is, for every 10 workers at the bottom, there is 1 supervisor; for every 10 of those supervisors, there is 1 supervisor of supervisors; for every one of those supervisors of supervisors, there is a supervisor of supervisors of supervisors and so on, all the way up the bureaucratic pyramid to the prime minister.   [LO5.1]

   a. How many supervisors will there be in each supervisory layer of the federal bureaucracy? Start with the layer of supervisors directly above the 1 million workers at the bottom.

   b. How many supervisors are there in total at all levels of the federal bureaucratic pyramid, including the prime minister?

2. Consider a corrupt provincial government in which each housing inspector examines two newly built structures each week. All the builders in the province are unethical and want to increase their profits by using substandard construction materials, but they can't do that unless they can bribe a housing inspector into approving a substandard building.   [LO5.2]

   a. If bribes cost $1000 each, how much will a housing inspector make each year in bribes? (Assume that each inspector works 52 weeks a year and gets bribed for every house he inspects.)

   b. There is a provincial construction supervisor who gets to hire all of the housing inspectors. He himself is corrupt and expects his housing inspectors to share their bribes with him. Suppose that 20 inspectors work for him and that each passes along half the bribes collected from builders. How much will the construction supervisor collect each year?

   c. Corrupt officials may have an incentive to reduce the provision of government services to help line their own pockets. Suppose that the provincial construction supervisor decides to cut the total number of housing inspectors from 20 to 10 in order to decrease the supply of new housing permits. This decrease in the supply of permits raises the equilibrium bribe from $1000 to $2500. How much per year will the construction supervisor now receive if he is still getting half of all the bribes collected by the 10 inspectors? How much more is the construction supervisor getting now than when he had 20 inspectors working in part (b)? Will he personally be happy with the reduction in government services?

   d. What if reducing the number of inspectors from 20 to 10 only increased the equilibrium bribe from $1000 to $1500? In this case, how much per year would the construction supervisor collect from his 10 inspectors? How much less is the construction supervisor getting than when he had 20 inspectors working in part (b)? In this case, will the construction supervisor be happy with the reduction in government services? Will he want to go back to using 20 inspectors?

Public Choice Theory and Voting Paradoxes

LOA5.1 Explain the difficulties of conveying economic preferences through majority voting.

A5.1 / Public Choice Theory

Market failures, such as public goods and externalities, impede economic efficiency and justify government intervention in the economy. But the government's response to market failures is not without its own problems and pitfalls. In fact, government can sometimes fail as badly or even worse than markets in terms of delivering economic efficiency and directing resources to the uses where they will bring the largest net benefits.

That is why it is important to study **public choice theory**—the economic analysis of government decision-making, politics, and elections. Just as the study of *market failure* helps us to understand how regulating markets may help to improve the allocation of resources, the study of *government failure* can help us to understand how changes in the way government functions might help it to operate more efficiently.

As we will discuss shortly, many instances of government failure can be traced to incentive structures that lead political representatives to pursue policies that go against the preferences of the people that they are representing. But an even more fundamental problem exists: The majority voting systems that we rely upon may make it difficult or even impossible to discern voter preferences correctly. In such cases, it is not surprising that government fails to deliver what the voters actually want.

ORIGIN OF THE IDEA A5.1 Public Choice Theory

Revealing Preferences Through Majority Voting

Society must decide in some way which public goods and services it wants and in what amounts. It also must determine the extent to which it wants government to intervene in private markets to correct externalities. Decisions needed to be made about how much regulation of business is necessary, the amount of income redistribution that is desirable, what policies the government might enact to mitigate asymmetric information problems, and more. Furthermore, society must determine the set of taxes it thinks is best for financing government. How should the total tax burden be apportioned (divided) among the public?

Decisions such as these are made collectively in Canada through a democratic process that relies heavily on majority voting. Candidates for office offer alternative policy packages, and citizens elect the people they think will make the best decisions on their collective behalf. Voters retire officials who do not adequately represent their collective wishes. Citizens also periodically have opportunities at the provincial and municipal levels to vote directly on public expenditures or new legislation.

Although the democratic process does a reasonably good job of revealing society's preferences, it is imperfect. Public choice theory demonstrates that majority voting can produce inefficiencies and inconsistencies.

Inefficient Voting Outcomes

Society's well-being is enhanced when government provides a public good whose total benefit exceeds its total cost. Unfortunately, majority voting does not always deliver that outcome.

INEFFICIENT "NO" VOTE

Assume that the government can provide a public good, say, national defence, at a total expense of $900. Assume there are only three individuals—Adams, Benson, and Conrad—in the society and that they will share the $900 tax expense equally, with each being taxed $300 if the proposed public good is provided. And assume, as Figure A5-1a illustrates, that Adams would receive $700 worth

| **FIGURE A5-1** | **Inefficient Voting Outcomes** |

Majority voting can produce inefficient decisions. (a) Majority voting leads to rejection of a public good that has greater total benefit than total cost. (b) Majority voting results in acceptance of a public good that has a higher total cost than total benefit.

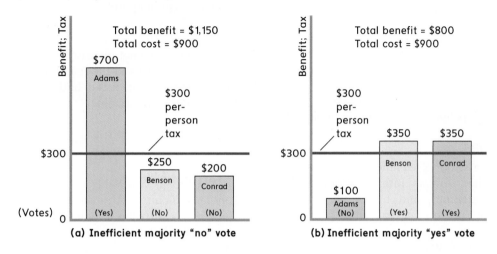

of benefits from having this public good, Benson $250, and Conrad $200.

What will be the result if a majority vote determines whether this public good is provided? Although people do not always vote strictly according to their own economic interest, it is likely that Benson and Conrad will vote no because they will incur tax costs of $300 each while gaining benefits of only $250 and $200, respectively. Adams will vote yes. So the majority vote will defeat the proposal even though the total benefit of $1150 (= $700 for Adams + $250 for Benson + $200 for Conrad) exceeds the total cost of $900.

INEFFICIENT "YES" VOTE

Now consider a situation in which the majority favours a public good even though its total cost *exceeds* its total benefit. Figure A5-1b shows the details. Again, Adams, Benson, and Conrad will equally share the $900 cost of the public good; they will each be taxed $300. But since Adams's benefit now is only $100 from the public good, she will vote against it. Meanwhile, Benson and Conrad will benefit by $350 each. They will vote for the public good because that benefit ($350) exceeds their tax payments ($300). The majority vote will provide a public good costing $900 that produces total benefits of only $800 (= $100 for Adams + $350 for Benson + $350 for Conrad). Society's resources will be inefficiently allocated to this public good, and there will be too much of it.

IMPLICATIONS

The point is that an inefficient outcome may occur as either an overproduction or an underproduction of a specific public good and, therefore, as an overallocation or underallocation of resources for that particular use. In Chapter 5 we saw that government can improve economic efficiency by providing public goods that the market system will not make available. Now we have extended that analysis to reveal that government might fail to provide some public goods whose production is economically justifiable while providing other goods that are not economically warranted.

In our examples, each person has only a single vote, no matter how much he or she might gain or lose from a public good. In the first example (inefficient "no" vote), Adams would be willing to purchase a vote from either Benson or Conrad if buying votes were legal. That way Adams could be assured of obtaining the national defence she so highly values. But since buying votes is illegal, many people with strong preferences for certain public goods may have to go without them.

When individual consumers have a strong preference for a specific *private good*, they usually can find that good in the marketplace even though it may be unpopular with the majority of consumers. But a person cannot easily buy a *public good* such as national defence once the majority has decided against it.

Conversely, a consumer in the marketplace can decide against buying a particular product, even a popular one. But although you may not want national defence, you must pay for it through your taxes when it is favoured by the majority.

Because majority voting fails to incorporate the *strength* of the preferences of the individual voter, it may produce economically inefficient outcomes.

Interest Groups and Logrolling

Some, but not all, of the inefficiencies of majority voting get resolved through the political process. Two examples follow.

INTEREST GROUPS

Those who have a strong preference for a public good may band together into an interest group and use advertisements, mailings, and direct persuasion to convince others of the merits of that public good. Adams might try to persuade Benson and Conrad that it is in their best interests to vote for national defence–that national defence is much more valuable to them than their $250 and $200 valuations. Such appeals are common in democratic politics. Sometimes they are successful; sometimes they are not.

POLITICAL LOGROLLING

Perhaps surprisingly, **logrolling**–the trading of votes to secure favourable outcomes–can also turn an inefficient outcome into an efficient one. In our first example (Figure A5-1), perhaps Benson has a strong preference for a different public good–for example, a new road–which Adams and Conrad do not think is worth the tax expense. That would provide an opportunity for Adams and Benson to trade votes to ensure provision of both national defence

and the new road. That is, Adams and Benson would each vote "yes" on both measures. Adams would get the national defence and Benson would get the road. Without the logrolling, both public goods would have been rejected. Logrolling will add to society's well-being if, as was true for national defence, the road creates a greater overall benefit than cost.

Logrolling need not increase economic efficiency. Even if national defence and the road each cost more than the total benefit they produced, both might still be provided because of the vote trading.

ORIGIN OF THE IDEA A5.2   Paradox of Voting

Paradox of Voting

Another difficulty with majority voting is the **paradox of voting**, a situation in which society may not be able to rank its preferences consistently through paired-choice majority voting.

PREFERENCES

Consider Table A5-1, in which we again assume a community of three voters: Adams, Benson, and Conrad. Suppose the community has three alternative public goods from which to choose: national defence, a road, and a weather warning system. We expect that each member of the community prefers the three alternatives in a certain order. For example, one person might prefer national defence to a road, and a road to a weather warning system. We can attempt to determine the preferences of the community through paired-choice majority voting. Specifically, a vote can be held between any two of the public goods, and the winner of that vote can then be matched against the third public good in another vote.

TABLE A5-1	Paradox of Voting		
	PREFERENCES		
Public good	**Adams**	**Benson**	**Conrad**
National defence	1st choice	3rd choice	2nd choice
Road	2nd choice	1st choice	3rd choice
Weather warning system	3rd choice	2nd choice	1st choice
Election	**Voting outcomes: Winner**		
1. National defence versus road	National defence (preferred by Adams and Conrad)		
2. Road vs. weather warning system	Road (preferred by Adams and Benson)		
3. National defence vs. weather warning system	Weather warning system (preferred by Benson and Conrad)		

The three goods and the assumed individual preferences of the three voters are listed in the top part of Table A5-1. The data indicate that Adams prefers national defence to the road and the road to the weather warning system. This implies also that Adams prefers national defence to the weather warning system. Benson values the road more than the weather warning system and the weather warning system more than national defence. Conrad's order of preference is weather warning system, national defence, and road.

VOTING OUTCOMES

The lower part of Table A5-1 shows the outcomes of three hypothetical decisions of the majority vote. In the first, national defence wins against the road because a majority of voters (Adams and Conrad) prefer national defence to the road. In the second election to see whether this community wants a road or a weather warning system, a majority of voters (Adams and Benson) prefer the road. We have determined that the majority of people in this community prefer national defence to a road and prefer a road to a weather warning system. It seems logical to conclude that the community prefers national defence to a weather warning system, but the community does not!

To demonstrate this conclusion, we hold a direct election between national defence and the weather warning system. Row (3) shows that a majority of voters (Benson and Conrad) prefer the weather warning system to national defence. As listed in Table A5-1, then, the three paired-choice majority votes imply that this community is irrational: it seems to prefer national defence to a road and a road to a weather warning system, but would rather have a weather warning system than national defence.

The problem is not irrational community preferences but rather a flawed procedure for determining those preferences. We see that the outcome from paired-choice majority voting may depend on the order in which the votes are taken. Different sequences of majority votes can lead to different outcomes, many of which may fail to reflect the electorate's underlying preferences. As a consequence, government may find it difficult to provide the "correct" public goods by acting in accordance with majority voting. One important note: this critique is not meant to suggest that some better procedure exists. Majority voting is much more likely to reflect community preferences than decisions made by, say, a dictator or a group of self-appointed leaders.

Median-Voter Model

One other aspect of majority voting reveals further insights into real-world phenomena. The **median-voter model** suggests that, under majority rule and consistent voting preferences, the median voter will, in a sense, determine the outcomes of elections. The median voter is the person holding the middle position on an issue; half the other voters have stronger preferences for a public good, amount of taxation, or degree of government regulation, while half have weaker or negative preferences. The extreme voters on each side of an issue prefer the median choice rather than the other extreme position, so the median voter's choice predominates.

EXAMPLE

Suppose a society composed of Adams, Benson, and Conrad has reached agreement that as a society it needs a weather warning system. Independently each is to submit a total dollar amount he or she thinks should be spent on the weather warning system, assuming each will be taxed one-third of that amount. An election will determine the size of the system. Because each person can be expected to vote for his or her own proposal, no majority will occur if all the proposals are placed on the ballot at the same time. Thus, the group decides on a paired-choice vote: they will first vote between two of the proposals and then match the winner of that vote against the remaining proposal.

The three proposals are as follows: Adams desires a $400 system; Benson wants an $800 system; Conrad opts for a $300 system. Which proposal will win? The median-voter model suggests it will be the $400 proposal submitted by the median voter, Adams. Half the other voters favour a more costly system; half favour a less costly system. To understand why the $400 system will be the outcome, let's conduct the two elections.

First, suppose that the $400 proposal is matched against the $800 proposal. Adams naturally votes for her $400 proposal, and Benson votes for his own $800 proposal. Conrad, who proposed the $300 expenditure for the weather warning system, votes for the $400 proposal because it is closer to his own. So Adams's $400 proposal is selected by a 2-to-1 majority vote.

Next, we match the $400 proposal against the $300 proposal. Again the $400 proposal wins. It gets a vote from Adams and one from Benson, who proposed the $800 expenditure and for that reason prefers a $400 expenditure to a $300 one. Adams, the median voter in this case, is in a sense the person who has decided the level of expenditure on a weather warning system for this society.

REAL-WORLD APPLICABILITY

Although our illustration is simple, it explains a great deal. We do note a tendency for public choices to match the median view most closely. Political candidates, for example, take one set of positions to win the nomination of their political parties; in so doing, they tend to

CONSIDER THIS   Voter Failure

Inefficient voting outcomes and the paradox of voting imply that governments may sometimes fail to deliver the best combination of public goods because it may be very difficult for politicians to discern what voters actually want. In other cases, though, economists worry that governments may end up failing to deliver allocative and productive efficiency, not because politicians can't tell what people want—but because they *can*.

The problem is that voters sometimes support policies that reduce rather than enhance allocative and productive efficiency. Examples include several types of wage and price controls, punitive tariffs on foreign products, and various industrial and agricultural subsidies.

These policies almost always reduce economic efficiency, but they are also extremely popular with voters in many countries. Faced with that reality, a politician may well end up supporting such policies even if he personally understands that they will create more economic harm than benefit.

That behaviour makes some observers wish for braver politicians who might be willing to oppose these instances of "voter failure." But others argue that it is too much to hope for braver politicians. Instead, efforts should be directed toward educating the public and convincing them to support government policies that are economically efficient.

appeal to the median voter within their party to get the nomination. They then shift their views more closely to the political centre when they square off against opponents from the opposite political party. In effect, they redirect their appeal toward the median voter within the total population. They also try to label their opponents as being too liberal, or too conservative, and out of touch with mainstream Canada. They then conduct polls and adjust their positions on issues accordingly.

IMPLICATIONS

The median-voter model has two important implications:

1. At any point in time, many people will be dissatisfied by the extent of government involvement in the economy. The size of government will largely be determined by the median preference, leaving many people desiring a much larger, or a much smaller, public sector. In the marketplace you can buy no zucchinis, two zucchinis,

or 200 zucchinis, depending on how much you enjoy them. In the public sector you will tend to get the public health funding that the median voter prefers.

2. Some people may "vote with their feet" by moving into political jurisdictions where the median voter's preferences are closer to their own. They may move from one province to another where the level of government services, and therefore taxes, is lower. Or they may move into an area known for its excellent but expensive school system. Some may move to other provinces; a few may even move to other countries.

For these reasons, and because our personal preferences for publicly provided goods and services are not static, the median preference shifts over time. Moreover, information about people's preferences is imperfect, leaving much room for politicians to misjudge the true median position. When they misjudge, they may have a difficult time getting elected or re-elected.

APPENDIX / Summary

LOA5.1 Explain the difficulties of conveying economic preferences through economic preferences through majority voting

- Public choice theory suggests that governments may sometimes suffer from government failures because majority voting fails to correctly indicate voter preferences.

- Majority voting creates the possibility of (a) underallocations or overallocations of resources to particular public goods and

(b) inconsistent voting outcomes that make it impossible for a democratic political system to definitively determine the will of the people.

- The median-voter model predicts that, under majority rule, the person holding the middle position on an issue will determine the outcome of an election involving that issue.

APPENDIX / Terms and Concepts

public choice theory
logrolling

paradox of voting
median-voter model

APPENDIX / Discussion Questions

1. Explain how affirmative and negative majority votes can some-times lead to inefficient allocations of resources to public goods. Is this problem likely to be greater under a benefits-received or an ability-to-pay tax system? Use the information in both panels of Figure A5-1 to show how society might be better off if Adams were allowed to buy votes.   [LOA5.1]

2. Discuss the following: Majority voting ensures that government will produce only those public goods for which benefits exceed costs.   [LOA5.1]

3. Critique this statement: The problem with our democratic institutions is that they don't correctly reflect the will of the people! If the people—rather than self-interested politicians or lobbyists—had control, we wouldn't have to worry about government taking actions that don't maximize allocative and productive efficiency.   [LOA5.1]

APPENDIX / Review Questions

1. Explain the paradox of voting through reference to the accom-panying table, which shows the ranking of three public goods by voters Jay, Dave, and Conan: [LOA5.1]

Public good	RANKINGS		
	Jay	Dave	Conan
Courthouse	2nd choice	1st choice	3rd choice
School	3rd choice	2nd choice	1st choice
Park	1st choice	3rd choice	2nd choice

2. We can apply voting paradoxes to the highway construction example of Chapter 4. Suppose there are only five people in a society and each favours one of the five highway construction options listed in Table 4.4. ("No new construction" is one of the five options.) Explain which of these highway options will be selected using a majority paired-choice vote. Will this option be the optimal size of the project from an economic perspective?   [LOA5.1]

3. True or False? The median-voter model explains why politicians so often stake out fringe positions that appeal only to a small segment of the electorate.   [LOA5.1]

APPENDIX / Problems

1. Look back at Figures A5-1a and b, which show the costs and benefits to voters Adams, Benson, and Conrad of two different public goods that the government will produce if a majority of Adams, Benson, and Conrad support them. Suppose that Adams, Benson, and Conrad have decided to have one single vote at which the funding for both public goods will be decided simultaneously.   [LOA5.1]

   a. Given the $300 cost per person of each public good, what are Adams' net benefits for each public good individually and for the two combined? Will he want to vote yes or no on the proposal to fund both projects simultaneously?

   b. What are Conrad's net benefits for each public good indi-vidually and for the two combined? Will he want to vote yes or no on the proposal to fund both projects simultaneously?

   c. What are Benson's net benefits for each public good indi-vidually and for the two combined? Will he want to vote yes or no on the proposal to fund both projects simultaneously—or will he be indifferent?

d. Who is the median voter here? Who will the two other voters be attempting to persuade?

2. Political advertising is often directed at winning over so-called swing voters, whose votes might go either way. Suppose that two political parties—the Freedom Party and the Liberty Party—disagree on whether to build a new road. Polling shows that of 1000 total voters, 450 are firmly for the new road and 450 are firmly against the new road. Thus, each party will try to win over a majority of the 100 remaining swing voters.   [LOA5.1]

a. Suppose that each party spends $5000 on untargeted TV, radio, and newspaper ads that are equally likely to reach any and all voters. How much per voter will be spent by both parties combined?

b. Suppose that, instead, each party could direct all of its spending towards just the swing voters by using targeted ads that exploit social media. If all of the two parties' combined spending was targeted at just swing voters, how much would be spent per swing voter?

c. Suppose that only the Freedom Party knows how to target voters using social media. How much per swing voter will it be spending? If at the same time the Liberty Party is still using only untargeted TV, radio, and newspaper ads, what portion of its total spending is likely to be reaching the 100 swing voters? How much per swing voter does that portion amount to?

d. Looking at your answers to part (c), how much more per swing voter will the Freedom Party be spending than the Liberty Party? If spending per swing voter influences elections, which party is more likely to win?

CHAPTER 6

An Introduction to Macroeconomics

LEARNING OBJECTIVES

LO6.1 Explain why economists focus on GDP, unemployment, and inflation when assessing the health of an entire economy.

LO6.2 Discuss why sustained increases in living standards are historically recent phenomena.

LO6.3 Identify why saving and investment are key factors in promoting rising living standards.

LO6.4 Describe why expectations, shocks, and sticky prices are responsible for short-run fluctuations in output and employment.

LO6.5 Characterize the degree to which various prices in the economy are sticky.

LO6.6 Explain why the greater flexibility of prices as time passes causes economists to use different macroeconomic models for different time horizons.

Macroeconomics focuses its attention on national economies while seeking answers to the largest of economic questions. For instance, why are some countries really rich while others are really poor? Why do some countries enjoy sustained, long-run increases in living standards, while other countries simply stagnate? Why do all countries–even the richest–go through alternating boom and bust periods? And is there anything that governments can do to improve living standards or fight recessions? This chapter provides an overview of the data that macroeconomists use to measure the status and growth of an entire economy as well as a preview of the models that they use to help explain both long-run growth and short-run fluctuations. Because it is an overview chapter, it raises many unanswered questions. Subsequent chapters will explain these topics in much greater detail.

6.1 Assessing the Health of the Economy: Performance and Policy

LO6.1 Explain why economists focus on GDP, unemployment, and inflation when assessing the health of an entire economy.

As you know from Chapter 1, macroeconomics studies the behaviour of the economy as a whole. It is primarily concerned with two topics: long-run economic growth and the short-run fluctuations in output and employment that are often referred to as the **business cycle**. These phenomena are closely related because they happen simultaneously. Economies show a distinct growth trend that leads to higher output and higher standards of living in the long run, but in the short run there is considerable variability. Sometimes growth proceeds more rapidly and sometimes it proceeds more slowly. It may even turn negative for a while so that output and living standards actually decline, a situation referred to as a **recession**. That is precisely what happened in 2008–2009, when the Canadian economy experienced what has come to be called the Great Recession.

To understand how economies operate and how their performance might be improved, economists collect and analyze economic data. Just as you keep tabs on the instrument panel of your car to make sure that it is functioning properly, economists collect data about the economy to measure how well or poorly it is running. An almost infinite number of data items can be examined, including the amount of new construction taking place each month, how many ships laden with cargo are arriving at Canadian ports each year, and how many new inventions have been patented in the last few weeks. But macroeconomists tend to focus on just a few statistics when trying to assess the health and development of an economy. Chief among these are real GDP, unemployment, and inflation.

- **Real GDP (real gross domestic product)** measures the value of final goods and services produced within the borders of a country during a specific time period, typically a year. This statistic is very useful because it can tell us whether an economy's output is growing. For instance, if Canada's real GDP in one year is larger than the previous year, we know that Canada's output increased from the first year to the next. To determine real GDP, government statisticians first calculate **nominal GDP**, which totals the dollar value of all goods and services produced within the borders of a country using the country's *current prices during the year the goods and services were produced*. But because nominal GDP uses the prices in place in the year the output was produced, it suffers from a major problem: it can increase from one year to the next even if no increase in output has occurred. To see how, consider a commercial blacksmith who produced 10 iron spiral staircases last year and 10 identical staircases this year. Clearly, the blacksmith's output did not change. But if the price of the staircases rose from $10,000 last year to $20,000 this year, nominal GDP increased from $100,000 (= 10 × $10,000) to $200,000 (= 10 × $20,000). Without knowing about the price increase, we might unwisely conclude that the output of staircases increased from 10 to 20. Real GDP statistically eliminates these kinds of price changes. As a result, we can compare real GDP numbers from one year to the next and know if there has been a change in output (rather than prices). Because more output means greater consumption possibilities–including the chance to consume not only more fun things (such as movies, vacations, and video games) but also more serious things (such as better health care and safer roads)– economists and policymakers are deeply concerned with encouraging a large and growing real GDP.

- **Unemployment** is the state a person is in if he or she cannot get a job despite being willing to work and actively seeking work. High rates of unemployment are undesirable because they indicate that a nation is not using a large portion of its most important resource–the talents and skills of its people. Unemployment is a waste because we must count as a loss all the goods and services that unemployed workers could have produced if they had been working. Researchers have drawn links between higher rates of unemployment and major social problems like higher crime rates and greater political unrest, as well as higher rates of depression, heart disease, and other illnesses among unemployed individuals.

- **Inflation** is an increase in the overall level of prices. As an example, consider all the goods and services bought by a typical family over the course of one year. If the economy is experiencing inflation, it will cost the family more money to buy those goods and services this year than it cost to buy them last year. This can be troublesome for several reasons. First, if the family's income does not rise as fast as the prices of the goods and services that it consumes, it won't be able to purchase as much as it used to and its standard of living will fall. Along the same lines, a surprise jump in inflation reduces the purchasing power of people's savings. Savings a family believed would buy a specific amount of goods and services will turn out to buy less than expected due to the higher-than-expected prices.

Because these statistics are the standards by which economists keep track of long-run growth and short-run fluctuations, we spend substantial time in the next few chapters examining how these statistics are computed, how accurately they capture the well-being of actual people, and how they vary both across countries and over time. Once these statistics are understood, we will build upon them in subsequent chapters by developing macroeconomic models of both long-run growth and short-run fluctuations. These models help us understand how policymakers attempt to maximize growth while minimizing unemployment and inflation.

Macroeconomic models also clarify many important questions about the powers and limits of government economic policy, including the following:

- Can governments promote long-run economic growth?

- Can governments reduce the severity of recessions by smoothing out short-run fluctuations?

- Are certain government policy tools, such as manipulating interest rates (monetary policy), more effective at mitigating short-run fluctuations than other government policy tools, such as making changes to tax rates or government spending (fiscal policy)?

- Is there a trade-off between lower rates of unemployment and higher rates of inflation?

- Does government policy work best when it is announced in advance or when it is a surprise?

The answers to these questions are of crucial importance because of the vast differences in economic performance seen across various economies at different times. For instance, the output generated by the Canadian economy grew at an average rate of 1.7 percent per year between 2001 and 2011, while the output generated by the Japanese economy grew at an average rate of less than 1 percent per year over the same period. In 2008–2009, the Canadian economy lost over 400,000 jobs, and the unemployment rate rose from 6.1 percent to as high as 8.3 percent. A couple of years later, in 2014, unemployment in Canada was only 6.9 percent of the labour force, while it was 5.0 percent in Germany, 8.6 percent in India, 8.7 percent in Poland, and more than 90 percent in Zimbabwe. At the same time, the inflation rate in Canada was 2.0 percent and in the United States it was 1.6 percent, compared with 0.9 percent in Germany, and 69 percent in Venezuela.

Our models will help us understand why such large differences in rates of growth, unemployment, and inflation exist among countries and why those rates can change so substantially from one period to another. These models will also provide significant insight into how government policies can influence rates of growth, unemployment, and inflation.

6.2 / The Miracle of Modern Economic Growth

LO6.2 Discuss why sustained increases in living standards are historically recent phenomena.

Rapid and sustained economic growth is a relatively recent phenomenon. Before the Industrial Revolution began in the late 1700s in England, standards of living showed virtually no growth over hundreds or even thousands of years. For instance, the standard of living of the average Roman peasant was virtually the same at the start of the Roman Empire, around the year 500 BC, as it was at the end of the Roman Empire about 1000 years later. Similarly, historians and archaeologists have estimated that the standard of living enjoyed by the average Chinese peasant was essentially the same in the year 1800 AD as it was in the year 100 AD.

This is not to say that the Roman and Chinese economies did not expand over time. They did. In fact, their total outputs of goods and services increased many times over. The problem was that as output increased, their populations went up by similar proportions so that the amount of output *per person* remained virtually unchanged. This historical pattern continued until the start of the Industrial Revolution, which ushered in not only factory production and automation but also increases in research and development so that new and better technologies were constantly being invented. The result was that output began to grow faster than the population, and living standards began to rise as the amount of output *per person* increased.

Not all countries experienced this phenomenon, but those that did were experiencing **modern economic growth** (in which output per person rises) as compared with earlier times in which output (but not output per person) increased. Under modern economic growth, the annual increase in output per person is often not large, perhaps 2 percent per year in the countries such as England that were the first to industrialize. But when compounded over time, an annual growth rate of 2 percent adds up very rapidly. Indeed, it implies that standards of living will double every 35 years. So if the average citizen of a country enjoying 2 percent growth begins this year with an income of $10,000, in 35 years that person will have an income of $20,000. And 35 years after that there will be another doubling so that the income of the average citizen in 70 years will be $40,000. And 35 years after that, income will double again to $80,000. Such high rates of growth are amazing when compared to the period before modern economic growth, when standards of living remained unchanged century after century.

 PRODUCTION AND THE STANDARD OF LIVING

The vast differences in living standards seen today between rich and poor countries are almost entirely the result of the fact that only some countries have experienced modern economic growth. Indeed, before the start of the Industrial Revolution in the late 1700s, living standards around the world were very similar–so much so that the average standard of living in the richest parts of the world was at most only two or three times higher than the standard of living in the poorest parts of the world. By contrast, the citizens of the richest nations today have material standards of living that are on average more than fifty times higher than those experienced by citizens of the poorest nations, as can be seen by the GDP per person data for the year 2014 given in Global Perspective 6.1.

Global Perspective 6.1 facilitates international comparisons of living standards by making three adjustments to each country's GDP. First, it converts each country's GDP from its own currency into U.S. dollars so no confusion exists about the values of different currencies. Second, it divides each country's GDP measured in dollars by the size of its population. The resulting number, *GDP per capita*, is the average amount of output each person in each country could have if each country's total output were divided equally among its citizens; it is a measure of each country's average standard of living. Third, a method called *purchasing power parity* adjusts for the fact that prices are much lower in some countries than others. By making this adjustment, we can trust that $1 of GDP per person in Canada represents about the same quantity of goods and services as $1 of GDP per person in any of the other countries. The resulting numbers–GDP per person adjusted for purchasing power parity–are presented in Global Perspective 6.1.

6.1 GLOBAL PERSPECTIVE

GDP per Person, Selected Countries

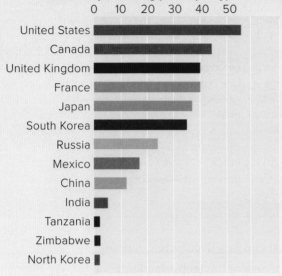

GDP per capita, 2014 (current international dollars
based on purchasing power parity) in thousands

Source: International Monetary Fund, www.imf.org, for all countries except North Korea (2013), the data for which come from the
CIA World Factbook, www.cia.gov.

QUICK REVIEW 6.2

- Before the Industrial Revolution, living standards did not show any sustained increases over time because any increase in output tended to be offset by an equally large increase in population.

- Since the Industrial Revolution, many nations have experienced modern economic growth in which output grows faster than population, so that living standards rose over time.

6.3 Saving, Investment, and Choosing Between Present and Future Consumption

LO6.3 Identify why saving and investment are key factors in promoting rising living standards.

At the heart of economic growth is the principle that, in order to raise living standards over time, an economy must devote at least some fraction of its current output to increasing future output. As implied in Chapter 1, this process requires flows of both saving and investment, which we will define before returning to discuss why they are so important for economic growth.

CONSIDER THIS   Economic versus Financial Investment

Economics students are often confused by how the word *investment* is used in economics. This is understandable, because economists make a distinction between financial investment and economic investment.

Financial investment captures what ordinary people mean when they say "investment," namely the purchase of assets like stocks, bonds, and real estate in the hope of reaping a financial gain. Anything of monetary value is an asset and, in everyday usage, people purchase—or invest in—assets hoping to receive a financial gain, either by eventually selling them at higher prices than they paid for them or by receiving a stream of payments from others who are allowed to use the assets.

By contrast, when economists say "investment," they are referring to **economic investment**, which relates to the creation and expansion of business enterprises. Specifically, economic investment only includes spending on the production and accumulation of newly created capital goods such as machinery, tools, factories, and warehouses.

For economists, purely financial transactions, such as swapping cash for a stock or a bond, are not investment. Neither are the purchases of factories or apartment buildings built in previous years. These transactions simply transfer the ownership of financial assets or existing real assets from one party to another. They do not purchase newly created capital goods. As such, they are great examples of financial investment but not of economic investment.

So now that you know the difference, remember that purely financial transactions like buying BlackBerry Limited stock or a five-year-old factory are indeed referred to as investments—except in economics!

* **Saving** occurs when current consumption is less than current output.

* **Investment** occurs when resources are devoted to increasing future output–for instance, by building a new research facility in which scientists invent the next generation of fuel-efficient automobiles, or by constructing a super-efficient factory. (Caution: In economics, the term *investment* differs from common usage. Be sure to read the Consider This . . . Economic versus Financial Investment box, where the difference is explained.)

The key point to understanding why saving and investment are so important for economic growth is that the amount of investment is ultimately limited by the amount of saving. The only way that more output can be directed at investment activities is if saving increases. But that, in turn, implies that individuals and society as a whole must make trade-offs between current and future consumption.

This is true because the only way to pay for more investment–and the higher levels of future consumption that more investment can generate–is to increase present saving. But increased saving can come only at the price of reduced current consumption. Individuals and society as a whole must therefore wrestle with a choice between present consumption and future consumption, deciding how to balance the reductions in current consumption that are necessary to fund current investment against the higher levels of future consumption that can result from more current investment.

Banks and Other Financial Institutions

Households are the principal source of savings, but businesses are the main economic investors. The pool of savings generated by households when they spend less than they consume gets transferred to businesses so that they can purchase newly created capital goods. The transfer mechanism is banks and other financial institutions such as mutual funds, pension plans, and insurance companies. These institutions collect the savings of households, rewarding savers with interest, dividends and sometimes capital gains (increases in asset values). The banks and other financial institutions then lend the funds to businesses, which invest in equipment, factories, and other capital goods.

Macroeconomics devotes considerable attention to money, banking, and financial institutions because a well-functioning financial system helps to promote economic growth and stability by encouraging saving and by properly directing those savings into the most productive possible investments. In contrast, a poorly functioning financial system can create serious problems for an economy.

- An economy can only grow if it invests, and it can only invest if it saves some of its current output. Thus, saving is crucial to increasing investment and, consequently, future output.

- Banks and other financial institutions channel household savings toward businesses, which invest in equipment, factories, and other capital goods.

6.4 | Uncertainty, Expectations, Shocks, and Short-Run Fluctuations

LO6.4 Describe why expectations, shocks, and sticky prices are responsible for short-run fluctuations in output and employment.

Decisions about saving and investment are complicated by the fact that the future is uncertain. Investment projects sometimes produce disappointing results or even fail totally. As a result, firms spend considerable time trying to predict future trends so that they can, ideally, invest only in projects that are likely to succeed. This implies that macroeconomics has to take into account **expectations** about the future.

The Importance of Expectations and Shocks

Expectations are hugely important for two reasons. The more obvious reason involves the effect that changing expectations have on current behaviour. If firms grow more pessimistic about the future returns likely to come from current investments, they are going to invest less today than they would if they were more optimistic. Expectations therefore have a large effect on economic growth since increased pessimism will lead to less current investment and, subsequently, less future consumption.

The less obvious reason expectations are so important has to do with what happens when expectations are unmet. Firms are often forced to cope with **shocks**–situations in which they were expecting one thing to happen but then something else happens. For instance, consider a situation in which a firm decides to build a high-speed railroad that will shuttle passengers between Windsor and Toronto. The firm expects it to be very popular and make a handsome profit. But if it unexpectedly turns out to be unpopular and loses money, the railroad must figure out how to respond. Should the railroad go out of business completely? Should it attempt to see if it can turn a profit by hauling cargo instead of passengers? Is there a possibility that the venture might succeed if the firm borrows $30 million from a bank to pay for a massive advertising campaign? These sorts of decisions are necessitated by the shock and surprise of having to deal with an unexpected situation.

Economies are exposed to both demand shocks and supply shocks. **Demand shocks** are unexpected changes in the demand for goods and services. **Supply shocks** are unexpected changes in the supply of goods and services. The word *shock* reveals only that something unexpected has happened, not whether it is unexpectedly good or unexpectedly bad. Economists use even more specific terms. A *positive demand shock* is a situation in which demand turns out to be higher than expected, while a *negative demand shock* is when demand turns out to be lower than expected.

Demand Shocks and Sticky Prices

Economists believe that most short-run fluctuations are the result of demand shocks. Supply shocks do happen in some cases and are very important when they occur. But we will focus most of our attention in this chapter and subsequent chapters on demand shocks, how they affect the economy, and how government policy may be able to help the economy adjust to them. But why are demand shocks such a big problem? Why would we have to consider calling in the government to help deal with them? And why can't firms deal with demand shocks on their own?

The answer to these questions is that the prices of many goods and services are inflexible (slow to change, or *sticky*) in the short run. As we will explain, this implies that price changes do not quickly equalize the quantities demanded of such goods and services with their respective quantities supplied. Instead, because prices are inflexible, the economy is forced to respond in the short run to demand shocks primarily through changes in output and employment rather than through changes in prices.

Example: A Single Firm Dealing with Demand Shocks and Sticky Prices

Although an economy as a whole is vastly more complex than a single firm, an analogy that uses a single car factory will be helpful in explaining why demand shocks and inflexible prices are so important to understanding most of the short-run fluctuations that affect the entire economy. Consider a car manufacturing company named Buzzer Auto. Like most companies, Buzzer Auto is in business to try to make a profit. Part of turning a profit involves trying to develop accurate expectations about future market conditions. Consequently, Buzzer constantly does market research to estimate future demand conditions so that it will, ideally, only build cars that people are going to want to buy.

SETTING EXPECTATIONS

After extensive market research, Buzzer concludes that it can likely earn a modest profit if it builds and staffs an appropriately sized factory to build an environmentally friendly car, which it decides to call the Prion. Buzzer's marketing economists collaborate with Buzzer's engineers and conclude that expected profits will be maximized if the firm builds a factory that has an optimal output rate of 900 cars per week. If the factory operates at this rate, it can produce Prions for only $36,500 per vehicle. This is terrific because the firm's estimates for demand indicate that a supply of 900 vehicles per week can be sold at a price of $37,000 per vehicle–meaning that if everything goes according to plan, Buzzer Auto should make an accounting profit of $500 on each Prion that it produces and sells. Expecting these future conditions, Buzzer decides to build the factory, staff it with workers, and begin making the Prion.

Look at Figure 6-1a, which shows the market for Prions when the vertical supply curve for Prions is fixed at the factory's optimal output rate of 900 cars per week. Notice that we have drawn three possible demand curves. D_L corresponds to low demand for the Prion, D_M corresponds to the medium level of demand that Buzzer's marketing economists are expecting to materialize, and D_H corresponds to high demand for the Prion. Figure 6-1a is consistent with the marketing economists' expectations; if all goes according to plan and the actual demand that materializes is D_M, the equilibrium price will in fact be $37,000 per Prion and the equilibrium quantity demanded will be 900 cars per week. Thus, if all goes according to expectations, the factory will have exactly the right capacity to meet the expected quantity demanded at the sales price of $37,000 per vehicle. In addition, the firm's books will show a profit of $500 per vehicle on each of the 900 vehicles that it builds and expects to sell each week at that price.

FULL EMPLOYMENT IF THERE ARE NO SHOCKS

Here is the key point: If expectations are always fulfilled, Buzzer Auto will never contribute to any of the short-run fluctuations in output and unemployment that affect real-world economies. If everything always goes according to plan and Buzzer Auto's expectations always come true, then the factory will always produce and sell at its optimal output rate of 900 cars per week. This would mean that it would never experience any fluctuations in output–either in the short run or in the long run. At the same time, since producing a constant output of 900 cars each week will always require the same number of workers, the factory's labour demand and employment should never vary. So if everything always goes according to plan, Buzzer Auto will never have any effect on unemployment because it will always hire a constant number of workers.

These facts imply that the short-run fluctuations in output and unemployment that we see in the real world must be the result of shocks and things *not* going according to plan. In particular, business cycle fluctuations typically arise because the actual demand that materializes ends up being either lower or

FIGURE 6-1   The Effect of Unexpected Changes in Demand Under Flexible and Fixed Prices

(a) If prices are flexible, then no matter what demand turns out to be, Buzzer Auto can continue to sell its optimal output of 900 cars per week since the equilibrium price will adjust to equalize the quantity demanded with the quantity supplied. (b) By contrast, if Buzzer Auto sticks with a fixed price policy, the quantity demanded will vary with the level of demand. At the fixed price of $37,000 per vehicle, the quantity demanded will be 700 cars per week if demand is D_L, 900 cars per week if demand is D_M, and 1150 cars per week if demand is D_H.

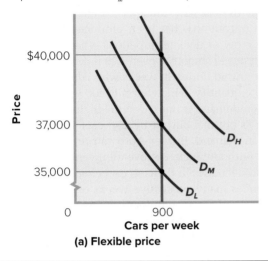

(a) Flexible price

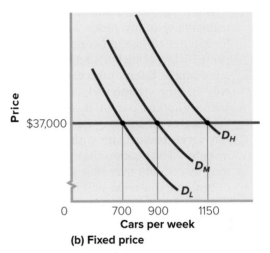

(b) Fixed price

higher than what firms were expecting. When this occurs, adjustments are needed to bring quantity demanded and quantity supplied back into alignment. As we are about to explain, the nature of these adjustments varies hugely depending on whether prices are flexible or inflexible.

PRICE CHANGES IF THERE ARE DEMAND SHOCKS AND FLEXIBLE PRICES

Figure 6-1a illustrates the case of adjusting to unexpected changes in demand *when prices are flexible*. Here, if demand is unexpectedly low at D_L, the market price can adjust downward to $35,000 per vehicle so that the quantity demanded at that price will still be equal to the factory's optimal output rate of 900 cars per week. On the other hand, if demand is unexpectedly high at D_H, the market price can adjust upward to $40,000 per vehicle so that the quantity demanded will still be equal to the factory's optimal output rate of 900 cars per week. These adjustments imply that *if* the price of Prions is free to quickly adjust to new equilibrium levels in response to unexpected changes in demand, the factory could always operate at its optimal output rate of 900 cars per week. Only the amount of profit or loss will vary with demand.

Applying this logic to the economy as a whole, *if* the prices of goods and services could always adjust quickly to unexpected changes in demand, then the economy could always produce at its optimal capacity since prices would adjust to ensure that the quantity demanded of each good and service would always equal the quantity supplied. Simply put, if prices were fully flexible, there would be no short-run fluctuations in output. Production levels would remain relatively constant and unemployment levels would not change much because firms would always need the same number of workers to produce the same amount of output.

OUTPUT CHANGES IF THERE ARE DEMAND SHOCKS AND STICKY PRICES

In reality, many prices in the economy are inflexible and are not able to change rapidly when demand changes unexpectedly. Consider the extreme case shown in Figure 6-1b, in which the price of Prions is totally inflexible, fixed at $37,000 per Prion. Here, if demand unexpectedly falls from D_M to D_L, the quantity demanded at the fixed price of $37,000 will be only 700 cars per week, which is 200 cars fewer than the factory's optimal output of 900 cars per week. On the other hand, if demand is unexpectedly high at D_H, the quantity demanded at the fixed price of $37,000 will be 1150 cars per week, which is 250 cars more than the factory's optimal output of 900 cars per week.

One way for companies to deal with these unexpected shifts in quantity demanded would be to try to adjust the factory's output to match them. That is, during weeks of low demand Buzzer Auto could attempt to produce only 700 Prions, while during weeks of high demand it could try to produce 1150 Prions. But this sort of flexible output strategy is very expensive because factories operate at their lowest costs when they are producing constantly at their optimal output levels; operating at either a higher or a lower production rate results in higher per-unit production costs.[1]

Knowing this, manufacturing firms typically attempt to deal with unexpected changes in demand by maintaining an inventory. An **inventory** is a store of output that has been produced but not yet sold. Inventories are useful because they can be allowed to grow or decline in periods when demand is unexpectedly low or high—thereby allowing production to proceed smoothly even when demand is variable. In our example, Buzzer Auto will maintain an inventory of unsold Prions. In weeks when demand is unexpectedly low, the inventory will increase by 200 Prions as the quantity demanded falls 200 vehicles short of the factory's optimal output. By contrast, during weeks when demand is unexpectedly high, the inventory will decrease as the quantity demanded exceeds the factory's optimal output by 250 cars. By allowing inventory levels to fluctuate with these unexpected shifts in demand, Buzzer Auto can respond by adjusting inventory levels rather than output levels. In addition, with any luck, the overall inventory level will stay roughly constant over time as unexpected increases and decreases in demand cancel each other out.

But consider what will happen if the firm experiences many successive weeks of unexpectedly low demand. For each such week, the firm's inventory of unsold Prions will increase by 200 cars. The firm's managers will not mind if this happens for a few weeks, but if it continues for many weeks the managers will be forced to cut production—because, among other things, there simply will be no place to park so many unsold vehicles. More importantly, holding large numbers of unsold cars in inventory is unprofitable because while costs must be incurred to build an unsold car, an unsold car obviously brings in no revenue. Constantly rising inventories hurt firm profits, and management will want to reduce output if it sees inventories rising week after week due to unexpectedly low demand.

CONSIDER THIS   The Great Recession

In late 2008 and 2009, Canada and many other countries (particularly the United States) encountered their worst financial and economic crisis since the Great Depression of the 1930s. The recession, so severe that it has been dubbed the Great Recession, was triggered by a steep decline in U.S. housing prices and a crisis involving mortgage loans and the financial securities built on them. Several key U.S. financial institutions collapsed or nearly failed, and lending markets largely froze. The financial crisis eventually spread to practically the entire global economy, including Canada, where employment fell by over 400,000 workers between late 2008 and May of 2009, and the unemployment rate rose from 6.1 percent to 8.3 percent over that same period. Economic growth slumped; in the last quarter of 2008 the Canadian economy shrank at an annual rate of 3.4 percent per annum, while in the first quarter of 2009 it shrank by a steep annual rate of 5.4 percent.

And this is where Buzzer Auto comes into the picture. The situation in Figure 6.1b, where the price of Buzzer's autos is inflexible, is highly relevant to the Great Recession. Like Buzzer, actual auto producers such as GM, Ford, and Chrysler, as well as thousands of producers of other products across the economy, established their production capacity and set their expectations of product demand on the basis of normal times. But demand for their goods and services fell unexpectedly because of greater consumer difficulty in getting loans, declining consumer confidence, and eventually declining income. The economy's price level (essentially a weighted average of all prices) declined only slightly, and that was after the recession was well underway. Therefore, real output (not prices) took the major brunt of the decline of total demand in the economy. Output dropped, employment plummeted, and unemployment soared.

---

[1] If you have studied microeconomics, you will recognize that the firm's optimal output level of 900 cars per week is the level that minimizes the factory's average total cost (ATC) per vehicle of producing the Prion. Producing either more or fewer Prions will result in higher per-vehicle production costs.

Generalizing from a Single Firm to the Entire Economy

This simplified story about a single car company explains why economists believe that a combination of unexpected changes in demand and inflexible prices is the key to understanding the short-run fluctuations that affect real-world economies. If prices were flexible, then the firm could always operate at the factory's optimal output level because prices would always adjust to ensure that it could sell its optimal output of 900 cars per week no matter what happened to demand. But if prices are inflexible, then an unexpected decline in demand that persists for any length of time will result in increasing inventories that will eventually force the firm's management to cut production to less than the optimal output level of 900 cars per week. When this happens, not only will output fall, but unemployment will also rise. The firm will lay off workers because fewer employees will be needed to produce fewer cars.

Generalizing this story to the economy as a whole, if demand falls for many goods and services across the entire economy for an extended period of time, then many firms will find inventories piling up and will be forced to cut production. As they do, the economy will go into recession, with GDP falling and unemployment rising.

On the other hand, if demand is unexpectedly high for a prolonged period of time, the economy will boom and unemployment will fall. In the case of our Prion example, for each week that demand is unexpectedly high inventories will fall by 250 cars. If this keeps happening week after week, inventories will start to run out and the firm will have to react by increasing production to more than the optimal output rate of 900 cars per week so that orders do not go unfilled. When this happens, GDP will increase as more cars per week are produced and unemployment will fall because the factory will have to hire more workers in order to produce the larger number of cars.

QUICK REVIEW 6.4

- Economic shocks occur when events unfold in ways that people were not expecting.

- Demand and supply shocks take place when demand or supply ends up being either higher or lower than expected.

- Real-world prices are often inflexible or *sticky* in the short run.

- When prices are sticky, the economy adjusts to demand shocks mostly through changes in output and employment (rather than through changes in prices).

6.5 | How Sticky Are Prices?

LO6.5 Characterize the degree to which various prices in the economy are sticky.

We have just shown that **inflexible prices**—or **sticky prices**, as economists are fond of saying—help to explain how unexpected changes in demand lead to the fluctuations in GDP and employment that occur over the course of the business cycle. Of course, not all prices are sticky. Indeed, the markets for many commodities and raw materials such as corn, oil, and natural gas have extremely **flexible prices** that react within seconds to changes in supply and demand. By contrast, the prices of most of the final goods and services people consume are quite sticky, with the average good or service going 4.3 months between price changes. To get a better appreciation for the fact that price stickiness varies greatly by product or service, look at Table 6-1, which gives the average number of months between price changes for various common goods and services. The prices of some products like gasoline and airline tickets can change very rapidly. By contrast, haircuts and newspapers average more than two years between price changes. And coin-operated laundry machines average nearly four years between price changes!

TABLE 6-1	Average Number of Months Between Price Changes for Selected Goods and Services	
Item		**Months**
Coin-operated laundry machines		46.4
Newspapers		29.9
Haircuts		25.5
Taxi fares		19.7
Veterinary services		14.9
Magazines		11.2
Computer software		5.5
Beer		4.3
Microwave ovens		3.0
Milk		2.4
Electricity		1.8
Airline tickets		1.0
Gasoline		0.6

Source: Mark Bils and Peter J. Klenow, "Some Evidence on the Importance of Sticky Prices," *Journal of Political Economy*, October 2004, pp. 947–85.

An important recent study has found that product prices are particularly sticky in response to widespread macroeconomic and monetary disturbances.[2] In later chapters, we will identify and discuss several factors that cause short-run price stickiness. But to keep the current discussion brief, let's focus on just two factors here.

One factor is that companies selling final goods and services know that consumers prefer stable, predictable prices that do not fluctuate rapidly with changes in demand. Consumers would be annoyed if the same bottle of pop or shampoo cost one price one day, a different price the next day, and yet another price a week later. Volatile prices make planning more difficult, and in addition, consumers who come in to buy the product on a day when the price happens to be high will likely feel they are being taken advantage of. To avoid this, most firms try to maintain stable prices that do not change very often. Firms do have occasional sales where they lower prices, but on the whole they tend to try to keep prices stable and predictable—with the result being price inflexibility.

Another factor that causes sticky prices has to do with the fact that in certain situations a firm may be afraid that cutting its price may be counterproductive because its rivals might simply match the price cut—a situation often referred to as a *price war*. This possibility is common among firms that have only one or two major rivals. Consider Coca-Cola and Pepsi. If Coca-Cola faces unexpectedly low demand for its product, it might be tempted to reduce its price in the hope that it can steal business away from Pepsi. But such a strategy would work only if Pepsi left its price alone when Coca-Cola cut its price. That, of course, is not likely. If Coca-Cola cuts its price, Pepsi will very likely cut its price in retaliation, doing its best to make sure that Coca-Cola doesn't steal any of its customers. Thus, if Pepsi retaliates, Coca-Cola will only be made worse off by its decision to cut its price; it will not pick up any more business (due to the fact that Pepsi also cut its price) and it will also be receiving less money for each bottle of Coke that it sells because it cut its price. Thus, firms that have to deal with the possibility of price wars often have sticky prices.

---

[2] Jean Boivin, Marc P. Giannoni, and Illan Mihov, "Sticky Prices and Monetary Policy: Evidence from Disaggregated US Data," *American Economic Review*, March 2009, pp. 350-384.

QUICK REVIEW 6.5

- Many commodity prices are extremely flexible and change constantly, but other prices in the economy change only very infrequently.
- Some prices are inflexible in order to please retail customers, others because rival firms are afraid that price changes may trigger a price war.

- Prices tend to become more flexible over time, so that as time passes, the economy can react to demand shocks with price changes as well as with output and employment changes.

6.6 / Categorizing Macroeconomic Models Using Price Stickiness

LO6.6 Explain why the greater flexibility of prices as time passes causes economists to use different macroeconomic models for different time horizons.

We have now demonstrated why price stickiness is believed to have such a large role in short-run economic fluctuations. Note, however, that price stickiness moderates over time. This is true because firms that choose to use a fixed-price policy in the short run do not have to use that policy permanently. In particular, if unexpected changes in demand begin to look permanent, many firms will allow their prices to change so that price changes (in addition to quantity changes) can help to equalize quantities supplied with quantities demanded.

For this reason, economists speak of *sticky* prices rather than *stuck* prices. Only in the very short run are prices totally inflexible. As time passes and prices are revised, the world looks much more like Figure 6-1a, in which prices are fully flexible, rather than Figure 6-1b, in which prices are totally inflexible. Indeed, the totally inflexible case shown in the latter graph can be thought of as the extremely short-run response to an unexpected change in demand, while the fully flexible case shown in the former graph can be thought of as a longer-run response to an unexpected change in demand. In terms of time durations, the extreme short run can be thought of as the first few weeks and months after a demand shock, while the long run can be thought of as extending from many months to several years after a demand shock happens.

This realization is very useful when categorizing and understanding the differences among the various macroeconomic models that we will be presenting in subsequent chapters. For instance, the aggregate expenditures model presented in Chapter 11 assumes perfectly inflexible prices (and wages) and thus is a model in which prices are not just sticky but completely stuck. By contrast, the aggregate demand–aggregate supply model presented in Chapter 12 allows for flexible prices (with or without flexible wages) and is therefore useful for understanding how the economy behaves over longer periods of time.

As you study these various models, keep in mind that we need different models precisely because the economy behaves differently depending on how much time has passed after a demand shock. The differences in behaviour result from the fact that prices go from stuck in the extreme short run to fully flexible in the long run. Using different models for different stages in this process gives us much better insights into not only how economies actually behave but also how various government and central bank policies may have different effects in the short run, when prices are fixed, versus the long run, when prices are flexible.

Where will we go from here? In the remainder of Part 2, we examine how economists measure GDP and why GDP has expanded over time. Then we discuss the terminology of business cycles and explore the measurement and types of unemployment and inflation. At that point you will be well prepared to examine the economic models, monetary considerations, and stabilization policies that lie at the heart of macroeconomics.

- Different macroeconomics models are required for the short run, during which prices are inflexible (so that demand shocks lead almost exclusively to output and employment changes), and for longer periods, during which prices become increasingly flexible (so that demand shocks lead more to price changes rather than output and employment changes).

The **LAST WORD**   Debating the Great Recession

Economists disagree vigorously about both the causes of the Great Recession and the best ways to speed a recovery.

The Great Recession of 2008–2009 was the worst economic downturn since the Great Depression of the 1930s. The government intervened massively to help promote recovery, but the subsequent recovery was the weakest since the Great Depression. Explanations about what caused the Great Recession differ sharply among economists. Here are two of the more popular hypotheses.

The Minsky Explanation: Euphoric Bubbles Economist Hyman Minsky believed that severe recessions are often preceded by asset-price bubbles—periods during which euphoria and debt-fueled speculation cause the price of one or more financial assets to irrationally skyrocket before collapsing to more realistic levels. Those who apply his ideas to the Great Recession note that easily obtained home-mortgage loans drove a massive bubble in housing prices in the U.S. When the bubble eventually collapsed, a financial crisis ensued that swept around the globe. Investors lost trillions of dollars in wealth. As a result, the demand for goods and services fell dramatically and unexpectedly. When combined with sticky prices, that leftward shift in demand forced many companies to reduce output and lay off workers (as in our Buzzer Auto example in this chapter). The weakest firms went bankrupt and had to permanently fire all of their workers.

The Austrian Explanation: Excessively Low Interest Rates Economists of the so-called Austrian School also blame bubbles for severe recessions, but they put the blame for bubbles not on euphoria but on government actions that they say keep interest rates too low. Their contention is that excessively low interest rates induce firms and individuals to borrow excessively. Individuals borrow excessively to fund consumption. Firms borrow excessively for construction and investment. When the bubble pops, society has too many factories (as a result of the massive increase in construction and investment on the part of firms) combined with too little demand (as consumers struggle to repay all the money they borrowed to fund their consumption).

In terms of this chapter's Buzzer Auto example, it would be as though Buzzer borrowed lots of money to build several factories only to discover that demand was much lower than expected because consumers were cutting back on spending in order to repay debt. With demand shifting left and prices sticky, Buzzer and other companies are forced to reduce output and lay off workers. Thus begins the recession.

Because economists did not have a consensus about what caused the Great Recession, it should not be surprising that they were also divided over the best policies for fighting the recession and improving upon the sluggish recovery that began in 2009. For simplicity, the wide variety of opinions can be grouped into two broad camps promoting two very different solutions.

The Stimulus Solution The majority of economists argued that the solution to the collapse in demand was to have the government take actions to shift demand curves rightward. For instance, the government could lower interest rates so that consumers and businesses would borrow and spend more. The government could also massively increase its purchases of goods and services so that a rightward shift in the government's demand for output could help to make up for the leftward shift in the private-sector demand for output.

This opinion in favour of government stimulus was the most commonly held view among economists, and the government did, in fact, push interest rates very low while also massively increasing government spending.

The Structural Solution A vocal minority of economists rejected the stimulus policies. They argued that the economy required a structural adjustment. In their opinion, the bubble period before the recession had seen a major misallocation of resources toward inefficient firms that generated net losses for society (MB < MC). The only way to redirect the resources that those firms were using back toward productive activities would be to let the inefficient firms go bankrupt. The resources would then flow toward efficient firms whose output generated net benefits for society (MB > MC).

Under this way of thinking, government stimulus efforts delayed recovery by keeping many wasteful firms on life support. Those who took that opinion wanted the government to mostly hang back, let inefficient firms go bankrupt, and allow the invisible hand to reallocate resources.

This debate over government stimulus was ongoing and continual during the sluggish recovery from the Great Recession. Those in favour of stimulus argued that the sluggish recovery was the result of too little stimulus. Those against stimulus argued that the sluggish recovery was the result of too much stimulus.

One of your tasks as you work your way through the subsequent chapters will be to understand the nature of this debate and the arguments and evidence on both sides. But don't look for a definitive answer. The complexities of giant national economies are only partly understood and the best policy may turn out to be something unseen by either of the two camps.

Question

How do the Minsky and Austrian explanations for the causes of the Great Recession differ? Explain how the proponents of government stimulus believe that it will affect aggregate demand and employment (be specific!). How might government stimulus possibly slow rather than accelerate a recovery?

Chapter Summary

LO6.1   EXPLAIN WHY ECONOMISTS FOCUS ON GDP, INFLATION, AND UNEMPLOYMENT WHEN ASSESSING THE HEALTH OF AN ENTIRE ECONOMY.

- Macroeconomics studies long-run economic growth and short-run economic fluctuations.

- Macroeconomists focus their attention on three key economic statistics: GDP, unemployment, and inflation. GDP is the dollar amount of all final goods and services produced in a country during a given period of time. The unemployment rate measures the percentage of all workers who are not able to find paid employment despite being willing and able to work. The inflation rate measures the extent to which the overall price level is rising in the economy.

LO6.2   DISCUSS WHY SUSTAINED INCREASES IN LIVING STANDARDS ARE HISTORICALLY RECENT PHENOMENA.

- Before the Industrial Revolution, living standards did not show any sustained increases over time. Economies grew, but any increase in output tended to be offset by an equally large increase in population, so that the amount of output per person did not rise. By contrast, since the Industrial Revolution began in the late 1700s, many nations have experienced modern economic growth in which output has grown faster than population, so that standards of living have risen over time.

LO6.3   IDENTIFY WHY SAVING AND INVESTMENT ARE KEY FACTORS IN PROMOTING RISING LIVING STANDARDS.

- Macroeconomists believe that one of the keys to modern economic growth is the promotion of saving and investment (for economists, the purchase of capital goods). Investment activities increase the economy's future potential output level. But investment must be funded by saving. This is possible only if people are willing to reduce current consumption, since the only way to increase future consumption is by reducing current consumption in order to gather the savings necessary to fund that investment. Consequently, individuals and society face a trade-off between current consumption and future consumption. Banks and other financial institutions help to convert saving into investment by taking the savings generated by households and lending them to businesses that wish to make investments.

LO6.4   DESCRIBE WHY EXPECTATIONS, SHOCKS, AND STICKY PRICES ARE RESPONSIBLE FOR SHORT-RUN FLUCTUATIONS IN OUTPUT AND EMPLOYMENT.

- Expectations have an important effect on the economy for two reasons. First, if people and businesses are more positive about the future, they will save and invest more. Second, individuals and firms must adjust to shocks—situations in which expectations are unmet and the future does not turn out the way people were expecting. In particular, shocks often imply situations where the quantity supplied of a given good or service does not equal the quantity demanded of that good or service.

- If prices were always flexible and capable of rapid adjustment, then dealing with situations in which quantities demanded did not equal quantities supplied would always be easy since prices could simply adjust to the market equilibrium price at which quantities demanded do equal quantities supplied. Unfortunately, real-world prices are often inflexible (or sticky) in the short run so that the only way for the economy to adjust is through changes in output levels.

- Sticky prices combine with shocks to drive short-run fluctuations in output and employment. Consider a negative demand shock in which demand is unexpectedly low. Because prices are fixed, the lower-than-expected demand will result in unexpectedly slow sales. This will cause inventories to increase. If demand remains low for an extended period of time, inventory levels will become too high and firms will have to cut output and lay off workers. Thus, when prices are inflexible, the economy adjusts to unexpectedly low demand through changes in output and employment rather than through changes in prices (which are not possible when prices are inflexible).

LO6.5   CHARACTERIZE THE DEGREE TO WHICH VARIOUS PRICES IN THE ECONOMY ARE STICKY.

- Prices are inflexible in the short run for various reasons, two of which are discussed in this chapter. First, firms often attempt to set and maintain stable prices in order to please customers (who like predictable prices because they make for easy planning, and who might become upset if prices were volatile). Second, a firm with just a few competitors may be reluctant to cut its price due to the fear of starting a price war, a situation in which its competitors retaliate by cutting their prices as well—thereby leaving the firm worse off than it was to begin with.

LO6.6   EXPLAIN WHY THE GREATER FLEXIBILITY OF PRICES AS TIME PASSES CAUSES ECONOMISTS TO USE DIFFERENT MACROECONOMIC MODELS FOR DIFFERENT TIME HORIZONS.

- Price stickiness moderates over time. As a result, economists have found it sensible to build separate economic models for different time horizons. For instance, some models are designed to reflect the high degree of price inflexibility that occurs in the immediate short run, while other models reflect the high degree of price flexibility that occurs in the long run. The different models allow economists to have a better sense for how various government policies will affect the economy in the short run when prices are inflexible versus the long run when prices are flexible.

Terms and Concepts

business cycle	modern economic growth	shocks
recession	saving	demand shocks
real GDP (real gross domestic product)	financial investment	supply shocks
nominal GDP	economic investment	inventory
unemployment	investment	inflexible prices (sticky prices)
inflation	expectations	flexible prices

Discussion Questions

1. Why do macroeconomists focus on just a few key statistics when trying to understand the health and trajectory of an economy? Would it be better to try to examine all possible data? [LO6.1]

2. Consider a nation in which the volume of goods and services is growing by 5 percent per year. What is the likely impact of this high rate of growth on the power and influence of its government relative to other countries experiencing slower rates of growth? What about the effect of this 5 percent growth on the nation's living standards? Will these also necessarily grow by 5 percent per year, given population growth? Why or why not? [LO6.2]

3. Did economic output start growing faster than population from the beginning of human existence? When did modern economic growth begin? Have all of the world's nations experienced the same extent of modern economic growth? [LO6.2]

4. Why is there a trade-off between the amount of consumption that people can enjoy today and the amount that they can enjoy in the future? Why can't people enjoy more of both? How does saving relate to investment and thus to economic growth? What role do banks and other financial institutions play in aiding the growth process? [LO6.3]

5. How does investment as defined by economists differ from investment as defined by the general public? What would happen to the amount of economic investment made today if firms expected the future returns to such investment to be very low? What if firms expected future returns to be very high? [LO6.3]

6. Why, in general, do shocks force people to make changes? Give at least two examples from your own experience. [LO6.4]

7. Catalogue companies have the classic example of perfectly inflexible prices because once they print and distribute their catalogues, they are committed to selling at the prices as printed. [LO6.4]

   a. If a catalogue company finds its inventory of sweaters rising, what does that say about the demand for sweaters? Was it unexpectedly high, unexpectedly low, or as expected? If the company *could* change the price of sweaters, would it raise the price, lower the price, or keep the price the same?

   b. Given that the company cannot change the price of sweaters, consider the number of sweaters it orders each month from the company that makes them. If inventories become very high, will the catalogue company increase, decrease, or keep orders the same? Given what the catalogue company does with its orders, what is likely to happen to employment and output at the sweater manufacturer?

8. Are all prices in the economy equally inflexible? Which ones show large amounts of short-run flexibility? Which ones show a great deal of inflexibility even over months and years? [LO6.5]

9. Why do many firms strive to maintain stable prices? [LO6.5]

10. Do prices tend to become more or less flexible as time passes? If there is a trend, how does it affect macroeconomists' choice of models? [LO6.6]

Review Questions

1. An increase in _____ GDP guarantees that more goods and services are being produced by an economy. [LO6.1]

   a. Nominal

   b. Real

2. True or False? The term *economic investment* includes purchasing stocks, bonds, and real estate. [LO6.3]

3. If an economy has sticky prices and demand unexpectedly increases, you would expect the economy's real GDP to [LO6.4]

   a. Increase

   b. Decrease

   c. Remain the same

4. If an economy has fully flexible prices and demand unexpectedly increases, you would expect that the economy's real GDP would tend to [LO6.4]

   a. Increase

   b. Decrease

   c. Remain the same

5. If the demand for a firm's output unexpectedly decreases, you would expect that its inventory would [LO6.4]

   a. Increase

   b. Decrease

   c. Remain the same

   d. Increase or remain the same, depending on whether prices are sticky

6. True or False? Because price stickiness only matters in the short run, economists are comfortable using just one macroeconomic model for all situations. [LO6.6]

Problems

1. Suppose that the annual rates of growth of real GDP of Econoland over a five-year period were as follows: 3 percent, 1 percent, −2 percent, 4 percent, and 5 percent. What was the average of these growth rates in Econoland over these five years? What term would economists use to describe what happened in year 3? If the growth rate in year 3 had been a positive 2 percent rather than a negative 2 percent, what would have been the average growth rate?   [LO6.1]

2. Suppose that Glitter Gulch, a gold mining firm, increased its sales revenues on newly mined gold from $100 million to $200 million between one year and the next. Assuming that the price of gold increased by 100 percent over the same period, by what numerical amount did Glitter Gulch's real output change? If the price of gold had not changed, what would have been the change in Glitter Gulch's real output?   [LO6.1]

3. A mathematical approximation called the *Rule of 70* tells us that the number of years it will take something that is growing to double in size is approximately equal to the number 70 divided by its percentage rate of growth. Thus, if Mexico's real GDP per person is growing at 7 percent per year, it will take about 10 years (= 70 ÷ 7) to double. Apply the Rule of 70 to solve the following problem. If real GDP per person in Mexico was $11,000 in 2008, while it was $44,000 per person in Canada, and if real GDP per person in Mexico grows at a rate of 5 percent per year, how long will it take Mexico's real GDP per person to reach the level that Canada was at in 2008? (*Hint:* How many times would Mexico's 2008 real GDP per person have to double in order to reach Canada's 2008 real GDP per person?)   [LO6.2]

4. Assume that a national restaurant firm called BBQ builds 10 new restaurants at a cost of $1 million per restaurant. It outfits each restaurant with an additional $200,000 of equipment and furnishings. To partially defray the cost of this expansion, BBQ issues and sells 200,000 shares of stock at $30 per share. What is the amount of economic investment that has resulted from BBQ's actions? How much purely financial investment took place?   [LO6.3]

5. Refer to Figure 6.1b and assume that price is fixed at $37,000 and that Buzzer Auto needs five workers for every automobile produced. If demand is D_M and Buzzer wants to perfectly match its output and sales, how many cars will Buzzer produce and how many workers will it hire? If, instead, demand unexpectedly falls from D_M to D_L, how many fewer cars will Buzzer sell? How many fewer workers will it need if it decides to match production to these lower sales?   [LO6.4]

CHAPTER 7

Measuring the Economy's Output

LEARNING OBJECTIVES

LO7.1 Explain how gross domestic product (GDP) is defined and measured.

LO7.2 Describe how expenditures on goods and services can be summed to determine GDP.

LO7.3 Explain how GDP can be determined by summing all of the incomes that were derived from producing the economy's output of goods and services.

LO7.4 Discuss the nature and function of a GDP price index, and describe the difference between *nominal GDP* and *real GDP*.

LO7.5 List and explain some limitations of the GDP measure.

Disposable Income Flat. Personal Consumption Surges. Investment Spending Stagnates. GDP Up 4 Percent. These headlines, typical of Yahoo! Finance or the *National Post*, give knowledgeable readers valuable information on the state of the economy. This chapter will help you interpret such headlines and understand the stories reported under them. Specifically, it will help you become familiar with the vocabulary and methods of national income accounting. Such accounting enables economists to measure the long-run rate of economic growth and identify the recessions and expansions associated with the economic ups and downs known as the *business cycle*. The terms and ideas in this chapter provide a foundation for the macroeconomic models in subsequent chapters.

7.1 / Measuring the Economy's Performance: GDP

LO7.1 Explain how gross domestic product (GDP) is defined and measured.

National income accounting measures the economy's overall performance. It does for the economy as a whole what private accounting does for the individual firm or household. (In Canada, all major national economic indicators are computed by Statistics Canada, our national statistics agency.) A firm measures its flows of income and expenditures regularly—usually every three months or once a year—to gauge its economic health. If things are going well and profits are good, the accounting data can be used to explain that success. Were costs down? Was output up? Have market prices risen? If things are going badly and profits are poor, the firm may be able to identify the cause by studying the record over several accounting periods. All of this information helps the firm's managers to plot their future strategy.

National income accounting operates in much the same way for the economy as a whole. Statistics Canada compiles the national income accounts for the Canadian economy. This accounting allows economists and policymakers to

- Assess the health of the economy by comparing levels of production at regular intervals
- Track the long-run course of the economy to see whether it has grown, been constant, or declined
- Formulate policies that will maintain and improve the economy's health

Gross Domestic Product

The main measure of the economy's performance is its annual total output of goods and services—or, as it is called, *aggregate output*. Aggregate output can be measured in several ways depending upon how an economy is defined. For instance, should the value of the cars produced at a Toyota plant in Ontario count as part of the output of the Canadian economy because they are made within Canada, or as part of the Japanese economy because Toyota is a Japanese company? The most common measure of aggregate output, **gross domestic product (GDP)**, clarifies this and other issues since it defines aggregate output as the dollar value of all final goods and services produced within the borders of a country during a specific period of time, typically a year. Under this definition, the value of the cars produced at the Toyota factory in Ontario clearly counts as part of Canadian aggregate output rather than Japanese aggregate output because the cars are made within the borders of Canada.[1]

A Monetary Measure

By necessity, GDP is a *monetary measure*. To see why, suppose that the economy produces three sofas and two computers in year 1 and two sofas and three computers in year 2. In which year is output greater? We can't answer that question until we attach a price tag to each of the two products to indicate how society evaluates their relative worth.

That's what GDP does. It measures the value of output in monetary terms. Without such a measure we would have no way to compare the relative values of the vast number of goods and services produced in different years. In Table 7-1 the price of sofas is $500 and the price of computers is $2000. GDP gauges the output of year 2 ($7000) as greater than the output of year 1 ($5500) because society places a higher monetary value on the output of year 2. Society is willing to pay $1500 more for the combination of goods produced in year 2 than for the combination of goods produced in year 1.

Avoiding Multiple Counting

To measure aggregate output accurately, all goods and services produced in a particular year must be counted only once. Because most products go through a series of production stages before they reach the market, some of their components are bought and sold many times. To avoid counting those components

---

[1] In contrast to GDP, Canadian gross *national* product (GNP) consists of the total value of all the final goods and services produced by Canadian-supplied resources, whether those goods and services are produced within the borders of Canada or abroad. Statistics Canada switched from GNP to GDP accounting in 1986 to match the type of accounting used by other countries worldwide.

TABLE 7-1	Comparing Heterogeneous Outputs by Using Money Prices	
Year	Annual output	Market value
1	3 sofas and 2 computers	3($500) + 2($2000) = $5500
2	2 sofas and 3 computers	2($500) + 3($2000) = $7000

more than once, GDP includes only the market value of *final goods* and ignores *intermediate goods* altogether. **Intermediate goods** are products that are purchased for resale or further processing or manufacturing. **Final goods** are products that are purchased by their end users. Crude oil is an intermediate good; gasoline used for personal transportation is a final good. Steel beams are intermediate goods; completed high-rise apartments are final goods. Lettuce, carrots, and vinegar in restaurant salads are intermediate goods; restaurant salads are final goods. Other examples of final goods are sunglasses bought by consumers, assembly machinery purchased by businesses, surveillance satellites bought by government, and smart phones purchased by foreign buyers.

Why is the value of final goods included in GDP but the value of intermediate goods is excluded? Because the value of final goods includes the value of all intermediate goods used in producing them. To include the value of intermediate goods would amount to **multiple counting**, and that would distort the value of GDP.

To see why, suppose there are five stages to manufacturing a woollen coat and getting it to the consumer—the final user. Table 7-2 shows that firm A, a sheep ranch, sells $120 worth of wool to firm B, a wool processor. Firm A pays out the $120 in wages, rent, interest, and profit. Firm B processes the wool and sells it to firm C, a coat manufacturer, for $180. What does firm B do with the $180 it receives? It pays $120 to firm A for the wool and uses the remaining $60 to pay wages, rent, interest, and profit for the resources used in processing the wool. Firm C, the manufacturer, sells the coat to firm D, a wholesaler, who sells it to firm E, a retailer. Then at last a consumer, the final user, comes in and buys the coat for $350.

How much of these amounts should we include in GDP to account for the production of the coat? Just $350, the value of the final product. The $350 includes all the intermediate transactions leading up to the product's final sale. To include the sum of all the intermediate sales, $1140, in GDP would amount to multiple counting. The production and sale of the final coat generated just $350, not $1140.

Alternatively, we could avoid multiple counting by measuring and cumulating only the *value added* at each stage. **Value added** is the market value of a firm's output *less* the value of the inputs the firm bought from others. At each stage, the difference between what a firm pays for inputs and what it receives from selling the product made from those inputs is paid out as wages, rent, interest, and profit. Column 3 of Table 7-2 shows that the value added by firm B is $60, the difference between the $180 value of its

TABLE 7-2	Value Added in a Five-Stage Production Process	
(1) Stage of production	(2) Sales value of materials or product	(3) Value added
	0	
Firm A, sheep ranch	$ 120	$120 (= $ 120 − $ 0)
Firm B, wool processor	180	60 (= 180 − 120)
Firm C, coat manufacturer	220	40 (= 220 − 180)
Firm D, clothing wholesaler	270	50 (= 270 − 220)
Firm E, retail clothier	350	80 (= 350 − 270)
Total sales value	$ 1140	
Value added (total income)		$350

output and the $120 it paid for the input from firm A. We find the total of the coat by adding together all the values added by the five firms. Similarly, by calculating and summing the values added to all the goods and services produced by all firms in the economy, we can find the market value of the economy's total output–its GDP.

GDP Excludes Nonproduction Transactions

Although many monetary transactions in the economy involve final goods and services, many others do not. These nonproduction transactions must be excluded from GDP because they have nothing to do with the production of final goods. *Nonproduction transactions* are of two types: purely financial transactions and second-hand sales.

FINANCIAL TRANSACTIONS

Purely financial transactions include the following:

- *Public Transfer Payments* These are the social insurance payments–for example, welfare and employment insurance–that the government makes directly to households. Since the recipients contribute nothing to *current production* in return, including such payments in GDP would overstate the year's output.

- *Private Transfer Payments* Such payments include, for example, money that parents give their children or the cash gifts given during the holidays. They produce no output. They simply transfer funds from one individual to another and consequently do not enter into GDP.

- *Stock Market Transactions* The buying and selling of stocks (and bonds) is just a matter of swapping bits of paper. Stock market transactions do not directly contribute to current production and are not included in GDP. Payments for the services provided by a stockbroker *are* included, however, because their services are currently provided and are thus a part of the economy's current output of goods and services.

SECOND-HAND SALES

Second-hand sales contribute nothing to current production and for that reason are excluded from GDP. Suppose you sell your 2007 Ford Mustang to a friend; that transaction would not be included in calculating this year's GDP because it generates no current production. The same would be true if you sold a brand-new Mustang to a neighbour a week after you purchased it.

Two Ways of Calculating GDP: Expenditures and Income

Let's look again at how the market value of total output is measured. Given the data listed in Table 7-2, how can we measure the market value of a coat? One way is to see how much the final user paid for it. That will tell us the market value of the final product. Or we can add up the entire wage, rental, interest, and profit incomes that were created in producing the coat.

The expenditures and income approaches are two ways of looking at the same thing: What is spent on making a product is income to those who helped to make it. If $350 is spent on manufacturing a coat, then $350 is the total income derived from its production. (See this chapter's Last Word for a third way in which Statistics Canada computes GDP: the value-added approach.)

We can look at GDP in the same two ways. We can view GDP as the sum of all the money spent in buying final goods and services, called the **expenditures approach**. Or we can view GDP in terms of the income derived or created from producing final goods and services, called the **income approach**. Buying (spending money) and selling (receiving income) are two aspects of the same transaction. On the expenditures side of GDP, all final goods produced by the economy are bought either by three domestic sectors (households, businesses, and government) or by buyers abroad. On the income side (once certain statistical adjustments are made), the total receipts from the sale of that total output go to the suppliers of factors of production as wages, rent, interest, and profit.

7.2 / The Expenditures Approach

LO7.2 Describe how expenditures on goods and services can be summed to determine GDP.

To determine GDP using the expenditures approach, we add up all the spending on final goods and services that has taken place throughout the year. Precise terms for the types of spending are listed in Table 7-3.

Personal Consumption Expenditures (C)

What we have called *consumption expenditures by households,* the national income accountants call **personal consumption expenditures**. This term covers all expenditures by households on goods and services.

In a typical year, roughly 10 percent of these personal consumption expenditures are on **durable goods**–products that have expected lives of three years or more. Such goods include new automobiles, furniture, and refrigerators. Another 30 percent are on **nondurable goods**–products with less than three years of expected life. Included are goods like food, clothing, and gasoline. About 60 percent of personal consumption expenditures are on **services**–the work done by lawyers, hair stylists, doctors, mechanics, and other service providers. Because of this high percentage, economists sometimes refer to the Canadian economy as a *service economy.*

National income accountants combine the household spending on durable goods, nondurable goods, and services and use the symbol C to designate the personal consumption expenditures component of GDP.

Gross Investment (I_g)

Gross investment (I_g) includes (1) all final purchases of machinery, equipment, and tools by firms; (2) all construction; (3) changes in inventories; and (4) intellectual property products (money spent on research and development (R&D) or the creation of new works of art, music, writing, and so on).

Notice that, except for the first item, this list includes more than we have meant by "investment" so far. The second item includes residential construction as well as the construction of new factories, warehouses, and stores. Why is residential construction regarded as investment rather than consumption? Because apartment buildings and houses, like factories and stores, earn income when they are rented or leased. Owner-occupied houses are treated as investment goods because they *could be* rented to bring in an income return. So, the national income accountants treat all residential construction as investment. Increases in inventories (unsold goods) are considered to be investment because they represent, in effect, unconsumed output. For economists, all new output that is not consumed is, by definition, capital. An increase in inventories is an addition (although perhaps temporary) to the stock of capital goods, and such additions are precisely how we define investment.

TABLE 7-3	Calculating GDP in 2014: The Expenditures Approach (billions of dollars)	
	GDP	**Percent of GDP**
Personal consumption expenditures (C)	1073	54.3
Gross investment (I_g)	467	23.6
Government current purchases of goods and services (G)	417	21.1
Net exports (X_n)	+18	+1.0
Gross domestic product at market prices*	**1975**	100.0

*Includes adjustments and statistical discrepancy. Numbers have been rounded.
Source: Statistics Canada Gross Domestic Product, expenditure-based. Accessed May 30, 2015. Updates at http://www.statcan.gc.ca/tables-tableaux/sum-som/l01/cst01/econ04-eng.htm

GDP statistics also include expenditures on R&D as well as money spent to develop new works of writing, art, music, and software as a form of investment. They do so because a country's stock of capital goods useful in producing output can be thought of as including not only tangible pieces of physical capital, such as fiber optic networks and factories, but also useful ideas that increase the economy's ability to produce goods and services. Software is a great example, as it is merely a set of instructions for telling computers what to do. But without those instructions, computers would be useless, so spending on software as well as on R&D and other intellectual activities that improve the economy's stock of "know-how" are now counted as investment.

Increases in inventories (unsold goods) are considered to be investment because they are unconsumed output.

POSITIVE AND NEGATIVE CHANGES IN INVENTORIES

Inventories can either increase or decrease over some period. Suppose they increased by $10 billion between December 31, 2014 and December 31, 2015. Thus, the economy produced $10 billion more output than was purchased in 2015. We need to count all output produced in 2015 as part of that year's GDP, even though some of it remained unsold at the end of the year. This is accomplished by including the $10 billion increase in inventories as investment in 2015. That way, the expenditures in 2015 will correctly measure the output produced that year.

Alternatively, suppose that inventories decreased by $10 billion in 2015. This "drawing down" of inventories means that the economy sold $10 billion more of output in 2015 than it produced that year. It did this by selling goods produced in prior years–goods already counted as GDP in those years. Unless corrected, expenditures in 2015 will overstate GDP for 2015. So, in 2015 we consider the $10 billion decline in inventories as *negative investment* and subtract it from total investment that year. Thus, expenditures in 2015 will correctly measure the output produced in 2015.

NONINVESTMENT TRANSACTIONS

So much for what investment is. You also need to know what it isn't. Investment does not include noninvestment transactions such as the transfer of paper assets (stocks, bonds) or the resale of tangible assets (houses, jewellery, boats). Such financial transactions merely transfer the ownership of existing assets. The investment in the GDP accounts is economic investment–the creation of *new* capital assets. The transfer (sale) of claims to existing capital goods does not produce new capital goods. Therefore such transactions (so-called financial investments) are not included as investment in the GDP accounts.

GROSS INVESTMENT VERSUS NET INVESTMENT

As we have seen, the category *gross investment*, or *gross capital formation*, includes (1) all final purchases of machinery, equipment, and tools; (2) all construction; (3) changes in inventories; and (4) spending on R&D and other activities that expand the economy's stock of technology and know-how. The word *gross* means that we are referring to all investment goods–both those that replace machinery, equipment, and buildings that were used up (worn out or made obsolete) in producing the current year's output and any net additions to the economy's stock of capital. Gross investment includes investment in replacement capital *and* in added capital.

In contrast, **net investment** includes *only* investment of added capital. The amount of capital that is used up over the course of a year is called **capital consumption allowance**, or simply *depreciation*. So

Net investment = gross investment − depreciation

In typical years, gross investment exceeds depreciation. Thus net investment is positive and the nation's stock of capital rises by the amount of net investment. As illustrated in Figure 7-1, the stock of

FIGURE 7-1

Gross Investment, Depreciation, Net Investment, and the Stock of Capital

When gross investment exceeds depreciation during a year, net investment occurs. This net investment expands the stock of private capital from the beginning of the year to the end of the year by the amount of the net investment. Other things equal, the economy's production capacity expands.

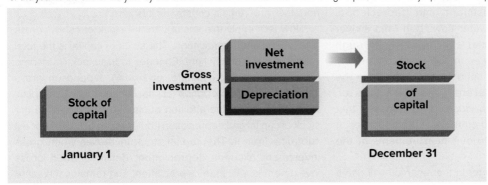

capital at the end of the year exceeds the stock of capital at the beginning of the year by the amount of net investment.

Gross investment need not always exceed depreciation, however. When gross investment and depreciation *are equal*, net investment is zero and there is no change in the size of the **capital stock**. When gross investment *is less than* depreciation, net investment is negative. The economy then is *disinvesting*–using up more capital than it is producing–and the nation's stock of capital shrinks. That happened in the Great Depression of the 1930s.

National income accountants use the symbol I for private domestic investment spending. To differentiate between gross investment and net investment, they add either a subscript g or a subscript n. But it is gross investment, I_g, that they use when tallying up GDP.

Government Purchases (G)

The third category of expenditures in the national income accounts is **government purchases**, officially labelled "general government final consumption expenditures" and "general government gross fixed capita formation gross investment" expenditures. These expenditures have two components: (1) expenditures for goods and services that government consumes in providing public services; (2) expenditures for *publicly owned capital*, such as schools and highways, which have long lifetimes; and (3) government expenditures on R&D and other activities that increase the economy's stock of know-how. Government purchases (federal, provincial, and municipal) include all government expenditures on final goods, investment goods, and all direct purchases of resources, including labour. Government purchases do *not* include *government transfer payments* because, as we have seen, they merely transfer government receipts to certain households and generate no production of any sort. Examples of government transfer payments are employment insurance benefits, welfare payments, and Canada Pension Plan benefits. National income accountants use the symbol G to signify government purchases.

Net Exports (X_n)

International trade transactions are a significant item in national income accounting. But when calculating Canadian GDP, we must keep in mind that we want to total up only those expenditures used to purchase goods and services produced within Canada. Thus, we must add in the value of exports, X, since exports are, by definition, goods and services produced *within the borders of Canada*. Don't be confused by the fact that the expenditures to buy our exports are made by foreigners. The definition of GDP does not care about *who* is making expenditures on Canadian-made goods and services–only that the goods and services they buy are made within Canada. Thus, foreign spending on our exports *must* be included in GDP.

CONSIDER THIS   Stocks versus Flows

A reservoir may be a helpful analogy in thinking about a nation's capital stock, investment, and depreciation. Picture a reservoir that has water flowing in from a river and flowing out from an outlet after it passes through turbines. The volume of water in the reservoir *at any particular time* is a "stock." In contrast, the inflow from the river and outflow from the outlet are "flows." Such flows are always measured over *some period of time*. Suppose that we measure these inflows and outflows at the end of each week and compare them with our measurements at the beginning of the week.

The volume, or stock, of water in the reservoir will rise if the weekly inflow exceeds the weekly outflow. It will fall if the inflow is less than the outflow. And it will remain constant if the two flows are equal.

We could simplify further by thinking in terms of the *net inflow* (inflow *minus* outflow) into the reservoir, where the net inflow can be positive or negative. The volume of water in the reservoir will rise if the net inflow is positive, decline if it is negative, and remain constant if it is zero.

Now let's apply this analogy to the stock of capital, gross investment, and depreciation. The stock of capital is the total capital in place at any time. Changes in this stock over some period of time (for example, one year) depend on gross *investment* and *depreciation* (capital consumption allowance). Gross investment (the addition of capital goods) adds to the stock of capital and depreciation (the using up of capital goods) subtracts from it. The capital stock increases when gross investment exceeds depreciation, declines when gross investment is less than depreciation, and remains the same when gross investment and depreciation are equal.

Alternatively, the stock of capital increases when *net investment* (gross investment *minus* depreciation) is positive. When net investment is negative, the stock of capital declines, and when net investment is zero, the stock of capital remains constant.

At this point, you might incorrectly think that GDP should be equal to the sum of $C + I_g + G + X$. But this sum overstates GDP. The problem is that, once again, we must consider only expenditures made on *domestically produced* goods and services. As it stands, C, I_g, and G count up expenditures on consumption, investment, and government purchases *regardless* of where those goods and services are made. Crucially, not all of the C, I_g, or G expenditures are for domestically produced goods and services. Some of the expenditures are for imports—goods and services produced outside of Canada. Thus, since we wish to count *only* the part of C, I_g, and G that goes to purchasing domestically produced goods and services, we must subtract the spending that goes to imports, M. Doing so yields the correct formula for calculating gross domestic product: $GDP = C + I_g + G + X - M$.

Accountants simplify this formula for GDP by defining **net exports**, X_n, to be equal to exports minus imports:

Net exports (X_n) = exports (X) − imports (M)

Using this definition of net exports, the formula for gross domestic product simplifies to

$$GDP = C + I_g + G + X_n$$

Table 7-3 shows that in 2014 Canada exported more to other countries than Canada imported from them. That is, net exports in 2014 were a positive $18 billion. In another year, net exports could be negative: imports would be greater than exports in that case.

Putting It All Together: GDP = $C + I_g + G + X_n$

Taken together, the four categories of expenditures provide a measure of the market value of a certain year's total output—its GDP.

For Canada in 2014 (in billions, from Table 7-3)

$$GDP = \$1073 + \$467 + \$417 + \$18 = \$1975$$

Global Perspective 7.1 lists the GDPs of several countries (values are converted to U.S. dollars using international exchange rates).

7.1 GLOBAL PERSPECTIVE

Comparative GDPs of Selected Nations, 2013 (trillions of dollars)

In 2013, Canada had the world's tenth highest GDP. The GDP data charted here have been converted to U.S. dollars using international exchange rates.

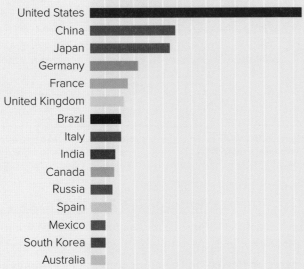

GDP in trillions of dollars

Source: World Bank. http://hdl.handle.net/123123123123/123. License: Creative Commons Attribution license (CC BY 3.0 IGO). The World Bank authorizes the use of this material subject to the terms and conditions on its website, http://www.worldbank.org/terms

7.3 / The Income Approach

LO7.3 Explain how GDP can be determined by summing all of the incomes that were derived from producing the economy's output of goods and services.

Table 7-4 shows how 2014's $1975 billion of expenditures were allocated as income to those producing the output. It would be simple if we could say that the entire amount of expenditures flowed back to them in the form of wages, rent, interest, and profit. But some expenditures flow to other recipients (such as the government) or to other uses (such as paying to replace the capital goods that have worn out while producing this year's GDP). These must be accounted for in order to balance the expenditure and income sides of the account. We will begin by looking at the items that make up **national income**.

Wages, Salaries, and Supplementary Labour Income

The largest income category is made up primarily of the wages and salaries paid by businesses and government to suppliers of labour. It also includes wage and salary supplements, in particular payments by employers of employment insurance premiums, workers' compensation premiums, and employer contributions to a variety of private and public pension funds for workers. Economists abbreviate all these as "wages."

TABLE 7-4	Calculating GDP in 2014: 1: The Income Approach (billions of dollars)	

	Percentage of GDP	
Wages, salaries, and supplementary labour income	$ 994	50.3
Profits of corporations and government enterprises before taxes	278	14.0
Interest and investment income	169	8.5
Net income of farm and unincorporated businesses	55	2.8
Taxes less subsidies on factors of production	77	3.9
Indirect taxes less subsidies on products*	121	6.1
Capital consumption allowances	280	14.1
Statistical discrepancy	1	0.3
Gross domestic product at market prices	**1975**	100.0

*Includes inventory valuation adjustment, which adjusts for price changes to corporate inventories carried from one year to the next. Numbers have been rounded.
Source: Statistics Canada Gross Domestic Product, ependiture-based. Accessed May 30, 2015. Updates at http://www.statcan.gc.ca/tables-tableaux/sum-som/l01/cst01/econ03-eng.htm

Profits of Corporations and Government Enterprises Before Taxes

Corporate profits are the earnings of government enterprises and the owners of corporations. Private corporations' profits are divided into three categories:

- *Corporate Income Taxes* These taxes are levied on the corporation's net earnings and flow to the government.

- *Dividends* These are the part of corporate profits that are paid to the corporate shareholders and thus flow to households–the ultimate owners of all corporations.

- *Undistributed Corporate Profits* This is money saved by the corporation to be invested later in new plant and equipment, also called *retained earnings*.

Interest and Investment Income

Interest income consists of money paid by private businesses to the suppliers of capital. This income includes interest on bonds and loans of capital. Investment income includes rental income received by households and imputed rent, that is, the estimated rent on housing that households use for their own purpose.

Net Income from Farms and Unincorporated Businesses

This is the earnings of farmers and proprietors from their own businesses. These earnings represent a mixture of labour income and investment income that is impossible to segregate. Farm and nonfarm proprietors supplying their own capital earn profits (or losses), interest, and rents mixed in with their labour income.

Adding Up Domestic Income

When we add up wages, salaries and supplementary labour income, corporate and government enterprise profits, interest and investment income, and income of farm and nonfarm unincorporated businesses, and make the appropriate inventory valuation adjustment, we get the *net domestic income at factor cost,* which is all the income earned by Canadian-supplied factors of production as wages, interest, rent, and profit. But to arrive at GDP we have to make two adjustments.

INDIRECT TAXES

The first adjustment is to add to net domestic income *indirect taxes,* less subsidies, which include general *sales taxes* (including GST), business property taxes, and customs duties.

Why do national income accountants add these indirect business taxes to wages, rent, interest, and profit in determining national income? They do this to account for expenditures that are diverted to the government. Consider an item that would otherwise sell for $1, but costs $1.05 because the government has imposed a 5 percent sales tax. When this item is purchased, consumers will expend $1.05 to buy it. But only $1 will go to the seller (who will then distribute it as income in the form of wages, rent, interest, and profit in order to compensate resource providers). The remaining 5 cents will flow as revenue to the government. The GDP accountants handle the extra 5 cents by placing it in the category called Taxes on Production and Imports and loosely consider it to be "income" to government.

DEPRECIATION: CAPITAL CONSUMPTION ALLOWANCE

The useful life of capital equipment (such as bakery ovens or automobile assembly lines) extends far beyond the year in which it was produced. To avoid understating profit and income in the year of purchase, and to avoid overstating profit and income in succeeding years, the cost of such capital must be allocated over its lifetime. The amount allocated is an estimate of the capital being used up each year in production, called *depreciation.*

The depreciation charge against gross investment is the capital consumption allowance–the allowance for capital goods consumed in producing this year's GDP. It is the portion of GDP that must be set aside to pay for the replacement of the capital goods used up in production. That part of this charge is the difference between gross investment, I_g, and net investment, I_n.

The money allocated to **consumption of fixed capital** (the depreciation allowance) is a cost of production and thus included in the gross value of output. But this money is not available for other purposes, and, unlike other costs of production, it does not add to anyone's income. So it is not included in national income. We must therefore add it to national income to achieve balance with the economy's expenditures, as in Table 7-4.

WORKED PROBLEM 7.1 Measuring Output and Income

Statistical Discrepancy

As you know, it should be possible to calculate GDP either by totaling expenditures or by summing incomes. Either method should give the same result. In practice, however, it is not possible to measure every input into either set of calculations with total precision. Difficulties arise due to a wide range of factors, including people misreporting their incomes on tax returns and the difficulty involved with accurately estimating depreciation. As a result, the GDP number produced by the income method always differs by a small percentage from the GDP number produced by the expenditures method. To account for this difference, national income accountants add a *statistical discrepancy* to national income. The addition of that number equalizes the GDP totals produced by the two methods. In 2014 the discrepancy value was $1 billion or 0.3 percent of GDP.

There are two more national income accounts concepts that will be useful for later chapters: personal income and disposable income. **Personal income (PI)** is the earned and unearned income available to resource suppliers and others before the payment of personal income taxes. **Disposable income (DI)** is personal income less personal taxes. As we will see in Chapter 9, disposable income is the main determinant of consumer spending.

7.4 / Nominal GDP versus Real GDP

LO7.4 Discuss the nature and function of a GDP price index, and describe the difference between nominal GDP and real GDP.

Recall that GDP is a measure of the market or money value of all final goods and services produced by the economy in a given year. We use money or nominal values to sum that heterogeneous output into a meaningful total. But, as alluded to in Chapter 6, that raises a question: How can we compare the market values of GDP from year to year if the value of money itself changes because of inflation (rising prices) or deflation (falling prices)? After all, we determine the value of GDP by multiplying total output (Q) by market prices (P).

Whether there is a 5 percent increase in output (Q) with no change in prices (P), or a 5 percent increase in prices (P) with no change in output (Q), the change in the value of GDP will be the same. And yet it is the *quantity* (Q) of goods that gets produced and distributed to households that affects our standard of living, not the price (P) of the goods. The hamburger that sold for $3 in 2015 yields the same satisfaction as an identical hamburger that sold for 50 cents in 1970.

The way around this problem is to *deflate* GDP when prices rise and to *inflate* GDP when prices fall. These adjustments give us a measure of GDP for various years, as if the value of the dollar had always been the same as in some reference (base) year. A GDP based on prices when the output was produced is called unadjusted GDP, or **nominal GDP**. A GDP that has been deflated or inflated to reflect changes in the price level is called adjusted GDP, or **real GDP**. Note that throughout the remaining chapters anytime we refer to GDP, it is always real GDP, unless otherwise stated.

Adjustment Process in a One-Product Economy

There are two ways to adjust nominal GDP to reflect price changes. For simplicity, let's assume that the economy produces only one good, pizza, in the amount indicated in Table 7-5 for years 1, 2, and 3. Suppose we gather revenue data directly from the financial reports of the pizza business to measure nominal GDP in various years. After completing our effort we will have calculated nominal GDP for each year, as shown in column 4 of Table 7-5. But we will have no way of knowing to what extent changes in price and/or changes in quantity of output account for the increases or decreases in nominal GDP that we observe.

PRICE INDEX

How can we calculate real GDP in our pizza economy? One way is to assemble data on the price changes that occurred over various years (column 2) and use them to establish an overall price index for the entire period. Then we can use the index in each year to adjust nominal GDP to real GDP for that year.

A **price index** is a measure of the price of a specified collection of goods and services, called a "market basket," in a specific year as compared to the price of an identical (or highly similar) collection of goods and

TABLE 7-5		Calculating Real GDP (base year = year 1)			
Year	(1) Units of output (Q)	(2) Price of pizza per unit (P)	(3) Price index (year 1 = 100)	(4) Unadjusted, or nominal, GDP (Q) × (P)	(5) Adjusted, or real, GDP
1	5	$10	100	$ 50	$50
2	7	20	200	140	70
3	8	25	250	200	80
4	10	30	—	—	—
5	11	28	—	—	—

services in a reference year. That point of reference, or benchmark, is known as the base period, **the base year**, or simply, the reference year. More formally,

$$\text{Price index in specific year} = \frac{\text{price of market basket in specific year}}{\text{price of same market basket in base year}} \times 100 \qquad (1)$$

By convention, the price ratio between a given year and the base year is multiplied by 100 to facilitate computation. For example, a price ratio of 2/1 (= 2) is expressed as a price index of 200. A price ratio of 1/3 (= 0.33) is expressed as a price index of 33.

In our pizza-only example, of course, our market basket consists of only one product. Column 2 of Table 7-5 reveals that the price of pizza was $10 in year 1, $20 in year 2, $25 in year 3, and so on. Let's select year 1 as our base year. Now we can express the successive prices of the contents of our market basket in, say, years 2 and 3 as compared to the price of the market basket in year 1:

$$\text{Price index, year 2} = \frac{\$20}{\$10} \times 100 = 200$$

$$\text{Price index, year 3} = \frac{\$25}{\$10} \times 100 = 250$$

For year 1, the base year, the price index is 100.

The index numbers tell us that the price of pizza rose from year 1 to year 2 by 100 percent [= (200 − 100)/100 × 100] and from year 1 to year 3 by 150 percent [= (250 − 100)/100 × 100].

DIVIDING NOMINAL GDP BY THE PRICE INDEX

We can now use the index numbers shown in column 3 to deflate or inflate the nominal GDP figures in column 4. The simplest and most direct method of deflating (or inflating) is to divide the price index into the corresponding nominal GDP. That gives us real GDP:

$$\text{Real GDP} = \frac{\text{nominal GDP}}{\text{price index}} \times 100 \qquad (2)$$

Column 5 of Table 7-5 shows the results. These figures for real GDP measure the market value of the output of pizza in years 1, 2, and 3 as though the price of pizza had been a constant $10 throughout the three-year period.

To test your understanding, extend Table 7-5 to years 4 and 5, using equation (2). Then run through the entire deflating procedure, using year 3 as the base period. This time you will have to inflate some of the nominal GDP data, using the same procedure as we used in the examples.

An Alternative Method

Another way to calculate real GDP is to gather separate data on physical outputs (*Q*) (as in column 1 of Table 7-5) and their prices (*P*) (as in column 2). We could then determine the market value of outputs in successive years *if the base-year price ($10) had prevailed*. In year 2, the seven units of pizza would have a value of $70 (= 7 units × $10). As column 5 confirms, that $70 worth of output is year 2's real GDP. Similarly, we could determine the real GDP for year 3 by multiplying the eight units of output that year by the $10 price in the base year.

Once we have determined real GDP through this method, we can identify the *implicit price index*, or **GDP deflator**, for a given year simply by dividing the nominal GDP by the real GDP for that year.

$$\text{GDP deflator} = \frac{\text{nominal GDP}}{\text{real GDP}} \times 100 \qquad (3)$$

WORKED PROBLEM 7.2   Real GDP and Price Indexes

For example, in year 2 we get a GDP deflator of 200, which equals the nominal GDP of $140 divided by the real GDP of $70 (× 100). Note that equation (3) is simply a rearrangement of equation (2). Table 7-6 summarizes the two methods of determining real GDP in our single-good economy.

Real-World Considerations and Data

In the real world of many goods and services, of course, determining GDP and constructing a reliable price index are far more complex matters than in our pizza-only economy. The national income accountants must assign a "weight" to each of the 380 categories of goods and services based on the relative proportion of each category in total output. They update the weights annually as expenditure patterns change, and roll the base year forward year by year using a moving average of expenditure patterns. The GDP price index used in the United States is called the *chain-type annual-weights price index*—which hints at its complexity.

Up to 2001, Statistics Canada established weights, based on price, for a base year for the 380 categories it uses in calculating the implicit price index, and changed these weights approximately every 10 years. Statistics Canada currently uses 2007 as the base year. This *fixed base price index* method, which we just studied, worked well as long as the weights remained relatively constant from year to year. But with the rapid expansion of the information technology (IT) sector, many prices for the outputs of this sector fell dramatically. Using 2007 prices as weights for the outputs of the IT sector would result in "overweighting"

TABLE 7-6   Steps for Deriving Real GDP from Nominal GDP

Method 1

1. Find nominal GDP for each year.
2. Compute a price index.
3. Divide each year's nominal GDP by that year's price index, then multiply by 100 to determine real GDP.

Method 2

1. Break down nominal GDP into physical quantities of output and prices for each year.
2. Find real GDP for each year by determining the dollar amount that each year's physical output would have sold for if base-year prices had prevailed. (The implicit price index, or GDP deflator, can then be found by dividing nominal GDP by real GDP, and then multiplying by 100.)

these goods and services. Since the output of the IT sector has grown rapidly in the last 20 years, such overweighting in essence overestimated GDP growth during this time period. Thus, in May 2001 Statistics Canada began to calculate a *chain-weighted index*, or chain Fisher index, which is adjusted annually to better represent the weight of each category, particularly the IT sector.

To better understand why Statistics Canada now calculates a chain-weighted index, let's look at an example. Consider an economy that has only two sectors, computers and pears, and consumers spend half of their income on pears and the other half on computers. We assume that the output of computers is rising at a very rapid 10 percent per year, while pear production is stagnant, remaining the same from year to year. We further assume that the price of computers falls relative to the price of pears over time, due to the rapid expansion of computer production. If we construct a fixed weighted index using prices (weights) prevailing in, say, 2015, the rapid output growth of computers will also translate into a very rapid growth rate of GDP. But that very rapid GDP growth rate is actually overstated because the price (the weight) of computers is falling. Moreover, consumers have not changed the proportion of their income that they spend on pears and computers. So, in situations where prices of some goods in the economy are falling, as has been the case in Canada in the IT sector in the last 20 years or so, the traditional fixed weight index to calculate real GDP is inadequate.

Rather than using only a base year, the new Statistics Canada method of calculating GDP considers both quantities and prices in the base year and the following year, and then averages the two. For example, if using 2015 prices as weights yields a real GDP increase of 4 percent in 2014, but using 2015 prices yields a GDP increase of 3 percent because some prices in the economy declined, the new chain-weighted index would give an increase of real GDP in 2015 of 3.5 percent (= (4 + 3)/2). You can see in this simple example that falling prices for some output in 2015 have reduced the growth rate of GDP compared to the fixed weighted method of calculating GDP.

The new index used by Statistics Canada is referred to as a chain-weighted index because it links each year to the previous year through the use of both the prior-year prices and current-year prices. For example, the calculation of the chain-weighted index would use both 2014 and 2015 prices to calculate real GDP growth in 2015. Since the 2014 chain-weighted index was arrived at using both 2013 and 2012 prices, the year 2013 is linked back—as the links of a chain are—to 2012, 2010, and previous years as well.

Table 7-7 shows some of the real-world relationships between nominal GDP, real GDP, and the GDP price index. Here the reference year is 2007, the base year Statistics Canada currently uses, and the index is set at 100. Because the price level has been rising over the long run, the pre-2007 values of real GDP (column 3) are higher than the nominal values of GDP for those years (column 2). This upward adjustment

TABLE 7-7	Nominal GDP, Real GDP, and the GDP Deflator*, Selected Years		
(1) **Year**	**(2)** **Nominal GDP**	**(3)** **Real GDP**	**(4)** **GDP deflator 2007 = 100**
1981	366.6	778.8	—
1985	495.6	859.0	57.7
1990	690.8	989.5	69.8
1995	826.2	—	76.6
2000	1098.2	—	82.9
2007	1565.9	1565.9	100.0
2010	1662.8	1593.4	—
2014	1974.8	1747.2	113.0

*Chain-type annual-weights price index.
Source: Statistics Canada. Gross GDP at: http://www.statcan.gc.ca/tables-tableaux/sum-som/l01/cst01/econ04-eng.htm, and Real GDP, expenditure-based, at http://www.statcan.gc.ca/tables-tableaux/sum-som/l01/cst01/econ05-eng.htm

means that prices were lower in the years before 2007, and thus nominal GDP understated the real output of those years and must be inflated.

Conversely, the rising price level on the post-2007 years caused nominal GDP figures for those years to over-state real output. So statisticians deflate those figures to determine what real GDP would have been in other years if 2007 prices had prevailed. Doing so reveals that real GDP has been less than nominal GDP since 2007.

By inflating the nominal pre-2007 GDP data and deflating the post-2007 data, government accountants determine annual real GDP, which can then be compared with the real GDP of any other year in the series of years. So the real GDP values in column 3 are directly comparable with one another.

Once we have determined nominal GDP and real GDP, we can calculate the GDP deflator. And once we have determined nominal GDP and the price index, we can calculate real GDP. For example, nominal GDP in 2014 was $1974.8 billion and real GDP was $1747.2 billion. So the price level in 2014 was 113.0 (= $1974.8/$1747.2 × 100), or 13 percent higher than in 2007. To find real GDP for 2014 we divide the nominal GDP of $1974.8 by the 2014 GDP deflator, and multiply by 100.

To test your understanding of the relationships between nominal GDP, real GDP, and the GDP deflator, determine the values of the GDP deflator for 1981 and 2010 in Table 7-7 and determine real GDP for 1995 and 2000. We have left those figures out on purpose.

QUICK REVIEW 7.2

- Nominal GDP is output valued at current prices. Real GDP is output valued at constant base-year prices.

- A price index compares the price (market value) of a basket of goods and services in a given year to the price of the same market basket in a reference year.

- Nominal GDP can be transformed into real GDP by dividing the nominal GDP by the GDP deflator and then multiplying by 100.

7.5 / Shortcomings of GDP

LO 7.5 List and explain some limitations of the GDP measure.

GDP is a reasonably accurate and highly useful measure of how well or how poorly the economy is performing. But it has several shortcomings as a measure of total output and of well-being (total utility).

Measurement Shortcomings

Although GDP is the best measure of overall output in an economy, it suffers from a number of omissions that tend to understate total output.

NONMARKET ACTIVITIES

Certain production transactions do not take place in any market—the services of stay-at-home parents, for example, and the labour of carpenters who repair their own homes. Such activities never show up in GDP because the accountants who tally up GDP only get data on economic transactions involving *market activities*—that is, transactions in which output or resources are traded for money. Consequently, GDP understates a nation's total output because it does not count *unpaid work*. The portion of farmers' output that farmers consume themselves is estimated and included in GDP.

7.2 GLOBAL PERSPECTIVE

The Underground Economy as a Percentage of GDP, Selected Nations

Underground economies vary in size worldwide. Three factors that help explain the variation are (1) the extent and complexity of regulation, (2) the type and degree of taxation, and (3) the effectiveness of law enforcement.

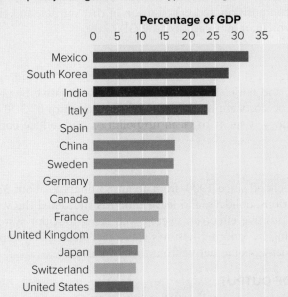

Percentage of GDP

Source: Friedrich Schneider, "Shadow Economies and Corruption All Over the World: New Estimates for 145 Countries," *Economics: The Open-Access, Open-Assessment E-Journal*, Vol. 1, 2007–9. http://www.economics-ejournal.org/economics/journalarticles/2007-9.

THE UNDERGROUND ECONOMY

In the Canadian economy there is a flourishing, productive underground sector. Some of the people who conduct business there are gamblers, smugglers, prostitutes, "fences" of stolen goods, drug growers, and drug dealers. They have good reason to conceal their income.

Most participants in the underground economy, however, engage in perfectly legal activities but choose (illegally) not to report their full income to the Canada Revenue Agency. A barista at a coffee shop may report just a portion of the tips received from customers. Storekeepers may report only a portion of their sales receipts. Unemployed workers who want to hold on to their employment insurance benefits may take an "off the books" or "cash only" job. A brick mason may agree to rebuild a neighbour's fireplace in exchange for the neighbour's repairing his boat engine. The value of such transactions does not show up in GDP, but is estimated to be about 15 percent of the recorded GDP in Canada–meaning that GDP in 2014 was understated by about $320 billion. Global Perspective 7.2 shows estimates of the relative sizes of underground economies in selected nations.

IMPROVED PRODUCT QUALITY

Because GDP is a quantitative measure rather than a qualitative measure, it fails to capture the full value of improvements in product quality. There is a very real difference in quality between a $200 cellphone purchased today and a cellphone that cost that same amount just five years ago. Today's cellphone is digital and has greater storage capacity, a clearer screen, and quite likely a camera and a music player.

Obviously quality improvement has a great effect on economic well-being, as does the quantity of goods produced. Although Statistics Canada adjusts GDP for quality improvements for selected items, the vast majority of such improvements for the entire range of goods and services do not get reflected in GDP.

Shortcomings of the Well-Being Measure

Although the output of goods and services is an important aspect of the well-being of the citizens of a nation, it is not the only factor. We must also consider environmental degradation caused by the production of goods and services, the composition and distribution of that output, and the importance of nonmaterial sources of well-being, which are not captured by GDP.

GDP AND THE ENVIRONMENT

The growth of GDP is inevitably accompanied by "gross domestic by-products," including dirty air and polluted water, toxic waste, congestion, and noise. The social costs of those negative by-products reduce our economic well-being. And since those costs are not deducted from total output, GDP overstates our national well-being. Ironically, when money is spent to clean up pollution and reduce congestion, those expenses are added to GDP!

LEISURE

The average workweek in Canada has declined since 1900–from about 53 hours to about 35 hours. Moreover, the greater frequency of paid vacations, holidays, and leave time has shortened the work year itself. This increase in leisure time has had a positive effect on overall well-being. But our system of national income accounting understates well-being by ignoring leisure's value. Nor does the system measure the satisfaction–the "psychic income"–that many people derive from their work.

COMPOSITION AND DISTRIBUTION OF OUTPUT

The composition of output is undoubtedly important for well-being. But GDP does not tell us whether the mix of goods and services is enriching or potentially detrimental to society. GDP assigns equal weight to an assault rifle and a computer, so long as both sell for the same price. Moreover, GDP reveals nothing about the way the output is distributed. Does 90 percent of the output go to 10 percent of the households, for example, or is the output more evenly distributed? The distribution of output may make a big difference for society's overall well-being.

NONMATERIAL SOURCES OF WELL-BEING

Finally, the connection between GDP and well-being is problematic for another reason. Just as a household's income does not measure its total happiness, a nation's GDP does not measure its total well-being. Many things could make a society better off without necessarily raising GDP: a reduction of crime and violence, peaceful relations with other countries, greater civility toward one another, better understanding between parents and children, and a reduction of drug and alcohol abuse.

The LAST WORD · Value Added and GDP

The third method by which Statistics Canada arrives at GDP is through the value-added approach. In this piece, Statistics Canada compares and contrasts the value-added approach with the expenditure-and-income approach in computing GDP in Canada.

Gross domestic product (GDP) by industry is one of the three GDP series produced by the Canadian System of National Accounts (CSNA). It is also known as the output-based GDP, because it sums the value added (output less intermediate consumption of goods and services) of all industries in Canada. This GDP series is published on a monthly basis and thus delivers the earliest and most up-to-date information on current developments in the economy. The other two GDP series are the income-based GDP, which tallies earnings that are generated by productive activity, and the expenditure-based GDP, which is equal to final expenditure on goods and services produced. Both the income-based and expenditure-based GDP measures are published on a quarterly basis.

The meaning of the word *output* in "output-based GDP" needs further explanation to avoid any confusion between its present definition in the International System of National Accounts 1993 (SNA 1993) and its earlier use. The output of an economy was always meant to be equal to *net output* (gross output of goods and services less the intermediate use of goods and services in its production). This net output is now called "value added" and the terms *gross output* and *net output* are no longer used in the SNA 1993. The three alternative GDPs are designed to independently but equivalently portray the production activity of the country, seen from different perspectives. With information on the sources of goods, services, and incomes generated by processes of production, the output-based GDP and the income-based GDP provide a comprehensive and detailed description of the supply side of domestic production.

Expenditure-based GDP, on the other hand, traces the disposition of the output produced among the various categories of demand, and thus offers a demand-side view of the Canadian economy. Changes in the level of production are key indicators of economic activity. Evaluating production, therefore, is fundamental in monitoring the behaviour of the economy. For this reason GDP is an indispensable tool for a broad range of analytical, modelling, and policy-formulation purposes. Governments, businesses, trade and labour organizations, academic researchers, journalists, and the general public use GDP figures to evaluate the performance of the economy, to appraise the success of monetary and industrial policies, to explore past trends in production, to forecast future prospects for economic growth, to carry out international comparisons, and so on.

Since economic activity is one of the several major factors influencing welfare policy, movements in GDP may also play a role in the assessment of the general well-being of the country. Estimates of the three GDP series are produced within the highly integrated conceptual and statistical framework of the CSNA, sharing a consistent set of concepts, definitions, and classifications. On an annual basis, the growth rates of the income-based and expenditure-based GDP are identical, and the year-to-year movements of the output-based GDP deviate only slightly. The small discrepancies in growth rates (less than two-tenths of one percent in any of the years between 1990 and 1998) are caused primarily by differences in the treatment of taxes and subsidies.

Source: Statistics Canada, Gross Domestic Product by Industry: Sources and Methods, 2002, p. 7, Catalogue No. at-547-XIE.

Question

Distinguish between (a) the value-added approach, (b) the expenditure approach, and (c) the income approach to calculating GDP.

Chapter Summary

LO7.1 EXPLAIN HOW GROSS DOMESTIC PRODUCT (GDP) IS DEFINED AND MEASURED.

- Gross domestic product (GDP), a basic measure of economic performance, is the market value of all final goods and services produced within the borders of a nation in a year.

- Final goods are those purchased by end users, whereas intermediate goods are those purchased for resale or for further processing or manufacturing. Intermediate goods, nonproduction transactions, and second-hand sales are purposely excluded when calculating GDP.

LO7.2   DESCRIBE HOW EXPENDITURES ON GOODS AND SERVICES CAN BE SUMMED TO DETERMINE GDP.

- GDP may be calculated by summing total expenditures on all final output or by summing the income derived from the production of that output.

- By the expenditures approach, GDP is determined by adding consumer purchases of goods and services, gross investment spending by businesses, government purchases, and net exports: $GDP = C + I_g + G + X_n$.

- Personal consumption expenditures consist of expenditures on goods (durable goods and nondurable goods) and services. About 60 percent of consumer expenditures in Canada are on services, leading economists to refer to the Canadian economy as a *service economy.*

- Gross investment is divided into (a) replacement investment (required to maintain the nation's stock of capital at its existing level), and (b) net investment (the net increase in the stock of capital). In most years, net investment is positive and therefore the economy's stock of capital and production capacity increase.

LO7.3   EXPLAIN HOW GDP CAN BE DETERMINED BY SUMMING ALL OF THE INCOMES THAT WERE DERIVED FROM PRODUCING THE ECONOMY'S OUTPUT OF GOODS AND SERVICES.

- By the income approach, GDP is calculated as the sum of wages and salaries, profits of corporations and government enterprises before taxes, interest and investment income, net income of farmers and unincorporated businesses, and the two noninvestment transactions (indirect taxes less subsidies and capital consumption allowances).

LO7.4   DISCUSS THE NATURE AND FUNCTION OF A GDP PRICE INDEX, AND DESCRIBE THE DIFFERENCE BETWEEN NOMINAL GDP AND REAL GDP.

- Price indexes are computed by dividing the price of a specific collection or market basket of output in a particular period by the price of the same market basket in a base period and multiplying the result (the quotient) by 100.

- The implicit price index, or GDP deflator, is used to adjust nominal GDP for inflation or deflation and thereby obtain real GDP.

- Nominal (current-dollar) GDP measures each year's output valued in terms of the prices prevailing in that year. Real (constant-dollar) GDP measures each year's output in terms of the prices that prevailed in a selected base year. Because real GDP is adjusted for price-level changes, differences in real GDP are due only to differences in production activity.

- A chain-weighted index to compute real GDP is constructed using an average of current and past prices as weights. It is particularly useful in an economy in which the prices of some outputs are declining.

LO 7.5   LIST AND EXPLAIN SOME LIMITATIONS OF THE GDP MEASURE.

- GDP is a reasonably accurate and very useful indicator of a nation's economic performance, but it has limitations. It fails to account for nonmarket and illegal transactions, changes in leisure and in product quality, the environmental effects of production, and the composition and distribution of output. GDP should not be interpreted as a complete measure of well-being.

Terms and Concepts

national income accounting	durable goods	national income
gross domestic product (GDP)	nondurable goods	consumption of fixed capital
intermediate goods	services	personal income
final goods	gross investment	disposable income
multiple counting	net investment	nominal GDP
value added	capital consumption allowance	real GDP
expenditures approach	capital stock	price index
income approach	government purchases	base year
personal consumption expenditures	net exports	GDP deflator

Discussion Questions

1. In what ways are national income statistics useful?   [LO7.1]

2. Why do national income accountants compare the market value of the total outputs in various years rather than actual physical volumes of production? What problem is posed by any comparison over time of the market values of various total outputs? How is this problem resolved?   [LO7.1]

3. Which of the following goods are usually intermediate goods and which are usually final goods: running shoes, cotton fibres, watches, textbooks, coal, sunscreen lotion, lumber? [LO7.1]

4. Why do economists include only final goods when measuring GDP for a particular year? Why don't they include the value of

the stocks and bonds bought and sold? Why don't they include the value of the used furniture bought and sold?   [LO7.1]

5. Explain why an economy's output, in essence, is also its income.   [LO7.1]

6. Provide three examples of each: consumer durable goods, consumer nondurable goods, and services.   [LO7.2]

7. Why are changes in inventories included as part of investment spending? Suppose inventories declined by $1 billion during 2012. How would this affect the size of gross investment and gross domestic product in 2012? Explain.   [LO7.2]

8. What is the difference between gross investment and net investment?   [LO7.2]

9. Use the concepts of gross investment and net investment to distinguish between an economy that has a rising stock of capital and one that has a falling stock of capital. Explain: "Though net investment can be positive, negative, or zero, it is impossible for gross investment to be less than zero."   [LO7.2]

10. Define net exports. Explain how Canadian exports and imports each affect domestic production. How are net exports determined? Explain how net exports might be a negative amount.   [LO7.2]

11. Contrast the ideas of nominal GDP and real GDP. Why is one more reliable than the other for comparing changes in the standard of living over a series of years? What is the GDP price index and what is its role in differentiating nominal GDP and real GDP?   [LO7.4]

12. Which of the following are actually included in deriving this year's GDP? Explain your answer in each case.   [LO7.5]

a. Interest on a Rogers Communications corporate bond

b. Canada Pension Plan payments received by a retired factory worker

c. The unpaid services of a painter in painting the family home

d. The income of a dentist from the dental services provided

e. The monthly allowance a college/university student receives from home

f. The money received by Josh when he resells his nearly brand-new Honda automobile to Kim

g. The publication and sale of a new college/university textbook

h. An increase in leisure resulting from a two-hour decline in the length of the workweek, with no reduction in pay

i. A $2 billion increase in business inventories

j. The purchase of 100 shares of Bank of Montreal stock

Review Questions

1. Tina walks into Ted's sporting goods store and buys a punching bag for $100. That $100 payment counts as _____ for Tina and _____ for Ted.   [LO7.1]

a. Income; expenditure

b. Value added; multiple counting

c. Expenditure; income

d. Rents; profits

2. Which of the following transactions would count in GDP? *Select one or more answers from the choices shown.*   [LO7.1]

a. Kerry buys a new sweater to wear this winter.

b. Patricia receives a Canada Pension Plan cheque.

c. Roberto gives his daughter $50 for her birthday.

d. Latika sells $1000 of Tim Hortons stock.

e. Karen buys a new car.

f. Amy buys a used car.

3. A small economy starts the year with $1 million in capital. During the course of the year, gross investment is $150,000 and depreciation is $50,000. How big is the economy's stock of capital at the end of the year?   [LO7.2]

a. $1,150,000

b. $1,100,000

c. $1,000,000

d. $850,000

e. $800,000

4. Suppose that this year a small country has a GDP of $100 billion. Also assume that I_g = $30 billion, C = $60 billion, and X_n = −$10 billion. How big is G?   [LO7.3]

a. $0

b. $10 billion

c. $20 billion

d. $30 billion

5. Suppose that Alberta imposes a sales tax of 10 percent on all goods and services. An Albertan named Ralph then goes into a home improvement store in the provincial capital of Edmonton and buys a leaf blower that is priced at $200. With the 10 percent sales tax, his total comes to $220. How much of the $220 paid by Ralph will be counted in the national income and product accounts as private income (employee compensation, rents, interest, proprietor's income, and corporate profits)?   [LO7.3]

a. $220

b. $200

c. $180

d. None of the above

6. Suppose that this year's nominal GDP is $1.6 trillion. To account for the effects of inflation, we construct a price-level index in which an index value of 100 represents the price level five years ago. Using that index, we find that this year's real GDP is $1.5 trillion. Given those numbers, we can conclude that the current value of the index is   [LO7.4]

a. Higher than 100

b. Lower than 100

c. Still 100

7. Which of the following items will be included in official Canadian GDP statistics? *Select **one** or **more** answers from the choices shown.*   [LO7.5]

a. Revenue generated by illegal marijuana growers in British Columbia

b. Money spent to clean up a local toxic waste site in Ontario

c. Revenue generated by legal medical marijuana sales in British Columbia

d. The dollar value of the annoyance felt by local citizens living near a noisy airport in Saskatoon

e. Robert paying Ted for a haircut in Winnipeg

f. Emily and Rhonda trading an hour of dance lessons for a haircut in Halifax

Problems

1. Suppose that annual output in year 1 in a three-good economy is 3 litres of ice cream, 1 bottle of shampoo, and 3 jars of peanut butter. In year 2, the output mix changes to 5 litres of ice cream, 2 bottles of shampoo, and 2 jars of peanut butter. If the prices in both years are $4 per litre for ice cream, $3 per bottle of shampoo, and $2 per jar of peanut butter, what was the economy's GDP in year 1? What was its GDP in year 2? [LO7.1]

2. Assume that a grower of flower bulbs sells its annual output of bulbs to an Internet retailer for $70,000. The retailer, in turn, brings in $160,000 from selling the bulbs directly to final customers. What amount would these two transactions add to personal consumption expenditures and thus to GDP during the year? [LO7.1]

3. If in some country personal consumption expenditures in a specific year are $50 billion, purchases of stocks and bonds are $30 billion, net exports are –$10 billion, government purchases are $20 billion, sales of second-hand items are $8 billion, and gross investment is $25 billion, what is the country's GDP for the year? [LO7.2]

4. Using the following national income accounting data, compute GDP by the expenditures approach. All figures are in billions. [LO7.3]

Wages, salaries, and supplementary labour income	$194.2
Canadian exports of goods and services	17.8
Capital consumption allowances (depreciation)	11.8
Government current purchases of goods and services	59.4
Net investment (net capital formation)	52.1
Canadian imports of goods and services	16.5
Personal consumption expenditures	219.1

5. Using the following national income accounting data, compute GDP by both the expenditures and income approaches. All figures are in billions.   [LO7.2, 7.3]

Profits of corporations and government enterprises before taxes	$ 46
Exports	94
Capital consumption allowances	65
Government current purchases of goods and services	113
Net income of farm and unincorporated businesses	24
Taxes less subsidies on factors of production	75
Wages, salaries, supplementary labour income	371
Gross investment	167
Indirect taxes less subsidies on products	11
Interest and investment income	59
Personal consumption expenditures	284
Imports	7

6. Suppose that in 1984 the total output in a single-good economy was 7000 buckets of chicken. Also suppose that in 1984 each bucket of chicken was priced at $10. Finally, assume that in 2005 the price per bucket of chicken was $16 and that 22,000 buckets were produced.   [LO7.4]

a. Determine the GDP price index for 1984, using 2005 as the base year. By what percentage did the price level, as measured by this index, rise between 1984 and 2005?

b. What were the amounts of real GDP in 1984 and 2005?

7. The following table shows nominal GDP and an appropriate price index group of selected years. Compute real GDP. Indicate in each calculation whether you are inflating or deflating the nominal GDP data. [LO7.4]

Year	Nominal GDP (billions)	GDP deflator (2007 = 100)	Real GDP (billions)
1981	366.6	47.1	$ _____
1991	696.9	71.8	$ _____
2001	1134.8	84.5	$ _____
2008	1646.0	103.9	$ _____
2011	1770.0	108.3	$ _____
2014	1974.8	113.0	$ _____

8. Assume that the total value of the following items is $600 billion in a specific year for Upper Mongoose: [LO7.5]

- net exports = $50 billion
- value of new goods and services produced in the underground economy = $75 billion
- personal consumption expenditures = $300 billion
- value of the services of stay-at-home parents = $25 billion
- gross domestic investment = $100 billion
- government purchases = $50 billion

    a. What is Upper Mongoose's GDP for the year?

    b. What is the size of the underground economy as a percentage of GDP?

    c. By what percentage would GDP be boosted if the value of the services of stay-at-home parents were included in GDP?

CHAPTER 8

Economic Growth

LEARNING OBJECTIVES

LO8.1 List two ways that economic growth is measured.

LO8.2 Define modern economic growth and explain the institutional structures an economy needs in order to experience it.

LO8.3 Identify the general supply, demand, and efficiency forces that give rise to economic growth.

LO8.4 Describe growth accounting and specific factors accounting for economic growth in Canada.

LO8.5 Explain why the trend rate of productivity growth in Canada has increased since the earlier 1973–1995 period.

LO8.6 Discuss differing perspectives on whether growth is desirable and sustainable.

People living in rich countries tend to take economic growth and rising standards of living for granted. Recessions–periods during which growth declines–are normally infrequent and temporary, usually lasting less than a year. Once they pass, market economies return to growing and living standards continue their seemingly inexorable rise.

But a look back at history or around the world today quickly dispels any confidence that economic growth and rising standards of living are automatic or routine. Looking back at history reveals that continually rising living standards are a recent phenomenon, seen only during the last century or two; before that, living standards barely rose from one generation to the next, if at all. And examining the modern world reveals huge differences in standards of living resulting from the disturbing fact that some countries have enjoyed decades or even centuries of steadily rising per capita income levels while others have experienced hardly any growth at all.

This chapter investigates the causes of economic growth, what government policies appear to promote economic growth, and the controversies surrounding the benefits and costs of economic growth. As you will see, economic growth has been perhaps the most revolutionary and powerful force in history. Consequently, no study of economics is complete without a thorough understanding of the causes and consequences of economic growth.

8.1 / Economic Growth

LO8.1 List two ways that economic growth is measured.

Economists define and measure **economic growth** as one of the following:

- An increase in real GDP occurring over some time period
- An increase in real GDP per capita occurring over some time period

With either definition, economic growth is calculated as a percentage rate of growth per quarter (three-month period) or per year. For the first definition, for example, real GDP in Canada was $1705.6 billion in 2013 and $1747.2 billion in 2014. So the rate of economic growth in Canada for 2014 was 2.4 percent, calculated as follows:

$$\text{Percent change in growth} = [(2014 \text{ real GDP} - 2013 \text{ real GDP})/2013 \text{ GDP}] \times 100$$
$$= [(\$1747.2 \text{ billion} - \$1705.6 \text{ billion})/\$1705.6 \text{ billion}] \times 100$$
$$= 2.4\%$$

The second definition takes into consideration the size of the population. **Real GDP per capita** (or *per capita output*) is the amount of real output per person in a country. It is calculated as follows:

$$\text{Real GDP per capita} = \frac{\text{real GDP}}{\text{population}}$$

For example, real GDP in Canada was $1705.6 billion in 2013 and population was 35.3 million. So real GDP per capita was $48,315. In 2014, real GDP per capita rose to $48,941. Therefore Canada's rate of growth of real GDP per capita for 2014 was 1.3 percent {= [($48,941 − $48,315)/$48,315] × 100}. In contrast, real GDP per capita fell by 2.8 percent in recession year 2009.

Unless specified otherwise, growth rates reported in the news and by international agencies use the growth of real GDP. For comparing living standards, however, the second definition is superior. While China's GDP in 2012 was U.S. $12,380 billion compared with Denmark's $332 billion, Denmark's real GDP per capita was $37,700 compared with China's hugely lower $9,100. And, in some cases, growth of real GDP can be misleading. The African nation of Eritrea had real GDP growth of 1.3 percent per year from 2000 to 2008, but over the same period its annual growth of population was 3.8 percent, resulting in a decline in real GDP per capita of roughly 2.5 percent per year.

Growth as a Goal

Growth is a widely held economic goal. The expansion of total output relative to population results in rising real wages and incomes and thus higher standards of living. An economy that is experiencing economic growth is better able to meet people's wants and resolve socioeconomic problems. Rising real wages and income provide richer opportunities to individuals and families–a vacation trip, a personal computer, a higher education–without sacrificing other opportunities and pleasures. With a growing economy a government can undertake new programs to alleviate poverty, embrace diversity, cultivate the arts, and protect the environment without impairing existing levels of consumption, investment, and public goods production. In short, *growth lessens the burden of scarcity.*

Arithmetic of Growth

Why do economists pay so much attention to small changes in the rate of growth? Because such changes really matter! For Canada, with a current real GDP of over $1 trillion, the difference between a 3 percent and a 4 percent rate of growth is more than $10 billion of output each year. For a poor country, a difference of one-half percentage point in the rate of growth may mean the difference between hunger and starvation.

The mathematical approximation called the **Rule of 70** provides a quantitative grasp of the effect of economic growth. It tells us that we can find the number of years it will take for some measure to double, given its annual percentage increase, by dividing that percentage increase into the number 70:

$$\text{Approximate number of years required to double real GDP} = \frac{70}{\text{annual percentage rate of growth}}$$

WORKED PROBLEM 6.1   GDP Growth

So, a 3 percent annual rate of growth will double real GDP in about 23 years (= 70 ÷ 3). Growth of 8 percent per year will double real GDP in about 9 years (= 70 ÷ 8). The Rule of 70 is applicable generally. For example, it also works for estimating how long it will take a price level or a savings account to double at various percentage rates of inflation or interest. When compounded over many years, an apparently small difference in the rate of growth thus becomes highly significant. Suppose China and Italy start with identical GDPs, but then China grows at an 8 percent yearly rate, while Italy grows at 2 percent. China's GDP would double in about 9 years but Italy's GDP would double in 35 years.

Growth in Canada

Table 8-1 gives an overview of economic growth in Canada over past years. Column 2 reveals strong growth as measured by increases in real GDP. Note that between 1961 and 2014 real GDP increased five-fold. But the Canadian population also increased. Nevertheless, in column 4 we find that real GDP per capita rose almost threefold over these years.

What has been the *rate* of growth in Canada? Real GDP grew at an annual rate of almost 3.3 percent between 1961 and 2014. Real GDP per capita increased at 2.1 percent per year over that time. But we must qualify these numbers in several ways.

- *Improved Products and Services* Since the numbers in Table 8-1 do not fully account for the improvements in products and services, they understate the growth of economic well-being. Such purely quantitative data do not fully compare an era of vacuum-tube computers and low-efficiency V8 hotrods with an era of digital cellphone networks and fuel-sipping hybrid-drive vehicles.

- *Added Leisure*   The increases in real GDP and per capita GDP identified in Table 8-1 were accomplished despite large increases in leisure. The standard workweek, once 50 hours, is now about 35 hours. Again, the raw growth numbers understate the gain in economic well-being.

- *Other Impacts*   These measures of growth do not account for any effects growth may have had on the environment and the quality of life. If growth debases the physical environment, excessively warms the planet, and creates a stressful work environment, the bare growth numbers will overstate the gains in well-being that result from growth. On the other hand, if growth leads to stronger environmental protections or a more secure and stress-free lifestyle, these numbers will understate the gains in well-being.

In Chapter 6, we made two other key points about Canada's growth rates. First, they are not constant or smooth over time. Like those of other countries, Canadian growth rates vary quarterly and annually depending on a variety of factors such as the introduction of major new inventions and the economy's current position in the business cycle. Second, although many countries share the Canadian experience of positive and ongoing economic growth, sustained growth is both a historically new occurrence and a phenomenon that is not shared equally by all countries.

TABLE 8-1   Real GDP and Per Capita GDP, 1961–2014

(1) Year	(2) GDP (billions of 2007 $)	(3) Population (millions)	(4) Per capita GDP (2007 $) (2) ÷ (3)
1961	322.7	18.3	17,633
1966	439.1	20.1	21,845
1971	534.0	22.0	24,272
1976	668.9	23.2	28,831
1981	789.8	24.9	31,171
1986	888.9	26.2	33,965
1991	977.3	28.1	34,779
1996	1116.8	29.7	37,602
2001	1348.3	31.1	43,353
2006	1541.6	32.7	47,143
2014	1747.2	35.7	48,941

Source: GDP: Canada. Canadian Economic Observer: Historical Statistical Supplement, accessed June 4, 2015 and CANSIM Table 380-0064. http://www5.statcan.gc.ca/cansim/a26?lang=eng&retrLang=eng&id=3800064&paSer=&pattern=&stByVal=1&p1=1&p2=-1&tabMode=dataTable&csid=, accessed June 9, 2015. The data from 1961 to 1976 have been converted from the 2002 base year to the 2007 base year by a factor of 1.22. Accessed June 4, 2015.Population data is from CANSIM Table 051-0005 http://www5.statcan.gc.ca/cansim/a26, accessed June 10, 2015

8.2 / Modern Economic Growth

LO8.2 Define modern economic growth and explain the institutional structures an economy needs in order to experience it.

We live in an era of wireless high-speed Internet connections, genetic engineering, and space exploration. New inventions and new technologies drive continual economic growth and ongoing increases in living standards. But it wasn't always like this. Economic growth and sustained increases in living standards are a historically recent phenomenon that started with the Industrial Revolution of the late 1700s. Before the Industrial Revolution, living standards were basically flat over long periods of time, so that, for instance, Greek peasants living in the year 300 BC had about the same material standard of living as Greek peasants living in the year 1500 AD. By contrast, our current era of **modern economic growth** is characterized by sustained and ongoing increases in living standards that can cause dramatic increases in the standard of living within less than a single human lifetime.

Economic historians informally date the start of the Industrial Revolution to the 1770s, when the Scottish inventor James Watt perfected a powerful and efficient steam engine. The steam engine–which could be used to drive industrial factory equipment, steamships, and steam locomotives–inaugurated the modern era. New industrial factories mass-produced goods for the first time, with nearly all manufacturing shifting to factories rather than being produced by hand by local craftsmen. The new steamships and steam locomotives meant that resources could easily flow to factories and that the products of factories could be shipped to distant consumers at low cost. The result was a huge increase in long-distance trade and a major population shift as people left farms to work in the towns and cities where the new industrial factories were concentrated. Steam power later would largely be replaced by electric power, and many more inventions followed the steam engine. These included railroads, motorized vehicles, telephones, airplanes, container ships, computers, the Internet, to name just a few. But the key point to remember is that the last 200 or so years of history have been fundamentally different from anything that went before.

 PRODUCTION AND THE STANDARD OF LIVING

The biggest change has been change itself. Whereas in earlier times material standards of living and the goods and services that people produced and consumed changed very little over the course of an entire human lifespan, today people living in countries experiencing economic growth are constantly exposed to new technologies, new products, and new services.

What is more, economic growth has vastly affected cultural, social, and political arrangements:

- Culturally, the vast increases in wealth and living standards have, for the first time in history, allowed ordinary people to have significant time for leisure activities and the arts.

- Socially, countries experiencing modern economic growth have instituted universal public education and have largely eliminated ancient social norms and legal restrictions preventing women and minorities from doing certain jobs or holding certain positions.

- Politically, countries experiencing modern economic growth have tended to move toward democracy, a form of government that was extremely rare before the start of the Industrial Revolution.

In addition, the average human lifespan has more than doubled, from an average of less than 30 years before economic growth began in the late 1700s to a worldwide average of over 67 years today. Thus, for the first time in world history, the average person can expect to live into old age. These and other changes speak to the truly revolutionary power of economic growth and naturally lead economists to consider the causes of economic growth and what policies could be pursued to sustain and promote it. Their desire is intensified by the reality that economic growth is distributed very unevenly around the world.

The Uneven Distribution of Growth

Modern economic growth has spread only slowly from its British birthplace. It first advanced to France, Germany, and other parts of Western Europe in the early 1800s before spreading to Canada, the United States, and Australia by the late 1800s. Japan began to industrialize in the 1870s, but the rest of Asia did not follow until the early to mid 1900s, at which time large parts of Central and South America, as well as the Middle East, also began to experience economic growth. Africa, for the most part, did not experience sustained economic growth until the past twenty years. Some parts of the world have yet to experience economic growth at all.

The different starting dates for modern economic growth in different parts of the world are the main cause of the vast differences in per capita GDP levels seen today. The huge divergence in living standards is best seen in Figure 8-1, which shows how GDP per capita has evolved since 1820 in Canada and the United States, Western Europe, Latin America, Asia, and Africa.

To make comparisons easy to interpret, income levels have been converted into 1990 U.S. dollars. Using this convention, it is clear that in 1820 per capita incomes in all areas were quite similar, with the richest area in the world in 1820, Western Europe, having an average per capita income of $1232, while the poorest area of the world at that time, Africa, had an average per capita income of $418. Thus, in 1820, average incomes in the richest area were only about three times larger than those in the poorest area.

But because Western Europe and North America started experiencing modern economic growth earlier than other areas, they have now ended up vastly richer than other areas, despite the fact that per capita incomes in nearly all places have increased at least a bit. For instance, per capita GDP in Canada in 1998 was $20,559, while it was only $1368 in Africa. Thus, because economic growth has occurred for nearly two centuries in Canada compared to a few decades in Africa, average living standards in Canada in 1998 were 15 times higher than those in Africa.

Catching Up Is Possible

Do not get the wrong impression from Figure 8-1. Countries that started to experience modern economic growth more recently are *not* doomed to be permanently poorer than the countries that began earlier. This is true because people can adopt technology more quickly than they can invent it. Broadly speaking, the richest countries today have achieved that status because they have the most advanced technology. But because rich countries already have the most advanced technology, they must invent new technology to get even richer. Because inventing and implementing new technology is slow and costly, real GDP per capita in the richest **leader countries** typically grows by an average annual rate of just 2 to 3 percent per year.

By contrast, poorer **follower countries** can grow much more quickly because they can simply adopt existing technologies from rich leader countries. For instance, in many places in Africa today, the first telephones most people have ever been able to use are cellphones. These countries have not bothered to install the copper wires necessary for land-line telephones, which are basically a 19th-century technology. Instead, they have gone directly for Internet-capable mobile phone networks, a 21st-century technology. By doing so, follower countries can skip past many stages of technology and development that Canada and other currently rich countries had to pass through. In effect, follower countries jump directly to the most up-to-date, most highly productive technology. The result is that, under the right circumstances, it is possible for poorer countries to experience extremely rapid increases in living standards that can continue until follower countries are caught up with the leader countries and become leader countries themselves. Once that happens, their growth rates typically fall down to the 2 to 3 percent rate typical of leader countries. This occurs because once follower countries become rich and are using the latest technology, their growth rates are limited by the rate at which new technology can be invented and applied.

Table 8-2 shows both how the growth rates of leader countries are constrained by the rate of technological progress and how certain follower countries have been able to catch up by adopting more advanced

---

FIGURE 8-1   **The Great Divergence in Living Standards**

Income levels around the world were very similar in 1820. But they are now very different because certain areas including Canada, the United States, and Western Europe began experiencing modern economic growth much earlier than other areas.

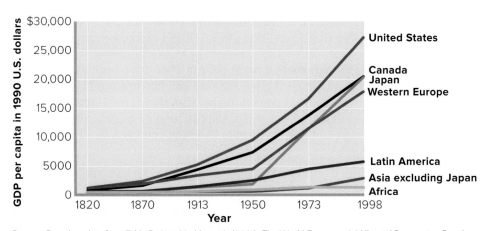

Source: Based on data from Table B–21 in Maddison, A. (2001), *The World Economy: A Millennial Perspective*, Development Centre Studies, OECD Publishing.http://dx.doi.org/10.1787/9789264189980-en

TABLE 8-2	Real GDP per Capita in 1960 and 2010 plus average annual growth rates of GDP per capita 1960–2010 for eight selected countries (figures are in 2005 dollars)		
Country	Real GDP per capita, 1960	Real GDP per capita, 2010	Average annual growth rate, 1960–2010
United States	14,776	41,365	2.1
Canada	12,901	37,110	2.1
United Kingdom	11,257	34,268	2.2
France	9,347	31,299	2.4
Ireland	6,666	34,877	3.3
Japan	5,472	31,477	3.5
Singapore	4,149	55,862	5.2
Hong Kong	3,849	38,865	4.6
South Korea	1,765	26,609	5.4

Source: Penn World Table version 7.1, pwt.econ.upenn.edu. Used by permission of the Center for International Comparisons at the University of Pennsylvania.
Note: GDP figures for all countries are measured in "international dollars" of equal value to U.S. dollars in 2005.

technologies and growing rapidly. Table 8-2 shows real GDP per capita in 1960 and 2010, as well as the average annual growth rate of real GDP per capita between 1960 and 2010, for four countries–the United States, Canada, the United Kingdom, and France–that were already rich leader countries in 1960, as well as for five other nations that were relatively poor follower countries at that time. To make comparisons easy, the GDP and GDP per capita for all countries are expressed in terms of 2005 U.S. dollars. The countries are in order according to their respective GDP per capita in 1960, so that the richest country in the world at the time, the United States, is listed first, while the poorest of the eight selected countries at the time, South Korea, is listed last.

First, notice that the average annual growth rates of the four leader countries have all been between 2.1 percent and 2.5 percent per year; their growth is limited by the rate at which new technologies can be invented and applied. By contrast, the five countries that were follower countries in 1960 have been able to grow much more quickly, between 3.5 percent per year and 5.4 percent per year. This has had remarkable effects on their standards of living relative to the leader countries. For instance, Ireland's GDP per capita was only about 60 percent of its neighbour, the United Kingdom, in 1960. But because Ireland grew at a 3.3 percent rate for the next 50 years while the United Kingdom grew at only a 2.2 percent rate, by 2010 Irish GDP per capita was actually higher than United Kingdom GDP per capita. Ireland had become a leader country, too.

The growth experiences of the other four nations that were poor in 1960 have been even more dramatic. Hong Kong, for instance, moved from a GDP per capita that was less than one-third of that enjoyed by the United Kingdom in 1960 to a GDP per capita 13 percent higher than that of the United Kingdom in 2010. The Consider This . . . Economic Growth Rates Matter! box emphasizes how quickly small differences in growth rates can change both the level of real GDP per capita and how countries stand in relation to each other in terms of real GDP per capita.

Institutional Structures That Promote Modern Economic Growth

Table 8-2 demonstrates that poor follower countries can catch up and become rich leader countries by growing rapidly. But how does a country start that process and begin to experience modern economic growth, and how does it keep the process going?

CONSIDER THIS | Economic Growth Rates Matter!

When compounded over many decades, small differences in rates of economic growth add up to substantial differences in real GDP and standards of living. Consider three hypothetical countries—Eclanum, Cumae, and Baiae. Suppose that in 2016 these countries had identical levels of real GDP ($6 trillion), population (200 million), and real GDP per capita ($30,000). Also assume that annual real GDP growth is 2 percent in Eclanum, 3 percent in Cumae, and 4 percent in Baiae.

How will these alternative growth rates affect real GDP and real GDP per capita over a long period, say, a 70-year life span? By 2086, the 2 percent, 3 percent, and 4 percent growth rates would boost real GDP from $1 trillion to approximately

- $24 trillion in Eclanum
- $47 trillion in Cumae
- $93 trillion in Baiae

For illustration, let's assume that each country experienced an average annual population growth of 1 percent over the 70 years. Then, in 2086 real GDP per capita would be about

- $60,000 in Eclanum
- $118, 000 in Cumae
- $233,000 in Baiae

Even small differences in growth rates matter!

Economic historians have identified several institutional structures that promote and sustain economic growth. Some structures increase the savings and investment that are needed to fund the construction and maintenance of the huge amounts of infrastructure required to run economies. Other institutional structures promote the development of new technologies. And still others act to ensure that resources flow efficiently to their most productive uses. These growth-promoting institutional structures include:

- **Strong Property Rights**   These appear to be absolutely necessary for rapid and sustained economic growth. People will not invest if they believe that thieves, bandits, or a rapacious and tyrannical government will steal their investments or their expected returns.

- **Patents and Copyrights**   Before patents and copyrights were first issued and enforced, inventors and authors usually saw their ideas stolen before they could profit from them. By giving inventors and authors the exclusive right to market and sell their creations, patents and copyrights give a strong financial incentive to invent and create.

- **Efficient Financial Institutions**   These are needed to channel the savings generated by households toward the businesses, entrepreneurs, and inventors who do most of society's investing and inventing. Banks as well as stock and bond markets appear to be institutions crucial to economic growth.

- **Literacy and Education**   Without highly educated inventors, new technologies do not get developed. And without a highly educated workforce, it is impossible to implement those technologies and put them to productive use.

- **Free Trade**   Free trade promotes economic growth by allowing countries to specialize so that different types of output can be produced where they can be made at the lowest opportunity cost. In addition, free trade promotes the rapid dissemination of new ideas so that innovations made in one country quickly spread to other countries.

- **Competitive Market System**   Under a market system, prices and profits serve as the signals that tell firms what to make, and in what quantity. Rich leader countries vary substantially in terms of how much government regulation they impose on markets, but in all cases, firms have substantial autonomy to follow market signals not only in terms of current production but also in terms of the investments they will currently make to produce what they believe consumers will demand in the future.

CONSIDER THIS   Patents and Innovation

It costs North American and European drug companies about $1 billion to research, patent, and safety-test a new drug because literally thousands of candidate drugs fail for each drug that succeeds. The only way to cover these costs is by relying on patent protections that give a drug's developer the exclusive monopoly right to market and sell the new drug for 20 years following the patent application. It is hoped that the revenues over that time period will be enough to cover the drug's development costs and—if the drug is popular—generate a profit for the drug company. Once the 20 years are over, however, the drug will go off patent and anyone will be able to manufacture and sell it.

Leader and follower countries have gotten into heated disputes over patented drugs, however, because the follower countries have often refused to recognize the patents granted to pharmaceutical companies in rich countries. India, for instance, has allowed local drug companies to copy and sell drugs that were developed by American companies and that are still under patent protection in the United States.

That policy benefits Indian consumers because competition among the local drug companies drives down the price to below the monopoly price that would be charged by the patent owner. But the weak patent protections in India have a side effect. They make it completely unprofitable for local drug producers to try to develop innovative new drugs. Local rivals would simply copy the new drugs and sell them at very low prices. So, India has recently moved to strengthen its patent protections to try to provide financial incentives to transform its local drug companies from copycats into innovators. But note that the innovative new drugs that may result from the increased patent protections are not without a cost. As patent protections in India are improved, inexpensive copycat drugs from leader countries will no longer be available to Indian consumers.

Several other difficult-to-measure factors also influence a nation's capacity for economic growth. For example, Canada's overall social, cultural, and political environment has encouraged economic growth. Beyond the market system that has prevailed, Canada has also had a stable political system characterized by democratic principles, internal order, the right of property ownership, the legal status of enterprise, and the enforcement of contracts. Economic freedom and political freedom have been "growth friendly."

In addition, and unlike some nations, virtually no social or moral taboos on production and material progress exist in Canada. The nation's social philosophy has embraced wealth creation as an attainable and desirable goal and the inventor, the innovator, and the business person are accorded high degrees of prestige and respect in Canadian society. Finally, Canadians have a positive attitude toward work and risk taking, resulting in an ample supply of willing workers and innovative entrepreneurs. A flow of energetic immigrants has greatly augmented that supply.

The Consider This . . . Patents and Innovation box deals with how fast-growing follower countries such as India sometimes alter their growth-related institutional structures as they grow richer. Chapter 17B looks at the special problems of economic growth in developing nations.

  PRODUCTION AND THE STANDARD OF LIVING

QUICK REVIEW 8.2

- Before the advent of modern economic growth in the late 1700s, starting in England, living standards showed no sustained increases over time.

- Large differences in standards of living exist today because certain areas of the world have experienced nearly 200 years of economic growth, while other areas have had only a few decades of economic growth.

- Poor follower countries can catch up with and even surpass the living standards of rich leader countries by adopting the cutting-edge technologies and institutions already developed by rich leader countries.

- Institutional structures that promote growth include strong property rights, patents and copyrights, efficient financial institutions, literacy and education, free trade, and a competitive market system.

8.3 / Determinants of Growth

LO8.3 Identify the general supply, demand, and efficiency forces that give rise to economic growth.

Our discussion of economic growth and the institutional structures that promote it has purposely been general. We now want to focus our discussion on six factors that directly affect the *rate* and quality of economic growth. These determinants of economic growth can be grouped into four supply factors, one demand factor, and one efficiency factor.

Supply Factors

The first four determinants of economic growth relate to the physical ability of the economy to expand:

- Increases in the quantity and quality of natural resources
- Increases in the quantity and quality of human resources
- Increases in the supply (or stock) of capital goods
- Improvements in technology

ORIGIN OF THE IDEA 8.1 Growth Theory

Any increases or improvements in these **supply factors** will increase the potential size of an economy's GDP. The remaining two factors are necessary for that potential to be fulfilled, not just in terms of the overall quantity of output but also in terms of the quality of that output and whether it is properly directed toward producing the items most highly valued by society.

Demand Factor

The fifth determinant of economic growth is the **demand factor**:

- To actually achieve the higher production potential created when the supply factors increase or improve, households, businesses, and the government must also expand their purchases of goods and services so as to provide a market for all the new output that can potentially be produced.

If that occurs, there will be no unplanned increases in inventories, and resources will remain fully employed. The demand factor acknowledges that economic growth requires increases in total spending if we are to actually realize the output gains made available by increased production capacity.

Efficiency Factor

The sixth determinant of economic growth is the **efficiency factor**:

- To reach its full production potential, an economy must achieve economic efficiency as well as full employment. The economy must use its resources in the least costly way (productive efficiency) to produce the specific mix of goods and services that maximize people's well-being (allocative efficiency). The ability to expand production, together with the full use of available resources, is not sufficient for achieving maximum possible growth. Also required is the efficient use of those resources.

The supply, demand, and efficiency factors in economic growth are related. Unemployment caused by insufficient total spending (the demand factor) may lower the rate of new capital accumulation (a supply factor) and delay expenditures on research (also a supply factor). Conversely, low spending on investment (a supply factor) may cause insufficient spending (the demand factor) and unemployment. Widespread inefficiency in the use of resources (the efficiency factor) may translate into higher costs of goods and services and thus lower profits, which in turn may slow innovation and reduce the accumulation of capital (supply factors). Economic growth is a dynamic process in which the supply, demand, and efficiency factors all interact.

Production Possibilities Analysis

To put the six factors affecting the rate of economic growth into better perspective, let's use the production possibilities analysis introduced in Chapter 1.

GROWTH AND PRODUCTION POSSIBILITIES

Recall that a curve like *AB* in Figure 8-2 is a production possibilities curve. It indicates the various *maximum* combinations of products an economy can produce with its fixed quantity and quality of natural, human, and capital resources and its associated stock of technological knowledge. An improvement in any of the supply factors will push the production possibilities curve outward, as from *AB* to *CD*.

But the demand factor reminds us that an increase in total spending is needed to move the economy from a point like *a* on curve *AB* to any of the points on the higher curve *CD*. And the efficiency factor reminds us that the location on *CD* must be optimal for the resources to make their maximum possible dollar contribution to total output. You will recall from Chapter 1 that this "best allocation" is determined by expanding production of each good until its marginal benefit equals its marginal cost. Here, we assume that this optimal combination of capital and consumer goods occurs at point *b*. If the efficiency factor is in full effect, then the economy will produce at point *b* rather than at any other point along curve CD.

For example, the net increase in the size of the labour force in Canada in recent years has been 250,000 to 300,000 workers per year. That increment raises the economy's production capacity. But obtaining the extra output that these added workers could produce depends on their success in finding jobs. It also depends on whether the jobs are in firms and industries where the workers' talents are fully and optimally used. Society does not want new labour-force entrants to be unemployed. Nor does it want pediatricians working as plumbers, or pediatricians producing pediatric services for which marginal costs exceed marginal benefits.

Normally, increases in total spending match increases in production capacity and the economy moves from a point on the previous production possibilities curve to a point on the expanded curve. Moreover, the competitive market system tends to drive the economy toward productive and allocative efficiency. Occasionally the curve may shift outward but leave the economy behind at some level of operation, such as *c* in Figure 8-2. Occasionally, however, the economy may end up at some point such as *c*. That kind of outcome occurred in Canada during the severe recession of 2008–2009. Real output fell far below the

---

FIGURE 8-2   **Economic Growth and the Production Possibilities Curve**

Economic growth is made possible by the four supply factors that shift the production possibilities curve outward, as from *AB* to *CD*. Economic growth is realized when the demand factor and the efficiency factor move the economy from points such as *a* and *c* that are inside *CD*, to the optimal output point, which is assumed to be point *b* in this figure.

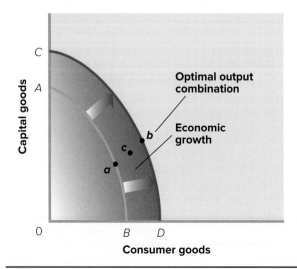

amount of output that the economy could have produced if it had achieved full employment and operated on its production possibilities curve.

LABOUR AND PRODUCTIVITY

Although demand and efficiency factors are important, discussions of economic growth focus primarily on supply factors. Society can increase its real output and income in two fundamental ways: (1) by increasing its inputs of resources, and (2) by raising the productivity of those inputs. Figure 8-3 focuses on the input of *labour* and provides a useful framework for discussing the role of supply factors in growth. A nation's real GDP in any year depends on the input of labour (measured in worker-hours) multiplied by **labour productivity** (measured as real output per worker per hour).

Real GDP = worker-hours × labour productivity

Or, expressed in terms of percentage change

% change in GDP = % change in worker-hours + % change in productivity

WORKED PROBLEM 8.2   Productivity and Economic Growth

Thought of in this way, a nation's economic growth from one year to the next depends on its *increase* in labour inputs (if any) and its *increase* in labour productivity (if any). As an illustration, suppose the hypothetical economy of Ziam has 10 workers in year 1, each working 2000 hours per year (50 weeks at 40 hours per week). The total input of labour, therefore, is 20,000 hours. If productivity (average real output per worker hour) is $10 per hour, then real GDP in Ziam will be $200,000 (= 20,000 × $10) per year. If worker-hours rise to 20,200 and labour productivity rises to $10.40 per hour, Ziam's real GDP will increase to $210,080 in year 2. Ziam's rate of economic growth will be about 5 percent [= ($210,080 − $200,000)/$200,000] for the year.

- ***Hours of Work*** What determines the number of hours worked each year? As shown in Figure 8-3, the hours of labour input depend on the size of the employed labour force and the length of the average workweek. Not shown, labour-force size depends on the size of the working-age population and the **labour force participation rate**–the percentage of the working-age population actually in the labour force. The length of the average workweek is governed by legal and institutional considerations and by collective bargaining agreements negotiated between unions and employers.

FIGURE 8-3   The Supply Determinants of Real Output

Real GDP is usefully viewed as the product of the quantity of labour inputs (worker-hours) multiplied by labour productivity.

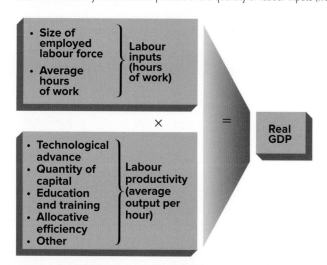

- *Labour Productivity* Figure 8-3 tells us that labour productivity is determined by technological progress, the quantity of capital goods available to workers, the quality of labour itself, and the efficiency with which inputs are allocated, combined, and managed. Productivity rises when the health, training, education, and motivation of workers improve, when workers have more and better machinery and natural resources with which to work, when production is better organized and managed, and when labour is reallocated from less efficient industries to more efficient industries.

8.4 / Accounting for Growth in Canada

LO8.4 Describe growth accounting and specific factors accounting for economic growth in Canada.

Output growth in Canada has been considerably greater in the last half century than can be attributed solely to increases in the inputs of labour and capital. Two other causes are involved.

The first cause is interindustry shifts from lower- to higher-productivity occupations. The best-known example is the shift of workers out of relatively low-productivity farming to higher-productivity urban industry.

The second cause is multifactor productivity (MFP), the efficiency with which factors are used together in the production process. It includes technological progress, organizational structure, economies of scale, regulation, entrepreneurship and risk taking, labour-management relations, capacity utilization, and the efficiency with which resources are allocated. MFP growth is output growth less input growth. Table 8-3 shows the annual growth rate of productivity in Canada in the post-World War II period. The output of the Canadian economy grew at almost 4 percent per year during the entire period, while employment increased by 1.7 percent. Output growth per worker averaged 2 percent per year for the 65-year period. We also show **productivity growth** rates for a number of sub-periods. What stands out is the rapid growth of output and productivity for the period up to 1973 compared to the subsequent sub-periods. Let's briefly take a look at the sources of growth in Canada.

Inputs versus Productivity

About two-thirds of Canada's growth rate in the last half century has been due to the use of more inputs and about one-third to rising productivity—getting more output per unit of labour and capital input. Thus, productivity growth has been a significant force underlying the growth of our real GDP.

Quantity of Labour

The Canadian population and the size of the labour force have both expanded significantly. Between 1945 and 2014, total population grew from 12 million to over 35 million, and the labour force increased from

TABLE 8-3	Annual Average Growth Rates of Productivity in Canada, 1946–2011*				
Years	Output	Employment	Hours worked	Output per worker	Output per hour
1946–2014	3.8	1.7	1.2	2.0	2.5
1946–1973	5.0	1.6	0.9	3.3	4.0
1973–1981	3.5	2.7	2.0	0.8	1.4
1981–1989	3.3	1.8	1.8	1.4	1.5
1989–2014	2.3	1.3	1.0	1.0	1.3

* The business sector
Source: Centre for the Study of Living Standards, http://www.csls.ca/data/ipt1.asp. Accessed May 31, 2015.

4.5 million to over 18 million workers. Reductions in the length of the workweek reduced the growth of labour inputs before World War II, but the workweek has remained relatively stable since then. Falling birth rates over the past 30 years have slowed the growth of the citizen-born population, but increased immigration has offset that slowdown. Of greatest significance has been the surge of women's participation in the labour force. Partly because of that increased participation, Canadian labour force growth has averaged over 200,000 workers per year during the past few decades.

Because increases in labour productivity are so important to economic growth, economists go to the trouble of investigating and assessing the relative importance of the factors that contribute to productivity growth. Five factors appear to explain changes in productivity growth rates: (1) technological advance, (2) the amount of capital each worker has to work with, (3) education and training, (4) economies of scale, and (5) resource allocation. We will examine each factor in turn, noting how much each factor contributes to productivity growth.

Technological Advance

The largest contributor to productivity growth is technological advance, which is thought to account for about 40 percent of productivity growth. As economist Paul Romer stated, "Human history teaches us that economic growth springs from better recipes, not just from more cooking."

Technological advance includes not only innovative production techniques, but also new managerial methods and new forms of business organization that improve the process of production. Generally, technological advance is generated by the discovery of new knowledge, which allows for resources to be combined in new ways that increase output. Once discovered and implemented, new knowledge soon becomes available to entrepreneurs and firms at relatively low cost. Technological advance therefore eventually spreads through the entire economy, boosting productivity and economic growth.

Technological advance and capital formation (investment) are closely related, since technological advance usually promotes investment in new machinery and equipment. In fact, technological advance is often *embodied* within new capital. For example, the purchase of new computers brings into industry speedier, more powerful computers that incorporate new technology.

Technological advance has been both rapid and profound. Gas and diesel engines, conveyor belts, and assembly lines were significant developments of the past. So, too, were fuel-efficient commercial aircraft, integrated microcircuits, personal computers, digital photography, and containerized shipping. More recently, technological advance has exploded, particularly in the areas of wireless communication, computers, photography, and the Internet. Other fertile areas of recent innovation are medicine and biotechnology. Government investment in basic research has facilitated technological advance in Canada.

Quantity of Capital

A key determinant of productivity growth is the amount of capital goods available *per worker*. If both the aggregate stock of capital goods and the size of the labour force increase rapidly over a given period, the individual worker is not necessarily better equipped and productivity will not necessarily rise. But the quantity of capital equipment available per worker in Canada has increased greatly over time.

Public investment in Canada's **infrastructure** (highways and bridges, public transit systems, wastewater treatment facilities, water systems, airports, educational facilities, and so on) has also grown. This publicly owned capital complements private capital. Investments in new highways promote private investment in new factories and retail stores along their routes. Industrial parks developed by local governments attract manufacturing and distribution firms.

Education and Training

Education and training contribute to a worker's stock of **human capital**–the knowledge and skill that make for a productive worker. Perhaps the simplest measure of labour quality is the level of educational attainment. Investment in human capital includes not only formal education but also on-the-job training.

Like investment in physical capital, investment in human capital is an important means of increasing labour productivity and earnings. An estimated 15 percent of productivity growth derives from investments in people's education and skills. An indication of educational attainment is the number of students attending university in Canada. In the academic year 2005-2006, the number of students enrolled at Canadian universities surpassed the 1 million mark for the first time. The fact that post-secondary education is subsidized in Canada is certainly a contributing factor for the rapid increase in the number of university students.

Economies of Scale and Resource Allocation

Economies of scale and improved resource allocation are a fourth and fifth source of productivity growth, and together are estimated to account for about 15 percent of productivity growth.

Education and training contribute to a worker's stock of human capital.

ECONOMIES OF SCALE

Reductions in per-unit production costs that result from the increases in output levels are called **economies of scale**. Markets have increased in size over time, allowing firms to increase output levels and thereby achieve production advantages associated with greater size. As firms expand, they use more efficient plants, equipment, and methods of manufacturing and delivery that result in greater productivity. They also are better able to recoup substantial investments in developing new products and production methods. Here are some examples. A large manufacturer of autos can use elaborate assembly lines with computerization and robotics, while smaller producers must settle for less advanced technologies using more labour inputs. And large pharmaceutical firms greatly reduce the average amount of labour (researchers, production workers) needed to produce each pill as they increase the number of pills produced. Accordingly, economies of scale enable greater real GDP and thus contribute to economic growth.

IMPROVED RESOURCE ALLOCATION

Improved resource allocation means that workers have moved over time from low-productivity employment to high-productivity employment. Historically, many workers have shifted from agriculture, where labour productivity is low, to manufacturing, where it is quite high. More recently, labour has shifted away from manufacturing industries to even higher-productivity industries such as computer software, business consulting, and pharmaceuticals. As a result of such shifts, the average productivity of Canadian workers has increased.

Also, discrimination in education and the labour market has historically deterred some women and minorities from entering high-productivity jobs. With the decline of such discrimination over time, many members of those groups have shifted from low-productivity jobs to higher-productivity jobs. The result has been higher overall labour productivity and real GDP.

Finally, tariffs, import quotas, and other barriers to international trade tend to relegate resources to relatively unproductive pursuits. Both here and abroad, the long-run movement toward liberalized international trade has improved the allocation of resources, increased labour productivity, and expanded real output.

QUICK REVIEW 8.3

- Institutional structures that promote growth include strong property rights, patents, efficient financial institutions, education, and a competitive market system.

- The determinants of economic growth include four supply factors (increases in the quantity and quality of natural resources, increases in the quantity and quality of human resources, increases in the stock of capital goods, and improvements in technology); a demand factor (increases in total spending); and an efficiency factor (achieving allocative and productive efficiency).

- Improvements in labour productivity have been an important contributor to increases in Canadian real GDP.

- Improved technology, more capital, greater education and training, economies of scale, and better resource allocation have been the main contributors to Canadian productivity growth and thus to Canadian economic growth.

8.5 / The Rise in the Average Rate of Productivity Growth

LO8.5 Explain why the trend rate of productivity growth in Canada has increased since the earlier 1973–1995 period.

The rise in productivity seen in the last decade is believed by many economists to be due to a significant new wave of technological advance coupled with global competition. Some economists are hopeful that the higher trend rates of productivity growth may be permanent.

Productivity growth is important because real output, real income, and **real wages** are linked to labour productivity. To see why, suppose you are alone on an uninhabited island. The number of fish you can catch or coconuts you can pick per hour–your productivity–is your real wage (or real income) per hour. By *increasing* your productivity, you can improve your standard of living because greater output per hour means there are more fish and coconuts (goods) available to consume.

So it is for the economy as a whole: Over long periods, the economy's labour productivity determines its average real hourly wage. The economy's income per hour is equal to its output per hour. Productivity growth is therefore the economy's main means of increasing its standard of living, since it allows firms to pay higher wages without lowering their business profits.

Reasons for the Rise in the Average Rate of Productivity Growth

Why has productivity growth increased relative to earlier periods?

THE MICROCHIP AND INFORMATION TECHNOLOGY

The core element of the productivity speedup is an explosion of entrepreneurship and innovation based on the microprocessor, or *microchip,* which bundles transistors on a piece of silicon. Some observers liken the invention of the microchip to that of electricity, the automobile, air travel, the telephone, and television in importance and scope.

The microchip has found its way into thousands of applications. It has helped create a wide array of new products and services as well as new ways of doing business. Its immediate results were the pocket calculator, the bar code scanner, the personal computer, the laptop computer, and more powerful business computers. But the miniaturization of electronic circuits also advanced the development of other products such as cellphones and pagers, computer-guided lasers, global positioning equipment, energy conservation systems, Doppler radar, digital cameras, and machines to decipher the human genome.

Perhaps of greatest significance, the widespread availability of personal and notebook computers stimulated the desire to tie them together. That desire promoted rapid development of the Internet and all its many manifestations such as business-to-household and business-to-business electronic commerce (e-commerce). The combination of the computer, fibre-optic cable, wireless technology, and the Internet constitute a spectacular advance in **information technology**, which has been used to connect all parts of the world.

NEW FIRMS AND INCREASING RETURNS

Hundreds of new **start-up firms** advanced various aspects of the new information technology. Many of these businesses created more hype than goods and services and quickly fell by the wayside. But a number of firms flourished, eventually to take their places among the nation's largest companies. Examples of those firms include BlackBerry (mobile communications), Rogers Communications (cable Internet provider and wireless phone service), Intel (microchips), Apple and Dell (personal computers), Microsoft and Oracle (computer software), Cisco Systems (Internet switching systems), Yahoo and Google (Internet search engines), and eBay, PayPal, and Amazon.com (electronic commerce). There are scores more! Most of these firms were not on the radar–or were just a small blip on the radar–30 years ago. Today each of them has large annual revenue and employs thousands of workers.

Successful new firms often experience **increasing returns**, a situation in which a given percentage increase in the amount of inputs a firm uses leads to an even larger percentage increase in the amount of output the firm produces. For example, suppose that a company called Techco decides to double the size of its operations to meet the growing demand for its services. After doubling its plant and equipment and doubling its workforce–say, from 100 workers to 200 workers–it finds that its total output has tripled, from 8000 units to 24,000 units. Techco has experienced increasing returns; its output has increased by 200 percent while its inputs have increased by only 100 percent. Consequently, its labour productivity has gone up from 80 units per worker (= 8000 units/100 workers) to 120 units per worker. Increasing returns boost labour productivity and lower per-unit production costs. Since these cost reductions result from increases in output levels, they are examples of economies of scale.

Both emerging firms and established firms can exploit several different sources of increasing returns and economies of scale:

- *More Specialized Inputs* Firms can use more specialized and thus more productive capital and workers as they expand their operations. A growing new e-commerce business, for example, can purchase highly specialized inventory management systems and hire specialized personnel, such as accountants, marketing managers, and system maintenance experts.

- *Spreading of Development Costs* Firms can spread high product development costs over greater output. For example, suppose that a new software product cost $100,000 to develop and only $2 per unit to manufacture and sell. If the firm sells 1000 units of the software its per-unit cost will be $102 [= ($100,000 + $2000)/1000], but if it sells 500,000 units that cost will drop to only $2.20 [= $100,000 + $1 million)/500,000].

- *Simultaneous Consumption* Many recently developed products and services can satisfy large numbers of customers at the same time. Unlike a litre of gas that needs to be produced for each buyer, a software program needs to be produced only once. It then becomes available at very low expense to thousands or even millions of buyers. The same is true of books delivered to electronic reading devices, movies distributed on DVDs, and information disseminated through the Internet.

- *Network Effects* Software and Internet services become more beneficial to a buyer when greater numbers of households and businesses buy them. When others have Internet service, you can send email messages to them. When they also have software to display documents and photos, you can attach those items to your email messages. These systems advantages are called **network effects**, increases in the value of the product to each user, including existing users, as the total number of users rises. The domestic and global expansion of the Internet in particular has produced network effects, as have cellphones, pagers, tablet computers, and other aspects of wireless communication. Network effects magnify the value of output well beyond the costs of inputs.

- *Learning-by-Doing* Finally, firms that produce new products or pioneer new ways of doing business ultimately experience increasing returns through **learning-by-doing**. Tasks that initially took hours may take only minutes once the methods are perfected.

Whatever the particular source of increasing returns, the result is higher productivity, which tends to reduce the per-unit cost of producing and delivering products.

GLOBAL COMPETITION

The Canadian economy is now characterized not only by information technology and increasing returns, but also by heightened global competition. The collapse of the socialist economies in the late 1980s and early 1990s, together with the success of market systems, has led to a reawakening of capitalism throughout the world. The new information technologies have "shrunk the globe" and made it imperative for all firms to lower their costs and prices, and to innovate to remain competitive. Free-trade zones such as NAFTA and the European Union (EU), along with trade liberalization through the World Trade Organization (WTO), have also heightened competition internationally by removing trade protection from domestic firms. The larger geographic markets, in turn, have enabled firms to expand beyond the borders of Canada. Global Perspective 8.1 shows the global competitiveness index for 2011-2012. Canada slipped a little in the last few years, but still ranks as the 12th most competitive nation in the world.

Implications of Economic Growth

Other things equal, stronger productivity growth and heightened global competition allow the economy to achieve a higher rate of economic growth. A glance back at Figure 8-2 will help make this point. Suppose the shift of the production possibilities curve from *AB* to *CD* reflects annual changes in potential output levels before the recent increase in growth rates. Then the higher growth rates of the more recent period of accelerated productivity growth would be depicted by a *larger* outward shift of the economy's production possibilities from *AB* to a curve beyond *CD*. When coupled with economic efficiency and increased total spending, the economy's real GDP would rise by more than that shown.

8.1 GLOBAL PERSPECTIVE

Global Competitiveness Index

The World Economic Forum annually compiles a global competitiveness index, which uses various factors (such as innovativeness, effective transfer of technology among sectors, efficiency of the financial system, rates of investment, and degree of integration with the rest of the world) to measure the ability of a country to achieve economic growth over time. Here is its latest top 10 list for 2014–2015, plus Canada, which ranks 15th.

Country	Global competitiveness ranking, 2014–2015
Switzerland	1
Singapore	2
United States	3
Finland	4
Germany	5
Japan	8
Hong Kong	7
Netherlands Denmark	8
United Kingdom	9
Sweden	10
Canada	15

Source: World Economic Forum, www.weforum.org.

Two cautions are in order, however: (1) Although the current productivity growth seems to be slightly faster than in the past and bodes well for long-term economic growth, fluctuations of the rate of economic growth will still occur. Because of demand factors, real output periodically deviates below and above the growth trend–as it certainly did during the very severe recession of 2008–2009. (2) You need to know that the growth of the Canadian labour force may decline in the not too distant future. If so, that slowing may offset some or all of the extra potential for economic growth that would arise from greater productivity growth.

Skepticism About Longevity

Although most macroeconomists have revised their forecasts for long-term productivity growth upward, at least slightly, others are still skeptical and urge a wait-and-see approach. These macroeconomists acknowledge that the economy has experienced a rapid advance of new technology, some new firms have experienced increasing returns, and global competition has increased. But they wonder if these factors are sufficiently profound to produce a long-lasting new era of substantially higher rates of productivity growth and real GDP growth.

What Can We Conclude?

Given the different views on the recent productivity acceleration, what should we conclude? Perhaps the safest conclusions are these:

- The prospects for a lasting increase in productivity growth are good. Studies indicate that productivity increases related to information technology have spread to a wide range of industries, including services.

- Time will tell. Not for several more years will economists be ready to declare the recent productivity acceleration a long-run, sustainable trend.

QUICK REVIEW 8.4

- Over long time periods, labour productivity growth determines an economy's growth of real wages and its standard of living.

- Many economists believe that Canada has entered a period of faster productivity growth and possibly higher rates of economic growth.

- The rise in the average rate of productivity growth is based on rapid technological change in the form of the microchip and information technology, increasing

returns and lower per-unit costs, and heightened global competition that helps hold down prices.

- More rapid productivity growth means the Canadian economy can grow at higher annual rates than it could with less rapid productivity growth, other things equal. Nonetheless, many economists caution that it is still too early to determine whether the higher rates of productivity growth are a lasting long-run trend or a short-lived occurrence.

8.6 / Is Economic Growth Desirable and Sustainable?

LO8.6 Discuss differing perspectives on whether growth is desirable and sustainable.

Economists usually take for granted that economic growth is desirable and sustainable. But not everyone agrees.

The Anti-Growth View

Critics of growth say industrialization and growth result in pollution, climate change, ozone depletion, and other environmental problems. These adverse spillover costs occur because inputs in the production process re-enter the environment as some form of waste. The more rapid our growth and the higher our standard of living, the more waste the environment must absorb—or attempt to absorb. In an already wealthy society, further growth usually means satisfying increasingly trivial wants at the cost of mounting threats to the ecological system.

Critics also argue that there is little compelling evidence for economic growth's having solved sociological problems such as poverty, homelessness, and discrimination. Consider poverty. In the anti-growth view, Canadian poverty is a problem of distribution, not production. The solution to the problem requires commitment and political courage to redistribute wealth and income, not further increases in output.

Anti-growth sentiment also says that although growth may permit us to make a better *living*, it does not give us a good *life*. We may be producing more and enjoying it less. Growth means assembly-line jobs, worker burnout, and alienated employees who have little or no control over decisions affecting their lives. High-growth economies are high-stress economies, which may impair our physical and mental health.

Finally, critics of high rates of growth doubt that they are sustainable. The planet Earth has finite amounts of natural resources available, and they are being consumed at alarming rates.

In Defence of Growth

The primary defence of growth is that it is the path to the greater material abundance and higher living standards desired by the vast majority of people. Rising output and incomes allow people to buy more of the goods and services they want. Growth also enables society to improve the nation's infrastructure, improve the care of the sick and elderly, provide greater access for the disabled, and provide more police and fire protection. Economic growth may be the only realistic means of reducing poverty, since little political support exists for greater redistribution of income. The way to improve the economic position of the poor is to increase household incomes through higher productivity and economic growth. Also, a no-growth policy among industrial nations might severely limit growth in poor nations. Foreign investment and development assistance in those nations would fall, keeping the world's poor in poverty longer.

Economic growth has not made labour more unpleasant or hazardous, as critics suggest. New machinery is usually less taxing and less dangerous than the machinery it replaces. Air-conditioned workplaces are more pleasant than steamy workshops.

Does growth threaten the environment? The connection between growth and environment is tenuous, say growth proponents. Increases in economic growth need not mean increases in pollution. Pollution is not so much a by-product of growth as it is a "problem of the commons." Much of the environment—streams, lakes, oceans, and the air—is treated as common property, with insufficient or no restrictions on its use. The commons have become our dumping grounds; we have overused and debased them. Environmental pollution is a case of spillover or external costs, and correcting this problem involves regulatory legislation or specific taxes (effluent charges) to remedy misuse of the environment.

Those who support growth admit that there are serious environmental problems. But they say that limiting growth is the wrong solution. Growth has allowed economies to reduce pollution, be more sensitive to environmental considerations, preserve wilderness, create national parks, and clean up hazardous waste, while still enabling rising household incomes.

Is growth sustainable? Yes, say its proponents. If depletion of natural resources was outpacing their discovery, we would see the prices of those resources rise. That has not been the case for most natural resources, and in fact the prices of many of them have declined. And if one natural resource becomes too expensive, another resource will be substituted for it. Moreover, say economists, economic growth has more to do with the expansion and application of human knowledge and information than with extractable natural resources. Economic growth is limited only by human imagination.

QUICK REVIEW 8.5

- Critics of growth argue that it adds to environmental degradation, increases human stress, and exhausts the earth's finite supply of natural resources.

- Defenders of growth say that it is the primary path to the rising living standards, that it need not debase the environment, and that there are no indications that we are running out of resources.

- Defenders of growth argue that it is sustainable because growth is based on the expansion and application of human knowledge, which is limited only by human imagination.

The **LAST WORD**   Can Economic Growth Survive Population Decline?

The demographic transition is causing greying populations, shrinking labour forces, and overall population decreases in many nations. Can economic growth survive?

As you know from this chapter, Real GDP = hours of work × labour productivity. The number of hours of work depends heavily, however, on the size of the working-age population. If it begins to shrink, the number of hours of work almost always falls. In such cases, the only way real GDP can rise is if labour productivity increases faster than hours of work decreases. The world is about to see if that can happen in countries that have populations that are greying and shrinking.

The historical background has to do with the fact that as nations industrialize their economies shift from agriculture to industry. As that happens, fertility levels plummet because the shift to modern technology transforms children from being economically essential farm hands who can contribute to their families' incomes from a young age to expensive investment goods that require many years of costly schooling before they can support themselves.

As people react to this change, birthrates tend to fall quite dramatically. The key statistic is the total fertility rate that keeps track of the average number of births that women have during their lifetimes. To keep the population stable in modern societies, the total fertility rate must be about 2.1 births per woman per lifetime (= 1 child to replace mom, 1 child to replace dad, and 0.1 child to compensate for those people who never end up reproducing as adults).

Every rich industrial nation has now seen its total fertility rate drop below the replacement level of 2.1 births per woman per lifetime. In Japan and many Eastern European countries, the number has been so low for so long that there are no longer enough children being born each year to replace the old folks who are dying. As a result, their overall populations are shrinking.

Economists only expect that pattern to become more common and more rapid, so that by the year 2050 the majority of nations will have decreasing populations. But decades before a nation's overall population begins to decrease, it faces a situation in which the labour force shrinks while the elderly population swells.

That pattern is the result of each generation being smaller than the one before. As an example, the Baby Boom generation, born between 1946 and 1964, is much larger than the Baby Bust generation that followed it. So as the Boomers retire over the next two decades, there will be a lot of retirees as compared to working-age adults.

This trend can be quantified by the inverse dependency ratio, which is defined as the number of people of working age (ages 20 to 64) divided by the number of dependents (seniors over age 65 plus youths under age 20). In Canada, the inverse dependency ratio is set to fall from about 1.5 people of working age per dependent in 2010 to just 1.16 people of working age per dependent in 2050. That is extremely problematic because it implies that worker productivity will have to rise dramatically just to make up for the relative decline in the number of workers as compared to dependents. If productivity doesn't keep up with the fall in the inverse dependency ratio, living standards will have to decline because there will simply be too many nonworking consumers relative to working-age producers.

The place where this problem is likely to show up first is Social Security. In 2013, for the first time in Canadian history, the number of retirees outnumbered young people in the 15–24 age group.

Statistics Canada projects that the working population will continue to drop while the number of seniors collecting pension is expected to rise. Clearly, worker productivity would have to increase to keep up with the decline in the number of workers relative to retirees.

Economists are uncertain about whether such large productivity increases will be forthcoming. The problem is that consumption competes with investment. A society with a larger fraction of dependents is a society that is likely to devote an increasingly high fraction of total output toward consumption rather than investment. If so, productivity growth may slow considerably.

Another possible problem is that, historically, most transformative new technologies and businesses have been created by energetic young people under the age of 40. With each generation getting smaller, there will be fewer people in that age range and thus, possibly, less innovation and slower productivity growth.

Other economists are more hopeful, however. They view old people as consumers and demanders. As their numbers swell, inventors may simply switch from inventing products for young people to inventing products for old people. If so, productivity growth and living standards could keep on rising at the rates we have come to expect. Moreover, Canada brings in about 250,000 new immigrants each year, which at least partially offsets the lower birth rate.

Question

Would you expect a country with a total fertility rate of 2.7 to have a growing or a shrinking population over the long run? What about a country with a total fertility rate of 1.2? In twenty years, will Canada have more or fewer workers per retiree than it does today? Why does a falling inverse dependency ratio make it harder for real GDP to continue growing?

Chapter Summary

LO8.1 LIST TWO WAYS THAT ECONOMIC GROWTH IS MEASURED.

- A nation's economic growth can be measured either as an increase in real GDP over time or as an increase in real GDP per capita over time. Real GDP in Canada has grown at an average annual rate of about 3.3 percent since 1961; real GDP per capita has grown at roughly a 2.1 percent annual rate over that same period.

LO8.2 DEFINE MODERN ECONOMIC GROWTH AND EXPLAIN THE INSTITUTIONAL STRUCTURES NEEDED FOR AN ECONOMY TO EXPERIENCE IT.

- Sustained increases in real GDP per capita did not happen until the late 1700s, when England, and then other countries, began to experience modern economic growth, which is characterized by institutional structures that encourage savings, investment, and the development of new technologies. Institutional structures that promote growth include strong property rights, patents, efficient financial institutions, education, and a competitive market system.

- Because some nations have experienced more than two centuries of economic growth while others have begun to experience economic growth only recently, today some countries are much richer than other countries.

- It is possible, however, for countries that are currently poor to grow more quickly than countries that are currently rich because the growth rates of GDP per capita in rich countries are limited to about 2 percent per year. In order to continue growing, rich countries must invent and apply new technologies. By contrast, poor countries can grow much more quickly because they can simply adopt the institutions and cutting-edge technologies already developed by the rich countries.

LO8.3 IDENTIFY THE GENERAL SUPPLY, DEMAND, AND EFFICIENCY FORCES THAT GIVE RISE TO ECONOMIC GROWTH.

- The determinants of economic growth responsible for changes in growth rates include four supply factors (increases in the quantity and quality of natural resources, increases in the quantity and quality of human resources, increases in the supply (or stock) of capital goods, and improvements in technology); one demand factor (increases in total spending); and one efficiency factor (increases in how well an economy achieves allocative and productive efficiency).

- The growth of a nation's capacity to produce output can be illustrated graphically by an outward shift of its production possibilities curve.

LO8.4 DESCRIBE GROWTH ACCOUNTING AND SPECIFIC FACTORS ACCOUNTING FOR ECONOMIC GROWTH IN CANADA.

- Growth accounting attributes increases in real GDP to increases in either the amount of labour being employed or in the productivity of the labour being employed. Increases in Canada's real GDP are mostly the result of improvements in labour productivity. The increases in labour productivity can be attributed to technological progress, increases in the quantity of capital per worker, improvements in the education and training of workers, the exploitation of economies of scale, and improvements in the allocation of labour across different industries.

LO8.5 EXPLAIN WHY THE TREND RATE OF PRODUCTIVITY GROWTH IN CANADA HAS INCREASED SINCE THE EARLIER 1973–1995 PERIOD.

- Over long time periods, the growth of labour productivity underlies an economy's growth of real wages and its standard of living.

- Canada's real GDP has grown partly because of increased inputs of labour and primarily because of increases in the productivity of labour. The increases in productivity have resulted mainly from technological progress, increases in the quantity of capital per worker, improvements in the quality of labour, economies of scale, and an improved allocation of labour.

- Over long time periods, the growth of labour productivity underlies an economy's growth of real wages and its standard of living.

- The post-1995 productivity growth is based on rapid technological change in the form of the microchip and information technology; new firms, increasing returns, and lower per-unit costs; and heightened global competition that holds down prices.

- The main sources of increasing returns in recent years are (a) use of more specialized inputs as firms grow, (b) the spreading of development costs, (c) simultaneous consumption by consumers, (d) network effects, and (e) learning-by-doing. Increasing returns mean higher productivity and lower per-unit production costs.

LO8.6 DISCUSS DIFFERING PERSPECTIVES AS TO WHETHER GROWTH IS DESIRABLE AND SUSTAINABLE.

- Skeptics wonder if the rise in the average rate of productivity growth is permanent. They point out that surges in productivity and real GDP growth have previously occurred but do not necessarily represent long-lived trends.

- Critics of rapid growth say that it adds to environmental degradation, increases human stress, and exhausts the Earth's finite supply of natural resources. Defenders of rapid growth say that it is the primary path to the rising living standards nearly universally desired by people, that it need not debase the environment, and that there are no indications we are running out of resources. Growth is based on the expansion and application of human knowledge, which is limited only by human imagination.

Terms and Concepts

economic growth
real GDP per capita
Rule of 70
modern economic growth
leader countries
follower countries
supply factors

demand factor
efficiency factor
labour productivity
labour force participation rate
productivity growth
infrastructure
human capital

economies of scale
real wage
information technology
start-up firm
increasing returns
network effects
learning-by-doing

Discussion Questions

1. How is economic growth measured? Why is economic growth important? Why could the difference between a 2.5 percent and a 3 percent annual growth rate be of great significance over several decades?   [LO8.1]

2. When and where did modern economic growth first happen? What are the major institutional factors that form the foundation for modern economic growth? What do they have in common?   [LO8.2]

3. Why are some countries today much poorer than other countries? Are today's poor countries destined always to be poorer than today's rich countries? If so, explain why. If not, explain how today's poor countries can catch up to or even pass today's rich countries.   [LO8.2]

4. What are the four supply factors of economic growth? What is the demand factor? What is the efficiency factor? Illustrate these factors in terms of the production possibilities curve.   [LO8.3]

5. Suppose that Alpha and Omega have identically sized working-age populations but that annual hours of work are much greater in Alpha than in Omega. Provide two possible explanations.   [LO8.3]

6. What is growth accounting? To what extent have increases in Canadian real GDP resulted from more labour inputs? From greater labour productivity? Rearrange the following contributors to the growth of productivity in order of their quantitative importance: economies of scale, quantity of capital, improved resource allocation, education and training, technological advance.   [LO8.4]

7. Is each of the following statements true or false? If the statement is false, explain why.   [LO8.4]

   a. Technological advance, which to date has played a relatively small role in Canadian economic growth, is destined to play a more important role in the future.

   b. Many public capital goods are complementary to private capital goods.

   c. Immigration has slowed economic growth in Canada.

8. Explain why there is such a close relationship between changes in a nation's rate of productivity growth and changes in its average real hourly wage.   [LO8.5]

9. Relate each of the following to the recent productivity acceleration: [LO8.5]

   a. Information technology

   b. Increasing returns

   c. Network effects

   d. Global competition

10. What, if any, are the benefits and costs of economic growth, particularly as measured by real GDP per capita?   [LO8.6]

Review Questions

1. If real GDP grows at 7 percent per year, then real GDP will double in approximately_____ years.   [LO8.1]

   a. 70

   b. 14

   c. 10

   d. 7

2. In 1820 living standards in various places around the globe were_____ they are today.   [LO8.2]

   a. More widely varying than

   b. Just as widely varying as

   c. Less widely varying than

3. True or False? Countries that currently have low real GDPs per capita are destined to always have lower living standards than countries that currently have high real GDPs per capita.   [LO8.2]

4. Identify each of the following situations as something that either promotes growth or retards growth.   [LO8.2]

   a. Increasing corruption allows government officials to steal people's homes.

   b. A nation introduces patent laws for the first time.

   c. A court order shuts down all banks permanently.

   d. A poor country extends free public schooling from 8 years to 12 years.

   e. A nation adopts a free-trade policy.

   f. A formerly communist country adopts free markets.

5. Real GDP equals_____times _____.   [LO8.4]

   a. Average hours of work; quantity of capital

   b. Average hours of work; allocative efficiency

   c. Labour input; labour productivity

   d. Natural resources; improvements in technology

6. Suppose that just by doubling the amount of output that it produces each year, a firm's per-unit production costs fall by 30 percent. This is an example of   [LO8.4]

   a. Economies of scale

   b. Improved resource allocation

   c. Technological advance

   d. The demand factor

7. True or False? Computers and increased global competition have retarded economic growth in recent decades.   [LO8.5]

8. Identify the following arguments about economic growth as being either anti-growth or pro-growth.   [LO8.6]

   a. Growth means worker burnout and frantic schedules.

   b. Rising incomes allow people to buy more education, medical care, and recreation.

   c. The Earth has only finite amounts of natural resources.

   d. We still have poverty, homelessness, and discrimination even in the richest countries.

   e. Richer countries spend more money protecting the environment.

   f. Natural resource prices have fallen rather than increased over time.

Problems

1. Suppose an economy's real GDP is $30,000 in year 1 and $31,200 in year 2. What is the growth rate of its real GDP? Assume that population is 100 in year 1 and 102 in year 2. What is the growth rate of real GDP per capita?   [LO8.1]

2. What annual growth rate is needed for a country to double its output in 7 years? In 35 years? In 70 years? In 140 years?   [LO8.1]

3. Assume that a leader country has real GDP per capita of $40,000, whereas a follower country has real GDP per capita of $20,000. Next, suppose that the growth of real GDP per capita falls to zero percent in the leader country and rises to 7 percent in the follower country. If these rates continue for long periods of time, how many years will it take for the follower country to catch up to the living standard of the leader country?   [LO8.2]

4. Refer to Figure 8-2 and assume that the values for points a, b, and c are $10 billion, $20 billion, and $18 billion respectively.

If the economy moves from point a to point b over a 10-year period, what must have been its annual rate of economic growth? If, instead, the economy was at point c at the end of the 10-year period, by what percentage did it fall short of its production capacity?   [LO8.3]

5. Suppose that work hours in New Zombie are 200 in year 1 and productivity is $8 per hour worked. What is New Zombie's real GDP? If work hours increase to 210 in year 2 and productivity rises to $10 per hour, what is New Zombie's rate of economic growth?   [LO8.4]

6. The per-unit cost of an item is its total average cost (= total cost/quantity). Suppose that a new cellphone application costs $100,000 to develop and only $0.50 per unit to deliver to each cellphone customer. What will be the per-unit cost of the application if it sells 100 units? 1000 units? 1 million units?   [LO8.5]

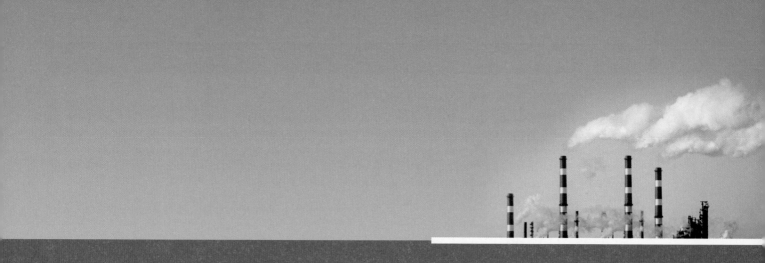

CHAPTER 9

Business Cycles, Unemployment, and Inflation

LEARNING OBJECTIVES

LO9.1 Describe the business cycle and its primary phases.

LO9.2 Illustrate how unemployment is measured and explain the different types of unemployment.

LO9.3 Explain how inflation is measured and distinguish between cost–push inflation and demand–pull inflation.

LO9.4 Understand how unanticipated inflation can redistribute real income.

LO9.5 Discuss how inflation may affect the economy's level of real output.

As indicated in Chapter 8, the Canadian economy has experienced remarkable economic growth over time. But this growth has not been smooth, steady, and predictable from year to year. At various times Canada has experienced recessions, high unemployment rates, or high inflation rates. For example, unemployment in Canada rose by 430,000 workers from the third quarter of 2008 to the third quarter of 2009, and the unemployment rate increased from 6.1 percent to 8.7 percent during the same period, which was the depth of the Great Recession. By the end of 2014 the unemployment rate was back down to 6.5 percent. Other nations have also suffered high unemployment rates at times. As just one example, Spain's unemployment rate exceeded 26 percent in 2012. Also, inflation has occasionally plagued Canada and other nations. For instance, the inflation rate in Canada in 1980 was 12.4 percent. Zimbabwe's inflation soared to 26,000 percent in 2007!

Our goal in this chapter is to examine the concepts, terminology, and facts relating to macroeconomic instability. Specifically, we want to discuss the business cycle, unemployment, and inflation. The concepts discussed are extremely important for understanding subsequent chapters on economic theory and economic policy.

9.1 / The Business Cycle

LO9.1 Describe the business cycle and its primary phases.

The long-run trend of the Canadian economy is one of economic growth, as indicated by the upsloping line labelled Growth Trend in Figure 9-1. But growth has been interrupted by periods of economic fluctuations usually associated with business cycles. The term **business cycle** refers to alternating increases and decreases in the level of economic activity, sometimes over several years. Individual cycles (one up followed by one down) vary substantially in duration and intensity.

ORIGIN OF THE IDEA 9.1   Business Cycles

Phases of the Business Cycle

Figure 9-1 shows the four phases of a generalized business cycle. At a **peak**, such as the middle peak shown in Figure 9-1, business activity has reached a temporary maximum. Here the economy is near or at full employment and the level of real output is at or very close to the economy's capacity. The price level is likely to rise during this phase.

A **recession** is a period of decline in total output, income, and employment. This downturn, which lasts six months or more, is marked by the widespread contraction of business activity in many sectors of the economy. Along with declines in real GDP, significant increases in unemployment occur. Table 9-1 documents the seven recessions that have occurred in Canada since 1930.

In the **trough** of the recession or depression, output and employment bottom out at their lowest levels. The trough phase may be either short-lived or quite long. A recession is usually followed by a recovery and **expansion**, a period in which real GDP, income, and employment rise. At some point the economy again approaches full employment. If spending then expands more rapidly than does production capacity, prices of nearly all goods and services will rise. In other words, inflation will occur.

Although business cycles all pass through the same phases, they vary greatly in duration and intensity. That is why many economists prefer to talk of business *fluctuations* rather than cycles, because cycles imply regularity but fluctuations do not. The Great Depression of the 1930s resulted in a 27.5 percent decline in real GDP over a three-year period in Canada and seriously impaired business activity for a decade. By comparison, more recent Canadian recessions, detailed in Table 9-1, were less severe in both intensity and duration, including the recession of 2008–2009 brought about by a global financial crisis.

FIGURE 9-1   The Business Cycle

Economists distinguish four phases of the business cycle; the duration and strength of each phase may vary.

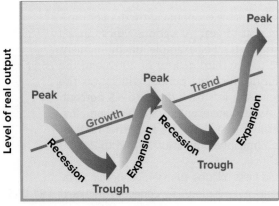

TABLE 9-1	Canadian Recessions Since 1930
Year	**Depth (decline in real GDP, %)**
1930–1933	−27.5
1945	−2.4
1946	−2.2
1954	−1.1
1982	−2.2
1991	−1.9
2009	−3.3

Source: Statistics Canada.

Recessions occur in other countries too, of course. For example, nearly all industrial nations and many developing nations have suffered recessions in the past several years.

Provincial Variations

National GDP data for Canada conceal significant differences in economic fluctuations among Canada's provinces and territories. Table 9-2 gives a breakdown of economic growth.

TABLE 9-2	Percentage Change in Real GDP for Provinces and Territories, 2013
	2013
CANADA	2.0
Newfoundland and Labrador	7.2
Prince Edward Island	2.0
Nova Scotia	0.2
New Brunswick	−0.5
Quebec	0.9
Ontario	1.2
Manitoba	2.2
Saskatchewan	4.9
Alberta	3.8
British Columbia	1.9
Yukon	−0.8
Northwest Territories	3.5
Nunavut	11.1

Source: Statistics Canada. http://www.statcan.gc.ca/tables-tableaux/sum-som/l01/cst01/econ50-eng.htm. Accessed May 31, 2015.

Causation: A First Glance

The long-run trend of the Canadian economy is toward expansion and growth. That is why the stylized business cycles in Figure 9-1 are drawn against a trend of economic growth. A key issue in macroeconomics is why the economy sees business cycle fluctuations rather than slow, smooth growth. In terms of Figure 9-1, why does output move up and down rather than just staying on the smooth growth trend line?

Economists have developed several possible explanations. But before turning to them, it is important to recall that in Chapter 6 we explained that theories are founded on the idea that fluctuations are driven by shocks—unexpected events that individuals and firms may have trouble adjusting to. Also recall that short-run price stickiness is widely believed to be a major factor in preventing the economy from rapidly adjusting to shocks. With prices sticky in the short run, price changes cannot quickly equalize the quantities demanded of goods and services with their respective quantities supplied after a shock has happened. Instead, the economy is forced to respond to shocks in the short run primarily through changes in output and employment rather than through changes in prices.

Economists cite several possible general sources of shocks that can cause business cycles.

- *Irregular Innovation* Significant new products or production methods, such as those associated with the railroad, automobile, computer, and Internet, can rapidly spread through the economy, sparking sizeable increases in investment, consumption, output, and employment. After the economy has largely absorbed the new innovation, the economy may for a time slow down or possibly decline. Because such innovations occur irregularly and unexpectedly, they may contribute to the variability of economic activity.

- *Productivity Changes* When productivity—output per unit of input—unexpectedly increases, the economy booms; when productivity unexpectedly decreases, the economy recedes. Such changes in productivity can result from unexpected changes in resource availability (of, say, oil or agricultural commodities) or from unexpected changes in the general rate of technological advance.

- *Monetary Factors* Some economists see business cycles as purely monetary phenomena. When a nation's central bank shocks the economy by creating more money than people were expecting, an inflationary boom in output occurs. By contrast, printing less money than people were expecting triggers an output decline and, eventually, a price-level fall.

- *Political Events* Unexpected political events such as peace treaties, new wars, or terrorist attacks can create economic opportunities or strains. In adjusting to these shocks, the economy may experience upswings or downswings.

- *Financial Instability* Unexpected financial bubbles (rapid asset price increases) or bursts (abrupt asset price decreases) can spill over to the general economy and create economic booms and busts.

The severe recession of 2008-2009 was precipitated by a combination of excessive money and a financial frenzy in the United States that led to overvalued real estate there and unsustainable mortgage debt. Institutions bundled this debt into new securities (derivatives), which were sold to financial investors all over the world. Some of the investors, in turn, bought insurance against losses that might arise from the securities. As real estate prices plummeted in the United States and mortgage defaults unexpectedly rocketed, the securitization and insurance structure buckled and nearly collapsed. The U.S. financial crisis quickly spread across the globe. Credit markets froze, pessimism prevailed, and spending by businesses and households tanked. Whatever the source of economic shocks, most economists agree that the *immediate* cause of the large majority of cyclical changes in the levels of real output and employment is unexpected changes in the level of total spending. If total spending unexpectedly sinks and firms cannot lower prices, firms will find themselves selling fewer units of output (since, with prices fixed, a decreased amount of spending implies fewer items purchased). Slower sales will cause firms to cut back on production. As they do, GDP will fall. And because fewer workers are needed to produce less output, employment will also fall. The economy will contract and enter a recession.

By contrast, if the level of spending unexpectedly rises, output, employment, and incomes will rise. This is true because with sticky prices the increased spending will mean that consumers will be buying a larger volume of goods and services (since, with prices fixed, more spending means more items purchased). Firms will respond by increasing output, and thus GDP will also rise. And because firms will need to hire more workers to produce the larger volume of output, employment will also increase. The economy will boom and enjoy an expansion. Eventually, as time passes and prices become more flexible, prices are also likely to rise as a result of the increased spending.

Cyclical Impact: Durables and Nondurables

Although the business cycle is felt everywhere in the economy, it affects different segments in different ways and to different degrees.

Firms and industries producing *capital goods* (for example, housing, commercial buildings, heavy equipment, and farm implements) and *consumer durables* (for example, automobiles and refrigerators) are affected most by the business cycle. Within limits, firms can postpone the purchase of capital goods. As the economy recedes, producers frequently delay the purchase of new equipment and the construction of new plants. The business outlook simply does not warrant increases in the stock of capital goods. In good times, capital goods are usually replaced before they depreciate completely. But when recession strikes, firms patch up their old equipment and make do. As a result, investment in capital goods declines sharply. Firms that have excess plant capacity may not even bother to replace all the capital that is depreciating. For them, net investment may be negative. The pattern is much the same for consumer durables such as automobiles and major appliances. When recession occurs and households must trim their budgets, purchases of these goods are often deferred. Families repair their old cars and appliances rather than buying new ones, and the firms producing these products suffer. (Of course, producers of capital goods and consumer durables also benefit most from expansions.)

In contrast, *service* industries and industries that produce *nondurable consumer goods* are somewhat insulated from the most severe effects of recession. People find it difficult to cut back on needed medical and legal services, for example. And a recession actually helps some service firms, such as pawnbrokers and law firms that specialize in bankruptcies. Nor are the purchases of many nondurable goods such as food and clothing easy to postpone. The quantity and quality of purchases of nondurables will decline, but not as much as will purchases of capital goods and consumer durables.

QUICK REVIEW 9.1

- The typical business cycle goes through four phases: peak, recession, trough, and expansion.
- Fluctuations in output and employment are caused by economic shocks combined with sticky prices.
- Sources of shocks that cause recessions include irregular innovation, productivity changes, monetary factors, political events, and financial instability.

- During recessions, industries that produce capital goods and consumer durables normally suffer greater output and employment declines than industries that produce services and nondurable consumer goods.

9.2 / Unemployment

LO9.2 Illustrate how unemployment is measured and explain the different types of unemployment.

Two problems arise over the course of the business cycle: unemployment and inflation. Let's look at unemployment first.

Measurement of Unemployment

To measure the unemployment rate we must first determine who is eligible and available to work. Figure 9-2 provides a helpful starting point. It divides the total Canadian population into three groups. One group is made up of people under 15 years of age and individuals who are institutionalized, for example in psychiatric hospitals or correctional facilities. Such people are not considered potential members of the labour force.

A second group, labelled "Not in labour force," is composed of adults who are potential workers but are not employed and are not seeking work. For example, they are homemakers, full-time students, or retirees.

The third group is the **labour force**, which constituted just over 50 percent of the total population in 2014. The labour force consists of people who are able and willing to work, and includes both those who are employed and those who are unemployed but actively seeking work. The labour force *participation rate* is defined as the percentage of the population 15 years and over (about 66.0 percent in 2014) that is currently employed or unemployed, but looking for work. The **unemployment rate** is the percentage of the labour force that is unemployed:

$$\text{Unemployment rate} = \frac{\text{unemployed}}{\text{labour force}} \times 100\%$$

| **FIGURE 9-2** | **The Labour Force, Employment, and Unemployment, 2014** |

The labour force consists of persons 15 years of age or older who are not in institutions and who are (1) employed or (2) unemployed but seeking employment.

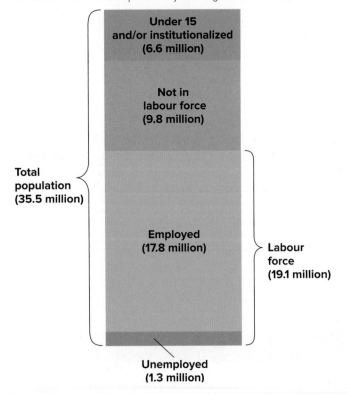

Source: Statistics Canada. The Labour Force, Employment, and Unemployment, 2014. Retrieved from http://www.statcan.gc.ca/tables-tableaux/sum-som/l01/cst01/labor07a-eng.htm, on May 31, 2015.

The statistics included in Figure 9-2 show that in 2014 the unemployment rate was 1.32 million/ 19.1 million = 6.9%.

WORKED PROBLEM 9.1   Unemployment Rate

Each month, Statistics Canada conducts a nationwide random survey of some 54,000 households to determine who is employed and who is not employed. In a series of questions, it asks which members of the household are working, unemployed and looking for work, not looking for work, and so on. From the answers, it determines an unemployment rate for the entire nation. Despite the use of scientific sampling and interviewing techniques, the data collected in this survey are subject to criticism.

- ***Part-Time Employment Statistics*** Canada fails to distinguish between fully and partially employed workers. In 2014, about 3.4 million people worked part-time. By counting them as fully employed, say critics, the official Statistics Canada data understate the unemployment rate.

- ***Discouraged Workers*** An individual must be actively seeking employment to be counted as unemployed. An unemployed person who is not actively seeking work is classified as "not in the labour force." The problem is that many people, after unsuccessfully seeking employment for a time, become discouraged and drop out of the labour force. The number of such **discouraged workers** is larger during recession than during prosperity. By not counting discouraged workers as unemployed, say critics, the official Statistics Canada data understate the unemployment problem.

Types of Unemployment

There are four types of unemployment: frictional, structural, cyclical, and seasonal.

FRICTIONAL UNEMPLOYMENT

At any particular time some workers are "between jobs." Some are moving voluntarily from one job to another. Others have been fired and are seeking re-employment. Still others have been laid off temporarily because of seasonal demand. In addition to those between jobs, many young workers are searching for their first job. As these unemployed people find jobs or are called back from temporary layoffs, other job

---

CONSIDER THIS | Downwardly Sticky Wages and Unemployment

Labour markets have an important quirk that helps to explain why unemployment goes up so much during a recession. The quirk is that wages are flexible upward but sticky downward. On the one hand, workers are perfectly happy to accept wage increases. So when the economy is booming and firms start bidding for the limited supply of labour, wages rise—sometimes quite rapidly. On the other hand, workers deeply resent pay cuts. So if the economy goes into a recession and firms need to reduce labour costs, managers almost never cut wages because doing so would only lead to disgruntled employees, low productivity, and—in extreme cases—workers stealing supplies or actively sabotaging their own firms.

Instead, managers usually opt for layoffs. The workers who are let go obviously don't like being unemployed. But those who remain get to keep their old wages and, consequently, keep on being as productive and cooperative as they were before.

This preference that firms show for layoffs over wage cuts results in downwardly sticky wages and an informal price floor that helps to explain why unemployment goes up so much during a recession. The problem is that when the demand for labour falls during a recession, the informal price floor prevents wages from falling. As a result, there is no way for falling wages to help entice at least some firms to hire a few more workers. Thus, when a recession hits, employment falls more precipitously than it would if wages were downwardly flexible and falling wages could help to increase hiring.

seekers and laid-off workers will replace them in the unemployment pool. A crucial point to keep in mind is that while the pool itself persists because there are always newly unemployed workers flowing into it, most workers do not stay in the pool for very long. Indeed most unemployed workers find new jobs within a couple of months. There is some evidence that the Internet has reduced the cost of finding employment and thus has probably reduced the amount of time workers are between jobs. Do not make the mistake of confusing the permanence of the pool itself with the false idea that the pool's membership is permanent, too.

Economists use the term **frictional unemployment**–consisting of search unemployment and wait unemployment–for workers who are either searching for jobs or waiting to take jobs in the near future. The word *frictional* implies that the labour market does not operate perfectly and instantaneously (without friction) in matching workers and jobs.

Frictional unemployment is inevitable and, at least in part, desirable. Many workers who are voluntarily between jobs are moving from low-paying, low-productivity jobs to higher-paying, higher-productivity positions. That means greater income for the workers, a better allocation of labour resources, and a larger real GDP for the economy.

STRUCTURAL UNEMPLOYMENT

Frictional unemployment blurs into a category called **structural unemployment**. Here, economists use *structural* in the sense of *compositional*. Changes over time in consumer demand and in technology alter the "structure" of the total demand for labour, both occupationally and geographically.

Occupationally, the demand for certain skills (for example, sewing clothes or working on farms) may decline or even vanish. The demand for other skills (for example, designing software or maintaining computer systems) will intensify. Unemployment results because the composition of the labour force does not respond immediately or completely to the new structure of job opportunities. Workers whose skills and experience have become obsolete thus find that they have no marketable talents. They are structurally unemployed until they adapt or develop skills that employers want.

Geographically, the demand for labour also changes over time. For example, industry and thus employment opportunities have migrated from the Maritimes to Central Canada over the past few decades. Migration of labour has also occurred in Western Canada to Alberta. Another example is the movement of jobs from inner-city factories to suburban industrial parks. And a final example is the *offshoring* of jobs that occurs when the demand for a particular type of labour shifts from domestic firms to foreign firms. As job opportunities shift from one place to another, some workers become structurally unemployed.

The distinction between frictional and structural unemployment is hazy at best. The key difference is that *frictionally* unemployed workers have saleable skills and either live in areas where jobs exist or are able to move to areas where they do. *Structurally* unemployed workers find it hard to find new jobs without retraining, gaining additional education, or relocating. Frictional unemployment is short-term; structural unemployment is more likely to be long-term and consequently more serious.

CYCLICAL UNEMPLOYMENT

Unemployment caused by a decline in total spending is called **cyclical unemployment** and typically begins in the recession phase of the business cycle. As the demand for goods and services decreases, employment falls and unemployment rises. Cyclical unemployment results from insufficient demand for goods and services. The 20 percent unemployment rate in the depth of the Great Depression in 1933 reflected mainly cyclical unemployment, as did significant parts of the 11 percent unemployment rate during the recession year 1982 and the 11.3 percent rate in the recession year 1991. The unemployment rate rose from 6.1 percent in the early fall of 2008 to 8.7 percent in August 2009. Since August 2009 the unemployment rate slowly dropped to 6.5 percent by the end of 2014.

Cyclical unemployment is a very serious problem when it occurs. We will say more about its high costs later, after we define *full employment*.

SEASONAL UNEMPLOYMENT

Most parts of Canada have quite severe winters during which some sectors (for example, building construction and farming) come to a virtual stop. These sectors experience substantial **seasonal unemployment**, as many workers are temporarily laid off due to seasonal factors. Another example of seasonal unemployment is ski resort workers laid off during summer months.

Definition of Full Employment

Because frictional and structural unemployment are largely unavoidable in a dynamic economy, *full employment* is something less than 100 percent employment of the labour force. Economists say that the economy is fully employed when it is experiencing only frictional, structural, and seasonal unemployment. That is, full employment occurs when no cyclical unemployment exists.

Economists describe the unemployment rate that is consistent with full employment as the *full-employment rate of unemployment,* or the **natural rate of unemployment (NRU),** sometimes referred to as the *non-inflationary rate of unemployment.* At the NRU, the economy is said to be producing its non-inflationary **potential GDP.** This is the real GDP that the economy would produce at full employment. In terms of the production possibilities curve, potential GDP means the economy would be operating on the curve. Recall from Figure 1-2 that points inside the production possibilities curve represent unemployed resources in an economy.

When the economy is operating at NRU, the number of *job seekers* equals the number of *job vacancies.* Also, it takes time for the structurally unemployed to achieve the skills and geographic relocation needed for re-employment.

However, "natural" does not mean that the economy will always operate at this rate and thus realize its potential output. When cyclical unemployment occurs, the economy has much more unemployment than that which would occur at the NRU. Moreover, the economy can operate for a while at an unemployment rate *below* the NRU. At times, the demand for labour may be so great that firms take a stronger initiative to hire and train the structurally unemployed. Also, some homemakers, teenagers, college and university students, and retirees who were casually looking for just the right part-time or full-time jobs may quickly find them. Thus the unemployment rate temporarily falls below the natural rate.

The NRU also can vary over time as demographic factors, job-search methods, and public policies change. In the 1980s, the NRU was about 7.5 percent. Today, it is estimated to be 6 to 7 percent.

Economic Costs of Unemployment

Unemployment that is above the natural rate involves great economic and social costs.

GDP GAP AND OKUN'S LAW

The basic economic cost of unemployment is forgone output. When the economy fails to create enough jobs for all who are able and willing to work, potential production of goods and services is irretrievably lost. In terms of the analysis in Chapter 1, unemployment above the natural rate means that society is operating at some point inside its production possibilities curve. Economists call this sacrifice of output a **GDP gap**– the difference between actual and potential GDP. That is,

GDP gap = actual GDP − potential GDP

The GDP gap can be either negative (actual GDP < potential GDP) or positive (actual GDP > potential GDP). In the case of unemployment above the natural rate, it is negative because actual GDP falls short of potential GDP.

Potential GDP is determined by assuming that the natural rate of unemployment prevails. The growth of potential GDP is simply projected forward on the basis of the economy's "normal" growth rate of real GDP. Figure 9-3 shows the GDP gap for recent years in Canada. It also indicates the close correlation between the actual unemployment rate (Figure 9-3b) and the GDP gap (Figure 9-3a). The higher the unemployment rate, the larger the GDP gap.

FIGURE 9-3   ## Actual and Potential GDP and the Unemployment Rate

(a) The difference between actual and potential GDP is the GDP gap. A negative GDP gap measures the output the economy sacrifices when actual GDP falls short of potential GDP. A positive GDP gap indicates that actual GDP is above potential GDP. (b) A high unemployment rate means a large GDP gap (negative), and a low unemployment rate means a small or even positive GDP gap.

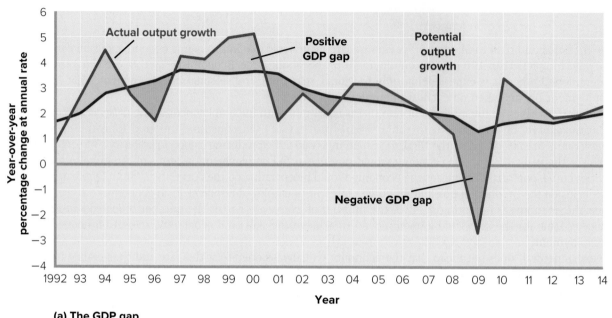

(a) The GDP gap

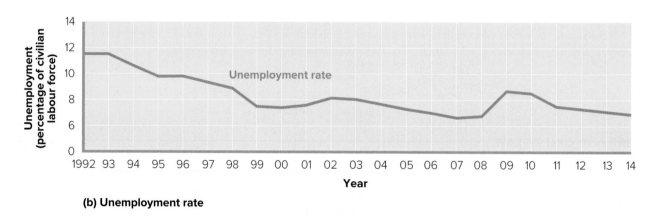

(b) Unemployment rate

Source: (a) Adapted from the Bank of Canada, Monetary Policy Report, October, 2014; (b) Statistics Canada, at www.stats.gov.nl.ca/statistics/Labour/PDF/UnempRate.pdf. Accessed June 10, 2015.

Macroeconomist Arthur Okun was the first to quantify the relationship between the unemployment rate and the GDP gap. Based on recent estimates, **Okun's law** indicates that *for every one percentage point by which the actual unemployment rate exceeds the natural rate, a GDP gap (shortfall) of about 2 percent occurs.* With this information, we can calculate the absolute loss of output associated with any above-natural unemployment rate. For example, in 2009 the average annual unemployment rate was 8.3 percent, or 1.8 percentage points above the 6.5 percent natural rate of unemployment. Multiplying this 1.8 percent by Okun's 2 percent indicates that 2009's GDP gap was 3.6 percent of potential GDP (in real terms). By applying this 3.6 percent loss to 2009 potential GDP of $1360 billion, we find that the economy sacrificed $49 billion of real output because the natural rate of unemployment was not achieved.

Sometimes the economy's actual output will exceed its potential GDP, or full-employment GDP, creating a positive GDP gap. Potential GDP can occasionally be exceeded, but the excess of actual over potential GDP eventually causes inflation and cannot be sustained indefinitely.

WORKED PROBLEM 9.2   Okun's Law

UNEQUAL BURDENS

An increase in the unemployment rate–say, from 8 to 9 or 10 percent–might be more tolerable to society if every worker's hours of work and wage income were reduced proportionately. But this is not the case. Part of the burden of unemployment is that its cost is unequally distributed.

Table 9-3 examines unemployment rates for various labour market groups for two years. Recession pushed the unemployment rate to as high as 8.7 percent in August 2009. In the early part of 2008 the Canadian economy was at full employment, with a rate of 5.8 percent unemployment. By observing the large variations in unemployment rates for the different groups within each year and comparing the rates between the two years, we can generalize as follows.

- *Occupation* Workers in lower-skilled occupations have higher unemployment rates than workers in higher-skilled occupations. Lower-skilled workers have more and longer spells of structural unemployment than higher-skilled workers. Moreover, lower-skilled workers usually bear the brunt of recessions. Businesses usually retain most of their higher-skilled workers, in whom they have invested the expense of training.

- *Age* Teenagers have much higher unemployment rates than adults. Teenagers have lower skill levels, quit their jobs more frequently, are more frequently fired, and have less geographic mobility than adults. Many unemployed teenagers are new in the labour market, searching for their first job. Male aboriginal teenagers, in particular, have very high unemployment rates. The unemployment for all teenagers rises during recessions.

- *Gender* The unemployment rates for men and women are usually similar. But in the recent Great Recession of late 2008 and 2009, the unemployment rate for men exceeded that for women.

TABLE 9-3	Unemployment by Demographic Group: Full Employment (2008) and Recession (2009)	
Demographic group	**Unemployment rate, February 2008**	**Unemployment rate, August 2009**
Overall	5.8%	8.7%
Age		
15–24 years	11.4	16.2
25 years and over	4.7	7.2
Sex		
Male	4.9	8.4
Female	4.5	6.0

Source: Statistics Canada.

- ***Education*** Less-educated workers, on average, have higher unemployment rates than workers with more education. Less education is usually associated with lower-skilled, less permanent jobs, more time between jobs, and jobs that are more vulnerable to cyclical layoff.

- ***Duration*** The number of persons unemployed for long periods–15 weeks or more–as a percentage of the labour force is much lower than the overall unemployment rate. But that percentage rises significantly during recessions.

Noneconomic Costs of Unemployment

Severe cyclical unemployment is more than an economic malady; it is a social catastrophe. Unemployment means idleness. And idleness means loss of skills, loss of self-respect, plummeting morale, family disintegration, and sociopolitical unrest. Widespread joblessness increases poverty, heightens racial and ethnic tensions, and reduces hope for material advancement. History demonstrates that severe unemployment can lead to rapid and sometimes violent social and political change. At the individual level, research links higher unemployment to increases in suicide, homicide, fatal heart attacks and strokes, and mental illness.

Regional Variations

The national unemployment rate in Canada does not reveal the significant diversity in regional unemployment. Table 9-4 gives both the national unemployment rate and a provincial breakdown. For 2014 the national rate was 6.9 percent, but rates went as high as 11.9 percent in Newfoundland and Labrador and as low as 3.8 percent in Saskatchewan.

International Comparisons

Unemployment rates differ greatly among nations at any given time. One reason is that nations have different natural rates of unemployment. Another is that nations may be in different phases of their business cycles. Global Perspective 9.1 shows unemployment rates for six industrialized nations in recent years. Between 2000 and 2008, the Canadian unemployment rate came down steadily, to reach a 30-year low of 5.8 percent by early 2008. In the autumn of 2008 Canada entered a recession that saw the unemployment

TABLE 9-4	Provincial Breakdown of the Unemployment Rate, 2014
Region	**Unemployment rate (%)**
CANADA	6.9
Newfoundland and Labrador	11.9
Prince Edward Island	10.6
Nova Scotia	9.0
New Brunswick	9.9
Quebec	7.7
Ontario	7.3
Manitoba	5.4
Saskatchewan	3.8
Alberta	4.7
British Columbia	6.1

Source: Statistics Canada. Updates at: http://www.statcan.gc.ca/tables-tableaux/sum-som/l01/cst01/labor07a-eng.htm. Accessed May 31, 2015.

9.1 GLOBAL PERSPECTIVE

Unemployment Rates in Six Industrial Nations, 2002–2012

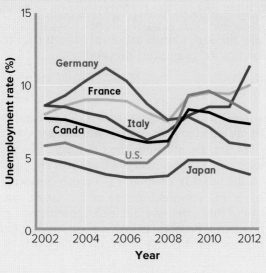

Source: U.S. Bureau of Labour Statistics, www.bls.gov.

rate rise to a post-recession peak of 8.7 percent. Still, Canada's economy did relatively well during the global recession of 2008–2009. While Canada has had a higher unemployment rate compared to the United States in the last 30 years, by January 2012 it was lower by a full percentage point. By the end of 2014, however, the unemployment rate in the U.S. once again dropped below the Canadian rate as it fell below 6 percent toward the end of 2014. In recent years the unemployment rate in Canada has been lower than in most European countries.

QUICK REVIEW 9.2

- Unemployment is of four general types: frictional, structural, cyclical, and seasonal.
- The natural unemployment rate (frictional plus structural) is currently 6 to 7 percent.
- Society loses real GDP when cyclical unemployment occurs: according to Okun's law, for each one

percentage point of unemployment above the natural rate, the Canadian economy suffers a 2 percent shortfall in real GDP below its potential GDP.

- Lower-skilled workers, teenagers, and less-educated workers bear a disproportionate burden of unemployment.

9.3 / Inflation

We now turn to inflation, another aspect of macroeconomic fluctuation. The problems inflation poses are more subtle than those created by unemployment.

MONEY AND INFLATION

Meaning of Inflation

LO9.3 Explain how inflation is measured and distinguish between cost–push inflation and demand–pull inflation.

Inflation is a continual rise in the *general level of prices*. When inflation occurs, each dollar of income will buy fewer goods and services than before. Inflation reduces the purchasing power of money. But inflation does not mean that *all* prices are rising. Even during periods of rapid inflation, some prices may be relatively constant and others may even fall. For example, although Canada experienced high rates of inflation in the 1970s and early 1980s, the price of digital watches and calculators declined.

Measurement of Inflation

The main measure of inflation in Canada is the **Consumer Price Index (CPI)**, compiled by Statistics Canada. The government uses this index to report inflation rates each month and each year. It also uses the CPI to adjust social benefits and income tax brackets for inflation. The CPI reports the price of a "market basket" of about 600 consumer goods and services in 175 commodity classes that are purchased by a typical Canadian consumer. (The GDP price index discussed in Chapter 7 is a much broader measure of inflation, since it includes not only consumer goods and services but also capital goods, goods and services purchased by government, and goods and services that enter world trade.) Generally, the price samples are collected during the first three weeks of the month. Gasoline prices are collected in four weeks of the month. Most of the price quotes (over 90 percent) used in the index are collected by Statistics Canada personnel at selected retail outlets.

The composition of the CPI market basket is based on spending patterns of Canadian consumers in a specific period, currently 2002. Statistics Canada sets the CPI for 2002 equal to 100. So, the CPI for any particular year is found as follows:

$$CPI = \frac{\text{Price of the 2002 basket in the particular year}}{\text{Price of the same basket in the base year (2002)}} \times 100\%$$

The rate of inflation for a certain year (say, 2014) is found by comparing, in percentage terms, that year's index with the index in the previous year. For example, the CPI was 125.2 in 2014, up from 122.8 in 2013. So the rate of inflation for 2014 is calculated as follows:

$$\text{Rate of inflation} = \frac{125.2 - 122.8}{122.8} \times 100\% = 2.0\%$$

In Chapter 8 we discussed the mathematical approximation called the *Rule of 70*, which tells us that we can find the number of years it will take for some measure to double, given its annual percentage increase, by dividing that percentage increase into the number 70. So, with a 3 percent annual rate of inflation, the price level will double in about 23 years (= 70 ÷ 3). Inflation of 8 percent per year will double the price level in about 9 years (= 70 ÷ 8).

Facts of Inflation

Figure 9-4 shows the December-to-December rates of annual inflation in Canada between 1960 and 2011. Observe that inflation reached double-digit rates in the 1970s and early 1980s, but has since declined and recently has been relatively mild.

In recent years, inflation in Canada has been unusually low relative to inflation in several other industrial countries (see Global Perspective 9.2); some nations (not shown) have had double-digit, triple-digit, or even higher annual rates of inflation. In 2009, for example, the annual inflation rate in the Democratic Republic of Congo was 46 percent; in Eritrea, 35 percent; Afghanistan, 31 percent; and Venezuela, 27 percent. Zimbabwe's inflation rate was 14.9 billion percent in 2008, before Zimbabwe did away with its existing currency.

FIGURE 9-4

Annual Inflation Rates in Canada, 1960–2014 (December to December changes in the CPI)

The major periods of inflation in Canada in the past half century were in the 1970s and 1980s.

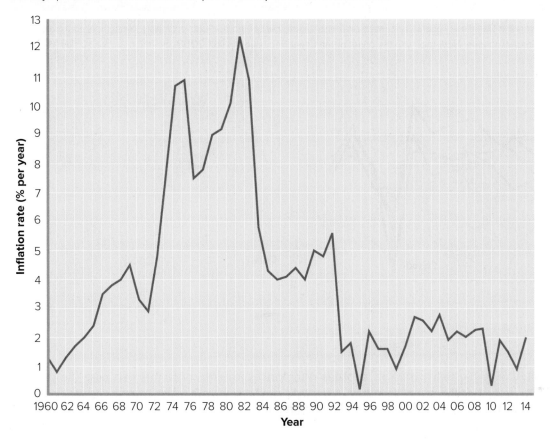

Source: Statistics Canada. Updates at: http://www.statcan.gc.ca/tables-tableaux/sum-som/l01/cst01/econ163a-eng.htm. Accessed June 1, 2015.

Types of Inflation

Nearly all prices in an economy are set by supply and demand. If the economy is experiencing inflation and the overall level of prices is rising, we need to look for an explanation in terms of demand and supply. *Demand-pull inflation* explains situations in which inflation is caused by an increase in demand. *Cost-push inflation* explains situations in which inflation is caused by a decrease in supply.

DEMAND–PULL INFLATION

Usually, increases in the price level are caused by an excess of total spending beyond the economy's capacity to produce. When resources are already fully employed, the business sector cannot respond to this excess demand by expanding output. So the excess demand bids up the prices of the limited real output, causing **demand-pull inflation.** The essence of this type of inflation is "too much spending chasing too few goods."

COST–PUSH INFLATION

Inflation may also arise on the supply, or cost, side of the economy. During some periods in Canadian economic history, including the mid-1970s, the price level increased even though total spending was not excessive.

9.2 GLOBAL PERSPECTIVE

Inflation Rates in Six Industrial Nations, 2002–2012

Inflation rates in Canada in recent years were neither extraordinarily high nor extraordinarily low compared to rates in other industrial nations. Note that with the onset of the Great Recession in late 2008, the inflation rate quickly fell.

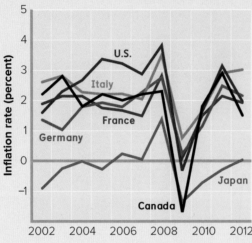

Source: U.S. Bureau of Labour Statistics, www.bls.gov.

The theory of **cost-push inflation** explains rising prices in terms of factors that raise the **per-unit production cost** at each level of spending. A per-unit production cost is the average cost of a particular level of output. This average cost is found by dividing the total cost of all resource inputs by the amount of output produced:

$$\text{Per-unit production cost} = \frac{\text{total input cost}}{\text{units of output}}$$

Rising per-unit production costs reduce profits and reduce the amount of output firms are willing to supply at the existing price level. As a result, the economy's supply of goods and services declines and the price level rises. In this scenario, costs are *pushing* the price level upward, whereas in demand–pull inflation demand is *pulling* it upward.

The major sources of cost-push inflation have been so-called *supply shocks*. Specifically, abrupt increases in the costs of raw materials or energy inputs have on occasion driven up per-unit production costs and thus product prices. The rocketing prices of imported oil in 1973–1974 and again in 1979–1980 are good illustrations. As energy prices surged upward during these periods, the costs of producing and transporting virtually every product in the economy rose, and cost-push inflation ensued.

Complexities

It is often difficult to distinguish between demand–pull and cost-push inflation unless the original source of inflation is known. For example, suppose a significant increase in total spending occurs in a fully employed economy, causing demand-pull inflation. But as the demand-pull stimulus works its way through various product and factor markets, individual firms find their wage costs, material costs, and fuel prices rising. Firms must raise their prices because production costs (someone else's prices) have risen. Although this inflation is clearly demand-pull in origin, it may mistakenly appear to be cost-push inflation to business

CONSIDER THIS | Clipping Coins

Loosely defined, demand–pull inflation is "too much money chasing too few goods." Some interesting early episodes of demand–pull inflation occurred in Europe during the 9th to 15th centuries, under feudalism. In that economic system lords (or princes) ruled individual fiefdoms and their vassals (or peasants) worked the fields. The peasants initially paid parts of their harvest as taxes to the princes. Later, when the princes began issuing "coins of the realm," peasants began paying their taxes with gold coins.

Some princes soon discovered a way to transfer purchasing power from their vassals to themselves without explicitly increasing taxes. As gold coins came into the treasury, princes clipped off parts, making them slightly smaller. From the clippings they minted new coins and used them to buy more goods for themselves. This practice of clipping coins was a subtle form of taxation. The quantity of goods being produced in the fiefdom remained the same, but the number of gold coins increased.

With too much money chasing too few goods, inflation occurred. Each gold coin earned by the peasants therefore had less purchasing power than previously because prices were higher. The increase of the money supply shifted purchasing power away from the peasants and toward the princes just as surely as if the princes had increased taxation of the peasants.

In more recent eras some dictators have simply printed money to buy more goods for themselves, their relatives, and their key loyalists. These dictators, too, have levied hidden taxes on their populations by creating inflation.

The moral of the story is quite simple: A society that values price-level stability should not entrust the control of its money supply to people who benefit from inflation.

firms and to government. Without proper identification of the source of the inflation, the Bank of Canada may be slow to enact policies to reduce excessive total spending.

Another complexity is that cost-push inflation and demand-pull inflation differ in their persistence. Demand-pull inflation will continue as long as there is excess total spending. Cost-push inflation is automatically self-limiting; it will die out by itself. Increased per-unit costs will reduce supply, which means lower real output and employment. Those decreases will constrain further per-unit cost increases. In other words, cost-push inflation generates a recession. And in a recession households and businesses concentrate on keeping their resources employed, not on pushing up the prices of those resources.

CORE INFLATION

Another complication relating to inflation (regardless of type) is noteworthy. Some price-flexible items within the Consumer Price Index–particularly food and energy–experience rapid changes in supply and demand, and therefore considerable price volatility from month to month and year to year. For example, the prices of grain, fruit, vegetables, and livestock sometimes move rapidly in one direction or the other, leading to sizeable changes in prices of food items such as bread, oranges, lettuce, and beef. Also, prices of energy items such as gasoline and natural gas can rise or fall rapidly from period to period. These ups and downs of food and energy prices usually are temporary and often cancel each other out over longer periods.

In tracking inflation, policymakers want to avoid being misled by rapid but temporary price changes that may distort the inflation picture. They are mainly interested in how rapidly the prices of the typically more stable components of the CPI are rising. By stripping volatile food and energy prices from the CPI, policymakers isolate **core inflation**–the underlying increases in the CPI after volatile food and energy prices are removed.

If core inflation is low and stable, policymakers may be satisfied with current policy even though changes in the overall CPI may be suggesting a rising rate of inflation. But policymakers become greatly concerned when core inflation is high and rising, and take deliberate measures to try to halt it. We discuss these policies in later chapters.

- Inflation is a rising general level of prices and is measured as the percentage change in a price index such as the Consumer Price Index (CPI).

- For the past several years, the inflation rate in Canada has been within the lower range of rates compared to other advanced industrial nations and far below the rates experienced by some nations.

- Demand–pull inflation occurs when total spending exceeds the economy's ability to provide goods and

services at the existing price level; total spending pulls the price level upward.

- Cost–push inflation occurs when factors such as rapid increases in the prices of raw materials drive up per-unit production costs at each level of output; higher costs push the price level upward.

- Core inflation is the underlying inflation rate after volatile food and energy prices have been removed.

9.4 / Redistribution Effects of Inflation

LO9.4 Understand how unanticipated inflation can redistribute real income.

Inflation hurts some people, leaves others unaffected, and actually helps still others by redistributing real income from some people to other people. Who gets hurt? Who benefits? Before we can answer, we need to discuss some terminology.

Nominal Income and Real Income

There is a difference between money (or nominal) income and real income. **Nominal income** is the number of dollars received as wages, rent, interest, or profits. **Real income** is a measure of the amount of goods and services nominal income can buy; it is the purchasing power of nominal income, or income adjusted for inflation. That is,

$$\text{Real income} = \frac{\text{nominal income}}{\text{price index}} \times 100\%$$

Inflation need not alter an economy's overall real income. It is evident from the above equation that real income will remain the same when nominal income rises at the same rate as the price index.

But when inflation occurs, not everyone's nominal income rises at the same pace as the price level. Therein lies the potential for redistribution of real income from some to others. If the change in the price level differs from the change in a person's nominal income, his or her real income will be affected. The following approximation (shown by the ≅ sign) tells us roughly how much real income will change:

Percentage change in real income	≅	Percentage change in nominal income	−	Percentage change in price

WORKED PROBLEM 9.3   Nominal and Real Income

For example, suppose the price level rises by 6 percent in some period. If Bob's nominal income rises by 6 percent, his real income will *remain unchanged*. But if his nominal income instead rises by 10 percent, his real income will *increase* by about 4 percent. And if Bob's nominal income rises by only 2 percent, his real income will *decline* by about 4 percent.[1]

EXPECTATIONS

The redistribution effects of inflation depend upon whether or not it is expected. We will first discuss situations involving **unanticipated inflation**. As you will see, these cause real income and wealth to be redistributed, harming some and benefiting others. We will then discuss situations involving **anticipated inflation**. These are situations in which people see inflation coming in advance. With the ability to plan ahead, people are able to avoid or lessen the redistribution effects associated with inflation.

Who Is Hurt by Inflation?

Unanticipated inflation hurts people with fixed incomes, savers, and creditors. It redistributes real income away from them and toward others.

- **Those with Fixed Incomes** People whose income is fixed see their real income fall when inflation occurs. The classic case is the elderly couple living on a private pension or annuity that provides a fixed amount of nominal income each month. They may have retired in, say, 1991 on what appeared to be an adequate pension. However, by 2008 they would have discovered that inflation has cut the purchasing power of that pension–their real income–by about one-third. Similarly, landlords who receive lease payments of fixed dollar amounts will be hurt by inflation as they receive dollars of declining value over time. Public-sector workers whose incomes are dictated by fixed pay schedules may also suffer under inflation. The fixed "steps" (the upward yearly increases) in their pay schedules may not keep up with inflation. Minimum-wage workers and families living on fixed welfare incomes will also be hurt by inflation.

- **Savers** Unanticipated inflation hurts savers. As prices rise, the real value, or purchasing power, of an accumulation of savings deteriorates. Paper assets such as savings accounts, insurance policies, and annuities that were once adequate to meet rainy-day contingencies or provide for a comfortable retirement, decline in real value during inflationary periods. For example, a household may save $1000 in a guaranteed investment certificate (GIC) in a chartered bank at 6 percent annual interest. But if inflation is 13 percent, the real value or purchasing power of that $1000 will be cut to about $938 by the end of the year. Although the saver will receive $1060 (equal to $1000 plus $60 of interest), deflating that $1060 for 13 percent inflation means that its real value is only about $938 (= $1060 ÷ 1.13).

- **Creditors** Unanticipated inflation harms creditors (lenders). Suppose Manitoba Bank lends Bob $1000, to be repaid in two years. If in that time the price level doubles, the $1000 that Bob repays will have only half the purchasing power of the $1000 he borrowed. Because of inflation, each of those dollars will buy only half as much as it did when the loan was negotiated. As prices go up, the value of the dollar goes down. Thus, the borrower is lent "dear" dollars but, because of inflation, pays back "cheap" dollars. The owners of Manitoba Bank suffer a loss of real income.

Who Is Unaffected or Helped by Inflation?

Some people are unaffected by inflation and others may actually be helped by it. For the second group, inflation redistributes real income toward them and away from others.

---

[1] A more precise calculation uses our equation for real income. In our first illustration above, if nominal income rises by 10 percent from $100 to $110 and the price level (index) rises by 6 percent from 100 to 106, then real income has increased as follows:

$$\frac{\$110}{106} \times 100 = 103.77$$

The 4 percent increase in real income shown by the simple formula in the text is a reasonable approximation of the 3.77 percent yielded by our more precise formula.

CONSIDER THIS   Could a Little Inflation Help Reduce Unemployment?

Economists have debated whether a little inflation—say two or three percent per year—might help to reduce the unemployment rate during recessions. Proponents argue that a little inflation might have this beneficial effect by boosting firms' profits and their demand for labour. Their argument goes like this: If wages and other costs were to remain fixed while inflation increased the prices at which firms could sell their output, firms would see their profitability increase. That in turn would cause firms to want to hire more workers.

The economists who disagree argue that it is implausible to assume that wages and other costs would remain fixed while inflation drives up the price of output. They point out that wages and other costs may well rise as fast or possibly even faster than output prices rise. If so, firms would not see any increase in their profitability—and thus they would not see any reason to hire more workers.

In addition, the economists who disagree also point out that even if inflation did lower unemployment, it would do so at the cost of lowering real wages. That's because if wages stay fixed while output prices rise, workers' fixed paycheques would only be able to purchase a smaller amount of goods and services. So while more workers might have jobs, all workers would have a lower standard of living.

- ***Those with Flexible Incomes*** Individuals who derive their income solely from social programs are largely unaffected by inflation, because payments are indexed to the CPI. Benefits automatically increase when the CPI increases, preventing erosion of benefits from inflation. Some union workers also get automatic **cost-of-living adjustments (COLAs)** in their pay when the CPI rises, although such increases rarely equal the full percentage rise in inflation.

  Rapid inflation may cause some nominal incomes to spurt ahead of the price level, thereby enhancing their real incomes. For some, the 3 percent increase in nominal income that occurs when inflation is 2 percent may become a 7 percent increase when inflation is 5 percent. As an example, property owners faced with an inflation-induced real-estate boom may be able to raise rents more rapidly than the rate of inflation. Also, some business owners may benefit from inflation. If product prices rise faster than factor prices, business revenues will grow more rapidly than costs. In those cases, the growth rate of profit incomes will outpace the rate of inflation.

- ***Debtors*** Unanticipated inflation benefits debtors (borrowers). In our previous example, Manitoba Bank's loss of real income from inflation is Bob's gain of real income. Debtor Bob borrows "dear" dollars but, because of inflation, pays back the principal and interest with "cheap" dollars of which purchasing power has been eroded by inflation. Real income is redistributed away from the owners of Manitoba Bank toward borrowers such as Bob.

Anticipated Inflation

The redistribution effects of inflation are less severe or are eliminated altogether if people anticipate inflation and can adjust their nominal incomes to reflect the expected price-level rises. The prolonged inflation that began in the late 1960s prompted many labour unions in the 1970s to insist on labour contracts with cost-of-living adjustment clauses.

Similarly, if inflation is anticipated, the redistribution of income from lender to borrower may be altered. Suppose a lender (perhaps a chartered bank or a credit union) and a borrower (a household) both agree that 5 percent is a fair rate of interest on a one-year loan provided the price level is stable. But assume that inflation has been occurring and is expected to be 6 percent over the next year. If the bank lends the household $100 at 5 percent interest, the bank will be paid back $105 at the end of the year. But if 6 percent inflation does occur during that year, the purchasing power of the $105 will have been reduced to about $99. The lender will in effect have paid the borrower $1 for the use of the lender's money for a year.

The lender can avoid this subsidy by charging an *inflation premium*–that is, by raising the interest rate by 6 percent, the amount of the anticipated inflation. By charging 11 percent, the lender will receive back $111 at the end of the year. Adjusted for the 6 percent inflation, that amount will have the purchasing power of today's $105. The result then will be a mutually agreeable transfer of purchasing power from borrower to lender of $5, or 5 percent, for the use of $100 for one year. Financial institutions have also developed variable-interest-rate mortgages to protect themselves from the adverse effects of inflation. (Incidentally, this example points out that, rather than being a *cause* of inflation, high nominal interest rates are a *consequence* of inflation.)

ORIGIN OF THE IDEA 9.2 Real Interest Rates

Our example reveals the difference between the real rate of interest and the nominal rate of interest. The **real interest rate** is the percentage increase in *purchasing power* that the borrower pays the lender. In our example the real interest rate is 5 percent. The **nominal interest rate** is the percentage increase in *money* that the borrower pays the lender, including that resulting from the built-in expectation of inflation, if any. In equation form

Nominal interest rate = real interest rate + inflation premium (the expected rate of inflation)

As illustrated in Figure 9-5, the nominal interest rate in our example is 11 percent.

Other Redistribution Issues

We end our discussion of the redistribution effects of inflation by making three final points.

- **Deflation** The effects of unanticipated **deflation**–declines in the price level–are the reverse of those of inflation. People with fixed nominal incomes will find their real incomes enhanced. Creditors will benefit at the expense of debtors. As prices and wages fall, fixed debt obligations actually rise as a percentage of disposable income. And savers will discover that the purchasing power of their savings has grown because of the falling prices.

- **Mixed Effects** A person who is simultaneously an income earner, a holder of financial assets, and a debtor will probably find that the redistribution impact of inflation is cushioned. If the person owns

---

| **FIGURE 9-5** | The Inflation Premium, and Nominal and Real Interest Rates |

The inflation premium—the expected rate of inflation—gets built into the nominal interest rate. Here, the nominal interest rate of 11 percent comprises the real interest rate of 5 percent plus the inflation premium of 6 percent.

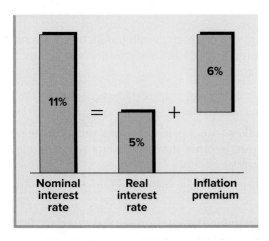

fixed-value monetary assets (savings accounts, bonds, and insurance policies), inflation will lessen their real value. But that same inflation may produce an increase in the person's nominal wage. Also, if the person holds a fixed-interest-rate mortgage, the real burden of that debt will decline. In short, many individuals are simultaneously hurt and benefited by inflation. All these effects must be considered before we can conclude that any particular person's net position is better or worse because of inflation.

- *Arbitrariness* The redistribution effects of inflation occur regardless of society's goals and values. Inflation lacks a social conscience and takes from some and gives to others, whether they are rich, poor, young, old, healthy, or infirm.

QUICK REVIEW 9.4

- Inflation harms those who receive relatively fixed nominal incomes and either leaves unaffected or helps those who receive flexible nominal incomes.

- Unanticipated inflation hurts savers and creditors while benefiting debtors.

- The nominal interest rate equals the real interest rate plus the inflation premium (the expected rate of inflation).

9.5 / Does Inflation Affect Output?

LO9.5 Discuss how inflation may affect the economy's level of real output.

Thus far, our discussion has focused on how inflation redistributes a given level of total real income. But inflation may also affect an economy's level of real output (and thus its level of real income). The direction and significance of this effect on output depends on the type of inflation and its severity.

 MONEY AND INFLATION

Cost–Push Inflation and Real Output

Recall that abrupt and unexpected rises in key resource prices can drive up overall production costs sufficiently to cause cost-push inflation. As prices rise, the quantity of goods and services demanded falls. So, firms respond by producing less output, and unemployment goes up.

Demand–Pull Inflation and Real Output

Economists do not fully agree on the effects of mild inflation (less than 3 percent) on real output. One perspective is that even low levels of inflation reduce real output, because inflation diverts time and effort toward activities designed to hedge against inflation. For example,

- Businesses must incur the cost of changing thousands of prices on their shelves and in their computers simply to reflect inflation.

- Households and businesses must spend time and effort obtaining the information they need to distinguish between real and nominal values such as prices, wages, and interest rates.

- To limit the loss of purchasing power from inflation, people try to limit the amount of money they hold in their wallets and chequing accounts at any one time and instead put more money into interest-bearing accounts and stock and bond funds. But cash and cheques are needed in even greater amounts to buy the higher-priced goods and services, so banking transactions become more frequent.

Without inflation, these uses of resources, time, and effort would not be needed and they could be diverted toward producing more valuable goods and services. Proponents of *zero inflation* bolster their case by pointing to cross-country studies that indicate an association between lower rates of inflation and higher rates of economic growth.

In contrast, other economists point out that full employment and economic growth depend on strong levels of total spending. Such spending creates high profits, strong demand for labour, and a powerful incentive for firms to expand their plants and equipment. In this view, the mild inflation that is a by-product of this strong spending is a small price to pay for full employment and continued economic growth. Moreover, a little inflation may have positive effects because it makes it easier for firms to adjust real wages downward when the demands for their products fall. With mild inflation, firms can reduce real wages by holding nominal wages steady. With zero inflation, firms would need to cut nominal wages to reduce real wages. Such cuts in nominal wages are highly visible and may cause considerable worker resistance and labour strife.

Finally, defenders of mild inflation say that it is much better for an economy to err on the side of strong spending, full employment, economic growth, and mild inflation than on the side of weak spending, unemployment, recession, and deflation.

Hyperinflation

All economists agree that **hyperinflation**, which is extraordinarily rapid inflation, can have a devastating impact on real output and employment.

As prices shoot up sharply and unevenly during hyperinflation, people begin to anticipate even more rapid inflation, and normal economic relationships are disrupted. Business owners do not know what to charge for their products. Consumers do not know what to pay. Resource suppliers want to be paid with actual output, rather than with rapidly depreciating money. Money eventually becomes almost worthless and ceases to do its job as a medium of exchange. To hedge against inflation, businesses and individual savers may decide to buy nonproductive wealth—jewels, gold and other precious metals, real estate, and so forth—rather than invest in capital equipment. The economy may be thrown into a state of barter, and production and exchange drop further. The net result is economic collapse and, often, political chaos.

Examples of hyperinflation occurred in Germany after World War I and Japan after World War II. In Germany, "prices increased so rapidly that waiters changed the prices on the menu several times during the course of a lunch. Sometimes customers had to pay double the price listed on the menu when they ordered."[2] In post-war Japan, in 1947 "fisherman and farmers . . . used scales to weigh currency and change, rather than bothering to count it."[3]

There are also more recent examples: Between June 1986 and March 1991, the cumulative inflation in Nicaragua was 11,895,866,143 percent. From November 1993 to December 1994, the cumulative inflation rate in the Democratic Republic of Congo was 69,502 percent. From February 1993 to January 1994, the cumulative inflation rate in Serbia was 156,312,790 percent.[4]

Such dramatic hyperinflations are always the consequence of highly imprudent expansions of the money supply by government. The rocketing money supply produces frenzied total spending and severe demand-pull inflation. Zimbabwe's 14.9 billion percent inflation in 2008 is just the latest example.

---

[2] Theodore Morgan, *Income and Employment*, 2nd ed. (Englewood Cliffs, NJ: Prentice-Hall, 1952), p. 361.

[3] Raburn M. Williams, *Inflation! Money, Jobs, and Politicians* (Arlington Heights, IL: AHM Publishing Corporation, 1980), p. 2.

[4] Stanley Fischer, Ratna Sahay, and Carlos Végh, "Modern Hyper- and High Inflations," *Journal of Economic Literature* (September 2002), p. 840.

The LAST WORD   Unemployment After the Great Recession: Canada versus the U.S.

Economists have been vigorously debating why employment recovered so slowly after the Great Recession of 2007-2009.

The Great Recession started in Canada in late 2008 and ended by the third quarter of 2009. GDP declined by 3.3 percent during that time, the worst contraction since the 1930s. In all, the Great Recession lasted only seven months in Canada. The unemployment rate increased from 6.1 to 8.7. What stood out about the Great Recession in Canada was the sudden drop in exports, which decreased 16 percent over the duration of the recession, and a 22 percent drop in investments. But despite the rapid slowdown the recovery was quicker, even more so than from the post-World War II recession. Many attribute the relatively good performance of the Canadian economy to a strong banking sector and the fact that it did not endure a housing bubble. The experience of our neighbours to the south was much worse.

The Great Recession began in the U.S. in December 2007 and ended in June 2009. The downturn was the most severe since the Great Depression of the 1930s, with real GDP falling 4.7 percent from peak to trough. After growth returned in mid-2009, real GDP increased slowly, taking until October 2011 to pass its prerecession peak.

Employment showed a similar pattern of rapid decline followed by slow recovery: 8.7 million people lost their jobs after employment peaked in January 2008. Employment began to expand again in early 2010, but job growth was so slow that in December 2012—more than three years after the recession ended and more than a year after real GDP had passed its prerecession high—employment was still 3.4 million less than it had been at the start of the recession.

The recession also dramatically increased the average length of time that workers spent unemployed before finding a new job. The typical (median) spell of unemployment went from 7.7 weeks in June 2007 to a peak of 24.8 weeks in June 2010. By way of comparison, the highest previous measurement for this statistic had been 12.3 weeks during the 1981–1982 recession. Thus, the Great Recession saw not only the loss of 8.7 million jobs, but unprecedentedly long wait times for unemployed workers to find new jobs.

When real GDP initially fell by 4.7 percent, it was easy to understand why employers might have shed 8.7 million jobs: fewer workers were needed to produce less output. But after real GDP recovered fully and passed its prerecession peak, economists began to debate why employment was still millions of jobs lower than it had been before the recession began.

Here are a few of the possible culprits for the relatively deeper recession and slower recovery of the U.S. economy.

Higher Federal Minimum Wage   It is widely acknowledged that raising the minimum wage may increase unemployment by pricing low-productivity workers out of the labour market. Thus, one potential culprit for the slow recovery in employment was the July 2009 increase in the federal minimum wage from $6.55 to $7.25. But, at any given time, fewer than 3 percent of workers are employed at minimum-wage jobs. So it would be hard to blame the increase in the minimum wage for more than a very small fraction of the slow post-recession recovery in employment.

Longer Unemployment Benefits   In November 2009, the U.S. Congress decided to extend the maximum period of time that unemployed workers could draw unemployment benefits from 26 weeks to 99 weeks. That decision is believed by many economists to have affected a large enough fraction of unemployed workers to have contributed to the slow recovery in employment. Congress had two intents when it extended the maximum draw period for unemployment benefits. The first was to help unemployed workers financially. The second was to help keep the economy moving by giving unemployed workers money to spend on goods and services.

One unintended consequence, however, was "inefficiently long search," meaning that many unemployed workers used the extended period during which they could survive on unemployment benefits to keep searching for perfect jobs even after they had been offered several so-so jobs. As a result, the unemployment rate stayed higher than it would have if benefits had continued to end after just 26 weeks and workers had felt financial pressure at an earlier date to accept so-so jobs rather than to keep on searching for perfect jobs.

Structural Adjustments   Another explanation for the slow recovery in employment was that the economy required *structural adjustments*—changes in the basic structure of what was being produced and thus which industries needed workers. Consider the housing bubble that preceded the Great Recession. After the housing bubble collapsed, the economy needed to transition several million unemployed construction workers into other lines of work. Creating that many new jobs in other industries was going to take time. Thus, it was to be expected that employment was slow to recover after the recession ended.

Higher Labour Costs   Other economists argued that worries about higher labour costs also contributed to the slow recovery in employment. In particular, they argued that several provisions of the 2010 health care reform law commonly known as Obamacare discouraged firms from hiring workers. One provision was an increase in the Medicare payroll tax. Another was the requirement that by 2014 any firm with more than 50 employees would have to provide health insurance coverage for all of its full-time workers.

That insurance provision was problematic because health insurance is very costly. In 2012, for example, the average cost for family coverage was $15,745 per worker. So, as the economy was making its way out of recession in 2010, it was the case that forward-looking employers may have reduced their hiring so as to have fewer full-time workers on the payroll when that provision of the law went into effect in 2014.

Still, despite the slow recovery of the U.S. economy, by the end of 2014 the unemployment rate had fallen slightly below 6 percent, lower than what it was in Canada. All told, it took longer for the U.S. economy to recover from the Great Recession compared to Canada, but this is not surprising given that it experienced a deeper recession caused primarily from a the burst of a housing bubble that set off a financial crisis.

Question

Why was the 2009 hike in the minimum wage in the U.S. probably not responsible for much of the slow growth in employment in the American economy after the Great Recession? What is "inefficiently long search" and how is it affected by the duration of unemployment benefits? How might Obamacare have discouraged hiring? Why was the Great Recession more severe in the U.S.?

Chapter Summary

LO9.1   DESCRIBE THE BUSINESS CYCLE AND ITS PRIMARY PHASES.

- Canada and other industrial economies have gone through periods of fluctuations in real GDP, employment, and price level. Although they have certain phases in common—peak, recession, trough, expansion—business cycles vary greatly in duration and intensity.

- Although economists explain the business cycle in terms of underlying causal factors such as major innovations, productivity shocks, money creation, and financial crises, they generally agree that the level of total spending is the immediate determinant of real output and employment.

- The business cycle affects all sectors of the economy, though in varying ways and degrees. The cycle has greater effects on output and employment in the capital goods and durable consumer goods industries than in the services and nondurable goods industries.

LO9.2　ILLUSTRATE HOW UNEMPLOYMENT IS MEASURED AND EXPLAIN THE DIFFERENT TYPES OF UNEMPLOYMENT.

- Economists distinguish among frictional, structural, cyclical, and seasonal unemployment. The full-employment or natural rate of unemployment, which is made up of frictional and structural unemployment, is currently 6 to 7 percent. The presence of part-time and discouraged workers makes it difficult to measure unemployment accurately.

- The GDP gap, which can be either a positive or a negative value, is found by subtracting potential GDP from actual GDP. The economic cost of unemployment, as measured by the GDP gap, consists of the goods and services forgone by society when its resources are involuntarily idle. Okun's law suggests that every increase in unemployment by 1 percent above the natural rate causes an additional 2 percent negative GDP gap.

- Unemployment rates vary widely globally. Unemployment rates differ because nations have different natural rates of unemployment and often are in different phases of their business cycles.

LO9.3　EXPLAIN HOW INFLATION IS MEASURED AND DISTINGUISH BETWEEN COST–PUSH INFLATION AND DEMAND–PULL INFLATION

- Inflation is a rise in the general price level and is measured in Canada by the Consumer Price Index (CPI). When inflation occurs, each dollar of income will buy fewer goods and services than before. That is, inflation reduces the purchasing power of money.

- Economists distinguish between demand–pull and cost–push (supply-side) inflation. Demand–pull inflation results from an excess of total spending relative to the economy's capacity to produce. The main source of cost–push inflation is abrupt and rapid increases in the prices of key resources. These supply shocks push up per-unit production costs and ultimately the prices of consumer goods.

LO9.4　UNDERSTAND HOW UNANTICIPATED INFLATION CAN REDISTRIBUTE REAL INCOME.

- Unanticipated inflation arbitrarily redistributes real income at the expense of people with a fixed income, creditors, and savers. If inflation is anticipated, individuals and businesses may be able to take steps to lessen or eliminate adverse redistribution effects.

- When inflation is anticipated, lenders add an inflation premium to the interest rate charged on loans. The nominal interest rate thus reflects the real interest rate plus the inflation premium (the expected rate of inflation).

LO9.5　DISCUSS HOW INFLATION MAY AFFECT THE ECONOMY'S LEVEL OF REAL OUTPUT.

- Cost–push inflation reduces real output and employment. Proponents of zero inflation argue that even mild demand–pull inflation (1 to 3 percent) reduces the economy's real output. Other economists say that mild inflation may be a necessary by-product of the high and growing spending that produces high levels of output, full employment, and economic growth.

- Hyperinflation, caused by highly imprudent expansions of the money supply, may undermine the monetary system and cause severe declines in real output.

Terms and Concepts

business cycle	seasonal unemployment	nominal income
peak	natural rate of unemployment (NRU)	real income
recession	potential GDP	unanticipated inflation
trough	GDP gap	anticipated inflation
expansion	Okun's law	deflation
labour force	inflation	cost-of-living adjustment (COLA)
unemployment rate	Consumer Price Index (CPI)	subsidy
discouraged workers	demand–pull inflation	real interest rate
frictional unemployment	cost–push inflation	nominal interest rate
structural unemployment	per-unit production cost	hyperinflation
cyclical unemployment	core inflation	

Discussion Questions

1. What are the four phases of the business cycle? How long do business cycles last? How do seasonal variations and long-run trends complicate measurement of the business cycle? Why does the business cycle affect output and employment in capital goods industries and consumer durable goods industries more severely than in industries producing consumer nondurables? [LO9.1]

2. How, in general, can a financial crisis lead to a recession? How, in general, can a major new invention lead to an expansion? [LO9.1]

3. How is the labour force defined and who measures it? How is the unemployment rate calculated? Does an increase in the unemployment rate necessarily mean a decline in the size of the labour force? Why is a positive unemployment rate—more than zero percent—fully compatible with full employment? [LO9.2]

4. How, in general, do unemployment rates vary by gender, occupation, and education? Why does the average length of time people are unemployed rise during a recession? [LO9.2]

5. Why is it difficult to distinguish between frictional, structural, seasonal, and cyclical unemployment? Why is unemployment an economic problem? What are the consequences of a negative GDP gap? What are the noneconomic effects of unemployment? [LO9.2]

6. Since Canada has an employment insurance program that provides income for those who are out of work, why should we worry about unemployment? [LO9.2]

7. What is the Consumer Price Index (CPI) and how is it determined each month? How does Statistics Canada calculate the rate of inflation from one year to the next? What effect does inflation have on the purchasing power of a dollar? What effect does inflation have on the gap, if any, between nominal and real interest rates? How does deflation differ from inflation? [LO9.3]

8. Distinguish between demand–pull and cost–push inflation. Which of the two types is most likely to be associated with a negative GDP gap? Which of the two types is most likely to be associated with a positive GDP gap (in which actual GDP exceeds potential GDP)? What is core inflation? Why is it calculated? [LO9.3]

9. Explain how an increase in your nominal income and a decrease in your real income might occur simultaneously. Who loses from inflation? Who gains? [LO9.4]

10. Explain how hyperinflation might lead to a severe decline in total output. [LO9.5]

Review Questions

1. Place the phases of the business cycle in order. [LO9.1]

   Recession   Trough   Peak   **Expansion**

2. Most economists agree that the immediate cause of the large majority of cyclical changes in the levels of real output and employment is unexpected changes in_____. [LO9.1]

   a. The level of total spending

   b. The level of the stock market

   c. The level of the trade deficit

   d. The level of unemployment

3. Suppose that an economy has 9 million people working full-time. It also has 1 million people who are actively seeking work but currently unemployed as well as 2 million discouraged workers who have given up looking for work and are currently unemployed. What is this economy's unemployment rate? [LO9.2]

   a. 10 percent

   b. 15 percent

   c. 20 percent

   d. 25 percent

4. Label each of the following scenarios as either frictional unemployment, structural unemployment, or cyclical unemployment. [LO9.2]

   a. Tim just graduated and is looking for a job.

   b. A recession causes a local factory to lay off 30 workers.

   c. Thousands of bus and truck drivers permanently lose their jobs when driverless, computer-driven vehicles make human drivers redundant.

   d. Hundreds of Toronto legal jobs permanently disappear when a lot of legal work gets outsourced to lawyers in India.

5. The unemployment rate that is consistent with full employment is known as_____. [LO9.2]

   a. The natural rate of unemployment

   b. The unnatural rate of unemployment

   c. The status quo rate of unemployment

   d. Cyclical unemployment

   e. Okun's rate of unemployment

6. A country's current unemployment rate is 11 percent. Economists estimate that its natural rate of unemployment is 6 percent. About how large is this economy's negative GDP gap? [LO9.2]

   a. 1 percent

   b. 3 percent

   c. 6 percent

   d. 10 percent

7. Cost–push inflation occurs when there is_____. [LO9.3]

   a. Excess inventory

   b. A trade deficit

   c. Rising per-unit production costs

   d. Excess demand for goods and services

8. Jimmer's nominal income will go up by 10 percent next year. Inflation is expected to be 22 percent next year. By approximately how much will Jimmer's real income change next year?   [LO9.3]

   a. 22 percent

   b. 8 percent

   c. 10 percent

   d. 12 percent

9. Kaitlin has $10,000 of savings that she may deposit with her local bank. Kaitlin wants to earn a real rate of return of at least 4 percent and she is expecting inflation to be exactly 3 percent. What is the lowest nominal interest rate that Kaitlin would be willing to accept from her local bank?   [LO9.4]

   a. 4 percent

   b. 5 percent

   c. 6 percent

   d. 7 percent

10. True or False? Lenders are helped by unanticipated inflation.   [LO9.4]

11. Economists agree that _____ inflation reduces real output.   [LO9.5]

   a. Cost–push

   b. Demand–pull

   c. Push–pull

Problems

1. Suppose that a country's annual growth rates were as follows over a 10-year period.

Year	Growth rate (%)
1	5
2	3
3	4
4	−1
5	−2
6	2
7	3
8	4
9	6
10	3

What was the country's trend rate of growth over this period? Which set of years most clearly demonstrates an expansionary phase of the business cycle? Which set of years best illustrates a recessionary phase of the business cycle?   [LO9.1]

2. Assume the following data for a country: total population, 500; population under 15 years of age or institutionalized, 120; not in labour force, 150; unemployed, 23; part-time workers looking for full-time jobs, 10. What is the size of the labour force? What is the official unemployment rate?   [LO9.2]

3. Suppose that the natural rate of unemployment in a particular year is 5 percent and the actual rate of unemployment is 9 percent. Use Okun's law to determine the size of the GDP gap in percentage-point terms. If the potential GDP is $500 billion in that year, how much output is being forgone because of cyclical unemployment?   [LO9.2]

4. If the CPI was 110 last year and is 121 this year, what is this year's rate of inflation? In contrast, suppose that the CPI was 110 last year and is 108 this year. What is this year's rate of inflation? What term do economists use to describe this second outcome?   [LO9.3]

5. How long would it take for the price level to double if inflation persisted at (a) 2, (b) 5, and (c) 10 percent per year?   [LO9.3]

6. If your nominal income rose by 5.3 percent and the price level rose by 3.8 percent in some year, by what approximate percentage would your real income increase? If your nominal income rose by 2.8 percent and your real income rose by 1.1 percent in some year, what was the approximate rate of inflation?   [LO9.4]

7. Suppose that the nominal rate of inflation is 4 percent and the inflation premium is 2 percent. What is the real interest rate? Alternatively, assume that the real interest rate is 1 percent and the nominal interest rate is 6 percent. What is the inflation premium?   [LO9.4]

PART 4 | MACROECONOMIC MODELS AND FISCAL POLICY

CHAPTER 10

Basic Macroeconomic Relationships*

LEARNING OBJECTIVES

LO10.1 Describe how changes in income affect consumption (and saving).

LO10.2 List and explain factors other than income that can affect consumption.

LO10.3 Explain how changes in real interest rates affect investment.

LO10.4 Identify and explain factors other than the real interest rate that can affect investment.

LO10.5 Illustrate how changes in investment (or one of the components of total spending) increase or decrease real GDP by a multiple amount.

In Chapter 9 we discussed the business cycle, unemployment, and inflation. Our eventual goal is to build economic models that can explain these phenomena. This chapter begins that process by examining basic relationships between three different pairs of economic aggregates. (Recall that, to economists, *aggregate* means "total" or "combined.") Specifically, this chapter looks at the relationships between

- Income and consumption (and income and saving)
- The interest rate and investment
- Changes in spending and changes in output

What explains the trends in consumption (consumer spending) and saving reported in the news? How do changes in interest rates affect investment? How can initial changes in spending ultimately produce multiplied changes in GDP? The basic macroeconomic relationships discussed in this chapter answer these questions.

---

* Note to instructors: If you wish to bypass the aggregate expenditures model covered in full in Chapter 11, assigning the present chapter will provide a seamless transition to the AD-AS model of Chapter 12 and the chapters beyond. If you want to cover the aggregate expenditures model, this chapter provides the necessary building blocks.

10.1	The Income–Consumption and Income–Saving Relationships

LO10.1   Describe how changes in income affect consumption (and saving).

The other-things-equal relationship between income and consumption is one of the best-established relationships in macroeconomics. In examining that relationship, we are also exploring the relationship between income and saving. Economists define *personal saving* as "not spending" or as "that part of disposable (after-tax) income not consumed." Saving (*S*) equals disposable income (DI) *minus* consumption (*C*). Disposable income, or after-tax income, is available to either *spend* or *save*.

FIGURE 10-1	Consumption and Disposable Income, 1990–2014

Each dot in this figure shows consumption and disposable income in a specific year. The line *C*, which generalizes the relationship between consumption and disposable income, indicates a direct relationship and shows that households consume most of their income.

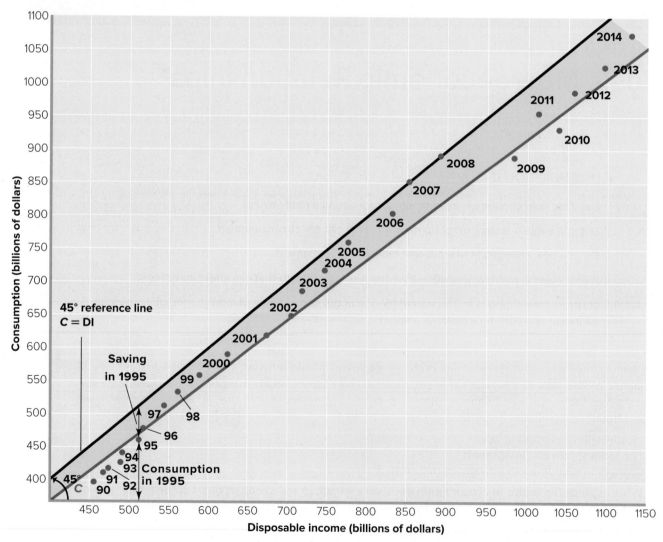

Source: Statistics Canada, CANSIM Tables 380-0073 http://www5.statcan.gc.ca/cansim/a26?lang=eng&retrLang=eng&id=3800073 and 380-0064: http://www5. statcan.gc.ca/cansim/a26?lang=eng&retrLang=eng&id=3800064. Accessed June 10, 2015.

Many factors determine a nation's levels of consumption and saving, but the most significant is disposable income. Consider some recent historical data for Canada. In Figure 10-1, each dot represents consumption and disposable income for one year since 1990. The line *C* fitted to these points shows that consumption is directly (positively) related to disposable income; moreover, households spend a large part of their income.

But we can say more. The **45° (degree) line** is a reference line. Because it bisects the 90° angle formed by the two axes of the graph, each point on it is equidistant from the two axes. At each point on the 45° line consumption equals disposable income, or *C* = DI. Therefore the vertical distance between the 45° line and any point on the horizontal axis measures either consumption *or* disposable income. If we let it measure disposable income, the vertical distance between it and the line labelled *C* represents the amount of saving (*S*) in that year.

Saving is the amount by which actual consumption in any year falls short of the 45° line (*S* = DI − *C*). For example, in 2014 disposable income was $1129 billion and consumption was $1074 billion, so saving was $55 billion. Observe that the vertical distance between the 45° line and line *C* increases as we move rightward along the horizontal axis and decreases as we move leftward. Like consumption, saving varies directly with the level of disposable income: as DI rises, saving increases; as DI falls, saving decreases.

ORIGIN OF THE IDEA 10.1   Income–Consumption Relationship

The Consumption Schedule

The dots in Figure 10-1 represent the actual amounts of DI, *C*, and *S* in Canada over a period of years. But, because we want to understand how the economy would behave under different possible scenarios, we need a schedule that shows the various amounts that households would plan to consume at each of the various levels of disposable income that might prevail at some time. Columns 1 and 2 of Table 10-1, represented in **Figure 10-2a (Key Graph)**, show a hypothetical consumption schedule of the type we

TABLE 10-1	**Consumption and Saving Schedules and Propensities to Consume and Save (billions of dollars)**					
(1) Level of output and income (GDP = DI)	(2) Consumption (C)	(3) Saving (S) (1) − (2)	(4) Average propensity to consume (APC) (2)/(1)	(5) Average propensity to save (APS) (3)/(1)	(6) Marginal propensity to consume (MPC) Δ(2)/Δ(1)*	(7) Marginal propensity to save (MPS) Δ(3)/Δ(1)*
(1) $370	$375	$−5	1.01	−0.01		
					0.75	0.25
(2) 390	390	0	1.00	0.00		
					0.75	0.25
(3) 410	405	5	0.99	0.01		
					0.75	0.25
(4) 430	420	10	0.98	0.02		
					0.75	0.25
(5) 450	435	15	0.97	0.03		
					0.75	0.25
(6) 470	450	20	0.96	0.04		
					0.75	0.25
(7) 490	465	25	0.95	0.05		
					0.75	0.25
(8) 510	480	30	0.94	0.06		
					0.75	0.25
(9) 530	495	35	0.93	0.07		
					0.75	0.25
(10) 550	510	40	0.93	0.07		

* The Greek letter Δ, delta, means "the change in."

KEY GRAPH

FIGURE 10-2 Consumption and Saving Schedules

The two parts of this figure show the income–consumption and income–saving relationships in Table 10-1 graphically. (a) Consumption rises as income increases. Saving is negative (dissaving occurs) when the consumption schedule is above the 45° line, and saving is positive when the consumption schedule is below the 45° line. (b) Like consumption, saving increases as income goes up. The saving schedule is found by subtracting the consumption schedule in the top graph vertically from the 45° line. For these hypothetical data, saving is −$5 billion at $370 billion of income, zero at $390 billion of income, and $5 billion at $410 of income. Saving is zero where consumption equals disposable income.

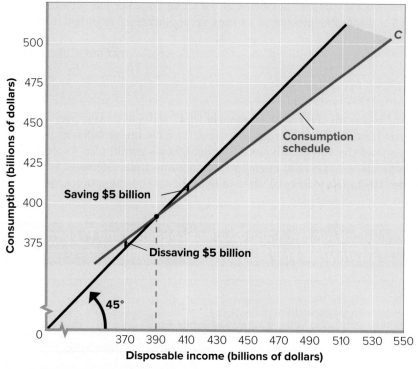

(a) Consumption schedule

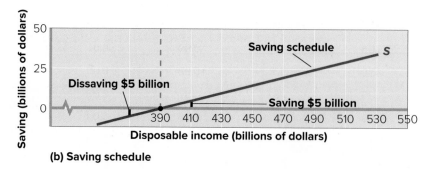

(b) Saving schedule

Quick Quiz

1. **The slope of the consumption schedule in this figure is 0.75. Thus the**
   a. Slope of the saving schedule is 1.33
   b. Marginal propensity to consume is 0.75
   c. Average propensity to consume is 0.25
   d. Slope of the saving schedule is also 0.75

2. **In this figure, when consumption is a positive amount, saving**
   a. Must be a negative amount
   b. Must also be a positive amount
   c. Can be either a positive or a negative amount
   d. Is zero

3. **In this figure**
   a. The marginal propensity to consume is constant at all levels of income
   b. The marginal propensity to save rises as disposable income rises
   c. Consumption is inversely (negatively) related to disposable income
   d. Saving is inversely (negatively) related to disposable income

4. **When consumption equals disposable income**
   a. The marginal propensity to consume is zero
   b. The average propensity to consume is zero
   c. Consumption and saving must be equal
   d. Saving must be zero

require. This **consumption schedule** (or *consumption function*) reflects the direct consumption–disposable income relationship. Note that, in the aggregate, households increase their spending as their disposable income rises and spend a larger proportion of a smaller disposable income than a larger disposable income.

The Saving Schedule

It is relatively simple to derive a **saving schedule** (or *saving function*). Because saving equals disposable income less consumption ($S = DI - C$), we need only subtract consumption (Table 10-1, column 2) from disposable income (column 1) to find the amount saved (column 3) at each DI. Thus, columns 1 and 3 in Table 10-1 are the saving schedule, represented in Figure 10-2b. The graph shows that there is a direct relationship between saving and DI but that saving is a smaller proportion of a small DI than of a large DI.

Since at each point on the 45° line consumption equals DI, we see *dissaving* at relatively low DIs, such as $370 billion (row 1, Table 10-1), at which consumption is $375 billion. Households can consume more than their current income by liquidating (selling for cash) accumulated wealth or by borrowing. Graphically, dissaving is shown as the vertical distance of the consumption schedule above the 45° line or as the vertical distance of the saving schedule below the horizontal axis. We have marked the dissaving at the $370 billion level of income in Figures 10-2a and b. Both vertical distances measure the $5 billion of dissaving that occurs at $370 billion of income.

In our example, the **break-even income** is $390 billion (row 2). This is the income level at which households plan to consume their entire incomes ($C = DI$). Graphically, the consumption schedule cuts the 45° line, and the saving schedule cuts the horizontal axis (saving is zero) at the break-even income level.

At all higher incomes, households plan to save part of their income. Graphically, the vertical distance of the consumption schedule below the 45° line measures this saving, as does the vertical distance of the saving schedule above the horizontal axis. For example, at the $410 billion level of income (row 3), both these distances indicate $5 billion of saving (also see Figures 10-2a and b).

Average and Marginal Propensities

Columns 4 to 7 in Table 10-1 show additional characteristics of the consumption and saving schedules.

10.1 GLOBAL PERSPECTIVE

Average Propensities to Consume, Selected Nations

There are surprisingly large differences in average propensities to consume (APCs) among nations. In 2011, Italy, the United States, Canada, and Netherlands in particular had substantially higher APCs, and thus lower APSs, than several other advanced economies.

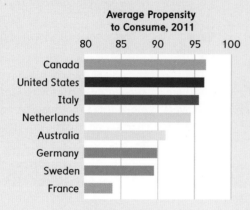

Source: Organization for Economic Cooperation and Development, OECD, www.oecd.org. Derived from OECD household saving rates as percentages of disposable income. Econ Outlook 86, Annex Table 23, extracted March 2013.

APC AND APS

The fraction, or percentage, of total income that is consumed is the **average propensity to consume (APC)**. The fraction of total income that is saved is the **average propensity to save (APS)**. That is,

$$APC = \frac{consumption}{income}$$

and

$$APS = \frac{saving}{income}$$

For example, at $470 billion of income (row 6) in Table 10-1, the APC is 450/470 = 45/47, or about 0.96 (= 96 percent), and the APS is 20/470 = 2/47, or about 0.04 (= 4 percent). Columns 4 and 5 in Table 10-1 show the APC and APS at each of the 10 levels of DI. As implied by our previous discussion, the APC falls as DI increases, while the APS rises as DI goes up.

Because disposable income is either consumed or saved, the fraction of any DI consumed plus the fraction saved (not consumed) must exhaust that income. Mathematically, APC + APS = 1 at any level of disposable income, as columns 4 and 5 in Table 10-1 illustrate. So, if 0.96 of the $470 billion of income in row 6 is consumed, 0.04 must be saved. That is why APC + APS = 1.

Global Perspective 10.1 shows APCs for several countries.

MPC AND MPS

The proportion, or fraction, of any change in income consumed is called the **marginal propensity to consume (MPC)**, with *marginal* meaning *extra* or *a change in*. The MPC is the ratio of a change in consumption to the change in the income that caused the consumption change:

$$MPC = \frac{\text{change in consumption}}{\text{change in income}}$$

Similarly, the fraction of any change in income saved is the **marginal propensity to save (MPS)**. The MPS is the ratio of a change in saving to the change in income that brought it about:

$$MPS = \frac{\text{change in saving}}{\text{change in income}}$$

If disposable income is $470 billion (row 6 horizontally in Table 10-1) and household income rises by $20 billion to $490 billion (row 7), households will consume $\frac{15}{20}$, or $\frac{3}{4}$, and save $\frac{5}{20}$, or $\frac{1}{4}$, of that increase in income. In other words, the MPC is $\frac{3}{4}$ or 0.75, and the MPS is $\frac{1}{4}$ or 0.25, as shown in columns 6 and 7.

The sum of the MPC and the MPS for any change in disposable income must always be 1. Neither MPC or MPS can be greater than 1. If you earn an extra $10 and spend it all, MPC would be equal to 1, and you would not save anything from the extra $10 you earned. Consuming or saving out of extra income is an either/or proposition; the fraction of any change in income not consumed is, by definition, saved. If 0.75 of extra disposable income is consumed, 0.25 must be saved. The fraction consumed (MPC) plus the fraction saved (MPS) must exhaust the whole change in income: MPC + MPS = 1. In our example, 0.75 plus 0.25 equals 1.

WORKED PROBLEM 10.1   Consumption and Saving

MPC AND MPS AS SLOPES

The MPC is the numerical value of the slope of the consumption schedule, and the MPS is the numerical value of the slope of the saving schedule. We know from the appendix to Chapter 1 that the slope of any line is the ratio of the vertical change to the horizontal change.

Figure 10-3 shows how the slopes of the consumption and saving lines are calculated, using enlarged portions of Figures 10-2a and 10-2b. Observe that consumption changes by $15 billion (vertical change) for each $20 billion change in disposable income (horizontal change). The slope of the consumption line is thus 0.75 (= $15/$20)–the value of the MPC. Saving changes by $5 billion (vertical change) for every $20 billion change in disposable income (horizontal change). The slope of the saving line therefore is 0.25 (= $5/$20), which is the value of the MPS.

FIGURE 10-3   **The Marginal Propensity to Consume and the Marginal Propensity to Save**

In the two parts of this figure, the Greek letter delta (Δ) means *the change in.* (a) The MPC is the slope (ΔC/ΔDI) of the consumption schedule. (b) The MPS is the slope (ΔS/ΔDI) of the saving schedule.

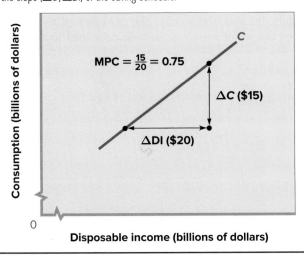

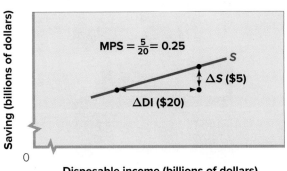

10.2 / Non-income Determinants of Consumption and Saving

LO10.2 List and explain factors other than income that can affect consumption.

The amount of disposable income is the main determinant of the amounts households will consume and save. But certain determinants other than income will cause households to consume more or less at each possible level of income and thereby shift the consumption and saving schedules. Those other determinants are wealth, borrowing, expectations, and real interest rates.

WEALTH

A household's wealth is the dollar amount of all the assets that it owns minus the dollar amount of its liabilities (all the debt that it owes). Households build wealth by saving money out of current income. The point of building wealth is to increase consumption possibilities. The larger the stock of wealth that a household can build up, the larger will be its present and future consumption possibilities.

Events sometimes suddenly boost the value of existing wealth. When this happens, households tend to increase their spending and reduce their saving. This so-called **wealth effect** shifts the consumption schedule upward and the saving schedule downward. They move in response to households taking advantage of the increased consumption possibilities afforded by the sudden increase in wealth. For example, in the late 1990s skyrocketing stock values expanded the value of household wealth by increasing the value of household assets. Predictably, households spent more and saved less. In contrast, a strong *reverse* wealth effect occurred in 2008. Plunging market prices joined together to erase billions of dollars of household wealth. Consumers quickly reacted by reducing their consumption spending. The consumption schedule shifted downward.

BORROWING

Household borrowing also affects consumption. When a household borrows, it can increase current consumption beyond what would be possible if its spending were limited to its DI.[1] By allowing households to spend more, borrowing shifts the current consumption schedule upward. But note that "there's no free lunch." While borrowing in the present allows for higher consumption in the present, it necessitates lower consumption in the future when the debts must be repaid. Stated a bit differently, increased borrowing increases debt (liabilities), which in turn reduces household wealth (since wealth = assets − liabilities). This reduction in wealth reduces future consumption possibilities in much the same way that a decline in asset values would. But note that the term *reverse wealth effect* is reserved for situations in which wealth unexpectedly changes because asset values unexpectedly change. It is not used to refer to situations such as the one being discussed here, where wealth is intentionally reduced by households through borrowing and piling up debt in order to increase current consumption. As of 2014, Canadian households had the dubious distinction of having one of the highest debt loads in the world. The governor of the Bank of Canada repeatedly warned Canadians of the potential danger of a high household debt load to the fragile recovery from the Great Recession of 2008–2009.

Expectations of rising prices tomorrow may trigger more spending and less saving today.

---

[1] Households can also maintain or increase current consumption by dipping into past savings.

EXPECTATIONS

Household expectations about future prices and income affect current spending and saving. For example, expectations of higher prices tomorrow may cause households to buy more today while prices are still low. Thus, the current consumption schedule shifts upward and the current saving schedule shifts downward. Or, expectations of lower income in the future may result in less consumption and more saving today. Households' greater present saving will help build wealth that will help them ride out the expected bad times. The consumption schedule will therefore shift downward and the saving schedule will shift upward.

REAL INTEREST RATES

When real interest rates (those adjusted for inflation) fall, households tend to borrow more, consume more, and save less. A lower interest rate, for example, decreases monthly loan payments and induces consumers to purchase automobiles and other goods bought on credit. A lower interest rate also diminishes the incentive to save because of the reduced interest "payment" to the saver. These effects on consumption and saving, however, are very modest. Lower interest rates shift the consumption schedule slightly upward and the saving schedule slightly downward. Higher interest rates do the opposite.

Other Important Considerations

There are several additional important points about the consumption and saving schedules.

- ***Switching to Real GDP*** When developing macroeconomic models, economists change their focus from the relationship between consumption (and saving) and disposable income to the relationship between consumption (and saving) and real domestic output (real GDP), since they want to know how changes in consumption and saving affect the output of the entire economy, not just disposable income. That modification is reflected in Figures 10-4a and 10-4b, where the horizontal axes measure real GDP.

KEY GRAPH

FIGURE 10-4 **Shifts in the Consumption and Saving Schedules**

Normally, if households consume more at each level of real GDP, they are necessarily saving less. Graphically this means that an upward shift of the consumption schedule (C_0 to C_1) entails a downward shift of the saving schedule (S_0 to S_1). If households consume less at each level of real GDP, they are saving more. A downward shift of the consumption schedule (C_0 to C_2) is reflected in an upward shift of the saving schedule (S_0 to S_2). (This pattern breaks down, however, when taxes change; then the consumption and saving schedules shift in the same direction—opposite to the direction of the tax change.)

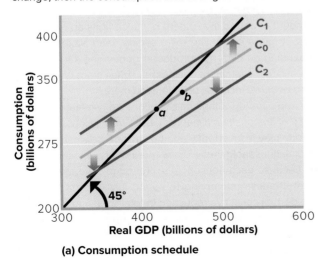

(a) Consumption schedule

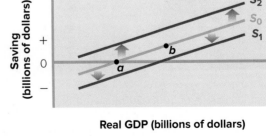

(b) Saving schedule

- *Changes Along Schedules* The movement from one point to another on a consumption schedule (for example, from a to b on C_0 in Figure 10-4a)–a change in the amount consumed–is solely caused by a change in disposable income (or GDP). On the other hand, an upward or downward shift of the entire schedule–for example, a shift from C_0 to C_1 or C_2 in Figure 10-4a–is a shift of the consumption schedule and is caused by changes in any one or more of the four non-income determinants of consumption just discussed.

  A similar distinction in terminology applies to the saving schedule in Figure 10-4b.

- *Simultaneous Shifts* Changes in wealth, borrowing, expectations, and real interest rates will shift the consumption schedule in one direction and the saving schedule in the opposite direction. If households decide to consume more at each possible level of real GDP they must save less, and vice versa. (Even when they spend more by borrowing, they are in effect reducing their current saving by the amount borrowed since borrowing is, effectively, negative saving.) Graphically, if the consumption schedule shifts from C_0 to C_1 in Figure 10-4a, the saving schedule will shift downward, from S_0 to S_1 in Figure 10-4b. Similarly, a downward shift of the consumption schedule from C_0 to C_2 means an upward shift of the saving schedule from S_0 to S_2.

- *Taxation* In contrast, a change in taxes shifts the consumption and saving schedules in the same direction. Taxes are paid partly at the expense of consumption and partly at the expense of saving. So an

---

CONSIDER THIS   The Great Recession and the Paradox of Thrift

The Great Recession of 2008–2009 altered the prior consumption and saving behaviour in the economy. Concerned about reduced wealth, high debt, and potential job losses, households increased their saving and reduced their consumption at each level of after-tax income (or each level of GDP). In Figure 10.4, this outcome is illustrated as the downward shift of the consumption schedule in the top graph and the upward shift of the saving schedule in the lower graph.

This change of behaviour illustrates the so-called **paradox of thrift**, which refers to the possibility that a recession can be made worse when households become more thrifty and save in response to the downturn. The paradox of thrift rests on two major ironies.

One irony is that saving more is *good* for the economy in the long run, as noted in Chapter 1. It finances investment and therefore fuels subsequent economic growth. But saving more can be *bad* for the economy during a recession, when the increased saving is not likely to be matched by an equal amount of added investment because firms are pessimistic about future sales. The extra saving, then, simply reduces spending on currently produced goods and services. That means that even more businesses suffer, more layoffs occur, and people's incomes decline even more.

The paradox of thrift has a second irony related to the *fallacy of composition* (Chapter 1, Last Word): Households as a group may inadvertently end up saving less when each individual household tries to save more during a recession. This is because each household's attempt to save more implies that it is also attempting to spend less. Across all households, that collective reduction in total spending in the economy creates more job losses and further drives down total income. The decline in total income reduces the ability of households as a group to save as much as they did before their spending reduction and subsequent income declines.

increase in taxes will reduce both consumption and saving, shifting the consumption schedule in Figure 10-4a and the saving schedule in Figure 10-4b downward. Conversely, households will partly consume and partly save any decrease in taxes. Both the consumption schedule and saving schedule will shift upward.

- **Stability** The consumption and saving schedules are usually relatively stable unless altered by major tax increases or decreases. Their stability may be because consumption-saving decisions are strongly influenced by long-term considerations such as saving to meet emergencies or saving for retirement. It may also be because changes in the non-income determinants frequently work in opposite directions and therefore may cancel each other out.

QUICK REVIEW 10.1

- Both consumption and saving rise when disposable income increases; both fall when disposable income decreases.

- The average propensity to consume (APC) is the fraction of disposable income that is spent on consumer goods; the average propensity to save (APS) is the fraction of disposable income that is saved. The APC falls and the APS rises as disposable income increases.

- The marginal propensity to consume (MPC) is the fraction of a change in disposable income that is consumed and is the slope of the consumption schedule; the marginal propensity to save (MPS) is the fraction of a change in disposable income that is saved and is the slope of the saving schedule.

- Changes in consumer wealth, consumer expectations, real interest rates, household debt, and taxes can shift the consumption and saving schedules (as they relate to real GDP).

10.3 / The Interest Rate–Investment Relationship

LO10.3 Explain how changes in real interest rates affect investment.

Recall that investment consists of expenditures on new plants, capital equipment, machinery, inventories, and so on. The investment decision is a marginal-benefit–marginal-cost decision: the marginal benefit from investment is the expected rate of return businesses hope to realize. The marginal cost is the interest rate that must be paid for borrowing funds. Businesses will invest in all projects for which the expected rate of return exceeds the interest rate. Expected returns (profits) and the interest rate therefore are the two basic determinants of investment spending.

Expected Rate of Return

Investment spending is guided by the profit motive; businesses buy capital goods only when such purchases will be profitable. Suppose the owner of a small cabinet-making shop is considering whether to invest in a new sanding machine that costs $1000 and has a useful life of only one year. The new machine will increase the firm's output and sales revenue. Suppose the net expected revenue from the machine (that is, after such operating costs as power, lumber, labour, and certain taxes have been subtracted) is $1100. Then, after the $1000 cost of the machine is subtracted from the net expected revenue of $1100, the firm will have an expected profit of $100. Dividing this $100 profit by the $1000 cost of the machine, we find that the **expected rate of return**, r, on the machine is 10 percent (= $100/$1000). Note that this is an *expected* rate of return, not a *guaranteed* rate of return. The investment may or may not generate as much revenue or as much profit as anticipated. Investment involves risk.

The Real Interest Rate

One important cost associated with investing that our example has ignored is interest–the financial cost of borrowing the *money* capital required to purchase the *real* capital (the sanding machine).

The interest cost is computed by multiplying the interest rate, i, by the $1000 amount borrowed to buy the machine. If the interest rate is, say, 7 percent, the total interest cost will be $70. This compares favourably with the net expected return of $100, which produced the 10 percent rate of return. We can generalize as follows: If the expected rate of return (say, 10 percent) exceeds the interest rate (say, 7 percent), the investment will be profitable. But if the interest rate (say, 12 percent) exceeds the expected rate of return (10 percent), the investment will be unprofitable. The firm undertakes all profitable investment projects. This means that the firm should array its prospective investment projects from the highest expected rate of return, r, downward, and then invest in all projects for which r exceeds i. The firm, therefore, should invest right to the very point where $r = i$ because then it will have undertaken all investments for which r is greater than i. The *real* rate of interest, rather than the *nominal* rate, is crucial in making investment decisions. Recall from Chapter 9 that the nominal interest rate is expressed in dollars of current value, but the real interest rate is stated in dollars of constant or inflation-adjusted value. The *real interest rate* is the nominal rate less the rate of inflation. In our sanding machine illustration, our implicit assumption of a constant price level ensures that all our data, including the interest rate, are in real terms.

Investment Demand Curve

We now move from a single firm's investment decision to total demand for investment goods by the entire business sector. Assume that every firm has estimated the expected rates of return from all investment projects and has recorded those data. We can cumulate–successively sum–these data by asking the following: How many dollars' worth of investment projects have an expected rate of return of, say, 16 percent or more? Of 14 percent or more? Of 12 percent or more? And so on.

Suppose no prospective investments yield an expected return of 16 percent or more. But suppose there are $5 billion of investment opportunities with expected rates of return of 14–16 percent, an additional $5 billion yielding 12–14 percent, still an additional $5 billion yielding 10–12 percent, and an additional $5 billion in each successive 2 percent range of yield down to and including the 0–2 percent range.

To cumulate these figures for each rate of return, r, we add the amounts of investment that will yield each particular rate of return r or higher. In this way we obtain the data in the table in Figure 10-5, shown graphically in **Figure 10-5 (Key Graph)**. In the table, the number opposite 12 percent, for example, tells us there are $10 billion of investment opportunities that will yield an expected rate of return of 12 percent or more. The $10 billion includes the $5 billion of investment expected to yield a return of 14 percent or more plus the $5 billion expected to yield 12–14 percent.

MATH 10.1   Investment Demand Curve

We know from our example of the sanding machine that an investment project will be profitable, and will be undertaken, if its expected rate of return, r, exceeds the real interest rate, i. Let's first suppose that i is 12 percent. Businesses will undertake all investments for which r is equal to or exceeds 12 percent. Figure 10-5 reveals that $10 billion of investment spending will be undertaken at a 12 percent interest rate; that means $10 billion of investment projects have an expected rate of return of 12 percent or more.

ORIGIN OF THE IDEA 10.2   Interest-Rate–Investment Relationship

By applying the marginal-benefit–marginal-cost rule that investment projects should be undertaken up to the point where $r = i$, we see that we can add the real interest rate to the vertical axis in Figure 10-5. The curve in Figure 10-5 shows not only rates of return, but also the quantity of investment demanded at each "price" i (interest rate) of investment. The vertical axis in Figure 10-5 shows the various possible real interest rates, and the horizontal axis shows the corresponding quantities of investment demanded. The inverse (downward-sloping) relationship between the interest rate (price) and dollar quantity of investment demanded conforms with the law of demand discussed in Chapter 3. The curve *ID* in Figure 10-5 is the economy's **investment demand curve**. It shows the amount of investment forthcoming at each real interest rate.

KEY GRAPH

FIGURE 10-5 The Investment Demand Curve

The investment demand curve is constructed by arraying all potential investment projects in descending order of their expected rates of return. The curve is downsloping, reflecting an inverse relationship between the real interest rate (the financial "price" of each dollar of investing) and the quantity of investment demanded.

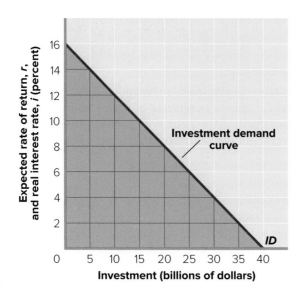

REAL INTEREST RATE (*I*), EXPECTED RATE OF RETURN (*R*), AND INVESTMENT

Expected rate of return (*r*)	Cumulative amount of investment having this rate of return or higher (billions per year)
16%	$ 0
14	5
12	10
10	15
8	20
6	25
4	30
2	35
0	40

Quick Quiz

1. The investment demand curve
   a. Reflects a direct (positive) relationship between the real interest rate and investment
   b. Reflects an inverse (negative) relationship between the real interest rate and investment
   c. Shifts to the right when the real interest rate rises
   d. Shifts to the left when the real interest rate rises

2. In this figure
   a. Greater cumulative amounts of investment are associated with lower expected rates of return on investment
   b. Lesser cumulative amounts of investment are associated with lower expected rates of return on investment
   c. Higher interest rates are associated with higher expected rates of return on investment, and therefore greater amounts of investment

   d. Interest rates and investment move in the same direction

3. In this figure, if the real interest rate falls from 6 percent to 4 percent
   a. Investment will increase from 0 to $30 billion
   b. Investment will decrease by $5 billion
   c. The expected rate of return will rise by $5 billion
   d. Investment will increase from $25 billion to $30 billion

4. In this figure, investment will be
   a. Zero if the real interest rate is zero
   b. $40 billion if the real interest rate is 16 percent
   c. $30 billion if the real interest rate is 4 percent
   d. $20 billion if the real interest rate is 12 percent

Answers: 1. b; 2. a; 3. d; 4. c

10.4 / Shifts in the Investment Demand Curve

LO10.4 Identify and explain factors other than the real interest rate that can affect investment.

Figure 10-5 shows the relationship between the interest rate and the amount of investment demanded, other things equal. When other things change, the investment demand curve shifts. In general, any factor that leads businesses collectively to expect greater rates of return on their investments increases investment demand; that factor shifts the investment demand curve to the right, as from ID_0 to ID_1 in Figure 10-6. Any factor that leads businesses collectively to expect lower rates of return on their investments shifts the curve to the left, as from ID_0 to ID_2. What are those non–interest rate determinants of investment demand?

Acquisition, Maintenance, and Operating Costs

The initial costs of capital goods, and the estimated costs of operating and maintaining those goods, affect the expected rate of return on investment. When costs fall, the expected rate of return from prospective investment projects rises, shifting the investment demand curve to the right. For example, lower electricity costs associated with operating equipment shift the investment demand curve to the right. Higher costs, in contrast, shift the curve to the left.

Business Taxes

When government is considered, firms look to expected returns *after taxes* in making their investment decisions. An increase in business taxes lowers the expected profitability of investments and shifts the investment demand curve to the left; a reduction of business taxes shifts it to the right.

Technological progress stimulates investment.

Technological Change

Technological progress–the development of new products, improvements in existing products, and the creation of new machinery and production processes–stimulates investment. The development of a more efficient machine, for example, lowers production costs or improves product quality and increases the expected rate of return from investing in the machine. Profitable new products (for example, cholesterol medications, Internet services, high-resolution televisions, cellphones, and so on) induce a flurry of investment as firms tool up for expanded production. A rapid rate of technological progress shifts the investment demand curve to the right.

Stock of Capital Goods on Hand

The stock of capital goods on hand, relative to output and sales, influences investment decisions by firms. When the economy is overstocked with production facilities and when firms have excessive inventories of finished goods, the expected rate of return on new investment declines. Firms with excess production capacity have little incentive to invest in new capital. Therefore, less investment is forthcoming at each real interest rate; the investment demand curve shifts leftward.

When the economy is understocked with production facilities, and when firms are selling their output as quickly as they can produce it, the expected rate of return on new investment increases and the investment demand curve shifts rightward.

| FIGURE 10-6 | **Shifts in the Investment Demand Curve** |

Increases in investment demand are shown as rightward shifts in the investment demand curve; decreases in investment demand are shown as leftward shifts in the investment demand curve.

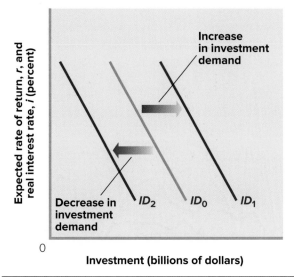

Planned Inventory

Recall from Chapter 7 that the definition of investment includes changes in inventories of unsold goods. An increase in inventories is counted as positive investment, while a decrease is counted as negative investment. It is important to remember that some inventory changes are planned, while others are unplanned. Since the investment demand curve deals only with *planned* investment, it is affected only by *planned* changes that firms desire to make to their inventory levels. If firms plan to increase their inventories, the investment demand curve shifts to the right. If firms plan to decrease their inventories, the investment demand curve shifts to the left.

Firms make planned changes to their inventory levels mostly because they are expecting either faster or slower sales. A firm that expects its sales to double in the next year will want to keep more inventory in stock, thereby increasing its investment demand. By contrast, a firm that is expecting slower sales will plan on reducing its inventory, thereby reducing its overall investment demand. But because life often does not turn out as expected, firms often find that the actual amount of inventory investment that they end up making is either more or less than what they had planned. The size of the gap is, naturally, the dollar amount of their *unplanned* inventory changes. These unplanned inventory adjustments will play a large role in the aggregate expenditures model studied in Chapter 11.

Expectations

We noted that business investment is based on expected returns (expected additions to profit). Most capital goods are durable, with a life expectancy of ten or twenty years. Thus, the expected rate of return on capital investment depends on the firm's expectations of future sales, future operating costs, and future profitability of the product that the capital helps to produce. These expectations are based on forecasts of future business conditions as well as on such elusive and difficult-to-predict factors as changes in the domestic political climate, the thrust of foreign affairs, population growth, and consumer tastes. If executives become more optimistic about future sales, costs, and profits, the investment demand curve will shift to the right; a pessimistic outlook will shift it to the left.

Global Perspective 10.2 compares investment spending relative to GDP for several nations in a recent year. Domestic real interest rates and investment demand determine the levels of investment relative to GDP.

| FIGURE 10-7 | The Volatility of Investment, 1973–2014 |

Annual percentage changes in investment spending are often several times greater than the percentage changes in GDP. (Data are in real terms. Investment is gross private domestic investment.)

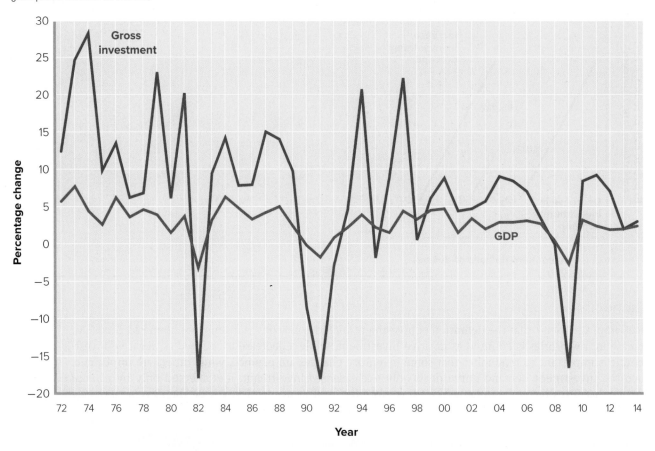

| CONSIDER THIS | The Great Recession and the Investment Riddle | |

During the Great Recession of 2008–2009, real interest rates declined essentially to zero. Figure 10-5 suggests that this drop in interest rates should have boosted investment spending. But gross fixed investment declined substantially—by 16 percent—between 2008 and 2009. Does this combination of lower real interest rates and reduced investment make Figure 10-5 irrelevant?

Definitely not! The key to the investment riddle is that during the recession the investment demand curve shifted inward, as from ID_0 to ID_2 in Figure 10-6, so much that this shift overwhelmed any investment-increasing effects of the decline of real interest rates. The net result turned out to be less investment, not more.

The leftward shift of the investment demand reflected a decline in the expected returns from investment. Firms envisioned zero or negative returns on investment in new capital because they were facing an overstock of existing capital relative to their current sales. Understandably, they were therefore not inclined to invest. Also, firms were extremely pessimistic about when the economy would regain its strength. This pessimism also contributed to low expected rates of return on investment and thus to exceptionally weak investment demand. Further, even though the interest rate was so low, firms that wanted to borrow and invest found that lenders were very reluctant to lend them money for fear that they would not be able to pay back the loans.

10.2 GLOBAL PERSPECTIVE

Gross Investment Expenditures as a Percentage of GDP, Selected Nations

As a percentage of GDP, investment varies widely by nation. These differences can, of course, change from year to year.

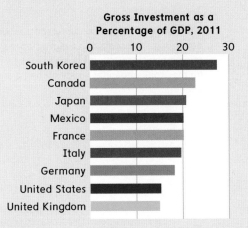

Gross Investment as a Percentage of GDP, 2011

Source: Gross fixed capital formation data from International Financial Statistics, International Monetary Fund, www.lmf.org.

Fluctuations of Investment

In contrast to the consumption schedule, the investment schedule fluctuates quite a bit. Investment is, in fact, the most volatile component of total spending–so much so that most of the fluctuations in output and employment that happen over the course of the business cycle can be attributed to demand shocks relating to unexpected increases and decreases in investment. Figure 10-7 shows just how volatile investment in Canada has been. Notice that the swings in investment in real terms are greater than the swings in real GDP. Several interrelated factors drawn from our previous discussion explain the variability of investment.

- **Variability of Expectations** Business expectations can change quickly when some event suggests a significant possible change in future business conditions. Changes in exchange rates, trade barriers, legislative actions, stock market prices, government economic policies, the outlook for war or peace, court decisions in key labour or antitrust cases, and a host of similar considerations may cause substantial shifts in business expectations.

- **Durability** Because of their durability, capital goods have indefinite useful lifespans. Within limits, purchases of capital goods are discretionary and therefore can be postponed. Firms can scrap or replace older equipment and buildings, or they can patch them up and use them for a few more years. Optimism about the future may prompt firms to replace their older facilities and such modernizing will call for a high level of investment. A less optimistic view, however, may lead to smaller amounts of investment as firms repair older facilities and keep them in use.

- **Irregularity of Innovation** New products and processes stimulate investment. Major innovations such as railroads, electricity, airplanes, automobiles, computers, the Internet, and cellphones induce vast upsurges or "waves" of investment spending that in time recede. But such innovations occur quite irregularly, adding to the volatility of investment.

- **Variability of Profits** High current profits often generate optimism about the future profitability of new investments, whereas low current profits or losses spawn considerable doubt about the wisdom of new investments. Additionally, firms often save a portion of current profits as retained earnings and use these funds (as well as borrowed funds) to finance new investments. So current profits affect both the incentive and ability to invest. But profits themselves are highly variable from year to year, contributing to the volatility of investment.

In terms of our previous analysis, we would represent volatility of investment as occasional and substantial unexpected shifts of the investment demand curve (as in Figure 10-6), which cause significant changes in investment spending (as in Figure 10-7). These demand shocks can contribute to cyclical fluctuations.

10.5 / The Multiplier Effect*

10.5 Illustrate how changes in investment (or one of the components of total spending) increase or decrease real GDP by a multiple amount.

A final basic relationship that merits discussion is the relationship between changes in spending and changes in real GDP. Assuming that the economy has room to expand–so that increases in spending do not lead to increases in prices–a direct relationship exists between these two aggregates. More spending results in a higher GDP; less spending results in a lower GDP. But there is much more to this relationship. A change in spending–say, investment–ultimately changes output and income by more than the initial change in investment spending. That surprising result is called the *multiplier effect:* a change in a component of total spending leads to a larger change in GDP. The **multiplier** determines how much larger that change will be; it is the ratio of a change in GDP to the initial change in spending (in this case, investment). Stated generally,

$$\text{Multiplier} = \frac{\text{change in real GDP}}{\text{initial change in spending}}$$

By rearranging this equation, we can also say that

Change in GDP = multiplier × initial change in spending

Note these four points about the multiplier:

1. The *initial change in spending* is usually associated with investment spending because of investment's volatility. But changes in consumption (unrelated to changes in income), net exports, and government purchases also lead to the multiplier effect.

2. The initial change in spending associated with investment spending results from a change in the real interest rate and/or a shift of the investment demand curve.

3. Implicit in the preceding point is that the multiplier works in both directions. An increase in initial spending will create a multiple increase in GDP; a decrease in spending will create a larger decrease in GDP.

---

*Note to instructors: If you cover the full aggregate expenditures model (Chapter 11) rather than moving directly to aggregate demand and aggregate supply (Chapter 12), you may choose to defer this discussion until after the analysis of equilibrium real GDP.

4. This is the *simple multiplier,* or closed economy multiplier. The open economy multiplier will be discussed in Chapter 11.

Rationale

The multiplier effect, which is similar to a "snowball effect," follows from two facts. First, the economy supports repetitive, continuous flows of expenditures and income through which dollars spent by Smith are received as income by Chin and then spent by Chin and received as income by Dubois, and so on. Second, any change in income will vary both consumption and saving in the same direction as, and by a fraction of, the change in income.

It follows that an initial change in spending will set off a spending chain throughout the economy. That chain of spending, although of diminishing magnitude at each successive step, will cumulate to a multiple change in GDP. Initial changes in spending produce magnified changes in output and income.

The table in Figure 10-8 illustrates the rationale underlying the multiplier effect. Suppose a $5 billion increase in investment spending occurs. We assume that the MPC is 0.75, the MPS is 0.25, and prices remain constant. That is, neither the initial increase in spending nor any of the subsequent increases in spending will cause prices to rise.

The initial $5 billion increase in investment generates an equal amount of wage, rent, interest, and profit income, because spending income and receiving income are two sides of the same transaction. How much consumption will be induced by this $5 billion increase in the incomes of households? We find the answer by applying the marginal propensity to consume of 0.75 to this change in income. Thus, the $5 billion increase in income initially raises consumption by $3.75 billion (= 0.75 × $5 billion) and saving by $1.25 billion (= 0.25 × $5 billion), as shown in columns 2 and 3 in the table.

Other households receive as income (in round 2) the $3.75 billion of consumption spending. Those households consume 0.75 of this $3.75 billion, or $2.81 billion, and save 0.25 of it, or $0.94 billion. The $2.81 billion that is consumed flows to still other households as income to be spent or saved (in round 3). And the process continues, with the added consumption and income becoming less in each round. The process ends when there is no additional income to spend.

The bar chart in Figure 10-8 shows several rounds of the multiplier process of the table graphically. As shown by rounds 1 to 5, each round adds a smaller and smaller orange block to national income and GDP. The process continues beyond the five rounds shown (for convenience we have simply cumulated the subsequent declining blocks into a single block labelled "All other rounds"). The accumulation of the additional income in each round–the sum of the orange blocks–is the total change in income or GDP resulting from the initial $5 billion change in spending. Because the spending and re-spending effects of the increase in investment diminish with each successive round of spending, the cumulative increase in output and income eventually ends. In this case, the ending occurs when $20 billion of additional income accumulates. Thus, the multiplier is 4 (= $20 billion/$5 billion).

The Multiplier and the Marginal Propensities

You may sense from the table in Figure 10-8 that the fraction of an increase in income consumed (MPC) and saved (MPS) determines the cumulative re-spending effects of any initial change in spending and therefore determines the size of the multiplier. *The MPC and the multiplier are directly related, and the MPS and the multiplier are inversely related.* The precise formulas are as shown in the following two equations:

$$\text{Multiplier} = \frac{1}{1 - \text{MPC}}$$

Recall, too, that MPC + MPS = 1. Therefore MPS = 1 − MPC, which means we can also write the multiplier formula as

$$\text{Multiplier} = \frac{1}{\text{MPS}}$$

FIGURE 10-8   ## The Multiplier Process (MPC = 0.75)

An initial change in investment spending of $5 billion creates an equal $5 billion of new income in round 1. Households spend $3.75 billion (= 0.75 × $5 billion) of this new income, creating $3.75 billion of added income in round 2. Of this $3.75 billion of new income, households spend $2.81 billion (= 0.75 × $3.75 billion), and income rises by that amount in round 3. The cumulation of such income increments over the entire process eventually results in a total change of income and GDP of $20 billion. The multiplier therefore is 4 (= $20 billion ÷ $5 billion).

THE MULTIPLIER: A TABULAR ILLUSTRATION (IN BILLIONS)			
	(1) Change in income	**(2)** Change in consumption (MPC = 0.75)	**(3)** Change in saving (MPS = 0.25)
Round 1: Increase in investment of **$5.00**	$ 5.00	$ 3.75	$ 1.25
Round 2	3.75	2.81	0.94
Round 3	2.81	2.11	0.70
Round 4	2.11	1.58	0.53
Round 5	1.58	1.19	0.39
All other rounds	4.75	3.56	1.19
Total	**$20.00**	$15.00	$5.00

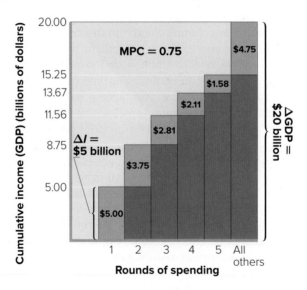

This latter formula is a quick way to determine the multiplier. All you need to know is the MPS.

The smaller the fraction of any change in income saved, the greater the re-spending at each round and, therefore, the greater the multiplier. When the MPS is 0.25, as in our example, the multiplier is 4. If the MPS were 0.2, the multiplier would be 5. If the MPS were 0.33, the multiplier would be 3. Let's see why.

Suppose the MPS is 0.2 and businesses increase investment by $5 billion. In the first round of the table in Figure 10-8, consumption will rise by $4 billion (= MPC of 0.8 × $5 billion) rather than by $3.75 billion because saving will increase by $1 billion (= MPS of 0.2 × $5 billion) rather than $1.25 billion. The greater rise in consumption in Round 1 will produce a greater increase in income in Round 2. The same will be true for all successive rounds. If we worked through all rounds of the multiplier, we would find that the process ends when income has cumulatively increased by $25 billion, not the $20 billion shown in the table. When the MPS is 0.2 rather than 0.25, the multiplier is 5 (= $25 billion/$5 billion) as opposed to 4 (= $20 billion/$5 billion).

FIGURE 10-9 The MPC and the Multiplier

The larger the MPC (the smaller the MPS), the greater the size of the multiplier.

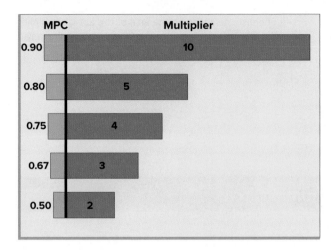

If the MPS were 0.33 rather than 0.25, the successive increases in consumption and income would be less than those in the table in Figure 10-8. We would discover that the process ended with a $15 billion increase in income rather than the $20 billion shown. When the MPS is 0.33, the multiplier is 3 (= $15 billion/$5 billion). The mathematics works such that the multiplier is equal to the reciprocal of the MPS. The reciprocal of any number is the quotient you obtain by dividing 1 by that number.

WORKED PROBLEM 10.2   Multiplier Effect

A large MPC (small MPS) means the succeeding rounds of consumption spending shown in Figure 10-9 diminish slowly and thereby cumulate to a large change in income. Conversely, a small MPC (a large MPS) causes the increases in consumption to decline quickly, so the cumulative change in income is small. The relationship between the MPC (and thus the MPS) and multiplier is summarized in Figure 10-9.

How Large Is the Actual Multiplier Effect?

The multiplier we have just described is based on simplifying assumptions. Consumption of domestic output rises by the increases in income minus the increases in saving. But in reality, consumption of domestic output increases in each round by a lesser amount than implied by the MPS alone. In addition to saving, households use some of the extra income in each round to purchase additional goods from abroad (imports) and pay additional taxes. Because spending on imports and taxes does not directly create new income in the Canadian economy, the 1/MPS formula for the multiplier overstates the actual size of the multiplier effect. We can correct this problem by changing the multiplier equation to read, "1 divided by the fraction of the change in income that is not spent on domestic output."

Also, we will find in later chapters that an increase in spending may be partly dissipated as inflation rather than realized fully as an increase in real GDP. This happens when increases in spending drive up prices. The multiplier process still happens, but it induces a much smaller change in real output because at higher prices any given amount of spending buys less real output. Economists disagree on the size of the actual multiplier in Canada. Estimates by the Department of Finance range from 1.6 to as low as 0.1. So keep in mind throughout later discussions that the actual multiplier is much lower than the multipliers in our simple explanatory examples. As will be discussed in the next chapter, the size of the multiplier also depends on the openness of the economy.

- The multiplier effect reveals that an initial change in spending can cause a larger change in domestic income and output. The multiplier is the factor by which the initial change is magnified: multiplier = change in real GDP/initial change in spending.

- The higher the marginal propensity to consume (the lower the marginal propensity to save), the larger the multiplier: multiplier = 1/MPS.

- Economists disagree on the size of the actual multiplier in the Canadian economy; estimates range all the way from 0.1 to 1.6.

The **LAST WORD**   Squaring the Economic Circle

Humorist Art Buchwald examines the multiplier.

The recession hit so fast that nobody knows exactly how it happened. One day we were the land of milk and honey and the next day we were the land of sour cream and food stamps.

This is one explanation.

Hofberger, the Ford salesman, called up Littleton, of Littleton Menswear & Haberdashery, and said, "Good news, the new [Fords] have just come in and I've put one aside for you and your wife."

Littleton said, "I can't, Hofberger, my wife and I are getting a divorce."

"I'm sorry," Littleton said, "but I can't afford a new car this year. After I settle with my wife, I'll be lucky to buy a bicycle."

Hofberger hung up. His phone rang a few minutes later.

"This is Bedcheck the painter," the voice on the other end said. "When do you want us to start painting your house?"

"I changed my mind," said Hofberger, "I'm not going to paint the house."

"But I ordered the paint," Bedcheck said. "Why did you change your mind?"

"Because Littleton is getting a divorce and he can't afford a new car."

That evening when Bedcheck came home his wife said, "The new color television set arrived from Gladstone's TV shop."

"Take it back," Bedcheck told his wife.

"Why?" she demanded.

"Because Hofberger isn't going to have his house painted now that the Littletons are getting a divorce."

The next day Mrs. Bedcheck dragged the TV set in its carton back to Gladstone. "We don't want it."

Gladstone's face dropped. He immediately called his travel agent, Sandstorm. "You know that trip you had scheduled for me to the Virgin Islands?"

"Right, the tickets are all written up."

"Cancel it. I can't go. Bedcheck just sent back the color TV set because Hofberger didn't sell a car to Littleton because they're going to get a divorce and she wants all his money."

Sandstorm tore up the airline tickets and went over to see his banker, Gripsholm. "I can't pay back the loan this month because Gladstone isn't going to the Virgin Islands."

Gripsholm was furious. When Rudemaker came in to borrow money for a new kitchen he needed for his restaurant, Gripsholm turned him down cold. "How can I loan you money when Sandstorm hasn't repaid the money he borrowed?"

Rudemaker called up the contractor, Eagleton, and said he couldn't put in a new kitchen. Eagleton laid off eight men.

Meanwhile, Ford announced it was giving a rebate on its new models. Hofberger called up Littleton immediately. "Good news," he said, "even if you are getting a divorce, you can afford a new car."

"I'm not getting a divorce," Littleton said. "It was all a misunderstanding and we've made up."

"That's great," Hofberger said. "Now you can buy the [Ford]."

"No way," said Littleton. "My business has been so lousy I don't know why I keep the doors open."

"I didn't realize that," Hofberger said.

"Do you realize I haven't seen Bedcheck, Gladstone, Sandstorm, Gripsholm, Rudemaker or Eagleton for more than a month? How can I stay in business if they don't patronize my store?"

Source: Art Buchwald, "Squaring the Economic Circle," *Cleveland Plain Dealer*, February 22, 1975. Reprinted by permission.

Question

What is the central economic idea humorously demonstrated in Art Buchwald's piece, "Squaring the Economic Circle"? How does the central idea relate to recessions, on the one hand, and vigorous expansion on the other?

Chapter Summary

LO10.1 DESCRIBE HOW CHANGES IN INCOME AFFECT CONSUMPTION (AND SAVING).

- Other things equal, a direct (positive) relationship exists between income and consumption and income and saving. The consumption and saving schedules show the various amounts that households intend to consume and save at the various income and output levels, assuming a fixed price level.

- The average propensities to consume and save show the fractions of any total income that are consumed and saved: APC + APS = 1. The marginal propensities to consume and save show the fractions of any change in total income that is consumed and saved: MPC + MPS = 1.

LO10.2 LIST AND EXPLAIN FACTORS OTHER THAN INCOME THAT CAN AFFECT CONSUMPTION.

- The locations of the consumption and saving schedules (as they relate to real GDP) are determined by (a) the amount of wealth owned by households, (b) expectations of future prices and incomes, (c) real interest rates, (d) household debt, and (e) tax levels. The consumption and saving schedules are relatively stable.

LO10.3 EXPLAIN HOW CHANGES IN REAL INTEREST RATES AFFECT INVESTMENT.

- The immediate determinants of investment are (a) the expected rate of return and (b) the real interest rate. The economy's investment demand curve is found by cumulating investment projects, arraying them in descending order according to their expected rates of return, graphing the result, and applying the

rule that investment will be profitable up to the point at which the real interest rate, i, equals the expected rate of return, r. The investment demand curve reveals an inverse relationship between the interest rate and the level of aggregated investment.

LO10.4 IDENTIFY AND EXPLAIN FACTORS OTHER THAN THE REAL INTEREST RATE THAT CAN AFFECT INVESTMENT.

- Shifts in the investment demand curve can occur as the result of changes in (a) the acquisition, maintenance, and operating costs of capital goods; (b) business taxes; (c) technology; (d) the stocks of capital goods on hand; and (e) expectations.

- Either changes in interest rates or shifts in the investment demand curve can shift the investment schedule.

- The durability of capital goods, the variability of expectations, and the irregular occurrence of major innovations all contribute to the high fluctuations in investment spending.

LO10.5 ILLUSTRATE HOW CHANGES IN INVESTMENT (OR ONE OF THE COMPONENTS OF TOTAL SPENDING) INCREASE OR DECREASE REAL GDP BY A MULTIPLE AMOUNT.

- Through the multiplier effect, an increase in investment spending (or consumption spending, government purchases, or net export) ripples through the economy, ultimately creating a magnified increase in real GDP. The multiplier is the ultimate change in GDP divided by the initiating change in investment or some other component of spending.

- The multiplier is equal to the reciprocal of the marginal propensity to save: the greater the marginal propensity to save, the smaller the multiplier. Also, the greater the marginal propensity to consume, the larger the multiplier.

- Economists disagree on the size of the actual multiplier in Canada, with estimates ranging all the way from 1.6 to 0.1. But all estimates or real-world multipliers are less than the multiplier in our simple text illustrations.

Terms and Concepts

45° (degree) line
consumption schedule
saving schedule
break-even income
average propensity to consume (APC)

average propensity to save (APS)
marginal propensity to consume (MPC)
marginal propensity to save (MPS)
wealth effect
paradox of thrift

expected rate of return
investment demand curve
multiplier

Discussion Questions

1. Precisely how do the MPC and APC differ? How does the MPC differ from the MPS? Why must the sum of the MPC and the MPS equal 1?   [LO10.1]

2. Why does a downward shift of the consumption schedule typically involve an equal upward shift of the saving schedule? What is the exception to this relationship?   [LO10.1]

3. Why will a reduction in the real interest rate increase investment spending, other things equal?   [LO10.3]

4. In what direction will each of the following occurrences shift the investment demand curve, other things equal?   [LO10.3]

   a. An increase in unused production capacity occurs.

   b. Business taxes decline.

   c. The costs of acquiring equipment fall.

   d. Widespread pessimism arises about future business conditions and sales revenues.

   e. A major new technological breakthrough creates prospects for a wide range of profitable new products.

5. How is it possible for investment spending to increase even in a period in which the real interest rate rises?   [LO10.4]

6. Why is investment spending unstable?   [LO10.4]

7. Is the relationship between changes in spending and changes in real GDP in the multiplier effect a direct (positive) relationship or is it an inverse (negative) relationship? How does the size of the multiplier relate to the size of the MPC? The MPS? What is the logic of the multiplier–MPC relationship?   [LO10.5]

8. Why is the actual multiplier in the Canadian economy less than the multiplier in this chapter's examples?   [LO10.5]

Review Questions

1. What are the variables (the items measured on the axes) in a graph of the (a) consumption schedule and (b) saving schedule? Are the variables inversely (negatively) related or are they directly (positively) related? What is the fundamental reason that the levels of consumption and saving in Canada are each higher today than they were a decade ago?   [LO10.1]

2. In year one, Adam earns $1000 and saves $100. In year 2, Adam gets a $500 raise so that he earns a total of $1500. Out of that $1500, he saves $200. What is Adam's MPC out of his $500 raise?   [LO10.1]

   a. 0.50

   b. 0.75

   c. 0.80

   d. 1.00

3. If the MPS rises, then the MPC will   [LO10.1]

   a. Fall

   b. Rise

   c. Stay the same

4. In what direction will each of the following occurrences shift the consumption and saving schedules, other things equal?   [LO10.2]

   a. A large decrease in real estate values, including private homes

   b. A sharp, sustained increase in stock prices

   c. A 5-year increase in the minimum age for collecting Social Security benefits

d. An economy-wide expectation that a recession is over and that a robust expansion will occur

e. A substantial increase in household borrowing to finance auto purchases

5. Irving owns a chain of movie theatres. He is considering whether he should build a new theatre downtown. The expected rate of return is 15 percent per year. He can borrow money at a 12 percent interest rate to finance the project. Should Irving proceed with this project?   [LO10.3]

a. Yes

b. No

6. Which of the following scenarios will shift the investment demand curve right? *Select one or more answers from the choices shown.*   [LO10.4]

a. Business taxes increase.

b. The expected return on capital increases.

c. Firms have a lot of unused production capacity.

d. Firms are planning on increasing their inventories.

7. True or False? Real GDP is more volatile (variable) than gross investment.   [LO10.4]

8. If a $50 billion initial increase in spending leads to a $250 billion change in real GDP, how big is the multiplier?   [LO10.5]

a. 1.0

b. 2.5

c. 4.0

d. 5.0

9. True or False? Larger MPCs imply larger multipliers.   [LO10.5]

Problems

1. Refer to the following table: [LO10.1]

Level of output and income (GDP = DI)	Consumption	Saving	APC	APS	MPC	MPS
$240	$_____	−$4	____	____	____	____
260	_____	0	____	____	____	____
280	_____	4	____	____	____	____
300	_____	8	____	____	____	____
320	_____	12	____	____	____	____
340	_____	16	____	____	____	____
360	_____	20	____	____	____	____
380	_____	24	____	____	____	____
400	_____	28	____	____	____	____

a. Fill in the missing numbers in the table.

b. What is the break-even level of income in the table? What term do economists use for the saving situation shown at the $240 level of income?

c. For each of the following items, indicate whether the value in the table is either constant or variable as income changes: MPS, APC, MPC, APS.

2. Suppose that disposable income, consumption, and saving in some country are $200 billion, $150 billion, and $50 billion, respectively. Next, assume that disposable income increases by $20 billion, consumption rises by $18 billion and saving goes up by $2 billion. What is the economy's MPC? What is its MPS? What was the APC before the increase in disposable income? After the increase?   [LO10.1]

3. **Advanced Analysis** Suppose that the linear equation for consumption in a hypothetical economy is $C = 40 + 0.8Y$. Also suppose that income (Y) is $400. Determine: (a) the marginal propensity to consume, (b) the marginal propensity to save, (c) the level of consumption, (d) the average propensity to consume, (e) the level of saving, and (f) the average propensity to save.   [LO10.1]

4. **Advanced Analysis** Linear equations for the consumption and saving schedules take the general form $C = a + bY$ and $S = -a + (1 - b)Y$, where C, S, and Y are consumption, saving, and national income, respectively. The constant a represents the vertical intercept, and b is the slope of the consumption schedule. [LO10.1, 10.2]

a. Use the following data to determine numerical values for a and b in the consumption and saving equations:

National income (Y)	Consumption (C)
$ 0	$ 80
100	140
200	200
300	260
400	320

b. What is the economic meaning of *b*? Of (1 − *b*)?

c. Suppose the amount of saving that occurs at each level of national income falls by $20, but that the values of *b* and (1 − *b*) remain unchanged. Restate the saving and consumption equations for the new numerical values, and cite a factor that might have caused the change.

5. Use your completed table for Problem 1 to solve this problem: Suppose the wealth effect is such that $10 changes in wealth produce $1 changes in consumption at each level of income. If real estate prices tumble such that wealth declines by $80, what will be the new level of consumption at the $340 billion level of disposable income? The new level of saving?   [LO10.2]

6. Suppose a handbill publisher can buy a new duplicating machine for $500 and the duplicator has a one-year life. The machine is expected to contribute $550 to the year's net revenue. What is the expected rate of return? If the real interest rate at which funds can be borrowed to purchase the machine is 8 percent, will the publisher choose to invest in the machine? Will it invest in the machine if the real interest rate is 9 percent? If it is 11 percent?   [LO10.3]

7. Assume there are no investment projects in the economy that yield an expected rate of return of 25 percent or more. But suppose there are $10 billion of investment projects yielding expected returns of 20–25 percent; another $10 billion yielding 15–20 percent; another $10 billion yielding 10–15 percent; and so forth. Cumulate these data and present them graphically, putting the expected rate of return (and the real interest rate) on the vertical axis and the amount of investment on the horizontal axis. What will be the equilibrium level of aggregate investment if the real interest rate is (a) 15 percent, (b) 10 percent, and (c) 5 percent?   [LO10.3]

8. Refer to the table in Figure 10-5 and suppose that the real interest rate is 6 percent. Next, assume that some factor changes such that the expected rate of return declines by 2 percentage points at each prospective level of investment. Assuming no change in the real interest rate, by how much and in what direction will investment change? Which of the following might cause this change: (a) a decision to increase inventories, (b) an increase in excess production capacity?   [LO10.4]

9. What will the multiplier be when the MPS is zero, 0.4, 0.6, and 1? What will it be when the MPC is 1, 0.90, 0.67, 0.50, and zero? How much of a change in GDP will result if firms increase their level of investment by $8 billion and the MPC is 0.80? If the MPC is 0.67?   [LO10.5]

10. Suppose that an initial $10 billion increase in investment spending expands GDP by $10 billion in the first round of the multiplier process. If consumption and GDP both rise by $6 billion in the second round of the process, what is the MPC in this economy? What is the size of the multiplier? If, instead, consumption and GDP both rose by $8 billion in the second round, what would have been the size of the multiplier?   [LO10.5]

CHAPTER 11

The Aggregate Expenditures Model

LEARNING OBJECTIVES

LO11.1 Explain how sticky prices relate to the aggregate expenditures model.

LO11.2 Explain how an economy's investment schedule is derived from the investment demand curve and an interest rate.

LO11.3 Illustrate how economists combine consumption and investment to depict an aggregate expenditures schedule and equilibrium output for a private closed economy.

LO11.4 Discuss the two other ways to characterize the equilibrium level of real GDP in a private closed economy: (1) saving = investment and (2) unplanned changes in inventories.

LO11.5 Analyze how changes in equilibrium GDP can occur in the aggregate expenditures model and how those changes relate to the multiplier.

LO11.6 Explain how economists integrate the international sector (exports and imports) into the aggregate expenditures model.

LO11.7 Explain how economists integrate the public sector (government expenditures and taxes) into the aggregate expenditures model.

LO11.8 Differentiate between equilibrium GDP and full-employment GDP, and identify and describe the nature and causes of *recessionary expenditure gaps* and *inflationary expenditure gaps*.

In previous chapters we answered in detail two of the most important questions in macroeconomics: How is an economy's output measured? and Why does an economy grow? But we have been relatively general in addressing two other important questions: (1) What determines the level of GDP, given a nation's production capacity? (2) What causes real GDP to rise in one period and to fall in another? To provide more thorough answers to these two questions, we construct the aggregate expenditures (AE) model, which has its origins in the 1936 writings of the British economist John Maynard Keynes (pronounced *Caines*). The basic premise of the aggregate expenditures model–also known as the *Keynesian cross model*– is that the amount of goods and services produced, and therefore the level of employment, depends directly on the level of aggregate expenditures (total spending). Business will produce only a level of output it thinks it can profitably sell; it will idle workers and machinery when no markets exist for their goods and services.

11.1   The Aggregate Expenditures Model: Consumption and Saving

LO11.1 Explain how sticky prices relate to the aggregate expenditures model.

We now turn to investigate the details of the aggregate expenditures model. But first, let's look at the assumptions underlying the model.

Assumptions and Simplifications

The simplifying assumptions underpinning the aggregate expenditures model reflect the economic conditions prevalent during the Great Depression. As discussed in this chapter's Last Word, Keynes created the model during the middle of the Great Depression in the hope of understanding both why the Great Depression had happened and how it might be ended.

The most fundamental assumption behind the aggregate expenditures model is that prices in the economy are fixed. In the terminology of Chapter 4, the aggregate expenditures model is an extreme version of a sticky price model. In fact, it is a stuck price model because the price level cannot change at all.

ORIGIN OF THE IDEA 11.1   Aggregate Expenditures Model

Keynes made this simplifying assumption because he had observed that prices had not declined sufficiently during the Great Depression to boost spending and maintain output and employment at their pre-Depression levels. Such price declines had been predicted by macroeconomic theories that were popular before the Great Depression, but actual prices did not fall sufficiently during the Great Depression, and the economy sank far below its potential output. Real GDP in Canada declined by 27 percent from 1929 to 1933 and the unemployment rate rose to 25 percent. Thousands of factories sat idle, gathering dust and producing nothing because nobody wanted to buy their output. To Keynes, this massive unemployment of labour and capital resulted from firms reacting to information about how much they should produce. As households and businesses greatly reduced their spending, inventories of unsold goods burgeoned. Unable or unwilling to slash their prices, firms could not sell all the goods they had already produced, so they greatly reduced their current production. This meant discharging workers, idling production lines, and even closing entire factories. Keynes thought that a new economic model was needed to show how all this could have happened and how it might be reversed.

The Keynesian aggregate expenditures model is not just of historical interest. It is still insightful today because many prices in the modern economy are inflexible downward over relatively short periods of time. The aggregate expenditures model, therefore, can help us understand how the modern economy is likely to adjust initially to various economic shocks over shorter periods of time. For example, it clarifies aspects of the severe 2008-09 recession, such as why unexpected initial declines in spending caused even larger declines in real GDP. It also illuminates the thinking underlying the stimulus programs (e.g., tax cuts, government spending increases) enacted by the government during the recession.

We will build up the aggregate expenditures model in simple stages. Let's first look at aggregate expenditures and equilibrium GDP in a *private closed economy*–one without international trade or government.

Then we will open the closed economy to exports and imports, and also convert our private economy to a more realistic mixed economy that includes government purchases (or, more loosely, *government spending*) and taxes.

In addition, until we introduce taxes into the model, we will assume that real GDP equals disposable income (DI). For instance, if $500 billion of output is produced as GDP, households will receive exactly $500 billion of disposable income that they can then consume or save. And finally, unless specified otherwise, we will assume (as Keynes did) that the economy has excess production capacity and unemployed labour, so an increase in aggregate expenditures will increase real output and employment without raising the price level.

11.2 | Consumption and Investment Schedules

LO11.2 Explain how an economy's investment schedule is derived from the investment demand curve and an interest rate.

In the private closed economy, the two components of **aggregate expenditures** are consumption, C, and gross investment, I_g. Because we examined the *consumption schedule* (Figure 10-2a) in the previous chapter, there is no need to repeat that analysis here. But to add the investment decisions of businesses to the consumption plans of households, we need to construct an investment schedule showing the amounts business firms collectively intend to invest–their **planned investment**–at each possible level of GDP. Such a schedule represents the investment plans of businesses in the same way as the consumption schedule represents the consumption plans of households. In developing the investment schedule, we will assume that this planned investment is independent of the level of current disposable income or real output.

Suppose the investment demand curve is as shown in Figure 11-1a and the current real interest rate is 8 percent. This means that firms will find it profitable to spend $20 billion on investment goods. The line I_g (*gross* investment) in Figure 11-1b shows the economy's **investment schedule**. Do not confuse

---

FIGURE 11-1   The Investment Demand Curve and the Investment Schedule

(a) The level of investment spending (here, $20 billion) is determined by the real interest rate (here, 8 percent) together with the investment demand curve *ID*.
(b) The investment schedule I_g relates the amount of investment ($20 billion) determined in part (a) to the various levels of GDP.

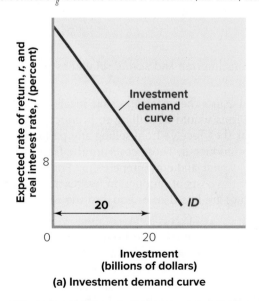

(a) Investment demand curve

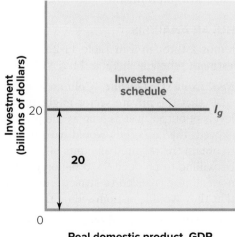

(b) Investment schedule

TABLE 11-1	The Investment Schedule (in billions)
(1) Level of real output and income	**(2) Investment (I_g)**
$370	$20
390	20
410	20
430	20
450	20
470	20
490	20
510	20
530	20
550	20

this investment schedule I_g with the investment demand curve *ID* in Figure 11-1a. The investment schedule shows the amount of investment forthcoming at each level of GDP. As indicated in Figure 11-1, this amount ($20 billion) is determined by the real interest rate together with the location of the investment demand curve. Table 11-1 shows the investment schedule in tabular form. Note that investment (I_g) in column 2 is $20 billion at all levels of real GDP.

11.3 / Equilibrium GDP: $C + I_g = $ GDP

LO11.3 Illustrate how economists combine consumption and investment to depict an aggregate expenditures schedule and equilibrium output for a private closed economy.

Now let's combine the consumption and investment schedules to explain the equilibrium levels of output, income, and employment.

TABULAR ANALYSIS

Columns 2 through 5 in Table 11-2 repeat the consumption and saving schedules in Table 10-1 and the investment schedule in Table 11-1.

- **Real Domestic Output**   Column 2 in Table 11-2 lists the various possible levels of total output–of real GDP–that the private sector might produce. Firms would be willing to produce any one of these 10 levels of output just as long as the revenue that they receive from selling any particular level equals or exceeds the costs they would have to incur to produce it. Those costs are the factor payments needed to obtain the required amounts of land, labour, capital, and entrepreneurship. For example, firms would be willing to produce $370 billion of output if the costs of production (wages, rents, interest, plus the normal profit needed to attract entrepreneurship) are less than or equal to the $370 billion in revenue that they would get from selling the output.

- **Aggregate Expenditures**   In the private closed economy of Table 11-2, aggregate expenditures consist of consumption (column 3) plus investment (column 5). Their sum is shown in column 6, which along with column 2 makes up the **aggregate expenditures schedule** for the economy. This schedule shows the amount ($C + I_g$) that will be spent at each possible output or income level. At this point we are working with *planned investment*–the data in column 5, Table 11-2. These data show the amounts

TABLE 11-2	Determination of the Equilibrium Levels of Employment, Output, and Income: A Private Closed Economy						
(1) Possible levels of employment (millions)	(2) Real domestic output (and income) (GDP = DI) (billions)	(3) Consumption (C) (billions)	(4) Saving (S) (billions)	(5) Investment (I_g) (billions)	(6) Aggregate expenditures $(C + I_g)$ (billions)	(7) Unplanned changes in inventories (+) or (−)	(8) Tendency of employment, output, and income
(1) 2.5	$370	$375	$−5	$20	$395	$−25	Increase
(2) 5.0	390	390	0	20	410	−20	Increase
(3) 7.5	410	405	5	20	425	−15	Increase
(4) 10.0	430	420	10	20	440	−10	Increase
(5) 12.5	450	435	15	20	455	−5	Increase
(6) 15.0	**470**	**450**	**20**	**20**	**470**	**0**	**Equilibrium**
(7) 17.5	490	465	25	20	485	+5	Decrease
(8) 20.0	510	480	30	20	500	+10	Decrease
(9) 22.5	530	495	35	20	515	+15	Decrease
(10) 25.0	550	510	40	20	530	+20	Decrease

firms intend to invest, not the amounts they actually will invest if there are unplanned changes in inventories—we'll say more about that shortly.

- **Equilibrium GDP**   Of the 10 possible levels of GDP in Table 11-2, which is the equilibrium level? Which total output is the economy capable of sustaining? The equilibrium output creates total spending just sufficient to produce that output. So the equilibrium level of GDP is the level at which the total quantity of goods produced (GDP) equals the total quantity of goods purchased $(C + I_g)$. In the private closed economy, the **equilibrium GDP** is where $C + I_g$ = GDP. If you look at the domestic output levels in column 2 and the aggregate expenditures level in column 6, you will see that this equality exists only at $470 billion of GDP (row 6). There is no overproduction, which would result in a piling up of unsold goods and consequently cutbacks in the production rate. Nor is there an excess of total spending, which would draw down inventories of goods and prompt increases in the rate of production. In short, there is no reason for businesses to alter this rate of production; $470 billion is the equilibrium GDP.

- **Disequilibrium**   No level of GDP other than the equilibrium level can be sustained. At levels of GDP less than equilibrium, spending always exceeds GDP. If, for example, firms produced $410 billion of GDP (row 3 in Table 11-2), this would yield $405 billion in consumer spending. Supplemented by $20 billion of planned investment, aggregate expenditures $(C + I_g)$ would be $425 billion, as shown in column 6. The economy would provide an annual rate of spending more than sufficient to purchase the $410 billion of annual production. Because buyers would be taking goods off the shelves faster than firms could produce them, an unintended decline in business inventories of $15 billion would occur (column 7). But businesses can adjust to such an imbalance between aggregate expenditures and real output by stepping up production. Greater output will increase employment and total income. This process will continue until the equilibrium level of GDP is reached ($470 billion). The reverse is true at all levels of GDP greater than the $470 billion equilibrium level. Businesses will find that these total outputs fail to generate the spending needed to clear the shelves of goods.

KEY GRAPH

FIGURE 11-2   Equilibrium GDP in a Private Closed Economy

The aggregate expenditures schedule, $C + I_g$, is determined by adding the investment schedule I_g to the upsloping consumption schedule C. Since investment is assumed to be the same at each level of GDP, the vertical distances between C and $C + I_g$ do not change. Equilibrium GDP is determined where the aggregate expenditures schedule intersects the 45° line, in this case at $470 billion.

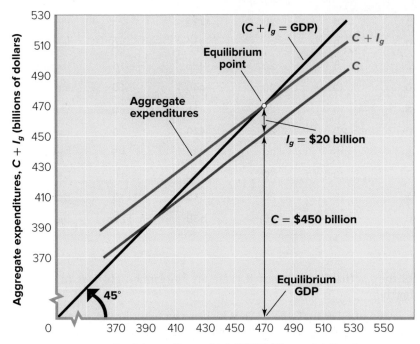

Quick Quiz

1. In this figure, the slope of the aggregate expenditures schedule $C + I_g$
   a. Increases as real GDP increases
   b. Decreases as real GDP increases
   c. Is constant and equals the MPC
   d. Is constant and equals the MPS

2. At all points on the 45° line
   a. Equilibrium GDP is possible
   b. Aggregate expenditures exceed real GDP
   c. Consumption exceeds investment
   d. Aggregate expenditures are less than real GDP

3. The $490 billion level of real GDP is not at equilibrium because
   a. Investment exceeds consumption
   b. Consumption exceeds investment
   c. Planned $C + I_g$ exceeds real GDP
   d. Planned $C + I_g$ is less than real GDP

4. The $430 billion level of real GDP is not at equilibrium because
   a. Investment exceeds consumption
   b. Consumption exceeds investment
   c. Planned $C + I_g$ exceeds real GDP
   d. Planned $C + I_g$ is less than real GDP

GRAPHICAL ANALYSIS

We can demonstrate the same analysis graphically in **Figure 11-2 (Key Graph)**. Recall that at any point on the 45° line, the value of what is being measured on the horizontal axis (here, GDP) is equal to the value of what is being measured on the vertical axis (here, aggregate expenditures, or $C + I_g$). Having discovered in our tabular analysis that the equilibrium level of domestic output is determined where $C + I_g$ equals GDP, we can say that the 45° line in Figure 11-2 is a graphical statement of that equilibrium condition.

Now we must graph the aggregate expenditures schedule onto Figure 11-2. To do this we duplicate the consumption schedule C in Figure 10-2a and add to it vertically the constant $20 billion amount of investment I_g from Figure 11-1b. This $20 billion is the amount we assumed firms plan to invest at all levels of GDP. Or, more directly, we can plot the $C + I_g$ data in column 6, Table 11-2.

Observe in Figure 11-2 that the aggregate expenditures line $C + I_g$ shows that total spending rises with income and output (GDP), but not as much as income rises. That is true because the marginal propensity to consume–the slope of line C–is less than 1. A part of any increase in income will be saved rather than spent. And because the aggregate expenditures line $C + I_g$ is parallel to the consumption line C, the slope of the aggregate expenditures line also equals the MPC for the economy and is less than 1. For our particular data, aggregate expenditures rise by $15 billion for every $20 billion increase in real output and income because $5 billion of each $20 billion increment is saved. Therefore, the slope of the aggregate expenditures line is 0.75 ($= \Delta\$15/\Delta\$20$).

The equilibrium level of GDP is determined by the intersection of the aggregate expenditures schedule and the 45° line. This intersection is the only point at which aggregate expenditures (on the vertical axis) are equal to GDP (on the horizontal axis). Because Figure 11-2 is based on the data in Table 11-2, we once again find that equilibrium output is $470 billion. Observe that consumption at this output is $450 billion and investment is $20 billion.

WORKED PROBLEM 11.1   Equilibrium GDP

It is evident from Figure 11-2 that no levels of GDP *above* the equilibrium level are sustainable because at those levels $C + I_g$ falls short of GDP. Underspending causes inventories to rise, prompting firms to readjust production downward, in the direction of the $470 billion output level.

Conversely, at levels of GDP *below* $470 billion, $C + I_g$ exceeds total output. This overspending causes inventories to decline, prompting firms to adjust production upward, in the direction of the $470 billion output level. Once production reaches that level, it will be sustained there indefinitely unless some change occurs in the location of the aggregate expenditures line.

11.4 / Other Features of Equilibrium GDP

LO11.4 Discuss the two other ways to characterize the equilibrium level of real GDP in a private closed economy: (1) saving = investment and (2) unplanned changes in inventories.

We have seen that $C + I_g$ = GDP at equilibrium in the private closed economy. A closer look at Table 11-2 reveals two more characteristics of equilibrium GDP:

(1)   Saving and *planned* investment are equal ($S = I_g$).
(2)   No *unplanned* changes in inventories occur.

SAVING EQUALS PLANNED INVESTMENT

As shown by row 6 in Table 11-2, saving and planned investment are both $20 billion at the $470 billion equilibrium level of GDP. Saving is a **leakage** or withdrawal of spending from the income–expenditures stream. Saving is what causes consumption to be less than total output or GDP. As a result of saving, consumption is insufficient to take all domestic output off the shelves, setting the stage for a decline in total output.

However, firms do not intend to sell their entire output to consumers; some domestic output will consist of capital goods sold within the business sector. Investment can therefore be thought of as an

injection of spending into the income-expenditures stream. Investment is thus a potential replacement for the leakage of saving.

If the leakage of saving at a certain level of GDP exceeds the injection of investment, then $C + I_g$ will fall short of GDP and that level of GDP cannot be sustained. Any GDP for which saving exceeds investment is an above-equilibrium GDP. This spending deficiency will reduce real GDP.

Conversely, if the injection of investment exceeds the leakage of saving, then $C + I_g$ will be greater than GDP and drive GDP upward. Any GDP for which investment exceeds saving is a below-equilibrium GDP. Only where $S = I_g$–where the leakage of saving of $20 billion is exactly offset by the injection of investment of $20 billion–will aggregate expenditures equal real output. And that $C + I_g$ = GDP equality is what defines the equilibrium GDP.

NO UNPLANNED CHANGES IN INVENTORIES

As part of their investment plans, firms may decide to increase or decrease their inventories. But, as confirmed in row 6 in Table 11-2, no **unplanned changes in inventory** occur at equilibrium GDP. This fact, along with $C + I_g$ = GDP, and $S = I_g$, is a characteristic of equilibrium GDP in the private closed economy.

Unplanned changes in inventory play a major role in achieving equilibrium GDP. Consider, as an example, the $490 billion *above-equilibrium* GDP shown in row 7 of Table 11-2. What happens if firms produce that output, thinking they can sell it? Households save $25 billion of their $490 billion DI, so consumption is only $465 billion. Planned investment–which includes *planned* changes in inventories–is $20 billion (column 5). This means that aggregate expenditures ($C + I_g$) are $485 billion and sales fall short of production by $5 billion. Firms retain that extra $5 billion of goods as an *unplanned* increase in inventories (column 7). It results when total spending is less than the amount needed to remove total output from the shelves.

Because changes in inventories are a part of investment, we note that *actual investment* is $25 billion. It consists of $20 billion of planned investment *plus* the $5 billion unplanned increase in inventories. Actual investment exactly equals the saving of $25 billion, even though saving exceeds planned investment by $5 billion. Because firms cannot earn profits by accumulating unwanted inventories, they will cut back production. GDP will fall to its equilibrium level of $470 billion, at which changes in inventories are zero.

Now look at the *below-equilibrium* $450 billion output (row 5, Table 11-2). Because households save only $15 billion of their $450 billion DI, consumption is $435 billion. Planned investment by firms is $20 billion, so aggregate expenditures are $455 billion. Sales exceed production by $5 billion. This is so only because a $5 billion unplanned decrease in business inventories has occurred. Firms must *disinvest* $5 billion in inventories (column 7). Note again that actual investment is $15 billion ($20 billion planned *minus* the $5 billion decline in inventory investment) and is equal to a saving of $15 billion, even though planned investment exceeds saving by $5 billion. The unplanned decline in inventories, resulting from the excess of sales over production, will encourage firms to expand production. GDP will rise to $470 billion, at which unplanned changes in inventories are zero.

When economists say differences between investment and saving can occur and bring about changes in equilibrium GDP, they are referring to planned investment and saving. Equilibrium occurs only when planned investment and saving are equal. *But when unplanned changes in inventories are considered, investment and saving are always equal, regardless of the level of GDP.* That is true because actual investment consists of planned investment and unplanned investment (unplanned changes in inventories). Unplanned changes in inventories act as a balancing item that equates the actual amounts saved and invested in any period.

11.5 / Changes in Equilibrium GDP and the Multiplier

LO11.5 Analyze how changes in equilibrium GDP can occur in the aggregate expenditures model and how those changes relate to the multiplier.

In the previous chapter, we established that an initial change in spending can cause a greater change in real output through the multiplier effect. In equation form

$$\text{Multiplier} = \frac{\text{change in real GDP}}{\text{initial change in spending}}$$

Further, we discovered that the size of the multiplier depends on the size of the MPS in the economy:

$$\text{Multiplier} = \frac{1}{\text{MPS}}$$

(Because the multiplier is such an important element of the aggregate expenditures model, we highly recommend that you quickly review Figure 10-8 at this time.)

In a private closed economy, the equilibrium GDP will change in response to changes in either the investment schedule or the consumption schedule. Because changes in the investment schedule are the main sources of instability, we will direct our attention toward them.

Figure 11-3 shows the effect of changes in investment spending on the equilibrium real GDP. Suppose the expected rate of return on investment rises or that the real interest rate falls such that investment spending increases by $5 billion. We would show this increase as an upward shift of the investment schedule in Figure 11-1b. In Figure 11-3, the $5 billion increase of investment will shift the aggregate expenditures schedule upward from $(C + I_g)_0$ to $(C + I_g)_1$. Equilibrium real GDP will rise from $470 billion to $490 billion.

If the expected rate of return on investment decreases or if the real interest rate rises, investment spending will decline by, say, $5 billion. That would be shown as a downward shift of the investment schedule in Figure 11-1b and a downward shift of the aggregate expenditures schedule from $(C + I_g)_0$ to $(C + I_g)_2$ in Figure 11-3. Equilibrium GDP will fall from $470 billion to $450 billion.

MATH 11.1   The Multiplier

FIGURE 11-3   ## Changes in the Aggregate Expenditure Schedule and the Multiplier Effect

An upward shift of the aggregate expenditures schedule from $(C + I_g)_0$ to $(C + I_g)_1$ will increase the equilibrium GDP. A downward shift from $(C + I_g)_0$ to $(C + I_g)_2$ will lower the equilibrium GDP.

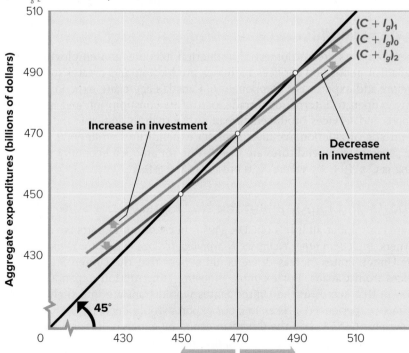

In our examples, a \$5 billion change in investment spending leads to a \$20 billion change in output and income. So the *multiplier* is 4 (= \$20/\$5). Recall that the simple multiplier equals 1/MPS. In our example the MPS is 0.25, meaning that for every \$1 billion of new income, \$0.25 billion of new saving occurs. Therefore, \$20 billion of new income is needed to generate \$5 billion of new saving. Once that increase in income and saving occurs, the economy is back in equilibrium–where $C + I_g$ = GDP; saving and investment are equal, and there are no unintended changes in inventories. You can see, then, that the multiplier process is an integral part of the aggregate expenditures model.

11.6 / Adding International Trade

LO11.6 Explain how economists integrate the international sector (exports and imports) into the aggregate expenditures model.

We next move from a closed economy to an open economy that incorporates exports (X) and imports (M). Our focus will be **net exports** (exports minus imports, or X_n), which may be positive or negative.

Net Exports and Aggregate Expenditures

Like consumption and investment, exports create domestic production, income, and employment for a nation. Foreign spending on Canadian goods and services increases production and creates jobs and incomes in Canada. We must therefore add exports as a component of Canada's aggregate expenditures.

Conversely, when an economy is open to international trade, part of its consumption and investment spending will be for imports–goods and services produced abroad rather than in domestic industries. To avoid overstating the value of domestic production, we must subtract expenditures on imports.

In short, for a closed economy, aggregate expenditures are $C + I_g$. But, for an open economy with international trade, aggregate spending is $C + I_g + X_n$, where X_n represents $(X - M)$.

The Determinants of Imports and Exports and the Net Export Schedule

Note in Table 11-3 that exports are constant at all levels of GDP. This is because our exports are dependent on the GDPs of our trading partners. *If GDP in other countries is growing, we can expect the demand for our exports to increase.* If GDP in the United States increased, we could expect that the United States would purchase more goods and services from Canada. For example, housing construction expands with the economy and, thus, an expansion in that sector in the United States would translate into higher sales of Canadian lumber. If the United States experienced a recession, our exports would decrease.

Our imports are dependent on our own GDP. When the Canadian economy expands, imports also rise. As the Canadian business sector expands and GDP rises, it will require machines and materials from abroad. Likewise, as consumer spending rises, some of it will go to imports.

Imports and exports are also affected by trade policies and the rate at which the Canadian dollar can be exchanged for other currencies. More will be said about trade policy and exchange rates later in this chapter.

TABLE 11-3	Net Export Schedule			
(1) Domestic output (and income) (GDP = DI) (billions)	(2) Exports (X) (billions)	(3) Imports (M) (billions)	(4) Net exports (X_n) (billions) (2) − (3)	(5) Marginal propensity to import (MPM) $\Delta(3)/\Delta(1)$
$370	$40	$15	$25	0.25
390	40	20	20	0.25
410	40	25	15	0.25
430	40	30	10	0.25
450	40	35	5	0.25
470	40	40	0	0.25
490	40	45	−5	0.25
510	40	50	−10	0.25
530	40	55	−15	0.25
550	40	60	−20	0.25

Imports and the Multiplier

A hypothetical *net export schedule* is shown in columns 1 to 4 of Table 11-3. Note that although exports are constant at all levels of GDP, imports, and therefore *net* exports (X − M), change by $5 billion for every $20 billion change in GDP. The change in imports divided by a change in GDP is called the **marginal propensity to import (MPM)**. In our example, the marginal propensity to import is 0.25 (= $5 billion/$20 billion). Just as the marginal propensity to consume is the slope of the consumption schedule, so the marginal propensity to import is the slope of the net export schedule.

For convenience, let's call this new multiplier an *open-economy multiplier*. Why does it differ from the multiplier of 4 in the closed economy? Recall that for the closed economy the multiplier is 1/MPS–or, for our data, 1/0.25, or 4. The multiplier is the reciprocal of the MPS, where the MPS is the fraction of any change in national income that "leaks" into saving. Moving to an open economy we add a second leakage–expenditures on imports. Since the marginal propensity to import (MPM) is the fraction of any change in disposable income spent on imports, we must add the MPM to the MPS in the denominator of the multiplier formula. The multiplier for an open economy (without a government sector) is therefore

$$\text{Open economy multiplier} = \frac{1}{\text{MPS} + \text{MPM}}$$

For the data of Table 11-3, the MPM is 5/20, or 0.25, and the open-economy multiplier is

$$\frac{1}{\text{MPS} + \text{MPM}} = \frac{1}{0.25 + 0.25} = \frac{1}{0.5} = 2$$

Note that the open economy multiplier applies to any change in expenditure, whether it originates in the domestic economy, such as a change in I_g, or a change in net exports (X_n). In the next section we investigate the impact of government expenditures and taxation on equilibrium GDP, changes that originate in the domestic economy. Keep in mind that in an open economy any change in either government spending or taxation is subject to the open economy multiplier. (Also, it should be noted that with the introduction of the open economy multiplier, the slope of the AE line actually changes, but we will continue to assume that the slope remains as it was before the introduction of the MPM, for simplicity).

| TABLE 11-4 | Determinants of the Equilibrium Levels of Output and Income in an Open Economy (Without Government) | | | | |

(1) Domestic output (and income) (GDP = DI) (billions)	(2) Aggregate expenditures for closed economy, without government (C + I_g) (billions)	(3) Exports (X) (billions)	(4) Imports (M) (billions)	(5) Net exports (X_n) (billions) (3) − (4)	(6) Aggregate expenditures for open economy, without government (C + I_g + X_n) (billions) (2) + (5)
$370	$395	$40	$15	$25	$420
390	410	40	20	20	430
410	425	40	25	15	440
430	440	40	30	10	450
450	455	40	35	5	460
470	**470**	**40**	**40**	**0**	**470**
490	485	40	45	−5	480
510	500	40	50	−10	490
530	515	40	55	−15	500
550	530	40	60	−20	510

Net Exports and Equilibrium GDP

Let's now include exports and imports in our discussion of income determination. Columns 1 and 2 of Table 11-4 repeat columns 2 and 6 from Table 11-2, where the equilibrium GDP for a closed economy is $470 billion. Columns 3 to 5 of Table 11-4 repeat columns 2 to 4 of Table 11-3. In column 6, we have adjusted the domestic aggregate expenditures of column 2 for net exports, giving us aggregate expenditures for an open economy.

The export and import figures we have selected are such that foreign trade leaves the equilibrium GDP unchanged. Net exports are zero at the closed economy's equilibrium GDP of $470 billion, so aggregate expenditures for the open economy (column 6) equal domestic output (column 1) at $470 billion.

Figure 11-4 shows these results. The $(C + I_g + X_n)_0$ schedule is aggregate expenditures for the open economy. In this case, aggregate expenditures for the open economy intersect domestic output at the same point as do aggregate expenditures for the closed economy, and therefore the $470 billion equilibrium GDP is unchanged by world trade.

POSITIVE NET EXPORTS

But there is no reason why net exports will have a neutral effect on equilibrium GDP. For example, by either increasing exports by $10 billion (from $40 billion to $50 billion) or decreasing imports by $10 billion at each GDP level, net exports become plus $10 billion at the original $470 billion GDP. With an open economy multiplier of 2, an increase in net exports of $10 billion results in a $20 billion increase in GDP. The recalculation of aggregate expenditures in column 6 of Table 11-4 reveals that the equilibrium GDP will shift from $470 to $490 billion.

In Figure 11-4b, the new open economy aggregate expenditures line is $(C + I_g + X_n)_2$, which lies $10 billion above $(C + I_g + X_n)_0$ because of the $10 billion increase in net exports. This creates a $10 billion gap at the original $470 billion equilibrium GDP, and as a result the equilibrium GDP *increases* to $490 billion.

| FIGURE 11-4 | Net Exports and the Equilibrium GDP |

(a) Net exports can be either positive, as shown by the net export schedule X_{n1}, or negative, as depicted by net export schedule X_{n2}. (b) Positive net exports elevate the aggregate expenditure schedule from the closed-economy level of $C + I_g$ to the open-economy level of $C + I_g + X_{n1}$. Negative net exports lower the aggregate expenditures schedule from the closed-economy level of $C + I_g$ to the open-economy level of $C + I_g + X_{n2}$.

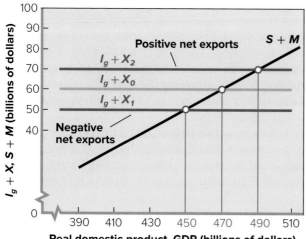

(a) Investment/export schedule

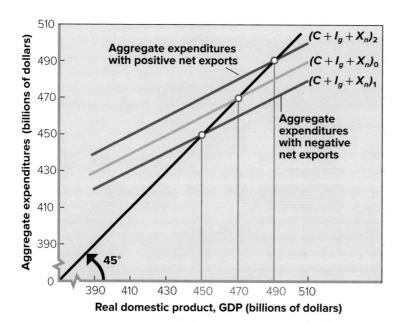

(b) Aggregate expenditures schedule

Figure 11-4a shows the same result. The new $I_g + X_2$ schedule (a $10 billion increase in exports: $I_g + X$ increases from $60 billion to $70 billion) intersects the $S + M$ schedule at the new equilibrium GDP of $490 billion.

Notice that the increase in GDP by $10 billion is the result of exports being larger than imports. This is true because exports and imports have opposite effects on domestic output. Exports increase real GDP by increasing expenditures on domestically produced output. Imports reduce real GDP by directing expenditures toward output produced abroad. It is only because net exports are positive in this example–so that the expansionary effect of exports outweighs the contractionary effect of imports–that we get the overall increase in real GDP. As the next section shows, if net exports are negative then the contractionary effect of imports will outweigh the expansionary effect of exports and domestic real GDP will decrease.

NEGATIVE NET EXPORTS

By reducing net exports by $10 billion, GDP will fall by $20 billion, given an open economy multiplier of 2. Recalculating aggregate expenditures in column 6 of Table 11-4, the resulting net equilibrium GDP will be $450 billion.

Graphically, the new open economy aggregate expenditures schedule is shown by $(C + I_g + X_n)_1$ in Figure 11-4b. This schedule lies $10 billion below $(C + I_g + X_n)_0$, reflecting the $10 billion decline in net exports. Thus, at the original $470 billion equilibrium GDP, a spending gap of $10 billion exists, which causes GDP to *decline* to $450 billion.

Figure 11-4a shows the same result. Note that the $I_g + X_0$ schedule intersects the leakages $S + M$ schedule at the equilibrium GDP of $470 billion. The new $I_g + X_1$ schedule intersects the $S + M$ schedule at the new equilibrium GDP of $450 billion. When imports exceed exports, the contractionary effect of the larger amount of imports outweighs the expansionary effect of the smaller amount of exports, and equilibrium real GDP decreases.

This allows us to generalize as follows: Other things equal, a decline in net exports decreases aggregate expenditures and reduces a nation's GDP; conversely, a rise in net exports increases aggregate expenditures and raises a nation's GDP.

Net exports vary greatly among the major industrial nations, as shown in Global Perspective 11.1.

International Economic Linkages

Our analysis of net exports and real GDP reveals how circumstances or policies abroad can affect Canadian GDP.

11.1 GLOBAL PERSPECTIVE

Net Exports of Goods, Selected Nations, 2014

Some nations, such as Canada, China, and Germany, have positive net exports; other countries, such as the United States and the United Kingdom, have negative net exports.

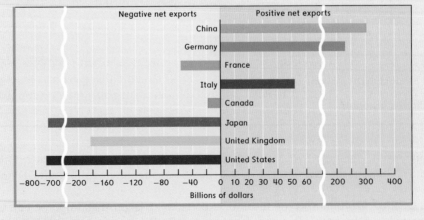

Source: *CIA World Factbook*, www.cia.gov

CONSIDER THIS | The Transmission of the Recession During the Global Economic Downturn of 2008–2009

The severe downturn in the United States reduced U.S. imports (other nations' exports). Countries such as Canada and Japan—whose economies depend highly on exports to the United States—therefore were negatively affected by the U.S. recession. Canada, along with many other nations, suffered its own financial crisis, albeit one less severe than in the U.S. The ensuing domestic economic weaknesses, and the decline in export sales to the United States, helped push the Canadian economy into recession. As our own recession made us poorer, we cut back on our purchases of U.S. exports. That, in turn, further lowered real GDP in the United States.

Global recessions typically shrink the volume of international trade. This reduces the output gains from specialization and exchange, and therefore lowers global output and income. That is precisely what happened during the recession of 2008–2009. The World Trade Organization reported that world trade shrank by a whopping 9 percent in 2009, the largest drop since the Second World War.

Nations experiencing painful declines in employment often are tempted to impose tariffs on imports to protect domestic production and employment. But when one trading partner increases trade barriers, other partners normally retaliate. To keep recessions from worsening, trading partners need to resist trade restrictions as well as other protectionist behaviours, such as enacting laws requiring their governments to buy goods only from domestic producers. These policies may for a time be good politics, but they are bad economics. They result in even greater unemployment and hardship.

PROSPERITY ABROAD

A rising level of real output, and thus income among our trading partners, enables Canada to sell more goods abroad, raising Canadian net exports and increasing our real GDP. We should be interested in the prosperity of our trading partners because if they do well they buy more of our exports, increasing our income and making it possible for us to buy more of their imports. Prosperity abroad transfers some of that prosperity to Canadians.

EXCHANGE RATES

Depreciation of the Canadian dollar relative to other currencies means the price of Canadian goods in terms of these currencies will fall, stimulating purchases of our exports. Also, Canadian consumers will find foreign goods more expensive and, consequently, will reduce their spending on imports. If the economy has the available capacity, the increased Canadian exports and decreased imports will increase Canada's net exports and expand the nation's GDP.

This last example has been cast only in terms of depreciation of the dollar. Now think through the impact that *appreciation* of the dollar would have on net exports and equilibrium GDP.

A CAUTION ON TARIFFS AND DEVALUATIONS

Because higher net exports increase real GDP, countries often look for ways to reduce imports and increase exports during recessions or depressions. Thus, a recession might tempt the Canadian federal government to increase tariffs and devalue the international value of the Canadian dollar (say, by supplying massive amounts of dollars in the foreign exchange market) to try to increase net exports. Such an increase of net exports would expand domestic production, reduce domestic unemployment, and help the economy recover.

But this interventionist thinking is too simplistic. Suppose that Canada imposes high tariffs on foreign goods to reduce our imports and thus increase our domestic production and employment. Our imports are, however, our trading partners' exports. So when we restrict our imports to stimulate our economy, we depress the economies of our trading partners. They are likely to retaliate against us by imposing tariffs on our products. If so, our exports to them will decline and our net exports may in fact fall. With retaliation in the picture, it is possible that tariffs may decrease, not increase, our net exports.

That unfortunate possibility became a sad reality during the Great Depression of the 1930s, when various nations, including Canada and the United States, imposed trade barriers as a way of reducing domestic unemployment. The result was many rounds of retaliation that simply throttled world trade, worsened the Depression, and increased unemployment. Abetting the problem were attempts by some nations to increase their net exports by devaluing their currencies. The international exchange rate system collapsed and world trade spiralled downward. Economic historians agree that tariffs and devaluations during the 1930s were huge policy mistakes!

Nations are tempted to use tariffs and currency devaluations because, *other things equal*, these policies *do* increase net exports and real GDP. But keep in mind that other things aren't likely to stay equal. In particular, other nations will almost certainly retaliate with their own tariffs and devaluations—with the final result being lower net exports and lower GDP for those countries and for our own.

11.7 / Adding the Public Sector

LO11.7 Explain how economists integrate the public sector (government expenditures and taxes) into the aggregate expenditures model.

Our final step in constructing the aggregate expenditures model is to move the analysis from that of a private (no government) open economy to a mixed open economy that has a public sector. This means adding government spending and taxes to the model.

For simplicity, we assume that government purchases do not cause any upward or downward shifts in the consumption and investment schedules. Thus, government expenditures are independent of the level of GDP. Also, we assume that government's net tax revenues—total tax revenues less "negative taxes" in the form of transfer payments—are derived entirely from personal taxes. Finally, we assume that a fixed amount of taxes is collected regardless of the level of GDP.

Government Purchases and Equilibrium GDP

Suppose that government decides to purchase $40 billion of goods and services regardless of the level of GDP.

TABULAR EXAMPLE

Table 11-5 shows the impact of this purchase on the equilibrium GDP. Columns 1 to 7 are carried over from Tables 11-2 and 11-4 for the open economy in which the equilibrium GDP is $470 billion. The only new items are exports and imports in columns 5 and 6, and government purchases in column 8. By adding government purchases to private spending ($C + I_g + X_n$), we get a new, higher level of aggregate expenditures, as shown in column 9. Comparing columns 1 and 9, we find that aggregate expenditures and real output are equal at a higher level of GDP. Without government spending, equilibrium GDP is $470 billion

TABLE 11-5   The Impact of Government Purchases on Equilibrium GDP

(1) Domestic output (and income) (GDP = DI) (billions)	(2) Consumption (C) (billions)	(3) Saving (S) (billions)	(4) Investment (I_g) (billions)	(5) Exports (X) (billions)	(6) Imports (M) (billions)	(7) Net exports (X_n) (billions) (5) − (6)	(8) Government purchases (G) (billions)	(9) Aggregate expenditures (C + I_g + X_n + G) (billions) (2) + (4) + (7) + (8)
(1) $370	$375	$−5	$20	$40	$15	$25	$40	$460
(2) 390	390	0	20	40	20	20	40	470
(3) 410	405	5	20	40	25	15	40	480
(4) 430	420	10	20	40	30	10	40	490
(5) 450	435	15	20	40	35	5	40	500
(6) 470	450	20	20	40	40	0	40	510
(7) 490	465	25	20	40	45	−5	40	520
(8) 510	480	30	20	40	50	−10	40	530
(9) 530	495	35	20	40	55	−15	40	540
(10) 550	510	40	20	40	60	−20	40	550

(row 6); with government spending, aggregate expenditures and real output are equal at $550 billion (row 10). Increases in public spending, like increases in private spending, shift the aggregate expenditures schedule upward and result in a higher equilibrium GDP.

MATH 11.2 Government

Note, too, that government spending is subject to the open economy multiplier. A $40 billion increase in government purchases has increased equilibrium GDP by $80 billion (from $470 billion to $550 billion). We have implicitly assumed that the $40 billion in government expenditure has all gone to purchase domestic output.

This $40 billion increase in government spending is *not* financed by increased taxes. Soon we will find that increased taxes *reduce* equilibrium GDP.

GRAPHICAL ANALYSIS

In Figure 11-5 we add $40 billion of government purchases, G, vertically to the level of private spending, $C + I_g + X_n$. That increases the aggregate expenditures schedule (private plus public) to $C + I_g + X_n + G$, resulting in the $80 billion increase in equilibrium GDP shown, from $470 billion to $550 billion.

A decline in government spending G will lower the aggregate expenditures schedule, and the result is a multiplied decline in the equilibrium GDP. Verify, using Table 11-5, that if government spending were to decline from $40 billion to $20 billion, the equilibrium GDP would fall by $40 billion.

Taxation and Equilibrium GDP

Government spends taxes, but it also collects them. Suppose it imposes a **lump-sum tax**, which is a tax yielding the same amount of tax revenue at all levels of GDP. For simplicity, we suppose this lump-sum tax is $40 billion, so government obtains $40 billion of tax revenue at each level of GDP. Generally, government revenues rise with GDP.

| FIGURE 11-5 | Government Spending and the Equilibrium GDP |

The addition of government purchases, G, raises the aggregate expenditures ($C + I_g + X_n + G$) schedule and increases the equilibrium level of GDP, as would an increase in C, I_g, or X_n.

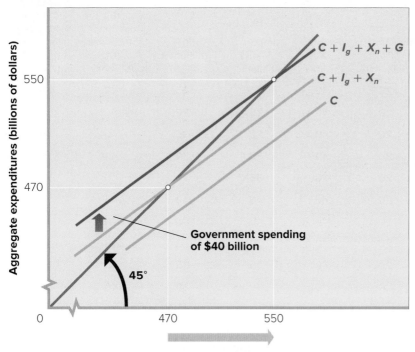

TABULAR EXAMPLE

In Table 11-6, which continues our example, we find taxes in column 2, and we see in column 3 that disposable (after-tax) income is lower than GDP (column 1) by the $40 billion amount of the tax. Because disposable income is used for consumer spending and saving, the tax lowers both consumption and saving. But, by how much will each decline as a result of the $40 billion in taxes? The MPC and MPS hold the answer: The MPC tells us what fraction of a decline in disposable income will come out of consumption, and the MPS indicates what fraction will come out of saving. Since the MPC is 0.75, if government collects $40 billion in taxes at each possible level of GDP, domestic consumption will drop by $30 billion (= 0.75 × $40 billion). Since the MPS is 0.25, saving will fall by $10 billion (= 0.25 × $40 billion).

We must make one more refinement to the new lower consumption level brought about by the tax increase. In an open economy such as Canada's, consumption consists of both domestic and imported commodities. Of the $30 billion drop in total consumption, there will be a $10 billion (= 0.25 × $40 billion) decrease in M since the MPM equals 0.25. The remaining $20 billion therefore comes out of domestic consumption.

Columns 4 and 5 of Table 11-6 list the amounts of consumption and saving *at each level of GDP*, which are $30 billion and $10 billion smaller, respectively, than those in Table 11-5. After taxes are imposed, DI is $410 billion, $40 billion short of the $450 billion GDP, with the result that consumption is only $405 billion, saving is $5 billion, and imports are $25 billion (row 5 of Table 11-6).

Taxes reduce disposable income by the amount of the taxes. This decline in DI reduces consumption, saving, and imports at each level of GDP. The sizes of the declines in C, S, and M are determined by the MPC, the MPS, and the MPM, respectively.

| TABLE 11-6 | Determination of the Equilibrium Levels of Employment, Output, and Income (in billions): Private and Public Sectors | | | | | | | | |

(1) Real domestic output (and income) (GDP = DI)	(2) Taxes (T)	(3) Disposable income (DI) (1) − (2)	(4) Consumption (C_a)	(5) Saving (S_a) (3) − (4)	(6) Investment (I_g)	(7) Net exports (X_n)			(8) Government purchases (G)	(9) Aggregate expenditures ($C_a + I_g + X_{na} + G$) (4) + (6) + (8) + (9)
						X	M_a	X_{na}		
(1) $370	$40	$330	$345	$215	$20	$40	$5	$35	$40	$440
(2) 390	40	350	360	210	20	40	10	30	40	450
(3) 410	40	370	375	25	20	40	15	25	40	460
(4) 430	40	390	390	0	20	40	20	20	40	470
(5) 450	40	410	405	5	20	40	25	15	40	480
(6) 470	40	430	420	10	20	40	30	10	40	490
(7) 490	40	450	435	15	20	40	35	5	40	500
(8) 510	40	470	450	20	20	40	40	0	40	510
(9) 530	40	490	465	25	20	40	45	25	40	520
(10) 550	40	510	480	30	20	40	50	210	40	530

To find out the effect of taxes on equilibrium GDP, we calculate aggregate expenditures once again, as shown in column 9 of Table 11-6. Aggregate spending is $20 billion less at each level of GDP than it was in Table 11-5. The reason is that after-tax consumption, C_a, is $30 billion less, and M_a is $10 billion less (therefore, X_{na} is $10 billion more) at each level of GDP. Comparing real output and aggregate expenditures in columns 1 and 9, we see that the aggregate amounts produced and purchased are equal only at the $510 billion level of GDP (row 8). The $40 billion lump-sum tax has reduced equilibrium GDP from $550 billion (row 10 in Table 11-5) to $510 billion (row 8 in Table 11-6), not back to $470 billion.

GRAPHICAL ANALYSIS

In Figure 11-6, the $40 billion increase in taxes shows up as a $20 billion (not $40 billion) decline in the aggregate expenditures ($C_a + I_g + X_{na} + G$) schedule. This decline in aggregate expenditures results solely from a decline in the consumption component C of the aggregate expenditures. The equilibrium GDP falls from $550 billion to $510 billion because of this tax-induced drop in consumption. Increases in taxes lower the aggregate expenditures schedule relative to the 45° line and reduce the equilibrium GDP.

In contrast to our previous case, a *decrease* in existing taxes will raise the aggregate expenditures schedule in Figure 11-6 as a result of an increase in the consumption at all GDP levels. You should confirm that a tax reduction of $20 billion (from the present $40 billion to $20 billion) will increase the equilibrium GDP from $510 billion to $530 billion.

DIFFERENTIAL IMPACTS

You may have noted that equal changes in government purchases and taxes do not have equivalent impacts on GDP. The $40 billion increase in G in our illustration, subject to the multiplier of 2, produced an $80 billion increase in real GDP. But the $40 billion increase in taxes reduced GDP by only $40 billion. Given an MPC of 0.75, the tax increase of $40 billion reduced consumption by only $30 billion (not $40 billion) and domestic consumption by $20 billion because savings fell by $10 billion and imports fell by $10 billion. Subjecting the $20 billion decline in consumption to the multiplier of 2, we find that the tax increase of $40 billion reduced GDP by $40 billion (not $80 billion).

FIGURE 11-6   **Taxes and Equilibrium GDP**

If the MPC is 0.75, the $40 billion of taxes will lower the domestic consumption schedule by $20 billion and cause a decline in the equilibrium GDP. In the open economy with government, with C_a representing after-tax income, equilibrium GDP occurs where $C_a + I_g + X_n + G =$ GDP.

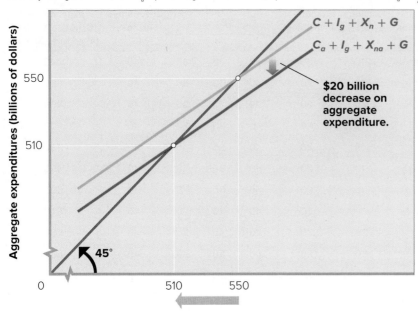

Table 11-6 and Figure 11-6 constitute the complete aggregate expenditures model for an open economy with government. When total spending equals total production, the economy's output is in equilibrium. In the open mixed economy, equilibrium GDP occurs where

$$C_a + I_g + X_{na} + G = \text{GDP}$$

INJECTIONS, LEAKAGES, AND UNPLANNED CHANGES IN INVENTORIES

The related characteristics of equilibrium that we noted for the private closed economy also apply to the full model. In particular, it is still the case that injections into the income–expenditures stream equal leakages from the income stream. For the private closed economy, $S = I_g$. For the expanded economy, imports and taxes are added leakages. Saving, importing, and paying taxes are all uses of income that subtract from potential consumption. Consumption will now be less than GDP–creating a potential spending gap–in the amount of after-tax saving (S_a), imports (M), and taxes (T). But exports (X) and government purchases (G), along with investment (I_g), are injections into the income–expenditures stream. At the equilibrium GDP, the sum of the leakages equals the sum of the injections. In symbols

$$S_a + M + T = I_g + X + G$$

WORKED PROBLEM 11.2   Complete Aggregate Expenditures Model

You should use the data in Table 11-6 to confirm this equality between leakages and injections at the equilibrium GDP of $510 billion. Also, verify that a lack of such an equality exists at all other possible levels of GDP.

Although not directly shown in Table 11-6, the equilibrium characteristic of "no unplanned changes in inventories" will also be fulfilled at the $510 billion GDP. Because aggregate expenditures equal GDP, all the goods and services produced will be purchased. There will be no unplanned increase in inventories, so firms will have no incentive to reduce their employment and production. Nor will they experience an unplanned decline in their inventories, which would prompt them to expand their employment and output to replenish their inventories.

11.8 / Equilibrium versus Full-Employment GDP

LO11.8 Differentiate between equilibrium GDP and full-employment GDP, and identify and describe the nature and causes of *recessionary expenditure gaps* and *inflationary expenditure gaps*.

A key point about the equilibrium GDP of the aggregate expenditures model is that it need not equal the economy's full-employment GDP. In fact, Keynes specifically designed the model so that it could explain situations like the Great Depression, during which the economy was seemingly stuck at a bad equilibrium where real GDP was far below potential output. As we will show you in a moment, Keynes also used the model to suggest policy recommendations for moving the economy back toward potential output and full employment.

The fact that equilibrium and potential GDP in the aggregate expenditures model need not match also reveals essential insights about the causes of demand-pull inflation. We will first examine the "expenditure gaps" that give rise to differences between equilibrium and potential GDP.

Recessionary Expenditure Gap

Suppose in **Figure 11-7a (Key Graph)** that the full-employment level of GDP is $510 billion and the aggregate expenditures schedule is AE_1. This schedule intersects the 45° line to the left of the full-employment output, at $490 billion, so the economy's aggregate production is $20 billion short of its full-employment output of $510 billion. According to column 1 in Table 11-2, employment at full-employment GDP is 22.5 million workers. But the economy depicted in Figure 11-7a is employing only 20 million workers; 2.5 million workers are unemployed. For that reason, the economy is sacrificing $20 billion of output.

The amount by which aggregate expenditures fall short of those required to achieve the full-employment GDP (also called potential GDP) is called the **recessionary expenditure gap**. In Table 11-6, assuming full-employment GDP to be $510 billion, the corresponding recessionary expenditure gap is $10 billion. The aggregate expenditures schedule would have to shift upward to realize the full-employment GDP. Because the multiplier is 2, there is a $20 billion differential ($10 billion times the multiplier of 2) between aggregate expenditures at the equilibrium GDP and those required to attain full-employment GDP. This $20 billion difference is a negative *GDP gap*—an idea you first encountered in our discussion of cyclical unemployment (Chapter 9).

KEYNES'S SOLUTION TO A RECESSIONARY EXPENDITURE GAP

Keynes pointed to two different policies that a government might pursue to close a recessionary expenditure gap and achieve full employment: (1) increase government spending or (2) lower taxes. Both work by increasing aggregate expenditures.

Look back at Figure 11-5. There we showed how an increase in government expenditures G will increase overall aggregate expenditures and, consequently, the equilibrium real GDP. Applying this strategy to the situation in Figure 11-7a, government could completely close the $20 billion negative GDP gap and the economy's potential output (full employment GDP) of $510 billion if it increased spending by the $10 billion amount of the recessionary expenditure gap. Given the economy's multiplier of 2, the $10 billion increase in G would create a $20 billion increase in equilibrium real GDP, thereby bringing the economy to full employment.

Government could also lower taxes to close the recessionary expenditure gap and thus eliminate the negative GDP gap. Look back at Figure 11-6, in which an *increase* in taxes resulted in lower after-tax consumption spending and a smaller equilibrium real GDP. Keynes simply suggested a reversal of this process: Since an increase in taxes lowers equilibrium real GDP, a decrease in taxes will raise equilibrium GDP. The decrease in taxes will leave consumers with higher after-tax income. That will lead to higher consumption expenditures and an increase in equilibrium real GDP.

KEY GRAPH

FIGURE 11-7   Recessionary and Inflationary Expenditure Gaps

The equilibrium and full-employment GDPs may not coincide. (a) A recessionary expenditure gap is the amount by which aggregate expenditures fall short of those required to achieve full-employment GDP. Here, the recessionary expenditure gap is $10 billion, causes a $20 billion shortfall of aggregate expenditures. (b) An inflationary expenditure gap is the amount by which aggregate expenditures exceed those just sufficient to achieve full-employment GDP. Here, the inflationary expenditure gap is $10 billion; this overspending produces demand–pull inflation.

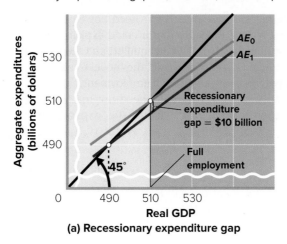

(a) Recessionary expenditure gap

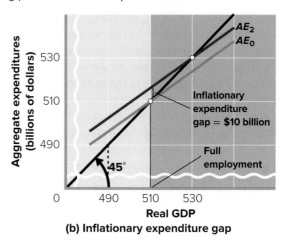

(b) Inflationary expenditure gap

Quick Quiz

1. **In the economy depicted**
   a. The MPS is 0.20
   b. The multiplier is 2
   c. The potential GDP level of real GDP is $530 billion
   d. Nominal GDP always equals real GDP

2. **The inflationary expenditure gap depicted will cause**
   a. Demand–pull inflation
   b. Cost–push inflation
   c. Cyclical unemployment
   d. Frictional unemployment

3. **The recessionary expenditure gap depicted will cause**
   a. Demand–pull inflation
   b. Cost–push inflation

   c. Cyclical unemployment
   d. Frictional unemployment

4. **In the economy depicted, the $20 billion inflationary expenditure gap**
   a. Expands full-employment real GDP to $530 billion
   b. Leaves full-employment real GDP at $510 billion, but causes inflation
   c. Could be remedied by equal $20 billion increases in taxes and government spending
   d. Implies that real GDP exceeds nominal GDP

Answers: 1. b; 2. a; 3. c; 4. b

But, by how much should the government cut taxes? By $13.33 billion, because the MPC is 0.75. The tax cut of $13.33 billion will increase consumers' after-tax income by $13.33 billion. They will then increase consumption spending by 0.75 of that amount, or $10 billion. This will increase aggregate expenditures by the $10 billion needed to close the recessionary expenditure gap. The economy's equilibrium real GDP will rise to its potential output of $510 billion.

But a big warning is needed here: As the economy moves closer to its potential output, it becomes harder to justify Keynes's assumption that prices are stuck. As the economy closes its negative GDP gap, nearly all workers are employed and nearly all factories are operating at or near full capacity. In such a situation, there is no massive oversupply of productive resources to keep prices from rising. In fact, economists know from real-world experience that in such situations prices are not fully stuck. Instead, they become increasingly flexible as the economy moves nearer to potential output.

This fact is one of the major limitations of the aggregate expenditures model and is the reason why in the next chapter we develop a different model that can handle inflation. Nevertheless, the aggregate expenditures model is very useful despite its inability to handle flexible prices. For instance, as we explained in Chapter 4, an economy operating near full employment will show sticky or even stuck prices in the short run. In such situations, the intuitions of the aggregate expenditures model will still hold true. The benefit of the aggregate demand–aggregate supply model that we develop in the next chapter is that it can also show us what happens in the longer run, as prices become more flexible and are increasingly able to adjust.

Inflationary Expenditure Gap

Economists use the term **inflationary expenditure gap** to describe the amount by which an economy's aggregate expenditures exceed those just necessary to achieve the full-employment level of GDP. In Figure 11-7b, a $10 billion inflationary expenditure gap exists at the $530 billion GDP. This is shown by the vertical distance between the actual aggregate expenditures schedule AE_2 and the hypothetical schedule AE_0, which would be just sufficient to achieve the $510 billion full-employment GDP. Thus, the inflationary expenditure gap is the amount by which the aggregate expenditures schedule would have to shift downward to realize equilibrium at the full-employment GDP.

WORKED PROBLEM 11.3   Expenditure Gaps

But why does the term *inflationary expenditure gap* contain the word "inflationary"? In particular, what does the situation depicted in Figure 11-7b have to do with inflation? The answer lies in the answer to a different question: *Could the economy actually achieve and maintain an equilibrium real GDP that is substantially above the full-employment output level?*

The unfortunate answer is no. It is unfortunate because if such a thing were possible, then the government could make real GDP as high as it wanted by simply increasing G to an arbitrarily high number. Graphically, it could raise the AE_2 curve in Figure 11-7b as far as it wanted, thereby raising equilibrium real GDP as high as it wanted. Living standards would skyrocket! But this is not possible because, by definition, all the workers in the economy are fully employed at the full-employment output level. Producing a bit more than the full-employment output level for a few months might be possible if you could convince all the workers to work overtime day after day. But there simply isn't enough labour to have the economy produce at much more than potential output for any extended period of time.

So what *does* happen in situations in which aggregate expenditures are so high that the model predicts an equilibrium level of GDP beyond potential output? The answer is twofold. First, the economy ends up producing either at potential output or just above potential output due to the limited supply of labour. Second, the economy experiences demand–pull inflation. With the supply of output limited by the supply of labour, high levels of aggregate expenditures simply act to drive up prices. Nominal GDP will increase because of the higher price level, but real GDP will not.

Application: The Recession of 2008–2009

In late 2008, the Canadian economy entered one of the deepest recessions since the Great Depression of the 1930s. We will defer discussion of the underlying financial crisis until later chapters, but the ultimate effect of the crisis is easily portrayed through the aggregate expenditures model. We know that the AE_0 line in Figure 11-7a consists of the combined amount of after-tax consumption expenditures (C_a), gross investment expenditures (I_g), net export expenditures (X_n), and government purchases (G) planned at each level of real GDP. During the recession, both after-tax consumption and investment expenditures declined, with planned investment expenditures suffering the largest drop.

Aggregate expenditures thus declined, as from AE_0 to AE_1 in Figure 11-7a. This set off a multiple decline in real GDP, illustrated in the figure by the decline from \$510 billion to \$490 billion. In the language of the aggregate expenditures model, a recessionary expenditure gap produced one of the largest negative GDP gaps since the Great Depression. Within a period of only eight months, employment sank by more than 400,000 people and the unemployment rate rose from 6.1 percent to over 8 percent.

The federal government undertook various Keynesian policies in 2008 and 2009 to try to eliminate the recessionary expenditure gap facing the economy. The foremost defensive move was a spending spree intended to stimulate private spending and investment to reduce the recessionary expenditure gap and, through the multiplier effect, increase real GDP and employment. This was expensive the federal government's annual budget quickly went from a surplus to a deficit of almost \$50 billion, and did not get back to balance until 2015.

ORIGIN OF THE IDEA 11.2   Say's law

We will defer discussion and further assessment of these stimulus attempts, but Figure 11-7a clearly illuminates their purpose. If the government could drive up aggregate expenditures, such as from AE_1 to AE_0, the recession would come to an end and the recovery phase of the business cycle would begin.

QUICK REVIEW 11.3

- Government purchases shift the aggregate expenditures schedule upward and raise the equilibrium GDP.

- Taxes reduce disposable income, lower consumption spending on domestically produced goods and saving, shift the imported and aggregate expenditures schedules downward, and reduce the equilibrium GDP.

- A recessionary expenditure gap is the amount by which GDP falls short of potential GDP; the inflationary expenditure gap is the amount by which GDP exceeds potential GDP.

The LAST WORD   Say's Law, the Great Depression, and Keynes

The aggregate expenditures theory emerged as a critique of classical economics and as a response to the Great Depression.

Until the Great Depression of the 1930s, many prominent economists, including David Ricardo (1772–1823) and John Stuart Mill (1806–73), believed that the market system would ensure full employment of an economy's resources. These so-called *classical economists* acknowledged that, now and then, abnormal circumstances such as wars, political upheavals, droughts, speculative crises, and gold rushes would occur, deflecting the economy from full-employment status. But when such deviations occurred, conditions would automatically adjust and soon restore the economy to

full-employment output. For example, a slump in output and employment would result in lower prices, wages, and interest rates, which in turn would increase consumer spending, employment, and investment spending. Any excess supply of goods and workers would soon be eliminated.

Classical macroeconomists denied that the level of spending in an economy could be too low to bring about the purchase of the entire full-employment output. They based their denial of inadequate spending in part on Say's law, attributed to the nineteenth-century French economist J. B. Say (1767–1832). This law is the disarmingly simple idea that the very act of producing goods generates income equal to the value of the goods produced. The production of any output automatically provides the income needed to buy that output. More succinctly stated, *supply creates its own demand*.

Say's law can best be understood in terms of a barter economy. A woodworker, for example, produces or supplies furniture as a means of buying or demanding the food and clothing produced by other workers. The woodworker's supply of furniture is the income that he will "spend" to satisfy his demand for the other goods. The goods he buys (demands) will have a total value exactly equal to the goods he produces (supplies). And so it is for other producers and for the entire economy. Demand must be the same as supply!

Assuming that the composition of output is in accord with consumer preferences, all markets would be cleared of their outputs. It would seem that all firms need to do to sell a full-employment output is to produce that level of output. Say's law guarantees there will be sufficient spending to purchase it all.

The Great Depression of the 1930s called into question the theory that supply creates its own demand (Say's law). In Canada, real GDP declined by almost 30 percent and the unemployment rate rocketed to nearly 20 percent. Other nations experienced similar impacts. And cyclical unemployment lingered for a decade. An obvious inconsistency exists between a theory that says unemployment is virtually impossible and the actual occurrence of a 10-year siege of substantial unemployment.

In 1936, British economist John Maynard Keynes (1883–1946) explained why cyclical employment could occur in a market economy. In his *General Theory of Employment, Interest, and Money*, Keynes attacked the foundations of classical theory and developed the ideas underlying the aggregate expenditures model. Keynes disputed Say's law, pointing out that not all income need be spent in the same period that it is produced. In fact, some income is always saved. In normal times, that saving is borrowed by businesses to buy capital goods—thereby boosting total spending in the economy. But if expectations about the future grow pessimistic, businesses will slash investment spending and a lot of that saving will not be put to use. The result will be insufficient total spending. Unsold goods will accumulate in producers' warehouses

and producers will respond by reducing their output and discharging workers. A recession or depression will result, and widespread cyclical unemployment will occur. Moreover, said Keynes, recessions or depressions are not likely to correct themselves. In contrast to the more laissez-faire view of the classical economists, Keynes argued that government should play an active role in stabilizing the economy.

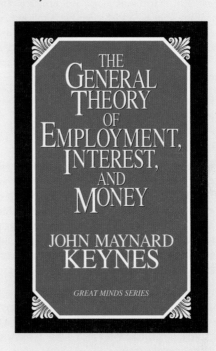

Today, most economists embrace the idea of fiscal stimulus in an economic downturn. The recession in Canada of 2008–2009 brought about by the global financial crisis is easily portrayed through the aggregate expenditures model, which John Maynard Keynes created to explain the Great Depression of the 1930s. Examine Figure 11-7a. Recall that the AE_0 line in this figure consists of the combined amount of after-tax consumption expenditures (C_a), gross investment expenditures (I_g), net export expenditures (X_n), and government purchases (G) planned at each level of real GDP. During the relatively severe recession of 2008–2009, both after-tax consumption and investment expenditures declined, with the largest drop being investment expenditures.

Question

What is Say's law? How does it relate to the view held by classical economists that the economy generally will operate at a position on its production possibilities curve (Chapter 1)? Use production possibilities analysis to demonstrate Keynes's view on this matter.

Chapter Summary

LO11.1   EXPLAIN HOW STICKY PRICES RELATE TO THE AGGREGATE EXPENDITURES MODEL.

- The aggregate expenditures model views the total amount of spending in the economy as the primary factor determining the level of real GDP that the economy will produce. The model assumes that the price is fixed. Keynes made this assumption to reflect the reality of the Great Depression, in which declines in output and employment rather than declines in prices were the dominant adjustments made by firms when they faced huge declines in their sales.

LO11.2   EXPLAIN HOW AN ECONOMY'S INVESTMENT SCHEDULE IS DERIVED FROM THE INVESTMENT DEMAND CURVE AND AN INTEREST RATE.

- An investment schedule shows how much investment the firms in an economy are collectively planning to make at each possible level of GDP. In this chapter, we utilize a simple investment schedule in which investment is a constant value and therefore the same at all levels of GDP. That constant value is derived from the investment demand curve by determining what quantity of investment will be demanded at the economy's current real interest rate.

LO11.3   ILLUSTRATE HOW ECONOMISTS COMBINE CONSUMPTION AND INVESTMENT TO DEPICT AN AGGREGATE EXPENDITURES SCHEDULE AND EQUILIBRIUM OUTPUT FOR A PRIVATE CLOSED ECONOMY.

- For a private closed economy, the equilibrium level of GDP occurs when aggregate expenditures and real output are equal—or, graphically, where the $C + I_g$ line intersects the 45° line. At any GDP greater than equilibrium GDP, real output will exceed aggregate spending, resulting in unintended investment in inventories and eventual declines in output and income (GDP). At any below-equilibrium GDP, aggregate expenditures will exceed real output, resulting in unintended declines in inventories and eventual increases in GDP.

LO11.4   DISCUSS THE TWO OTHER WAYS TO CHARACTERIZE THE EQUILIBRIUM LEVEL OF REAL GDP IN A PRIVATE CLOSED ECONOMY: (1) SAVING = INVESTMENT AND (2) UNPLANNED CHANGES IN INVENTORIES.

- At equilibrium GDP, the amount households save (leakages) and the amount businesses plan to invest (injections) are equal. Any excess of saving over planned investment will cause a shortage of total spending, forcing GDP to fall. Any excess of planned investment over saving will cause an excess of total spending, inducing GDP to rise. The change in GDP will in both cases correct the discrepancy between saving and planned investment.

- At equilibrium GDP, no unplanned changes in inventories occur. When aggregate expenditures diverge from GDP, an unplanned change in inventories occurs. Unplanned increases in inventories are followed by a cutback in production and a decline of real GDP. Unplanned decreases in inventories result in an increase in production and a rise of GDP.

- Actual investment consists of planned investment plus unplanned changes in inventories and is always equal to saving.

LO11.5   ANALYZE HOW CHANGES IN EQUILIBRIUM GDP CAN OCCUR IN THE AGGREGATE EXPENDITURES MODEL AND HOW THOSE CHANGES RELATE TO THE MULTIPLIER.

- The simple multiplier is equal to the reciprocal of the marginal propensity to save: the greater the marginal propensity to save, the smaller the multiplier. The greater the marginal propensity to consume, the larger the multiplier.

- A shift in the investment schedule (caused by changes in expected rates of return or changes in interest rates) shifts the aggregate expenditures curve and causes a new equilibrium level of real GDP. Real GDP changes by more than the amount of the initial change in investment. This multiplier effect ($\Delta GDP/\Delta I_g$) accompanies both increases and decreases in aggregate expenditures and also applies to changes in net exports (X_n) and government purchases (G).

LO11.6   EXPLAIN HOW ECONOMISTS INTEGRATE THE INTERNATIONAL SECTOR (EXPORTS AND IMPORTS) INTO THE AGGREGATE EXPENDITURES MODEL.

- The net export schedule relates net exports (exports minus imports) to levels of real GDP. For simplicity, we assume the level of exports is the same at all levels of real GDP.

- Positive net exports increase aggregate expenditures to a higher level than they would reach if the economy were closed to international trade. They raise equilibrium real GDP by a multiple of the net exports. Negative net exports decrease aggregate expenditures relative to those in a closed economy, decreasing equilibrium real GDP by a multiple of their amount. Increases in exports or decreases in imports have an expansionary effect on real GDP, but decreases in exports or increases in imports have a contractionary effect.

LO 11.7 EXPLAIN HOW ECONOMISTS INTEGRATE THE PUBLIC SECTOR (GOVERNMENT EXPENDITURES AND TAXES) INTO THE AGGREGATE EXPENDITURES MODEL.

- Government purchases shift the aggregate expenditures schedule upward and raise GDP.

- Taxation reduces disposable income, lowers consumption spending and saving, shifts the aggregate expenditures curve downward, and reduces equilibrium GDP.

- In the complete aggregate expenditures model, equilibrium GDP occurs where $C_a + I_g + X_n + G =$ GDP. At the equilibrium GDP, leakages of after-tax saving (S_a), imports (M), and taxes (T) equal injections of investment (I_g), exports (X), and government purchases (G). Also, there are no unplanned changes in inventories.

LO11.8 DIFFERENTIATE BETWEEN EQUILIBRIUM GDP AND FULL-EMPLOYMENT GDP, AND IDENTIFY AND DESCRIBE THE NATURE AND CAUSES OF RECESSIONARY EXPENDITURE GAPS AND INFLATIONARY EXPENDITURE GAPS.

- The equilibrium GDP and the full-employment GDP may differ. The recessionary expenditure gap is the amount by which aggregate expenditures fall short of those required to achieve full-employment GDP. This gap produces a negative GDP gap (actual GDP minus potential GDP). The inflationary expenditure gap is the amount by which aggregate expenditures exceed those needed to achieve full-employment GDP. This gap causes demand–pull inflation.

- Keynes suggested that the solution to the large negative GDP gap that occurred during the Great Depression was for government to increase aggregate expenditures. It could do this by increasing its own expenditures (G) or by lowering taxes (T) to increase after-tax consumption expenditures (C_a) by households. Because the economy had millions of unemployed workers and massive amounts of unused production capacity, government could boost aggregate expenditures without worrying about creating inflation.

- The stuck-price assumption of the aggregate expenditures model is not credible when the economy approaches or attains its full-employment output. With unemployment low and excess production capacity small or nonexistent, an increase in aggregate expenditures will cause inflation along with any increase in real GDP.

Terms and Concepts

aggregate expenditures
planned investment
investment schedule
aggregate expenditures schedule
equilibrium GDP

leakage
injection
unplanned changes in inventory
net exports
marginal propensity to import (MPM)

lump-sum tax
recessionary expenditure gap
inflationary expenditure gap
Say's law

Discussion Questions

1. What is the investment schedule and how does it differ from an investment demand curve? [LO11.2]

2. Why does equilibrium real GDP occur where $C + I_g =$ GDP in a private closed economy? What happens to real GDP when $C + I_g$ exceeds GDP? When $C + I_g$ is less than GDP? What two expenditure components of real GDP are purposely excluded in a private closed economy? [LO11.3]

3. Why is saving called a *leakage*? Why is planned investment called an *injection*? Why must saving equal planned investment at equilibrium GDP in a private, closed economy? Are unplanned changes in inventories rising, falling, or constant at equilibrium GDP? Explain. [LO11.4]

4. Other things equal, what effect will each of the following changes independently have on the equilibrium level of real GDP in a private closed economy? [LO11.5]

   a. A decline in the real interest rate

   b. An overall decrease in the expected rate of return on investment

   c. A sizeable, sustained increase in stock prices

5. Depict graphically the aggregate expenditures model for a private closed economy. Now show a decrease in the aggregate expenditures schedule and explain why the decline in real GDP in your diagram is greater than the initial decline in aggregated expenditures. What would be the ratio of a decline in real GDP to the initial drop in aggregate expenditures if the slope of your aggregate expenditures schedule was 0.8?   [LO11.5]

6. Assuming the economy is operating below its potential output, what is the impact of an increase in net exports on real GDP? Why is it difficult, if not impossible, for a country to boost its net exports by increasing its tariffs during a global recession?   [LO11.6]

7. What is a recessionary expenditure gap? An inflationary expenditure gap? Which is associated with a positive GDP gap? A negative GDP gap?   [LO11.8]

Review Questions

1. True or False? The aggregate expenditures model assumes flexible prices.   [LO11.1]

2. If total spending is just sufficient to purchase an economy's output, then the economy is   [LO11.3]

   a. In equilibrium

   b. In recession

   c. In debt

   d. In expansion

3. True or False? If spending exceeds output, real GDP will decline as firms cut back on production.   [LO11.3]

4. If inventories unexpectedly rise, then production _____ sales and firms will respond by_____ output.   [LO11.3]

   a. Trails; expanding

   b. Trails; reducing

   c. Exceeds; expanding

   d. Exceeds; reducing

5. If the multiplier is 5 and investment increases by $3 billion, equilibrium real GDP will increase by   [LO11.5]

   a. $2 billion

   b. $3 billion

   c. $8 billion

   d. $15 billion

   e. None of the above

6. A depression abroad will tend to _____ our exports, which in turn will _____ net exports, which in turn will _____ equilibrium real GDP.   [LO11.6]

   a. Reduce; reduce; reduce

   b. Increase; increase; increase

   c. Reduce; increase; increase

   d. Increase; reduce; reduce

7. Explain graphically the determination of equilibrium GDP for a private economy through the aggregate expenditures model. Now add government purchases (any amount you choose) to your graph, showing its impact on equilibrium GDP. Finally, add taxation (any lump-sum tax amount you choose) to your graph and show its effect on equilibrium GDP. Looking at your graph, determine whether equilibrium GDP has increased, decreased, or stayed the same given the sizes of the government purchases and taxes that you selected.   [LO11.7]

8. The economy's current level of equilibrium GDP is $780 billion. The full employment level of GDP is $800 billion. The multiplier is 4. Given those facts, we know that the economy faces _____expenditure gap of _____.   [LO11.8]

   a. An inflationary; $5 billion

   b. An inflationary; $10 billion

   c. An inflationary; $20 billion

   d. A recessionary; $5 billion

   e. A recessionary; $10 billion

   f. A recessionary; $20 billion

9. If an economy has an inflationary expenditure gap, the government could attempt to bring the economy back toward the full-employment level of GDP by _____ taxes or _____ government expenditures.   [LO11.8]

   a. Increasing; increasing.

   b. Increasing; decreasing

   c. Decreasing; increasing

   d. Decreasing; decreasing

Problems

1. Assuming the level of investment is $16 billion and independent of the level of total output, complete the following table and determine the equilibrium levels of output and employment that this private closed economy would provide. What are the sizes of the MPC and MPS?   [LO11.3]

Possible levels of employment (millions)	Real domestic output (GDP = DI) (billions)	Consumption (billions)	Saving (billions)
40	$240	$244	$_____
45	260	260	_____
50	280	276	_____
55	300	292	_____
60	320	308	_____
65	340	324	_____
70	360	340	_____
75	380	356	_____
80	400	372	_____

2. Using the consumption and saving data in problem 1 and assuming investment is $16 billion, what are saving and planned investment at the $380 billion level of domestic output? What are saving and actual investment at that level? What are saving and planned investment at the $300 billion level of domestic output? What are the levels of saving and actual investment? In which direction and by what amount will unplanned investment change as the economy moves from the $380 billion level of GDP to the equilibrium level of real GDP? From the $300 billion level of real GDP to the equilibrium level of GDP?   [LO11.4]

3. By how much will GDP change if firms increase their investment by $8 billion when the MPC is 0.80? When the MPC is 0.67?   [LO11.5]

4. Suppose a certain country has an MPC of 0.9 and a real GDP of $400 billion. If its investment spending decreases by $4 billion, what will be its new level of real GDP in the aggregate expenditures model?   [LO11.5]

5. The data in columns 1 and 2 in the table below are for a private closed economy.   [LO11.6]

   a. Use columns 1 and 2 to determine the equilibrium GDP for this hypothetical economy.

   b. Now open up this economy to international trade by including the export and import figures of columns 3 and 4. Fill in columns 5 and 6 and determine the equilibrium GDP for the open economy. What is the change in equilibrium GDP caused by the addition of net exports?

   c. Given the original $20 billion level of exports, what would be the equilibrium GDP if imports were $10 billion greater at each level of GDP?

   d. What is the multiplier in this example?

(1) Real domestic output (GDP = DI) (billions)	(2) Aggregate expenditures, private closed economy (billions)	(3) Exports (billions)	(4) Imports (billions)	(5) Net exports (billions)	(6) Aggregate expenditures, private open economy (billions)
$200	$240	$20	$30	$_____	$_____
250	280	20	30	_____	_____
300	320	20	30	_____	_____
350	360	20	30	_____	_____
400	400	20	30	_____	_____
450	440	20	30	_____	_____
500	480	20	30	_____	_____
550	520	20	30	_____	_____

6. Assume that, without taxes, the consumption schedule of an economy is as shown in the table below.   [LO11.7]

   a. Graph this consumption schedule and determine the MPC.

   b. Assume now that a lump-sum tax is imposed such that the government collects $10 billion in taxes at all levels of GDP. Graph the resulting consumption schedule, and compare the MPC and the multiplier with those of the pretax consumption schedule.

GDP (billions)	Consumption (billions)
$100	$120
200	200
300	280
400	360
500	440
600	520
700	600

7. Refer to columns 1 and 6 in the table for problem 5. Incorporate government into the table by assuming that it plans to tax and spend $20 billion at each possible level of GDP. Also assume that the tax is a personal tax and that government spending does not induce a shift in the private aggregate expenditures schedule. What is the change in equilibrium GDP caused by the addition of government?   [LO11.7]

8. **Advanced Analysis** Assume the consumption schedule for a private open economy is $C = 50 + 0.8Y$. Assume further that planned investment I_g and net exports X_n are independent of the level of real GDP and constant at $I_g = 30$ and $X_n = 10$. Recall that, in equilibrium, the real output produced (Y) is equal to aggregate expenditures: $Y = C + I_g + X_n$.   [LO11.7]

   a. Calculate the equilibrium level of income or real GDP for this economy. Check your work by expressing the consumption, investment, and net export schedules in tabular form and determining the equilibrium GDP.

   b. What happens to equilibrium Y if I_g changes to 10? What does this outcome reveal about the size of the multiplier?

9. Refer to the table below in answering the questions that follow: [LO11.8]

(1) Possible levels of employment (millions)	(2) Real domestic output (billions)	(3) Aggregate expenditures ($C_a + I_g + X_n + G$) (billions)
9	$500	$520
10	550	560
11	600	600
12	650	640
13	700	680

   a. If full employment in this economy is 13 million, will there be an inflationary or a recessionary expenditure gap? What will be the consequence of this gap? By how much would aggregate expenditures in column 3 have to change at each level of GDP to eliminate the inflationary or the recessionary gap? What is the multiplier in this example?

   b. Will there be an inflationary expenditure gap or a recessionary expenditure gap if the full-employment level of output is $500 billion? By how much would aggregate expenditures in column 3 have to change at each level of GDP to eliminate the inflationary or the recessionary gap? What is the multiplier in this example?

   c. Assuming that investment, net exports, and government expenditures do not change with changes in real GDP, what are the sizes of the MPC, the MPS, and the multiplier?

10. Answer the following questions relating to the aggregate expenditures model: [LO11.8]

   a. If C_a is $100, I_g is $50, X_n is $–10, and G is $30, what is the economy's equilibrium GDP?

   b. If real GDP in an economy is currently $200, C_a is $100, I_g is $50, X_n is $–10, and G is $30, will its real GDP rise, fall, or stay the same?

   c. Suppose that full-employment (and full-capacity) output in an economy is $200. If C_a is $150, I_g is $50, X_n is $–10, and G is $30, what will be the macroeconomic result?

Math Appendix to Chapter 11

A11.1 / The Math Behind the Aggregate Expenditures Model

We begin with an explanation of the symbols we use:

- Aggregate expenditures, AE
- Real GDP, Y
- Disposable income, Y_d
- Consumption expenditure, C
- Autonomous consumption expenditure, a
- Investment expenditure, I_a
- Government expenditure, G_a
- Exports, X_a
- Imports, M
- Autonomous taxes, T_a
- Marginal tax rate, t
- Marginal propensity to consume, b
- Marginal propensity to import, m
- Autonomous expenditure, A
- Marginal propensity to withdraw, W

Aggregate Expenditures

We know that $AE = C + I + (X - M) + G$. Let's look at each component of aggregate expenditures in more detail.

CONSUMPTION EXPENDITURES

The consumption function is given by the linear equation $C = a + bY_d$. This means that consumption consists of an "autonomous" amount, a, plus a portion of disposable income Y_d, the portion being the product of Y_d and the marginal propensity to consume, b. To arrive at disposable income Y_d we must deduct net taxes. So far we have assumed that taxes are a lump sum, an assumption that made the exposition easier. We now assume that taxes consist of an autonomous amount T_a, plus an induced portion of Y, which is the marginal tax rate, t. So the consumption function becomes

$$C = a + b(Y - T_a - tY)$$
$$= a - bT_a + b(1 - t)Y$$

INVESTMENT

We assume investment spending (I_a) to be autonomous, or a constant amount.

NET EXPORTS

Recall that in our expenditures model, exports (X_a) are determined abroad, so they are autonomous. Imports are determined by the level of our own GDP multiplied by the marginal propensity to import (m):

$$M = mY$$

GOVERNMENT EXPENDITURES

Our expenditure model assumes that government expenditures (G_a) are autonomous, or independent of GDP.

We can now put all the terms together to get

$$AE = a - bT_a + b(1 - t)Y + I_a + G_a + X_a - mY \quad (1)$$

AGGREGATE EXPENDITURES AND EQUILIBRIUM GDP

Equilibrium expenditures occur when planned aggregate expenditures (AE) equal real GDP (Y):

$$Y = AE \quad (2)$$

Substituting (2) into (1), we get

$$Y = a - bT_a + b(1 - t)Y + I_a + G_a + X_a - mY$$

We now solve for the value of Y that satisfies both equations (1) and (2). To do so, we group the Y terms that are on the right-hand side of the previous equation:

$$Y = Y[b(1 - t) - m] + a - bT_a + I_a + G_a + X_a$$

Bringing the Y terms to the left-hand side of the equation leads us to the equilibrium condition:

$$Y = \frac{a - bT_a + I_a + G_a + X_a}{1 - [b(1 - t) - m]} \quad (3)$$

Note that in the denominator, $[b(1 - t) - m]$ is the equivalent of the marginal propensity to consume, but that this term refers to the marginal propensity to spend out of national income, rather than just consumption. Note that the denominator $1 - [b(1 - t) - m]$ is a leakage, or a withdrawal from domestic expenditures, which apart from savings also includes taxes and imports. We can simplify equation (3) by denoting the numerator, which consists of autonomous expenditures, by the letter A, and using the letter W for the marginal propensity to withdraw from domestic expenditures, to give us

$$Y = A/W$$

GRAPHICAL ILLUSTRATION

In Figure A11-1a the slope of the aggregate expenditures curve, equal to the term $b(1 - t) - m$, is the marginal propensity to spend. Autonomous expenditure, A, is equal to the sum of $a - bT_a + I_a + G_a + X_a$.

Figure A11-1b shows that equilibrium in the aggregate expenditures model occurs where planned expenditure is equal to actual output.

NUMERICAL EXAMPLE

Let's look at a concrete example to calculate equilibrium income. Suppose you are given the following information:

$$C = 60 + 0.6\,Y_d \qquad G_a = 70$$

$$T = 40 + 0.25Y \qquad X_a = 44$$

$$I_a = 60 \qquad M = 0.15Y$$

There are two ways you can arrive at the result. The first is to substitute the numbers into equation (1). At equilibrium, $Y = AE$, or

$$Y = C + I + (X - M) + G$$

Substituting each of the components into the equation, we get

$$Y = 60 + 0.6(Y - 40 - 0.25Y) + 60 + (44 - 0.15Y) + 70$$

Collecting the terms gives us

$$Y = 210 + 0.3Y$$

Subtracting $0.3Y$ from each side yields

$$0.7Y = 210$$

Dividing both sides of the equation by 0.7 gives us the equilibrium real GDP:

$$Y = 300$$

The second way is to substitute the numbers into equation (3):

$$Y = \frac{a - bT_a + I_a + G_a + X_a}{1 - [b(1 - t) - m]}$$

$$Y = \frac{60 - 0.6(40) + 60 + 70 + 44}{1 - [0.6(1 - 0.25) - 0.15]}$$

$$Y = \frac{210}{1 - 0.3}$$

$$Y = \frac{210}{0.7}$$

$$Y = 300$$

FIGURE A11-1   **The Aggregate Expenditures Curve**

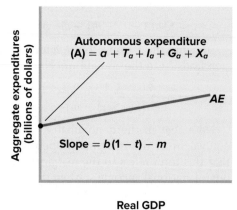

(a) The AE curve

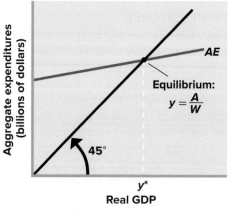

(b) Equilibrium expenditure

CHAPTER 12

Aggregate Demand and Aggregate Supply

LEARNING OBJECTIVES

LO12.1 Define aggregate demand (AD) and explain how its downward slope is the result of the real-balances effect, the interest-rate effect, and the foreign-trade effect.

LO12.2 Explain the factors that cause changes (shifts) in AD.

LO12.3 Define aggregate supply (AS) and explain how it differs in the immediate short run, the short run, and the long run.

LO12.4 Explain the factors that cause changes (shifts) in AS.

LO12.5 Discuss how AD and AS determine an economy's equilibrium price level and level of real GDP.

LO12.6 Describe how the AD–AS model explains periods of demand–pull inflation, cost–push inflation, and recession.

LOA12.1 (Appendix) Identify how the aggregate demand curve relates to the aggregate expenditures model.

During the recession of 2008-2009, the economic terms *aggregate demand* and *aggregate supply* moved from the obscurity of economic journals and textbooks to the spotlight of national newspapers, websites, radio, and television.

The media and public wanted to know why *aggregate demand* had declined, producing the deepest recession and highest rate of unemployment since 1982. Why hadn't the reductions in interest rates by the Bank of Canada boosted aggregate demand? Would the federal government's fiscal stimulus increase aggregate demand and reduce unemployment, as intended? Would a resurgence of oil prices and other energy prices reduce aggregate supply, choking off an economic expansion?

Aggregate demand and aggregate supply are the featured elements of the **aggregate demand–aggregate supply model (AD–AS model)**–the focus of this chapter. The aggregate expenditures model of the previous chapter is an immediate-short-run model because prices are assumed to be fixed. In contrast, the AD–AS model in this chapter is a variable price–variable output model that allows both the price level and level of real GDP to change. It also puts time elements into the picture, distinguishing between the immediate short run, the short run, and the long run. Further, in subsequent chapters we will see that the AD–AS model easily depicts fiscal and monetary policies such as those used in 2008 and 2009 to try to halt the downward slide of the economy and promote its recovery.

12.1 / Aggregate Demand

LO12.1 Define aggregate demand (AD) and explain how its downward slope is the result of the real-balances effect, the interest-rate effect, and the foreign-trade effect.

Aggregate demand is a schedule or curve that shows the amounts of a nation's output (real GDP) that buyers collectively desire to purchase at each possible price level. These buyers include the nation's households, businesses, and government, along with consumers located abroad (households, businesses, and governments in other nations). The relationship between the price level (as measured by the GDP price index) and the amount of real GDP demanded is inverse or negative: when the price level rises, the quantity of real GDP demanded decreases; when the price level falls, the quantity of real GDP demanded increases.

Aggregate Demand Curve

The inverse relationship between the price level and real GDP is shown in Figure 12-1, where the aggregate demand curve AD slopes downward, as does the demand curve for an individual product. Why the downward slope? The explanation rests on three effects of a price-level change.

FIGURE 12-1   **The Aggregate Demand Curve**

The downsloping aggregate demand curve AD indicates an inverse relationship between the price level and the amount of real output purchased. It slopes downward because of (1) the real-balances effect, (2) the interest-rate effect, and (3) the foreign-trade effect.

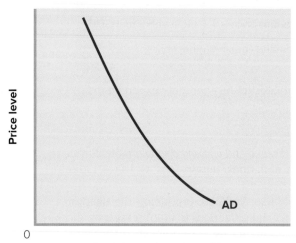

Real domestic output, GDP

ORIGIN OF THE IDEA 12.1   Real-Balances Effect

REAL-BALANCES EFFECT

A change in the price level produces a **real-balances effect**. Here is how it works. A higher price level reduces the purchasing power of the public's accumulated saving balances. In particular, the real value of assets with fixed money values, such as savings accounts or bonds, diminishes. Because a higher price level erodes the purchasing power of such assets, the public is poorer in real terms and will reduce its spending. A household might buy a new car or a plasma TV if the purchasing power of its financial asset balances is, say, $50,000. But if inflation erodes the purchasing power of its asset balances to $30,000, the family may defer its purchase. So a higher price level means less consumption spending.

INTEREST-RATE EFFECT

The aggregate demand curve also slopes downward because of the **interest-rate effect**. When we draw an aggregate demand curve, we assume that the supply of money in the economy is fixed. But when the price level rises, consumers need more money for purchases, and businesses need more money to meet their payrolls and to buy other resources. A $10 bill will do when the price of an item is $10, but a $10 bill plus a loonie is needed when the item costs $11. In short, a higher price level increases the demand for money. So, given a fixed supply of money, an increase in money demand will drive up the price paid for its use. The price of money is the interest rate.

Higher interest rates restrain investment spending and interest-sensitive consumption spending. Firms that expect a 6 percent rate of return on a potential purchase of capital will find that investment profitable when the interest rate is, say, 5 percent. But the investment will be unprofitable and will not be made when the interest rate has risen to 7 percent. Similarly, consumers may decide not to purchase a new house or automobile when the interest rate on loans goes up. So, by increasing the demand for money and consequently the interest rate, a higher price level reduces the amount of real output demanded.

FOREIGN-TRADE EFFECT

The final reason why the aggregate demand curve slopes downward is the **foreign-trade effect**. When the Canadian price level rises relative to foreign price levels, foreigners buy fewer Canadian goods and Canadians buy more foreign goods. Therefore, Canadian exports fall and Canadian imports rise. In short, the rise in the price level reduces the quantity of Canadian goods demanded as net exports.

These three effects work in the opposite directions for a decline in the price level, of course. A decline in the price level increases consumption through the real-balances effect and interest-rate effect, increases investment through the interest-rate effect, and raises net exports by increasing exports and decreasing imports through the foreign-trade effect.

12.2 / Changes in Aggregate Demand

LO12.2 Explain the factors that cause changes (shifts) in AD.

Other things equal, a change in the price level will change the amount of aggregate spending and therefore change the amount of real GDP demanded by the economy. Movements along a fixed aggregate demand curve represent these changes in real GDP. However, if one or more of those other things changes, the entire aggregate demand curve will shift. We call these other things **determinants of aggregate demand**. They are listed in Figure 12-2.

In Figure 12-2, the rightward shift of the curve from AD$_1$ to AD$_2$ shows an increase in aggregate demand. At each price level, the amount of real goods and services demanded is larger than before. The leftward shift of the curve from AD$_1$ to AD$_3$ shows a decrease in aggregate demand; the amount of real GDP demanded at each price level is lower.

Let's examine each determinant of aggregate demand that is listed in Figure 12-2.

| **FIGURE 12-2** | **Changes in Aggregate Demand** |

A change in one or more of the listed determinants of aggregate demand will change aggregate demand. An increase in aggregate demand is shown as a rightward shift of the AD curve, here from AD_1 to AD_2; a decrease in aggregate demand is shown as a leftward shift, here from AD_1 to AD_3.

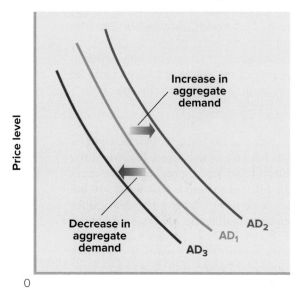

Determinants of aggregate demand: factors that shift the aggregate demand curve

1. Change in consumer spending
   a. Consumer wealth
   b. Consumer expectations
   c. Household borrowing
   d. Personal taxes
2. Change in investment spending
   a. Interest rates
   b. Expected returns
      • Expected future business conditions
      • Technology
      • Degree of excess capacity
      • Business taxes
3. Change in government spending
4. Change in net export spending
   a. National income abroad
   b. Exchange rates

CONSUMER SPENDING

Even when the Canadian price level is constant, domestic consumers may change their purchases of Canadian-produced real output. If those consumers decide to buy more output at each price level, the aggregate demand curve will shift to the right, as from AD_1 to AD_2 in Figure 12-2. If they decide to buy less output, the aggregate demand curve will shift to the left, as from AD_1 to AD_3.

Several factors other than a change in the price level may change consumer spending and thus shift the aggregate demand curve. As Figure 12-2 shows, those factors are real consumer wealth, consumer expectations, household borrowing, and taxes.

Consumer Wealth   Consumer wealth is the total dollar value of all assets owned by consumers in the economy less the dollar value of their liabilities (debts). Assets include stocks, bonds, and real estate. Liabilities include mortgages, car loans, and credit card balances. Consumer wealth sometimes changes suddenly and unexpectedly due to surprising changes in asset values. An unforeseen increase in the stock market is a good example. The increase in wealth prompts pleasantly surprised consumers to save less and buy more out of their current incomes than they had previously been planning. The resulting increase in consumer spending—the so-called wealth effect—shifts the aggregate demand curve to the right. In contrast, an unexpected decline in asset values will cause an unanticipated reduction in consumer wealth at each price level. As consumers tighten their belts in response to the bad news, a *reverse wealth effect* sets in. Unpleasantly surprised consumers increase savings and reduce consumption, thereby shifting the aggregate demand curve to the left.

Household Borrowing   Consumers can increase their consumption spending by borrowing. Doing so shifts the aggregate demand curve to the right. By contrast, a decrease in borrowing for consumption purposes shifts the aggregate demand curve to the left. The aggregate demand curve will also shift to the left if consumers increase their saving rates in order to pay off their debts. With more money flowing to debt repayment, consumption expenditures decline and the AD curve shifts left.

Consumer Expectations   Changes in expectations about the future may change consumer spending. When people expect their future real income to rise, they spend more of their current income. Thus current consumption spending increases (current saving falls), and the aggregate demand curve shifts to the right. Similarly, a widely held expectation of surging inflation in the near future may increase aggregate demand today because consumers will want to buy products before their prices rise. Conversely, expectations of lower future income or lower future prices may reduce current consumption and shift the aggregate demand curve to the left.

Personal Taxes   A reduction in personal income tax rates raises take-home income and increases consumer purchases at each possible price level. Tax cuts shift the aggregate demand curve to the right. Tax increases reduce consumption spending and shift the curve to the left.

INVESTMENT SPENDING

Investment spending (the purchase of capital goods) is a second major determinant of aggregate demand. A decline in investment spending at each price level will shift the aggregate demand curve to the left, while an increase in investment spending will shift it to the right.

Real Interest Rates   Other things equal, an increase in interest rates will raise borrowing costs, lower investment spending, and reduce aggregate demand. We are not referring here to the interest-rate effect resulting from a change in the price level. Instead, we are identifying a change in the interest rate that results from, say, a change in the nation's money supply. An increase in the money supply lowers the interest rate, thereby increasing investment and aggregate demand. A decrease in the money supply raises the interest rate, reduces investment, and decreases aggregate demand.

Expected Returns   Higher expected returns on investment projects will increase the demand for capital goods and shift the aggregate demand curve to the right. Declines in expected returns will decrease investment and shift the curve to the left. Expected returns are influenced by several factors:

- *Expectations About Future Business Conditions*   If firms are optimistic about future business conditions, they are more likely to invest more today. If they think the economy will deteriorate in the future, they will invest less today.

- *Technology*   New and improved technologies increase expected returns on investment and thus increase aggregate demand. For example, recent advances in microbiology have motivated pharmaceutical companies to establish new labs and production facilities.

- *Degree of Excess Capacity*   Other things equal, firms operating factories at well below capacity have little incentive to build new factories. But when firms discover that their excess capacity is dwindling or has completely disappeared, their expected returns on new investment in factories and capital equipment rise. They increase their investment spending and the aggregate demand curve shifts to the right.

- *Business Taxes*   An increase in business taxes will reduce after-tax profits from capital investment and lower expected returns. So investment and aggregate demand will decline. A decrease in business taxes will have the opposite effect.

The variability of interest rates and investment expectations makes investment quite volatile. In contrast to consumption, investment spending rises and falls quite often, independent of changes in total income. Investment, in fact, is the least stable component of aggregate demand.

GOVERNMENT SPENDING

Government purchases are the third determinant of aggregate demand. An increase in government purchases (for example, more computers for government agencies) will shift the aggregate demand curve to the right, provided tax collections and interest rates do not change as a result. In contrast, a reduction in government spending (for example, fewer transportation projects) will shift the curve to the left.

NET EXPORT SPENDING

The final determinant of aggregate demand is net export spending. Other things equal, a rise of Canadian *exports* means increased foreign demand for Canadian goods, whereas a decrease in Canadian *imports* implies that Canadian consumers have decreased their demand for foreign-produced products. So a rise in net exports (higher exports and/or lower imports) shifts the aggregate demand curve to the right. In contrast, a decrease in Canadian net exports shifts the aggregate demand curve leftward. (These changes in net exports are *not* those prompted by a change in the Canadian price level–those associated with the foreign-trade effect. The changes here explain shifts of the AD curve, not movements along the AD curve.)

What might cause net exports to change, other than the price level? Two possibilities are changes in national income abroad and changes in exchange rates.

National Income Abroad   Rising national income abroad encourages foreigners to buy more products, some of which are made in Canada. Canadian net exports thus rise and the Canadian aggregate demand curve shifts to the right. Declines in national income abroad, of course, do the opposite: they reduce Canadian net exports and shift the aggregate demand curve in Canada to the left. For example, in 2008 the economy of the U.S., Canada's largest trading partner, slowed down perceptibly and our exports to the U.S. declined.

Exchange Rates   Changes in the dollar's exchange rates–the prices of foreign currencies in terms of the Canadian dollar–may affect Canadian net exports and therefore aggregate demand. Suppose the Canadian dollar depreciates in terms of the euro (the euro appreciates in terms of the dollar). The new relative lower value of dollars and higher value of euros make Canadian goods less expensive, so European consumers buy more Canadian goods and Canadian exports rise. But Canadian consumers now find European goods more expensive, so reduce their imports from Europe. Canadian exports rise and Canadian imports fall. Therefore we conclude that dollar depreciation increases net exports (imports go down; exports go up) and increases aggregate demand. Dollar *appreciation* has the opposite effects: net exports fall (imports go up; exports go down) and aggregate demand declines.

- Aggregate demand reflects an inverse relationship between the price level and the amount of real output demanded.
- Changes in the price level create real-balances, interest-rate, and foreign-trade effects that explain the downward slope of the aggregate demand curve.
- Changes in one or more of the determinants of aggregate demand (Figure 12-2) alter the amounts of real

GDP demanded at each price level; they shift the aggregate demand curve.
- An increase in aggregate demand is shown as a rightward shift of the aggregate demand curve, a decrease, as a leftward shift of the curve.

12.3 / Aggregate Supply

LO12.3 Define *aggregate supply* (AS) and explain how it differs in the immediate short run, the short run, and the long run.

Aggregate supply is a schedule or curve showing the relationship between a nation's price level of output and the amount of real domestic output that firms in the economy produce. This relationship varies depending on the time horizon and how quickly output prices and input prices can change. We will define three time horizons.

- In the *immediate short run*, both input prices and output prices are fixed.
- In the *short run*, input prices are fixed but output prices can vary.
- In the *long run*, input prices as well as output prices can vary.

In Chapter 6, we discussed both the immediate short run and the long run in terms of how an automobile maker named Buzzer Auto responds to changes in the demand for its new car, the Prion. Here we extend the logic of that chapter to the economy as a whole in order to discuss how total output varies with the price level in the immediate short run, the short run, and the long run. As you will see, the relationship between the price level and total output is different in each of the three time horizons because input prices are stickier than output prices. While both become more flexible as time passes, output prices usually adjust more rapidly.

Aggregate Supply in the Immediate Short Run

Depending on the type of firm, the immediate short run can last anywhere from a few days to a few months. It lasts as long as *both* input prices and output prices stay fixed. Input prices are fixed in both the immediate short run and the short run by contractual agreements. In particular, 75 percent of the average firm's costs are wages and salaries–and these are almost always fixed by labour contracts for months or years at a time. As a result, they are usually fixed for a much longer duration than output prices, which can begin to change within a few days or a few months depending upon the type of firm.

Output prices are also typically fixed in the immediate short run. This is most often caused by firms setting fixed prices for their customers and then agreeing to supply whatever quantity demanded results at those fixed prices. For instance, once an appliance manufacturer sets its annual list prices for refrigerators, stoves, and microwaves, it is obligated to supply however many or few appliances customers want to buy at those prices. Similarly, a catalogue company is obliged to sell however many of its products customers want to buy at the prices listed in its current catalogue. And it is stuck supplying those quantities demanded until it sends out its next catalogue.

With output prices fixed and firms selling as much as customers want to purchase at those fixed prices, the **immediate-short-run aggregate supply curve** AS_{ISR} is a horizontal line, as shown in Figure 12-3. The AS_{ISR} curve is horizontal at the overall price level P_1, which is calculated from all of the individual prices set by the various firms in the economy. Its horizontal shape implies that the total amount of output supplied in the economy depends directly on the volume of spending that results at price level P_1. If total spending is low at price level P_1, firms will supply a small amount to match the low level of spending. If total spending is high at price level P_1, they will supply a high level of output to match the high level of spending. The amount of output that results may be higher than or lower than the economy's full-employment output level, GDP_f.

| FIGURE 12-3 | Aggregate Supply in the Immediate Short Run |

In the immediate short run, the aggregate supply curve AS_{ISR} is horizontal at the economy's current price level, P_1. With output prices fixed, firms collectively supply the level of output that is demanded at those prices.

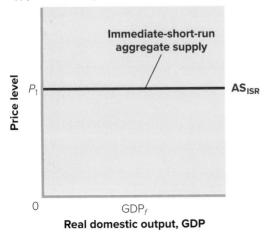

Notice, however, that firms will respond in this manner to changes in total spending only as long as output prices remain fixed. As soon as firms are able to change their product prices, they can respond to changes in consumer spending not only by increasing or decreasing output but also by raising or lowering prices. This is the situation that leads to the upsloping short-run aggregate supply curve, which we discuss next.

Aggregate Supply in the Short Run

The short run begins after the immediate short run ends. As it relates to macroeconomics, the short run is a period of time during which output prices are flexible but input prices are either totally fixed or highly inflexible.

These assumptions about output prices and input prices are general–they relate to the economy in the aggregate. Naturally, some input prices are more flexible than others. Since gasoline prices are quite flexible, a package delivery firm like UPS that uses gasoline as an input will have at least one very flexible input price. On the other hand, wages at UPS are set by multi-year labour contracts negotiated with its drivers' union. Because wages are the firm's largest and most important input cost, it is the case that, overall, UPS faces input prices that are inflexible for several years at a time. Thus, its short run–during which it can change the shipping prices that it charges its customers but during which it must deal with substantially fixed input prices–is actually quite long. Keep this in mind as we derive the short-run aggregate supply for the entire economy. Its applicability does not depend on some arbitrary definition of how long the short run should be. Instead, the short run for which the model is relevant is any period of time during which output prices are flexible but input prices are fixed or nearly fixed.

As illustrated in Figure 12-4, the **short-run aggregate supply curve** AS slopes upward because with input prices fixed, changes in the price level will raise or lower real firm profits. To see how this works, consider an economy that has only a single multi-product firm called Mega Buzzer and in which the firm's owners must receive a real profit of $20 in order to produce the full-employment output of 100 units.

FIGURE 12-4   **Short-Run Aggregate Supply Curve**

The upsloping aggregate supply curve AS indicates a direct (or positive) relationship between the price level and the amount of real output that firms will offer for sale. The AS curve is relatively flat below the full-employment output because unemployed resources and unused capacity allow firms to respond to price-level rises with large increases in real output. It is relatively steep beyond the full-employment output because resource shortages and capacity limitations make it difficult to expand real output as the price level rises.

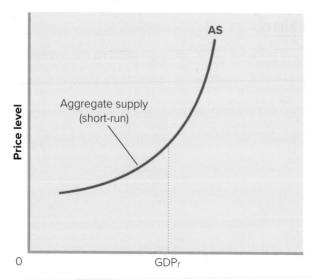

Real gross domestic output, GDP

Assume the owner's only input (aside from entrepreneurial talent) is 10 units of hired labour at $8 per worker, for a total wage cost of $80. Also assume that the 100 units of output sell for $1 per unit, so total revenue is $100. Mega Buzzer's nominal profit is $20 (= $100 − $80), and using the $1 price to designate the base-price index of 100, its real profit is also $20 (= $20/1.00). Under these circumstances, the full-employment output is produced.

Next, consider what will happen if the price of Mega Buzzer's output doubles. The doubling of the price level will boost total revenue from $100 to $200, but since we are discussing the short run, during which input prices are fixed, the $8 nominal wage for each of the 10 workers will remain unchanged so that total costs stay at $80. Nominal profit will rise from $20 (= $100 − $80) to $120 (= $200 − $80). Dividing that $120 profit by the new price index of 200 (= 2.0 in hundredths), we find that Mega Buzzer's real profit is now $60. The rise in the real reward from $20 to $60 prompts the firm (economy) to produce more output. Conversely, price-level declines reduce real profits and cause the firm (economy) to reduce its output. So, in the short run, there is a direct, or positive, relationship between the price level and real output. When the price level rises, real output rises and when the price level falls, real output falls. The result is an upsloping short-run aggregate supply curve. Notice, however, that the upslope of the short-run aggregate supply curve is not constant. It is flatter at outputs below the full-employment output level GDP$_f$ and steeper at outputs above it. This has to do with the fact that per-unit production costs underlie the short-run aggregate supply curve. Recall from Chapter 7 that

$$\text{Per-unit production cost} = \frac{\text{total input cost}}{\text{units of output}}$$

The per-unit production cost of any specific level of output establishes that output's price level because the associated price level must cover all the costs of production, including profit "costs."

As the economy expands in the short run, per-unit production costs generally rise because of reduced efficiency. But the extent of that rise depends on where the economy is operating relative to its capacity. When the economy is operating below its full-employment output, it has large amounts of unused machinery and equipment and large numbers of unemployed workers. Firms can put these idle human and property resources back to work with little upward pressure on per-unit production costs. And as output expands, few if any shortages of inputs or production bottlenecks will arise to raise per-unit production costs. That is why the slope of the short-run aggregate supply curve increases only slowly at output levels below the full-employment output level GDP$_f$.

On the other hand, when the economy is operating beyond GDP$_f$, the vast majority of its available resources are already employed. Adding more workers to a relatively fixed number of highly used capital resources, such as plant and equipment, creates congestion in the workplace and reduces the efficiency (on average) of workers. Adding more capital, given the limited number of available workers, leaves equipment idle and reduces the efficiency of capital. Adding more land resources when capital and labour are highly constrained reduces the efficiency of land resources. Under these circumstances, total input costs rise more rapidly than total output. The result is rapidly rising per-unit production costs that give the short-run aggregate supply curve its rapidly increasing slope at output levels beyond GDP$_f$.

Aggregate Supply in the Long Run

In macroeconomics, the long run is the time horizon over which both input prices and output prices are flexible. It begins after the short run ends. Depending on the type of firm and industry, this may be from a couple of weeks to several years in the future. But for the economy as a whole, it is the time horizon over which all output and input prices—including wage rates—are fully flexible.

The **long-run aggregate supply curve** AS$_{LR}$ is vertical at the economy's full-employment output GDP$_f$, as shown in Figure 12-5. The vertical curve means that in the long run the economy will produce the full-employment output level no matter what the price level is. How can this be? Shouldn't higher prices cause firms to increase output? The explanation lies in the fact that in the long run, when both input prices and output prices are flexible, profit levels will always adjust to give firms exactly the right profit incentive to produce exactly the full-employment output level GDP$_f$.

| FIGURE 12-5 | Aggregate Supply in the Long Run |

The long-run aggregate supply curve AS_{LR} is vertical at the full-employment level of real GDP (GDP_f) because in the long run wages and other input prices rise and match changes in the price level. So price-level changes do not affect firms' profits and thus create no incentive for firms to alter their output.

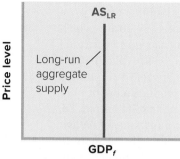

To see why this is true, look back at the short-run aggregate supply curve AS shown in Figure 12-4. Suppose the economy starts out producing at the full-employment output level GDP_f and that the price level at that moment has an index value of $P = 100$. Now suppose that output prices double, so that the price index goes to $P = 200$. We previously demonstrated for our single-firm economy that this doubling of the price level would cause profits to rise in the short run and that the higher profits would motivate the firm to increase output.

This outcome, however, is totally dependent upon the fact that input prices are fixed in the short run. Consider what will happen in the long run when they are free to change. Firms can produce beyond the full-employment output level only by running factories and businesses at extremely high rates of utilization. This creates a great deal of demand for the economy's limited supply of productive resources. In particular, labour is in great demand because the only way to produce beyond full employment is to have workers labouring overtime.

As time passes and input prices are free to change, the high demand will start to raise input prices. In particular, overworked employees will demand and receive raises as employers scramble to deal with the labour shortages that arise when the economy is producing at above its full-employment output level. As input prices increase, firm profits will begin to fall. And as they decline, so does the motive firms have to produce more than the full-employment output level. This process of rising input prices and falling profits continues until the rise in input prices exactly matches the initial change in output prices (in our example, they both double). When that happens, firm profits in real terms return to their original level so that firms are once again motivated to produce at exactly the full-employment output level. This adjustment process means that in the long run the economy will produce at full employment regardless of the price level (in our example, at either $P = 100$ or $P = 200$). That is why the long-run aggregate supply curve AS_{LR} is vertical above the full-employment output level. Every possible price level on the vertical axis is associated with the economy producing at the full-employment output level in the long run once input prices adjust to exactly match changes in output prices.

An aggregate supply curve refers to the combined output of all the goods and services in an economy.

Focusing on the Short Run

The immediate-short-run aggregate supply curve, the short-run aggregate supply curve, and the long-run aggregate supply curve are all important. Each curve is appropriate to situations that match its respective assumptions about the flexibility of input and output prices. In the remainder of the book, we will have several different opportunities to refer to each curve. But our focus in the rest of this chapter and the several chapters that immediately follow will be on short-run aggregate supply curves, such as the AS curve shown in Figure 12-4. Indeed, unless explicitly stated otherwise, all references to "aggregate supply" are to the AS curve in the short run.

Our emphasis on the short-run aggregate supply curve AS stems from our interest in understanding the business cycle in the simplest possible way. It is a fact that real-world economies typically manifest simultaneous changes in both their price levels and their levels of real output. The upsloping short-run AS curve is the only version of aggregate supply that can handle simultaneous movements in both of these variables. By contrast, the price level is assumed fixed in the immediate-short-run version of aggregate supply illustrated in Figure 12-3 and the economy's output is always equal to the full-employment output level in the long-run version of aggregate supply shown in Figure 12-5. This renders these versions of the aggregate supply curve less useful as part of a core model for analyzing business cycles and demonstrating the short-run government policies designed to deal with them. In our current discussion, we will reserve use of the immediate short run and the long run for specific, clearly identified situations. Later in the book we will explore how the short-run AS curve and long-run AS curve are linked, and how that linkage adds several additional macroeconomic insights about cycles and policy.

12.4 / Changes in Aggregate Supply

LO12.4 Explain the factors that cause changes (shifts) in AS.

An existing aggregate supply curve identifies the relationship between the price level and real output, other things equal. But when one or more of these "other things" change, the curve itself shifts. The rightward shift of the curve from AS_1 to AS_3 in Figure 12-6 represents an increase in aggregate supply, indicating that firms are willing to produce and sell more real output at each price level. The leftward shift of the curve from AS_1 to AS_2 represents a decrease in aggregate supply. At each price level, firms will not produce as much output as before.

FIGURE 12-6   Changes in Short-Run Aggregate Supply

A change in one or more of the listed determinants of aggregate supply will shift the aggregate supply curve. The rightward shift of the aggregate supply curve from AS_1 to AS_3 represents an increase in aggregate supply; the leftward shift of the curve from AS_1 to AS_2 shows a decrease in aggregate supply.

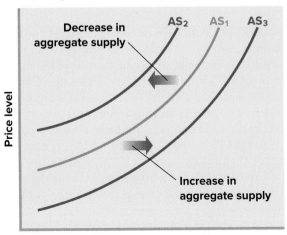

Determinants of the short-run aggregate supply: factors that shift the aggregate supply curve

1. Change in input prices
   a. Domestic resource price
   b. Price of imported resources
2. Change in productivity
3. Change in legal-institutional environment
   a. Business taxes and subsidies
   b. Government regulation

Figure 12-6 lists the "other things"–the **determinants of aggregate supply**–that collectively determine the location of the aggregate supply curve and shift the curve when they change. Changes in these determinants cause per-unit production costs to be either higher or lower than before *at each price level*. These changes in per-unit production cost affect profits, which leads firms to alter the amount of output they are willing to produce *at each price level*. For example, firms may collectively offer $1 trillion of real output at a price level of 1.0 (100 in index value), rather than $900 billion. Or they may offer $800 billion rather than $1 trillion. The point is that when one of the determinants listed in Figure 12-6 changes, the aggregate supply curve shifts to the right or left. Changes that reduce per-unit production costs shift the aggregate supply curve to the right, as from AS$_1$ to AS$_2$; changes that increase per-unit production costs shift it to the left, as from AS$_1$ to AS$_3$. When per-unit production costs change for reasons other than changes in real output, the aggregate supply curve shifts.

The determinants of aggregate supply listed in Figure 12-6 require more discussion.

INPUT PRICES

Input or factor (resource) prices–to be distinguished from the output prices that make up the price level–are a key determinant of aggregate supply. These resources can be either domestic or imported.

Domestic Factor Prices   As stated earlier, wages and salaries make up about 75 percent of all business costs. Other things equal, decreases in wages and salaries reduce per-unit production costs. So the aggregate supply shifts to the right. Increases in wages and salaries shift the curve to the left. For example:

- Labour supply increases because of substantial immigration. Wages and per-unit production costs fall, shifting the AS curve to the right.

- Labour supply decreases because a rapid increase in pension income causes many older workers to opt for early retirement. Wage rates and per-unit production costs rise, shifting the AS curve to the left.

Similarly, the aggregate supply curve shifts when the prices of land and capital inputs change. For example

- The price of capital (machinery and equipment) falls because of declines in the prices of steel and electronic components. Per-unit production costs decline and the AS curve shifts to the right.

- Land resources expand through discoveries of mineral deposits, irrigation of land, or technical innovations that transform non-resources (say, vast northern shrub lands) into valuable resources (productive lands). The price of land declines, per-unit production costs fall, and the AS curve shifts to the right.

Prices of Imported Resources   Just as foreign demand for Canadian goods contributes to Canadian aggregate demand, resources imported from abroad (such as oil, tin, and coffee beans) add to Canadian aggregate supply. Added resources–whether domestic or imported–boost production capacity. Generally, a decrease in the price of imported resources increases Canadian aggregate supply, and an increase in their price reduces Canadian aggregate supply.

A good example of the major effect that changing resource prices can have on aggregate supply is the oil price hikes of the 1970s. At that time, a group of oil-producing nations called the Organization of the Petroleum Exporting Countries (OPEC) worked in concert to decrease oil production in order to raise the price of oil. The tenfold increase in the price of oil that OPEC achieved during the 1970s drove up per-unit production costs and jolted the Canadian aggregate supply curve leftward. By contrast, a sharp decline in oil prices in the mid 1980s resulted in a rightward shift of the Canadian aggregate supply curve. In 1999, OPEC reasserted itself, raising oil prices and therefore per-unit production costs for some Canadian producers including airlines and shipping companies like FedEx and UPS. In 2007, the price of oil shot upward, but this increase was attributed to greater demand rather than to decreases in supply caused by OPEC. After the Great Recession of 2008–2009 the price of oil fell abruptly, only to rise again with the world economic recovery. But keep in mind that no matter what their cause, increases in the price of oil and other resources raise production costs and decrease aggregate supply.

Exchange-rate fluctuations are another factor that may change the price of imported resources. Suppose the Canadian dollar appreciates. This means that domestic producers face a lower *dollar* price of imported resources.

Canadian firms would respond by increasing their imports of foreign resources, thereby lowering their per-unit production costs at each level of output. Falling per-unit production costs would shift the Canadian aggregate supply curve to the right.

A depreciation of the dollar will have the opposite effects and will shift the aggregate supply to the left.

PRODUCTIVITY

The second major determinant of aggregate supply is **productivity**, which is a measure of the relationship between a nation's level of real output and the amount of resources used to produce it. Productivity is a measure of real output per unit of input:

$$\text{Productivity} = \frac{\text{total output}}{\text{total input}}$$

An increase in productivity enables the economy to obtain more real output from its limited resources. An increase in productivity affects aggregate supply by reducing the per-unit cost of output (per-unit production cost). Suppose, for example, that real output is 10 units, that 5 units of input are needed to produce that quantity, and that the price of each input unit is $2. Then

$$\text{Productivity} = \frac{\text{total output}}{\text{total input}} = \frac{10}{5} = 2$$

and

$$\text{Per-unit production cost} = \frac{\text{total input cost}}{\text{total output}} = \frac{(\$2 \times 5)}{10} = \$1$$

Note that we obtain the total input cost by multiplying the unit input cost by the number of inputs used.

WORKED PROBLEM 12.1 Productivity and Costs

Now suppose productivity increases so that real output doubles to 20 units, while the price and quantity of the input remain constant at $2 and 5 units. Using the above equations, we see that productivity rises from 2 to 4 and that the per-unit production cost of the output falls from $1 to $0.50. Doubled productivity has reduced the per-unit production cost by half.

By reducing the per-unit production cost, an increase in productivity shifts the aggregate supply curve to the right. The main source of productivity advance is improved production technology, often embodied within a new plant and equipment that replaces an old plant and equipment. Other sources of productivity increases are a better-educated and better-trained workforce, improved forms of business enterprises, and the reallocation of labour resources from lower productivity to higher productivity uses.

Much rarer are decreases in productivity that increase per-unit production costs and therefore reduce aggregate supply (shift the curve to the left).

LEGAL–INSTITUTIONAL ENVIRONMENT

Changes in the legal-institutional setting in which businesses operate are the final determinant of aggregate supply. Such changes may alter the per-unit costs of output and, in doing so, shift the aggregate supply curve. Two changes of this type are (1) changes in business taxes and subsidies, and (2) changes in the extent of regulation.

Business Taxes and Subsidies   Higher business taxes–corporate income taxes and capital, sales, excise, and payroll taxes–increase per-unit costs and reduce aggregate supply in much the same way that a wage increase does. An increase in such taxes paid by businesses will increase per-unit production costs and shift the aggregate supply curve to the left. Similarly, a business subsidy–a payment or tax break by government to producers– lowers production costs and increases aggregate supply. For example, Canada's corporate tax rate (combined provincial and federal) fell to 25 percent in 2011, the lowest rate in the G7 countries, and will contribute to an increase in aggregate supply. This favourable corporate tax rate no doubt contributed to the prestigious *Forbes* magazine proclaiming Canada to be the number one country in the world for business in 2011.

Government Regulation   It is usually costly for businesses to comply with government regulations. More regulation therefore tends to increase per-unit production costs and shift the aggregate supply curve to the left. Supply-side proponents of deregulation of the economy have argued forcefully that, by increasing efficiency and reducing the paperwork associated with complex regulations, deregulation will reduce per-unit costs and shift the aggregate supply curve to the right. For example, compared to Europe our labour laws currently place fewer restrictions on businesses. Corporations can more easily lay workers off when business conditions make it necessary. Also, hiring new employees does not saddle businesses with huge obligations, as it does in Europe, and thus unemployment rates are generally lower in Canada compared to European countries, contributing to the rightward shift of the aggregate supply curve. But environmental regulations of Canadian business–for example the oil sector in Western Canada–have added cost, contributing to a leftward shift of the aggregate supply curve.

- The immediate-short-run aggregate supply curve is horizontal; given fixed input and output prices, producers will supply whatever quantity of real output is demanded at the current price level.

- The short-run aggregate supply curve (or simply the *aggregate supply curve*) is upsloping; given fixed resource prices, higher output prices raise firms' profits and encourage them to increase their output levels.

- The long-run aggregate supply curve is vertical; given sufficient time, wages and other input prices rise or fall to match any change in the price level (that is, any change in the level of *output* prices).

- By altering the per-unit production cost independent of changes in the level of output, changes in one or more of the determinants of aggregate supply (Figure 12-6) shift the short-run aggregate supply curve.

- An increase in short-run aggregate supply is shown as a rightward shift of the curve; a decrease is shown as a leftward shift of the curve.

12.5 / Equilibrium in the AD–AS Model

LO12.5 Discuss how AD and AS determine an economy's equilibrium price level and level of real GDP.

Of all the possible combinations of price levels and levels of real GDP, which combination will the economy gravitate toward, at least in the short run? **Figure 12-7 (Key Graph)** and its accompanying table provide the answer. Equilibrium occurs at the price level that equalizes the amount of real output demanded and supplied. The intersection of the aggregate demand curve AD and the aggregate supply curve AS establishes the economy's **equilibrium price level** and **equilibrium real output**. So aggregate demand and aggregate supply jointly establish the price level and level of real GDP.

In Figure 12-7 the equilibrium price level and level of real output are 100 and $510 billion, respectively. To illustrate why, suppose the price level was 92 rather than 100. We see from the table that the lower price level would encourage businesses to produce real output of $502 billion. This is shown by point *a* on the AS curve in the graph. But, as revealed by the table and point *b* on the aggregate demand curve, buyers would want to purchase $514 billion of real output at price level 92. Competition among buyers to purchase the lesser available real output of $502 billion will eliminate the $12 billion (= $514 billion − $502 billion) shortage and pull up the price level to 100.

As the table and graph show, the excess demand for the output of the economy causes the price level to rise from 92 to 100, which encourages producers to increase their real output from $502 billion to $510 billion, thereby increasing GDP. In increasing their real output, producers hire more employees, reducing the unemployment level in the economy. When equality occurs between the amounts of real output produced and purchased, as it does at price level 100, the economy has achieved equilibrium (here at $510 billion of real GDP).

A final note: Although the equilibrium price level happens to be 100 in our example, nothing special is implied by that. Any price level can be an equilibrium price level.

KEY GRAPH

FIGURE 12-7 The Equilibrium Price Level and Equilibrium Real GDP

The intersection of the aggregate demand curve and the aggregate supply curve determines the economy's equilibrium price level. At the equilibrium price level of 100 (in index-value terms) the $510 billion of real output demanded matches the $510 billion of real output supplied. So the equilibrium GDP is $510 billion.

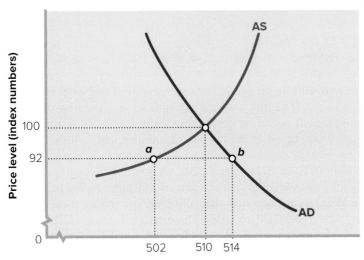

Real output demanded (billions)	Price level (index number)	Real output supplied (billions)
$506	108	$513
508	104	512
510	**100**	**510**
512	96	505
514	92	502

Quick Quiz

1. **The AD curve slopes downward because**
   a. Per-unit production costs fall as real GDP increases
   b. The income and substitution effects are at work
   c. Changes in the determinants of AD alter the amounts of real GDP demanded at each price level
   d. Decreases in the price level give rise to real-balances, interest-rate, and foreign-trade effects, which increase the amounts of real GDP demanded

2. **The AS curve slopes upward because**
   a. Per-unit production costs rise as real GDP expands toward and beyond its full-employment level
   b. The income and substitution effects are at work
   c. Changes in the determinants of AS alter the amounts of real GDP supplied at each price level
   d. Increases in the price level give rise to real-balances, interest-rate, and foreign-purchases

   effects, which increase the amounts of real GDP supplied

3. **At price level 92**
   a. A GDP surplus of $12 billion occurs that drives the price level up to 100
   b. A GDP shortage of $12 billion occurs that drives the price level up to 100
   c. The aggregate amount of real GDP demanded is less than the aggregate amount of real GDP supplied
   d. The economy is operating beyond its capacity to produce

4. **Suppose real output demanded rises by $4 billion at each price level. The new equilibrium price level will be**
   a. 108   c. 96
   b. 104   d. 92

12.6 / Changes in Equilibrium

LO12.6 Describe how the AD–AS model explains periods of demand–pull inflation, cost–push inflation, and recession.

Now let's apply the AD-AS model to various situations that can confront the economy. For simplicity we will use P and GDP as symbols rather than using actual numbers. Remember that these symbols represent, respectively, price index values and real amounts of GDP.

Increases in AD: Demand–Pull Inflation

Suppose households and businesses decide to increase their consumption and investment spending–actions that shift the aggregate demand curve to the right. Our list of determinants of aggregate demand (Figure 12-2) provides several reasons that this shift might occur. Perhaps consumers feel wealthier because of large gains in their stock holdings. As a result, consumers would consume more (save less) of their current income. Perhaps firms boost their investment spending because they anticipate higher future profits from investments in new capital. Those profits are based on having new equipment and facilities that incorporate a number of new technologies. And perhaps government increases spending in health care.

As shown by the rise in the price level from P_1 to P_2 in Figure 12-8, the increase in aggregate demand beyond the full-employment level of output causes inflation. This is *demand-pull inflation,* because the price level is being pulled up by the increase in aggregate demand. Also, observe that the increase in demand expands real output from the full-employment level GDP_f to GDP_1. The distance between GDP_1 and GDP_f is an **inflationary gap**, the amount by which equilibrium GDP exceeds potential GDP. An inflationary gap is also referred to as a *positive GDP gap.*

A careful examination of Figure 12-8 reveals an interesting point. The increase in aggregate demand from AD_1 to AD_2 increases real output only to GDP_1, not to GDP_2, because part of the increase in aggregate demand is absorbed as inflation as the price level rises from P_1 to P_2. Had the price level remained at P_1, the

---

FIGURE 12-8   An Increase in Aggregate Demand that Causes Demand–Pull Inflation

An increase in aggregate demand generally increases both the GDP and price level. The increase in aggregate demand from AD_1 to AD_2 is partly dissipated in inflation (P_1 to P_2) and real output increases only from GDP_f to GDP_1.

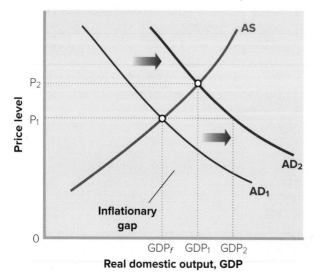

shift of aggregate demand from AD_1 to AD_2 would have increased real output to GDP_2. But in Figure 12-8 inflation reduced the increase in real output only to GDP_1. For any initial increase in aggregate demand, the resulting increase in real output will be smaller the greater the increase in the price level.

Decreases in AD: Recession and Cyclical Unemployment

Decreases in aggregate demand describe the opposite end of the business cycle: recession and cyclical unemployment (rather than above-full employment and demand-pull inflation). For example, in 2008 and 2009, investment spending in Canada greatly declined because of sharply lower expected returns on investment. These lower expectations resulted from the prospects of poor future business conditions and high degrees of current unused production capacity. In Figure 12-9 we show the resulting decline in aggregate demand as a leftward shift from AD_1 to AD_2.

But we now add an important twist to the analysis. *Deflation*—a decline in the price level—is not the norm in the Canadian economy. We discussed sticky prices in Chapter 4 and previously explained how fixed prices lead to horizontal intermediate-short-run aggregate supply curves. For reasons we will examine soon, many important prices in the Canadian economy are downwardly inflexible such that the price level is sticky downward even when aggregate demand substantially declines. Consider Figure 12-9 where the aggregate demand declines from AD_1 to AD_2. If the price level is stuck at P_1, the economy moves from a to b along the broken horizontal line rather than from a to c along the short-run aggregate supply curve AS.

The outcome is a decline of real output from GDP_f to GDP_1, with no change in the price level. It is as though the aggregate supply curve in Figure 12-9 is horizontal at P_1 leftward from GDP_f, as indicated by the dashed line. This decline of real output from GDP_f to GDP_1 constitutes a *recession*, and since fewer workers are needed to produce the lower output, *cyclical unemployment* arises. The distance between GDP_1 and GDP_f is a *recessionary gap*, the amount by which actual output falls short of the full-employment output. A recessionary gap is also referred to as a *negative GDP gap*.

All recent recessions in Canada have generally mimicked the "GDP gap but no deflation" scenario shown in Figure 12-9. Consider the recession of 2008–2009, which resulted from chaos in the financial markets in the U.S. that quickly led to significant declines in spending by businesses and households in Canada.

FIGURE 12-9 **A Decrease in Aggregate Demand that Causes a Recession**

If the price level is downwardly inflexible at P_1, a decline of aggregate demand from AD_1 to AD_2 will move the economy leftward from a to b along the horizontal broken-line segment and reduce real GDP from GDP_f to GDP_1. Idle production capacity, cyclical unemployment, and a recessionary GDP gap (of GDP_f minus GDP_1) will result. If the price level were flexible downward, the decline in aggregate demand would move the economy from a to c instead of from a to b.

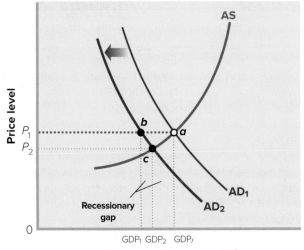

Because of the resulting decline in aggregate demand, real GDP fell short of potential real GDP in 2009. The nation's unemployment rate rose from 6.0 percent in December of 2008 to 8.7 percent in August of 2009. Still, deflation did not occur.

Real output takes the brunt of declines in aggregate demand in the Canadian economy because the price level tends to be downwardly inflexible in the immediate short run. There are several reasons for this downward price stickiness.

- **Fear of Price Wars** Some large firms may be concerned that if they reduce their prices, rivals not only will match their price cuts but also may retaliate by making even deeper cuts. An initial price cut may touch off an unwanted *price war*–successively deeper and deeper rounds of price cuts. In such a situation, each firm eventually ends up with far less profit or higher losses than would be the case if it had simply maintained its prices. For this reason, each firm may resist making the initial price cut, choosing instead to reduce production and lay workers off.

- **Menu Costs** Firms that think a recession will be relatively short lived may be reluctant to cut their prices. One reason is what economists metaphorically call **menu costs**, named after their most obvious example: the cost of printing new menus when a restaurant decides to change its prices. But lowering prices also creates other costs, including (1) estimating the magnitude and duration of the shift in demand to determine whether prices should be lowered, (2) re-pricing items held in inventory, (3) printing and mailing new catalogues, and (4) communicating new prices to customers, perhaps through advertising. When menu costs are present, firms may choose to avoid them by retaining current prices. That is, they may wait to see if the decline in aggregate demand is permanent.

- **Wage Contracts** It usually is not profitable for firms to cut their product prices if they cannot also cut their wage rates. Wages are usually inflexible downward because large parts of the labour force work under contracts prohibiting wage cuts for the duration of the contract. (It is not uncommon for collective bargaining agreements in major industries to run for three years.) Similarly, the wages and salaries of non-union workers are usually adjusted once a year, rather than quarterly or monthly.

- **Morale, Effort, and Productivity** Wage inflexibility downward is reinforced by the reluctance of many employers to reduce wage rates. Some current wages may be so-called **efficiency wages**– wages that elicit maximum work effort and thus minimize labour costs per unit of output. If worker

---

CONSIDER THIS The Ratchet Effect

A ratchet is a good analogy for the effects of changes in aggregate demand on the price level. A ratchet is a tool or mechanism such as a winch, car jack, or socket wrench that cranks a wheel forward but does not allow it to go backward. Properly set, each allows the operator to move an object (boat, car, or nut) in one direction while preventing it from moving in the opposite direction.

Product prices, wage rates, and per-unit production costs are highly flexible upward when aggregate demand increases along the aggregate

supply curve. In Canada, the price level has increased in 61 of the 62 years since 1950.

But when aggregate demand decreases, product prices, wage rates, and per-unit production costs are inflexible downward. The price level has declined in only a single year (1953) since 1950, even though aggregate demand and real output have declined in a number of years, such as 1946, 1954, 1982, and 1991.

In terms of our analogy, increases in aggregate demand ratchet the Canadian price level upward. Once in place, the higher price level remains until it is ratcheted up again. The higher price level tends to remain even with declines in aggregate demand.

productivity (output per hour of work) remains constant, lower wages *do* reduce labour costs per unit of output. But lower wages might lower worker morale and work effort, thereby reducing productivity. Considered alone, lower productivity raises labour costs per unit of output because less output is produced. If the higher labour costs resulting from reduced productivity exceed the cost savings from the lower wage, then wage cuts will increase rather than decrease labour costs per unit of output. In such situations, firms will resist lowering wages when they are faced with a decline in aggregate demand.

- *Minimum Wage* The minimum wage imposes a legal floor under the wages of the least skilled workers. Firms paying those wages cannot reduce that wage rate when aggregate demand declines.

ORIGIN OF THE IDEA 12.2   Efficiency Wages

Decreases in AS: Cost–Push Inflation

Suppose that tropical storms in areas where there are major oil facilities severely disrupt world oil supplies and drive up oil prices by, say, 300 percent. Higher energy prices would spread through the economy, driving up production and distribution costs on a wide variety of goods. The Canadian aggregate supply curve would shift to the left—say, from AS_1 to AS_2 in Figure 12-10. The resulting increase in price level would be *cost-push inflation.*

The effects of a leftward shift in aggregate supply are doubly bad. When aggregate supply shifts from AS_1 to AS_2, the economy moves from *a* to *b*. The price level rises from P_1 to P_2 and real output declines from GDP_f to GDP_2. Along with the cost-push inflation, a recession (and negative GDP gap) occurs. That is exactly what happened in Canada in the mid 1970s when the price of oil rocketed upward. Then, oil expenditures were about 10 percent of Canadian GDP, compared to only 3 percent today. So, as indicated in this chapter's Last Word, the Canadian economy is now less vulnerable to cost-push inflation arising from such aggregate supply shocks.

FIGURE 12-10   **A Decrease in Aggregate Supply that Causes Cost–Push Inflation**

A leftward shift of aggregate supply from AS_1 to AS_2 raises the price level from P_1 to P_2 and produces cost–push inflation. Real output declines and a negative GDP gap (of GDP_f minus GDP_2) occurs.

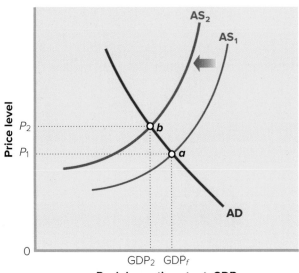

Increases in AS: Full Employment with Price-Level Stability

For the first time in more than a decade, in early 2000 Canada experienced full employment, strong economic growth, and very low inflation. Specifically, in 2000 the unemployment rate fell below 7 percent—a level not seen since 1975—and real GDP grew at 4.3 percent, *without igniting inflation*. At first thought, this "macroeconomic bliss" seems to be incompatible with the AD–AS model. An upsloping aggregate supply curve suggests that increases in aggregate demand that are sufficient for full employment (or overfull employment) will raise the price level. Higher inflation, it would seem, is the inevitable price paid for expanding output to and beyond the full-employment level.

But inflation remained very mild in the late 1990s and early 2000s. Figure 12-11 helps explain why. Let's first suppose that aggregate demand increased from AD_1 to AD_2 along the aggregate supply curve AS_1. Taken alone, that increase in aggregate demand would move the economy from a to b. Real output would rise from less than full-employment real output GDP_1 to full-capacity real output GDP_f. The economy would experience inflation as shown by the increase in the price level from P_1 to P_3. Such inflation had occurred at the end of previous vigorous expansions of aggregate demand in the late 1980s.

More recently, however, larger-than-usual increases in productivity occurred due to a burst of new technology relating to computers, the Internet, inventory management systems, electronic commerce, and so on. The quickened productivity growth reduced per-unit production cost and shifted the aggregate supply curve to the right, as from AS_1 to AS_2 in Figure 12-11. The relevant aggregate demand and aggregate supply curves thus became AD_2 and AS_2, not AD_2 and AS_1. Instead of moving from a to b, the economy moved from a to c. Real output increased from GDP_1 to GDP_3 and the price level rose only modestly (from P_1 to P_2). The shift of the aggregate supply curve from AS_1 to AS_2 increased the economy's full-employment output and its full-capacity output. That accommodated the increase in aggregate demand without causing inflation.

But in 2001 the macroeconomic bliss of the late 1990s came face to face with the old economic principles. Aggregate demand growth slowed because of a substantial fall in investment spending. The terrorist attacks of September 11, 2001 in the U.S. further dampened aggregate demand through lower exports to our largest trading partner. The unemployment rate rose from 6.8 percent in January 2001 to 7.7 percent in mid 2002.

| **FIGURE 12-11** | **Growth, Full Employment, and Relative Price Stability** |

Normally, an increase in aggregate demand from AD_1 to AD_2 would move the economy from a to b along AS_1. Real output would expand to its full-capacity level (GDP_f), and inflation would result (P_1 to P_3). But in the late 1990s, significant increases in productivity shifted the aggregate supply curve, as from AS_1 to AS_2. The economy moved from a to c rather than from a to b. It experienced strong economic growth (GDP_1 to GDP_3), full employment, and only very mild inflation (P_1 to P_2).

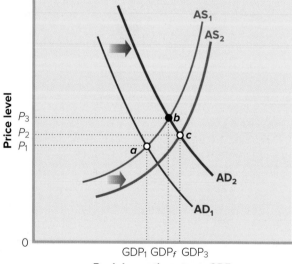

Productivity per worker will affect the aggregate supply curve. An increase in productivity will shift the aggregate supply curve to the right.

The economy rebounded between 2002 and 2008, eventually duplicating its earlier success of strong economic growth, low inflation, and low unemployment. By the early part of 2008, the unemployment rate reached a 37-year low of 5.8 percent. Some economists began to talk about The Great Moderation, the period since 1982 in which business cycles were longer and relatively mild. They implied that businesses and government had smoothed out the business cycle. Wrong! The severity of the recession that began late in 2008 and continued in 2009 was a huge surprise to most economists.

QUICK REVIEW 12.3

- The equilibrium price level and amount of real output are determined at the intersection of the aggregate demand and aggregate supply curves.

- Increases in aggregate demand beyond the full-employment level of real GDP cause demand–pull inflation.

- Decreases in aggregate demand cause recessions and cyclical unemployment, partly because the price level and wages tend to be inflexible in a downward direction.

- Decreases in aggregate supply cause cost–push inflation.

- Full employment, high economic growth, and price stability are compatible if productivity-driven increases in aggregate supply are sufficient to balance growing aggregate demand.

The LAST WORD | Stimulus and the Great Recession in the American versus the Canadian Economy

Aggregate demand stimulus helped to prevent the 2008–2009 downturn from becoming another Great Depression. But why was the stimulus-fueled recovery in the U.S. substantially weaker than expected? The Canadian economy fared much better.

In retrospect, it is clear that the U.S. economy was in a precarious position in 2006. Trillions of dollars had been borrowed to buy housing on the expectation that home prices would keep on rising. That expectation made borrowing seem like a "no brainer," as a potential buyer could anticipate that if she borrowed $200,000 to buy a house in one year, she would be able to sell it the next year for, say, $215,000. Selling at a higher price would allow her to pay off the $200,000 loan and keep the rest as pure profit. Unfortunately, home prices in the U.S. started to fall in 2006. When they did, many people who had borrowed to buy houses found themselves unable to pay off their loans. That in turn meant that many banks found themselves holding loans that would never be paid back. Soon, many banks teetered on bankruptcy, the financial markets began to freeze up, and it became clear by late 2007 that the overall economy would probably enter a recession as the result of the housing collapse.

When it was widely recognized in late 2008 that the downturn was going to be unusually severe, public officials took extraordinarily strong steps to stimulate aggregate demand. In terms of monetary policy, the Federal Reserve, the U.S. central bank lowered short-term interest rates to nearly zero in order to shift AD to the right by stimulating investment and consumption. In terms of fiscal policy, the federal government began the country's largest peacetime program of deficit-funded spending increases. Those spending increases also shifted AD to the right by increasing the total amount of government expenditures. Those actions were widely credited with preventing a much worse downturn. Real GDP did fall by 4.7 percent and the unemployment rate did rise from 4.6 to 10.1 percent. But those negative changes were much less severe than what had happened during the Great Depression of the 1930s, when real GDP fell by nearly 27 percent and the unemployment rate rose to nearly 25 percent.

The recession in Canada was much less pronounced. GDP fell by 2.7 percent in 2009 and unemployment rose from 6.1 percent to 8.7 percent from late 2008 to the peak of the unemployment rate in August of the following year.

As time passed, however, it became clear that the stimulus was having less of an effect on the American economy than many economists had anticipated. White House economists, for instance, had predicted that the stimulus begun in 2009 would reduce the unemployment rate to 5.2 percent by 2012. But three years later the unemployment rate was still at 7.8 percent despite the Federal Reserve continuing to keep interest rates extremely low and despite the federal government continuing to run massive deficits to fund huge amounts of government expenditures.

GDP growth was also disappointing. Real GDP expanded by only 2.4 percent in 2010, 1.8 percent in 2011, and 1.6 percent in 2012. By contrast, the period after the early 1980s recession had seen annual growth rates as high as 7.2 percent per year.

In Canada the recession was both less severe and the recovery more potent. In 2010 GDP rose 3.4 percent, 3.0 percent in 2011 and 1.9 percent in 2012. In the meantime, unemployment remained below the U.S. rate: it peaked in 2009 at 8.7 percent, to fall slowly to 8 percent in 2010, 7.4 percent in 2011 and 7.2 percent in 2012.

One explanation for the disappointing unemployment and GDP numbers in the U.S. was that it was hard for the stimulus to be very effective given the high debt levels that were built up during the bubble years. The lower interest rates engineered by the Federal Reserve, for instance, were probably not much of an inducement for consumers to increase their borrowing when so many of them were already heavily in debt.

A related problem was that savings rates in the U.S. economy had risen. When the government attempted to use deficit spending and fiscal policy to stimulate the economy, policy makers were hoping that each dollar of government spending would induce many dollars of consumer spending. But debt-strapped consumers were devoting large parts of their income to making interest payments on debt or paying off loans. So, when stimulus dollars came their way, they often short-circuited the spending process by saving a lot rather than spending a lot.

Another issue was that the stimulus was diffuse while the sectors of the economy in greatest need of stimulus were focused. In particular, the government's stimulus efforts shifted *aggregate* demand to the right. But not all sectors had been hit equally hard by the recession. Thus, when AD shifted right, a lot of the effect was felt in business sectors that hadn't been hurt that badly during the recession. Meanwhile, many sectors that had been hit hard only received a small portion of the total amount of stimulus that they would have needed to see a full recovery.

A related problem is that in some sectors of the U.S. economy, the government's stimulus may have resulted mostly in price increases rather than output gains. That is because the supply curves for many industries are steep. Consider dentists and jewelers. It takes many years to train competent dentists or skilled jewelers. So even if the demand for their services shifts right, there is a nearly fixed supply of dental services and jewelry services in the short run—meaning that any increase in demand will mostly cause higher prices rather than higher output. So when the government shifted *aggregate* demand to the right, certain sectors probably saw mostly price increases rather than output gains.

By the end of 2014 the U.S. economy had picked up steam and the unemployment rate fell below 6 percent for the first time since the Great Recession started. Indeed, in the last months of 2014 the unemployment in the U.S. was lower that the Canadian rate. In hindsight, it is clear that the severity of the housing bubble and the accompanying financial crisis in the U.S. explains the slow recovery compared to Canada. We did not endure a housing bubble and our banking system was solid. As a consequence we endured a less serious recession and enjoyed a quicker recovery.

Question

What were the monetary and fiscal policy responses to the Great Recession in the U.S.? What were some of the reasons suggested for why those policy responses didn't seem to have as large an effect as anticipated on unemployment and GDP growth in the American economy? Why was the recession less severe in Canada and the subsequent recovery more robust?

Chapter Summary

LO12.1 DEFINE *AGGREGATE DEMAND* (AD) AND EXPLAIN HOW ITS DOWNWARD SLOPE IS THE RESULT OF THE REAL-BALANCES EFFECT, THE INTEREST-RATE EFFECT, AND THE FOREIGN TRADE EFFECT.

- The aggregate demand–aggregate supply model (AD–AS model) is a variable-price model that enables analysis of simultaneous changes of real GDP and the price level.

- The aggregate demand curve shows the level of real output that the economy will purchase at each price level.

- The aggregate demand curve is downsloping because of the real-balances effect, the interest-rate effect, and the foreign-trade effect. The real-balances effect indicates that inflation reduces the real value or purchasing power of fixed-value financial assets held by households, causing them to retrench on their consumer spending. The interest-rate effect means that, with a specific supply of money, a higher price level increases the demand for money, raising the interest rate and reducing consumption and investment purchases. The foreign-trade effect suggests that an increase in one country's price level relative to other countries' reduces the net exports component of that nation's aggregate demand.

LO12.2 EXPLAIN THE FACTORS THAT CAUSE CHANGES (SHIFTS) IN AD.

- The determinants of aggregate demand are spending by domestic consumers, businesses, government, and foreign buyers. Changes in the factors listed in Figure 12-2 alter the spending by these groups and shift the aggregate demand curve.

LO12.3 DEFINE AGGREGATE SUPPLY (AS) AND EXPLAIN HOW IT DIFFERS IN THE IMMEDIATE SHORT RUN, THE SHORT RUN, AND THE LONG RUN.

- The aggregate supply curve shows the levels of real output that businesses will produce at various possible price levels. The slope of the aggregate supply curve depends upon the flexibility of input and output prices. Since these vary over time, aggregate supply curves are categorized into three time horizons that have different underlying assumptions about the flexibility of input and output prices.

- The *immediate-short-run aggregate supply curve* assumes that both input prices and output prices are fixed. With output prices fixed, the aggregate supply curve is a horizontal line at the current price level. The *short-run aggregate supply curve* assumes nominal wages and other input prices remain fixed while output prices vary. The aggregate supply curve is generally upsloping because per-unit production costs, and hence the prices that firms must receive, rise as real *output* expands. The aggregate supply curve is relatively steep to the right of the full-employment output level and relatively flat to the left of it. The *long-run aggregate supply curve* assumes that nominal wages and other input prices fully match any change in the price level. The curve is vertical at the full-employment output level.

- Because the short-run aggregate supply curve is the only version of aggregate supply that can handle simultaneous changes in the price level and real output, it serves well as the core aggregate supply curve for analyzing the business cycle and economic policy. Unless stated otherwise, all references to aggregate supply refer to the immediate-short-run aggregate supply and the short-run aggregate supply curve.

LO12.4 EXPLAIN THE FACTORS THAT CAUSE CHANGES (SHIFTS) IN AS.

- Figure 12-6 lists the determinants of aggregate supply: input prices, productivity, and the legal–institutional environment. A change in any one of these factors will change per-unit production costs at each level of output and therefore alter the location of the aggregate supply curve.

LO12.5 DISCUSS HOW AD AND AS DETERMINE AN ECONOMY'S EQUILIBRIUM PRICE LEVEL AND LEVEL OF REAL GDP.

- The intersection of the aggregate demand and aggregate supply curves determines an economy's equilibrium price level and real GDP. At the intersection, the quantity of real GDP demanded equals the quantity of real GDP supplied.

LO12.6 DESCRIBE HOW THE AD–AS MODEL EXPLAINS PERIODS OF DEMAND–PULL INFLATION, COST–PUSH INFLATION, AND RECESSION.

- Increases in aggregate demand to the right of the full-employment output cause inflation and positive GDP gaps (actual GDP exceeds potential GDP). An upward-sloping aggregate supply curve weakens the effect of an increase in aggregate demand because a portion of the increase in aggregate demand is dissipated in inflation.

- Shifts of the aggregate demand curve to the left of the full-employment output cause recession, negative GDP gaps, and cyclical unemployment. The price level may not fall during recessions because of downwardly inflexible prices and wages. This inflexibility results from fear of price wars, menu costs, wage contracts, efficiency wages, and minimum wages. When the price level is fixed, in essence there is a horizontal portion of the aggregate supply curve, referred to as the immediate-short-run aggregate supply curve.

- Leftward shifts of the aggregate supply curve reflect increases in per-unit production costs and cause cost–push inflation, with accompanying negative GDP gaps.

- Rightward shifts of the aggregate supply curve, caused by large improvements in productivity, help explain the simultaneous achievement of full employment, economic growth, and price stability that Canada experienced between 1996 and 2000, and 2002 and 2008, before giving way to the severe recession that started in late 2008 and continued into 2009.

Terms and Concepts

aggregate demand–aggregate supply model
  (AD–AS model)
aggregate demand
real-balances effect
interest-rate effect
foreign-trade effect

determinants of aggregate demand
aggregate supply
immediate-short-run aggregate supply curve
short-run aggregate supply curve
long-run aggregate supply curve
determinants of aggregate supply

productivity
equilibrium price level
equilibrium real output
menu costs
efficiency wages

Discussion Questions

1. Why is the aggregate demand curve downsloping? Specify how your explanation differs from that for the downsloping demand curve for a single product.   [LO12.1]

2. Distinguish between the *real-balances effect* and the *wealth effect* as the terms are used in this chapter. How does each relate to the aggregate demand curve?   [LO12.1]

3. What assumptions cause the immediate-short-run aggregate supply curve to be horizontal? Why is the long-run aggregate supply curve vertical? Explain the shape of the short-run aggregate supply curve. Why is the short-run aggregate supply curve relatively flat to the left of the full-employment output and relatively steep to its right?   [LO12.3]

4. Explain how an upsloping aggregate supply curve weakens the impact of a rightward shift of the aggregate demand curve.   [LO12.6]

5. Why does a reduction in aggregate demand in the actual economy reduce real output, rather than the price level? Why

might a full-strength multiplier apply to a decrease in aggregate demand?   [LO12.6]

6. Explain the following statement, and in each case specify the price-level outcomes: Unemployment can be caused by a decrease of aggregate demand or a decrease of aggregate supply.   [LO12.6]

7. Use shifts in the AD and AS curves to explain (a) the Canadian experience of strong economic growth, full employment, and price stability between 2006 and early 2008, and (b) how a strong negative wealth effect (from, say, a precipitous drop in the stock market) could cause a recession even though productivity is surging.   [LO12.6]

8. In late 2008 consumption and investment spending sharply declined in Canada because of the spread of the global financial crisis. Use AD–AS analysis to show the impact on real GDP.   [LO12.3]

Review Questions

1. Which of the following help to explain why the aggregate demand curve slopes downward?   [LO12.1]

   a. When the domestic price level rises, our goods and services become more expensive to foreigners.

   b. When government spending rises, the price level falls.

   c. There is an inverse relationship between consumer expectations and personal taxes.

   d. When the price level rises, the real value of financial assets (like stocks, bonds, and savings account balances) declines.

2. Which of the following will shift the aggregate demand curve to the left?   [LO12.2]

   a. The government reduces personal income taxes.

   b. Interest rates rise.

   c. The government raises corporate profit taxes.

   d. There is an economic boom overseas that raises the incomes of foreign households.

3. Label each of the following descriptions as being either an immediate-short-run aggregate supply curve, a short-run aggregate supply curve, or a long-run aggregate supply curve.   [LO12.3]

   a. A vertical line

   b. The price level is fixed

   c. Output prices are flexible, but input prices are fixed

   d. A horizontal line

   e. An upsloping curve

   f. Output is fixed

4. Which of the following will shift the aggregate supply curve to the right?   [LO12.4]

   a. A new networking technology increases productivity all over the economy.

   b. The price of oil rises substantially.

   c. Business taxes fall.

   d. The government passes a law doubling all manufacturing wages.

5. At the current price level, producers supply $375 billion of final goods and services while consumers purchase $355 billion of final goods and services. The price level is   [LO12.5]

   a. Above equilibrium

   b. At equilibrium

c. Below equilibrium

d. More information is needed

6. What effects would each of the following have on aggregate demand or aggregate supply, other things equal? In each case, use a diagram to show the expected effects on the equilibrium price level and the level of real output, assuming that the price level is flexible both upward and downward.   [LO12.5]

a. A widespread fear by consumers of an impending economic depression

b. A new national tax on producers based on the value added between the costs of the inputs and the revenue received from their output

c. A reduction in interest rates at each price level

d. A major increase in spending for health care by the federal government

e. The general expectation of coming rapid inflation

f. The complete disintegration of OPEC, causing oil prices to fall by one half

g. A 10 percent across-the-board reduction in personal income tax rates

h. A sizable increase in labour productivity (with no change in nominal wages)

i. A 12 percent increase in nominal wages (with no change in productivity)

j. An increase in exports that exceeds an increase in imports (not due to tariffs)

7. True or False? Decreases in AD normally lead to decreases in both output and the price level.   [LO12.6]

8. Assume that (a) the price level is flexible upward but not downward, and (b) the economy is currently operating at its full-employment output. Other things equal, how will each of the following affect the equilibrium price level and equilibrium level of real output in the short run?   [LO12.6]

a. An increase in aggregate demand

b. A decrease in aggregate supply, with no change in aggregate demand

c. Equal increases in aggregate demand and aggregate supply

d. A decrease in aggregate demand

e. An increase in aggregate demand that exceeds an increase in aggregate supply

9. True or False? If the price of oil suddenly increases by a large amount, AS will shift left, but the price level will not rise, thanks to price inflexibility.   [LO12.6]

Problems

1. Suppose that consumer spending initially rises by $5 billion for every 1 percent rise in household wealth and that investment spending initially rises by $20 billion for every one percentage point fall in the real interest rate. Also assume that the economy's multiplier is 4. If household wealth falls by 5 percent because of declining house values, and the real interest rate falls by two percentage points, in what direction and by how much will the aggregate demand curve initially shift at each price level? In what direction and by how much will it eventually shift?   [LO12.2]

2. Answer the following questions on the basis of the three sets of data for the country of North Vaudeville: [LO12.4]

A		B		C	
Price level	Real GDP	Price level	Real GDP	Price level	Real GDP
110	275	100	200	110	225
100	250	100	225	100	225
95	225	100	250	95	225
90	200	100	275	90	225

a. Which set of data illustrates aggregate supply in the immediate short run in North Vaudeville? The short run? The long run?

b. Assuming no change in hours of work, if real output per hour of work increases by 10 percent, what will be the new levels of real GDP in the right column of A? Does the new data reflect an increase in aggregate supply or does it indicate a decrease in aggregate supply?

3. Suppose that the aggregate demand and the aggregate supply schedules for a hypothetical economy are as shown below: [LO12.5]

Amount of real domestic output demanded (billions)	Price level (price index)	Amount of real domestic output supplied (billions)
$100	300	$450
200	250	400
300	200	300
400	150	200
500	100	100

a. Use these data to graph the aggregate demand and supply curves. What is the equilibrium price level and level of real output in this hypothetical economy? Is the equilibrium real output also the full-employment real output?

b. If the price level in this economy is 150, will quantity demanded equal, exceed, or fall short of quantity supplied? By what amount? If the price level is 250, will quantity demanded equal, exceed, or fall short of quantity supplied? By what amount?

c. Suppose that buyers desire to purchase $200 billion of extra real output at each price level. Sketch in the new aggregate demand curve as AD_1. What is the new equilibrium price level and the level of real output?

4. Suppose that the table below shows an economy's relationship between the real output and the inputs needed to produce that output: [LO12.4]

Input quantity	Real domestic output
150.0	400
112.5	300
75.0	200

a. What is productivity in this economy?

b. What is the per-unit cost of production if the price of each input unit is $2?

c. Assume that the input price increases from $2 to $3 with no accompanying change in productivity. What is the new

per-unit cost of production? In what direction would the $1 increase in input price push the aggregate supply curve? What effect would this shift of the short-run aggregate supply have on the price level and the level of real output?

d. Suppose that the increase in input price does not occur but instead productivity increases by 100 percent. What would be the new per-unit cost of production? What effect would this change in per-unit production cost have on the short-run aggregate supply curve? What effect would this shift of the short-run aggregate supply have on the price level and the level of real output?

5. Refer to the data in the table that accompanies problem 2. Suppose that the present equilibrium price level and level of real GDP are 100 and $225, and that data set B represents the relevant aggregate supply schedule for the economy. [LO12.6]

a. What must be the current amount of real output demanded at the 100 price level?

b. If the amount of output demanded declined by $25 at the 100 price levels shown in B, what would be the new equilibrium real GDP? In business cycle terminology, what would economists call this change in real GDP?

Appendix to Chapter 12

The Relationship of the Aggregate Demand Curve to the Aggregate Expenditures Model*

LOA12.1 Identify how the aggregate demand curve relates to the aggregate expenditures model.

Derivation of the Aggregate Demand Curve from the Aggregate Expenditures Model

We can directly connect the downsloping aggregate demand curve of Figure 12-1 to the aggregate expenditures model discussed in Chapter 11 by relating the various possible price levels to corresponding equilibrium GDPs. In Figure A12-1 we have stacked the aggregate expenditures model (Figure A12-1a) and the aggregate demand curve (Figure A12-1b) vertically. We can do this because the horizontal axes of both models measure real GDP. Now let's derive the AD curve in three distinct steps. (Throughout this discussion, keep in mind that price level P_1 < price level P_2 < price level P_3).

- First suppose that the economy's price level is P_1 and its aggregate expenditures schedule is AE_1, the top schedule in Figure A12-1a. The equilibrium GDP is then GDP_1 at point 1. So in Figure A12-1b we can plot the equilibrium real output GDP_1 and the corresponding price level P_1. This gives us point 1′ in Figure A12-1b.

- Now assume the price level rises from P_1 to P_2. Other things equal, this higher price level will (1) decrease the value of wealth, decreasing consumption expenditures; (2) increase the interest rate, reducing investment and interest-sensitive consumption expenditures; and (3) increase imports and decrease exports, reducing net export expenditures. The aggregate expenditures schedule will fall from AE_1 to, say, AE_2 in Figure A12-1a, giving us equilibrium GDP_2 at point 2. In Figure A12-1b we plot this new price-level–real-output combination, P_2 and GDP_2, as point 2′.

- Finally, suppose the price level rises from P_2 to P_3. The value of real wealth balances, the interest rate rises, exports fall, and imports rise. Consequently, the consumption, investment, and net export schedules fall,

shifting the aggregate expenditures schedule downward from AE_2 to AE_3, which gives us equilibrium GDP_3 at point 3. In Figure A12-1b, this enables us to locate point 3′, where the price level is P_3 and real output is GDP_3.

In summary, increases in the economy's price level will successively shift its aggregate expenditures schedule downward and will reduce real GDP. The resulting price level–real GDP combination will yield various points such as 1′, 2′, and 3′ in Figure A12-1b. Together, such points locate the downsloping aggregate demand curve for the economy.

Aggregate Demand Shifts and the Aggregate Expenditures Model

The determinants of aggregate demand listed in Figure 12-2 are the components of the aggregate expenditures model discussed in Chapter 11. When one of those determinants changes, the aggregate expenditures schedule shifts too. We can easily link such shifts in the aggregate expenditures schedule to shifts of the aggregate demand curve.

Let's suppose the price level is constant. In Figure A12-2 we begin with the aggregate expenditures schedule at AE_1 in diagram (a), yielding real output of GDP_1. Assume now that investment spending increases in response to more optimistic business expectations, so that the aggregate expenditures schedule rises from AE_1 to AE_2. (The notation "at P_1" reminds us that the price level is assumed to be constant.) The result will be a multiplied increase in real output from GDP_1 to GDP_2.

In Figure A12-2b, the increase in investment spending is reflected in the horizontal distance between AD_1 and the broken curve to its right. The immediate effect of the increase in investment is an increase in aggregate demand by the exact amount of the new spending. But then the multiplier process magnifies the initial increase in investment into successive rounds of consumption spending and an ultimate multiplied increase in aggregate demand from AD_1 to AD_2. Equilibrium real output

---

* This appendix presumes knowledge of the aggregate expenditures model discussed in Chapter 11 and should be skipped if Chapter 11 was not assigned.

| FIGURE A12-1 | Deriving the Aggregate Demand Curve from the Expenditures Model |

(a) Rising price levels from P_1 to P_2 to P_3 shift the aggregate expenditures curve downward from AE_1 to AE_2 to AE_3 and reduce real GDP from GDP_1 to GDP_2 to GDP_3. (b) The aggregate demand curve AD is derived by plotting the successively lower real GDPs from the upper graph against the P_1, P_2, and P_3 price levels.

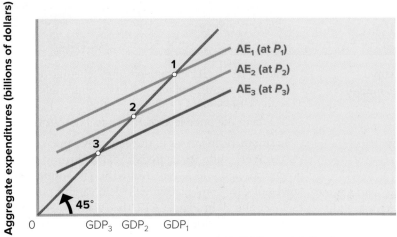

(a) Aggregate expenditures model

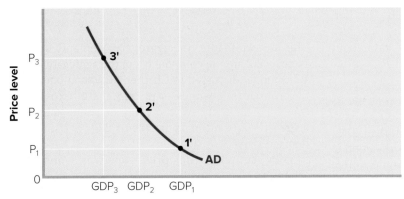

(b) Aggregate demand–aggregate supply model

rises from GDP_1 to GDP_2, the same multiplied increase in real GDP as that in Figure A12-2a. The initial increase in investment in part (a) has shifted the AD curve in part (b) by a horizontal distance equal to the change in investment times the multiplier. This particular change in real GDP is still associated with the constant price level P_1. To generalize

Shift of AD curve = initial change in spending × multiplier

FIGURE A12-2 Shifts in the Aggregate Expenditures Schedule and in the Aggregate Demand Curve

(a) A change in some determinant of consumption, investment, or net exports (other than the price level) shifts the aggregate expenditures schedule upward from AE_1 to AE_2. The multiplier increases real output from GDP_1 to GDP_2. (b) The counterpart of this change is an initial rightward shift of the aggregate demand curve by the amount of initial new spending (from AD_1 to the broken curve). This leads to a multiplied rightward shift of the curve to AD_2, which is just sufficient to show the same increase in GDP as in the aggregate expenditures model.

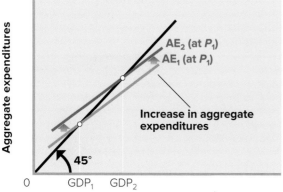

(a) Aggregate expenditures model

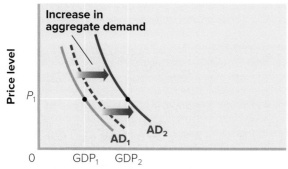

(b) Aggregate demand–aggregate supply model

APPENDIX / Summary

LOA12.1 Identify how the aggregate demand curve relates to the aggregate expenditures model.

- A change in the price level alters the location of the aggregate expenditures schedule through the real-balances, interest-rate, and foreign-trade effects. The aggregate demand curve is derived from the aggregate expenditures model by allowing the price level to change and observing the effect on the aggregate expenditures schedule and thus on equilibrium GDP.

- With the price level held constant, increases in consumption, investment, government, and net export expenditures shift the aggregate expenditures schedule upward and the aggregate demand curve to the right. Decreases in these spending components produce the opposite effects.

APPENDIX / Discussion Questions

1. Carefully explain the following: A change in the price level shifts the aggregate expenditures curve but not the aggregate demand curve.   [LOA12.1]

2. Suppose the price level is constant and investment spending decrease sharply. How would you show this increase in the aggregate expenditures model? What would be the outcome for real GDP? How would you show this fall in investment in the aggregate demand–aggregate supply model, assuming the economy is operating in what is, in effect, a horizontal range of the aggregate supply curve?   [LOA12.1]

APPENDIX / Review Questions

1. True or False? A higher price level increases aggregate expenditures.   [LOA12.1]

2. If the government decreases expenditures, the AE curve will shift _____ and the AD curve will shift _____.   [LOA12.1]

   a. Down; left

   b. Down; right

   c. Up; left

   d. Up; right

APPENDIX / Problems

1. Refer to Figure A12-1a and A12-1b. Assume that Q_1 is 300, Q_2 is 200, Q_3 is 100, P_3 is 120, P_2 is 100, and P_1 is 80. If the price level increases from P_1 to P_3 in Figure A12-1b, in what direction and by how much will real GDP change? If the slopes of the AE lines in Figure A12-1a are 0.8 and equal to the MPC, in what direction will the aggregate expenditures schedule in Figure A12-1a need to shift to produce the previously determined change in real GDP? What is the size of the multiplier in this example?   [LOA12.1]

2. Refer to Figure A12-2 and assume that Q_1 is \$400 and Q_2 is \$500, the price level is stuck at P_1, and the slopes of the AE lines in Figure A12-2a are 0.75 and equal to the MPC. In what direction and by how much does the aggregate expenditures schedule in Figure A12-2a need to shift in order to shift the aggregate demand curve in Figure A12-2b from AD_1 to AD_2? What is the multiplier in this example? Given the multiplier, what must be the distance between AD_1 and the broken line to its right at P_1?   [LOA12.1]

CHAPTER 13

Fiscal Policy, Deficits, Surpluses, and Debt

LEARNING OBJECTIVES

LO13.1 Identify and explain the purposes, tools, and limitations of fiscal policy.

LO13.2 Explain the role of built-in stabilizers in moderating business cycles.

LO13.3 Describe how the cyclically adjusted budget reveals the status of Canadian fiscal policy.

LO13.4 Summarize recent Canadian fiscal policy and the projections for Canadian fiscal policy over the next few years.

LO13.5 Discuss the problems that governments may encounter in enacting and applying fiscal policy.

LO13.6 Discuss the size, composition, and consequences of the Canadian public debt.

In the previous chapter we saw that an excessive increase in aggregate demand can cause demand-pull inflation, and that a significant decline in aggregate demand can cause recession and cyclical unemployment. For those reasons, central governments sometimes use budgetary actions to try to "stimulate the economy" or "rein in inflation." Such countercyclical **fiscal policy** consists of deliberate changes in government spending and tax collections designed to achieve full employment, control inflation, and encourage economic growth. (The adjective "fiscal" simply means "financial.") We begin this chapter by examining the logic behind fiscal policy, its current status, and its limitations. Then we examine a closely related topic: the Canadian public debt.

Our discussion of fiscal policy and public debt is very timely. In the last few years, since the Great Recession, the federal government has run annual deficits to keep aggregate demand buoyant. This fiscal policy contributed to the rising public debt for the first time in a decade.

13.1 / Fiscal Policy and the AD–AS Model

LO13.1 Identify and explain the purposes, tools, and limitations of fiscal policy.

Since 1945 one of the main tools used by government in stabilization policy has been fiscal policy, which includes changes in government spending and taxation designed to achieve full employment and a stable price level. In Canada, the idea that government fiscal actions can exert a stabilizing influence on the economy emerged from the Great Depression of the 1930s and the rise of Keynesian economics. Since then, macroeconomic theory has played a major role in the design of fiscal policy and the improved understanding of its limitations.

Fiscal policy is described as *discretionary* (or *active*) if the changes in government spending and taxes are *at the option* of the government. They do not occur automatically, independent of parliamentary action. Those changes are *nondiscretionary* (or *passive* or *automatic*), and we will examine them in the next section of this chapter.

Expansionary Fiscal Policy

When recession occurs, an **expansionary fiscal policy** may be in order. This policy consists of government spending increases, tax reductions, or both, designed to increase aggregate demand and therefore raise real GDP. (Note that we have assumed an MPC of 0.75, and thus a multiplier of 4. We pointed out that in the real world the multiplier is actually much lower. We use a multiplier of 4 for simplicity.) Consider Figure 13-1, where we suppose that a sharp decline in investment spending has shifted the economy's aggregate demand curve leftward from AD_1 to AD_2. Perhaps profit expectations on investment projects have dimmed, curtailing much investment spending and reducing aggregate demand. (Disregard the arrows and dashed downsloping line for now.)

ORIGIN OF THE IDEA 13.1   Fiscal Policy

FIGURE 13-1	**Expansionary Fiscal Policy**

Expansionary fiscal policy uses increases in government spending or tax cuts to push the economy out of recession. In an economy with an MPC of 0.75, a $5 billion increase in government spending or a $6.67 billion decrease in personal taxes (producing a $5 billion initial increase in consumption) expands aggregate demand from AD_2 to the downsloping dashed curve. The multiplier then magnifies this initial increase in spending to AD_1. So real GDP rises along the broken horizontal line by $20 billion.

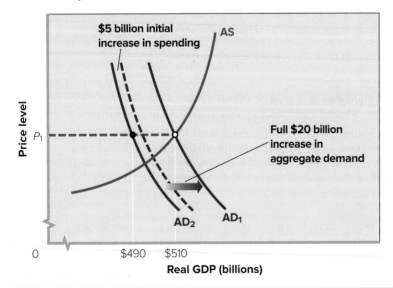

Suppose the economy's potential or full-employment output is $510 billion in Figure 13-1. If the price level is inflexible downward at P_1, the broken horizontal line becomes relevant to the analysis. The aggregate demand curve moves leftward and reduces real GDP from $510 billion to $490 billion. A negative GDP gap of $20 billion (= $490 billion − $510 billion) arises. An increase in unemployment accompanies this negative GDP gap because fewer workers are needed to produce the reduced output. In short, the economy depicted is suffering both recession and cyclical unemployment.

What fiscal policy should the federal government adopt to stimulate the economy? It has three main options: (1) increase government spending, (2) reduce taxes, or (3) some combination of the two. If the federal budget is balanced at the outset, expansionary fiscal policy will create a government **budget deficit**–annual government spending in excess of tax revenues.

INCREASED GOVERNMENT SPENDING

Other things equal, a sufficient increase in government spending will shift an economy's aggregate demand curve to the right, from AD_2 to AD_1 in Figure 13-1. To see why, suppose the recession prompts the government to initiate $5 billion of new spending on highways, education, and health care. We represent this new $5 billion of government spending as the horizontal distance between AD_2 and the dashed downsloping line immediately to its right. At each price level, the amount of real output that is demanded is now $5 billion greater than that demanded before the expansion of government spending.

If government initiates new spending on highways, airports, education, and health care, the amount of real output demanded rises.

But the initial increase in aggregate demand is not the end of the story. Through the multiplier effect, the aggregate demand curve shifts to AD_1, a distance exceeding that represented by the originating $5 billion increase in government purchases. This greater shift occurs because the multiplier process magnifies the initial change in spending into successive rounds of new consumption spending. If the economy's marginal propensity to consume (MPC) is 0.75, then the simple multiplier is 4. So the aggregate demand curve shifts rightward by four times the distance between AD_2 and the broken downsloping line.

Because this *particular* increase in aggregate demand occurs along the horizontal broken-line segment, real output rises by the full extent of the multiplier. Observe that real output rises to $510 billion, up $20 billion from its recessionary level of $490 billion. Concurrently, unemployment falls as firms increase their employment to the full-employment level that existed before the recession.

TAX REDUCTIONS

Alternatively, the government could reduce taxes to shift the aggregate demand curve to the right, as from AD_2 to AD_1. Suppose the government cuts personal income taxes by $6.67 billion, which increases disposable income by the same amount. Consumption will rise by $5 billion (= MPC of 0.75 × $6.67 billion) and saving will go up by $1.67 billion (= MPS of 0.25 × $6.67 billion). In this case the horizontal distance between AD_2 and the dashed downsloping line in Figure 13-1 represents only the $5 billion initial increase in consumption spending. Again, we call it "initial" consumption spending because the multiplier process yields successive rounds of increased consumption spending. The aggregate demand curve eventually shifts rightward by four times the $5 billion initial increase in consumption produced by the tax cut. Real GDP rises by $20 billion, from $490 billion to $510 billion, implying a multiplier of 4. Employment increases accordingly.

You may have noted that a tax cut must be somewhat larger than the proposed increase in government spending if it is to achieve the same amount of rightward shift in the aggregate demand curve. This is because part of a tax reduction increases saving, rather than consumption. To increase initial consumption by a specific amount, the government must reduce taxes by more than that amount. With an MPC of 0.75, taxes must fall by $6.67 billion for $5 billion of new consumption to be forthcoming because $1.67 billion is saved (not consumed). If the MPC had instead been, say, 0.6, an $8.33 billion reduction in tax collections would have been necessary to increase initial consumption by $5 billion. The smaller the MPC, the greater the tax cut needed to accomplish a specific initial increase in consumption and a specific shift in the aggregate demand curve.

COMBINED GOVERNMENT SPENDING INCREASES AND TAX REDUCTIONS

The government may combine spending increases and tax cuts to produce the desired initial increase in spending and eventual increase in aggregate demand and real GDP. In the economy depicted in Figure 13-1, the government might increase its spending by $1.25 billion while reducing taxes by $5 billion. As an exercise, explain why this combination will produce the targeted $5 billion initial increase in new spending.

If you were assigned Chapter 11, think through these three fiscal policy options in terms of the recessionary expenditure-gap analysis associated with the aggregate expenditures model (Figure 11-7). And recall from the appendix to Chapter 12 that rightward shifts of the aggregate demand curve relate directly to upward shifts of the aggregate expenditures schedule.

Contractionary Fiscal Policy

When demand-pull inflation occurs, a restrictive or **contractionary fiscal policy** may help control it. This policy consists of government spending reductions, tax increases, or both, designed to decrease aggregate demand and therefore lower or eliminate inflation. Look at Figure 13-2, where the full-employment level of real GDP is $510 billion. The economy starts at equilibrium at point a, where the initial aggregate demand curve AD_3 intersects aggregate supply curve AS. Suppose that after going through the multiplier process, a $5 billion initial increase in investment and net export spending shifts the aggregate demand curve to the right by $20 billion, from AD_3 to AD_4. (Ignore the downsloping dashed line for now.) Given the upsloping AS curve, however, the equilibrium GDP does not rise by the full $20 billion. It rises by only $12 billion, to $522 billion, creating an inflationary GDP gap of $12 billion ($522 billion − $510 billion).

The upward slope of the AS curve means that some of the rightward movement of the AD curve ends up causing demand-pull inflation rather than increased output. As a result, the price level rises from P_1 to P_2 and the equilibrium moves to point b.

Without a government response, the inflationary GDP gap will cause further inflation (as input prices rise in the long run to meet the increase in output prices). If the government looks to fiscal policy to eliminate the inflationary GDP gap, its options are the opposite of those used to combat recession. It can

CONSIDER THIS   **Canada's Economic Action Plan to Combat the Great Recession of 2009**

During the Great Recession, in early 2009, the Canadian federal government embarked on Canada's Economic Action Plan—essentially an expansionary fiscal policy—to fight the economic downturn. Under the plan, some 26,000 projects were funded using a $60 billion fiscal stimulus directed toward improving Canada's infrastructure, particularly at colleges and universities across the country. Also targeted were clean energy and the environment, improvement of federal laboratories (such as the Canadian Food Inspection Agency), and post-secondary education and research. As the Canadian economy recovered from the recession in 2010 and 2011, Canada's Economic Action Plan turned to measures to foster growth and balance the federal budget by 2016. The federal government achieved its goal by 2015 when it ran a small surplus.

FIGURE 13-2	**Contractionary Fiscal Policy**

Contractionary fiscal policy uses decreases in government spending, increases in taxes, or both, to reduce demand–pull inflation. Here, an increase in aggregate demand from AD_3 to AD_4 has driven the economy to point b and ratcheted the price level up to P_2, where it becomes inflexible downward. If the economy's MPC is 0.75 and the multiplier therefore is 4, the government can either reduce its spending by $3 billion or increase its taxes by $4 billion (which will decrease consumption by $3 billion) to eliminate the inflationary GDP gap of $12 billion (= $522 billion − $510 billion). Aggregate demand will shift leftward, first from AD_4 to the dashed downsloping curve to its left, and then to AD_5. With the price level remaining at P_2, the economy will move from point b to point c and the inflationary GDP gap will disappear.

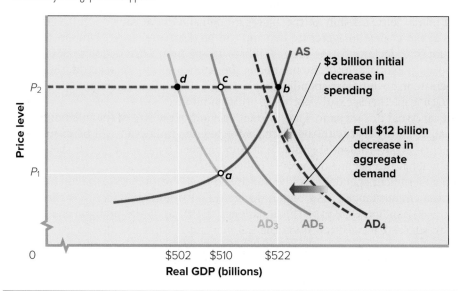

(1) decrease government spending, (2) raise taxes, or (3) use some combination of those two policies. When the economy faces demand-pull inflation, fiscal policy should move toward a government **budget surplus**–tax revenues in excess of government spending.

But before discussing how the government can either decrease government spending or increase taxes to move toward a government budget surplus and control inflation, we have to keep in mind that the price level is like a ratchet. While increases in aggregate demand that expand real output beyond the full-employment level tend to ratchet the price level upward, declines in aggregate demand do not seem to push the price level downward. This means that stopping inflation is a matter of halting the rise of the price level, not trying to lower it to the previous level. It also means that the government must take the ratchet effect into account when deciding how much it should decrease spending or increase taxes.

DECREASED GOVERNMENT SPENDING

Reduced government spending shifts the aggregate demand curve leftward to control demand-pull infla-tion. To see why the ratchet effect matters so much, look at Figure 13-2 and consider what would happen if the government ignored the ratchet effect and attempted to design a spending reduction policy to eliminate the inflationary GDP gap. Since the $12 billion gap was caused by the $20 billion rightward movement of the aggregate demand curve from AD_3 to AD_4, the government might naively think that it could solve the problem by causing a $20 billion leftward shift of the aggregate demand curve to move it back to where it originally was. It could attempt to do so by reducing government spending by $5 billion and then allowing the multiplier effect to expand that initial decrease into a $20 billion decline in aggre-gate demand. That would shift the aggregate demand curve leftward by $20 billion, putting it back at AD_3.

This policy would work fine if there were no ratchet effect and if prices were flexible. The economy's equilibrium would move back from point b to point a, with equilibrium GDP returning to the full-employment level of $510 billion and the price level falling from P_2 back to P_1. But because there *is* a ratchet effect, that scenario is not what will actually happen. Instead, the ratchet effect implies that the price level is stuck at P_2, so that the broken horizontal line at price level P_2 becomes important to the analysis. The fixed price level means that when the government reduces spending by $5 billion in order to shift the aggregate demand curve back to AD_3, it will actually cause a recession! The new equilibrium will not be at point a. It will be at point d, where aggregate demand curve AD_3 crosses the broken horizontal line. At point d, real GDP is only $502 billion, $8 billion below the full-employment level of $510 billion.

The problem is that with the price level downwardly inflexible at P_2, we have in essence an immediate-short-run AS curve and the multiplier is at full effect. With the price level fixed and the aggregate supply curve horizontal, the $20 billion leftward shift of the aggregate demand curve causes a full $20 billion decline in real GDP. None of the change in aggregate demand can be dissipated as a decline in the price level. As a result, equilibrium GDP declines by the full $20 billion, falling from $522 billion to $502 billion and putting it $8 billion below potential output. By not taking the ratchet effect into account, the government has overdone the decrease in government spending, replacing a $12 billion inflationary GDP gap with an $8 billion recessionary GDP gap. This is clearly not what it had in mind.

Here's how government can avoid this scenario. First, it takes account of the size of the inflationary GDP gap. It is $12 billion. Second, it knows that with the price level fixed, the multiplier will be in full effect. Thus, it knows that any decline in government spending will be multiplied by a factor of 4. It then reasons that government spending will have to decline by only $3 billion rather than $5 billion. Why? Because the $3 billion initial decline in government spending will be multiplied by 4, creating a $12 billion decline in aggregate demand. Under the circumstances, a $3 billion decline in government spending is the correct amount to exactly offset the $12 billion GDP gap. This inflationary GDP gap is the problem that government wants to eliminate. To succeed, it need not undo the full increase in aggregate demand that caused the inflation in the first place.

Graphically, the horizontal distance between AD_4 and the dashed downsloping line to its left represents the $3 billion decrease in government spending. Once the multiplier process is complete, this spending cut will shift the aggregate demand curve leftward from AD_4 to AD_5. With the price level fixed at P_2 the economy will come to equilibrium at point c. The economy will operate at its potential output of $510 billion. The inflationary GDP gap will be eliminated. And because the government took the ratchet effect correctly into account, the government will not accidentally push the economy into a recession by making an overly large initial decrease in government spending.

TAX INCREASES

Just as government can use tax reductions to increase consumption spending, it can use tax *increases* to *reduce* consumption spending. If the economy in Figure 13-2 has an MPC of 0.75, the government must raise taxes by $4 billion to achieve its fiscal policy objective. The $4 billion tax increase reduces saving by $1 billion (= the MPS of 0.25 × $4 billion). This $1 billion reduction in saving, by definition, is not a reduction in spending. But the $4 billion tax increase also reduces consumption spending by $3 billion (= the MPC of 0.75 × $4 billion), as shown by the distance between AD_4 and the dashed downsloping line to its left in Figure 13-2. After the multiplier process is complete, this initial $3 billion decline in consumption will cause aggregate demand to shift leftward by $12 billion (= multiplier of 4 × $3 billion) at each price level. With the economy moving to point c, the inflationary GDP gap will be closed and the inflation will be halted.

COMBINED GOVERNMENT SPENDING DECREASES AND TAX INCREASES

The government may choose to combine spending decreases and tax increases in order to reduce aggregate demand and check inflation. To check your understanding, determine why a $1.5 billion decline in government spending combined with a $2 billion increase in taxes would shift the aggregate demand curve from AD_4 to AD_5. Also, if you were assigned Chapter 11, explain the three fiscal policy options for fighting inflation by referring to the inflationary-expenditure-gap concept developed with the aggregate expenditures model (Figure 11-7). And recall from the appendix to Chapter 12 that leftward shifts of the aggregate demand curve are associated with downward shifts of the aggregate expenditures schedule.

Policy Options: *G* or *T*?

Which is preferable as a means of eliminating recession and inflation: government spending or taxes? The answer depends largely on whether one views the government as too large or too small. Economists who recognize many unmet social and infrastructure needs usually recommend that government spending be increased during recessions. In times of demand–pull inflation, they usually recommend tax increases. Both actions either expand or preserve the size of government. Economists who think that the government is too large and inefficient usually advocate tax cuts during recessions and cuts in government spending during times of demand–pull inflation. Both actions either restrain the growth of government or reduce its size. The point is that discretionary fiscal policy designed to stabilize the economy can be associated with either an expanding government or a contracting government.

QUICK REVIEW 13.1

- Discretionary fiscal policy is the deliberate change in government expenditures and tax collections by government to promote full employment, price stability, and economic growth.

- Expansionary fiscal policy consists of increases in government spending, decreases in taxes, or both, and is designed to expand real GDP by increasing aggregate demand.

- Contractionary fiscal policy consists of decreases in government spending, increases in taxes, or both, and is designed to reduce aggregate demand and slow or halt demand–pull inflation.

- To be implemented correctly, contractionary fiscal policy must account for the ratchet effect and the fact that prices will not fall as the government shifts the aggregate demand curve leftward.

13.2 / Built-in Stability

LO13.2 Explain the role of built-in stabilizers in moderating business cycles.

To some degree, government tax revenues change automatically over the course of the business cycle, in ways that stabilize the economy. This automatic response, or built-in stability, constitutes nondiscretionary budgetary policy. We did not include this built-in stability in our discussion of fiscal policy because we implicitly assumed that the same amount of tax revenue was being collected at each level of GDP. But the actual Canadian tax system is such that *net tax revenues* vary directly with GDP. (Net taxes are tax revenues less transfers and subsidies. From here on, we will use the simpler *taxes* to mean "net taxes.")

Virtually any tax will yield more tax revenue as GDP rises. In particular, personal income taxes have progressive rates and thus generate more than proportionate increases in tax revenues as GDP expands. Furthermore, as GDP rises and more goods and services are purchased, revenues from corporate income taxes and from sales taxes also increase. And similarly, revenues from employment insurance and Canada pension (compulsory) contributions rise as economic expansion creates more jobs. Conversely, when GDP declines, tax revenues from all these sources also decline.

Transfer payments (or "negative taxes") behave in the opposite way from tax revenues. Unemployment compensation payments and welfare payments decrease during economic expansion and increase during economic contraction.

Automatic or Built-in Stabilizers

A **built-in stabilizer** is a structure of taxation and spending that increases the government's budget deficit (or reduces its budget surplus) during a recession and increases its budget surplus (or reduces its budget deficit) during an expansion without requiring explicit action by policymakers. As Figure 13-3 reveals, this is precisely what the Canadian tax system does.

FIGURE 13-3   Built-in Stability

Tax revenues *T* vary directly with GDP, and government spending *G* is assumed to be independent of GDP. As GDP falls in a recession, deficits occur automatically and help alleviate the recession. As GDP rises during expansion, surpluses occur automatically and help offset possible inflation.

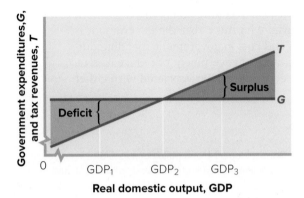

Government expenditures, *G*, are fixed and assumed to be independent of the level of GDP. Parliament decides on a particular level of spending, but it does not determine the magnitude of tax revenues. Instead, it establishes tax rates, and then tax revenues vary directly with the level of GDP that the economy achieves. Line *T* represents that direct relationship between tax revenues and GDP.

ECONOMIC IMPORTANCE

The economic importance of this direct relationship between tax receipts and GDP becomes apparent when we consider the following:

• Taxes reduce spending and aggregate demand.

• Reductions in spending are desirable when the economy is developing inflationary pressures, whereas increases in spending are desirable when the economy is slumping.

As shown in Figure 13-3, tax revenues automatically increase as GDP rises during prosperity, and since taxes reduce household and business spending, they restrain the economic expansion. That is, as the economy moves toward a higher GDP, tax revenues automatically rise and move the budget from deficit toward surplus. In Figure 13-3, observe that the high and perhaps inflationary income level GDP$_3$ automatically generates a contractionary budget surplus. Conversely, as GDP falls during recession, tax revenues automatically decline, increasing spending by households and businesses and thus cushioning the economic contraction. With a falling GDP, tax receipts decline and move the government's budget from surplus toward deficit. In Figure 13-3, the low level of income GDP$_1$ will automatically yield an expansionary budget deficit.

TAX PROGRESSIVITY

Figure 13-3 reveals that the size of the automatic budget deficits or surpluses—and therefore built-in stability—depends on the responsiveness of tax revenues to changes in GDP. If tax revenues change sharply as GDP changes, the slope of line *T* in the figure will be steep and the vertical distances between *T* and *G* (the deficits or surpluses) will be large. If tax revenues change very little when GDP changes, the slope will be gentle and built-in stability will be low.

The steepness of *T* in Figure 13-3 depends on the tax system itself. In a **progressive tax system**, the average tax rate (= tax revenue/GDP) rises with GDP. In a **proportional tax system**, the average tax rate remains constant as GDP rises. In a **regressive tax system**, the average tax rate falls as GDP rises. The progressive tax system has the steepest tax line *T* of the three. However, tax revenues will rise with GDP under both the progressive and proportional tax systems, and they may rise, fall, or stay the same under a regressive tax system. The main point is this: the more progressive the tax system, the greater the economy's built-in stability.

The built-in stability provided by the Canadian tax system has reduced the severity of business fluctuations. In recession year 2009, for example, revenues from the individual income tax fell. This decline helped keep household spending and real GDP from falling even more than they did. But built-in stabilizers can only dampen, not counteract, swings in real GDP. *Discretionary fiscal policy* (changes in tax rates and expenditures) or monetary policy (when the central bank changes in interest rates) therefore may be needed to try to counter a recession or inflation of any appreciable magnitude.

13.3 | Evaluating How Expansionary or Contractionary Fiscal Policy Is Determined

LO13.3 Describe how the cyclically adjusted budget reveals the status of Canadian fiscal policy.

How can we determine whether a government's discretionary fiscal policy is expansionary or contractionary? We cannot simply examine the actual budget deficits or surpluses that take place under the current policy because they will necessarily include the automatic changes in tax revenues that accompany every change in GDP. In addition, the expansionary or contractionary strength of any change in discretionary fiscal policy depends not on its absolute size but on how large it is relative to the size of the economy. So, in evaluating the status of fiscal policy, we must adjust deficits and surpluses to eliminate automatic changes in tax revenues and also compare the sizes of the adjusted budget deficits and surpluses to the level of potential GDP.

Cyclically Adjusted Budget

Economists use the **cyclically adjusted budget** (also called the *full-employment budget*) to adjust actual federal budget deficits and surpluses to account for the changes in tax revenues that happen automatically whenever GDP changes. The cyclically adjusted budget measures what the federal budget deficit or surplus would have been with existing tax rates and government spending levels if the economy had achieved its full-employment level of GDP (its potential output). The idea essentially is to compare *actual* government expenditures with the tax revenues *that would have occurred* if the economy had achieved full-employment GDP. That procedure removes budget deficits or surpluses that arise simply because of cyclical changes in GDP, which then tell us whether the government's current discretionary fiscal policy is fundamentally expansionary, contractionary, or neutral.

Consider Figure 13-4a, where line *G* represents government expenditures and line *T* represents tax revenues. In full-employment year 1, government expenditures of $500 billion equal tax revenues of $500 billion, as indicated by the intersection of lines *G* and *T* at point *a*. The cyclically adjusted budget deficit in year 1 is zero: government expenditures equal the tax revenues forthcoming at the full-employment output GDP_1. Obviously, the full-employment deficit *as a percentage of GDP* is also zero. The government's fiscal policy is neutral.

Now, suppose that a recession occurs and GDP falls from GDP_1 to GDP_2, as shown in Figure 13-4a. Let's also assume that the government takes no discretionary action, so that lines *G* and *T* remain as shown in the figure. Tax revenues automatically fall to $450 billion (point *c*) at GDP_2, while government spending remains unaltered at $500 billion (point *b*). A $50 billion budget deficit (represented by distance *bc*) arises. But this **cyclical deficit** is simply a by-product of the economy's slide into recession, not the result of discretionary fiscal actions by the government. We would be wrong to conclude from this deficit that the government is engaging in an expansionary fiscal policy. The government's fiscal policy has not changed. It is still neutral.

That fact is highlighted when we remove the cyclical part of the deficit and thus consider the cyclically adjusted budget deficit for year 2 in Figure 13-4a. The $500 billion of government expenditures in

FIGURE 13-4   ## Cyclically Adjusted Deficits

(a) The cyclically adjusted deficit is zero at the full-employment output GDP_1. But it is also zero at the recessionary output GDP_2, because the $500 billion of government expenditures at GDP_2 equals the $500 billion of tax revenues that would be forthcoming at the full-employment GDP_1. There has been no change in fiscal policy. (b) Discretionary fiscal policy, as reflected in the downward shift of the tax line from T_1 to T_2, has increased the cyclically adjusted budget deficit from zero in year 3 (before the tax cut) to $25 billion in year 4 (after the tax cut). This is found by comparing the $500 billion of government spending in year 4 with the $475 billion of taxes that would accrue at the full-employment GDP_3. Such a rise in cyclically adjusted deficits (as a percentage of GDP) identifies an expansionary fiscal policy.

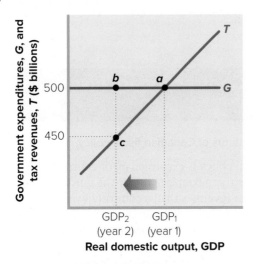

(a) Zero cyclically adjusted deficits, years 1 and 2

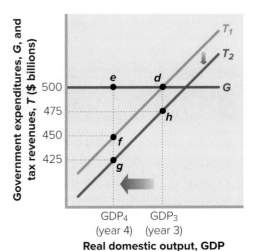

(b) Zero cyclically adjusted deficit, year 3; $25 billion full-employment deficit, year 4

year 2 are shown by *b* on line *G*. And, as shown by *a* on line *T*, $500 billion of tax revenues would have occurred if the economy had achieved its full-employment GDP. Because both *b* and *a* represent $500 billion, the cyclically adjusted budget deficit in year 2 is zero, as is this deficit as a percentage of GDP. Since the cyclically adjusted budget deficits are zero in both years, we know that government did not change its discretionary fiscal policy, even though a recession occurred and an actual deficit of $50 billion resulted.

Next, consider Figure 13-4b. Suppose that real output declined from full-employment GDP_3 to GDP_4. But also suppose the federal government responded to the recession by reducing tax rates in year 4, as represented by the downward shift of the tax line from T_1 to T_2. What has happened to the size of the cyclically adjusted deficit? Government expenditures in year 4 are $500 billion, as shown by *e*. We compare that amount with the $475 billion of tax revenues that would occur if the economy achieved its full-employment GDP. That is, we compare position *e* on line *G* with position *h* on line T_2. The $25 billion of tax revenues by which *e* exceeds *h* is the cyclically adjusted budget deficit for year 4. As a percentage of GDP, the cyclically adjusted budget deficit has increased from zero in year 3 (before the tax rate cut) to some positive percentage (= $25 billion/$GDP_4$ × 100%) in year 4. This increase in the relative size of the cyclically adjusted deficit between the two years reveals that the new fiscal policy is *expansionary*.

In contrast, if we observed a full-employment deficit (as a percentage of GDP) of zero in one year, followed by a cyclically adjusted budget surplus in the next, we could conclude that fiscal policy has changed from being neutral to being contractionary. Because the cyclically adjusted budget adjusts for automatic changes in tax revenues, the increase in the cyclically adjusted budget surplus reveals that government either decreased its spending (*G*) or increased tax rates such that tax revenues (*T*) increased. These changes in *G* and *T* are precisely the discretionary actions that we have identified as elements of a *contractionary* fiscal policy.

13.4 / Recent Canadian Fiscal Policy

LO13.4 Summarize recent Canadian fiscal policy and the projections for Canadian fiscal policy over the next few years.

Table 13.1 lists the actual federal budget deficits and surpluses (column 2) and the cyclically adjusted deficits and surpluses (column 3), as percentages of actual GDP and potential GDP, respectively, between 1995 and 2010. Observe that the cyclically adjusted deficits are generally smaller than the actual deficits. This is because the actual deficits include cyclical deficits, whereas the cyclically adjusted deficits eliminate them. Recall that the cyclically adjusted deficit or surplus is what the actual budget deficit or surplus would have been if the economy were at full employment, also referred to as potential GDP. Only cyclically adjusted surpluses and deficits as percentages of potential GDP (column 3) provide the information needed to assess discretionary fiscal policy and determine whether it is expansionary, contractionary, or neutral.

Column 3 shows that fiscal policy was contractionary from the late 1990s to 2007, leading to surpluses. Because of these surpluses, the federal government was better positioned to move toward an expansionary fiscal policy if the economy significantly weakened, as it did in the last quarter of 2008.

With the onset in 2008 of the global recession set off by the U.S. financial crisis, the federal government embarked on what it called Canada's Economic Action Plan and the federal budget moved quickly to a deficit. During 2009, $32 billion in stimulus spending and tax relief was put into place, and in 2010 an additional $28 billion in stimulus was added. The vast majority of the projects ended in March 2011. The federal government claimed that some 540,000 jobs would be created by Canada's Economic Action Plan and hoped to

TABLE 13-1	**Federal Deficits (−) and Surpluses (+) as Percentage of GDP, 2000–2013**	
(1) Year	**(2) Actual deficit or surplus**	**(3) Cyclically adjusted deficit or surplus**
2000	+1.4	+1.8
2001	+1.9	+1.1
2002	+0.7	+0.8
2003	+0.6	+1.2
2004	+0.7	+0.9
2005	+0.1	+0.9
2006	+0.9	+0.9
2007	+0.9	+0.5
2008	+0.6	0.0
2009	−0.3	−0.2
2010	−3.4	−0.8
2011	−1.9	−0.6
2012	−1.5	−0.9
2013	−1.0	−0.8

Source: Table 17 - Actual, cyclically adjusted and primary-cyclically adjusted budget balances as a percentage of potential GDP at market prices. www.fin.gc.ca/frt-trf/2013/frt-trf-1303-eng.asp. Department of Finance Canada, 2013. Reproduced with the permission of the Minister of Public Works and Government Services Canada, 2013.

13.1 GLOBAL PERSPECTIVE

Cyclically Adjusted Budget Deficits or Surpluses as a Percentage of Potential GDP, Selected Nations

In 2014, most nations had cyclically adjusted budget deficits. These deficits varied as a percentage of each nation's potential GDP. Generally, the deficits represented expansionary fiscal policy in place to fight the recession that ensued in many nations with the onset of the global financial crisis. These deficits persisted even after economic recovery began in 2010.

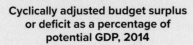

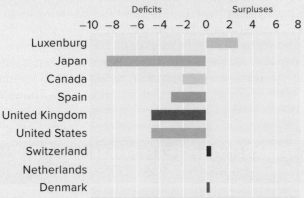

Source: Based on data from OECD (2014), "OECD Economic Outlook No. 96," OECD Economic Outlook: Statistics and Projections (database). http://dx.doi.org/10.1787/data-00717-en

move back to its pre-financial crisis budget surplus by 2016. Beginning in 2009, the federal government budget turned from surplus in the previous year to deficits as tax revenues dropped and automatic expenditures, such as employment insurance, increased. In 2009 we can see that the fiscal policy was definitely expansionary. The actual deficit was 2.5 percent of GDP, whereas the cyclically adjusted budget was 0.6 percent of potential GDP. In other words, if the Canadian economy had been at full employment in 2009, it would have had a budget surplus. Fiscal policy remained mildly expansionary up to 2013, by which time the federal government was close to balancing its budget. At the end of 2014 the finance minister announced a small surplus of $1.4 billion by the end of 2015, but that target became increasingly unlikely as the economy had slowed by mid 2015.

Global Perspective 13.1 shows the extent of the cyclically adjusted budget deficits or surpluses of a number of countries in 2014.

QUICK REVIEW 13.2

- Automatic changes in net taxes (taxes minus transfers) add a degree of built-in stability to the economy.

- Cyclical deficits arise from declines in net tax revenues that automatically occur as the economy recedes and incomes and profits fall.

- The cyclically adjusted budget eliminates cyclical effects on net tax revenues; it compares actual levels of government spending to the projected levels of net taxes that would occur if the economy were achieving its full-employment output.

13.5 Problems, Criticisms, and Complications of Implementing Fiscal Policy

LO13.5 Discuss the problems that governments may encounter in enacting and applying fiscal policy.

Economists recognize that governments may encounter a number of significant problems in developing and applying fiscal policy.

Problems of Timing

Several problems of timing may arise in connection with fiscal policy:

- *Recognition Lag* The recognition lag is the time between the beginning of recession or inflation and the certainty that it is actually happening. This lag arises because the economy does not move smoothly through the business cycle. Even during good times, the economy has slow months interspersed with months of rapid growth and expansion. This makes recognizing a recession difficult since several slow months will have to happen in succession before people can conclude with any confidence that the good times are over and a recession has begun. The same is true with inflation. Even periods of moderate inflation have months of high inflation—so that several high-inflation months must come in sequence before people can confidently conclude that inflation has moved to a higher level. Attempts to reduce the length of the recognition lag by trying to predict the future course of the economy have also proven to be highly difficult. As a result, the economy is often four to six months into a recession or inflation before the situation is clearly discernible in the relevant statistics. Due to this recognition lag, the economic downslide or the inflation may become more serious than it would have if the situation had been identified and acted on sooner.

- *Administration Lag* The wheels of democratic government turn slowly. There will typically be a significant lag between recognizing the need for fiscal action and taking action. Government sometimes takes so much time to adjust fiscal policy that the economic situation has changed in the interim, rendering the belated policy action inappropriate.

- *Operational Lag* A lag also occurs between the time fiscal action is taken and the time that action affects output, employment, or the price level. Although changes in tax rates can be put into effect relatively quickly once new laws are passed, government spending on public works—new dams, hospitals, and so on—requires long planning periods and even longer periods of construction. Such spending is of questionable use in offsetting short periods (for example, six to eighteen months) of recession. Consequently, discretionary fiscal policy has increasingly relied on tax changes rather than on changes in spending as its main tool.

Political Considerations

In the implementation of fiscal policy situations may arise that can reduce the policy's effectiveness, or in which the correct policies may not be implemented. For example, fiscal policy is conducted in a political arena. That reality may slow the enactment of fiscal policy, but it may also create the potential for political considerations to swamp economic considerations while the policy is being formulated. It is a human trait to rationalize actions and policies that are in one's self-interest. Politicians are very human—they want to be re-elected. A strong economy at election time will certainly help them, so they may favour large tax cuts under the guise of expansionary fiscal policy even though that policy is economically inappropriate. Similarly, they may rationalize increased government spending on popular items such as farm subsidies, health care, highways, and education.

At the extreme, elected officials and political parties might collectively "hijack" fiscal policy for political purposes, cause inappropriate changes in aggregate demand, and thereby cause (rather than avert) economic fluctuations. For instance, before an election they may try to stimulate the economy to improve their re-election hopes. After the election they may try to use contractionary fiscal policy to dampen the excessive aggregate demand that they caused with their pre-election stimulus. In short, elected officials may cause a so-called **political business cycle**–swings in overall economic activity and real GDP resulting from election-motivated fiscal policy, rather than from inherent instability in the private sector. Political business cycles are difficult to document and prove, but there is little doubt that political considerations weigh heavily in the formulation of fiscal policy. The question is, how often, if ever, do those political considerations run counter to sound economics?

Future Policy Reversals

Fiscal policy may fail to achieve its intended objectives if households expect future reversals of policy. Consider a tax cut, for example. If taxpayers believe that the tax reduction is temporary, they may save a large portion of their tax cut, reasoning that rates will go up again in the future. They save more now so that they will be able to draw on these extra savings to maintain their future consumption levels if taxes do indeed rise. The extra saving today will help them maintain their consumption at that time. But in the present, consumption spending and aggregate demand will not rise as much as our simple model (Figure 13-1) suggests.

The opposite may be true for a tax increase. If taxpayers think that it is temporary, they may reduce their saving to pay the tax while maintaining their present consumption. They may reason that they can increase their saving when the tax rate falls. So the tax increase will not reduce current consumption and aggregate demand by as much as policymakers intended.

To the extent that this so-called *consumption smoothing* occurs, fiscal policy will lose some of its strength. The lesson is that tax-rate changes viewed by households as permanent are more likely to alter consumption and aggregate demand than changes viewed as temporary.

Offsetting Provincial and Municipal Finance

The fiscal policies of provincial and municipal governments are frequently *pro-cyclical*, meaning that they worsen rather than correct recession or inflation. Like households and private businesses, provincial and municipal governments increase their expenditures during prosperity and cut them during recession. During the recession of 1990–1991, some provincial and municipal governments had to increase tax rates, impose new taxes, and reduce spending to offset falling tax revenues resulting from the reduced personal income and spending of their citizens.

Crowding-Out Effect

Another potential flaw of fiscal policy is the so-called **crowding-out effect**: An expansionary fiscal policy (deficit spending) may increase the interest rate and reduce investment spending, thereby weakening or cancelling the stimulus of the expansionary policy. The rising interest rate might also potentially crowd out interest-sensitive consumption spending (such as purchasing automobiles on credit). But since investment is the most volatile component of GDP, the crowding-out effect focuses its attention on investment and whether the stimulus provided by deficit spending may be partly or even fully neutralized by an offsetting reduction in investment spending.

ORIGIN OF THE IDEA 13.2   Crowding-out Effect

To see the potential problem, note that whenever the government borrows money (as it must if it is deficit spending) it increases the overall demand for money. If the monetary authorities are holding the money supply constant, this increase in demand will raise the price paid for borrowing money: the interest rate. Because investment spending varies inversely with the interest rate, some investment will be choked off or *crowded out*.

Economists vary in their opinions about how strong the crowding-out effect is. An important thing to keep in mind is that crowding out is likely to be less of a problem when the economy is in recession, because investment demand tends to be low. Because the sale of products slows down during recessions, most businesses end up with substantial amounts of excess capacity. As a result, they do not have much incentive to add new machinery or build new factories. After all, why should they add capacity when some of the capacity they already have is sitting idle?

With investment demand low during a recession, the crowding-out effect is likely to be very small. Simply put, there isn't much investment for the government to crowd out. Even if deficit spending does increase the interest rate, investment spending cannot fall by much for the simple reason that it is only a small number to begin with.

By contrast, when the economy is operating at or near full capacity, investment demand is likely to be quite high so that crowding out will probably be a much more serious problem. When the economy is booming, factories will be running at or near full capacity and firms will have high investment demand for two reasons. First, equipment running at full capacity wears out quickly, so that firms will be doing a lot of investment just to replace machinery and equipment that wears out and depreciates. Second, the economy is likely to be growing overall, so firms will be investing to *add* to their production capacity so they can meet anticipated demand.

GRAPHICAL PRESENTATION

An upsloping aggregate supply curve causes a part of the increase in aggregate demand, as in Figure 13-5, to be dissipated in higher prices, with the result that the increase in real GDP is diminished. The price level rises from P_0 to P_1 and real domestic output increases to only GDP_1, rather than GDP_f. As was noted earlier, the ratchet effect will mean that the price level will rise to P_1.

Fiscal Policy in the Open Economy

An additional complication when implementing fiscal policy arises from the fact that each national economy is a component of the world economy.

SHOCKS ORIGINATING FROM ABROAD

Events and policies abroad that affect a nation's net exports affect its own economy. Economies are open to unforeseen international *aggregate demand shocks* that can alter domestic GDP and make current domestic fiscal policy inappropriate. Suppose Canada is in a recession and has enacted an expansionary fiscal policy

---

FIGURE 13-5   **Fiscal Policy: The Effects of Crowding Out and the Net Export Effect**

With an upsloping aggregate supply curve, a part of the impact of an expansionary policy will be reflected in a rise in the price level rather than an increase in real output and employment.

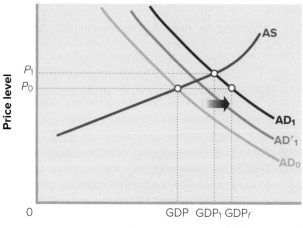

to increase aggregate demand and GDP without igniting inflation. Now suppose the economies of Canada's major trading partners unexpectedly expand rapidly. Greater employment and rising incomes in those nations mean more purchases of Canadian goods. Canadian net exports rise, aggregate demand increases rapidly and beyond its full employment level, and Canada experiences demand-pull inflation. If Canadian policymakers had known in advance that net exports might rise significantly, less-expansionary fiscal policy would have been enacted. We see, then, that participation in the world economy brings with it the complications of mutual interdependence along with the gains from specialization and trade.

An example of shocks coming from abroad is provided by the Great Recession of 2008–2009 when the Canadian economy suddenly took a nosedive as a result of the turmoil in the U.S. housing and financial markets. Between October 1, 2008, and May 31, 2009, GDP fell over 2 percent, unemployment climbed almost 3 percentage points, and exports to the U.S. took their steepest drop in at least a generation. Moreover, the Canadian dollar was almost at par with the U.S. dollar at the start of September 2008, but was below U.S. 80¢ by early March 2009. While economic conditions improved in both Canada and the U.S. later in 2009, the so-called global financial crisis that hit the Canadian economy in 2008–2009 was a textbook case of shocks emanating from abroad—in this case from the U.S., Canada's largest trading partner.

NET EXPORT EFFECT

The **net export effect** may also work through international trade to reduce the effectiveness of fiscal policy. We concluded in our discussion of the crowding-out effect that an expansionary fiscal policy might boost interest rates, reducing investment and weakening fiscal policy. Now we want to know what effect an interest-rate increase might have on a nation's *net exports* (exports minus imports).

Suppose Canada undertakes an expansionary fiscal policy that causes a higher Canadian interest rate. The higher interest rate will attract financial capital from abroad, where we assume interest rates are unchanged. But foreign financial investors must acquire Canadian dollars to invest in Canadian securities. We know that an increase in the demand for a commodity—in this case, dollars—will raise its price. So the price of the Canadian dollar rises in terms of foreign currencies—that is, the Canadian dollar appreciates.

The impact of this dollar appreciation on Canadian net exports is that the rest of the world will see Canadian exports as being more expensive, and Canadian exports will decline. Canadians, who can now exchange their dollars for more units of foreign currencies, will buy more imports. Consequently, with Canadian exports falling and imports rising, net export expenditures in Canada will diminish; this is a contractionary change, so Canada's expansionary fiscal policy will be partially cancelled.[1]

A return to our aggregate demand and supply analysis in Figure 13-5 will clarify this point. An expansionary fiscal policy aimed at increasing aggregate demand from AD_0 to AD_1 may hike the domestic interest rate and ultimately reduce net exports through the process just described. The decline in the net export component of aggregate demand will partially offset the expansionary fiscal policy. The aggregate demand curve will shift rightward from AD_0 to AD'_1, *not* to AD_1, and equilibrium GDP will not increase as much. Moreover, the price level in the economy will rise due to the ratchet effect. Thus, the net export effect of fiscal policy joins the problems of timing, politics, and crowding out in complicating the management of aggregate demand.

Table 13-2 summarizes the net export effect resulting from fiscal policy. Column 1 reviews the analysis just discussed. But note that the net export effect works in both directions. By reducing the domestic interest rate, a *contractionary* fiscal policy *increases* net exports. In this regard, you should follow through the analysis in column 2 in Table 13-2 and relate it to the aggregate demand–aggregate supply model.

Current Thinking on Fiscal Policy

Where do these complications leave us as to the advisability and effectiveness of discretionary fiscal policy? In view of the complications and uncertain outcomes of fiscal policy, some economists argue that it is better not to engage in it at all. They advocate monetary policy (changes in interest rates engineered by the Bank of Canada) as a stabilizing device or believe that most economic fluctuations tend to be mild and self-correcting.

[1] The appreciation of the dollar will also reduce the dollar price of foreign resources imported to Canada. As a result, aggregate supply will increase and part of the contractionary net export effect described here may be offset.

TABLE 13-2	Fiscal Policy and the Net Export Effect

(1) Expansionary fiscal policy	(2) Contractionary fiscal policy
Problem: Recession, slow growth	Problem: Inflation
↓	↓
Expansionary fiscal policy	Contractionary fiscal policy
↓	↓
Higher domestic interest rate	Lower domestic interest rate
↓	↓
Increased foreign demand for dollars	Decreased foreign demand for dollars
↓	↓
Dollar appreciates	Dollar depreciates
↓	↓
Net exports decline (aggregate demand decreases, partially offsetting the expansionary fiscal policy)	Net exports increase (aggregate demand increases, partially offsetting the contractionary fiscal policy)

However, most economists believe that fiscal policy remains an important, useful policy lever in the government's macroeconomic toolkit. The current popular view is that fiscal policy can help push the economy in a particular direction but cannot fine-tune it to a precise macroeconomic outcome. Mainstream economists generally agree that monetary policy is the best month-to-month stabilization tool for the Canadian economy. If monetary policy is doing its job, the government should maintain a relatively neutral fiscal policy, with a cyclically adjusted budget deficit or surplus of no more than 2 percent of potential GDP. It should hold major discretionary fiscal policy in reserve to help counter situations where recession threatens to be deep and long-lasting or where a substantial reduction in aggregate demand might help to eliminate a large inflationary gap and aid the Bank of Canada in its efforts to quell the major bout of inflation caused by that large inflationary gap.

Finally, economists agree that any proposed fiscal policy should be evaluated for its potential positive and negative impacts on long-run productivity growth. The short-run policy tools used for conducting active fiscal policy often have long-run impacts. Countercyclical fiscal policy should be shaped to strengthen, or at least not impede, the growth of long-run aggregate supply (shown as a rightward shift of the long-run aggregate supply curve in Figure 13-5). For example, a tax cut might be structured to enhance work effort, strengthen investment, and encourage innovation. Alternatively, an increase in government spending might center on preplanned projects for public capital (highways, mass transit, ports, airports), which are complementary to private investment and thus support long-term economic growth.

QUICK REVIEW 13.3

- Time lags, political problems, expectations, and provincial and municipal finance complicate fiscal policy.
- The crowding-out effect indicates that an expansionary fiscal policy may increase the interest rate and reduce investment spending.
- Fiscal policy may be weakened by the net export effect, which works through changes in (a) the interest rate, (b) exchange rates, and (c) exports and imports.

13.6 / Deficits, Surpluses, and the Federal Debt

LO13.6 Discuss the size, composition, and consequences of the Canadian public debt.

A *budget deficit* is the amount by which a government's expenditures exceed its revenues during a particular year. For example, during 1995–1996, the federal government spent $161 billion and its receipts were only $131 billion, resulting in a $30 billion deficit. In contrast, a *budget surplus* is the amount by which government revenues exceed government expenditures in a given year. For example, federal government revenues of $237 billion in 2011 exceeded expenditures of $270 billion, resulting in a $33 billion budget deficit.

The national or **public debt** is the total accumulation of the federal government's total deficits and surpluses that have occurred through time. It represents the total amount of money owed by the federal government to holders of Canadian government securities. In 2014 the net federal debt was $682 billion, or approximately 35 percent of GDP. These deficits have emerged mainly because of war financing, recessions, and fiscal policy.

- *Debt and GDP* A simple statement of the absolute size of the debt ignores the fact that the wealth and productive ability of our economy have also increased tremendously. A wealthy, highly productive nation can more easily incur and carry a large public debt than can a poor nation. It is more meaningful to measure changes in the public debt in relation to the economy's GDP. Figure 13-6 shows the size of the federal government public debt in relation to Canada's GDP. Notice that this percentage surged to

FIGURE 13-6   **The Net Federal Debt as a Percentage of GDP**

The net federal public debt as a percentage of GDP fell from the mid-1990s until 2008, and has since remained steady.

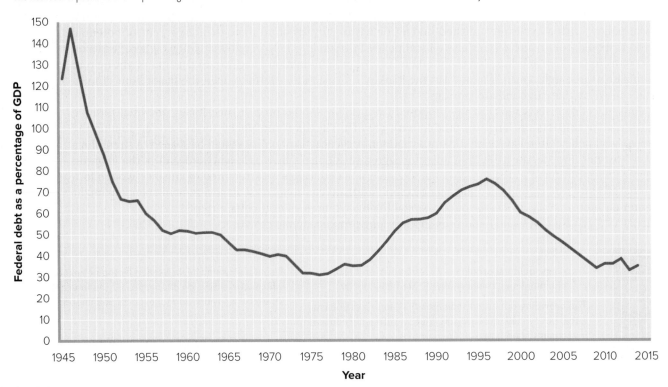

Source: Statistics Canada, CANSIM 380-0039, 380-0016, 385-0010 and Department of Finance http://www.fin.gc.ca/afr-rfa/2014/report-rapport-eng.asp#toc5, accessed May 27, 2015.

13.2 GLOBAL PERSPECTIVE

Publicly Held Debt: International Comparisons

Canada has one of the lowest public debts as a percentage of GDP among advanced industrial nations.

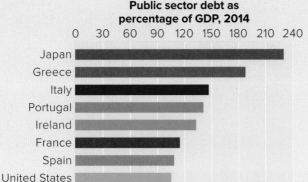

Public sector debt as percentage of GDP, 2014

Source: Based on data from OECD (2014), "Government debt," *Economics: Key Tables from OECD*, No. 21. Accessed on November 18, 2014, http://dx.doi.org/10.1787/gov-debt-table-2014-1-en

almost 150 percent right after World War II, receded to a low of just over 30 percent in the mid-1970s, and rose back up to 75 percent by the mid-1990s. The federal government public debt as a percentage of GDP took a fairly precipitous drop from the mid 1990s and 2008, but began to rise slightly in 2009 as the federal government ran deficits to fight the onset of the Great Recession.

- **International Comparisons** It is not uncommon for countries to have sizeable public debts. As shown in Global Perspective 13.2, the public debt as a percentage of real GDP in Canada is actually one of the lowest relative to such debt percentages in other advanced industrial nations.

- **Interest Charges** Many economists conclude that the primary burden of the debt is the annual interest charge accruing as a result. Interest payments increased significantly as a proportion of GDP beginning in the early 1980s, but have recently declined to historically low levels. This ratio reflects the level of taxation (the average tax rate) required to service the public debt. In 2014, government had to collect taxes equal to 1.4 percent of GDP to pay interest on its debt.

- **Ownership** Figure 13-7 shows that about 9 percent of the total public debt is held by the Bank of Canada, and 66 percent by private individuals, chartered banks, insurance companies, and corporations in Canada. About 25 percent of the total debt is held by foreigners. The vast majority of the gross federal debt is thus held internally, not externally.

Unfounded Concerns

You may wonder whether a large public debt might bankrupt Canada or at least place a burden on our children and grandchildren. Fortunately, these are largely unfounded concerns.

BANKRUPTCY

The public debt does not threaten to bankrupt the federal government, leaving it unable to meet its financial obligations, for two main reasons: refinancing and taxation.

| FIGURE 13-7 | Ownership of Canada's Net Public Debt in 2014 |

About 66 percent of the federal government debt is held by the public and the chartered banks. The Bank of Canada holds 9 percent of the federal debt, while 25 percent of it is foreign owned.

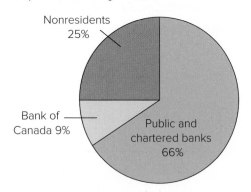

Nonresidents 25%

Bank of Canada 9%

Public and chartered banks 66%

Total debt = $682 billion

Source: Adapted from Bank of Canada, Banking and Financial Statistics, April 2015, http://www.bankofcanada.ca/wp-content/uploads/2015/04/bfs_april15.pdf, accessed May 27, 2015, , and the Department of Finance, Fiscal Reference Tables http://www.fin.gc.ca/afr-rfa/2014/report-rapport-eng.asp#toc5, accessed May 27, 2015.

- *Refinancing* As long as the Canadian public debt is viewed by lenders as manageable and sustainable, the public debt is easily refinanced. As portions of the debt come due each month, the government in Ottawa does not cut expenditures or raise taxes to provide the funds required for its operation. Rather, the federal government refinances the debt by selling new bonds and using the proceeds to pay off holders of the maturing bonds. The new bonds are in strong demand because lenders (purchasers of government bonds) can obtain a market-determined interest return with little risk of default by the federal government. Of course, refinancing could become an issue with a high enough debt-to-GDP ratio. Some countries, such as Greece, have run into this problem. High and rising ratios in Canada might raise fears that the Canadian government might be unable to pay back loans as they come due. But, with the present relatively low Canadian debt-to-GDP ratio and the prospects of long-term economic growth, this is not a concern for Canada.

- *Taxation* The federal government has the authority to levy and collect taxes. Parliament can impose a tax increase to pay interest and principal on the public debt. Financially distressed private households and corporations cannot resolve their financial difficulties by taxing the public. If their income or sales

CONSIDER THIS   The European Sovereign Debt Crisis

In early 2010 it became painfully clear that the global financial crisis had taken a huge toll on government finances in many countries, notably in Europe. Greece, in particular, found itself in dire straits as its deficit in 2009 reached 13 percent of GDP, an unsustainable level that would soon bankrupt the country. In February 2010 the Greek government announced an austerity plan to deal with the sovereign debt crisis. Ireland and Portugal also had unsustainable deficits and accumulated sovereign debt levels.

Surprisingly, in mid 2011 financial markets turned their attention to the sovereign debts of Italy and Spain, much larger and more robust economies. Throughout 2011 the ratings agency downgraded the sovereign debts of many European nations, including France. In the ensuing panic, interest rates on government borrowing skyrocketed. For example, the Italian government was paying only a small premium of just over 1 percent above the German government bonds at the beginning of 2011, but this rate shot up to over 7 percent by November 2011, a level many economists thought unsustainable in the long run.

Interest rates on government bonds were on their way down in by mid 2015 as governments scrambled to get their fiscal houses in order.

revenues fall short of their expenses, they can, indeed, go bankrupt. But the federal government has the option to impose new taxes or increase existing tax rates if necessary to finance its debt. Such tax hikes may be politically unpopular and may weaken incentives to work and invest, but they *are* a means of raising funds to finance the debt.

BURDENING FUTURE GENERATIONS

In 2014, public debt per capita was $19,198. Was each child born in 2014 handed a $19,198 bill from Ottawa? Not really. The public debt does not impose as much of a debt on future generations as is generally thought.

Canada owes a substantial portion of the public debt to itself. Over 80 percent of Government of Canada bonds are held by citizens and institutions–banks, businesses, insurance companies, government agencies, and pensions and trust funds–within Canada. While the public debt is a liability to Canadians (as taxpayers), part of the same debt is simultaneously an asset to Canadians (as bondholders).

To eliminate the Canadian-owned part of the public debt would require a gigantic transfer payment from Canadians to Canadians. Taxpayers would pay higher taxes and the government, in turn, would pay out those tax revenues to those same taxpaying individuals. Only the repayment of the approximately 20 percent of the public debt owned by foreigners would have a negative impact on Canadian purchasing power.

Substantive Issues

Although the above issues are of no real concern, there are a number of substantive issues relating to the public debt. Economists assign them varying degrees of importance.

INCOME DISTRIBUTION

The distribution of government securities ownership is uneven. Some people own much more than their $19,198 per capita share of government securities; others own less or none at all. The ownership of the public debt is concentrated among wealthier groups. Because the federal tax system is only mildly progressive, payment of interest on the public debt probably increases income inequality. If greater income equality is one of our social goals, then this redistributive effect is undesirable.

INCENTIVES

The current federal public debt necessitates an annual interest payment of almost $28 billion. This annual interest charge must be paid out of tax revenues. Higher taxes may dampen incentives to bear risk, to innovate, to invest, and to work. So, indirectly, the existence of a large debt may impair economic growth and therefore impose a burden of reduced output (and income) on future generations.

FOREIGN-OWNED PUBLIC DEBT

The 25 percent of Canada's debt held by citizens and institutions of foreign countries is an economic burden to Canadians. Because we do not owe that portion of the debt "to ourselves," the payment of interest and principal on this **external public debt** enables foreigners to buy some of our output. In return for the benefits derived from the borrowed funds, Canada transfers goods and services to foreign lenders. Of course, Canadians also own debt issued by foreign governments, so payment on principal and interest by these governments transfers some of their goods and services to Canadians.

CROWDING OUT REVISITED

A potentially more serious problem is the financing (and continual refinancing) of a large public debt, which can transfer a real economic burden to future generations by passing on a smaller stock of capital goods. This possibility involves the crowding-out effect: the idea that deficit financing will increase interest rates and thereby reduce private investment spending. As we mentioned earlier, if public borrowing happened only during recessions, crowding out would not likely be much of a problem. Because private investment demand tends to be low during recessions, any increase in interest rates caused by public borrowing will, at most, cause a small reduction in investment spending.

In contrast, the need to continuously finance a large public debt may be more troublesome. At times, that financing requires borrowing large amounts of money when the economy is near or at its full-employment output. This is usually when private investment demand is very high. In such situations, any increase in interest rates caused by the borrowing necessary to refinance the debt may result in a substantial decline in investment spending. If the amount of current investment crowded out is extensive, future generations will inherit an economy with a smaller production capacity and, other things equal, a lower standard of living.

A Graphical Look at Crowding Out   We know from Chapter 12 that the amount of investment spending is inversely related to the real interest rate. When graphed, that relationship is shown as a downsloping investment demand curve, such as either ID_1 or ID_2 in Figure 13-8. Let's first consider curve ID_1 (ignore curve ID_2 for now).

Suppose government borrowing increases the real interest rate from 6 percent to 10 percent. Investment spending will then fall from $25 billion to $15 billion, as shown by the economy's move from a to b. That is, the financing of the debt will compete with the financing of private investment projects and crowd out $10 billion of private investment. So the stock of private capital handed down to future generations will be $10 billion less than it would have been without the need to finance the public debt.

Public Investments and Public–Private Complementarities   But even with crowding out, two factors could partly or fully offset the net economic burden shifted to future generations. First, just as private expenditures may involve either consumption or investment, so it is with public goods. Part of the government spending enabled by the public debt is for public investment outlays (for example, highways, mass transit systems, and electric power facilities) and human capital (for example, investments in education, job training, and health). Like private expenditures on machinery and equipment, those **public investments** increase the economy's future production capacity. Because of the financing through debt, the stock of public capital passed on to future generations may be higher than otherwise. That greater stock of public capital may offset the diminished stock of private capital resulting from the crowding-out effect, leaving overall production capacity unimpaired.

FIGURE 13-8   **The Investment Demand Curve and the Crowding-Out Effect**

If the investment demand curve (ID_1) is fixed, the increase in the interest rate from 6 percent to 10 percent caused by financing a large public debt will move the economy from a to b and crowd out $10 billion of private investment and decrease the size of the capital stock inherited by future generations. However, if the government spending enabled by the debt improves the profit expectations of businesses, the private investment demand curve will shift rightward, as from ID_1 to ID_2. That shift may offset the crowding-out effect wholly or in part. In this case, it moves the economy from a to c.

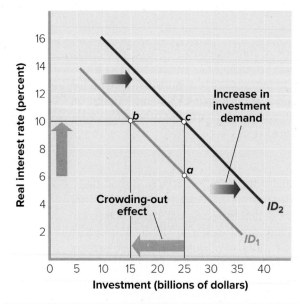

So-called public-private complementarities are a second factor that could reduce the crowding-out effect. Some public and private investments are complementary. Thus, the public investment financed through the debt could spur some private-sector investment by increasing its expected rate of return. For example, a federal building in a city may encourage private investment in the form of nearby office buildings, shops, and restaurants. Through its complementary effect, the spending on public capital may shift the private investment demand curve to the right, as from ID_1 to ID_2 in Figure 13-8. Even though the government borrowing boosts the interest rate from 6 percent to 10 percent, total private investment need not fall. In the case shown as the move from a to c in Figure 13-8, it remains at $25 billion.

QUICK REVIEW 13.4

- The Canadian federal public debt is essentially the total accumulation of federal budget deficits minus surpluses over time; about 25 percent of the public debt is held by foreigners.

- As a percentage of GDP, the debt is lower today than it was in the mid-1990s and is in the low range of such debts among major industrial nations.

- There is no danger of the federal government going bankrupt because it need only refinance (not retire) the public debt and can raise revenues, if needed, through higher taxes.

- The borrowing and interest payments associated with the public debt may (a) increase income inequality, (b) require higher taxes, which may dampen incentives, and (c) impede the growth of the nation's stock of capital through crowding out of private investment.

The LAST WORD — Federal and Provincial per Capita Net Debt, 2014

Significant variance in per capita net debt exists among Canadian provinces. The federal government has a per capita debt of about $19,198. Quebec, at more than $22,000, has the highest provincial per capita net debt among the provinces. Not far behind are Ontario, and Newfoundland and Labrador. The provinces with the least per capita debt are to be found in Western Canada. Saskatchewan's per capita debt, at $3,745, is about 17 percent that of Quebec. Alberta has the distinction of being the only province with a per capita credit of $$2,348! This distinction is attributable to the revenues the Alberta government gets from its oil and gas sector, which also give it the luxury of not having to charge a provincial sales tax.

Canada	$ 19,198
Quebec	22.150
Newfoundland and Labrador	17,112
Ontario	19,533
Nova Scotia	15,654
New Brunswick	15,439
Prince Edward Island	14,520
Manitoba	13,485
British Columbia	8,373
Saskatchewan	3,745
Alberta	−2,348

Source: Calculated from population figures from Statistics Canada and net debt from the Department of Finance, *Fiscal Reference Tables,* 2014. The Department of Finance website, http://www.fin.gc.ca/frt-trf/2014/frt-trf14-eng.pdf, accessed March 8, 2015. Statistics Canada website, http://www.statcan.gc.ca/tables-tableaux/sum-som/l01/cst01/demo02a-eng.htm, accessed March 8, 2015.

Question

Which provinces have the highest per capita debt. Which have the lowest.?

Chapter Summary

LO13.1   IDENTIFY AND EXPLAIN THE PURPOSES, TOOLS, AND LIMITATIONS OF FISCAL POLICY.

- Fiscal policy consists of deliberate changes in government spending, taxes, or some combination of both to promote full employment, price-level stability, and economic growth. Fiscal policy requires increases in government spending, decreases in taxes, or both—a budget deficit—to increase aggregate demand and push an economy from a recession. Decreases in government spending, increases in taxes, or both—a budget surplus—are appropriate fiscal policy for decreasing aggregate demand to try to slow or halt demand–pull inflation.

LO13.2   EXPLAIN THE ROLE OF BUILT-IN STABILIZERS IN MODERATING BUSINESS CYCLES.

- Built-in stability arises from net tax revenues, which vary directly with the level of GDP. During recession, the federal budget automatically moves toward a stabilizing deficit; during expansion, the budget automatically moves toward an anti-inflationary surplus. Built-in stability lessens, but does not fully correct, undesired changes in the real GDP.

LO13.3   DESCRIBE HOW THE CYCLICALLY ADJUSTED BUDGET REVEALS THE STATUS OF CANADIAN FISCAL POLICY.

- Actual federal budget deficits can go up or down because of changes in GDP, changes in fiscal policy, or both. Deficits caused by changes in GDP are called cyclical deficits. The cyclically adjusted budget removes cyclical deficits from the budget and therefore measures the budget deficit or surplus (if either) that would occur if the economy operated at its full-employment output throughout the year. Changes in the cyclical-budget deficit or surplus are those that result from changes in the real GDP.

- Changes in the cyclically adjusted deficit or surplus provide meaningful information as to whether the government's fiscal policy is expansionary, neutral, or contractionary. Changes in the actual budget deficit or surplus do not, since such deficits or surpluses can include cyclical deficits or surplus.

LO13.4   SUMMARIZE RECENT CANADIAN FISCAL POLICY AND THE PROJECTIONS FOR CANADIAN FISCAL POLICY OVER THE NEXT FEW YEARS.

- The Canadian federal government had a budgetary surplus from 2000 to 2008. With the onset of the Great Recession it ran budgetary deficits in an effort to stimulate the economy. By mid 2015 the federal government had a small budgetary surplus as the Canadian economy finally seemed to recover from the deep recession that started in later 2008. The slowdown of the Canadian economy due to the fall in oil prices threatened to create a budgetary deficit by the end of 2015.

LO13.5   DISCUSS THE PROBLEMS THAT GOVERNMENTS MAY ENCOUNTER IN ENACTING AND APPLYING FISCAL POLICY.

- Certain problems complicate the enactment and implementation of fiscal policy. They include (a) timing problems associated with recognition, administrative, and operational lags; (b) the potential for misuse of fiscal policy for political rather than economic purposes; (c) the tendency for provincial and municipal finances to be procyclical; (d) potential ineffectiveness if households expect future policy reversals; (e) the possibility of fiscal policy crowding out private investment; and (f) complications relating to the effects of fiscal policy on exchange rates and net exports.

- Most economists believe that fiscal policy can help move the economy in a desired direction but cannot reliably be used to fine-tune the economy to a position of price stability and full employment. Nevertheless, fiscal policy is a valuable backup tool for aiding monetary policy in fighting significant recession or inflation.

LO13.6   DISCUSS THE SIZE, COMPOSITION, AND CONSEQUENCES OF THE CANADIAN PUBLIC DEBT.

- The public debt is the total accumulation of all past federal government deficits and surpluses. Foreigners hold 25 percent of the Canadian portion of the federal debt. In 2014, interest payments as a percentage of GDP amounted to about 1.4 percent.

- The concern that a large public debt may bankrupt the Canadian government is generally a baseless worry because (a) the debt need only be refinanced rather than repaid and (b) the federal government has the power to increase taxes to make interest payments on the debt.

- In general, the public debt is not a vehicle for shifting economic burdens to future generations. Canadians inherit not only most of the public debt (a liability) but also most of the Canadian securities (an asset) that finance the debt.

- More substantive problems associated with public debt include the following: (a) payment of interest on the debt may increase income inequality, (b) interest payments on the debt require higher taxes, which may impair incentives, (c) paying interest or principal on the portion of the debt held by foreigners means a transfer of real output abroad, and (d) government borrowing to refinance or pay interest on the debt may increase interest rates and crowd out private investment spending, leaving future generations with a smaller stock of capital than they would have otherwise.

- The increase in investment in public capital that may result from debt financing may partly or wholly offset the crowding-out effect of the public debt on private investment. Also, the added public investment may stimulate private investment, where the two are complements.

Terms and Concepts

fiscal policy	progressive tax system	crowding-out effect
expansionary fiscal policy	proportional tax system	net export effect
budget deficit	regressive tax system	public debt
contractionary fiscal policy	cyclically adjusted budget	external public debt
budget surplus	cyclical deficit	public investments
built-in stabilizer	political business cycle	

Discussion Questions

1. What are the government's fiscal policy options for an inflationary gap caused by demand–pull inflation? Use the aggregate demand–aggregate supply model to show the impact of these policies on the price level. Which of these fiscal options do you think a person who wants to preserve the size of government might favour? A person who thinks the public sector is too large? How does the ratchet effect affect anti-inflationary fiscal policy?   [LO13.1]

2. (For students assigned Chapter 11) Use the aggregate expenditures model to show how government fiscal policy could eliminate either a recessionary gap or an inflationary gap (Figure 11-7). Explain how equal increases in G and T could eliminate a recessionary gap and how equal decreases in G and T could eliminate an inflationary gap.   [LO13.1]

3. Some politicians have suggested that Canada enact a constitutional amendment requiring the federal government to balance its budget annually. Explain why such an amendment, if strictly enforced, would compel the government to enact a contractionary fiscal policy whenever the economy experienced a severe recession.   [LO13.1]

4. Explain how built-in (or automatic) stabilizers work. What are the differences between proportional, progressive, and regressive tax systems as they relate to an economy's built-in stability?   [LO13.2]

5. Define the cyclically adjusted budget, explain its significance, and state why it may differ from the actual budget. Suppose the full-employment, noninflationary level of real output is GDP_3 (not GDP_2) in the economy depicted in Figure 13-3. If the economy is operating at GDP_2 instead of GDP_3, what is the status of its cyclically adjusted budget? The status of its current fiscal policy? What change in fiscal policy would you recommend? How would you accomplish that in terms of the G and T lines in the figure?   [LO13.3]

6. Briefly state and evaluate the problems of time lags in enacting and applying fiscal policy. Explain the idea of a political business cycle. How might expectations of a near-term policy reversal weaken fiscal policy based on changes in tax rates? What is the crowding-out effect and why might it be relevant to fiscal policy? In view of your answers, explain the following statement: Although fiscal policy clearly is useful in combatting severe recession and demand–pull inflation, it is impossible to use fiscal policy to fine-tune the economy to the full-employment, noninflationary level of real GDP and keep the economy there indefinitely.   [LO13.5]

7. How do economists distinguish between the absolute and relative sizes of the public debt? Why is the distinction important? Distinguish between refinancing the debt and retiring the debt. How does an internally held public debt differ from an externally held public debt? Contrast the effects of retiring an internally held debt and retiring an externally held debt.   [LO13.6]

8. Are the following statements true or false? If false, explain why.   [LO13.6]

   a. The total public debt is more relevant to an economy than the public debt as a percentage of GDP.

   b. An internally held public debt is like a debt of the left hand owed to the right hand.

   c. The Bank of Canada and the public and chartered banks hold 75 percent of the public debt.

9. Why might economists be quite concerned if the annual interest payments on the Canadian public debt sharply increased as a percentage of GDP?   [LO13.6]

10. Trace the cause-and-effect chain through which financing and refinancing of the public debt might affect real interest rates, private investment, the stock of capital, and economic growth. How might investment in public capital and complementarities between public capital and private capital alter the outcome of the cause–effect chain?   [LO13.6]

Review Questions

1. Which of the following would help a government reduce an inflationary output gap?   [LO13.1]

    a. Raising taxes

    b. Lowering taxes

    c. Increasing government spending

    d. Decreasing government spending

2. The economy is in a recession. A parliamentarian suggests increasing spending to stimulate aggregate demand but also at the same time raising taxes to pay for the increased spending. Her suggestion to combine higher government expenditures with higher taxes is   [LO13.1]

    a. The worst possible combination of tax and expenditure changes

    b. The best possible combination of tax and expenditure changes

    c. A mediocre and contradictory combination of tax and expenditure changes

    d. None of the above

3. During the recession of 2008–2009, the federal government's tax collections fell from about $245 billion down to about $222 billion while GDP declined by about 3 percent. Does the Canadian tax system appear to have built- in stabilizers?   [LO13.2]

    a. Yes

    b. No

4. Last year, while an economy was in a recession, government spending was $595 billion and government revenue was $505 billion. Economists estimate that if the economy had been at its full-employment level of GDP last year, government spending would have been $555 billion and government revenue would have been $550 billion. Which of the following statements about this government's fiscal situation is true?   [LO13.3]

    a. The government has a non–cyclically adjusted budget deficit of $595 billion.

    b. The government has a non–cyclically adjusted budget deficit of $90 billion.

    c. The government has a non–cyclically adjusted budget surplus of $90 billion.

    d. The government has a cyclically adjusted budget deficit of $555 billion.

    e. The government has a cyclically adjusted budget deficit of $5 billion.

    f. The government has a cyclically adjusted budget surplus of $5 billion.

5. Label each of the following scenarios in which there are problems enacting and applying fiscal policy as being an example of either recognition lag, administrative lag, or operational lag. [LO13.5]

    a. To fight a recession, Parliament has passed a bill to increase infrastructure spending—but the legally required environmental-impact statement for each new project will take at least two years to complete before any building can begin.

    b. Distracted by a conflict that is going badly, inflation reaches 8 percent before politicians take notice.

    c. A sudden recession is recognized by politicians, but it takes many months of political deal making before a stimulus bill is finally approved.

    d. To fight a recession, the prime minister orders federal agencies to get rid of petty regulations that burden private businesses—but the federal agencies begin by spending a year developing a set of regulations on how to remove petty regulations.

6. In January, the interest rate is 5 percent and firms borrow $50 billion per month for investment projects. In February, the federal government doubles its monthly borrowing from $25 billion to $50 billion. That drives the interest rate up to 7 percent. As a result, firms cut back their borrowing to only $30 billion per month. Which of the following is true?   [LO13.6]

    a. There is no crowding-out effect because the government's increase in borrowing exceeds firms' decrease in borrowing.

    b. There is a crowding-out effect of $20 billion.

    c. There is no crowding-out effect because both the government and firms are still borrowing a lot.

    d. There is a crowding-out effect of $25 billion.

Problems

1. Assume that a hypothetical economy with an MPC of 0.8 is experiencing severe recession. By how much would government spending have to rise to shift the aggregate demand curve rightward by $25 billion? How large a tax cut would be needed to achieve the same increase in aggregate demand? Determine one possible combination of government spending increases and tax decreases that would accomplish the same goal without changing the amount of outstanding debt.   [LO13.1]

2. Refer to the table in Figure 12-7 in Chapter 12. Suppose that aggregate demand increases such that the amount of real output demanded rises by $7 billion at each price level. By what percent will the price level increase? Will this inflation be demand–pull inflation or will it be cost–push inflation? If potential real GDP (= full-employment GDP) is $510 billion, what will be the size of the positive GDP after the change in aggregate demand? If government wants to use fiscal policy to counter the resulting inflation without changing tax rates, would it increase government spending or decrease it?   [LO13.1]

3. (For students assigned Chapter 11) Assume that the consumption schedule, without taxes, for an economy is as shown below: [LO13.2]

GDP (billions)	Consumption (billions)
$100	$120
200	200
300	280
400	360
500	440
600	520
700	600

a. Graph this consumption schedule. What is the size of the MPC?

b. Assume a lump-sum (regressive) tax is imposed such that the government collects $10 billion in taxes at all levels of GDP. Calculate the tax rate at each level of GDP. Graph the resulting consumption schedule and compare the MPC and the multiplier with that of the pretax consumption schedule.

c. Now suppose a proportional tax with a 10 percent tax rate is imposed instead of the regressive tax. Calculate the new consumption schedule, graph it, and note the MPC and the multiplier.

d. Finally, impose a progressive tax such that the tax rate is zero percent when GDP is $100, 5 percent at $200,

10 percent at $300, 15 percent at $400, and so forth. Determine and graph the new consumption schedule, noting the effect of this tax on the MPC and the multiplier.

e. Use a graph similar to Figure 13-3 to show why proportional and progressive taxes contribute to greater economic stability, while a regressive tax does not.

4. Refer to the accompanying table for Waxwania. What is the marginal tax rate in Waxwania? The average tax rate? Which of the following describes the tax system: proportional, progressive, or regressive?   [LO13.2]

Government expenditures, G	Tax revenues, T	Real GDP
$160	$100	$500
160	120	600
160	140	700
160	160	800
160	180	900

5. Refer to the table for Waxwania in Problem 4. Suppose Waxwania is producing $600 of real GDP, whereas the potential real GDP (= full-employment real GDP) is $700. How large is its budget deficit? Its cyclically adjusted budget deficit? Its cyclically adjusted budget deficit as a percentage of potential real GDP? Is Waxwania's fiscal policy expansionary?   [LO13.3]

6. Suppose that a country has no public debt in year 1, but experiences a budget deficit of $40 billion in year 2, a budget deficit of $20 billion in year 3, a budget surplus of $10 billion in year 3, and a budget deficit of $2 billion in year 4. What is the absolute size of its public debt in year 4? If its real GDP in year 4 is $104 billion, what is this country's public debt as a percentage of real GDP in year 4?   [LO13.6]

7. Suppose that the investment demand curve in a certain economy is such that investment declines by $100 billion for every 1 percentage point increase in the real interest rate. Also, suppose that the investment demand curve shifts rightward by $150 billion at each real interest rate for every 1 percentage point increase in the expected rate of return from investment. If stimulus spending (an expansionary fiscal policy) by government increases the real interest rate by 2 percentage points, but also raises the expected rate of return on investment by 1 percentage point, how much investment, if any, will be crowded out?   [LO13.6]

PART 5 | MONEY, BANKING, AND MONETARY POLICY

CHAPTER 14

Money, Banking, and Money Creation

LEARNING OBJECTIVES

LO14.1	Identify and explain the functions of money.
LO14.2	List and describe the components of the supply of money in Canada.
LO14.3	Describe what backs Canada's money supply, making us willing to accept it as payment.
LO14.4	Discuss the structure of the Canadian financial system.
LO14.5	Identify and explain the main factors that contributed to the U.S. financial crisis of 2007–2008.
LO14.6	Discuss why the Canadian banking system is called a *fractional reserve* system.
LO14.7	Explain the basics of a bank's balance sheet and the distinction between a bank's actual reserves and its desired reserves.
LO14.8	Describe how a chartered bank can create money.
LO14.9	Describe the multiple-deposit expansion of the entire chartered banking system.
LO14.10	Define the monetary multiplier, explain how to calculate it, and demonstrate its relevance.

Money is a fascinating aspect of the economy.

Money bewitches people. They fret for it and they sweat for it. They devise most ingenious ways to get it, and most ingenious ways to get rid of it. Money is the only commodity that is good for nothing but to be gotten rid of. It will not feed you, clothe you, shelter you, or amuse you unless you spend it or invest it.

It imparts value only in parting. People will do almost anything for money, and money will do almost anything for people. Money is a captivating, circulating, masquerading puzzle.[1]

In this chapter and the one that follows, we want to unmask the crucial role of money and the monetary system of the economy. When the monetary system is working properly, it provides the lifeblood of the circular flows of income and expenditure. A well-operating monetary system helps the economy achieve both full employment and the efficient use of resources. A malfunctioning monetary system distorts the allocation of resources and creates severe fluctuations in the economy's levels of output, employment, and prices.

In the first half of this chapter we will delve into the nature of money and its vital role in a modern economy. In the second half we investigate how money is created and how the Bank of Canada regulates the economy's money supply. We will see that Canada's central bank relies primarily on chartered banks to help expand the money supply to accommodate a growing economy.

14.1 / The Functions of Money

LO14.1 Identify and explain the functions of money.

Just what is money? There is an old saying that "Money *is* what money *does*." In a general sense, anything that performs the functions of money *is* money. Here are those functions.

- *Medium of Exchange* First and foremost, money is a **medium of exchange** that is used to buy and sell goods and services. A bakery worker in Montreal does not want to be paid 200 bagels per week. Nor does the bakery owner want to accept, say, halibut in exchange for bagels. Money, however, is readily acceptable as payment. As we saw in Chapter 2, money is a social invention with which resource suppliers and producers can be paid and that can be used to buy any of the full range of items available in the marketplace. As a medium of exchange, money allows society to escape the complications of barter. And, because it provides a convenient means of exchanging goods, money enables society to gain the advantages of geographic and human specialization.

- *Measure of Value* Money is also a measure of value, or, more formally, a **unit of account**. A monetary unit—the dollar, in Canada—is a yardstick for measuring the relative worth of a wide variety of goods, services, and resources. Just as we measure distance in kilometres, we measure the value of goods and services in dollars.

With money as an acceptable unit of account, the price of each item need be stated only in terms of the monetary unit. We need not state the price of cows in terms of corn, crayons, and computers. Money allows buyers and sellers to easily compare the prices of various goods, services, and resources. It also permits us to define debt obligations, determine taxes owed, and calculate the nation's GDP.

- *Store of Value* Money also serves as a **store of value** that makes it possible to acquire goods and services at a future date. People normally do not spend all their income on the day they receive it. To buy things later, they store (save) some of their wealth as money. The money you place in a safe or a chequing account will still be available to you a few weeks or months from now. When inflation is nonexistent or mild, holding money is a relatively risk-free way to preserve your wealth for later use.

People can, of course, choose to hold some or all of their wealth in a wide variety of assets besides money—real estate, stocks, bonds, precious metals such as gold, and even collectible items like fine art or comic books. But a key advantage that money has over all other assets is that it has the most *liquidity*, or spendability.

An asset's **liquidity** is the ease with which it can be converted quickly into the most widely accepted and easily spent form of money—cash—with little or no loss of purchasing power. The more liquid an asset is, the more quickly it can be converted into cash and used for purchases of goods and services or other assets.

---

[1] "Creeping Inflation," *Business Review*, August 1957, p. 3. Federal Reserve Bank of Philadelphia. Used with permission.

Levels of liquidity vary radically. By definition, cash is perfectly liquid. By contrast, a house is highly illiquid for two reasons. First, it may take several months before a willing buyer can be found and a sale negotiated so that its value can be converted into cash. Second, there is a loss of purchasing power when the house is sold because numerous fees have to be paid to real estate agents and other individuals to complete the sale.

Money is a medium of exchange that is used to buy and sell goods and services.

As we are about to discuss, our economy uses several different types of money including cash, coins, chequing account deposits, savings account deposits, and even more exotic things like deposits to money market mutual funds. As we describe the various forms of money in detail, take the time to compare their relative levels of liquidity—both with each other and as compared to other assets like stocks, bonds, and real estate. Cash is perfectly liquid. Other forms of money are highly liquid, but less liquid than cash.

14.2 / The Components of the Money Supply

LO14.2 List and describe the components of the supply of money in Canada.

Money is a *stock* of some item or group of items (unlike income, for example, which is a *flow*). Societies have used many items as money, including whales' teeth, circular stones, elephant-tail bristles, gold coins, furs, cigarettes, playing cards, and pieces of paper. Anything that is widely accepted as a medium of exchange can serve as money. In Canada, currency is not the only form of money. As you will see, certain debts of government and financial institutions are also used as money.

Money Definition *M*1+

The narrowest definition of the Canadian money supply is called **M1+**. It consists of two components: (a) currency (coins and paper money) outside chartered banks, and (b) all **demand deposits**, meaning *chequing account deposits* in chartered banks.

Coins and paper money are issued by the Bank of Canada, and demand deposits are provided by chartered banks. When you deposit money into your chequing account, the chartered bank into which you deposited it "owes" you the amount of money you deposited. Your deposit is a chartered bank's debt.

CURRENCY: COINS AND PAPER MONEY

From nickels to toonies, coins are the small change of our money supply. It is worth noting that the Bank of Canada announced in early 2012 that it would eliminate the penny from the Canadian coinage system. Coins constitute a small portion of *M*1+. All coins that are in circulation in Canada are **token money**. This means that the *intrinsic value*, the value of the metal contained in the coin itself, is less than the face value of the coin. This is to prevent people from melting down the coins for sale as a commodity, in this case, the metal. If our 25¢ pieces each contained 50¢ worth of silver bullion, it would be profitable to melt them and sell the metal (although it is illegal to do so), and 25¢ pieces would disappear from circulation. This happened with our then-silver coins in the late 1960s and early 1970s; an 80 percent silver, pre-1967 quarter is now worth several dollars. Token money is minted by the Royal Canadian Mint.

Paper money and coins constitute about 10 percent of the economy's narrowly defined (*M*1+) money supply. Paper currency is in the form of **Bank of Canada notes**—the paper notes you carry in your wallet—issued by our government-owned central bank. Every bill has "Bank of Canada" printed at the top of the face of the bill.

FIGURE 14-1   Components of Money Supply *M*1+, *M*2, *M*2+, and *M*2++ in Canada

*M*1+ is a narrow definition of the money supply that includes currency (in circulation) and demand deposits. *M*2, *M*2+, and *M*2++ are broader definitions that include *M*1+ along with several other account balances.

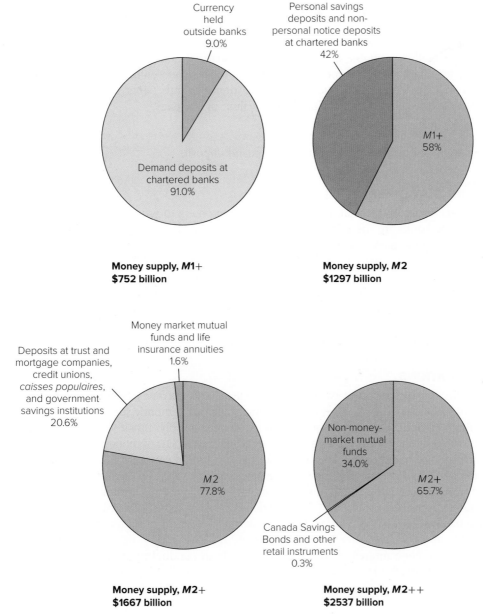

Source: Adapted from Bank of Canada, *Weekly Financial Statistics*, March 27, 2015; http://www.bankofcanada.ca/wp-content/uploads/2015/03/wfs270315.pdf, accessed June 29, 2015

Figure 14-1 shows that, together, coins and paper money amounted to $68 billion in December 2014, or 9 percent of *M*1+.

DEMAND DEPOSITS

The safety and convenience of cheques and debit cards have made them the largest component of the *M*1+ money supply. You would not think of stuffing $4896 in bills in an envelope and dropping it in a mailbox to pay a debt. But to write and mail a cheque or use a debit card for a large amount is commonplace. A cheque must be endorsed (signed on the reverse) by the person cashing it. Similarly, because a cheque requires endorsement, the theft or loss of a cheque is not nearly as unfortunate as losing an identical amount of currency. Finally, it is more convenient to write a cheque than to transport and count out a large sum of currency. For all these reasons, chequebook money, or demand deposits, is a large component of the stock of money. About 91 percent of $M1+$ is in the form of demand deposits, on which cheques can be drawn.

It might seem strange that chequing account balances are regarded as part of the money supply. But the reason is clear: Cheques are nothing more than a way to transfer the ownership of deposits in chartered banks and are generally acceptable as a medium of exchange. Although cheques are less generally accepted than currency for small purchases, for major purchases most sellers willingly accept cheques as payment. Moreover, people can convert chequable (demand) deposits into paper money and coins on demand; cheques drawn on those deposits are thus the equivalent of currency.

To summarize

Money, $M1+$ = currency in circulation + demand deposits

INSTITUTIONS THAT OFFER DEMAND DEPOSITS

In Canada, several types of financial institutions allow customers to write cheques on funds they have deposited. Chartered banks are the primary depository institutions. They accept the deposits of households and businesses, keep the money safe until it is demanded via cheques, and in the meantime use it to make available a wide variety of loans. Chartered bank loans provide short-term working capital to businesses, and finance consumer purchases of automobiles and other durable goods. There are six major chartered banks in Canada: the Royal Bank, the Canadian Imperial Bank of Commerce (CIBC), the Bank of Montreal, TD Canada Trust (TD), the Bank of Nova Scotia (Scotiabank), and the National Bank of Canada. Other institutions that offer chequing accounts in Canada are trust and mortgage loan companies, credit unions, and *caisses populaires* (the Quebec equivalent of credit unions).

TWO QUALIFICATIONS

We must qualify our discussion in two important ways. First, currency held by the Bank of Canada and chartered banks is excluded from $M1+$ and other measures of the money supply. A $5 bill in the wallet of, say, Emma Buck obviously constitutes just $5 of the money supply. But if we counted currency held by banks as part of the money supply, the same $5 would count for $10 of money supply when Emma deposited the currency into her chequing account in her bank. It would count for $5 of chequing deposit owned by Emma and also $5 of currency in the bank's cash drawer or vault. By excluding currency held by chartered banks when determining the total supply of money, we avoid this problem of double counting.

Also excluded from the money supply are any deposits of the federal government or the Bank of Canada that are held by chartered banks. This exclusion is designed to enable a better assessment of the amount of money available *to the private sector* for potential spending. The amount of money available to households and businesses is of keen interest to the Bank of Canada in conducting its monetary policy (a topic we cover in detail in Chapter 15).

Money Definition *M2*

A second and broader definition of money includes $M1+$ plus several near-monies. **Near-monies** are highly liquid financial assets that do not directly function as a medium of exchange but can be readily converted into currency or demand deposits. For example, you may withdraw currency from a *nonchequable savings account* at a chartered bank, or trust and mortgage loan company, credit union, or *caisse populaire*. Or you may request that funds be transferred from a nonchequable savings account to a chequable account.

You cannot withdraw funds quickly from *term deposits*, which become available to a depositor only at maturity. The difference between a savings account and a term account is that there is a penalty if you withdraw money from your term account. For example, a 90-day or 6-month term deposit is available

CONSIDER THIS   Are Credit Cards Money?

You may wonder if credit cards such as Visa and MasterCard are considered part of the money supply. After all, credit cards are a convenient means of making purchases. The answer is that a credit card is not really money but rather a means of obtaining a short-term loan from the chartered bank or other financial institution that issued the card.

What happens when you purchase an MP3 player with a credit card? The bank that issued the card will reimburse the seller by making a money payment and charging the establishment a transaction fee, and later you will reimburse the bank for its loan to you by also making a money payment. Credit cards are merely a means of deferring or postponing payment for a short period. You may have to pay an annual fee for the services provided, and, if you repay the bank in installments, you will pay a sizable interest charge on the loan. Your chequing account balance that you use to pay your credit card bill is money: the credit card is *not* money.*

Although credit cards are not money, they allow individuals and businesses to economize in the use of money. Credit cards enable people to hold less currency in their billfolds and, prior to payment due dates, fewer chequable deposits in their bank accounts. Credit cards also help people coordinate the timing of their expenditures with their receipt of income.

* A bank debit card, however, is very similar to a cheque in your chequebook. Unlike a purchase with a credit card, a purchase with a debit card creates a direct "debit" (a subtraction) from your chequing account balance. That chequing account balance is money—it is part of *M*1+.

when the designated period expires. Although term deposits are less liquid (spendable) than nonchequable savings accounts, they can be taken as currency or shifted into chequable accounts when they mature.

If these near-monies are added to *M*1+, we arrive at a broader definition of money. This is also set out in Table 14-1. Adding personal savings deposits and nonpersonal (business) notice deposits (requiring notice before withdrawal) to *M*1+ gives us **M2**, also shown in Figure 14-1. At the end of 2014, *M*2 in Canada was about $1297 billion.

Money Definition *M2+* and *M2++*

An even broader monetary aggregate is **M2+**, which is *M*2 plus deposits at credit unions, *caisses populaires*, trust companies, other nonbank deposit-taking institutions, and money market mutual funds. *M*2+ totalled about $1667 billion in December 2014.

Note the following about non-chartered banks and other financial institutions. Credit unions, *caisses populaires*, and trust companies gather the savings of households and businesses that are then used to finance housing mortgages and provide other loans. *Credit unions* accept deposits from, and lend to, "members"–usually a group of individuals who work for the same company or live in the same area. There are now some 450 credit unions of various sizes operating under the auspices of Credit Union Central of Canada. *Caisses populaires* can be found in Manitoba, Ontario, Quebec, and New Brunswick. The largest in Canada are those associated with the Caisses Desjardins. *Trust companies* are rapidly dwindling in number in Canada as they merge with chartered banks. For example, some years ago TD Bank merged with Canada Trust, to transform itself into TD Canada Trust.

Finally, the Bank of Canada's broadest monetary aggregate is **M2++**, which consists of *M*2+ plus Canada Savings Bonds and non-money-market mutual funds. At the end of 2014, *M*2++ totalled more than $2.5 trillion, as shown in Table 14-1.

Which definition of money shall we use? The simple *M*1+ includes only items *directly* and *immediately* usable as a medium of exchange. For this reason it is an oft-cited statistic in discussions of the money supply. However, for some purposes economists prefer the broader *M*2, *M*2+, or *M*2++ definitions.

TABLE 14-1	Money in Canada,* December 2014

Money	Billions of dollars
Currency held outside banks	$ 68
+ Demand deposits at chartered banks held by individuals and businesses	684
= *M*1+	$ 752
+ Personal savings deposits and nonpersonal notice deposits at chartered banks	545
= *M*2	$ 1297
+ Deposits at trust and mortgage companies, credit unions, *caisses populaires*, and government savings institutions	347
+ Money market mutual funds and life insurance annuities	23
= *M*2+	$ 1667
+ Canada Savings Bonds and other retail instruments	7
+ Non-money-market mutual funds	863
= *M*2++	$2537

* Seasonally adjusted average monthly data

Source: Adapted from Bank of Canada, *Weekly Financial Statistics*, March 27, 2015; http://www.bankofcanada.ca/wp-content/uploads/2015/03/wfs270315.pdf, accessed June 29, 2015

We will use the narrow *M*1 definition of money in our discussion and analysis, unless stated otherwise. The important principles that apply to *M*1 are also applicable to *M*2, *M*2+, and *M*2++, because *M*1 is a base component of these broader measures.

14.3 What Backs the Money Supply?

LO14.3 Describe what backs Canada's money supply, making us willing to accept it as payment.

The money supply in Canada essentially is backed (guaranteed) by government's ability to keep the value of money relatively stable. Nothing more!

Money as Debt

The major components of the money supply—paper money and demand deposits—are debts, or promises to pay. In Canada, paper money is the circulating debt of the Bank of Canada. Demand deposits are the debts of chartered banks.

Paper currency and demand deposits have no intrinsic value. A $5 bill is just an inscribed piece of paper. A demand deposit is merely a bookkeeping entry. And coins, we know, have less intrinsic value than their face value. Nor will government redeem the paper money you hold for anything tangible, such as gold.

To many people, the fact that the government does not back the currency with anything tangible seems implausible and insecure. But the decision not to back the currency with anything tangible was made for a very good reason. If the government backed the currency with something tangible like gold, then the supply of money would vary with the amount of gold available. By not backing the currency, the government avoids this constraint and indeed receives a key freedom—the ability to provide as much or as little money as needed to maintain the value of money and to best suit the economic needs of the country. In effect, by choosing not to back the currency, the government has chosen to give itself the ability to freely manage the nation's money supply. Its monetary authorities attempt to provide the amount of money needed for the particular volume of business activity that will promote full employment, price-level stability, and economic growth.

Most economists agree that managing the money supply is more sensible than linking it to gold or to some other commodity whose supply might change arbitrarily and capriciously. For instance, if we used gold to back the money supply so that gold was redeemable for money and vice versa, then a large increase in the nation's gold stock as the result of a new gold discovery might increase the money supply too rapidly and thereby trigger rapid inflation. Or a long-lasting decline in gold production might reduce the money supply to the point where recession and unemployment resulted.

In short, people cannot convert paper money into a fixed amount of gold or any other precious commodity. Money is exchangeable only for paper money. If you ask the Bank of Canada to redeem $5 of your paper money, it will swap one paper $5 bill for another bearing a different serial number. That is all you can get. Similarly, cheque money cannot be redeemed for gold but only for paper money—which, as we have just seen, the government will not redeem for anything tangible.

Value of Money

So why are currency and demand deposits money, whereas, say, "money" from a Monopoly game is not? What gives a $20 bill or a $100 chequing account entry its value? The answer to these questions has three parts.

 MONEY AND INFLATION

- *Acceptability* Currency and demand deposits are money because people accept them as money. By virtue of longstanding business practice, currency and demand deposits perform the basic function of money: they are acceptable as a medium of exchange. We accept paper money in exchange because we are confident it will be exchangeable for real goods, services, and resources when we spend it.

- *Legal Tender* Our confidence in the acceptability of paper money is strengthened because government has designated currency as **legal tender**. Specifically, each bill contains the statement "This note is legal tender." That means that paper currency must be accepted in payment of a debt that was contracted in dollars. (But private firms and government are not mandated to accept cash. It is not illegal for them to specify payment in noncash forms such as cheques, cashier's cheques, money orders, or credit cards.) The paper money in our economy is fiat money; it is money because the government has declared it so, not because it can be redeemed for precious metal.

The general acceptance of paper currency in exchange is more important than the government's decree that money is legal tender, however. The government has never decreed cheques to be legal tender, and yet they serve as such in many of the economy's exchanges of goods, services, and resources.

- *Relative Scarcity* The value of money, like the economic value of anything else, depends on its supply and demand. Money derives its value from its scarcity relative to its utility (its want-satisfying power). The utility of money lies in its capacity to be exchanged for goods and services, now or in the future. The economy's demand for money thus depends on the total dollar volume of transactions in any period plus the amount of money individuals and businesses want to hold for future transactions. With a reasonably constant demand for money, the supply of money provided by the monetary authorities will determine the value or "purchasing power" of the monetary unit (dollar, yen, peso, or whatever).

Money and Prices

The purchasing power of money is the amount of goods and services a unit of money will buy. When money rapidly loses its purchasing power, it loses its role as money.

THE PURCHASING POWER OF THE DOLLAR

The amount a unit of a currency—in our case, a dollar—will buy varies inversely with the price level; that is, a reciprocal relationship exists between the general price level and the purchasing power of the dollar. When the Consumer Price Index (or "cost of living" index) goes up, the purchasing power of the dollar goes down, and vice versa. Higher prices lower the purchasing power of the dollar, because more dollars are needed to buy a particular amount of goods, services, or resources. For example, if the price level doubles, the purchasing power of the dollar declines by one half, or 50 percent.

Conversely, lower prices increase the purchasing power of the dollar, because fewer dollars are needed to obtain a specific quantity of goods and services. If the price level falls by, say, one half, or 50 percent, the purchasing power of the dollar doubles.

In equation form, the relationship looks like this:

$$D = 1/P$$

To find the value of the dollar D, divide 1 by the price level P expressed as an index number (in hundredths). If the price level is 1.0, then the value of the dollar is 1. If the price level rises to, say, 1.20, D falls to 0.833; a 20 percent increase in the price level reduces the value of the dollar by 16.67 percent. Check your understanding of this reciprocal relationship by determining the value of D and its percentage rise when P falls by 20 percent to 0.80.

INFLATION AND ACCEPTABILITY

In Chapter 9 we noted situations in which a nation's currency became worthless and unacceptable in exchange. These instances of runaway inflation, or *hyperinflation*, happened when the government issued so many pieces of paper currency that the purchasing power of each of those units of money was almost totally undermined. The infamous post-World War I hyperinflation in Germany is an example. In December 1919 there were about 50 billion German marks in circulation—four years later, there were 496,585,345,900 billion! The result? The German mark in 1923 was worth a very small fraction of its 1919 value.[2]

Runaway inflation will significantly depreciate the value of money between the time it is received and the time it is spent. Rapid declines in the value of a currency may cause it to cease being used as a medium of exchange. Businesses and households may refuse to accept paper money in exchange because they do not want to bear the loss in its value that will occur while it is in their possession. Without an acceptable domestic medium of exchange, the economy may revert to barter. Alternatively, a more stable currency, such as the European euro, may come into widespread use. At the extreme, the economy may adopt a foreign currency as its own official currency as a way to counter hyperinflation.

Similarly, people will use money as a store of value only as long as there is no sizable deterioration in the value of that money because of inflation. And an economy can effectively employ money as a unit of account only when its purchasing power is relatively stable. When the value of the dollar is declining rapidly, sellers do not know what to charge and buyers do not know what to pay.

---

[2] Frank G. Graham, *Exchange, Prices, and Production in Hyperinflation Germany, 1920–1923* (Princeton, N.J.: Princeton University Press, 1930), p. 13.

STABILIZING THE PURCHASING POWER OF MONEY

Rapidly rising price levels (rapid inflation) and the consequent erosion of the purchasing power of money typically result from imprudent economic policies. Since the purchasing power of money and the price level vary inversely, stabilization of the purchasing power of a nation's money requires stabilization of the nation's price level. Such price-level stability (with 2 to 3 percent annual inflation) mainly necessitates prudent regulation of the nation's money supply and interest rates (*monetary policy*). It also requires appropriate *fiscal policy* supportive of the efforts of the nation's monetary authorities to hold down inflation. In Canada, a combination of legislation, government policy, and social practice inhibits imprudent expansion of the money supply that might jeopardize money's purchasing power. The critical role of the Canadian monetary authorities in maintaining the purchasing power of the dollar is the subject of Chapter 15. For now, simply note that the Bank of Canada makes available a particular quantity of money, such as *M*1 or *M*2 in Figure 14-1, and can change that amount through its policy tools.

QUICK REVIEW 14.2

- In Canada, all money consists essentially of the debts of the government and chartered banks.
- These debts efficiently perform the functions of money so long as their value, or purchasing power, is relatively stable.
- The value of money is rooted not in specified quantities of precious metals but in the amounts of goods, services, and resources that money will purchase.
- The value of the dollar (its domestic purchasing power) is inversely related to the price level.
- Government's responsibility in stabilizing the purchasing power of the monetary unit calls for (1) effective control over the supply of money by the monetary authorities, and (2) the application of appropriate fiscal policies by the federal government.

14.4 / The Canadian Financial System

LO14.4 Discuss the structure of the Canadian financial system.

The main component of the money supply–demand deposits–is created by and comes into circulation through the chartered banks. We now take a look at the framework of the Canadian banking system.

Money and banking are federal responsibilities. Under the Bank Act, each bank is incorporated under a separate Act of Parliament and granted a charter. This is why a Canadian commercial bank is called a **chartered bank**.

At Confederation in 1867, there were 28 chartered banks; this number grew in the following years to 41, before failures and mergers brought the number to eight in the 1960s. The late 1960s and 1970s brought the formation of new banks, and more amalgamations and two failures. With the 1980 Bank Act revisions, foreign banks were allowed to establish Canadian subsidiaries. By 2014, there were 29 domestic banks, 24 foreign bank subsidiaries (as well as 27 foreign bank branches), and 3 foreign lending branches in Canada. In total, the domestic and foreign banks had almost $4 trillion in assets at the end of 2014.

Canada's Chartered Banks

Table 14-2 sets out the balance sheet of the Canadian chartered banks. Their cash reserves are only a small percentage of deposits. As we will discuss later in this chapter, our banking system is a fractional reserve banking system–chartered banks loan out most of their deposits, keeping only a small percentage to meet everyday cash withdrawals. If depositors in the chartered banks were to come all at once to withdraw their money, there would not be enough cash reserves to meet their requests. In such an unlikely event, chartered banks borrow from the Bank of Canada, the *bankers' bank*.

TABLE 14-2	The Balance Sheet of Canadian Chartered Banks, December 2014 (billions of dollars)		
Assets		**Liabilities**	
Reserves (currency and chartered banks' deposits with Bank of Canada)	$ 0	Demand deposits	$ 232
Loans (determined in Canadian dollars)	879	Savings deposits	268
Canadian securities	287	Term deposits	312
Mortgages	994	Foreign-currency liabilities	61
		Government of Canada deposit	1
Other assets	166	Other liabilities	1452
Total	$2326	Total	$2326

Source: Adapted from Bank of Canada, *Weekly Financial Statistics,* March 27, 2015; http://www.bankofcanada.ca/wp-content/uploads/2015/03/wfs270315.pdf, accessed June 29, 2015.

Making Loans

Chartered banks are private companies owned by shareholders who seek a competitive return on their investments. Thus, the primary goal of chartered banks is to try to maximize profits. They loan out as much of their deposits as is prudently possible to increase profits. Those funds that cannot be safely loaned out are used to buy Government of Canada securities. The rate banks charge on loans to their best corporate customers is referred to as the *prime rate*. Banks earn a profit on the spread between deposit interest rates and loan interest rates.

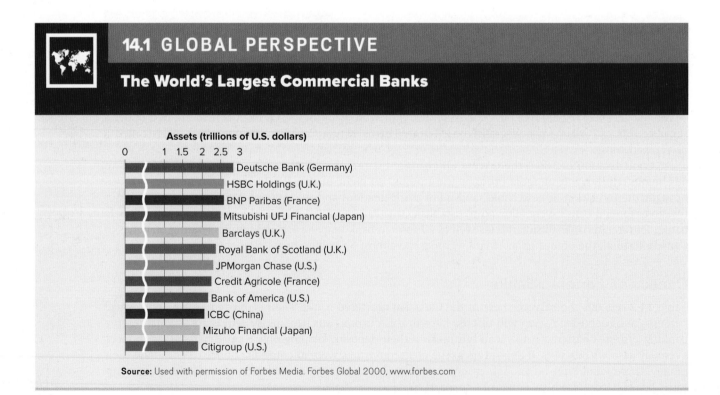

14.1 GLOBAL PERSPECTIVE

The World's Largest Commercial Banks

Assets (trillions of U.S. dollars)

Deutsche Bank (Germany)
HSBC Holdings (U.K.)
BNP Paribas (France)
Mitsubishi UFJ Financial (Japan)
Barclays (U.K.)
Royal Bank of Scotland (U.K.)
JPMorgan Chase (U.S.)
Credit Agricole (France)
Bank of America (U.S.)
ICBC (China)
Mizuho Financial (Japan)
Citigroup (U.S.)

Source: Used with permission of Forbes Media. Forbes Global 2000, www.forbes.com

Other Financial Intermediaries

Although the present analysis focuses on chartered banks, the banking system is supplemented by other financial intermediaries. These include trust companies, loan companies, credit unions, and *caisses populaires* that accept the funds of small savers and make them available to investors by extending mortgage loans or by purchasing marketable securities. Insurance companies accept large volumes of savings in the form of premiums on insurance policies and annuities, and use these funds to buy a variety of private, corporate, and government securities.

The Canadian financial system has been undergoing restructuring to permit more competition among the former "four pillars": the banking, insurance, trust, and securities industries.

Chartered banks and savings institutions have two basic functions: (1) they hold the money deposits of businesses and households, and (2) they make loans to the public in an effort to make profits. We will see in the next section that in doing so the intermediaries increase the economy's supply of money.

Cheque Clearing

A cheque is a written order that the drawer uses in making a purchase or paying a debt. A cheque is collected, or "cleared," when one or more banks transfer part of the drawer's chequing account to the chequing account of the recipient. If Jones and Smith have chequing accounts in the same bank and Jones gives Smith a $10 cheque, Smith can collect this cheque by taking it to the bank, where his account will be increased by $10 and Jones's reduced by $10. In most cases, however, the drawer and the receiver will be located in different towns or provinces and therefore have their accounts in bank branches far from each other. Under federal law, the Canadian Payments Association (CPA) was set up in 1982 to take over the interbank cheque clearing system, which had been run by the Canadian Bankers' Association. All of the chartered banks are members of the CPA. In recent years, the CPA has been transitioning to the digital age by adopting image-based clearing. Financial institutions will now capture images of each cheque, and these will then be transmitted between financial institutions electronically.

14.5 | ## The Importance of a Properly Functioning Financial System: The U.S. Financial Crisis of 2007–2008

LO14.5 Identify and explain the main factors that contributed to the U.S. financial crisis of 2007–2008.

As previously noted, a properly functioning monetary system supports the continuous circular flows of income and expenditures in the economy. In contrast, a malfunctioning monetary system causes major problems in credit markets and can cause severe fluctuations in the economy's levels of output, employment, and prices.

"Malfunctioning" is too gentle an adjective to describe the U.S. monetary system in late 2007 and 2008. In that period, the U.S. financial system faced its most serious crisis since the Great Depression of the 1930s. The financial crisis soon spread to practically the entire global economy, culminating in the relatively severe Canadian recession of 2008–2009. We discussed the recession in detail in previous chapters. Now we examine the global financial crisis that led up to it. What was the nature of the global financial crisis? What caused it? Given that the financial crisis had its start in the U.S., it will be worthwhile to examine it in some detail. The financial crisis occurred in a banking system that was *not* functioning properly.

The U.S. Mortgage Default Crisis

In 2007, a major wave of defaults on home mortgage loans threatened the health not only of the original mortgage lenders but of any financial institution in the U.S. and abroad that had made or invested in such loans either directly or indirectly. A majority of these mortgage defaults were on **subprime mortgage loans**–high-interest-rate loans to home buyers with higher-than-average credit risk. Many home owners purchased houses with very little down payment and took out *adjustable-rate mortgages* with a low fixed interest rate for an average length of two years, after which the interest rate would be adjusted to the market rate, usually at much higher rate. Ironically, the U.S. federal government had encouraged the banks to make these types of loans as part of an effort to broaden home ownership among Americans. But more to the point, several of the biggest indirect investors in these subprime loans were the commercial banks. The banks loaned money to investment companies that had purchased many of the mortgages from mortgage lenders. As housing prices began to fall, many homeowners found themselves with higher-interest mortgages and their down payment basically disappeared, thus many simply could not pay the higher mortgages and walked away from their homes. When the mortgages started to go bad, many investment funds "blew up" and could not repay the loans they had received from the banks. The banks thus had to write off (declare unrecoverable) the loans they had made to the investment funds, but doing that meant reducing their banks' cash reserves and limiting their ability to generate new loans. This greatly threatened the economy because both consumers and businesses rely on loans to finance consumption and investment expenditures.

A strange thing about the crisis was that before it happened, banks and government regulators mistakenly believed that an innovation known as the "mortgage-backed security" had eliminated most of the bank exposure to mortgage defaults. **Mortgage-backed securities** are bonds backed by mortgage payments. To create them, commercial banks and other mortgage lenders in the U.S. first made mortgage loans. But then instead of holding all of those loans as assets on their balance sheets and collecting the monthly mortgage payments, the banks and other mortgage lenders bundled hundreds or thousands of them together and sold them off as bonds–in essence selling the right to collect all the future mortgage payments. The banks obtained a single up-front cash payment for the bond and the bond buyer started to collect the mortgage payments as the return on the investment.

From the banks' perspective, this seemed like a smart business decision because it transferred any future default risk on those mortgages to the buyer of the bond. The banks thought that they were off the hook for these mortgages. Unfortunately for them, however, they loaned a substantial portion of the money they received from selling the bonds to investment funds that invested in mortgage-backed bonds. They also purchased large amounts of mortgage-backed securities as financial investments to help meet bank capital requirements set by U.S. bank regulators. So while the banks were no longer directly exposed to major portions of the mortgage default risk, they were still indirectly exposed to it. When many homebuyers started to default on their mortgages, the banks lost money on the mortgages they still held. The banks also lost money on the loans they had made to the investors who had purchased mortgage-backed securities and on the mortgage-backed securities the banks had purchased from investment firms.

But what had caused the skyrocketing mortgage default rates in the first place? There were many causes, including certain government programs that greatly encouraged and subsidized home ownership for former renters. Also contributing were declining real-estate values that arrived at the end of a long housing boom during which house prices had greatly increased. But an equally important factor was the bad incentives provided by the previously discussed mortgage-backed bonds. Since the banks and other mortgage lenders considered themselves immune to large portions of their mortgage default risk, they became very lax in their lending practices–so much so that people were granted subprime mortgage loans that they were very unlikely to be able to repay. Some mortgage companies were so eager to sign up new homebuyers (to bundle their loans together to sell bonds) that they stopped running credit checks and even allowed applicants to claim higher incomes than they were actually earning in order to qualify them for big loans. The natural result was that many people took on "too much mortgage" and were soon failing to make their monthly payments.

Securitization

The problems just described relate to **securitization**–the process of slicing up and bundling groups of loans, mortgages, corporate bonds, or other financial debts into distinct new securities. This process was not new and was viewed favourably by government regulators who thought securitization made the banking system safer by allowing banks to shed risk. As noted in our discussion of mortgages, these securities were sold to financial investors, who purchased them to obtain the interest payments and the eventual return of principal generated by the underlying securities. For example, the mortgage loans provided to the subprime borrowers were bundled together as mortgage-backed securities and sold to private investors, mutual fund firms, and pension funds. These securities were attractive to private investors and financial institutions alike because they offered higher interest returns than securities backed by less-risky mortgages or other safer investments.

Once created, loan-backed securities are bought and sold in financial markets just like other securities such as stocks and bonds. These sorts of securities can therefore end up worldwide in the investment portfolios of banks, thrift institutions, insurance companies, and pensions, as well as in personal accounts. To reduce the risk for holders of these securities, a few large insurance companies developed other securities that the holders of loan-backed securities could purchase to insure against losses from defaults. American International Group (AIG), in particular, issued billions of dollars of *collateralized default swaps*–essentially insurance policies–that were designed to compensate the holders of loan-backed securities if the loans underlying these investments went into default and did not pay off. Thus, collateralized default swaps became yet another category of investment security that was highly exposed to mortgage-loan risk.

Securitization was so widespread and so essential to the modern financial system that economists sometimes referred to it as the *shadow banking system*. All sorts of securities backed by loans or other securities were issued, bought, sold, and resold each day in a process that helped keep credit flowing to the households and businesses that relied on it for their personal and business needs. In general, securitization was therefore a positive financial innovation. But mortgage-backed securities, in particular, contained much more risk than most people thought.

Investors and U.S. government regulators failed to ask three related questions: (1) What would happen if the value of one of the types of loans (say, mortgages) that underlies part of the securitization process unexpectedly plunged? (2) What would happen if some of the largest holders of the securities based on these mortgages were major U.S. financial institutions vitally important to the day-to-day financing of the credit needed to keep the American economy running smoothly? (3) What would happen if the main insurer of these securities was the largest insurance company not only in the United States but in the world?

All three seemingly improbable scenarios occurred! As previously explained, interest rates on adjustable-rate mortgages increased and house prices fell. Borrowers who had made relatively small down payments on home purchases or had previously cashed out home equity through refinancing discovered that they owed more on their mortgages than their properties were worth. Their loans were said to be "underwater." As interest rates adjusted upward and the economy slowed, borrowers began falling behind on their monthly mortgage payments. Lenders began to foreclose on some borrowers' houses, while other borrowers literally handed in their house keys and walked away from their houses *and* their mortgages. This had disastrous consequences for mortgage lenders and commercial banks, many of which became insolvent and had to be rescued by the U.S. Treasury with taxpayer money. But this very fact demonstrates the problem of *moral hazard*. As it relates to financial investment, **moral hazard** is the tendency for financial investors and financial services firms to take on greater risks because they assume they are at least partially insured against losses.

Luckily, Canada's relatively conservative banking system was not much affected by the financial crisis in the U.S. However, the Canadian economy entered a recession in late 2008 as exports to the U.S. collapsed and apprehensive consumers cut back on purchases. The financial crisis that started in the U.S. made it abundantly clear that a well-functioning financial system is a necessary condition for a healthy economy.

QUICK REVIEW 14.3

- The Canadian financial system is dominated by the six major chartered banks.

- The financial crisis of 2007–2008 consisted of an unprecedented rise in mortgage loan defaults, the collapse or near collapse of several major financial institutions, and the generalized freezing up of credit availability. In 2007, a major wave of defaults on home mortgage loans threatened the health not only of the original mortgage lenders but of financial institutions both in the U.S. and around the world.

- The crisis resulted from bad mortgage loans together with declining real estate prices.

- The crisis exposed the underestimation of risk by holders of mortgage-backed securities as well as faulty insurance securities that had been designed to protect holders of mortgage-backed securities from the risk of default. The financial crisis in the U.S. spread to Canada and around the globe, leading to the relatively severe recession of 2008–2009.

14.6 / Chartered Banks and the Creation of Money

LO14.6 Discuss why the Canadian banking system is called a *fractional reserve* system.

Have you ever considered how money is created? You may believe that it is simply printed by the Bank of Canada. Although this is true, the creation of money is slightly more complex, and it is actually done with the help of Canada's chartered banks.

The Fractional Reserve System

Canada, like most other countries today, has a **fractional reserve banking system** in which only a portion (fraction) of demand deposits and cash reserves is held in chartered bank vaults. Our goal is to explain this system and show how chartered banks can create demand deposits by issuing loans. Our examples will involve chartered banks, but remember that credit unions, *caisses populaires*, and trust companies also provide deposits on which cheques can be written, though these institutions use the chartered banking system to clear the cheques written on their accounts.

Because of the public's acceptance of the goldsmiths' receipts as paper money, owners rarely redeemed the gold they had in storage with the goldsmiths.

Illustrating the Idea: The Goldsmiths

Here is the history behind the idea of the fractional reserve system. When early traders began to use gold in making transactions, they soon realized that it was both unsafe and inconvenient to carry gold and to have it weighed and assayed (judged for purity) every time they negotiated a transaction. So by the sixteenth century they had begun to deposit their gold with goldsmiths, who would store it in vaults for a fee. On receiving a gold deposit, the goldsmith would issue a receipt to the depositor. Soon people were paying for goods with goldsmiths' receipts, which served as one of the first types of paper money.

At this point the goldsmiths–budding bankers–used a 100 percent reserve system; they backed their circulating paper money receipts fully with the gold that they held "in reserve" in their vaults. But because of the public's acceptance of the goldsmiths' receipts as paper money, the goldsmiths soon realized that owners rarely redeemed the gold they had in storage. In fact, the goldsmiths observed that the amount of gold being deposited with them in any week or month was likely to exceed the amount that was being withdrawn.

Then some clever goldsmith hit on the idea that paper "receipts" could be issued in excess of the amount of gold held. Goldsmiths would put these receipts, which were redeemable in gold, into circulation by making interest-earning loans to merchants, producers, and consumers. A borrower might, for instance, borrow $10,000 worth of gold receipts today with the promise to repay $10,500 worth of gold receipts in one year (a 5 percent interest rate). Borrowers were willing to accept loans in the form of gold receipts because the receipts were accepted as a medium of exchange in the marketplace.

This was the beginning of the fractional reserve system of banking, in which cash reserves in bank vaults are a fraction of the total money supply. If, for example, the goldsmith issued $1 million in receipts for actual gold in storage and another $1 million in receipts as loans, then the total value of paper money in circulation would be $2 million–twice the value of the gold. Gold reserves would be a fraction (one half) of outstanding paper money.

Significant Characteristics of Fractional Reserve Banking

The goldsmith story highlights two significant characteristics of fractional reserve banking. First, banks can create money through lending. In fact, goldsmiths created money when they made loans by giving borrowers paper money that was not fully backed by gold reserves. The quantity of such money that goldsmiths could create depended on the amount of reserves they deemed it prudent to have available. The smaller the amount of reserves thought necessary, the larger the amount of paper money the goldsmiths could create. Today, gold is no longer used as bank reserves. Instead, currency itself serves as bank reserves so that the creation of demand deposit money by banks (via their lending) is limited by the amount of *currency reserves* that the banks feel obligated to keep.

A second reality is that banks operating on the basis of fractional reserves are vulnerable to "panics" or "runs." A goldsmith who issued paper money equal to twice the value of his gold reserves would be unable to convert all that paper money into gold in the event that all the holders of that money appeared at his door at the same time demanding their gold. In fact, many European, U.S., and Canadian banks were once ruined by just this unfortunate circumstance. However, this kind of bank panic is highly unlikely if the banker's reserve and lending policies are prudent. Indeed, one reason why banking systems are highly regulated industries is to prevent bank runs.

This is also why Canada has a system of deposit insurance. By guaranteeing deposits, deposit insurance helps to prevent the sort of bank runs that often happened before deposit insurance was available. By guaranteeing that depositors will always get their money, deposit insurance removes the incentive to try to withdraw one's deposit before anyone else can. It thus stops most bank runs.

14.7 / A Single Chartered Bank

LO14.7 Explain the basics of a bank's balance sheet and the distinction between a bank's actual reserves and its desired reserves.

To illustrate the workings of the modern fractional reserve banking system, we need to examine a chartered bank's **balance sheet**—its statement of assets and claims on assets (things owned by the bank or owed to the bank) that summarizes the financial position of the bank at a certain time. Every balance sheet must balance; this means that the value of *assets* must equal the amount of claims against those assets. The claims shown on a balance sheet are divided into two groups: the claims of non-owners of the bank against the firm's assets, called *liabilities*, and the claims of the owners of the firm against the firm's assets, called *net worth*. Liabilities are debts owed by the bank to depositors or others. A balance sheet is balanced because

Assets = liabilities + net worth

For every $1 change in assets, there must be an offsetting $1 change in liabilities plus net worth. For every $1 change in liabilities plus net worth, there must be an offsetting $1 change in assets.

Now let's work through a series of bank transactions involving balance sheets to establish how individual banks can create money.

Formation of a Chartered Bank

To see how individual banks create money we must understand the items a bank carries on its balance sheet and how certain transactions affect the balance sheet. We begin with the organization of a local chartered bank.

TRANSACTION 1: CREATING A BANK

Suppose some citizens of Vancouver decide a new chartered bank is needed to provide banking services for their growing city. Once they get Parliament to pass an act granting a charter for their bank, they then sell, say, $250,000 worth of capital stock (equity shares) to buyers both in and out of the province. The Bank of Vancouver now exists. What does the bank's balance sheet look like at this stage?

The owners of the new bank have sold $250,000 worth of shares of stock in the bank–some to themselves and some to other people. As a result, the bank now has $250,000 in cash on hand and $250,000 worth of capital stock outstanding. The cash is an asset to the bank. Cash held by a bank is sometimes called **vault cash** or "till money." The bank's balance sheet reads

Creating a Bank

Balance Sheet 1: Bank of Vancouver

Assets		Liabilities and net worth	
Cash	$250,000	Capital stock	$250,000

Each item listed in a balance sheet such as this is called an *account*.

TRANSACTION 2: ACQUIRING PROPERTY AND EQUIPMENT

The first step for the new bank will be to acquire property and equipment. The bank purchases buildings for $220,000 and buys $20,000 worth of office equipment. This transaction changes the composition of the bank's assets. The bank now has $240,000 less in cash and $240,000 of new property assets. The bank's balance sheet at the conclusion of Transaction 2 appears as follows:

Acquiring Property and Equipment

Balance Sheet 2: Bank of Vancouver

Assets		Liabilities and net worth	
Cash	$ 10,000	Capital stock	$250,000
Property	240,000		

Note that the balance sheet still balances, as it must.

TRANSACTION 3: ACCEPTING DEPOSITS

Chartered banks have two basic functions: to accept deposits of money, and to make loans. Now that our bank is in operation, suppose the citizens and businesses of Vancouver decide to deposit $100,000 in the Bank of Vancouver. What happens to the bank's balance sheet?

The bank receives cash, an asset to the bank. Suppose this money is placed in the bank as demand deposits (chequing accounts), rather than savings accounts or term deposits. These newly created *demand deposits* are claims that depositors have against the assets of the Bank of Vancouver, thus creating a new liability account. The bank's balance sheet now looks like this:

Accepting Deposits

Balance Sheet 3: Bank of Vancouver

Assets		Liabilities and net worth	
Cash	$ 110,000	Demand deposits	$ 100,000
Property	240,000	Capital stock	250,000

There has been no change in the economy's total supply of money, but a change has occurred in the composition of the money supply as a result of Transaction 3. Demand deposits have *increased* by $100,000 and currency in circulation has *decreased* by $100,000. Note that currency held by a bank is *not* part of the economy's money supply.

A withdrawal of cash will reduce the bank's demand deposit liabilities and its holdings of cash by the amount of the withdrawal. This, too, changes the composition–but not the total supply–of money in the economy.

Desired Cash Reserves

The Bank of Vancouver has to have sufficient *cash reserves* to serve the daily cash needs of the chartered bank's customers. Cash reserves are also called **desired reserves**. Generally, banks keep a minimum percentage of their holdings in cash reserves. We refer to the specified percentage of deposit liabilities the chartered bank chooses to keep as vault cash as the **desired reserve ratio**. Up to the mid 1990s the Bank of Canada actually required chartered banks to hold a specified percentage of demand, savings, and term deposits, and referred to this as *required reserves*. The desired reserve ratio is calculated as follows:

$$\text{Desired reserve ratio} = \frac{\text{chartered bank's desired reserves}}{\text{chartered bank's demand} - \text{deposit liabilities}}$$

If the desired reserve ratio is 20 percent, our bank, having accepted $100,000 in deposits from the public, would keep $20,000 as reserves to meet its daily cash needs.

There are two things to note about cash reserves:

1. **Excess Reserves** A bank's **excess reserves** are found by subtracting its desired reserves from its **actual reserves**.

   Excess reserves = actual reserves − desired reserves

   In this case

Actual cash reserves	$110,000
Desired reserves	−20,000
Excess reserves	$ 90,000

   The only reliable way of computing excess cash reserves is to multiply the bank's demand deposit liabilities by the desired reserve ratio to obtain desired cash reserves ($100,000 × 20 percent = $20,000) and then to subtract desired cash reserves from the actual cash reserves listed on the asset side of the bank's balance sheet.

   To test your understanding, compute the bank's excess cash reserves from Balance Sheet 3, assuming that the desired reserve ratio is (a) 5 percent, (b) 33.3 percent, and (c) 50 percent. We will soon demonstrate that the ability of a chartered bank to make loans depends on the existence of excess cash reserves. So, understanding this concept is crucial in seeing how the banking system creates money.

2. **Influence** Excess cash reserves are a means by which the Bank of Canada can influence the lending ability of chartered banks. The next chapter will explain in detail how the Bank of Canada can implement certain policies that either increase or decrease chartered bank cash reserves and affect the ability of banks to make loans. To the degree that these policies are successful in influencing the volume of chartered bank credit, the Bank of Canada can help the economy smooth out business fluctuations.

TRANSACTION 4: CLEARING A CHEQUE DRAWN AGAINST THE BANK

Assume that Clem Bradshaw, a Vancouver lumberyard owner, deposited a substantial portion of the $100,000 in demand deposits that the Bank of Vancouver received in Transaction 3. Suppose Bradshaw buys $50,000 worth of lumber from the Ajax Forest Products Company of Chilliwack. Bradshaw pays for this lumber by writing a $50,000 cheque against his deposit in the Bank of Vancouver. Ajax deposits the cheque in its account with the Bank of Manitoba, which has a branch in Chilliwack.

Note that the balance statements of the two banks will balance. The Bank of Vancouver will reduce both its assets and its liabilities by $50,000. The Bank of Manitoba will have $50,000 more in cash and in deposits. *Whenever a cheque is drawn against one bank and deposited in another bank, collection of that cheque will reduce both cash reserves and demand deposits by the bank on which the cheque is drawn.* In our example, the Bank of Vancouver loses $50,000 in both cash reserves and deposits to the Bank of Manitoba. But there is no loss of cash reserves or deposits for the banking system as a whole: what one bank loses, another bank gains.

If we bring all the other assets and liabilities back into the picture, the Bank of Vancouver's balance sheet looks like this at the end of Transaction 4:

Clearing a Cheque

Balance Sheet 4: Bank of Vancouver			
Assets		**Liabilities and net worth**	
Cash reserves	$ 60,000	Demand deposits	$ 50,000
Property	240,000	Capital stock	250,000

Verify that with a 20 percent desired reserve ratio, the bank's excess cash reserves now stand at $50,000.

14.8 / Money-Creating Transactions of a Chartered Bank

LO14.8 Describe how a chartered bank can create money.

The next two transactions are crucial because they explain (1) how a chartered bank can literally create money by making loans, and (2) how banks create money by purchasing government bonds from the public.

TRANSACTION 5: GRANTING A LOAN

Suppose the Grisley Meat Packing Company of Vancouver decides to expand. Suppose, too, that the company needs exactly $50,000–which just happens to be equal to the Bank of Vancouver's excess cash reserves–to finance this project.

Grisley requests a loan for this amount from the Bank of Vancouver. Convinced of Grisley's ability to repay, the bank grants the loan. Grisley hands a promissory note–a fancy IOU–to the bank. Grisley wants the convenience and safety of paying its obligations by cheque. So, instead of receiving cash from the bank, Grisley gets a $50,000 increase in its demand deposit account in the Bank of Vancouver.

The Bank of Vancouver has acquired an interest-earning asset (the promissory note) and has created a deposit (a liability) to pay for this asset. At the moment the loan is completed, the Bank of Vancouver's position is shown by Balance Sheet 5a:

When a Loan Is Negotiated

Balance Sheet 5a: Bank of Vancouver

Assets		Liabilities and net worth	
Cash reserves	$ 60,000	Demand deposits	$ 100,000
Loans	50,000	Capital stock	250,000
Property	240,000		

A close examination of the bank's balance sheet will reveal a startling fact: *When a bank makes loans, it creates money.* The president of Grisley went to the bank with something that is not money–her IOU–and walked out with something that *is* money–a demand deposit.

When banks lend, they create demand deposits (chequing accounts) that *are* money. By extending credit, the Bank of Vancouver has *monetized* an IOU. Grisley and the bank have created and then swapped claims. The claim created by the bank and given to the Grisley Company is money; cheques drawn against a deposit are acceptable as a medium of exchange. It is through the extension of credit by chartered banks that the bulk of the money used in our economy is created.

Bank creation of money raises an interesting question: If banks create demand deposit money when they lend their excess cash reserves, is money destroyed when borrowers pay off their loans? The answer is yes. When loans are paid off, the process just described works in reverse: demand deposits decline by the amount of the loan repayment.

Assume that Grisley awards a $50,000 building contract to the Quickbuck Construction Company of Kamloops. Quickbuck completes the expansion job and is paid with a cheque for $50,000 drawn by Grisley against its demand deposit in the Bank of Vancouver. Quickbuck, with headquarters in Kamloops, does *not* deposit this cheque back into the Bank of Vancouver but instead deposits it in a Kamloops branch of the Bank of Manitoba. The Bank of Manitoba now has a $50,000 claim against the Bank of Vancouver. As a result, the Bank of Vancouver *loses* both cash reserves and deposits equal to the amount of the cheque; the Bank of Manitoba *acquires* $50,000 of cash reserves and deposits.

In summary, assuming a cheque is drawn by the borrower for the entire amount of the loan ($50,000) and given to a firm that deposits it in another bank, the Bank of Vancouver's balance sheet will read as follows after the cheque has been cleared against it:

After a Cheque Is Drawn on the Loan

Balance Sheet 5b: Bank of Vancouver

Assets		Liabilities and net worth	
Cash reserves	$ 10,000	Demand deposits	$ 50,000
Loans	50,000	Capital stock	250,000
Property	240,000		

WORKED PROBLEM 14.1 Single Bank Accounting

After the cheque has been collected, the Bank of Vancouver is just barely meeting its desired reserve ratio of 20 percent. The bank has no excess cash reserves; it is fully "loaned up." The money supply has not decreased due to the cheque drawn on the Bank of Vancouver; the money is simply showing up in the Bank of Manitoba.

TRANSACTION 6: BUYING GOVERNMENT SECURITIES

When a chartered bank buys government bonds from the public, the effect is substantially the same as lending. New money is created.

Assume that the Bank of Vancouver's balance sheet initially stands as it did at the end of Transaction 4. Now suppose that instead of making a $50,000 loan, the bank buys $50,000 of government securities from a securities dealer. The bank receives the interest-bearing bonds, which appear on its balance statement as the asset "Securities" and give the securities dealer an increase in its deposit account. The bank's balance sheet appears as follows:

Buying Government Securities

Balance Sheet 6: Bank of Vancouver			
Assets		**Liabilities and net worth**	
Cash reserves	$ 60,000	Demand deposits	$100,000
Securities	50,000	Capital stock	250,000
Property	240,000		

Demand deposits–that is, the supply of money–have increased by $50,000, as in Transaction 5a. *Bond purchases from the public by chartered banks increase the supply of money in the same way as does lending to the public.*

Finally, the *selling* of government bonds to the public (including securities dealers) by a chartered bank–like the repayment of a loan–reduces the supply of money. The securities buyer pays by cheque and both "Securities" and "Demand deposits" (the latter being money) decline by the amount of the sale.

Profits, Liquidity, and the Overnight Lending Rate

The asset items on a chartered bank's balance sheet reflect the banker's pursuit of two conflicting goals:

1. ***Profit*** Chartered banks, like any other business, seek profits, which is why the bank makes loans and buys securities–the two major earning assets of chartered banks.

2. ***Liquidity*** For a bank, safety lies in liquidity, specifically such liquid assets as cash and excess cash reserves. A bank must be on guard for depositors who want to transform their demand deposits into cash. Bankers thus seek a balance between prudence and profit. The compromise is between assets that earn high returns and highly liquid assets.

An interesting way in which banks can partly reconcile the goals of profit and liquidity is to lend temporary excess cash reserves to other chartered banks. Normal day-to-day flows of funds to banks rarely leave all banks with their exact levels of desired cash reserves. Banks therefore lend these excess reserves to other banks on an overnight basis as a way to earn additional interest without sacrificing long-term liquidity. Banks that borrow in this market do so because they are temporarily short of the level of cash reserves they wish to hold. The interest rate paid on these overnight loans is called the **overnight lending rate**.

- Banks create money when they make loans; money vanishes when bank loans are repaid.

- New money is created when banks buy government bonds from the public; money disappears when banks sell government bonds to the public.

- Banks balance profitability and safety in determining their mix of earning assets and highly liquid assets.

- Although the Bank of Canada pays interest on excess reserves, chartered banks may be able to obtain higher interest rates by temporarily lending the reserves to other banks in the overnight loans market; the interest rate on such loans is the overnight lending rate.

14.9 / The Banking System: Multiple-Deposit Expansion

LO14.9 Describe the multiple-deposit expansion of the entire chartered banking system.

Thus far we have seen that a single bank in a banking system can lend one dollar for each dollar of its excess cash reserves. The situation is different for all chartered banks as a group. We will find that the chartered banking system can lend–that is, can create money–by a multiple of its excess cash reserves. This multiple lending is accomplished even though each bank in the system can lend only "dollar for dollar" with its excess cash reserves.

How do these seemingly paradoxical results come about? To answer this question succinctly, we will make three simplifying assumptions:

1. The desired reserve ratio for all chartered banks is 20 percent.

2. Initially all banks are meeting this 20 percent desired reserve ratio. No excess cash reserves exist; or, in the parlance of banking, they are "loaned up" (or "loaned out").

3. If any bank can increase its loans as a result of acquiring excess cash reserves, an amount equal to those excess cash reserves will be lent to one borrower, who will write a cheque for the entire amount of the loan and give it to someone else, who will deposit the cheque in another bank. This third assumption means that the worst thing possible happens to every lending bank–a cheque for the entire amount of the loan is drawn and cleared against it in favour of another bank.

The Banking System's Lending Potential

Suppose a junkyard owner in Moncton finds a $100 bill while dismantling a car that has been on the lot for years. He deposits the $100 in Bank A, which adds the $100 to its cash reserves. We will record only changes in the balance sheets of the various chartered banks. The deposit changes Bank A's balance sheet as shown by entries (a_1):

Multiple-Deposit Expansion Process

	Balance Sheet: Chartered Bank A		
Assets		**Liabilities and net worth**	
Cash reserves	$+100 ($a_1$)	Demand deposits	$+100 ($a_1$)
	−80 (a_3)		+80 (a_2)
Loans	+80 (a_2)		−80 (a_3)

Recall from Transaction 3 that this $100 deposit of currency does not alter the money supply. Although $100 of demand deposit money comes into being, it is offset by the $100 of currency no longer in the hands of the public (the junkyard owner). What has happened is that Bank A has acquired excess cash reserves of $80. Of the newly acquired $100 in cash reserves, 20 percent, or $20, is earmarked for the desired cash reserves on the new $100 deposit, and the remaining $80 becomes excess cash reserves. Since a single chartered bank can lend only an amount equal to its excess reserves, we conclude that Bank A can lend a maximum of $80. When a loan for this amount is made, Bank A's loans increase by $80 and the borrower gets an $80 demand deposit. We add these figures–entries (a_2)–to Bank A's balance sheet.

But now we make our third assumption: The borrower uses the full amount of the loan ($80) to write a cheque ($80) to someone else, and that person deposits the amount in Bank B, a different bank. As we saw in Transaction 6, Bank A loses both cash reserves and deposits equal to the amount of the loan, as indicated in entries (a_3). The net result of these transactions is that Bank A's cash reserves now stand at +$20 (= $100 − $80), loans at +$80, and demand deposits at +$100 (= $100 + $80 − $80). When the dust has settled, Bank A is just meeting the 20 percent reserve ratio.

Recalling our previous discussion, we know that Bank B acquires both the reserves and the deposits that Bank A has lost. Bank B's balance sheet is changed as in entries (b_1):

Multiple-Deposit Expansion Process

Balance Sheet: Chartered Bank B

Assets		Liabilities and net worth	
Cash reserves	$+80 (b_1)	Demand deposits	$+80 (b_1)
	−64 (b_3)		+64 (b_2)
Loans	+64 (b_2)		−64 (b_3)

When the borrower's cheque is drawn and cleared, Bank A loses $80 in cash reserves and deposits and Bank B gains $80 in cash reserves and deposits. But 20 percent, or $16, of Bank B's new cash reserves are kept against the new $80 in demand deposits. This means that Bank B has $64 (= $80 − $16) in excess reserves. It can therefore lend $64 [entries (b_2)]. When the new borrower writes a cheque for $64 to buy a product, and the seller deposits the cheque in Bank C, the cash reserves and deposits of Bank B both fall by $64 [entries (b_3)]. As a result of these transactions, Bank B's cash reserves now stand at +$16 (= $80 − $64), loans at +$64, and demand deposits at +$80 (= $80 + $64 − $64). After all this, Bank B is just meeting the 20 percent desired reserve ratio.

We are off and running again. Bank C acquires the $64 in cash reserves and deposits lost by Bank B. Its balance sheet changes as in entries (c_1):

Multiple-Deposit Expansion Process

Balance Sheet: Chartered Bank C

Assets		Liabilities and net worth	
Cash reserves	$+64.00 (c_1)	Demand deposits	$+64.00 (c_1)
	−51.20 (c_3)		+51.20 (c_2)
Loans	+51.20 (c_2)		−51.20 (c_3)

Exactly 20 percent, or $12.80, of these new cash reserves will be kept as reserves; the remaining $51.20 are excess reserves. Hence, Bank C can safely lend a maximum of $51.20. Suppose it does [entries (c_2)]. And suppose the borrower writes a cheque for the entire amount ($51.20) to a merchant, who deposits it in another bank [entries (c_3)].

We could go ahead with this procedure by bringing Banks D, E, F, G . . . J and so on into the picture. In fact, the process will go on almost indefinitely, just as long as banks farther down the line receive at least one penny in new cash reserves that they can use to back another round of lending and money creation. But we suggest that you work through the computations for Banks D, E, F, and G to be sure you understand the procedure.

The entire analysis is summarized in Table 14-3. Data for Banks D through J are supplied on their own rows so that you may check your computations. The last row of the table consolidates into one row everything that happens for all banks down the line after Bank J. Our conclusion is startling: On the basis of only $80 in excess cash reserves (acquired by the banking system when someone deposited $100 of currency in Bank A), the entire chartered banking system is able to lend $400, the sum of the amounts in column 4. The banking system can lend excess reserves by a multiple of 5 (= $400/$80) when the reserve ratio is 20 percent. Yet each single bank in the banking system is lending only an amount equal to its own excess reserves. How do we explain this? How can the banking system as a whole lend by a multiple of its excess cash reserves, when each individual bank can lend only "dollar for dollar" with its excess reserves?

The answer is that cash reserves lost by a single bank are not lost to the banking system as a whole. The reserves lost by Bank A are acquired by Bank B. Those lost by B are gained by C; C loses to D, D to E, E to F, and so forth. Although cash reserves can be, and are, lost by individual banks in the banking system, there is no loss of cash reserves for the banking system as a whole.

An individual bank can safely lend only an amount equal to its excess reserves, *but the chartered banking system can lend by a multiple of its collective excess cash reserves*. This contrast, incidentally, is an illustration of why it is imperative that we keep the fallacy of composition (The Last Word, Chapter 1) firmly in mind. Chartered banks as a group can create money by lending in a manner much different from that of the individual banks in that group.

TABLE 14-3   **Expansion of the Money Supply by the Chartered Banking System**

Bank	(1) Acquired cash reserves and deposits	(2) Desired reserves (reserve ratio = 0.2)	(3) Excess cash reserves, (1) − (2)	(4) Amount bank can lend; new money created = (3)
Bank A	$100.00 (a_1)	$20.00	*$80.00*	$ 80.00 (a_2)
Bank B	80.00 (a_3, b_1)	16.00	64.00	64.00 (b_2)
Bank C	64.00 (b_3, c_1)	12.80	51.20	51.20 (c_2)
Bank D	51.20	10.24	40.96	40.96
Bank E	40.96	8.19	32.77	32.77
Bank F	32.77	6.55	26.22	26.22
Bank G	26.21	5.24	20.97	20.97
Bank H	20.98	4.20	16.78	16.78
Bank I	16.78	3.36	13.42	13.42
Bank J	13.42	2.68	10.74	10.74
Other banks	53.68	10.74	42.94	42.94
Total amount of money created (sum of the amounts in column 4)				*$400.00*

14.10 / The Monetary Multiplier

LO14.10 Define the monetary multiplier, explain how to calculate it, and demonstrate its relevance.

The **monetary multiplier** defines the relationship between any new excess cash reserves in the banking system and the magnified creation of new demand deposit money by banks as a group. It is a separate idea from the spending-income multiplier of Chapter 10, but shares some mathematical similarities. The spending-income multiplier exists because the reserves and deposits lost by one bank are received by another bank. It magnifies excess cash reserves into a larger creation of demand deposit money. The monetary multiplier m is the reciprocal of the desired reserve ratio R (the leakage into cash reserves that occurs at each step in the lending process). In short

Monetary multiplier = 1/desired reserve ratio

or, in symbols,

$m = 1/R$

MATH 14.1   The Monetary Multiplier

In this formula, m represents the maximum amount of new demand deposits that can be created by a single dollar of excess cash reserves, given the value of R. By multiplying the excess reserves E by m, we can find the maximum amount of new demand deposit money, D, that can be created by the banking system. That is

Maximum demand deposit creation = excess cash reserves × monetary multiplier

or, more simply,

$D = E \times m$

In our example in Table 14-3, R is 0.20 so m is 5 (= 1/0.20). Then

$D = \$80 \times 5 = \$400$

WORKED PROBLEM 14.2   Money Creation

Figure 14-2 depicts the final outcome of our example of a multiple-deposit expansion of the money supply. The initial deposit of $100 of currency into the bank (lower right-hand box) creates new cash reserves of an equal amount (upper box). With a 20 percent desired reserve ratio, however, only $20 of currency reserves is needed to back up this $100 chequable (demand) deposit. The excess cash reserves of $80 permit the creation of $400 of new demand deposits via the making of loans, confirming a monetary multiplier of 5. The $100 of new cash reserves supports a total supply of money of $500, consisting of the $100 initial demand deposit plus $400 of demand deposits created through lending.

Higher desired reserve ratios mean lower monetary multipliers and therefore less creation of new demand deposit money via loans; smaller desired reserve ratios mean higher monetary multipliers and thus more creation of new demand deposit money via loans. With a high desired reserve ratio–say, 50 percent–the monetary multiplier would be 2 (= 1/0.5), and in our example the banking system could create only $100 (= $50 of excess reserves × 2) of new demand deposits. With a low desired reserve ratio–say, 5 percent–the monetary multiplier would be 20 (= 1/0.05), and the banking system could create $1900 (= $95 of excess reserves × 20) of new demand deposits. It should be noted that if there are

| FIGURE 14-2 | The Outcome of the Money Expansion Process, New Reserves |

A deposit of $100 of currency into a chequing account creates an initial demand deposit of $100. If the desired reserve ratio is 20 percent, only $20 of cash reserves is required to support the $100 demand deposit. The $80 of excess cash reserves allows the banking system to create $400 of demand deposits through making loans. The $100 of cash reserves supports a total of $500 of money ($100 + $400).

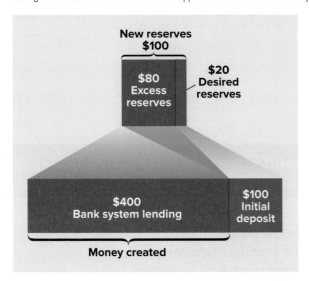

currency drains—that is, some borrowers do not deposit their loans in the bank—the multiplier will be reduced. During a financial crisis the multiplier may be reduced if the public wants to hold more cash and chartered banks more cash reserves as precautionary measures against borrowers not being able to pay back their loans.

Experiment with the following two brainteasers to test your understanding of multiple credit expansion by the banking system:

- Re-work the analysis in Table 14-3 (at least three or four steps of it) assuming the desired reserve ratio is 10 percent. What is the maximum amount of money the banking system can create upon acquiring $100 in new cash reserves and deposits? (The answer is not $800!)

- Suppose the banking system is loaned up and has a 20 percent desired reserve ratio. Explain how it might have to reduce its outstanding loans by $400 when a $100 cash withdrawal from a demand deposit account forces one bank to draw down its cash reserves by $100.

Reversibility: The Multiple Destruction of Money

The process we have described is reversible. Just as demand deposit money is created when banks make loans, demand deposit money is destroyed when loans are paid off. Loan repayment, in effect, sets off a process of multiple destruction of money, just the opposite of the multiple creation process. Because loans are both made and paid off in any period, the direction of the loans, demand deposits, and money supply in a given period will depend on the net effect of the two processes. If the dollar amount of loans made in some period exceeds the dollar amount of loans paid off, demand deposits will expand and the money supply will increase. But if the dollar amount of loans is less than the dollar amount of loans paid off, demand deposits will contract and the money supply will decline.

- A single bank in a multibank system can safely lend (create money) by an amount equal to its excess cash reserves; the banking system can lend (create money) by a multiple of its excess cash reserves.

- The monetary multiplier is the reciprocal of the desired reserve ratio; it is the multiple by which the banking

system can expand the money supply for each dollar of excess cash reserves.

- The monetary multiplier works in both directions; it applies to money destruction from the repayment of loans as well as to money creation from the making of loans.

The LAST WORD   Banking, Leverage, and Financial Instability in the U.S. Compared to Canada

Leverage boosts banking profits but makes the banking system less stable. Prior to the recession of 2007–2009 the banking system in the U.S. may have been over-leveraged. Time to reduce leverage?

The term *leverage* is used in finance to describe how the use of borrowed money can magnify both profits and losses. To see how leverage works, first consider an investment opportunity that produces a 10 percent positive return if things go well but a 5 percent loss if things go poorly. Those rates of return imply that if a person invests $100 of his own savings, he will end up with either $110 if things go well or $95 if things go badly. Put slightly differently, he will either gain $10 or lose $5 from where he started, with his own $100 being used to fund the $100 investment.

But now consider what happens to his potential returns if he uses borrowed money to provide leverage. In fact, let's have him use a lot of leverage. To make the $100 investment, he uses $10 of his own savings and $90 of borrowed money (which, for simplicity, we will assume that he can borrow at zero percent interest). If things go well, the investment will return $110. He then must repay the $90 loan. That will leave him with $20 (= $110 of investment return if things go well minus $90 to repay the loan). That means that he will end up with $20 if things go well and he uses leverage. Notice that this implies that if he uses leverage, he will get a 100 percent (= $20 divided by $10) return on the $10 of his own savings that he himself invested. That, of course, is much nicer than a 10 percent return. In fact, it is 10 times as large—hence the term *leverage*. The use of borrowed money has massively increased the percentage rate of return if things go well.

Unfortunately, however, nothing in life is free. Leverage also magnifies the investor's losses if things go wrong. To see this, note

that if things go wrong in this example, the investor will end up turning $100 into $95. But then he has to pay back the $90 that he borrowed. That will leave him with only $5 (= $95 investment return if things go badly minus $90 to repay the loan). That implies that the investor will lose $5 off of the $10 of his own savings that he himself originally put into the investment. That is a 50 percent loss—ten times as much as the 5 percent loss that he would have sustained if he had used only his own money to make the $100 investment. Thus, you can see that leverage increases both profits if things go well and losses if things go badly.

A modern chartered bank uses a lot of leverage. In fact, only about 5 percent of the money that it invests comes from its shareholders and the money they paid to purchase ownership shares in the bank. The other 95 percent comes from borrowing, either by issuing bonds (about 25 percent) or by taking in demand and savings deposits (about 70 percent). It surprises many people, but chequing and savings deposits are technically a type of loan made by depositors to their banks. So banks get 70 percent of their leverage and funding from money borrowed from depositors.

The problem with that much leverage is that it takes only very small losses to drive the bank into insolvency and a situation in which it cannot repay all of the money that it has borrowed because the value of the bank's assets has fallen below the value of the bank's liabilities. Consider what would happen if for every $100 invested by the bank only $94 returned. That, by itself, is a 6 percent rate of loss. But because the bank is borrowing $95 of every $100 that it invests, it will be driven into insolvency by that six percent loss because it is getting back less than the amount that it borrowed to fund the investment. With the investment returning only $94, there won't be enough money to pay off the $95 that the bank borrowed!

While in Canada the banking sector has been fairly conservative, it was not the case in the U.S. before the financial crisis of 2007–09. So why did some American banks use this much leverage? Because it is very profitable for the bankers who run the banks and also because they were not as closely regulated as in Canada. If things are going well, the leverage massively increases the banks' profit rates—and bankers get paid bonuses based on those profit rates. On the other hand, if things go badly, bankers have come to expect bailouts in which the government uses taxpayer money to ensure that all of a bank's liabilities are repaid. So from the perspective of the bankers, it's "heads I win, tails you lose."

One solution to these problems would be to require banks to use much less leverage. For every $100 that a bank wants to invest, the bank could be required to raise $30 from its shareholder owners so that it would only be borrowing the other $70 through issuing bonds or by taking in chequing and savings deposits. That would make the entire banking system much more stable because it would be very unlikely that for any $100 invested into projects by the bank, less than $70 would come back. Even if only $71 came back, there would still be enough money to pay back the $70 of borrowed money—and thus no need for the bank to go bankrupt or require a government bailout via the deposit insurance system.

Unfortunately, however, bankers in the U.S. have lobbied strongly and successfully against any legal attempts to require lower leverage levels. So the current regulatory system relies instead on bank supervisors who attempt to prevent the banks from making bad loans. That system was unable to prevent the 2007–2008 financial crisis and a number of economists argue that until leverage is reduced, no amount of bank supervision will be sufficient to prevent another financial crisis because with massive leverage even a small loss can destroy a bank.

Questions

Does leverage increase the total size of the gain or loss from an investment, or just the percentage rate of return on the part of the investment amount that was not borrowed? How would lowering leverage make the financial system more stable?

Chapter Summary

LO14.1   EXPLAIN THE FUNCTIONS OF MONEY.

- Anything that is accepted as (a) a medium of exchange, (b) a unit of monetary account, and (c) a store of value can be used as money.

LO14.2   LIST AND DESCRIBE THE COMPONENTS OF THE SUPPLY OF MONEY IN CANADA.

- Money is generally defined as demand deposits plus currency (coins and paper money) in circulation ($M1+$). Demand deposits, the largest component of the money supply, are money because they can be spent by writing cheques against them. Savings, term, and notice deposits—some chequable and some not—are also money and are added to more broadly defined monetary aggregates ($M2$, $M2+$, and $M2++$). In our analysis we concentrate on $M1+$ since its components are immediately spendable.

LO14.3   DESCRIBE WHAT BACKS CANADA'S MONEY SUPPLY, MAKING US WILLING TO ACCEPT IT AS PAYMENT.

- Money is the debts of government and depository institutions (chartered banks, trust companies, and credit unions) and has value because of goods, services, and resources it will command in the market. Maintaining the purchasing power of money depends largely on the government's effectiveness in managing the money supply.

LO14.4   DISCUSS THE STRUCTURE OF THE CANADIAN FINANCIAL SYSTEM.

- The Canadian banking system is composed of (a) the Bank of Canada and (b) twenty-nine Canadian-owned and twenty-seven foreign-owned banks. The chartered banks of the economy accept money deposits and make loans. The Canadian banking system is concentrated compared to other nations, particularly the United States.

LO14.5   IDENTIFY AND EXPLAIN THE MAIN FACTORS THAT CONTRIBUTED TO THE U.S. FINANCIAL CRISIS OF 2007–2008.

- The U.S. financial crisis of 2007–2008 consisted of an unprecedented rise in mortgage loan defaults, the collapse or near-collapse of several major financial institutions, and the generalized freezing up of credit availability. The crisis resulted from bad mortgage loans together with declining real estate prices. It also resulted from underestimation of risk by holders of mortgage-backed securities and faulty insurance securities designed to protect holders of mortgage-backed securities from the risk of default.

LO14.6   DISCUSS WHY THE CANADIAN BANKING SYSTEM IS CALLED A *FRACTIONAL RESERVE* SYSTEM.

- Modern banking systems are fractional reserve systems: only a fraction of deposits are backed by currency.

LO14.7   EXPLAIN THE BASICS OF A BANK'S BALANCE SHEET AND THE DISTINCTION BETWEEN A BANK'S ACTUAL RESERVES AND ITS DESIRED RESERVES.

- The operation of a chartered bank can be understood through its balance sheet, where assets equal liabilities plus net worth.

- Chartered banks keep cash reserves as vault cash and a small amount in the Bank of Canada for cheque-clearing purposes. This reserve is equal to a desired percentage of the chartered bank's deposit liabilities. Excess cash reserves are equal to actual reserves minus desired cash reserves.

- Banks lose both cash reserves and deposits when cheques are drawn against them.

- Chartered banks create money—create demand deposits, or deposit money—when they make loans. They convert IOUs, which are *not* money, into demand deposits, which *are* money. Money is destroyed when bank loans are repaid.

LO14.8   DESCRIBE HOW A CHARTERED BANK CAN CREATE MONEY.

- The ability of a single chartered bank to create money by lending depends on the size of its excess cash reserves. Generally speaking, a chartered bank lends only an amount equal to the amount of its excess cash reserves.

- Rather than making loans, chartered banks may decide to use excess cash reserves to buy bonds from the public. In doing so, banks merely credit the demand deposit accounts of the bond sellers, thus creating demand deposit money. Money vanishes when banks sell bonds to the public because bond buyers must draw down their demand deposit balances to pay for the bonds.

- Banks earn interest by making loans and by purchasing bonds; they maintain liquidity by holding excess cash reserves. Banks with temporary excess reserves often lend them overnight to banks that are short of desired cash reserves. The interest rate paid on loans in this market is called the overnight lending rate.

LO14.9   DESCRIBE THE MULTIPLE-DEPOSIT EXPANSION OF THE ENTIRE CHARTERED BANKING SYSTEM.

- The chartered banking system as a whole can lend by a multiple of its excess cash reserves because the banking system cannot lose cash reserves, although individual banks can lose cash reserves to other banks in the system.

LO14.10   DEFINE THE MONETARY MULTIPLIER, EXPLAIN HOW TO CALCULATE IT, AND DEMONSTRATE ITS RELEVANCE.

- The multiple by which the banking system could lend on the basis of each dollar of excess cash reserves is the reciprocal of the desired reserve ratio. This multiple credit expansion process is reversible.

Terms and Concepts

medium of exchange	M2	balance sheet
unit of account	M2+	vault cash
store of value	M2++	desired reserves
liquidity	legal tender	desired reserve ratio
M1+	chartered bank	excess reserves
demand deposit	subprime mortgage loans	actual reserves
token money	mortgage-backed securities	overnight lending rate
Bank of Canada notes	securitization	monetary multiplier
near-monies	moral hazard	
savings deposit	fractional reserve banking system	

Discussion Questions

1. What are the three functions of money? Describe how rapid inflation can undermine money's ability to perform each of its three functions.   [LO14.1]

2. What are the components of the *M*1+ money supply? What is the largest component? Which of the components of *M*1 is legal tender? Why is the face value of a coin greater than its intrinsic value? Distinguish between *M*2, *M*2+, and *M*2++. What are near-monies?   [LO14.2]

3. Explain and evaluate the following statements.   [LO14.2]

   a. The invention of money is one of the great achievements of humankind, for without it the enrichment that comes from broadening trade would have been impossible.

   b. Money is whatever society says it is.

   c. In Canada, the debts of government and chartered banks are used as money.

   d. People often say they would like to have more money, but what they usually mean is that they would like to have more goods and services.

   e. When the price of everything goes up, it is not because everything is worth more but because the currency is worth less.

   f. Any central bank can create money; the trick is to create enough, but not too much of it.

4. What backs the money supply in Canada? What determines the value (domestic purchasing power) of money? How does the purchasing power of money relate to the price level? Who is responsible for maintaining the purchasing power of money?   [LO14.3]

5. How do each of the following relate to the U.S. financial crisis of 2007–2008: declines in real estate values, subprime mortgage loans, mortgage-backed securities?   [LO14.5]

6. Explain why merchants accepted gold receipts as a means of payment even though the receipts were issued by goldsmiths, not the government. What risk did goldsmiths introduce into the payments system by issuing loans in the form of gold receipts?   [LO14.6]

7. Why is the banking system in Canada referred to as a fractional reserve banking system? What is the role of deposit insurance in a fractional reserve system?   [LO14.6]

8. What is the difference between an asset and a liability on a bank's balance sheet? How does net worth relate to each? Why must a balance sheet always balance? What are the major assets and claims on a chartered bank's balance sheet?   [LO14.7]

9. "Whenever currency is deposited in a chartered bank, cash goes out of circulation and, as a result, the supply of money is reduced." Do you agree? Explain why or why not.   [LO14.7]

10. "When a chartered bank makes loans, it creates money; when loans are repaid, money is destroyed." Explain.   [LO14.8]

11. Explain why a single chartered bank can safely lend only an amount equal to its excess cash reserves but the banking system as a whole can lend by a multiple of its excess reserves. What is the monetary multiplier, and how does it relate to the desired reserve ratio?   [LO14.9, 14.10]

12. How would a decrease in the desired reserve ratio affect the (a) size of the money multiplier, (b) amount of excess cash reserves in the banking system, and (c) extent to which the system could expand the money supply through the creation of demand deposits via loans?   [LO14.10]

Review Questions

1. The three functions of money are   [LO14.1]

   a. Liquidity, store of value, and gifting

   b. Medium of exchange, unit of account, and liquidity

   c. Liquidity, unit of account, and gifting

   d. Medium of exchange, unit of account, and store of value

2. Recall the formula that states that $V = 1/P$, where V is the value of the dollar and P is the price level. If the price level falls from 1 to 0.75, what will happen to the value of the dollar?   [LO14.3]

   a. It will rise by a third (33.3%).

   b. It will rise by a quarter (25%).

   c. It will fall by a quarter (225%).

   d. It will fall by a third (233.3%).

3. Alberta Bank is considering making a $50 million loan to a company named Sheet Oil that wants to commercialize a process for turning used blankets, pillowcases, and sheets into oil. This company's chances for success are dubious, but Alberta Bank makes the loan anyway because it believes that the government will bail it out if Sheet Oil goes bankrupt and cannot repay the loan. Alberta Bank's decision to make the loan has been affected by   [LO14.5]

   a. Liquidity

   b. Moral hazard

   c. Token money

4. True or False? The U.S. financial crisis hastened the ongoing process in which the financial services industry was transforming from having a few large firms to many small firms.   [LO14.5]

5. A goldsmith has $2 million of gold in his vaults. He issues $5 million in gold receipts. His gold holdings are what fraction of the paper money (gold receipts) he has issued?   [LO14.6]

   a. 1/10
   b. 1/5
   c. 2/5
   d. 5/5

6. A chartered bank has $100 million in demand-deposit liabilities and $12 million in actual reserves. The desired reserve ratio is 0.1. How big are the bank's excess reserves?   [LO14.7]

   a. $100 million
   b. $88 million
   c. $12 million
   d. $2 million

7. A single chartered bank in a multibank banking system can lend only an amount equal to its initial preloan _____.   [LO14.7]

   a. Total reserves
   b. Excess reserves
   c. Total deposits
   d. Excess deposits

8. The two conflicting goals facing chartered banks are   [LO14.8]

   a. Profit and liquidity
   b. Profit and loss

   c. Deposits and withdrawals
   d. Assets and liabilities

9. Suppose that the banking system in Canada has a desired reserve ratio of 10 percent while the banking system in the United States has a desired reserve ratio of 20 percent. In which country would $100 of initial excess reserves be able to cause a larger total amount of money creation?   [LO14.9]

   a. Canada
   b. United States

10. Suppose that the desired reserve is 10 percent and that chartered banks collectively have $2 billion in excess reserves. What is the maximum amount of new demand-deposit money that can be created by the banking system?   [LO14.10]

   a. $0
   b. $200 million
   c. $2 billion
   d. $20 billion

11. Suppose that last year $30 billion in new loans were extended by banks while $50 billion in old loans were paid off by borrowers. What happened to the money supply?   [LO14.10]

   a. Increased
   b. Decreased
   c. Stayed the same

Problems

1. Assume that the following asset values (in millions of dollars) exist in Ironmania: [LO14.1]

   Bank of Canada notes in circulation = $700

   Corporate bonds = $300

   Currency in chartered banks = $100

   Demand deposits = $1500

   Coins in circulation = $40

   Iron ore deposits = $50

   Personal savings deposits and nonpersonal notice deposits at chartered banks = $540

   a. What is $M1+$ in Ironmania?
   b. What is $M2$ in Ironmania?

2. Assume that Jimmy Cash has $2000 in his chequing account and uses his chequing account card to withdraw $200 of cash from the bank's automated teller machine. By what dollar amount did the $M1+$ money supply change as a result of this single transaction?   [LO14.2]

3. Suppose the price level and the value of the dollar in Year 1 are 1.0 and $1.00, respectively. If the price level rises to 1.25 in Year 2, what is the new value of the dollar? If instead the price level had fallen to 0.50, what would have been the value of the dollar? What generalization can you draw from your answers?   [LO14.3]

4. Assume that securitization combined with borrowing and irrational exuberance in Hyperville have driven up the value of existing financial securities at a geometric rate, specifically from $2 to $4 to $8 to $16 to $32 to $64 over a six-year time

period. Over the same period, the value of the assets underlying the securities rose at an arithmetic rate from $2 to $3 to $4 to $5 to $6 to $7. If these patterns hold for decreases as well as for increases, by how much would the value of the financial securities decline if the value of the underlying asset suddenly and unexpectedly fell by $5?   [LO14.4]

5. Suppose that Lady Gaga goes to Las Vegas to play poker and at the last minute her record company says it will reimburse her for 50 percent of any gambling losses that she incurs. Will Lady Gaga wager more or less as a result of the reimbursement offer? What economic concept does your answer illustrate? [LO14.5]

6. Suppose the assets of the Silver Lode Bank are $100,000 higher than on the previous day and its net worth is up $20,000. By how much and in what direction must its liabilities have changed from the day before?   [LO14.6]

7. Suppose that Serendipity Bank has excess cash reserves of $8000 and demand deposits of $150,000. If the desired reserve ratio is 20 percent, what is the size of the bank's actual cash reserves?   [LO14.6]

8. The Bank of Manitoba has cash reserves of $20,000 and demand deposits of $100,000. The desired reserve ratio is 20 percent. Households deposit $5000 in currency into the bank and that currency is added to cash reserves. What level of excess reserves does the bank now have?   [LO14.7]

9. Suppose again that the Bank of Manitoba has cash reserves of $20,000 and deposits of $100,000. The desired reserve ratio is 20 percent. The bank now sells $5000 in securities to the Bank of Canada, receiving a $5000 increase in its deposit there in return. How much in excess cash reserves does the bank now have? Why does your answer differ (yes, it does!) from the answer to Problem 8?   [LO14.8]

10. Suppose Yukon Bank has the following simplified balance sheet and that the desired reserve ratio is 20 percent.   [LO14.8]

Assets

	(1)	(2)
Cash reserves	$22,000	___	___
Securities	38,000	___	___
Loans	40,000	___	___

Liabilities and net worth

	(1)	(2)
Deposits	$100,000	___	___

a. What is the maximum amount of new loans this bank can make? Show in column 1 how the bank's balance sheet will appear after the bank has loaned this additional amount.

b. By how much has the supply of money changed?

c. How will the bank's balance sheet appear after cheques drawn for the entire amount of the new loans have been cleared against this bank? Show this new balance sheet in column 2.

d. Answer parts (a), (b), and (c) on the assumption that the desired reserve ratio is 15 percent.

11. Suppose the simplified consolidated balance sheet shown below is for the entire chartered banking system. All figures are in billions of dollars. The desired reserve ratio is 25 percent. [LO14.10]

Assets

	(1)	(2)
Cash reserves	$ 52	___	___
Securities	48	___	___
Loans	100	___	___

Liabilities and net worth

	(1)	(2)
Deposits	$200	___	___

a. How much in excess cash reserves does the chartered banking system have? What is the maximum amount the banking system might lend? Show in column 1 how the consolidated balance sheet would look after this amount has been lent. What is the size of the monetary multiplier?

b. Answer the questions in part (a) assuming that the desired reserve ratio is 20 percent. What is the resulting difference in the amount the chartered banking system can lend?

12. If the desired reserve ratio is 10 percent, what is the monetary multiplier? If the monetary multiplier is 4, what is the desired reserve ratio?   [LO14.10]

CHAPTER 15

Interest Rates and Monetary Policy

LEARNING OBJECTIVES

LO15.1 Discuss how the equilibrium interest rate is determined in the market for money.

LO15.2 List and explain the main functions of the Bank of Canada.

LO15.3 List and explain the goals and tools of monetary policy.

LO15.4 Describe the overnight lending rate and how the Bank of Canada directly influences it.

LO15.5 Identify the mechanisms by which monetary policy affects GDP and the price level.

LO15.6 Explain the effectiveness of monetary policy and its shortcomings.

LO15.7 Describe the effects of the international economy on the operation of monetary policy.

Recall from Chapter 9 that market economies are subject to fluctuations, often experiencing substantial unemployment and sometimes inflationary pressures. In this chapter you will learn that a change in the money supply affects interest rates, which influence the level of investment and real GDP. Thus the Bank of Canada, within limits, can help smooth out the fluctuations in the Canadian economy by influencing interest rates through its control of the money supply. The main goal of the Bank of Canada's **monetary policy** is to achieve and maintain price stability, but it would also like to see the economy achieve full employment. Price stability facilitates the ultimate aim of ensuring that a nation is employing all its resources–particularly its labour force–to their fullest extent.

15.1 / The Market for Money and the Determination of Interest Rates

LO15.1 Discuss how the equilibrium interest rate is determined in the market for money.

The Bank of Canada's primary influence on the economy in normal economic times is its ability to change the money supply ($M1+$) and therefore affect interest rates. Interest rates can be thought of in several ways. Most basically, **interest** is the price paid for the use of money. And it is the price that borrowers need to pay lenders for transferring purchasing power to the future. It can be thought of as the amount of money that must be paid for the use of $1 for one year. Although there is a full cluster of Canadian interest rates that vary by purpose, size, risk, maturity, and taxability, we will simply speak of *the* interest rate unless stated otherwise.

Let's see how the interest rate is determined. Because it is a *price*, we again turn to demand and supply analysis for the answer.

The Demand for Money

Why does the public want to hold some of its wealth as *money*? There are two main reasons: to make purchases with it, and to hold it as an asset.

TRANSACTIONS DEMAND, D_t

People hold money because it is convenient for purchasing goods and services. Households usually are paid once a week, every two weeks, or monthly, whereas their expenditures are less predictable and typically more frequent. So households must have enough money on hand to buy groceries and pay mortgage and utility bills. Revenues and expenditures are not simultaneous for businesses, either. Businesses need to have money available to pay for labour, materials, power, and other inputs. The demand for money as a medium of exchange is called the **transactions demand for money**.

The level of nominal GDP is the main determinant of the amount of money demanded for transactions. The larger the total money value of all goods and services exchanged in the economy, the larger the amount of money demanded for transactions. The transactions demand for money varies directly with nominal GDP. We specify *nominal* GDP because households and firms will want more money for transactions if prices rise or if real output increases. In both instances there will be a need for a larger dollar volume to accomplish the desired transactions.

In **Figure 15-1a (Key Graph)** we graph the quantity of money demanded for transactions against the interest rate. For simplicity, let's assume that the amount demanded depends exclusively on the level of nominal GDP and is independent of the interest rate. (In reality, higher interest rates are associated with slightly lower volumes of money demanded for transactions.) Our simplifying assumption allows us to graph the transactions demand, D_t, as a vertical line. This demand curve is positioned at $100 billion, on the assumption that each dollar held for transactions purposes is used in transactions on an average of three times per year and that nominal GDP is $300 billion. Thus the public needs $100 billion (= $300 billion/3) to purchase that GDP.

ASSET DEMAND, D_a

The second reason for holding money derives from money's function as a store of value. People may hold their financial assets in many forms, including corporate stocks, corporate or government bonds, or money. To the extent that they want to hold money as an asset, there is an **asset demand for money**.

People like to hold some of their financial assets as money (apart from using it to buy goods and services) because money is the most liquid of all financial assets: it is immediately usable for purchasing other assets when opportunities arise. Money is also an attractive asset to hold when the prices of other assets, such as bonds, are expected to decline. For example, when the price of a bond falls, the bondholder who sells the bond prior to the payback date of the full principal will suffer a loss (called a *capital loss*). That loss will partially or fully offset the interest received on the bond. Holding money presents no such risk of capital loss from changes in interest rates.

KEY GRAPH

FIGURE 15-1   The Demand for Money, the Supply of Money, and the Equilibrium Interest Rate

The total demand for money D_m is determined by horizontally adding the asset demand for money D_a to the transactions demand D_t. The transactions demand is vertical because it is assumed to depend on nominal GDP rather than on the interest rate. The asset demand varies inversely with the interest rate because of the opportunity cost involved in holding currency and chequable deposits that pay no interest or very low interest. Combining the money supply (stock) S_m with total money demand D_m portrays the money market and determines the equilibrium interest rate i_e.

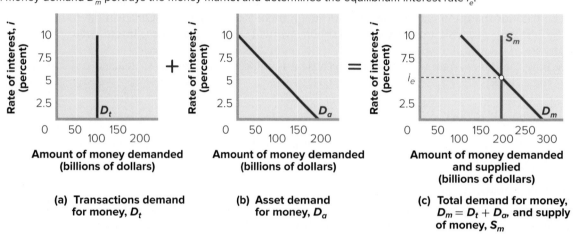

(a)   Transactions demand for money, D_t

(b)   Asset demand for money, D_a

(c)   Total demand for money, $D_m = D_t + D_a$, and supply of money, S_m

Quick Quiz

1. In this graph, at the interest rate i_e
    a. The amount of money demanded as an asset is $50 billion
    b. The amount of money demanded for transactions is $200 billion
    c. Bond prices will decline
    d. $100 billion is demanded for transactions, $100 billion is demanded as an asset, and the money supply is $200 billion

2. In this graph, at an interest rate of 10 percent
    a. No money will be demanded as an asset
    b. Total money demanded will be $200 billion
    c. The Bank of Canada will supply $100 billion of money
    d. There will be a $100 billion shortage of money

3. Curve D_a slopes downward because
    a. Lower interest rates increase the opportunity cost of holding money
    b. Lower interest rates reduce the opportunity cost of holding money

    c. The asset demand for money varies directly (positively) with the interest rate
    d. The transactions demand for money curve is perfectly vertical

4. Suppose the supply of money declines to $100 billion. The equilibrium interest rate would
    a. Fall, the amount of money demanded for transactions would rise, and the amount of money demanded as an asset would decrease
    b. Rise, and the amounts of money demanded both for transactions and as an asset would decrease
    c. Fall, and the amounts of money demanded both for transactions and as an asset would increase
    d. Rise, the amount of money demanded for transactions would be unchanged, and the amount of money demanded as an asset would decrease

Answers: 1. d; 2. a; 3. b; 4. d

The disadvantage of holding money as an asset is that it earns no or very little interest. Chequable deposits pay either no interest or lower interest rates than bonds. Currency itself earns no interest at all.

Knowing these advantages and disadvantages, the public must decide how much of its financial assets to hold as money, rather than other assets such as bonds. The answer depends primarily on the rate of interest. A household or a business incurs an opportunity cost when it holds money; in both cases, interest income is forgone or sacrificed. If a bond pays 6 percent interest, for example, holding $100 as cash or in a non-interest chequable account costs $6 per year of forgone income.

ORIGIN OF THE IDEA 15.1   Liquidity Preference

The amount of money demanded as an asset therefore varies inversely with the rate of interest (which is the opportunity cost of holding money as an asset). When the interest rate rises, being liquid and avoiding capital losses becomes more costly. The public reacts by reducing its holdings of money as an asset. When the interest rate falls, the cost of being liquid and avoiding capital losses also declines. The public therefore increases the amount of financial assets that it wants to hold as money. This inverse relationship is shown by D_a in Figure 15-1b.

TOTAL MONEY DEMAND, D_m

As shown in Figure 15-1c, we find the **total demand for money** D_m by horizontally adding the asset demand to the transactions demand. The resulting downsloping line in Figure 15-1c represents the total amount of money the public wants to hold, both for transactions and as an asset, at each possible interest rate.

Recall that the transactions demand for money depends on the nominal GDP. A change in the nominal GDP–working through the transactions demand for money–will shift the total money demand curve. Specifically, an increase in nominal GDP means that the public wants to hold a larger amount of money for transactions, and that extra demand will shift the total money demand curve to the right. In contrast, a decline in the nominal GDP will shift the total money demand curve to the left. As an example, suppose nominal GDP increases from $300 billion to $450 billion and the average dollar held for transactions is still spent three times per year. Then the transactions demand curve will shift from $100 billion (= $300 billion/3) to $150 billion (= $450 billion/3). The total money demand curve will then be $50 billion farther to the right at each possible interest rate.

WORKED PROBLEM 15.1   Demand for Money

The Equilibrium Interest Rate

We combine the demand for money with the supply of money to determine the equilibrium rate of interest. In Figure 15-1c, the vertical line S_m represents the money supply. It is a vertical line because the monetary authorities and financial institutions provide the economy with some particular stock of money. Here, it is $200 billion.

Just as in a product market or a factor market, the intersection of demand and supply determines the equilibrium price in the market for money. In Figure 15-1, this equilibrium price is the equilibrium interest rate, i_e. At this interest rate, the quantity of money demanded (= $200 billion) equals the quantity of money supplied (= $200 billion). The equilibrium interest rate can be thought of as the market-determined price that borrowers must pay for using someone else's money over some period of time. Changes in the demand for money, the supply of money, or both can change the equilibrium interest rate. For reasons that will soon become apparent, we are most interested in changes in the supply of money. The important generalization is this: An increase in the supply of money will lower the equilibrium interest rate; a decrease in the supply of money will raise the equilibrium interest rate.

Interest Rates and Bond Prices

Interest rates and bond prices are closely related. When the interest rate rises, bond prices fall; when the interest rate falls, bond prices rise. Why is this so? First understand that bonds are bought and sold in financial markets, and that the price of bonds is determined by bond demand and bond supply. Suppose that a bond with no expiration date (also called a *consol*) pays a fixed $50 in annual interest and is selling for its face value of $1000. The interest yield on this bond is 5 percent:

$$\frac{\$50}{\$1000} = 5\% \text{ interest yield}$$

Now suppose the interest rate in the economy rises to 7.5 percent from 5 percent. Newly issued bonds will pay $75 per $1000 lent. Older bonds paying only $50 will not be saleable at their $1000 face value. To compete with the 7.5 percent bond, the price of this bond will need to fall to $667 to remain competitive. The $50 fixed annual interest payment will then yield 7.5 percent to whoever buys the bond:

$$\frac{\$50}{\$667} = 7.5\%$$

WORKED PROBLEM 15.2   Bond Prices and Interest Rates

Next suppose that the interest rate falls to 2.5 percent from the original 5 percent. Newly issued bonds will pay $25 on $1000 loaned. A bond paying $50 will be highly attractive. Bond buyers will bid up its price to $2000, where the yield will equal 2.5 percent.

$$\frac{\$50}{\$2000} = 2.5\%$$

The point is that bond prices fall when the interest rate rises, and rise when the interest rate falls. There is an inverse relationship between the interest rate and bond prices.

QUICK REVIEW 15.1

- People demand money for transaction and asset purposes.
- The total demand for money is the sum of the transactions and asset demands; it is graphed as an inverse relationship (downsloping line) between the interest rate and the quantity of money demanded.
- The equilibrium interest rate is determined by money demand and supply; it occurs when people are willing to hold the exact amount of money being supplied by the monetary authorities.
- Interest rates and bond prices are inversely related.

15.2 / Functions of the Bank of Canada

LO15.2 List and explain the main functions of the Bank of Canada.

The functions of the Bank of Canada, the country's **central bank**, can be divided into five categories. We discuss the most important function last.

1. ***Acting as the "Bankers' Bank"*** You head for the nearest chartered bank if you want to deposit, withdraw, or borrow money; the chartered banks turn to the Bank of Canada as their bank. As such, the Bank of Canada is sometimes referred to as "the lender of last resort." There are times when the chartered banks need to borrow from the central bank. Chartered banks also keep minimal reserves with the Bank of Canada to settle bilateral payment balances among themselves.

2. *Issuing Currency* The Bank of Canada supplies the economy with paper currency–Bank of Canada notes–and coins. This involves designing notes and coins; printing, stamping, and distributing new notes and coins; and replacing worn currency.

3. *Acting as Fiscal Agent* The Bank of Canada acts as the fiscal agent (provider of financial services, including banking) for the federal government. The federal government collects funds through taxation, spends these funds on a variety of goods and services, and sells and redeems bonds. The federal government uses the Bank of Canada's facilities to carry out these activities.

4. *Supervising the Chartered Banks* The Department of Finance and the Bank of Canada supervise the operations of chartered banks and other nonbank financial institutions. The Bank of Canada makes periodic assessments of the banks' profitability, to check that the chartered banks perform in accordance with the many regulations to which they are subject, and to uncover questionable practices or fraud.

5. *Regulating the Supply of Money* Finally, and most important, the Bank of Canada has ultimate responsibility for regulating the supply of money, and this in turn enables it to influence interest rates. The major task of the central bank is to manage the money supply (and thus interest rates) according to the needs of the economy. This involves making available an amount of money consistent with high and steadily rising levels of output and employment, and a relatively constant price level. While all of the other functions of the Bank of Canada are routine or of a service nature, managing the money supply requires making basic, but unique, policy decisions.

Bank of Canada Independence

Parliament purposely established the Bank of Canada as an independent agency of government. The objective was to protect the Bank of Canada from political pressures so that it could effectively control the money supply and maintain price stability. Political pressure may at times lead to inflationary fiscal policies, including tax cuts and special-interest spending. If the federal government also controlled the nation's monetary policy, citizens and lobbying groups undoubtedly would pressure elected officials to keep interest rates low even though at times high interest rates are necessary to reduce aggregate demand and thus control inflation. An independent monetary authority (the Bank of Canada) can take actions to increase interest rates when necessary to reduce inflation. Studies show that countries with independent central banks like the Bank of Canada have lower rates of inflation, on average, than countries that have little or no central bank independence.

Consolidated Balance Sheet of the Bank of Canada

With this basic understanding of interest rates we can turn to monetary policy, which relies on changes in interest rates to be effective. The Bank of Canada balance sheet helps us consider how it conducts monetary policy. Table 15-1 consolidates the assets and liabilities of the Bank of Canada. You will see that some of the Bank of Canada's assets and liabilities differ from those found on the balance sheet of chartered banks.

Assets

The two main assets of the Bank of Canada are securities and (much smaller) advances to the chartered banks.

1. *Securities* The securities shown in Table 15-1 are Government of Canada bonds (long-term securities) and Treasury bills (short-term securities) issued by the Government of Canada to finance past and present budget deficits. These securities are part of the public debt–money borrowed by the federal government. Some were bought directly from the government, but most from the public (through investment dealers) and the chartered banks. Although they are an important source of interest income to the Bank of Canada, they are bought and sold primarily to influence the amount of chartered bank reserves, and therefore the banks' ability to create money by lending.

TABLE 15-1	Bank of Canada Statement of Assets and Liabilities, December 31, 2014 (in millions)		
Assets		**Liabilities**	
Advances to chartered banks	$ 26	Notes in circulation	$68,980
Treasury bills of Canada	19,998	Government of Canada deposits	21,874
Other securities issued or guaranteed by Canada	71,022	Chartered bank deposits	176
Securities purchased under resale agreement	1,397	Other liabilities	2,263
Other assets	850	Total	$ 93,293
Total	$ 93,293		

Source: Adapted from Bank of Canada, Weekly Financial Statistics, February 20, 2015, http://www.bankofcanada.ca/publications-research/periodicals/wfs/; accessed July 23, 2015.

2. *Advances to Chartered Banks* For reasons that will soon become clear, chartered banks occasionally borrow from the Bank of Canada. The promissory notes (IOUs) that the chartered banks give to the Bank of Canada in negotiating advances are listed as advances to chartered banks. These IOUs are assets to the Bank of Canada because they are claims against the chartered banks. To the chartered banks, these IOUs are liabilities. Through borrowing, the chartered banks obtain increases in their reserves. Advances to the chartered banks are not large, usually making up less than 2 percent of the Bank of Canada's assets.

Liabilities

On the liability side of the Bank of Canada's consolidated balance sheet, there are three main items: chartered bank deposits, Government of Canada deposits, and notes in circulation.

1. *Chartered Bank Deposits* These deposits are assets of the chartered banks but a liability to the Bank of Canada. Up to the early 1990s chartered banks were required by law to keep a specified percentage of their reserves with the Bank of Canada. Since the abolition of required reserves, these deposits have been considerably reduced because their only function is to permit cheque-clearing to settle payment balances among the chartered banks.

2. *Government of Canada Deposits* The federal government keeps deposits at the Bank of Canada and draws cheques on them to pay its obligations. To the government, all such deposits are assets, while to the banks, including the central bank, they are liabilities.

3. *Notes in Circulation* The supply of paper money in Canada consists of bank notes issued by the Bank of Canada. When this paper money is circulating outside the Bank of Canada, it is treated as claims against the assets of the Bank of Canada and is thus a liability.

QUICK REVIEW 15.2

- The two main assets of the Bank of Canada are securities and loans to chartered banks. Most of the securities are bills, notes, and bonds issued by the federal government to finance past federal budget deficits.

- The three major liabilities of the Bank of Canada are the reserves of chartered banks, the Government of Canada deposits, and outstanding Bank of Canada notes.

15.3 / Goals and Tools of Monetary Policy

LO15.3 List and explain the goals and tools of monetary policy.

With this look at the Bank of Canada's consolidated balance sheet, we can now explore how the Bank of Canada can influence the money-creating abilities of the commercial banking system. The Bank of Canada is responsible for supervising and controlling the operation of the Canadian financial system. (For the names of central banks in various nations, see Global Perspective 15.1.)

The objective of the Bank of Canada's monetary policy is to keep inflation low, stable, and predictable so as to help to moderate the business cycle and help the economy attain full employment and sustained economic growth. Monetary policy consists of altering the economy's money supply to influence interest rates, which indirectly affect the inflation rate, employment, and the level of economic activity in the Canadian economy. In a recession, or in anticipation of a slowdown, the Bank of Canada would increase the money supply, which decreases interest rates, to stimulate spending. At the present time the Bank of Canada has an inflation target range of 1–3 percent annually. If the Canadian economy were expanding too quickly and accompanied by inflation above 3 percent, the Bank of Canada would restrict the money supply to raise interest rates, which would help to slow the economy down.

The Bank of Canada alters the amount of the nation's money supply by manipulating the amount of excess reserves held by chartered banks. Excess reserves, you will recall, are crucial to the money-creating ability of the banking system. Once we see how the Bank of Canada controls excess reserves and the money supply, we will explain how changes in the stock of money affect interest rates, aggregate demand, and the economy.

Tools of Monetary Policy

The Bank of Canada implements monetary policy through its influence on short-term interest rates. We will see later in this chapter that monetary policy also affects the value of the Canadian dollar on foreign exchange markets. The Bank of Canada keeps a watchful eye on the Canadian-dollar exchange rate, the

15.1 GLOBAL PERSPECTIVE

Central Banks, Selected Nations

The monetary policies of the central banks in the world's nations are often in the international news. Here are some of their official names, along with a few of their popular nicknames.

Australia: Reserve Bank of Australia ("RBA")

Canada: Bank of Canada

Euro Zone: European Central Bank ("ECB")

Japan: The Bank of Japan ("BOJ")

Mexico: Banco de Mexico ("Mex Bank")

Russia: Central Bank of Russia

Sweden: Sveriges Riksbank

United Kingdom: Bank of England

United States: Federal Reserve System (the "Fed") (12 regional Federal Reserve Banks)

output performance of the Canadian economy, and the behaviour of the Consumer Price Index (CPI), and implements monetary policy accordingly. Monetary policy is implemented primarily by influencing chartered bank reserves.

ORIGIN OF THE IDEA 15.2   Tools of Monetary Policy

The Bank of Canada has one main instrument and one of lesser importance in influencing and changing chartered bank reserves: open-market operations and the bank rate.

Open-Market Operations

Bond markets are "open" to all buyers and sellers of corporate and government bonds (securities). The Bank of Canada is the largest single holder of Canadian government securities. The federal government, not the Bank of Canada, issues these Treasury bills and long-term bonds to finance past budget deficits. Over the decades, the Bank of Canada has purchased these securities from major financial institutions that buy and sell government and corporate securities for themselves or their customers.

The Bank of Canada's **open-market operations** consist of the buying of government bonds from, or the selling of government bonds to, chartered banks and the general public. (The Bank of Canada actually buys and sells the government bonds to chartered banks and the public through a few large financial firms called *primary dealers*.) Open-market operations are the Bank of Canada's most important day-to-day instrument for influencing the money supply.

BUYING SECURITIES

Suppose the Bank of Canada decides to buy government bonds. It can purchase these bonds from chartered banks or the general public. In both cases, reserves of the chartered banks will increase.

From Chartered Banks   When the Bank of Canada buys government bonds from chartered banks

(a) The chartered banks give up a part of their holdings of securities (the government bonds) to the Bank of Canada.

(b) The Bank of Canada, in paying for these securities, places newly created reserves in the accounts of the chartered banks at the Bank of Canada. (These reserves are created "out of thin air," so to speak!) The reserves of the chartered banks go up by the amount of the purchase of the securities.

We show these outcomes as (*a*) and (*b*) on the following consolidated balance sheet of the chartered banks and the Bank of Canada.

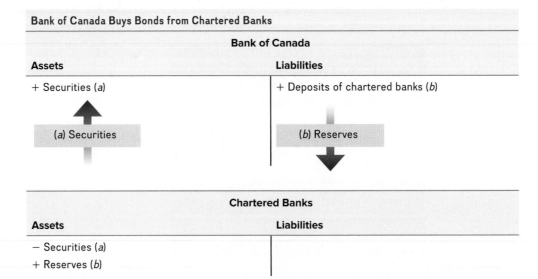

Bank of Canada Buys Bonds from Chartered Banks

Bank of Canada	
Assets	**Liabilities**
+ Securities (*a*)	+ Deposits of chartered banks (*b*)
(*a*) Securities	(*b*) Reserves

Chartered Banks	
Assets	**Liabilities**
− Securities (*a*)	
+ Reserves (*b*)	

The upward arrow shows that securities have moved from the chartered banks to the Bank of Canada. Therefore, we write "— Securities" (minus Securities) in the Assets column of the balance sheet of the chartered banks. For the same reason, we write "+ Securities" in the Assets column of the balance sheet of the Bank of Canada.

The downward arrow indicates that the Bank of Canada has provided reserves to the chartered banks. Therefore we write "+ Reserves" in the Assets column of the balance sheet of the chartered banks. The plus sign in the Liabilities column of the balance sheet of the Bank of Canada indicates that chartered bank deposits have increased; they are a liability to the Bank of Canada because the reserves are owned by the chartered banks.

What is most important about this transaction is that when the Bank of Canada purchases securities from chartered banks, it increases the reserves in the banking system, which then increases the lending ability of the chartered banks.

From the Public   The effect on chartered bank reserves is much the same when the Bank of Canada purchases securities from the public (through investment dealers). Suppose Mariposa Investments Limited (a large Toronto dealer representing the public) has Government of Canada bonds that it sells in the open market to the Bank of Canada. The transaction has several elements:

(a) Mariposa Investments gives up securities to the Bank of Canada and gets in payment a cheque drawn by the Bank of Canada on itself.

(b) Mariposa Investments promptly deposits this cheque into its account with the Bank of York.

(c) The Bank of York collects from the Bank of Canada and thus increases its reserves.

To keep things simple, we will dispense with showing the balance sheet changes resulting from the Bank of Canada's sale or purchase of bonds from the public. But two aspects of this transaction are particularly important. First, as with Bank of Canada purchases of securities directly from chartered banks, the purchase of securities increases the reserves and lending ability of the chartered banking system. Second, the supply of money is directly increased by the central bank's purchase of government bonds (aside from any expansion of the money supply that may occur from the increase in chartered bank reserves). This direct increase in the money supply has taken the form of an increased amount of chequing account money in the economy as a result of Mariposa's deposit.

There is a slight difference between the Bank of Canada's purchases of securities from the chartered banks and from the public. If we assume all chartered banks are "loaned up" initially, the Bank of Canada bond purchases *from chartered banks* increase actual reserves and excess reserves of chartered banks by the entire amount of the bond purchases. As shown in the left-hand panel of Figure 15-2, a $1000 bond purchase from a chartered bank would increase both the actual and excess reserves of the chartered bank by $1000.

In contrast, Bank of Canada purchases of bonds *from the public* increase actual reserves but also increase demand deposits. Thus, a $1000 bond purchase from the public would increase demand deposits and hence actual reserves of the "loaned up" banking system by $1000. But with a 20 percent desired reserve ratio applied to demand deposits, the excess reserves of the banking system would be only $800.

WORKED PROBLEM 15.3   Open Market Operations

However, in both transactions the end result is the same: *When the Bank of Canada buys securities (bonds) in the open market, chartered banks' reserves are increased.* When the chartered banks lend out an amount equal to their excess reserves, the nation's money supply will rise. Observe in Figure 15-2 that a $1000 purchase of bonds by the Bank of Canada results in a potential of $5000 of additional money, regardless of whether the purchase was made from the banks or from the general public.

SELLING SECURITIES

As you may suspect, when the Bank of Canada sells government bonds, chartered bank reserves are reduced. Let's see why.

FIGURE 15-2

The Bank of Canada's Purchase of Bonds and the Expansion of the Money Supply

Assuming all chartered banks are "loaned up" initially, a Bank of Canada purchase of a $1000 bond from either a chartered bank or the public can increase the money supply by $5000 when the desired reserve ratio is 20 percent. In the left-hand portion of the diagram, the purchase of a $1000 bond from a chartered bank creates $1000 of excess reserves that support an expansion of demand deposits of $5000 through making loans. In the right-hand portion, the purchase of a $1000 bond from the public creates only $800 of excess reserves, because $100 of reserves are needed to back up the $1000 new demand deposit in the banking system. The chartered banks can therefore expand the money supply by $4000 by making loans. This $4000 of chequing account money plus the initial new demand deposit of $1000 together equal $5000 of new money.

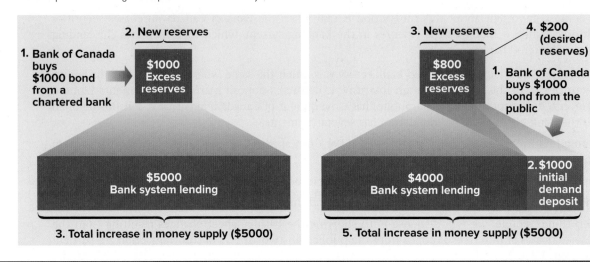

To Chartered Banks   When the Bank of Canada sells government bonds in the open market to chartered banks

(a) The Bank of Canada gives up securities that the chartered banks acquire.

(b) Chartered banks pay for those securities by drawing cheques against their deposits–that is, against their reserves–in the Bank of Canada. The Bank of Canada collects those cheques by reducing the chartered banks' reserves accordingly.

The balance sheet changes, again identified by (a) and (b), appear as follows:

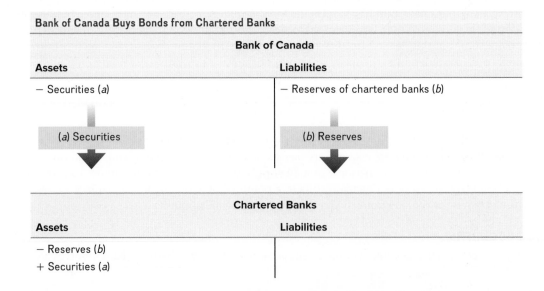

The reduction in chartered bank deposits in the Bank of Canada is indicated by the minus signs before these entries.

To the Public   When the Bank of Canada sells securities to the public, the outcome is much the same. Let's put Mariposa Investments Ltd. on the buying end of government bonds that the Bank of Canada is selling:

(a) The Bank of Canada sells Government of Canada bonds to Mariposa Investments, which pays with a cheque drawn on the Bank of York.

(b) The Bank of Canada clears this cheque against the Bank of York by reducing York's reserves.

(c) The Bank of York returns the cancelled cheque to Mariposa Investments, reducing the company's demand deposit accordingly.

The Bank of Canada bond sales of $1000 to the chartered banking system reduce the system's actual and excess reserves by $1000. But a $1000 bond sale to the public reduces excess reserves by $800, because demand deposit money is also reduced by $1000 in the sale. Since the chartered banking system has reduced its outstanding deposits by $1000 it need only keep $200 less in reserves.

Whether the Bank of Canada sells securities to the public or to chartered banks, the conclusion is the same: *When the Bank of Canada sells securities in the open market, chartered bank reserves are reduced.*

If all excess reserves are already lent out, this decline in chartered bank reserves will translate into a decline in the nation's money supply. In our example, a $1000 sale of government securities will result in a $5000 decline in the money supply, whether the sale was made to chartered banks or to the public. You can verify this by re-examining Figure 15-2 and tracing the effects of a sale of a $1000 bond by the Bank of Canada either to chartered banks or to the public.

What makes chartered banks and the public willing to sell government securities to, or buy them from, the Bank of Canada? The answer lies in the price of bonds and their interest yields. We know that bond prices and interest rates are inversely related. When the Bank of Canada buys government bonds, the demand for the bonds increases. Government bond prices rise and their interest yields decline. The higher bond prices and their lower yields prompt chartered banks, securities firms, and individual holders of government bonds to sell them to the Bank of Canada.

When the Bank of Canada sells government bonds, the additional supply of bonds in the bond market lowers bond prices and raises their yields, making government bonds attractive purchases for chartered banks and the public.

The Bank Rate and the Overnight Lending Rate

One of the functions of a central bank is to be a "lender of last resort," or as we noted earlier, "the bankers' bank." Occasionally, chartered banks have unexpected and immediate needs for additional funds. In such cases, the Bank of Canada will make short-term loans to chartered banks.

When a chartered bank borrows, it gives the Bank of Canada a promissory note (IOU) drawn against itself and secured by acceptable collateral—typically, Canadian government securities. Just as chartered banks charge interest on their loans, so too the Bank of Canada charges interest on loans it grants to chartered banks. The interest rate it charges is called the **bank rate**. The bank rate influences other interest rates in the economy, and thereby indirectly affects the amount of lending by chartered banks.

In providing the loan, the Bank of Canada increases the reserves of the borrowing chartered bank. All new reserves acquired by borrowing from the Bank of Canada are excess reserves. *In short, borrowing from the Bank of Canada by chartered banks increases the reserves of the chartered banks and enhances their ability to extend credit.*

Since February 1996, the bank rate has been set at the upper end of the Bank of Canada's **operating band** for the **overnight lending rate**, the interest rate at which chartered banks, investment dealers, and other financial market participants borrow and lend funds for one day. The Bank of Canada has a publicized target on the overnight lending rate and maintains it within a range of one-half of a percentage point (50 basis points) of the target range through open market operation, its main monetary policy tool. By lending and borrowing in the overnight market, the Bank of Canada affects the liquidity position of the chartered banks.

- The main objective of monetary policy is to achieve price stability and thereby help the economy achieve full employment.
- The Bank of Canada uses open-market operations to influence the overnight lending rate and the amount of

reserves in the banking system. The bank rate can also be used by the Bank of Canada to control reserves in the banking system, but is a more passive instrument.

15.4 / Targeting the Overnight Lending Rate

LO15.4 Describe the overnight lending rate and how the Bank of Canada directly influences it.

The Bank of Canada focuses monetary policy on the interest rate that it can directly influence: the overnight lending rate. This is the rate of interest that banks charge one another on overnight loans made from temporary excess reserves. The Bank of Canada sets a target level for the overnight rate, often referred to as the *key policy rate* or *key interest rate*. The Bank of Canada uses predetermined dates, known as *fixed announcement dates,* to communicate the target for the overnight interest rate.

Recall from Chapter 14 that each chartered bank has a desired reserve ratio that it targets. At the end of any business day, some banks temporarily have excess reserves (more actual reserves than they feel comfortable holding) and other banks have reserve deficiencies (fewer reserves than they want). To earn some interest, chartered banks prefer to lend out their temporary excess reserves overnight to other banks that temporarily need them to meet their desired reserve ratio. An equilibrium interest rate arises in this overnight market for bank reserves.

The Bank of Canada uses its status as a supplier of reserves to target the specific overnight lending rate that it deems appropriate based on the expected future performance of the Canadian economy. We demonstrate how this works in Figure 15-3, where we initially assume that the Bank of Canada desires a 4 percent overnight lending rate. The demand curve for reserves D_f slopes downward because lower interest rates give chartered banks with reserve deficiencies a greater incentive to borrow in the overnight market rather than reduce loans as a way to meet their desired reserve requirement. The supply curve for reserves, S_{f1}, is somewhat unusual. Specifically, it is horizontal at the targeted overnight rate, here 4 percent. (Disregard supply curves S_{f2} and S_{f3} for now.) It is horizontal because the Bank of Canada uses open-market operations to manipulate the supply of reserves so that the quantity supplied of reserves will exactly equal the quantity demanded of reserves at the targeted interest rate.

In this case, the Bank of Canada seeks to achieve an equilibrium overnight rate of 4 percent. In Figure 15-3 it is successful. Note that at the 4 percent overnight rate, the quantity of reserves supplied (Q_{f1}) equals the quantity of reserves demanded (also Q_{f1}). This 4 percent overnight rate will remain, as long as the supply curve of reserves is horizontal at 4 percent.

In recent years the overnight lending rate has been the primary vehicle through which the Bank of Canada has implemented monetary policy. It can enter the overnight loans market through a *special purchase and resale agreement* (SPRA), a transaction in which the Bank of Canada offers to purchase Government of Canada securities with an agreement to sell them back at a predetermined price the next business day. As you know by now, when the Bank of Canada buys bonds it puts downward pressure on short-term interest rates. Through SPRAs the Bank of Canada reinforces its target overnight rate.

Or the Bank of Canada can enter a *sale and repurchase agreement* (SRA), in which it offers to sell Government of Canada securities to designated counterparties with an agreement to buy them back at a

| FIGURE 15-3 | Targeting the Overnight Lending Rate |

In implementing monetary policy, the Bank of Canada determines a desired overnight lending rate and then uses open-market operations (buying and selling of securities) to add or subtract chartered bank reserves to achieve and maintain that targeted rate. In an expansionary monetary policy, the Bank of Canada increases the supply of reserves, for example, from S_{f1} to S_{f2} to move the overnight lending rate from 4 percent to 3.5 percent. In a restrictive monetary policy, it decreases the supply of reserves, say, from S_{f1} to S_{f3}. Here, the overnight lending rate rises from 4 percent to 4.5 percent.

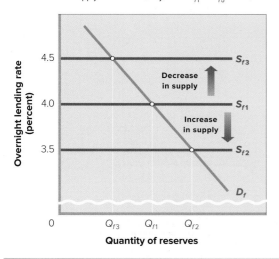

predetermined price the next business day. Selling securities puts upward pressure on interest rates; the Bank of Canada will enter into SRAs when it wants to see interest rates rise.

In Figure 15-3, if the demand for reserves increases (D_f shifts to the right along S_{f1}), the Bank of Canada will use its open-market operations to increase the availability of reserves through SPRAs (inject reserves) such that the 4 percent overnight rate is retained. If the demand for reserves in the overnight market declines (D_f shifts to the left along S_{f1}), the Bank of Canada will enter SRAs (withdrawn reserves) to keep the overnight rate at 4 percent.

Expansionary Monetary Policy

Suppose the economy faces recession and unemployment. How will the Bank of Canada respond? It will initiate an **expansionary monetary policy** (or *easy money policy*). This policy will lower interest rates to bolster borrowing and spending, which will increase aggregate demand and expand real output. The Bank of Canada's immediate step will be to announce a lower target for the overnight loans rate—say, 3.5 percent instead of 4 percent. To achieve that lower rate the Bank of Canada will use open-market operations to buy bonds from banks and the public, which increases the cash reserves in the banking system.

The greater cash reserves in the banking system produce two crucial results:

1. The supply of reserves in the overnight market increases, lowering the overnight rate to the new targeted rate. We show this in Figure 15-3 as a downshift of the horizontal supply curve from S_{f1} to S_{f2}. The equilibrium overnight rate falls to 3.5 percent, just as the Bank of Canada wanted. The equilibrium quantity of reserves in the overnight market for reserves rises from Q_{f1} to Q_{f2}.

2. A multiple expansion of the nation's money supply occurs (as we demonstrated in Chapter 14). Given the demand for money, the larger money supply places a downward pressure on other interest rates.

One such rate is the **prime interest rate**—the benchmark interest rate used by chartered banks as a reference point for a wide range of interest rates charged on loans to businesses and individuals. The prime interest rate is higher than the overnight rate because the prime rate involves longer, more risky loans than

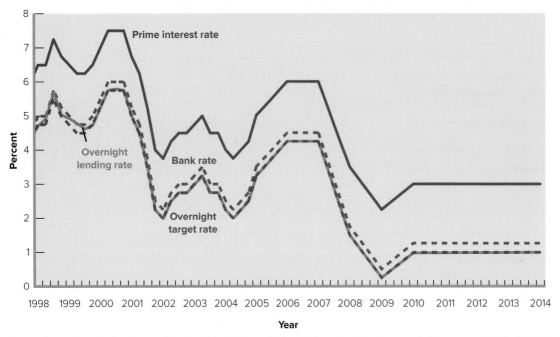

FIGURE 15-4

The Prime Interest Rate, the Bank Rate, the Overnight Target Rate, and the Overnight Lending Rate in Canada, 1998–2014

The prime interest rate rises and falls with changes in the bank rate, the overnight target rate, and the overnight lending rate.

Source: Adapted from Bank of Canada. Selected Historical Interest Rates. Retrieved from http://www.bankofcanada.ca/en/rates/sel_hist.html.

overnight loans between chartered banks. But the overnight rate, the prime interest rate, and the bank rate closely track one another, as is evident in Figure 15-4. Also evident are the changes in these rates over the period shown. We will address these changes later in our discussion of recent monetary policy.

Restrictive Monetary Policy

The opposite monetary policy is in order for periods of rising inflation. The Bank of Canada will then undertake a **restrictive monetary policy** (or *tight money policy*). This policy will increase the interest rate to reduce borrowing and spending, which will curtail the expansion of aggregate demand and hold down price-level increases. The Bank of Canada's immediate step will be to announce a higher target for the overnight rate—say, 4.5 percent instead of 4 percent. Through open-market operations, the Bank of Canada will sell bonds to the chartered banks and the public, and the sale of those bonds will absorb cash reserves in the banking system.

The smaller cash reserves in the banking system produce two results opposite those discussed for an expansionary monetary policy:

- The supply of overnight cash reserves decreases, raising the overnight lending rate to the new targeted rate. We show this in Figure 15-3 as an upshift of the horizontal supply curve from S_{f1} to S_{f3}. The equilibrium overnight rate rises to 4.5 percent, just as the Bank of Canada wanted, and the equilibrium quantity of reserves in this market falls to Q_{f3}.

- A multiple contraction of the nation's money supply occurs (as demonstrated in Chapter 14). Given the demand for money, the smaller money supply places an upward pressure on other interest rates. For example, the prime interest rate rises.

A good way to remember the role of the Bank of Canada in setting the overnight lending rate is to imagine a large bowl of water, with the amount of water in the bowl representing the stock of reserves in the banking system. Then think of the Bank of Canada as holding a large sponge, labelled "open-market operations." If the Bank of Canada wants to decrease the overnight lending rate, it uses the sponge—filled with reserves created by the Bank of Canada—to squeeze new reserves into the banking system's bowl. It continues this process until the greater supply of reserves reduces the overnight lending rate to the Bank of Canada's targeted level. If the Bank of Canada wants to increase the overnight rate, it uses the sponge to absorb cash reserves from the banking system. As the supply of reserves falls, the overnight rate rises to the Bank of Canada's targeted level.

The Taylor Rule

The proper overnight lending rate for a certain period is a matter of policy discretion by the Bank of Canada. It adheres to a strict inflationary target or monetary policy rule. And, as such, it appears to roughly follow a rule first established by economist John Taylor of Stanford University. The **Taylor Rule** assumes that the central bank is willing to tolerate a 2 percent target rate of inflation, and that the central bank follows three rules when setting its target for the overnight funds rate:

1. When real GDP is equal to potential GDP and inflation is equal to the target rate of 2 percent, the overnight lending rate should remain at about 4 percent, implying an overnight real lending rate of 2 percent (= 4 percent nominal overnight rate *minus* 2 percent inflation rate).

2. For each 1 percent increase of real GDP above potential GDP, the central bank should raise the *real* overnight rate by one-half a percentage point.

3. For each 1 percent increase in the inflation rate above its target of 2 percent, the central bank should raise the *real* overnight lending rate by one-half a percentage point. (Note, though, that in this case each 0.5-percentage-point increase in the real rate will require a 1.5-percentage-point increase in the nominal rate to account for the underlying 1 percent increase in the inflation rate.)

The last two rules are applied independently of each other so that, if real GDP is above potential output and at the same time inflation is above the 2 percent target rate, the Bank of Canada will apply both rules and raise real interest rates in response to both factors. For instance, if real GDP is 1 percent above potential output and inflation is simultaneously 1 percent above the 2 percent target rate, then the Bank of Canada will raise the *real* overnight lending rate by 1 percentage point (= one-half percentage point for the excessive GDP + one-half percentage point for the excessive inflation).

Also notice that the last two rules are reversed for situations in which real GDP falls below potential GDP or inflation falls below 2 percent. Each 1 percent decline in real GDP below potential GDP or fall in inflation below 2 percent calls for a decline of the *real* overnight lending rate by one-half percentage point.

WORKED PROBLEM 15.4 The Taylor Rule

We re-emphasize that the Bank of Canada has no official allegiance to the Taylor Rule. It changes the overnight lending rate to any level that it deems appropriate. During some periods, its policy has diverged significantly from the Taylor Rule.

- The Bank of Canada conducts its monetary policy by establishing a targeted overnight lending rate—the rate that chartered banks charge one another for overnight loans of reserves.

- An expansionary monetary policy (easy money policy) lowers the overnight rate, increases the money supply, and lowers other interest rates.

- A restrictive monetary policy (tight money policy) increases the overnight lending rate, reduces the money supply, and increases other interest rates.

- The Bank of Canada uses its discretion in setting the overnight lending rate, but its decisions regarding monetary policy and the target rate appear to be broadly consistent with the Taylor Rule over many time periods.

15.5 / Monetary Policy, Real GDP, and Price Level

LO15.5 Identify the mechanisms by which monetary policy affects GDP and the price level.

We have identified and explained the tools of expansionary and contractionary monetary policy. We now want to emphasize how monetary policy affects the economy's levels of investment, aggregate demand, real GDP, and prices.

Cause–Effect Chain: The Transmission Mechanism

The four diagrams in **Figure 15-5 (Key Graph)** will help you understand how monetary policy works toward the goal of achieving price stability and, indirectly, full employment.

MARKET FOR MONEY

Figure 15-5a represents the market for money, in which the demand curve for money and the supply curve for money are brought together. Recall that the total demand for money is made up of transactions demand and asset demand.

This figure also shows three potential money supply curves, S_{m1}, S_{m2}, and S_{m3}. In each case, the money supply is shown as a vertical line representing some fixed amount of money determined by the Bank of Canada.

The equilibrium interest rate is the interest rate at which the amount of money demanded and the amount supplied are equal. With money demand D_m in Figure 15-5a, if the supply of money is $125 billion ($S_{m1}$), the equilibrium interest rate is 10 percent. With a money supply of $150 billion ($S_{m2}$), the interest rate is 8 percent; with a money supply of $175 billion ($S_{m3}$), it is 6 percent.

You know that the real, not the nominal, rate of interest is crucial for investment decisions. So here we assume that Figure 15-5a portrays real interest rates.

INVESTMENT

These 10 percent, 8 percent, and 6 percent real interest rates are carried rightward to the investment demand curve of Figure 15-5b. This curve shows the inverse relationship between the interest rate—the cost of borrowing to invest—and the amount of investment spending. At the 10 percent interest rate it will be profitable for the nation's businesses to invest $15 billion; at 8 percent, $20 billion; at 6 percent, $25 billion.

Changes in the interest rate mainly affect the investment component of total spending, although they also affect spending on durable consumer goods (such as autos and furniture) that are purchased on credit. The impact of changing interest rates on investment spending is great because of the large cost and long-term nature of capital purchases. Capital equipment, factory buildings, and warehouses are tremendously expensive. In absolute terms, interest charges on funds borrowed for these purchases are considerable. Similarly, the interest cost on a house purchased on a long-term contract is very large: a one-half percentage point change in the interest rate could amount to a difference of thousands of dollars in the total cost of buying a home.

KEY GRAPH

FIGURE 15-5 Monetary Policy and Equilibrium GDP

An expansionary monetary policy that shifts the money supply curve rightward from S_{m1} to S_{m2} in panel (a) lowers the interest rate from 10 percent to 8 percent in panel (b). As a result, investment spending increases from $15 billion to $20 billion, shifting the aggregate demand curve rightward from AD_1 to AD_2 in panel (c) so that real output rises from the recessionary level of GDP_1 to the full-employment level at GDP_f along the horizontal line. In panel (d), the economy at point a has an inflationary gap, and thus GDP is above potential output. A restrictive monetary policy that shifts the money supply curve leftward from S_{m3} = $175 billion to just $162.5 billion in panel (a) will increase the interest rate from 6 percent to 7 percent. Investment spending thus falls from $25 billion to $22.5 billion in panel (b). The aggregate demand curve shifts leftward in panel (d) from AD_3 to AD_4, moving the economy along the horizontal line to equilibrium point b. This returns the economy to full-employment output and eliminates the inflationary gap.

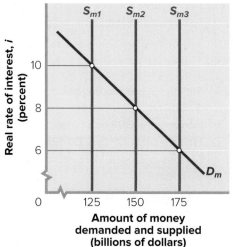

(a) The market for money

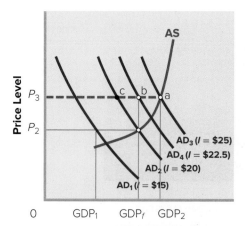

(b) Investment demand

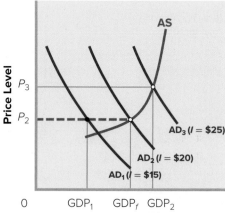

(c) Equilibrium real GDP and the price level

(d) Equilibrium real GDP and the price level

Quick Quiz

1. **The ultimate objective of an expansionary money policy is depicted by**
   a. A decrease in the money supply from S_{m3} to S_{m2}
   b. A reduction of the interest rate from 8 percent to 6 percent
   c. An increase in investment from $20 billion to $25 billion
   d. An increase in real GDP from GDP_1 to GDP_f

2. **A successful restrictive policy is shown as a shift in the money supply curve from**
   a. S_{m3} to a halfway point between S_{m2} and S_{m3}, a decrease in investment from $25 billion to $22.5 billion and a decline in aggregate demand from AD_3 to AD_4
   b. S_{m1} to S_{m2}, an increase in investment from $20 billion to $25 billion and an increase in real GDP from GDP_1 to GDP_f

   c. S_{m3} to S_{m2}, a decrease in investment from $25 billion to $20 billion and a decline in the price level from P_3 to P_2
   d. S_{m3} to S_{m2}, a decrease in investment from $25 billion to $20 billion and an increase in aggregate demand from AD_2 to AD_3

3. **The Bank of Canada could increase the money supply from S_{m1} to S_{m2} by**
   a. Increasing the bank rate
   b. Reducing taxes
   c. Buying government securities in the open market
   d. Selling government securities in the open market

4. **If the spending–income multiplier is 4 in the economy depicted, an increase in the money supply from $125 billion to $150 billion will**
   a. Shift the aggregate demand curve rightward by $20 billion
   b. Increase real GDP by $25 billion
   c. Increase real GDP by $100 billion
   d. Shift the aggregate demand curve leftward by $5 billion

Answers: 1.d; 2.a; 3.c; 4.a

In brief, the impact of changing interest rates is mainly on investment (and, through that, on aggregate demand, output, employment, and price level). Moreover, as Figure 15-5b shows, investment spending varies inversely with the interest rate.

Changes in the interest rate mainly affect the investment component of total spending.

EQUILIBRIUM GDP

Figure 15-5c shows the impact of our three interest rates and corresponding levels of investment spending on aggregate demand (ignore Figure 15-5d for the time being; we will return to it shortly). As noted, aggregate demand curve AD_1 is associated with the $15 billion level of investment, AD_2 with investment of $20 billion, and AD_3 with investment of $25 billion. That is, investment spending is one of the determinants of aggregate demand. Other things equal, the greater this investment spending, the farther to the right lies the aggregate demand curve.

Suppose the money supply in Figure 15-5a is $150 billion ($S_{m2}$), producing an equilibrium interest rate of 8 percent. In Figure 15-5b, we see that this 8 percent interest rate will bring forth $20 billion of investment spending. This $20 billion of investment spending joins with consumption spending, net exports, and government spending to yield aggregate demand curve AD_2 in Figure 15-5c. The equilibrium levels of real output and prices are GDP_f and P_2, as determined by the intersection of AD_2 and the aggregate supply curve AS.

To test your understanding of these relationships, explain why each of the other two levels of money supply in Figure 15-5a results in a different interest rate, level of investment, aggregate demand curve, and equilibrium real output and price level.

Effects of an Expansionary Monetary Policy

Recall that the inflationary ratchet effect discussed in Chapter 10 describes the fact that real-world price levels tend to be downwardly inflexible. Thus, with our economy starting from the initial equilibrium where AD_2 intersects AS, the price level will be downwardly inflexible at P_2 so that aggregate supply will be horizontal to the left of GDP_f. This means that if aggregate demand decreases, the economy's equilibrium will move leftward along the dashed horizontal line shown in Figure 15-5c.

Just such a decline would happen if the money supply fell to $125 billion ($S_{m1}$), shifting the aggregate demand curve leftward to AD_1 in Figure 15-5c. This results in a real output of GDP_1, less than the economy's full-employment GDP level. The economy will be experiencing recession, a negative GDP gap, and substantial unemployment. The Bank of Canada should therefore institute an expansionary monetary policy.

To increase the money supply, the Bank of Canada will buy government securities from chartered banks and the public in the open market, while at the same time decreasing the bank rate. The intended outcome will be an increase in excess cash reserves in the chartered banking system and a decline in the overnight rate. Because excess reserves are the basis on which chartered banks can earn profit by lending and thereby expand the money supply, the nation's money supply likely will rise. An increase in the money supply will lower the interest rate, increasing investment, aggregate demand, and equilibrium GDP.

For example, an increase in the money supply from $125 billion to $150 billion ($S_{m1}$ to S_{m2}) will reduce the interest rate from 10 percent to 8 percent, as indicated in Figure 15-5a, and increase investment from $15 billion to $20 billion, as shown in Figure 15-5b. This $5 billion increase in investment spending will shift the aggregate demand curve rightward from AD_1 to AD_2, as shown in Figure 15-5c. This rightward shift in the aggregate demand curve along the dashed horizontal line will increase from GDP_1 to the desired full-employment output at GDP_f, thereby closing the negative GDP gap.[1]

Column 1 of Table 15-2 summarizes the chain of events associated with an expansionary monetary policy.

Effects of a Restrictive Monetary Policy

Let's turn next to restrictive monetary policy. To prevent overcrowding, we will use parts (a), (b), and (d) {not part (c)} in Figure 15-5 to demonstrate the effects of a restrictive monetary policy on the economy. Figure 15-5d represents exactly the same economy as Figure 15-5c, but adds some extra curves that relate only to our explanation of restrictive monetary policy.

To see how restrictive monetary policy works, let us first consider a situation in which the economy moves from a full-employment equilibrium to operating at more than full employment so that inflation is a problem and restrictive monetary policy would be appropriate. Assume the economy begins at the full-employment equilibrium where AD_2 and AS intersect. The price level is P_2 at equilibrium GDP_f. Next, assume that the money supply expands from $150 billion to $175 billion ($S_{m3}$) in Figure 15-5a. This results in an interest rate of 6 percent, investment spending of $25 billion rather than $20 billion, and aggregate

---

[1] To keep things simple, we assume that the increase in real GDP does not increase the demand for money. In reality, the transactions demand for money would rise, slightly dampening the decline in the interest rate shown in Figure 15-5a.

TABLE 15-2	Monetary Policy: The Transmission Mechanism
(1) Expansionary monetary policy	**(2) Restrictive monetary policy**
Problem: Unemployment and recession	Problem: Inflation
↓	↓
Bank of Canada buys bonds and lowers the bank rate	Bank of Canada sells bonds and raises the bank rate
↓	↓
Excess cash reserves increase	Excess cash reserves decrease
↓	↓
Overnight rate falls	Overnight rate rises
↓	↓
Money supply rises	Money supply falls
↓	↓
Interest rate falls	Interest rate rises
↓	↓
Investment spending increases	Investment spending decreases
↓	↓
Aggregate demand increases	Aggregate demand decreases
↓	↓
Real GDP rises	Inflation declines

demand AD_3. As the AD curve shifts to the right from AD_2 to AD_3 in Figure 15-5d, the economy will move along the upsloping AS curve until it comes to an equilibrium at point a, where AD_3 intersects AS.

At the new equilibrium, the price level has risen to P_3 and the equilibrium level of real GDP is at GDP_1, indicating an inflationary GDP gap. Aggregate demand AD_3 is excessive relative to the economy's full-employment level of real output GDP_f. To rein in spending, the Bank of Canada will institute a restrictive monetary policy. The Bank of Canada will undertake to sell government bonds to chartered banks and to the public in the open market, while at the same time increasing the bank rate. Banks will then discover that their reserves are too low to meet possible cash withdrawals and therefore will need to reduce their demand deposits by refraining from issuing new loans as old loans are paid back. This will shrink the money supply and increase the interest rate. The higher interest rate will discourage investment, decreasing aggregate demand and restraining demand-pull inflation.

But the Bank of Canada must be careful about just how much to decrease the money supply. The problem is that the inflation ratchet will take effect at the new equilibrium point a, such that prices will be inflexible at price level P_3. As a result, the dashed horizontal line to the left of point a in Figure 15-5d will become relevant. This means that the Bank of Canada cannot simply lower the money supply to S_{m2} in Figure 15-5a. If it were to do that, investment demand would fall to $20 billion in Figure 15-5b, and the AD curve would shift to the left from AD_3 back to AD_2. But because of inflexible prices, the economy's equilibrium would move to point c, where AD_2 intersects the horizontal dashed line that represents aggregate supply to the left of point a. This would put the economy into a recession, with equilibrium output below the full-employment output level of GDP_f.

To achieve full employment, the Bank of Canada needs to move the AD curve back only from AD_3 to AD_4, so that the economy will come to equilibrium at point b. This will require a decrease in aggregate demand, so that equilibrium output falls from GDP_2 at point a to GDP_f at point b. The Bank of Canada can achieve this shift by setting the supply of money in Figure 15-5a at $162.5 billion.

To see how this works, draw a vertical money supply curve in Figure 15-5a at $162.5 billion and label it as S_{m4}. It will be exactly halfway between money supply curves S_{m2} and S_{m3}. Notice that the intersection of

S_{m4} with the money demand curve D_m will result in an interest rate of 7 percent. In Figure 15-5b, this interest rate of 7 percent will result in investment spending of $22.5 billion (halfway between $20 billion and $25 billion). Thus, by setting money supply at $162.5 billion, the Bank of Canada can reduce investment, lowering it to a level associated with AD_4. This shift will move the economy to equilibrium point b, returning output to the full employment level and eliminating the inflationary GDP gap.[2]

Column 2 of Table 15-2 summarizes the cause–effect chain of a restrictive monetary policy.

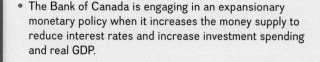

QUICK REVIEW 15.5

- The Bank of Canada is engaging in an expansionary monetary policy when it increases the money supply to reduce interest rates and increase investment spending and real GDP.

- The Bank of Canada is engaging in a restrictive monetary policy when it reduces the money supply to increase interest rates and reduce investment spending and inflation.

15.6 / Monetary Policy: Evaluation and Issues

LO15.6 Explain the effectiveness of monetary policy and its shortcomings.

Monetary policy has become the dominant component of Canadian national stabilization policy. It has two key advantages over fiscal policy: (1) speed and flexibility, and (2) isolation from political pressure.

Compared with fiscal policy, monetary policy can be quickly altered. Recall that government deliberations can delay the application of fiscal policy. In contrast, the Bank of Canada can buy or sell securities from day to day and thus affect the money supply and interest rates almost immediately.

Also, because the governor of the Bank of Canada is appointed and serves a seven-year term, the Bank of Canada is relatively isolated from lobbying and need not worry about being popular with voters. Thus, the Bank of Canada, more readily than the federal government, can engage in politically unpopular policies (higher interest rates) that may be necessary for the long-term health of the economy. Moreover, monetary policy is a subtler and more politically neutral measure than fiscal policy. Changes in government spending directly affect the allocation of resources, and changes in taxes can have extensive political ramifications. Because monetary policy works more subtly, it is more politically palatable.

Recent Monetary Policy in Canada

The Bank of Canada has been highly active in its use of monetary policy in recent decades. To demonstrate this fact, let's begin with the year 2000, in which the economy abruptly slowed from a five-year period of strong economic growth. Although inflation remained low in the late 1990s, in the last quarter of 2000 the economy began to slow. The Bank of Canada responded by cutting interest rates early in 2001. As it became evident that investment spending was dropping sharply, the Bank of Canada began cutting rates aggressively. The terrorist attacks on September 11, 2001, in the United States gave the Bank of Canada more reason to continue reducing interest rates. The overnight rate went from 5.75 percent in January 2001 to 2.0 percent by early 2002.

---

[2] Again, we assume for simplicity that the decrease in nominal GDP does not feed back to reduce the demand for money and thus the interest rate. In reality, this would occur, slightly dampening the increase in the interest rate shown in Figure 15-5a.

In 2002, the Canadian economy began to expand again, and the Bank of Canada responded by increasing the overnight rate to 2.75 percent by the end of the year. Despite the increase in interest rates in 2002, the Canadian economy did very well, adding more than 500,000 jobs and expanding the GDP at an annual rate of 3.1 percent. In 2003, the Bank of Canada left the overnight rate at 2.75 percent as the economy continued to expand at an unremarkable annual rate of 2 percent. In 2004, the Bank of Canada reduced the overnight rate to as low as 2 percent in an effort to stimulate the economy and then began to raise the overnight rate toward the end of 2004. Indeed, in 2004, GDP rose just under 3 percent. As the economy began to expand robustly in 2005, the Bank of Canada began a series of interest-rate hikes that saw the target overnight rate rise to 3.25 percent by the end of that year. The purpose of the rate hikes was to boost the prime interest rate (5.00 percent at the end of 2005) and other interest rates to make sure that aggregate demand continued to grow at a pace consistent with low inflation. In that regard, the Bank of Canada was successful.

The Bank of Canada continued to hike the overnight lending rate throughout 2006 and 2007 as the economy continued to expand and as the threat of inflation increased because of rising oil prices. But by early 2008 it became evident that the Canadian economy was slowing along with that in the U.S., where a housing bubble was unwinding and had created a financial crisis that spread across the globe. The overnight rate dropped to 1.5 percent by the end of 2008. In the first quarter of 2009, the global financial crisis that had engulfed most of the major economies of the world forced the Bank of Canada to drop the target overnight lending rate to a historic low of 0.25 percent, as the Canadian economy sank into a recession. The Bank of Canada felt that the global economic slowdown merited keeping interest rates at these historic lows until the middle of 2010. The uncertainty caused by the financial crisis made many financial institutions wary of lending for fear that borrowers would not be able to pay back the loans. In the initial stages of the financial crisis, Canada's chartered banks were even worried about lending to each other, not knowing which of them had exposure to the financial mess in the U.S., where the crisis had started. There was discussion about *quantitative easing* (or simply "credit easing"), which would have had the Bank of Canada purchase private sector assets (primarily bonds) to provide liquidity to a temporarily impaired financial system. Such purchases would have the effect of raising bond prices, and would thus reduce interest rates. The Bank of Canada was able to reduce interest rates through normal channels, and did not have to resort to direct quantitative easing. However, the financial crisis in the U.S. was of such magnitude that the Federal Reserve went through three rounds of quantitative easing, the last starting in September of 2012 and ending two years later.

As the Canadian economy returned to a normal growth rate, the Bank of Canada increased the overnight lending rate to 1 percent in the autumn of 2010, where it stayed until the end of 2014. When it became evident that the large drop in oil prices in 2014 would adversely impact the Canadian economy, the Bank of Canada reduced the overnight lending rate to 0.5 percent by the middle of 2015.

Problems and Complications

Despite its recent successes in Canada, monetary policy has certain limitations and faces actual-economy complications.

Lags

Recall that fiscal policy is hindered by three delays, or lags—a recognition lag, an administrative lag, and an operational lag. Monetary policy also faces a recognition lag and an operational lag, but because the Bank of Canada can construct and implement policy changes within days, it avoids the long administrative lag that hinders fiscal policy. A recognition lag affects monetary policy because normal monthly variations in economic activity and the price level mean that the Bank of Canada may not be able to quickly recognize when the economy is truly starting to recede or when inflation is really starting to rise. Once the Bank of Canada acts, an operational lag of three to six months affects monetary policy because that much time is typically required for interest-rate changes to have their full impacts on investment, aggregate demand, real GDP, and the price level. These two lags complicate the timing of monetary policy.

Cyclical Asymmetry and the Liquidity Trap

The metaphor of "pushing on a string" is often invoked to describe the problem of **cyclical asymmetry**, in which monetary policy may be more successful in slowing expansions and controlling inflation than in extracting the economy from severe recession. Imagine the Bank of Canada standing on the left-hand side of Figure 15.5d, holding one end of a "monetary-policy string." And imagine that the other end of the monetary-policy string is tied to the AD curve. Because the string would go taut if pulled on, monetary policy may be useful in *pulling* aggregate demand to the left. But because the string would go limp if pushed on, monetary policy will be rather ineffective at *pushing* aggregate demand to the right.

The reason for this asymmetry has to do with people's responses to changes in bank cash reserves. If pursued vigorously, a restrictive monetary policy can deplete bank reserves to the point where banks are forced to reduce the volume of loans. That means a contraction of the money supply, higher interest rates, and reduced aggregate demand. The Bank of Canada can absorb sufficient cash reserves and eventually achieve its goal. But the Bank of Canada cannot be certain of achieving its goal when it adds reserves to the banking system because of the so-called **liquidity trap**, in which adding more liquidity to banks has little or no additional positive effect on lending, borrowing, investment, or aggregate demand. For example, during the recent recession of 2008–2009, the Bank of Canada created billions of dollars of excess reserves that drove the overnight lending rate down to as low as 0.25 percent. The prime interest rate fell from 6.25 percent (July 2007) to 2.25 percent (April 2009). Nevertheless, lending by banks stalled at the start of the recession.

To switch analogies, an expansionary monetary policy suffers from a "You can lead a horse to water, but you can't make it drink" problem. The Bank of Canada can create excess reserves, but it cannot guarantee that the chartered banks will actually make additional loans and thus promote spending. If chartered banks seek liquidity and are unwilling to lend, the efforts of the Bank of Canada will be of little consequence. Similarly, households and businesses can frustrate the intentions of the Bank of Canada by not borrowing excess reserves being made available as loans. And when the Bank of Canada buys securities from the public, people may choose to pay off existing loans with the money received, rather than increase their spending on goods and services.

Furthermore, a severe recession may so undermine business confidence that the investment demand curve shifts to the left and overwhelms the lower interest rates associated with an expansionary monetary policy. That is what happened in the recession of 2008–2009. Although the Bank of Canada drove the real interest rate down to near zero percent, investment spending remained low and the economy remained mired in recession for the first part of 2009. The same happened in Japan in the 1990s and early 2000s. Although Japan's central bank drove the real interest rate to zero percent, investment spending remained low and the Japanese economy stayed mired in recession. The Japanese and Canadian experiences remind us that monetary policy is not an assured cure for the business cycle. Under some circumstances, implementing monetary policy may be like "pushing on a string."

Inflation Targeting

Some economists claim that the Bank of Canada's adoption of **inflation targeting**—the annual statement of a target range of inflation, currently 1–3 percent—for the economy is to be credited for its recent successes. The Bank of Canada now explains to the public how each monetary action fits within its overall strategy. If the Bank of Canada misses its target, it explains what went wrong. So inflation targeting has increased the "transparency" (openness) of monetary policy and increased the Bank of Canada's accountability. Proponents of inflation targeting say that, along with increasing transparency and accountability, it has focused Canada's central bank on what should be its main mission: controlling inflation. They say that an explicit commitment to price-level stability has created more certainty for households and firms about future product and input prices and created greater output stability. The setting and meeting of an inflation target has also achieved its important subsidiary goals of full employment and economic growth. Several other countries have adopted inflation targeting, including New Zealand, Sweden, and the United Kingdom.

- The Bank of Canada aggressively lowered the overnight lending rate following the Great Recession of 2008–2009. The overnight lending rate was increased in 2010 to 1 percent where it stayed for 4 years. It was reduced to 0.5 percent by mid 2015 to ward off the negative effects on the Canadian economy of the drop in world oil prices.

- Monetary policy's main strengths are (1) speed and flexibility, and (2) political acceptability. Monetary policy's main weaknesses are (1) time lags and (2) potential reduced effectiveness during recession.

15.7 / Monetary Policy and the International Economy

LO15.7 Describe the effects of the international economy on the operation of monetary policy.

In Chapter 11 we noted that linkages among the economies of the world complicate domestic fiscal policy. These linkages extend to monetary policy as well.

Net Export Effect

As we saw in Chapter 13, an expansionary fiscal policy (financed by government borrowing) may increase the domestic interest rate because the government competes with the private sector in obtaining loans. The higher interest rate causes the Canadian dollar to appreciate in the foreign exchange market. So imports rise and exports fall, and the resulting decline in net exports weakens the stimulus of the expansionary fiscal policy. This is the so-called *net export effect* of fiscal policy.

Will an expansionary monetary policy have a similar effect? The answer is no. As outlined in column 1 of Table 15-3, an expansionary monetary policy does indeed produce a net export effect, but its direction is opposite that of an expansionary fiscal policy. An expansionary monetary policy in, say, Canada reduces the domestic interest rate. The lower interest rate discourages the inflow of financial capital to Canada. The demand for dollars in foreign exchange markets falls, causing the Canadian dollar to depreciate in value.

TABLE 15-3	Monetary Policy and the Net Export Effect
(1) Expansionary monetary policy	**(2) Restrictive monetary policy**
Problem: Recession, slow growth	Problem: Inflation
↓	↓
Expansionary monetary policy (lower interest rate)	Restrictive monetary policy (higher interest rate)
↓	↓
Decreased foreign demand for dollars	Increased foreign demand for dollars
↓	↓
Dollar depreciates	Dollar appreciates
↓	↓
Net exports increase (aggregate demand increases, strengthening the expansionary monetary policy)	Net exports decrease (aggregate demand decreases, strengthening the restrictive monetary policy)

It takes more dollars to buy, for example, a Japanese yen or a euro. All foreign goods become more expensive to Canadian residents, and Canadian goods become cheaper to foreigners. Canadian imports thus fall, and Canadian exports rise, so Canada's net exports increase. As a result, aggregate expenditures and equilibrium GDP expand in Canada.

We conclude that, in contrast to an expansionary fiscal policy that reduces net exports, an expansionary monetary policy *increases* net exports and thus strengthens monetary policy. The depreciation of the Canadian dollar that results from the lower interest rate means that Canadian net exports rise along with domestic investment. Similarly, the net export effect strengthens a restrictive monetary policy. To see how this happens, follow through the analysis in column 2 of Table 15-3.

Macroeconomic Stability and the Trade Balance

Assume that, in addition to domestic macroeconomic stability, a widely held economic goal is that Canada should balance its exports and imports on goods and services. That is, Canadian net exports should be zero. In simple terms, Canada wants to "pay its own way" in international trade by earning from its exports an amount of money sufficient to finance its imports.

Consider column 1 in Table 15-3 once again, but now suppose Canada initially has a very large balance-of-international-trade *deficit*, which means its imports exceed its exports and so it is *not* paying its way in world trade. By following through the cause–effect chain in column 1, we find that an expansionary monetary policy lowers the international value of the dollar so that Canadian exports increase and Canadian imports decline. This increase in net exports works to correct the initial balance-of-trade deficit.

We conclude that *the expansionary monetary policy that is appropriate for the alleviation of unemployment and sluggish growth is compatible with the goal of correcting a balance-of-trade deficit.* Similarly, if the initial problem was a Canadian trade surplus, a restrictive monetary policy would tend to resolve that surplus.

Now consider column 2 in Table 15-3 and assume again that Canada has a large balance-of-trade deficit. In using a restrictive monetary policy to restrain inflation, the Bank of Canada would cause net exports to decrease–Canadian exports would fall and imports would rise. That would mean a larger trade deficit.

We conclude that *a restrictive monetary policy is used to alleviate inflation conflicts with the goal of correcting a balance-of-trade deficit.* However, if the initial problem was a trade surplus, a restrictive monetary policy would help to resolve it.

Overall we find that an expansionary monetary policy alleviates a trade deficit and aggravates a trade surplus; a restrictive monetary policy alleviates a trade surplus and aggravates a trade deficit. The point is that certain combinations of circumstances create conflicts or trade-offs between the use of monetary policy to achieve domestic stability and the realization of a balance in the nation's international trade.

QUICK REVIEW 15.7

- The effect of an expansionary monetary policy on domestic GDP is strengthened by the increase in net exports that results from a lower domestic interest rate.

- A restrictive monetary policy is strengthened by a decline in net exports. Depending on the situation, there may be a conflict or complementarity between monetary policy's effects on the domestic and international economies.

The LAST WORD   Worries about ZIRP, QE, and Twist

*ZIRP, QE, and Operation Twist provided massive economic stimulus
during and after the Great Recession. But there remain many worries
about unintended consequences.*

When the U.S. financial crisis reached its peak in 2008, the Fed acted aggressively to prevent bank runs and stabilize the financial system by acting as a lender of last resort. It also did its best to get the economy moving again by lowering short-term interest rates to nearly zero—a strategy that came to be known as the zero interest rate policy, or ZIRP.

When ZIRP by itself didn't seem to be causing enough stimulus, the Fed also began engaging in trillions of dollars' worth of bond purchases. Those purchases went by the name of quantitative easing, or QE, because the Fed printed up electronic money to pay for the purchases, thereby massively increasing (easing) the total quantity of money in circulation. The Fed's hope was that the additional money would lead to additional spending and lending that would boost aggregate demand by increasing consumption and investment. Later, the policy known as Operation Twist lowered longer-term interest rates.

One important effect of ZIRP and Operation Twist was to help the U.S. federal government engage in aggressive deficit-financed fiscal stimulus. Thanks to ZIRP and Operation Twist, the federal government was able to fund large deficits by issuing 10-year bonds at nominal interest rates of about 2 percent—substantially lower than the historical average of about 6 percent.

But the Federal Reserve didn't just help the U.S. federal government with low interest rates. It also served as the federal government's primary lender. In 2012, for instance, the Federal Reserve purchased over 70 percent of all U.S. government debt. Thus, 70 percent of the federal government's new borrowing came from the Federal Reserve in the form of newly printed money that the Fed created in order to fund its open-market purchases of U.S. government bonds.

The consensus among economists was that the Fed's aggressive use of ZIRP and QE were warranted by the severity of the financial crisis and the historically slow pace with which the economy recovered after the 2007–2009 recession. However, concerns were also raised about possible unintended consequences.

One worry had to do with the large annual budget deficits that the U.S. federal government was running. While many economists felt that the large deficits were appropriate given the sluggish economy, others believed that the U.S. federal government was overspending and taking resources away from the private sector. As a result, they felt that the Fed's use of ZIRP and QE was making it too easy for the U.S. Congress to overspend and run large budget

deficits because the Fed would always provide a ready buyer for the bonds that had to be issued to finance those large deficits.

A longer-term worry was that when ZIRP ended and interest rates began to rise again toward normal levels, the U.S. federal government would be suddenly confronted with huge interest costs. Consider the $16 trillion of debt that had accumulated by 2013: $16 trillion borrowed at 2 percent interest generates annual interest payments of $320 billion per year. But if the interest rate on U.S. government debt were to rise back to its historical average of 6 percent, the annual interest payments on $16 trillion would come to $960 billion per year. Such a huge increase in annual interest payments would likely require either massive budget cuts or even more borrowing, unless the economy began to grow so quickly that increased tax revenues were enough to compensate for the increased interest payments.

Another problem with extremely low interests rates is that they punish savers. A senior citizen who has saved for retirement will find that her investments yield very low rates of return when the Fed is keeping interest rates low. Instead of being able to live off of the interest generated by her investments, she may find herself spending down her accumulated wealth because the interest payments amount to nearly nothing.

On a larger scale, U.S. pension plans and retirement funds are also hit hard by low interest rates. Those institutions take deposits from current workers, invest those funds, and promise to pay out certain amounts when workers retire. Prior to the financial crisis, most of those institutions had assumed that they would be able to earn 8 percent per year on the retirement funds that they were entrusted with. But with the Fed keeping interest rates so low, the pension plans and retirement funds were not earning anywhere near 8 percent per year on their investments. As a result, the low interest rates engineered by the Fed made it very unlikely that pension plans and retirement funds would be able to keep their promises to retirees and deliver enough money in 20 or 30 years to pay each individual retiree what he or she had been promised.

Luckily, Canada weathered the financial crisis relatively well compared to its southern neighbour thanks to a robust banking system that was not faced with a housing bubble as in the U.S. and had been more conservative in its lending practices. Thus the Bank of Canada did not have to turn to the same extreme measures as the Federal Reserve. Still, to fight the Great Recession, the Bank of Canada dropped short-term interest rates to historic lows, and they have remained at historic lows through 2015. But, as in the U.S., pension plans and retirement funds may find it difficult to maintain their promises to retirees in 20 or 30 years unless interest rates return to their long-term levels.

Question

Did Operation Twist target long-term or short-term U.S. interest rates? How does ZIRP cause problems for savers and pension funds? How might low interest rates lead to problematic fiscal policy decisions?

Chapter Summary

LO15.1 DISCUSS HOW THE EQUILIBRIUM INTEREST RATE IS DETERMINED IN THE MARKET FOR MONEY.

- The total demand for money consists of the transactions demand and the asset demand for money. The amount of money demanded for transactions varies directly with the nominal GDP; the amount of money demanded as an asset varies inversely with the interest rate. The market for money combines the total demand for money with the money supply to determine equilibrium interest rates.

- Interest rates and bond prices are inversely related.

LO15.2 LIST AND EXPLAIN THE MAIN FUNCTIONS OF THE BANK OF CANADA.

- The major functions of the Bank of Canada are to (a) be a lender of last resort (bankers' bank) to the chartered banks, (b) supply the economy with paper currency, (c) act as the fiscal agent for the federal government, (d) supervise the operations of chartered banks (together with the Department of Finance), and (e) regulate the supply of money.

- The Bank of Canada's major asset is Government of Canada securities. Its three major liabilities are chartered bank reserves, Government of Canada deposits, and notes in circulation.

LO15.3 LIST AND EXPLAIN THE GOALS AND TOOLS OF MONETARY POLICY.

- The goal of monetary policy is price stability. Full employment and economic growth are secondary objectives that follow directly from price stability.

- In regard to monetary policy, the most important assets of the Bank of Canada are Government of Canada bonds and Treasury bills.

- The two instruments of monetary policy are open-market operations and the bank rate. The instrument used most often is open-market operations.

LO15.4 DESCRIBE THE OVERNIGHT LENDING RATE AND HOW THE BANK OF CANADA DIRECTLY INFLUENCES IT.

- The overnight lending rate is the interest rate that banks charge one another for overnight loans of reserves. The prime interest rate is the banks' benchmark rate for a wide range of interest rates on short-term loans to businesses and individuals.

- The Bank of Canada adjusts the overnight rate to a level appropriate for economic conditions. In an expansionary monetary policy it purchases securities from chartered banks and the general public to inject reserves into the banking system. This lowers the overnight rate to the targeted level and also reduces other interest rates (such as the prime rate). In a restrictive monetary policy the Bank of Canada sells securities to chartered banks and the general public via open-market operations. Consequently, reserves are removed from the banking system, and the overnight rate and other interest rates rise.

LO15.5   IDENTIFY THE MECHANISMS BY WHICH MONETARY POLICY AFFECTS GDP AND THE PRICE LEVEL.

- Monetary policy operates through a complex cause–effect chain: (a) policy decisions affect chartered bank reserves; (b) changes in reserves affect the supply of money; (c) changes in the money supply alter the interest rate; (d) changes in the interest rate affect investment; (e) changes in investment affect aggregate demand; (f) changes in aggregate demand affect equilibrium real GDP and the price level. Table 15-2 draws together all the basic notions relevant to the use of monetary policy.

LO15.6   EXPLAIN THE EFFECTIVENESS OF MONETARY POLICY AND ITS SHORTCOMINGS.

- The advantages of monetary policy include its flexibility and political acceptability. In the recent past, the Bank of Canada has adroitly used monetary policy to hold inflation in check as the economy boomed, avoided recession in the economic slowdown of 2001, and hastened economic recovery. During the Great Recession of 2008–2009, monetary policy in Canada prevented the recession from becoming more severe and adroitly nursed the Canadian economy back to health. Today, nearly all economists view monetary policy as a significant policy tool.

- Monetary policy has two limitations and potential problems: (1) recognition and operational lags complicate the timing of monetary policy; (2) in a severe recession, the reluctance of banks to lend excess reserves and firms to borrow money to spend on capital goods may contribute to a liquidity trap that limits the effectiveness of an expansionary monetary policy.

LO15.7   DESCRIBE THE EFFECTS OF THE INTERNATIONAL ECONOMY ON THE OPERATION OF MONETARY POLICY.

- The effect of an expansionary monetary policy on domestic GDP is strengthened by the increase in net exports that results from a lower domestic interest rate.

- A restrictive money policy is strengthened by a decline in net exports. Depending on the situation, there may be a conflict or complementarity between monetary policy's effects on the domestic and international economies.

Terms and Concepts

monetary policy	open-market operations	restrictive monetary policy
interest	bank rate	Taylor Rule
transactions demand for money	operating band	cyclical asymmetry
asset demand for money	overnight lending rate	liquidity trap
total demand for money	expansionary monetary policy	inflation targeting
central bank	prime interest rate	

Discussion Questions

1. What is the basic determinant of (a) the transactions demand and (b) the asset demand for money? Explain how these two demands can be combined graphically to determine total money demand. How is the equilibrium interest rate in the money market determined? Use a graph to show the impact of an increase in the total demand for money on the equilibrium interest rate (with no change in money supply). Use your general knowledge of equilibrium prices to explain why the previous interest rate is no longer sustainable.   [LO15.1]

2. What is the basic objective of monetary policy? What are the major strengths of monetary policy? Why is monetary policy easier to conduct than fiscal policy?   [LO15.3]

3. Distinguish between the overnight lending rate and the prime interest rate. Why is one higher than the other? Why do changes in the two rates closely track each other?   [LO15.4]

4. Why is a decrease in the supply of overnight funds shown as an upshift of the supply curve in Figure 15-3, whereas an increase in overnight funds is shown as a downshift of the supply curve?   [LO15.4]

5. Suppose you are the governor of the Bank of Canada. The economy is experiencing a sharp rise in the inflation rate. What changes in (a) open-market operations and (b) the bank rate would you consider? Explain in each case how the change you advocate would affect chartered bank cash reserves and influence the money supply.   [LO15.5]

6. Explain the links between changes in the nation's money supply, the interest rate, investment spending, aggregate demand, real GDP, and the price level.   [LO15.5]

7. What do economists mean when they say that monetary policy can exhibit cyclical asymmetry? How does the idea of a liquidity trap relate to cyclical asymmetry? Why is this possibility of a liquidity trap significant to policymakers?   [LO15.6]

8. Does an expansionary monetary policy on domestic GDP strengthen or weaken net exports? Explain.   [LO15.7]

Review Questions

1. When bond prices go up, interest rates go_____ [LO15.1]

   a. Up

   b. Down

   c. Nowhere

2. A chartered bank sells securities to the Bank of Canada for $100,000. The money supply [LO15.3]

   a. Increases by $100,000

   b. Decreases by $100,000

   c. Is unaffected by the transaction

3. Use chartered bank and Bank of Canada balance sheets to demonstrate the effect of each of the following transactions on chartered bank reserves: [LO15.3]

   a. The Bank of Canada purchases securities from banks.

   b. Chartered banks borrow from the Bank of Canada at the bank rate.

   c. The chartered banks reduce their desired reserve ratio.

   d. Chartered banks increase their reserves after the Bank of Canada increases the interest rate that it pays on reserves.

4. A bank currently has $100,000 in demand deposits and $15,000 in actual reserves. If the desired reserve ratio is 20 percent, the bank has_____ in money-creating potential. If the desired reserve ratio is 14 percent, the bank has _____in money-creating potential. [LO15.3]

   a. $20,000; $14,000

   b. $3,000; $2,100

   c. $25,000; $1,000

   d. $5,000; $1,000

5. A bank borrows $100,000 from the Bank of Canada, leaving $100,000 of securities on deposit with the Bank of Canada to serve as collateral for the loan. The bank rate that applies to the loan is 4 percent and the desired reserve ratio is 10 percent. How much of the $100,000 borrowed by the bank will it keep as desired reserves? [LO15.3]

   a. $0

   b. $4,000

   c. $10,000

   d. $100,000

6. Which of the following actions will increase bank lending? [LO15.3]

   *Select **one or more** answers from the choices shown.*

   a. The Bank of Canada raises the bank rate from 5 percent to 6 percent.

   b. The chartered banks raise the desired reserve ratio from 10 percent to 11 percent.

   c. The Bank of Canada buys $400 million worth of bonds from chartered banks.

   d. The Bank of Canada lowers the bank rate from 4 percent to 2 percent.

7. If the Bank of Canada wants to increase the overnight lending rate using open-market operations, it should _____ bonds. [LO15.4]

   a. Buy

   b. Sell

8. True or False? A liquidity trap occurs when expansionary monetary policy fails to work because an increase in chartered bank reserves by the Bank of Canada does not lead to an increase in bank lending. [LO15.6]

9. True or False? In Canada, monetary policy has two key advantages over fiscal policy: (1) isolation from political pressure and (2) speed and flexibility. [LO15.6]

10. True or False? A restrictive money policy is strengthened by a decline in net exports. [LO15.7]

Problems

1. Assume that the following data characterize the hypothetical economy of Trance: money supply = $200 billion; quantity of money demanded for transactions = $150 billion; quantity of money demanded as an asset = $10 billion at 12 percent interest, increasing by $10 billion for each 2-percentage-point fall in the interest rate. [LO15.1]

   a. What is the equilibrium interest rate in Trance?

   b. At the equilibrium interest rate, what are the quantity of money supplied, the total quantity of money demanded, the amount of money demanded for transactions, and the amount of money demanded as an asset in Trance?

2. Suppose a bond with no expiration date has a face value of $10,000 and annually pays a fixed amount of interest of $800. Compute and enter in the spaces provided in the table that follows either the interest rate that the bond would yield to a bond buyer at each of the bond prices listed or the bond price at each of the interest yields shown. What generalization can be drawn from the completed table? [LO15.1]

Bond price	Interest rate(s)
$ 8,000	_____
_____	8.9
$10,000	_____
$11,000	_____
_____	6.2

3. In the table below you will find simplified consolidated balance sheets for the chartered banking system and the Bank of Canada. Use columns 1–3 to indicate how the balance sheets would read after each transaction in parts (a) to (c) is completed. Do not accumulate your answers; analyze each transaction separately, starting in each case from the numbers provided. All accounts are in billions of dollars.   [LO15.3]

Consolidated Balance Sheet:
All chartered banks
(billions of dollars)

Assets	(1)	(2)	(3)
Cash reserves...............$33	____	____	____
Securities 60	____	____	____
Loans...................... 60	____	____	____

Liabilities	(1)	(2)	(3)
Demand deposits...........$150	____	____	____
Advances from the Bank of Canada 3	____	____	____
	____	____	____

Balance Sheet:
Bank of Canada
(billions of dollars)

Assets	(1)	(2)	(3)
Securities $60	____	____	____
Advances to chartered banks 3	____	____	____

Liabilities	(1)	(2)	(3)
Reserves of chartered banks...$33	____	____	____
Government of Canada deposits 3	____	____	____
Notes in circulation..........27	____	____	____

a. A decline in the bank rate prompts chartered banks to borrow an additional $1 billion from the Bank of Canada. Show the new balance-sheet figures in column 1 of each table.

b. The Bank of Canada sells $3 billion in securities to the public, who pay for the bonds with cheques. Show the new balance sheet figures in column 2 of each table.

c. The Bank of Canada buys $2 billion of securities from chartered banks. Show the new balance sheet numbers in column 3 of each table.

d. Now review all of the above three transactions, asking yourself these three questions: (1) What change, if any, took place in the money supply as a direct and immediate result of each transaction? (2) What increase or decrease in chartered banks' cash reserves took place in each transaction? (3) Assuming a desired reserve ratio of 20 percent, what change in the money-creating potential of the chartered banking system occurred as a result of each transaction?

4. Suppose that the demand for overnight loans curve is such that the quantity of funds demanded changes by $120 billion for each 1 percent change in the overnight interest rate. Also, assume that the current overnight lending rate is at the 3 percent rate that is targeted by the Bank of Canada. Now suppose that the Bank of Canada retargets the rate to 3.5 percent. Assuming no change in demand, will the Bank of Canada need to increase or decrease the supply of overnight loans? By how much will the quantity of overnight loans have to change for the equilibrium to occur at the new target rate?   [LO15.4]

5. Suppose that the inflation rate is 2 percent, the overnight lending rate is 4 percent, and real GDP falls 2 percent below potential GDP. According to the Taylor Rule, in what direction and by how much should the Bank of Canada change the real overnight lending rate?   [LO15.4]

6. Using the table that follows for the country of Moola, answer the following questions.   [LO15.5]

a. What is the equilibrium interest rate in Moola?

b. What is the level of investment at the equilibrium interest rate? Is there either a recessionary output gap (negative GDP gap) or an inflationary output gap (positive GDP gap) at the equilibrium interest rate, and, if either, what is the amount?

c. Given money demand, by how much would the Moola central bank need to change the money supply to close the output gap? What is the expenditure multiplier in Moola?

Money supply	Money demand	Interest rate	Investment at interest rate shown	Potential real GDP	Actual real GDP at interest rates shown
$500	$800	2%	$50	$350	$390
500	700	3	40	350	370
500	600	4	30	350	350
500	500	5	20	350	330
500	400	6	10	350	310

CHAPTER 16

Long-Run Macroeconomic Adjustments

LEARNING OBJECTIVES

LO16.1 Explain how the economy arrives at its long-run equilibrium.

LO16.2 Explain how to apply the long-run AD–AS model to explain inflation, recessions, and growth.

LO16.3 Explain the short-run trade-off between inflation and unemployment (the Phillips Curve).

LO16.4 Discuss why there is no long-run trade-off between inflation and unemployment.

LO16.5 Explain the relationship between tax rates, tax revenues, and aggregate supply.

During the early years of the Great Depression, many economists suggested that the economy would correct itself *in the long run* without government intervention. To this line of thinking, economist John Maynard Keynes remarked, "In the long run we are all dead!"

For several decades following the Great Depression, macroeconomists understandably focused on refining fiscal policy and monetary policy to smooth business cycles and address the problems of unemployment and inflation. The main emphasis was on short-run problems and policies associated with the business cycle. But over people's lifetimes, and from generation to generation, the long run is tremendously important for economic well-being. For that reason, macroeconomists have refocused attention on long-run macroeconomic adjustments, processes, and outcomes. The renewed emphasis on the long run has produced significant insights about aggregate supply, economic growth, and economic development. We will also see that it has renewed historical debates over the causes of macroeconomic instability and the effectiveness of stabilization policy.

Our goals in this chapter are to apply the long-run AD-AS model to analyze inflation and recession, examine the inflation–unemployment relationship, and assess the effect of taxes on aggregate supply. The latter is a key concern of so-called *supply-side economics*.

16.1 / From the Short Run to the Long Run

LO15.1 Explain how the economy arrives at its long-run equilibrium.

In Chapter 11, we noted that in macroeconomics the difference between the *short run* and the *long run* has to do with the flexibility of input prices. Input prices are inflexible or even totally fixed in the short run but fully flexible in the long run. (By contrast, output prices are assumed under these definitions to be fully flexible in both the short run *and* the long run.) The assumption that input prices are flexible only in the long run leads to large differences in the shapes and positions of both the short-run and the long-run aggregate supply curves. As explained in Chapter 12, the short-run aggregate supply curve is an upsloping line, whereas the long-run aggregate supply curve is a vertical line situated directly above the economy's full-employment output level, GDP_f.

We will begin this chapter by discussing how aggregate supply transitions *from* the short run *to* the long run. Once that is done, we will combine the short-run and long-run aggregate supply curves with the aggregate demand curve to form a single model that gives insight into how the economy adjusts to economic shocks and changes in monetary and fiscal policy in the short run and the long run. That will lead us to discuss how economic growth relates to long-run aggregate supply and how inflation and aggregate supply are related in the short run and the long run. We will conclude with a discussion of a particular set of economic policies that may help both short-run aggregate supply and long-run aggregate supply.

Short-Run Aggregate Supply

Our immediate objective is to demonstrate the relationship between short-run aggregate supply and long-run aggregate supply. We begin by briefly reviewing short-run aggregate supply.

Consider the short-run aggregate supply curve AS_1 in Figure 16-1a. This curve AS_1 is based on three assumptions: (1) the initial price level is P_1, (2) nominal wages have been established on the expectation that this price level will persist, and (3) the price level is flexible both upward and downward. Observe

---

FIGURE 16-1   **Short-Run and Long-Run Aggregate Supply**

(a) In the short run, nominal wages and other input prices do not respond to price-level changes because of the expectation that price level P_1 will continue. An increase in the price level from P_1 to P_2 increases profits and output, moving the economy from a_1 to a_2; a decrease in the price level from P_1 to P_3 reduces profits and real output, moving the economy from a_1 to a_3. The short-run aggregate supply curve therefore slopes upward. (b) In the long run, a price-level rise increases nominal wages and other input prices and thus shifts the short-run aggregate supply curve leftward. Conversely, a decrease in the price level reduces nominal wages and shifts the short-run aggregate supply curve rightward. After such adjustments, the economy reaches equilibrium at points such as b_1 and c_1. Thus, the long-run aggregate supply curve is vertical.

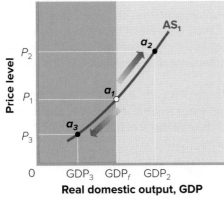

(a) Short-run aggregate supply

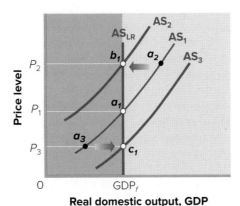

(b) Long-run aggregate supply

from point a_1 that at price level P_1 the economy is operating at its full-employment output GDP_f. This output is the real production forthcoming when the economy is operating at its natural rate of unemployment (or potential output).

Now let's review the short-run effects of changes in the price level–say, from P_1 to P_2 in Figure 16-1a. The higher prices associated with P_2 increase revenues to firms, and because the nominal wages the firms are paying their workers and other input prices remain unchanged, profits rise. Responding to the higher profits, firms collectively increase their output from GDP_f to GDP_2; the economy moves from a_1 to a_2 on curve AS_1. At GDP_2 the economy is operating beyond its full-employment output. Firms make this possible by extending the hours of part-time and full-time workers, enticing new workers such as homemakers and retirees into the labour force, and hiring and training the structurally unemployed. Thus, the nation's unemployment rate declines below its natural rate.

How will firms respond when the price level *falls*–say, from P_1 to P_3 in Figure 16-1a? Because the prices they receive for their products are lower while the nominal wages they pay workers remain unchanged, firms discover that their revenues and profits have diminished or disappeared. Under these circumstances, firms reduce their employment and production, and as shown by the movement from a_1 to a_3, real output falls to GDP_3. The decline in real output is accompanied by increased unemployment; at output GDP_3 the unemployment rate is greater than the full employment associated with output GDP_f.

Long-Run Aggregate Supply

The outcomes are different in the long run. To see why, we need to extend the analysis of aggregate supply to account for changes in nominal wages that occur in response to changes in the price level. That will enable us to derive the economy's long-run aggregate supply curve. We illustrate the implications for the aggregate supply curve in Figure 16-1b. Again suppose the economy is initially at point a_1 (P_1 and GDP_f). As we just demonstrated, an increase in the price level from P_1 to P_2 will move the economy from point a_1 to a_2 along the short-run aggregate supply curve AS_1. At a_2, the economy is producing at more than its potential output. This implies very high demand for productive inputs, so that input prices will begin to rise. In particular, the high demand for labour will drive up nominal wages, which will increase per-unit production costs. As a result the short-run supply curve then shifts leftward from AS_1 to AS_2, which now reflects the higher price level P_2 and the new expectation that P_2, not P_1, will continue. The leftward shift in the short-run aggregate supply curve to AS_2 moves the economy from a_2 to b_1. Real output returns to its full-employment level GDP_f, and the unemployment rate returns to its natural rate.

What is the long-run outcome of a *decrease* in the price level? Assuming downward wage flexibility, a decline in the price level from P_1 to P_3 in Figure 16-1b works in the opposite way from a price-level increase. At first the economy moves from point a_1 to a_3 on AS_1. Profits are squeezed or eliminated because prices have fallen and nominal wages have not. But this movement along AS_1 is the short-run response that results only while input prices remain constant. As time passes, input prices will begin to fall because the economy is producing at below its full-employment output level. With so little output being produced, the demand for inputs will be low and their prices will begin to decline. In particular, the low demand for labour will drive down nominal wages and reduce per-unit production costs. Lower nominal wages therefore shift the short-run aggregate supply curve rightward from AS_1 to AS_3. Real output returns to its full-employment level of GDP_f at point c_1.

By tracing a line between the long-run equilibrium points b_1, a_1, and c_1, we obtain a long-run aggregate supply curve. Observe that it is vertical at the full-employment level of real GDP. After long-run adjustments in nominal wages, real output is GDP_f, regardless of the specific price level.

Long-Run Equilibrium in the AD–AS Model

Figure 16-2 helps us understand the long-run equilibrium in the AD-AS model, now extended to include the distinction between short-run and long-run aggregate supply. In the short run, equilibrium occurs

| FIGURE 16-2 | Equilibrium in the Long-Run AD–AS Model |

The long-run equilibrium price level P_1 and level of real output GDP_f occur at the intersection of the aggregate demand curve AD_1, the long-run aggregate supply curve AS_{LR} (potential GDP), and the short-run aggregate supply curve AS_1.

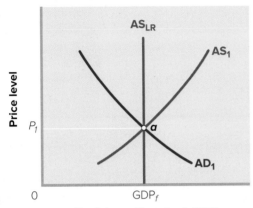

wherever the downsloping aggregate demand curve and upsloping short-run aggregate supply curve intersect. This can be at any level of output, not simply the full-employment level. Either a negative or a positive GDP gap is possible in the short run.

But in the long run, the short-run aggregate supply curve adjusts as we have just described. After those adjustments, long-run equilibrium occurs where the aggregate demand curve, vertical long-run aggregate supply curve, and short-run aggregate supply curve all intersect. Figure 16-2 shows the long-run outcome. Equilibrium occurs at point a, where AD_1 intersects both AS_{LR} and AS_1, and the economy achieves its full-employment (or potential) output, GDP_f. At long-run equilibrium price level P_1 and output level GDP_f, there is neither a negative GDP gap nor a positive GDP gap. The economy's *natural rate of unemployment* prevails, meaning that the economy achieves full employment.

In Canada, output GDP_f in Figure 16-2 implies a 6–7 percent unemployment rate. The natural rate of unemployment can vary from one time period to another and can differ between countries. But whatever the rate happens to be, it defines the level of potential output and establishes the location of the long-run AS curve.

FIGURE 16-3   Demand–Pull Inflation in the Long-Run AD–AS Model

An increase in aggregate demand from AD_1 to AD_2 drives up the price level and increases real output in the short run. But in the long run, nominal wages rise and the short-run aggregate supply curve shifts leftward, as from AS_1 to AS_2. Real output then returns to its prior level, and the price level rises even more. In this scenario, the economy moves from a to b and then eventually to c.

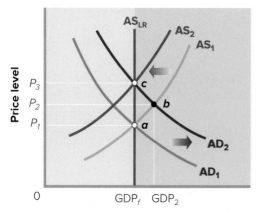

16.2 / Applying the Long-Run AD–AS Model

LO16.2 Explain how to apply the long-run AD–AS model to explain inflation, recessions, and growth.

The long-run AD–AS model helps clarify the long-run aspects of demand-pull inflation, cost-push inflation, and recession.

Demand–Pull Inflation in the Long-Run AD–AS Model

Recall that *demand-pull inflation* occurs when an increase in aggregate demand pulls up the price level. With a long-run aggregate supply, however, an increase in the price level will eventually produce an increase in nominal wages and thus a leftward shift of the short-run aggregate supply curve. This is shown in Figure 16-3, where we initially suppose the price level is P_1 at the intersection of aggregate demand curve AD_1, short-run aggregate supply curve AS_1, and long-run aggregate supply curve AS_{LR}. Observe that the economy is achieving its full-employment real output GDP_f at point a.

Now consider the effects of an increase in aggregate demand as represented by the rightward shift from AD_1 to AD_2. This shift can result from any one of a number of factors, including an increase in investment spending or a rise in net exports. Whatever its cause, the increase in aggregate demand boosts the price level from P_1 to P_2 and expands real output from GDP_f to GDP_2 at point b.

So far, none of this is new to you. But now we want to emphasize the distinction between short-run and long-run aggregate supply. With the economy producing above potential output, inputs will be in high demand. Input prices including nominal wages will rise. As they do, the short-run aggregate supply curve will eventually shift leftward until it intersects long-run aggregate supply at point c.[1] There, the economy has re-established long-run equilibrium, with the price level and real output now P_3 and GDP_f respectively.

---

[1] We say "eventually" because the initial leftward shift in short-run aggregate supply will intersect the long-run aggregate supply curve AS_{LR} at price level P_2 (review Figure 16-1). But the intersection of AD_2 and this new short-run aggregate supply curve (that is not shown in Figure 16-3) will produce a price level above P_2. (You may want to pencil this in to make sure you understand this point.) Again nominal wages will rise, shifting the short-run aggregate supply curve farther leftward. The process will continue until the economy moves to point c, where the short-run aggregate supply curve is AS_2, the price level is P_3, and real output is GDP_f.

Only at point c does the new aggregate demand curve AD_2 intersect both the short-run aggregate supply curve AS_2 and the long-run aggregate supply curve AS_{LR}.

In the short run, demand-pull inflation drives up the price level and increases real output; in the long run, only the price level rises. In the long run, the initial increase in aggregate demand has moved the economy *along* its vertical aggregate supply curve AS_{LR}. For a while, an economy can operate beyond its full-employment level of output. But the demand-pull inflation eventually causes adjustments of nominal wages that move the economy back to its full-employment output GDP_f.

Cost–Push Inflation in the Long-Run AD–AS Model

Cost-push inflation arises from factors that increase the cost of production at each price level—that is, factors that shift the aggregate supply curve leftward—and therefore increase the price level. But in our previous analysis we considered only short-run aggregate supply. We now want to examine cost-push inflation in its long-run context.

ANALYSIS

Look at Figure 16-4, in which we again assume that the economy is initially operating at price level P_1 and output level GDP_f (point *a*). Suppose that international oil producers get together and boost the price of oil by, say, 100 percent. As a result, the per-unit production cost of producing and transporting goods and services rises substantially in the economy represented by Figure 16-4. The increase in per-unit production cost shifts the short-run aggregate supply curve to the left, as from AS_1 to AS_2, and the price level rises from P_1 to P_2 (as seen by comparing points *a* and *b*). In this case, the leftward shift of the aggregate supply curve is not a *response* to a price-level increase, as it was in our previous discussions of demand-pull inflation; it is the initiating *cause* of the price-level increase.

POLICY DILEMMA

Cost-push inflation creates a dilemma for policymakers. Without expansionary stabilization policy, aggregate demand in Figure 16-4 remains at AD_1—the curve does not shift—and real output declines from GDP_f

---

FIGURE 16-4   **Cost–Push Inflation in the Long-Run AD–AS Model**

Cost–push inflation occurs when the short-run aggregate supply curve shifts leftward, as from AS_1 to AS_2. If government counters the decline in real output by increasing aggregate demand to the broken line, the price level rises even more. That is, the economy moves in steps from *a* to *b* to *c*. In contrast, if government allows a recession to occur, nominal wages eventually fall and the aggregate supply curve shifts back rightward to its original location. The economy moves from *a* to *b* and then eventually back to *a*.

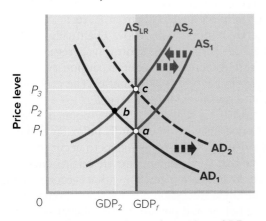

to GDP$_2$. Government can counter this recession and the attendant rise in unemployment by using fiscal policy and/or monetary policy to increase aggregate demand to AD$_2$. But there is a potential policy trap here: an increase in aggregate demand to AD$_2$ will further increase inflation by increasing the price level from P$_2$ to P$_3$ (a move from point b to point c).

Suppose government recognizes this policy trap and decides *not* to increase aggregate demand from AD$_1$ to AD$_2$ (so you can now disregard the dashed AD$_2$ curve). Instead, it implicitly decides to allow a cost-push created recession to run its course. How will that happen? Widespread layoffs, plant shutdowns, and business failures eventually occur. At some point the demands for oil, labour, and other inputs fall such that oil prices and nominal wages decline. When that happens, the initial leftward shift of the short-run aggregate supply curve is undone. In time the recession will shift the short-run aggregate supply curve rightward from AS$_2$ to AS$_1$. The price level will return to P$_1$, and the full-employment level of output will be restored at GDP$_f$ (point a on the long-run aggregate supply curve AS$_{LR}$).

This analysis yields two generalizations:

- If government attempts to maintain full employment when there is cost-push inflation, even more inflation will occur.

- If government takes a hands-off approach to cost-push inflation, the recession will linger. Although falling input prices will eventually undo the initial rise in per-unit production costs, the economy in the meantime will experience high unemployment and a loss of real output.

By far the most controversial application of the long-run AD–AS model is to recession.

Recession and the Long-Run AD–AS Model

By far the most controversial application of the long-run AD-AS model is to recession. We look at this controversy in detail in Bonus Chapter 16B; here we simply want to present the model and identify the key point of contention.

Suppose in Figure 16-5 that aggregate demand initially is AD$_1$ and that short-run and long-run aggregate supply curves are AS$_1$ and AS$_{LR}$, respectively. Therefore, as shown by point a, the price level is P$_1$ and output is GDP$_f$. Now suppose that investment spending dramatically declines, reducing aggregate demand to AD$_2$. Real output declines from GDP$_f$ to GDP$_1$, indicating that a recession has occurred. But if we make the assumption that prices and wages are flexible downward, the price level falls from P$_1$ to P$_2$. With the economy producing below potential output at point b, demand for inputs will be low. Eventually, nominal wages themselves fall to restore the previous real wage; when this happens, the short-run aggregate supply curve shifts rightward from AS$_1$ to AS$_2$. The negative GDP gap evaporates without expansionary fiscal or monetary policy, since real output expands from GDP$_1$ (point b) back to GDP$_f$ (point c). The economy is again located on its long-run aggregate supply curve AS$_{LR}$, but now at lower price level P$_3$.

There is disagreement among economists about this hypothetical scenario. The key point of dispute revolves around the degree to which both input and output prices may be downwardly inflexible and how long it would take in the actual economy for the necessary price and wage adjustments to occur to regain the full-employment level of output. Most economists believe that such adjustments are forthcoming, but will occur only after the economy has experienced a relatively long-lasting recession with its accompanying rise in unemployment and a loss of output. The severity of the Great Recession of 2008-2009 strengthened this view. Therefore, economists recommend active monetary policy, and perhaps fiscal policy, to counteract recessions.

FIGURE 16-5 Recession in the Long-Run AD–AS Model

A recession occurs when aggregate demand shifts leftward, as from AD_1 to AD_2. If prices and wages are downwardly flexible, the price level falls from P_1 to P_2. This decline in the price level eventually reduces nominal wages, which in turn shifts the aggregate supply curve from AS_1 to AS_2. The price level declines to P_3, and output increases back to GDP_f. The economy moves from a to b and then eventually to c.

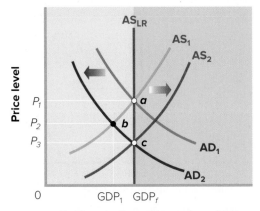

Economic Growth with Ongoing Inflation

In our analysis so far, we have seen how demand and supply shocks can cause, respectively, demand-pull inflation and cost-push inflation. But in these previous cases, the extent of the inflation was *finite* because the size of the initial movement in either the AD curve or the AS curve was *limited*. For instance, in Figure 16-3, the aggregate demand curve shifts rightward by a limited amount, from AD_1 to AD_2. As the economy's equilibrium moves from a, to b, to c, the price level rises from P_1, to P_2, to P_3. During this transition, inflation obviously occurs because the price level is rising. But once the economy reaches its new equilibrium at point c, the price level remains constant at P_3 and no further inflation takes place. That is, the limited movement in aggregate demand causes a limited amount of inflation that ends when the economy returns to full employment.

But the modern economy almost always experiences continuous, but usually mild, positive rates of inflation. That can only happen with ongoing shifts in either the aggregate demand or long-run aggregate supply curves because any single, finite shift will only cause inflation of limited duration. This insight is crucial to understanding why modern economies usually experience ongoing inflation while achieving economic growth. Both aggregate demand and long-run aggregate supply increase over time in the actual economy, and inflation occurs because the increases in aggregate demand generally exceed the increases in long-run aggregate supply. It will be helpful to examine this point graphically.

INCREASES IN LONG-RUN AGGREGATE SUPPLY

As discussed in Chapter 8, economic growth is driven by supply factors such as improved technologies and access to more or better resources. Economists illustrate economic growth as either an outward shift of an economy's production possibilities curve or a rightward shift of its long-run aggregate supply curve. As shown in Figure 16-6, the outward shift of the production possibilities curve from AB to CD in panel (a) is equivalent to the rightward shift of the economy's long-run aggregate supply curve from AS_{LR1} to AS_{LR2} in panel (b).

FIGURE 16-6   **Production Possibilities and Long-Run Aggregate Supply**

(a) Economic growth driven by supply factors (such as improved technologies or the use of more or better resources) shifts an economy's production possibilities curve outward, as from *AB* to *CD*. (b) Those same factors shift the economy's long-run aggregate supply curve to the right, as from AS_{LR1} to AS_{LR2}.

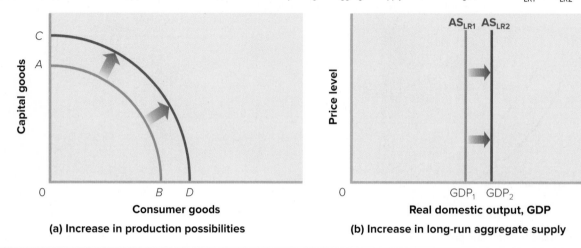

(a) Increase in production possibilities   **(b) Increase in long-run aggregate supply**

Let's simply transfer this rightward shift of the economy's long-run aggregate supply curve to Figure 16-7, which depicts economic growth in Canada in the context of the long-run aggregate demand–aggregate supply model. Suppose the economy's long-run aggregate supply curve initially is AS_{LR1}, while its aggregate demand curve and short-run aggregate supply curve are AD_1, and AS_1, as shown. The equilibrium price level is P_1 and the equilibrium level of real output is GDP_1.

FIGURE 16-7   **Depicting Canadian Growth in the Long-Run AD–AS Model**

Long-run and short-run aggregate supply have increased over time, as from AS_{LR1} to AS_{LR2} and AS_1 to AS_2. Simultaneously, aggregate demand has shifted rightward, as from AD_1 to AD_2. The actual outcome of these combined shifts has been economic growth, shown as the increase in real output from GDP_1 to GDP_2, accompanied by inflation, shown as the rise in the price level from P_1 to P_2.

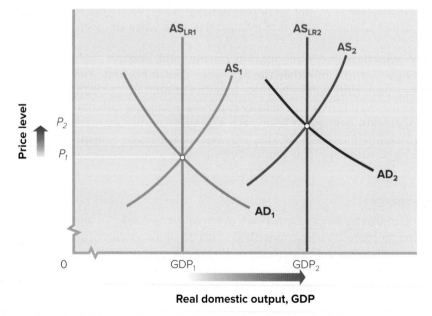

Real domestic output, GDP

Now let's assume that economic growth driven by changes in supply factors (quantity and quality of resources and technology) shifts the long-run aggregate supply curve rightward from AS_{LR1} to AS_{LR2} while the economy's aggregate demand curve remains at AD_1. Also, suppose that product and factor prices are flexible downward. The economy's potential output will expand, as reflected by the increase of available real output from GDP_1 to GDP_2. With aggregate demand constant at AD_1, the rightward shift of the long-run aggregate supply curve will lower the price level from P_1 to P_3. Taken alone, expansions of long-run aggregate supply in the economy are deflationary.

INCREASES IN AGGREGATE DEMAND AND INFLATION

But a decline in the price level such as the one from P_1 to P_3 in Figure 16-7 is not part of the long-run Canadian growth experience. Why not? The answer is that the nation's central bank–the Bank of Canada–engineers ongoing increases in the nation's money supply to create rightward shifts of the aggregate demand curve. These increases in aggregate demand would be highly inflationary absent the increases in long-run aggregate supply. But because the Bank of Canada usually makes sure that the inflationary rightward shifts of the aggregate demand curve are only slightly faster than the deflationary rightward shifts of the aggregate supply curve, only mild inflation occurs along with economic growth.

We illustrate this outcome in Figure 16-7, where aggregate demand shifts to the right from AD_1 to AD_2 at the same time as long-run aggregate supply shifts rightward from AS_{LR1} to AS_{LR2}. Real output expands from GDP_1 to GDP_2 and the price level increases from P_1 to P_2. At the higher price level P_2, the economy confronts a new short-run aggregate supply curve AS_2. The changes shown in Figure 16-7 describe the actual Canadian experience: economic growth, accompanied by mild inflation. Real output on average increases at about 3-4 percent annually and inflation averages 2-3 percent per year.

Of course, other long-term outcomes besides that depicted are entirely possible. Whether deflation, zero inflation, mild inflation, or rapid inflation accompanies economic growth depends on the extent to which aggregate demand increases relative to long-run aggregate supply. Over long periods, any inflation that accompanies economic growth is exclusively the result of aggregate demand increasing more rapidly than long-run aggregate supply. The expansion of long-run aggregate supply–of potential real GDP–is never the cause of inflation.

QUICK REVIEW 16.2

- In the short run, demand–pull inflation raises both the price level and real output; in the long run, nominal wages rise, the short-run aggregate supply curve shifts to the left, and only the price level increases.

- Cost–push inflation creates a policy dilemma for the government: If it engages in an expansionary policy to increase output, additional inflation will occur; if it does nothing, the recession will linger until input prices have fallen by enough to return the economy to producing at potential output.

- In the short run, a decline in aggregate demand reduces real output (creates a recession); in the long run, prices and nominal wages fall, the short-run aggregate supply curve shifts to the right, and real output returns to its full-employment level.

- The economy has ongoing inflation because the Bank of Canada uses monetary policy to shift the AD curve to the right faster than the supply factors shift the long-run AS curve to the right.

16.3 / The Inflation–Unemployment Relationship

LO16.3 Explain the short-run trade-off between inflation and unemployment (the Phillips Curve).

We have just seen that the Bank of Canada can determine how much inflation occurs in the economy by how much it causes aggregate demand to shift relative to aggregate supply. Given that low inflation and low unemployment rates are the Bank of Canada's major economic goals, its ability to control inflation brings up at least two interesting policy questions: (1) Are low unemployment and low inflation compatible goals or conflicting goals? (2) What explains situations in which high unemployment and high inflation coexist?

 INFLATION–UNEMPLOYMENT TRADE-OFF

The long-run AD–AS model supports three significant generalizations relating to these questions:

- Under normal circumstances, there is a short-run trade-off between the rate of inflation and the rate of unemployment.
- Aggregate supply shocks can cause both higher rates of inflation and higher rates of unemployment.
- There is no significant trade-off between inflation and unemployment over long periods of time.
- The first two generalizations are taken up in this section, and the third generalization is discussed in the next section.

ORIGIN OF THE IDEA 16.1   Phillips Curve

The Phillips Curve

We can demonstrate the short-run trade-off between the rate of inflation and the rate of unemployment through the **Phillips Curve**, named after A. W. Phillips, who developed the idea in Great Britain. This curve, generalized in Figure 16-8a, suggests an inverse relationship between the rate of inflation and the rate of unemployment. Lower unemployment rates (measured as leftward movements on the horizontal axis) are associated with higher rates of inflation (measured as upward movements on the vertical axis).

The underlying rationale of the Phillips Curve becomes apparent when we view the short-run aggregate supply curve in Figure 16-9 and perform a simple mental experiment. Suppose that in some short-run period aggregate demand expands from AD_0 to AD_2, either because firms decide to buy more capital goods

---

FIGURE 16-8   **The Phillips Curve: Concept and Canadian Empirical Data**

(a) The Phillips Curve relates annual rates of inflation and annual rates of unemployment for a series of years. Because this is an inverse relationship, there presumably is a trade-off between unemployment and inflation. (b) Data points for the 1960s seemed to confirm the Phillips Curve concept.

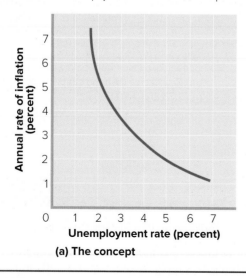

(a) The concept

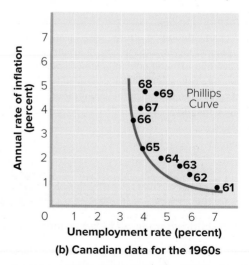

(b) Canadian data for the 1960s

FIGURE 16-9

The Short-Run Effect of Changes in Aggregate Demand on Real Output and the Price Level

Comparing the effects of various possible increases in aggregate demand leads to the conclusion that the larger the increase in aggregate demand, the higher the rate of inflation and the greater the increase in real output. Because real output and the unemployment rate move in opposite directions, we can generalize that, given short-run aggregate supply, high rates of inflation should be accompanied by low rates of unemployment.

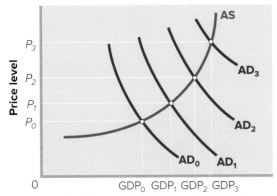

or the government decides to increase its expenditures. Whatever the cause, in the short run the economy experiences inflationary pressures. The price level thus rises from P_0 to P_2 and real output rises from GDP_0 to GDP_2. As real output rises, the unemployment rate falls.

Now let's compare what would have happened if the increase in aggregate demand had been larger—going, say, from AD_0 to AD_3. The equilibrium at P_3 and GDP_3 indicates that the amount of inflation and the growth of real output would both have been greater (and that the unemployment rate would have been lower). Similarly, suppose aggregate demand during the year had increased only modestly, from AD_0 to AD_1. Compared with our shift from AD_0 to AD_2, the amount of inflation and the growth of real output would have been smaller (and the unemployment rate higher).

The generalization we draw from this mental experiment is this: *Assuming a constant short-run aggregate supply curve,* high rates of inflation are accompanied by low rates of unemployment, and low rates of inflation are accompanied by high rates of unemployment. Other things equal, the expected relationship should look something like Figure 16-8a.

Figure 16-8b reveals that for Canada the facts for the 1960s nicely fit the theory. On the basis of that evidence and evidence from other countries, most economists working at the end of 1960s concluded that there was a stable, predictable trade-off between unemployment and inflation. Moreover, Canadian economic policy was built on that supposed trade-off. According to this thinking, it was impossible to achieve "full employment without inflation": Manipulation of aggregate demand through fiscal and monetary measures would simply move the economy along the Phillips Curve. An expansionary fiscal and monetary policy that boosted aggregate demand and lowered the unemployment rate would simultaneously increase inflation. Society had to choose between the incompatible goals of price stability and full employment; it had to decide where to locate on its Phillips Curve.

For reasons we will soon see, many of today's economists reject the idea of a stable, predictable Phillips Curve. Nevertheless, they agree that there is a short-run trade-off between unemployment and inflation. *Given short-run aggregate supply,* increases in aggregate demand boost real output and reduce the unemployment rate. As the unemployment rate falls and dips below the natural rate, the excessive spending produces demand–pull inflation. Conversely, when recessions set in and the unemployment rate increases, the weak aggregate demand that caused the recession also leads to lower inflation rates. For example, from April 2008 to May 2009, the unemployment rate increased from 6 percent to

FIGURE 16-10   Inflation Rates and Unemployment Rates in Canada, 1961–2014

A series of aggregate supply shocks in the 1970s resulted in higher rates of inflation and higher rates of unemployment. So, data points for the 1970s and 1980s tended to be above and to the right of the Phillips Curve for the 1960s. In the 1990s the inflation–unemployment data points slowly moved back toward the 1960s Phillips Curve. Points for the late 1990s and 2000s are similar to those from the 1960s. (*Note:* Inflation rates are on a December-to-December basis.)

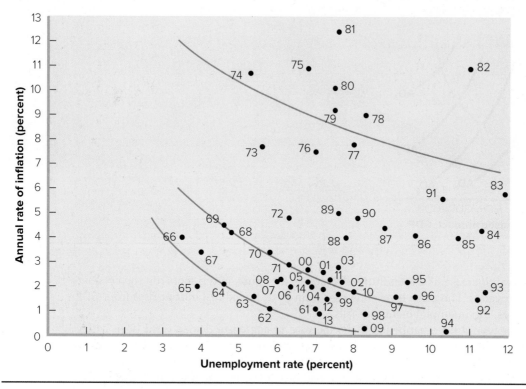

Source: Statistics Canada. For inflation see: http://www.statcan.gc.ca/tables-tableaux/sum-som/l01/cst01/econ163a-eng.htm For the unemployment rate see www.stats.gov.nl.ca/statistics/Labour/PDF/UnempRate.pdf

8.7 percent, but over the same time period the Consumer Price Index increased only 0.4 percent, compared to over 2 percent for all of 2008.

Aggregate Supply Shocks and the Phillips Curve

The unemployment-inflation experience of the 1970s and early 1980s demolished the idea of an always-stable Phillips Curve. In Figure 16-10 we show the Phillips Curve for the 1960s in green and then add the data points for 1970 through 2014. Observe that in most of the years of the 1970s and early 1980s the economy experienced both higher inflation rates and higher unemployment rates than in the 1960s. In fact, inflation and unemployment rose simultaneously in some of those years. This latter condition is called **stagflation**–a term that combines the words *stagnation* and *inflation*. If a Phillips Curve existed, it had clearly shifted outward, perhaps as shown.

ADVERSE AGGREGATE SUPPLY SHOCKS

The Phillips data points for the 1970s and early 1980s support our second generalization: *Aggregate supply shocks can cause both higher rates of inflation and higher rates of unemployment.* A series of adverse **aggregate supply shocks**–sudden, large increases in resource costs that jolt an economy's short-run aggregate supply curve leftward–hit the economy in the 1970s and early 1980s. The most significant of these shocks was a quadrupling of oil prices by the Organization of the Petroleum Exporting Countries (OPEC). Consequently, the cost of producing and distributing virtually every product and service rose rapidly.

These shocks shifted the aggregate supply curve to the left and distorted the usual inflation-unemployment relationship. Recall that we derived the inverse relationship between the rate of inflation and the unemployment rate shown in Figure 16-8a by shifting the aggregate demand curve along a stable short-run aggregate supply curve (Figure 16-9). But the cost-push inflation model shown in Figure 16-4 tells us that a *leftward shift* of the short-run aggregate supply curve increases the price level and reduces real output (and increases the unemployment rate). This, say most economists, is what happened in two periods in the 1970s. The unemployment rate shot up from 5.6 percent in 1973 to 8.0 percent in 1977, contributing to a significant decline in real GDP. In the same period, the price level rose by over 40 percent. The stagflation scenario recurred in 1978, when OPEC increased oil prices by more than 100 percent. The Canadian price level rose by 50 percent over the 1978–1982 period, while unemployment increased from 8.3 percent to 11.0 percent.

STAGFLATION'S DEMISE

Another look at Figure 16-10 reveals a generally inward movement of the inflation–unemployment points between 1983 and 1989. By 1989 the lingering effects of the earlier period had subsided. One precursor to this favourable trend was the deep recession of 1981–1982, largely caused by a restrictive money policy aimed at reducing inflation. The recession increased the unemployment rate to 11.9 percent in 1983. With so many workers unemployed, those who were working accepted smaller increases in their nominal wages— or in some cases wage reductions—to preserve their jobs. Firms, in turn, restrained their price increases to try to retain their relative shares of a diminished market.

Other factors were also at work. Foreign competition throughout this period held down wage and price hikes in several basic industries such as automobiles and steel. Deregulation of the airline and trucking industries also resulted in wage reductions or so-called "wage givebacks." A significant decline in OPEC's monopoly power and a greatly reduced reliance on oil in the production process produced a stunning fall in the price of oil and its derivative products, such as gasoline.

All these factors combined to reduce per-unit production costs and to shift the short-run aggregate supply curve rightward (as from AS_2 to AS_1 in Figure 16-4). Employment and output expanded and the unemployment rate fell from 11 percent in 1983 to 7.6 percent in 1989. Figure 16-10 reveals that the inflation–unemployment points for recent years are closer to the points associated with the Phillips Curve of the 1960s than to the points in the late 1970s and early 1980s. Even the recession of 2008–2009 did not greatly alter the recent inflation rate–unemployment rate pattern. In 2008, the unemployment rate was 6.1 percent but the inflation rate was 2.3 percent. The inflation–unemployment point for 2009, however, moved up and to the right relative to the point for 2008. In 2009, unemployment was 8.3 percent while the inflation rate on a December-to-December basis was 0.3 percent.

The media sometimes express the sum of the unemployment rate and the inflation rate as a very rough gauge of the economic discomfort that inflation and unemployment jointly impose on an economy in a particular year. The sum of the two rates is used to compute the *misery index*. For example, a nation with a 5 percent unemployment rate and a 5 percent inflation rate has a misery index number of 10, as does a nation with an 8 percent unemployment rate and a 2 percent inflation rate.

Global Perspective 16.1 shows the misery index for several nations between 2001 and 2012. (It uses average annual inflation rates, not the December-to-December inflation rates used to construct Figure 16-10.) The Canadian misery index number has been neither exceptionally low nor exceptionally high relative to the misery index numbers for the other major economies shown. But bear in mind that economists do not put much stock in the misery index since they do not view the national discomfort associated with a 1 percent change in inflation and a 1 percent change in unemployment as necessarily equivalent. In particular, the misery index can greatly disguise the extent of hardship during a recession. The rise in the unemployment rate in these circumstances causes a huge loss of national output and income (and huge gain in misery!), even if the higher unemployment rate is partially or fully offset with a decline in the rate of inflation.

16.1 GLOBAL PERSPECTIVE

The Misery Index, Selected Nations, 2001–2012

The Canadian misery index number (the sum of its unemployment rate and inflation rate) has generally been in the mid-range of such numbers relative to other major economies in recent years.

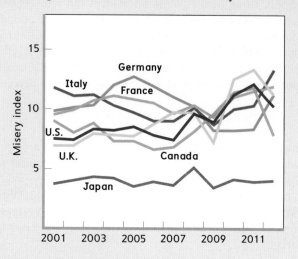

Source: Adapted from Bureau of Labor Statistics (www.bls.gov). Inflation rates and unemployment rates in this calculation are both on an average-annual basis.

16.4 / The Long-Run Phillips Curve

LO16.4 Discuss why there is no long-run trade-off between inflation and unemployment.

The overall set of data points in Figure 16-10 points to our third generalization relating to the inflation-unemployment relationship: There is no apparent *long-run* trade-off between inflation and unemployment. When decades as opposed to a few years are considered, any rate of inflation is consistent with the natural rate of unemployment prevailing at that time. We know from Chapter 9 that the natural rate of unemployment is the rate of unemployment that occurs when cyclical unemployment is zero; it is the rate of unemployment when the economy achieves its potential output.

How can there be a short-run inflation-unemployment trade-off but not a long-run trade-off? Figure 16-11 provides the answer.

The Short-Run Phillips Curve

Consider Phillips Curve PC_1 in Figure 16-11. Suppose the economy initially is experiencing a 3 percent rate of inflation and a 5 percent natural rate of unemployment. Such short-term curves as PC_1, PC_2, and PC_3 (drawn as straight lines for simplicity) exist because the actual rate of inflation is not always the same as the expected rate.

Establishing an additional point on Phillips Curve PC_1 will clarify this. We begin at a_1, where nominal wages are set on the assumption that the 3 percent rate of inflation will continue. That is, because workers expect output prices to rise by 3 percent per year, they negotiate wage contracts that feature 3 percent per

FIGURE 16-11 **The Long-Run Vertical Phillips Curve**

Increases in aggregate demand beyond those consistent with full-employment output may temporarily boost profits, output, and employment (as from a_1 to b_1). But nominal wages eventually will catch up so as to sustain real wages. When they do, profits will fall, negating the previous short-run stimulus to production and employment (the economy now moves from b_1 to a_2). Consequently, there is no trade-off between the rates of inflation and unemployment in the long run; that is, the long-run Phillips Curve is roughly a vertical line at the economy's natural rate of unemployment.

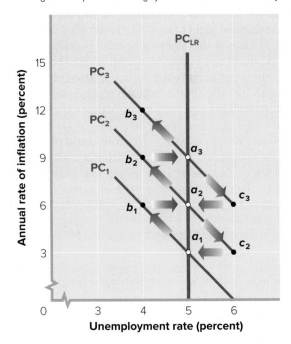

year increases in nominal wages so that these increases will exactly offset the expected rise in prices and thereby keep real wages the same.

But suppose the rate of inflation rises to 6 percent, perhaps because the Bank of Canada has decided to move the AD curve to the right even faster than it had been before. With a nominal wage rate set on the expectation that the 3 percent rate of inflation will continue, the higher product prices raise business profits. Firms respond to the higher profits by hiring more workers and increasing output. In the short run, the economy moves to b_1, which, in contrast to a_1, is at a lower rate of unemployment (4 percent) and a higher rate of inflation (6 percent). The movement from a_1 to b_1 is consistent with both an upsloping aggregate supply curve and the inflation–unemployment trade-off implied by the Phillips Curve analysis. But this short-run Phillips Curve simply is a manifestation of the following principle: *When the actual rate of inflation is higher than expected, profits temporarily rise and the unemployment rate temporarily falls.*

Expectation and the Long-Run Vertical Phillips Curve

But point b_1 is not a stable equilibrium. Workers will recognize that their nominal wages have not increased as quickly as inflation has and will therefore renegotiate their labour contracts so that they feature faster increases in nominal wages. These faster increases in nominal wages make up for the higher rate of inflation and restore the workers' lost purchasing power. As these new labour contracts kick in, business profits will fall to their prior level. The reduction in profits means that the original motivation to employ more workers and increase output has disappeared.

Unemployment then returns to its natural level at point a_2. Note, however, that the economy now faces a higher actual and expected rate of inflation—6 percent rather than 3 percent. This happens because the new labour contracts feature 6 percent per year increases in wages to make up for the 6 percent per year inflation rate. Because wages are a production cost, this faster increase in wage rates will imply faster future increases in output prices as firms are forced to raise prices more rapidly to make up for the faster future rate of wage growth. Stated a bit differently, the initial increase in inflation will become *persistent* because it leads to renegotiated labour contracts that will perpetuate the higher rate of inflation. In addition, because the new labour contracts are public, it will also be the case that the higher rates of inflation they will cause will be *expected* by everyone rather than being a surprise. In view of the higher 6 percent expected rate of inflation, the short-run Phillips Curve shifts upward from PC_1 to PC_2 in Figure 16-11. An "along-the-Phillips-curve" kind of movement from a_1 to b_1 on PC_1 is merely a short-run occurrence. As expectation of inflation adjusts in the long run, nominal wage contracts catch up with increases in the inflation rate, unemployment returns to its natural rate at a_2, and there is a new short-run Phillips Curve PC_2 at the higher expected rate of inflation.

The scenario repeats if aggregate demand continues to increase. Prices rise temporarily ahead of nominal wages, profits expand, and employment and output increase (as implied by the move from a_2 to b_2). But, in time, the expected rate of inflation changes, and nominal wages increase so as to restore real wages. Profits then fall to their original level, pushing employment back to the normal rate at a_3. The economy's "reward" for lowering the unemployment rate below the natural rate is a still higher (9 percent) rate of inflation.

ORIGIN OF THE IDEA 16.2   Long-Run Vertical Phillips Curve

Movements along the short-run Phillips Curve (a_1 to b_1 on PC_1) cause the curve to shift to a less favourable position (PC_2, then PC_3, and so on). A stable Phillips Curve with the dependable series of unemployment rate–inflation rate tradeoffs simply does not exist in the long run. The economy is characterized by a **long-run vertical Phillips Curve**.

The vertical line through a_1, a_2, and a_3 shows the long-run relationship between unemployment and inflation. Any rate of inflation is consistent with the 5 percent natural rate of unemployment.

Disinflation

The distinction between the short-run and long-run Phillips Curve also helps explain **disinflation**—reductions in the inflation rate from year to year. Suppose that in Figure 16-11 the economy is at a_3, where the inflation rate is 9 percent. And suppose that a decline in the rate at which aggregate demand shifts to the right faster than aggregate supply (as happened during the 2008–2009 recession) reduces inflation below the 9 percent expected rate to, say, 6 percent. Business profits fall, because prices are rising less rapidly than wages. The nominal wage increases, remember, were set on the assumption that the 9 percent rate of inflation would continue. In response to the decline in profits, firms reduce their employment and consequently the unemployment rate rises. The economy temporarily slides downward from point a_3 to c_3 along the short-run Phillips Curve PC_3. *When the actual rate of inflation is lower than the expected rate, profits temporarily fall and the unemployment rate temporarily rises.*

Firms and workers eventually adjust their expectations to the new 6 percent rate of inflation, and thus newly negotiated wage increases decline. Profits are restored, employment rises, and the unemployment rate falls back to its natural rate of 5 percent at a_2. Because the expected rate of inflation is now 6 percent, the short-run Phillips Curve PC_3 shifts leftward to PC_2.

If the rate at which aggregate demand shifts to the right faster than aggregate supply declines even more, the scenario will continue. Inflation declines from 6 percent to, say, 3 percent, moving the economy from a_2 to c_2 along PC_2. The lower-than-expected rate of inflation (lower prices) squeezes profits and reduces employment. But in the long run firms respond to the lower profits by reducing their nominal wage increases. Profits are restored and unemployment returns to its natural rate at a_1 as the short-run Phillips Curve moves from PC_2 to PC_1. Once again, the long-run Phillips Curve is vertical at the 5 percent natural rate of unemployment.

- As implied by the upsloping short-run aggregate supply curve, there may be a short-run trade-off between the rate of inflation and the rate of unemployment. This trade-off is reflected in the Phillips Curve, which shows that lower rates of inflation are associated with higher rates of unemployment.

- Aggregate supply shocks that produce severe cost–push inflation can cause stagflation—simultaneous increases in the inflation rate and the unemployment rate. Such stagflation occurred from 1973 to 1975 and

recurred from 1978 to 1982, producing Phillips Curve data points above and to the right of the Phillips Curve for the 1960s.

- After all nominal wage adjustments to increases and decreases in the rate of inflation have occurred, the economy ends up back at its full-employment level of output and its natural rate of unemployment. The long-run Phillips Curve therefore is vertical at the natural rate of unemployment.

16.5 / Taxation and Aggregate Supply

LO16.5 Explain the relationship between tax rates, tax revenues, and aggregate supply.

A final topic in our discussion of aggregate supply is taxation. Government policies can either impede or promote rightward shifts of the short-run and long-run aggregate supply curves shown in Figure 16-1. One such policy is taxation. The effects of taxation on the supply curves are a key concern of **supply-side economics**. Supply-side economists (or *supply-siders*) stress that changes in aggregate supply are an active force in determining the levels of inflation, unemployment, and economic growth.

These economists say that the enlargement of a nation's tax system influences the incentive to work, save, and invest. High tax rates impede productivity growth, hence the pace of expansion of long-run aggregate supply. By reducing the after-tax rewards of workers and producers, high tax rates reduce the financial attractiveness of work, saving, and investing. Particularly important are the *marginal tax rates*–the rates on extra dollars of income–because those rates affect the benefits from working, saving, and investing more.

Taxes and Incentives to Work

How long and how hard people work depends on the amount of additional after-tax earnings they derive from their efforts. Reductions in marginal tax rates on earned incomes induce more work and therefore increase aggregate inputs of labour. Lower marginal tax rates make leisure relatively more expensive and thus work more attractive. The higher opportunity cost of leisure encourages people to substitute work for leisure. This increase in productive effort could be achieved in many ways: by increasing the number of hours worked per day or week, by encouraging workers to postpone retirement, by inducing more people to enter the labour force, by motivating people to work harder, and by giving people the incentive to avoid long periods of unemployment.

Incentives to Save and Invest

The rewards for saving and investing have also been reduced by high marginal tax rates. For example, suppose that Tom saves $10,000 at 8 percent, bringing him $800 of interest per year. If his marginal tax rate is 40 percent, his after-tax interest earnings will be $480, not $800, and his after-tax interest rate will fall to 4.8 percent. Although Tom might be willing to save (forgo current consumption) for an 8 percent return on his saving, he might prefer to consume when the return is only 4.8 percent.

Saving, remember, is the prerequisite of investment. Thus supply-side economists recommend lower marginal tax rates on interest earned from saving. They also call for lower taxes on income from capital to ensure that there are ready investment outlets for the economy's enhanced pool of saving. A critical determinant of investment spending is the expected after-tax return on that spending.

The Laffer Curve

In the supply-side view, reductions in marginal tax rates increase the nation's aggregate supply and can leave the nation's tax revenues unchanged, or even enlarge them. Thus, supply-side tax cuts need not result in federal budget deficits.

This idea is based on the **Laffer Curve**, named after Arthur Laffer, who popularized it. As Figure 16-12 shows, the Laffer Curve depicts the relationship between tax rates and tax revenues. As tax rates increase from zero to 100 percent, tax revenues increase from zero to some maximum level (at *m*) and then fall to zero. Tax revenues decline beyond some point because higher tax rates discourage economic activity, thereby shrinking the tax base. This is easiest to see at the extreme, where the tax rate is 100 percent. Tax revenues here are, in theory, reduced to zero because the 100 percent tax rate has halted production. A 100 percent tax rate applied to a tax base of zero yields no revenue.

In the early 1980s, Laffer suggested that at a point (such as *n* on the curve in Figure 16-12) tax rates are so high that production is discouraged to the extent that tax revenues are below the maximum (at *m*). If the economy is at *n*, then lower tax rates can either increase tax revenues or leave them unchanged. For example, lowering the tax rate point *n* to point *l* would bolster the economy such that the government would bring in the same total amount of tax revenue as before.

Laffer's reasoning was that lower tax rates stimulate incentives to work, to save and invest, to innovate, and to take business risks, thus triggering an expansion of real output and income. That enlarged tax base sustains tax revenues even though tax rates are lowered. Indeed, between *n* and *m* lower tax rates result in *increased* tax revenue.

Also, when tax rates are lowered, tax avoidance (which is legal) and tax evasion (which is not) decline. High marginal tax rates prompt taxpayers to avoid taxes through various tax shelters. Lower tax rates reduce the inclination to engage in either tax avoidance or tax evasion.

The Laffer curve also implies that for any particular amount of tax revenue that the government can possibly collect, there will be both a high tax rate at which that amount of revenue can be collected as well as a low tax rate at which that amount of revenue can be collected. As an example, compare points *n* and *l* in Figure 16.12. Point *n* has a high tax rate and point *l* has a low tax rate, but they both collect the same amount of tax revenue.

FIGURE 16-12   **The Laffer Curve**

The Laffer Curve suggests that up to point *m*, higher tax rates will result in larger tax revenues. But higher tax rates will adversely affect incentives to work and produce, reducing the size of the base (output and income) to the extent that tax revenues will decline. It follows that if tax rates are above *m*, reductions in tax rates will produce increases in tax revenues.

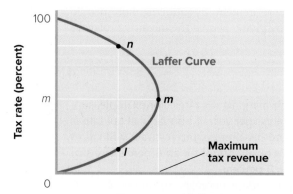

Criticisms of the Laffer Curve

The Laffer Curve and its supply-side implications have been subject to severe criticism.

TAXES, INCENTIVES, AND TIME

A fundamental criticism relates to the degree to which economic incentives are sensitive to changes in tax rates. Skeptics say that ample empirical evidence shows the impact of a tax cut on incentives to be small, of uncertain direction, and relatively slow to emerge.

INFLATION OR REAL INTEREST RATES

Most economists think that the demand-side effects of a tax cut are more immediate and certain than longer-term supply-side effects. Thus, tax cuts undertaken when the economy is at or near its full-employment level of output may produce increases in aggregate demand that overwhelm any increase in aggregate supply. Demand–pull inflation is the likely result. If so, the real interest rates will rise and investment will decline. That will defeat the purpose of the supply-side tax cut.

POSITION ON THE CURVE

Skeptics say the Laffer Curve is merely a logical proposition, and assert that there must be some level of tax rates between zero and 100 percent at which tax revenues will be at their maximum. Economists of all persuasions can agree with this. But the issue of where a particular economy is located on its Laffer Curve is an empirical question. If we assume that we are at point n in Figure 16-12, then tax cuts will increase tax revenues. But critics say that the economy's location on the Laffer Curve is undocumented and unknown. If the economy is at any point below m on the curve, then tax reductions will reduce tax revenues.

Rebuttal and Evaluation

Today, there is general agreement that the Canadian economy is operating at a point below m–rather than above m–on the Laffer Curve in Figure 16.12. In this zone, the overall effect is that personal tax-rate increases raise tax revenues while personal tax-rate decreases reduce tax revenues. But at the same time, economists recognize that, other things equal, cuts in tax rates reduce tax revenues in percentage terms by less than the tax-rate reductions. Similarly, tax-rate increases do not raise tax revenues by as much in percentage terms as the tax-rate increases. This is true because changes in marginal tax rates alter taxpayer behaviour and thus affect taxable income. Although these effects seem to be relatively modest, they need to be considered in designing tax policy. Thus, supply-side economics has contributed to how economists and policymakers design and implement fiscal policy.

The **LAST WORD**   Do Tax Increases Reduce Real GDP?*

Determining the relationship between changes in txes and permanent changes in real GDP is fraught with complexities and difficulties. University of California-Berkeley economists Christina Romer and David Romer have recently devised a novel way to approach the topic. Their findings suggest that tax increases reduce real GDP.[†]

How do changes in the level of taxation affect the level of economic activity? The simple correlation between taxation and economic activity shows that, on average, when economic activity rises more rapidly, tax revenues also are rising more rapidly. But this correlation almost surely does not reflect a positive effect of tax increases on output. Rather, under our tax system, any positive shock to output raises tax revenues by increasing income.

In "The Macroeconomic Effects of Tax Changes: Estimates Based on a New Measure of Fiscal Shocks," authors Christina Romer and David Romer observe that this difficulty is just one of many manifestations of a more general problem. Changes in taxes occur for many reasons. And, because the factors that give rise to tax changes often are correlated with other developments in the economy, disentangling the effects of the tax changes from the other effects of these underlying factors is inherently difficult.

To address this problem, Romer and Romer use the narrative record—U.S. presidential speeches, executive branch documents, U.S. congressional reports, and so on—to identify the size, timing, and principal motivation for all major tax policy actions in the post–World War II United States. This narrative analysis allows them to separate revenue changes resulting from legislation from changes occurring for other reasons. It also allows them to classify legislated changes according to their primary motivation.

Romer and Romer find that despite the complexity of the legislative process, most significant tax changes have been motivated by one of four factors: counteracting other influences in the economy; paying for increases in government spending (or lowering taxes in conjunction with reductions in spending); addressing an inherited budget deficit; and promoting long-run growth. They observe that legislated tax changes taken to counteract other influences on the economy, or to pay for increases in government spending, are very likely to be correlated with other factors affecting the economy. As a result, these observations are likely to lead to unreliable estimates of the effect of tax changes.

Tax changes that are made to promote long-run growth or to reduce an inherited budget deficit, in contrast, are undertaken for reasons essentially unrelated to other factors influencing output. Thus, examining the behaviour of output following these tax changes is likely to provide more reliable estimates of the output effects of tax changes. *The results of this more reliable test indicate that tax changes have very large effects: a tax increase of 1 percent of GDP lowers real GDP by roughly 2 to 3 percent.*

These output effects are highly persistent. The behaviour of inflation and unemployment suggests that this persistence reflects long-lasting departures of output from previous levels. Romer and Romer also find that output effects of tax changes are much more closely tied to the actual changes in taxes than news about future changes, and that investment falls sharply in response to tax changes. Indeed, the strong response of investment helps to explain why the output consequences of tax increases are so large.

Romer and Romer find suggestive evidence that tax increases to reduce an inherited budget deficit have much smaller output costs than other tax increases. This is consistent with the idea that deficit-driven tax increases may have important expansionary effects through [improved] expectations and [lower] long-term interest rates, or through [enhanced] confidence.

Question

On average, does an increase in taxes raise or lower real GDP? If taxes as a percent of GDP go up 1 percent, by how much does real GDP change? Are the decreases in real GDP caused by tax increases temporary or permanent? Does the intention of a tax increase matter?

---

* Abridged from Les Picker, "Tax Increases Reduce GDP," *The NBER Digest*, February/March 2008. The *Digest* provides synopses of research papers in progress by economists affiliated with the National Bureau of Economic Research (NBER).
[†] Christina Romer and David Romer, "The Macroeconomic Effects of Tax Changes: Estimates Based on a New Measure of Fiscal Shocks," *American Economic Review*, June 2010, pp. 763–801.

Chapter Summary

LO16.1   EXPLAIN HOW THE ECONOMY ARRIVES AT ITS LONG-RUN EQUILIBRIUM.

- In macroeconomics, the short run is a period in which nominal wages do not respond to changes in the price level. In contrast, the long run is a period in which nominal wages fully respond to changes in the price level.

- The short-run aggregate supply curve is upsloping. Because nominal wages are fixed, increases in the price level (prices received by firms) increase profits and real output. Conversely, decreases in the price level reduce profits and real output. However, the long-run aggregate supply curve is vertical. With sufficient time for adjustment, nominal wages rise and fall with the price level, moving the economy along a vertical aggregate supply curve at the economy's full-employment output.

LO16.2   EXPLAIN HOW TO APPLY THE LONG-RUN AD–AS MODEL TO EXPLAIN INFLATION, RECESSIONS, AND GROWTH.

- In the short run, demand–pull inflation raises the price level and real output. Once nominal wages have increased, the temporary increase in real output is reversed.

- In the short run, cost–push inflation raises the price level and lowers real output. Unless the government expands aggregate demand, nominal wages will eventually decline under conditions of recession and the short-run aggregate supply curve will shift back to its initial location. Prices and real output will eventually return to their original levels.

- If prices and wages are flexible downward, a decline in aggregate demand will lower output and the price level. The decline in the price level will eventually lower nominal wages and shift the short-run aggregate supply curve rightward. Full-employment output will thus be restored.

- One-time changes in AD and AS can only cause limited bouts of inflation. Ongoing mild inflation occurs because the Bank of Canada purposely increases AD slightly faster than the expansion of long-run AS (driven by the supply factors of economic growth).

LO16.3   EXPLAIN THE SHORT-RUN TRADE-OFF BETWEEN INFLATION AND UNEMPLOYMENT (THE PHILLIPS CURVE).

- Assuming a stable upsloping short-run aggregate supply curve, rightward shifts of the aggregate demand curve of various sizes yield the generalization that high rates of inflation are associated with low rates of unemployment, and vice versa. This inverse relationship is known as the Phillips Curve, and empirical data for the 1960s seem to be consistent with it.

- In the 1970s and early 1980s, the Phillips Curve apparently shifted rightward, reflecting stagflation—simultaneously rising inflation rates and unemployment rates. The standard interpretation is that the stagflation mainly resulted from huge oil price increases that caused large leftward shifts in the short-run aggregate supply curve (so-called supply shocks). The Phillips Curve shifted inward toward its original position in the 1980s. By 1989 stagflation had subsided, and the data points for the late 1990s and first half of the first decade of the 2000s were similar to those of the 1960s.

LO16.4   DISCUSS WHY THERE IS NO LONG-RUN TRADE-OFF BETWEEN INFLATION AND UNEMPLOYMENT.

- Although there is a short-run trade-off between inflation and unemployment, there is no such long-run trade-off. Workers will adapt their expectations to new inflation realities, and when they do, and nominal wages adjust proportionately with the price level, the unemployment rate will return to the natural rate. The long-run Phillips Curve is therefore vertical at the natural rate, meaning that higher rates of inflation do not "buy" the economy less unemployment.

LO16.5   EXPLAIN THE RELATIONSHIP BETWEEN TAX RATES, TAX REVENUES, AND AGGREGATE SUPPLY.

- Supply-side economists focus on government policies, such as high taxation, that impede the expansion of aggregate supply. The Laffer Curve relates tax rates to levels of tax revenue and suggests that, under some circumstances, cuts in tax rates can expand the tax base (output and income) and increase tax revenues. Most economists, however, believe that Canada is operating in the range of the Laffer Curve where tax rates and tax revenues move in the same, not the opposite, direction.

- Today's economists recognize the importance of considering supply-side effects in designing optimal fiscal policy.

Terms and Concepts

Phillips Curve	long-run vertical Phillips Curve	Laffer Curve
stagflation	disinflation	
aggregate supply shocks	supply-side economics	

Discussion Questions

1. Distinguish between the short run and the long run as they relate to macroeconomics. Why is the distinction important? [LO16.1]

2. Which of the following statements are true? Which are false? Explain why the false statements are untrue.   [LO16.1]

   a. Short-run aggregate supply curves reflect an inverse relationship between the price level and the level of real output.

   b. The long-run aggregate supply curve assumes that nominal wages are fixed.

   c. In the long run, an increase in the price level will result in an increase in nominal wages.

3. Suppose the government judges the natural rate of unemployment to be much lower than it actually is, and thus undertakes expansionary fiscal and monetary policies to try to achieve the lower rate. (a) Use the concept of the short-run Phillips Curve to explain why these policies might at first succeed. (b) Use the concept of the long-run Phillips Curve to explain the long-run outcome of these policies.   [LO16.4]

4. What do the distinctions between short-run aggregate supply and long-run aggregate supply have in common with the distinction between the short-run Phillips Curve and long-run Phillips Curve? Explain.   [LO16.4]

5. What is the Laffer Curve and how does it relate to supply-side economics? Why is determining the location of the economy on the curve so important in assessing tax policy?   [LO16.5]

6. Why might one person work more, earn more, and pay more income tax when his or her tax rate is cut, while another person might work less, earn less, and pay less income tax in the same circumstance?   [LO16.5]

Review Questions

1. Suppose the full-employment level of real output (Q) for a hypothetical economy is $250 and the price level (P) initially is 100. Use the short-run aggregate supply schedules below to answer the questions that follow.   [LO16.1]

AS P_{100}		AS P_{125}		AS P_{75}	
P	Q	P	Q	P	Q
125	280	125	250	125	310
100	250	100	220	100	280
75	220	75	190	75	250

   a. What will be the level of real output in the short run if the price level unexpectedly rises from 100 to 125 because of an increase in aggregate demand? What if the price level falls unexpectedly from 100 to 75 because of a decrease in aggregate demand? Explain each situation, using numbers from the table.

   b. What will be the level of real output in the long run when the price level rises from 100 to 125? When it falls from 100 to 75? Explain each situation.

   c. Show the circumstances described in parts (a) and (b) on graph paper, and derive the long-run aggregate supply curve.

2. Suppose that AD and AS intersect at an output level that is higher than the full-employment output level. After the economy adjusts back to equilibrium in the long run, the price level will be_____.   [LO16.2]

   a. Higher than it is now

   b. Lower than it is now

   c. The same as it is now

3. Suppose that an economy begins in long-run equilibrium before the price level and real GDP both decline simultaneously. If those changes were caused by only one curve shifting, then those changes are best explained as the result of   [LO16.2]

   a. The AD curve shifting right

   b. The AS curve shifting right

   c. The AD curve shifting left

   d. The AS curve shifting left

4. Identify the two descriptions below as being the result of either cost–push inflation or demand–pull inflation.   [LO16.2]

   a. Real GDP is below the full-employment level and prices have risen recently.

   b. Real GDP is above the full-employment level and prices have risen recently.

5. Use graphical analysis to show how each of the following would affect the economy first in the short run and then in the long run. Assume that Canada is initially operating at its full-employment level of output, that prices and wages are eventually flexible both upward and downward, and that there is no counteracting fiscal or monetary policy.   [LO16.2]

   a. Because of a war abroad, the oil supply to Canada is disrupted, sending oil prices rocketing upward.

b. Construction spending on new homes rises dramatically, greatly increasing total Canadian investment spending.

c. Economic recession occurs abroad, significantly reducing foreign purchases of Canadian exports.

6. Between 1990 and 2010, the Canadian price level rose by about 49 percent while real output increased by about 61 percent. Use the AD–AS model to illustrate these outcomes graphically. [LO16.2]

7. Assume there is a particular short-run aggregate supply curve for an economy and the curve is relevant for several years. [LO16.3]

a. Use the AD–AS analysis to show graphically why higher rates of inflation over this period would be associated with lower rates of unemployment, and vice versa.

b. What is this inverse relationship called?

8. Aggregate supply shocks can cause _____ rates of inflation that are accompanied by _____ rates of unemployment. [LO16.3]

a. Higher; higher

b. Higher; lower

c. Lower; higher

d. Lower; lower

9. Suppose that firms are expecting 6 percent inflation while workers are expecting 9 percent inflation. How much of a pay raise will workers demand if their goal is to maintain the purchasing power of their incomes? [LO16.4]

a. 3 percent

b. 6 percent

c. 9 percent

d. 12 percent

10. Suppose that firms were expecting inflation to be 3 percent, but then it actually turned out to be 7 percent. Other things equal, firm profits will be [LO16.4]

a. Smaller than expected

b. Larger than expected

Problems

1. Use the accompanying figure to answer the following questions. Assume that the economy is initially operating at price level 120 and real output level $870. This output level is the economy's potential (or full-employment) level of output. [LO16.1]

a. Suppose that the price level rises from 120 to 130. By how much will real output increase in the short run? In the long run?

b. Instead, now assume that the price level drops from 120 to 110. Assuming flexible product and resource prices, by how

much will real output fall in the short run? In the long run? What is the long-run level of output at each of the three price levels shown?

2. **Advanced Analysis** Suppose that the equation for a particular short-run AS curve is $P = 20 + 0.5Q$, where P is the price level and Q is real output in dollar terms. What is Q if the price level is 120? Suppose that the Q in your answer is the full-employment level of output. By how much will Q increase *in the short run* if the price level unexpectedly rises from 120 to 132? By how much will Q increase *in the long run* due to the price level increase? [LO16.1]

3. Suppose that over a 30-year period Buskerville's price level increased from 72 to 138 while its real GDP rose from $1.2 trillion to $2.1 trillion. Did economic growth occur in Buskerville? If so, by what average yearly rate? Did Buskerville experience inflation? If so, by what average yearly rate? Which shifted rightward faster in Buskerville: its long-run aggregate supply curve (AS$_{LR}$) or its aggregate demand curve (AD)? [LO16.2]

4. Suppose that for years East Confetti's short-run Phillips Curve was such that each 1 percentage point increase in its unemployment rate was associated with a 2 percentage point decline in its inflation rate. Then, during several recent years the short-run pattern changed such that its inflation rate rose by 3 percentage points for every 1 percentage point drop in its unemployment rate. Graphically, did East Confetti's Phillips Curve shift upward or did it shift downward? [LO16.3]

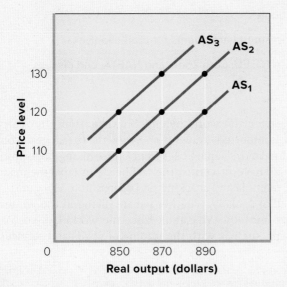

CHAPTER 17

International Trade*

LEARNING OBJECTIVES

LO17.1 List and discuss several key facts about Canada's international trade.

LO17.2 Define *comparative advantage*, and demonstrate how specialization and trade add to a nation's output.

LO17.3 Describe how differences between world prices prompt exports and imports.

LO17.4 Analyze the economic effects of tariffs and quotas.

LO17.5 Analyze the validity of the most frequently presented arguments for protectionism.

LO17.6 Identify and explain the objectives of GATT, WTO, EU, Euro Zone, and NAFTA, and discuss offshoring and those hurt by free trade.

Backpackers in the wilderness like to think they are leaving the world behind, but, like Atlas, they carry the world on their shoulders. Much of their equipment is imported–knives from Switzerland, rain gear from South Korea, cameras from Japan, aluminum pots from England, sleeping bags from China, hiking boots from Italy, and compasses from Finland. Moreover, they may have driven to the trailheads in Japanese-made Toyotas or German-made BMWs, sipping coffee from Colombia and snacking on bananas from Honduras.

International trade and the global economy affect all of us daily, whether we are hiking in the wilderness, driving our cars, listening to music, or working at our jobs. We cannot leave the world behind. We are enmeshed in a global web of economic relationships, such as with the trading of goods and services,

---

* Note to Instructors: If you prefer to cover international trade early in your course, you can assign this chapter at the end of either Part 1 or Part 2. This chapter builds on the introductory ideas of opportunity costs, supply and demand analysis, and economic efficiency but does not require an understanding of either market failures or government failures.

multinational corporations, cooperative ventures among the world's firms, and ties among the world's financial markets.

The focus of this chapter is the trading of goods and services. Then in Chapter 18 we examine exchange rates and the balance of payments. In bonus Chapter 18B on our website, we look at the economics of developing nations.

17.1 | Canada, International Linkages, and Globalization

LO17.1 List and discuss several key facts about Canada's international trade.

As identified in Figure 17-1, four economic flows link the Canadian economy and the economies of other nations:

- *Goods and Services Flows (Trade Flows)* Canada exports goods and services to other nations and imports goods and services from them.

- *Capital and Labour Flows (Resource Flows)* Canadian firms establish production facilities–new capital–in foreign countries and foreign firms establish production facilities in Canada. Labour also moves between nations. Each year many foreigners immigrate to Canada and some Canadians move to other nations.

- *Information and Technology Flows* Canada transmits information to other nations about Canadian products, prices, interest rates, and investment opportunities, and receives such information from abroad. Firms in other countries use technology created in Canada and Canadian businesses incorporate technology developed abroad.

- *Financial Flows* Money is transferred between Canada and other countries for several purposes: paying for imports, buying foreign assets, paying interest on debt, purchasing foreign currencies, and providing foreign aid.

Canada and World Trade

What is the extent and pattern of international trade, and how much has that trade grown? Who are the major participants? Global Perspective 17.1 suggests the importance of world trade for selected countries. Canada, with a limited domestic market, cannot efficiently produce the variety of goods its citizens want. So we must import goods from other nations. That, in turn, means that we must export, or sell abroad, some of our own products. For Canada, exports make up about 31 percent of gross domestic product (GDP)–the

---

FIGURE 17-1 **International Linkages**

The Canadian economy is intertwined with other national economies through goods and service flows (trade flows), capital and labour flows (resource flows), information and technology flows, and financial flows.

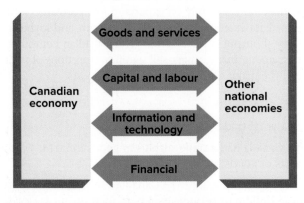

17.1 GLOBAL PERSPECTIVE

China has the largest share of world exports, followed by the United States and Germany. The eight largest export nations account for over 40 percent of world exports.

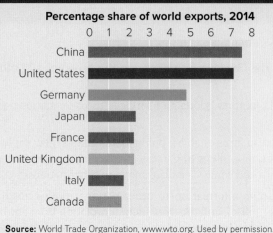

Percentage share of world exports, 2014

Source: World Trade Organization, www.wto.org. Used by permission.

market value of all goods and services produced in an economy. Other countries–the United States, for example–have a large internal market. Although the total volume of trade is huge in the United States, it constitutes about 14 percent of its GDP, a much smaller percentage than in a number of other nations.

VOLUME

For Canada and for the world as a whole, the volume of international trade has been increasing both absolutely and relative to GDP. A comparison of the data in Figure 17-2 reveals substantial growth in the dollar amount of Canadian exports and imports over the past several decades. The graph shows the growth of Canadian exports and imports of goods and services as percentages of GDP. Canadian exports are currently approximately 28 percent and imports are 29 percent of GDP–both higher than in 1971.

DEPENDENCE

Canada is almost entirely dependent on other countries for bananas, cocoa, coffee, spices, tea, raw silk, tin, and natural rubber. Imported goods compete with Canadian goods in many of our domestic markets: Japanese cars, French and American wines, and Swiss and Austrian snow skis are a few examples.

Of course, world trade is a two-way street. Many Canadian industries rely on exports to foreign markets. Almost all segments of Canadian agriculture rely on sales abroad; for example, exports of wheat, corn, and soybeans vary from one-tenth to more than three-quarters of the total output of those crops. The Canadian computer, chemical, aircraft, automobile, and machine tool industries, among many others, sell significant portions of their output in international markets. Table 17-1 shows some of the major Canadian exports and imports.

TRADE PATTERNS

The following facts will give you an overview of international trade:

- A *trade surplus* occurs when exports exceed imports. Canada had a trade surplus in goods in 2014, when Canadian exports of goods exceeded Canadian imports of goods by $5 billion.

- A *trade deficit* occurs when imports exceed exports. For example, in 2013 Canadian imports exceeded Canadian imports by $7 billion. Canada had a trade deficit in services (such as accounting services

FIGURE 17-2	Canadian Trade as Percentage of GDP

Canadian imports and exports of goods and services have increased both in volume and as a percentage of the GDP since 1971.

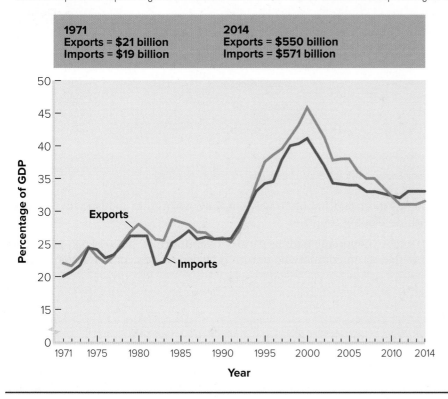

1971
Exports = $21 billion
Imports = $19 billion

2014
Exports = $550 billion
Imports = $571 billion

Source: Statistics Canada, http://www.statcan.gc.ca/tables-tableaux/sum-som/l01/cst01/econ05-eng.htm. Accessed March 8, 2015.

and financial services) in 2014. Canadian firms and citizens collectively supply (export) less transportation, banking, legal, and other services than they purchase (import) from foreign firms and citizens. Canadian imports of services exceeded exports of services by $23 billion.

- Canada imports some of the same categories of goods that it exports, specifically automotive products and machinery and equipment (see Table 17-1). This type of trade is called intra-industry trade.

TABLE 17-1	Principal Canadian Exports and Imports of Goods, 2014

Exports	% of total	Imports	% of total
Machinery and equipment	16	Machinery and equipment	10
Automotive products	22	Automotive products	17
Industrial goods and materials	18	Industrial goods and materials	10
Forestry products	7	Consumer goods	20
Energy products	24	Agricultural and fishing products	3
Agricultural and fishing products	7	Energy products	8

Source: Statistics Canada. At: http://www.statcan.gc.ca/tables-tableaux/sum-som/l01/cst01/gblec04-eng.htm and http://www.statcan.gc.ca/tables-tableaux/sum-som/l01/cst01/gblec05-eng.htm. Accessed May 28, 2015.

TABLE 17-2	Canadian Exports and Imports of Goods by Area, 2014		
Exports to	**Percentage of total**	**Imports from**	**Percentage of total**
United States	76	United States	67
European Union*	8	European Union*	9
United Kingdom	3	United Kingdom	2
Japan	2	Japan	2
Other countries	11	Other countries	20

* Excluding the U.K.

Source: Statistics Canada. http://www.statcan.gc.ca/tables-tableaux/sum-som/l01/cst01/gblec02a-eng.htm. Accessed May 28, 2015.

- As Table 17-2 shows, Canada's export and import trade is mainly with other industrially advanced nations. The remainder is with developing countries.

- The United States is Canada's most important trading partner quantitatively. In 2014, 76 percent of Canadian exported goods were sold to Americans, who in turn provided 67 percent of Canada's imports of goods (see Table 17-2).

Rapid Trade Growth

Several factors have propelled the rapid growth of international trade since World War II.

TRANSPORTATION TECHNOLOGY

High transportation costs are a barrier to any type of trade. But improvements in transportation have shrunk the globe and have fostered world trade. Container ships deliver self-contained boxcars of goods to ports, which offload them to waiting trucks and trains. We now routinely transport oil in massive tankers, significantly lowering the cost of transportation per barrel. Grain is loaded onto ocean-going ships at modern, efficient grain silos at Great Lakes and coastal ports. Natural gas flows through large-diameter pipelines from exporting to importing countries–for instance, from Russia to Germany and from Canada to the United States.

COMMUNICATIONS TECHNOLOGY

Dramatic improvements in communications technology have also advanced world trade. Computers, the Internet, telephones, and fax machines now directly link traders around the world, enabling exporters to assess overseas markets and to carry out trade deals. A distributor in Vancouver can get a price quotation on 1000 woven baskets in Thailand as quickly as a quotation on 1000 notebook computers in Ontario. Money moves around the world in the blink of an eye. Exchange rates, stock prices, and interest rates flash onto computer screens nearly simultaneously in Toronto, London, and Lisbon.

GENERAL DECLINE IN TARIFFS

Tariffs are excise taxes (duties) on imported products. They have had their ups and downs over the years, but since 1940 they have generally fallen. Canadian tariffs as a percentage of imports are now about 5 percent, down from over 20 percent in the mid-1930s. Many nations still maintain barriers to free trade, but on average tariffs have fallen significantly, thus increasing international trade.

Participants in International Trade

All the nations of the world participate to some extent in international trade. Global Perspective 17.2 lists the top participants in world trade by total dollar volume (as opposed to percentage of GDP, as in Global

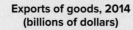

17.2 GLOBAL PERSPECTIVE

Comparative Exports

China, the United States, and Germany are the world's largest exporters. Canada is the world's ninth largest.

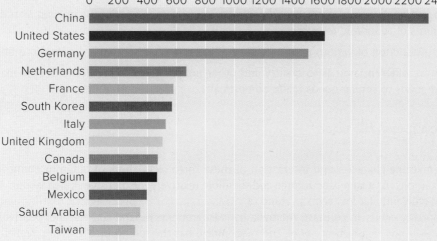

Exports of goods, 2014
(billions of dollars)

Source: Data used with permission of World Trade Organization, http://stat.wto.org/StatisticalProgram/WSDBViewData. aspx?Language=E.. Accessed May 28, 2015.

Perspective 17.1). Observe that China, the United States, and Germany had combined exports of over $5 trillion in 2014. Along with Germany, other Western European nations such as France, Britain, and Italy are major exporters. Canada is also a major exporter, ranking ninth in the world, and so are the Southeast Asian countries of South Korea, Taiwan, and Singapore, whose combined exports exceed those of France, Britain, or Italy. China, with its increased reliance on the market system and its reintegration of Hong Kong, has quickly emerged as a major international trader. In 1990, its exports were about $60 billion. In 2014, they were nearly $2.3 trillion.

QUICK REVIEW 17.1

- Four main categories of economic flows link nations: goods and services flows, capital and labour flows, information and technology flows, and financial flows.

- Advances in transportation and communications technology and declines in tariffs have all helped expand world trade.

- World trade has increased globally and nationally. In terms of volume, Canada is the world's ninth largest exporter. With exports and imports of about a third of GDP, Canada is more dependent on international trade than most other nations.

- Nearly all nations participate in world trade, but China, the United States, Germany, and the Western European nations dominate world trade by volume.

17.2 / The Economic Basis for Trade

LO17.2 Define *comparative advantage*, and demonstrate how specialization and trade add to a nation's output.

International trade enables nations to specialize their production, improve their resource productivity, and acquire more goods and services. Nations, like individuals and the regions of a nation, can gain by specializing in those products they can produce with greatest relative efficiency and trading them for those goods they cannot produce as efficiently. A more complete answer to the question "Why do nations trade?" hinges on three facts:

1. The distribution of natural, human, and capital resources among nations is uneven; nations differ in their endowments of economic resources.

2. Efficient production of various goods requires different technologies or combinations of resources.

3. Products are differentiated as to quality and other nonprice attributes. Some people may prefer certain imported goods to similar goods made domestically.

 SPECIALIZATION AND TRADE

To recognize the character and interaction of these three facts, think of different countries in the world. China, for example, has a large labour force and therefore relatively inexpensive skilled labour. As a result, China can produce efficiently (at low cost) a variety of **labour-intensive goods** such as textiles, electronics, apparel, toys, and sporting goods. In contrast, Australia has vast amounts of land and can inexpensively produce such **land-intensive goods** as wheat, wool, and meat. Brazil has the soil, tropical climate, rainfall, and ready supply of unskilled labour that are needed for the efficient, low-cost production of vegetables. And it is possible for industrially advanced economies with relatively large amounts of capital to inexpensively produce such **capital-intensive goods** as airplanes, automobiles, agricultural equipment, machinery, and chemicals.

Also, regardless of their resource intensities, nations can develop individual products that are in demand worldwide because of their special qualities. Examples include fashions from Italy, chocolates from Belgium, software from the United States, watches from Switzerland, and ice wine from Canada.

The distribution of resources, technology, and product distinctiveness among nations is relatively stable in short time periods but certainly can change over time. When that distribution changes, the relative efficiency and success that nations have in producing and selling goods also changes. For example, in the past few decades South Korea has upgraded the quality of its labour force and has greatly expanded its stock of capital. Although South Korea was primarily an exporter of agricultural products and raw materials a half century ago, it now exports large quantities of manufactured goods. Similarly, the new technologies that gave us synthetic fibres and synthetic rubber drastically altered the resource mix needed to produce these goods and changed the relative efficiency of nations in manufacturing them.

As national economies evolve, the size and quality of their labour forces may change, the volume and composition of their capital stocks may shift, new technologies may develop, and even the quality of land and the quantity of natural resources may be altered. As such changes take place, the relative efficiency with which a nation can produce specific goods will also change. As economists would say, comparative advantage can and does sometimes change.

Comparative Advantage

In an open economy (one with an international sector), a country produces more of certain goods (exports) and fewer of other goods (imports) than it would otherwise. Thus, the country shifts some labour and other resources toward export industries and away from import industries. For example, in the presence of international trade, Canada uses more resources to make telecommunications equipment and to grow wheat, and fewer resources to make television sets and sew clothes. So we ask, "Do such shifts of resources make economic sense? Do they enhance total output in Canada and thus the standard of living of Canadians?"

All nations, regardless of their labour, land, or capital intensity, can find special niches for products that are in demand worldwide.

The answers are affirmative. Specialization and international trade increase the productivity of Canadian resources and allow Canada to obtain greater total output than otherwise would be possible, and these benefits are the result of exploiting both *absolute advantages* and *comparative advantages*. A country is said to have an **absolute advantage** over other producers for a product if it is the most efficient producer of that product (by which we mean that it can produce more output of that product from any given amount of resource inputs than can any other producer). A country is said to have a **comparative advantage** over other producers of a product if it can produce the product at a lower opportunity cost (by which we mean that it must forgo less output of alternative products when allocating productive resources to producing the product in question).

In 1776, Adam Smith used the concept of absolute advantage to argue for international specialization and trade. His point was that nations would be better off if they each specialized in the production of those products in which they had an absolute advantage and were therefore the most efficient producers:

> It is the maxim of every prudent master of a family, never to attempt to make at home what it will cost him more to make than to buy. The tailor does not attempt to make his own shoes, but buys them of the shoemaker. The shoemaker does not attempt to make his own clothes, but employs a tailor. The farmer attempts to make neither the one nor the other, but employs those different artificers.
>
> What is prudence in the conduct of every private family, can scarce be folly in that of a great kingdom. If a foreign country can supply us with a commodity cheaper than we can make it, better buy it of them with some part of the produce of our own industry, employed in a way in which we have some advantage.[2]

In the early 1800s, David Ricardo extended Smith's idea by demonstrating that it is advantageous for a country to specialize and trade with another country even if it is more productive in all economic activities than that other country. Stated more formally, a nation does not need Smith's absolute advantage—total superiority in the efficiency with which it produces products—to benefit from specialization and trade. It needs only a comparative advantage.

The Basic Principle

The central concept underlying comparative advantage can be illustrated by posing a problem. Suppose that Madison, a chartered accountant, is a swifter painter than Mason, the professional painter she is thinking of hiring. Also assume that Madison can earn $50 per hour doing accounting and must pay Mason $15 per hour. And suppose that Madison would need 30 hours to paint her house but Mason would need 40 hours. Finally, assume Madison receives no special pleasure from painting.

Should Madison take time off from accounting to paint her own house or should she hire the painter? Madison's opportunity cost of painting her house is $1500 (= 30 hours × $50 per hour of sacrificed income). The cost of hiring Mason is only $600 (= 40 hours × $15 per hour paid to the painter). Although Madison is better at both accounting and painting, she will get her house painted at lower cost by specializing in accounting and using some of the proceeds to hire a house painter.

Note that Madison has an absolute advantage in both accounting and painting: she can do accounting and paint more efficiently than our hypothetical house painter. Despite this, Madison should hire a house painter because of her *comparative advantage*.

[2] Adam Smith, *The Wealth of Nations* (originally published, 1776; New York: Modern Library, 1937), p. 424.

Similarly, Mason can reduce his cost of obtaining accounting services by specializing in painting and using some of his income to hire Madison to prepare his income tax forms. Suppose Mason would need 10 hours to prepare his income tax return, but Madison could handle this task in 2 hours. Mason would sacrifice $150 of income (= 10 hours × $15 per hour of Mason's sacrificed time) to get a task done that he could hire out for $100 (= 2 hours × $50 per hour of an accountant's time). By specializing in painting and hiring Madison to prepare his tax return, Mason *lowers his cost of getting the tax return prepared.*

We will see that what is true for our chartered accountant and house painter is also true for nations. Specializing on the basis of comparative advantage enables nations to reduce the cost of obtaining goods and services they desire.

With this simple example in mind, let's turn to an international trade model to understand the gains from international specialization and trade.

Two Isolated Nations

Our goal is to place the idea of comparative advantage into the context of trading nations. Our method is to build a simple model that relies on the familiar concepts of production possibilities curves. Suppose the world economy has just two nations, Canada and Brazil. For simplicity, assume the labour forces in Canada and Brazil are of equal size. Each can produce both steel and soybeans, but at differing levels of economic efficiency. Suppose Canadian and Brazilian domestic production possibilities curves for soybeans and steel are as shown in Figures 17-3a and 17-3b. Note three realities relating to the production possibilities curves in the two graphs:

- **Constant Costs**   The "curves" are drawn as straight lines, in contrast to the concave-from-the-origin production possibilities frontiers introduced in Chapter 1. This means the law of increasing costs has been replaced with the assumption of constant costs. This substitution simplifies our discussion but does not change our analysis and conclusions. Later we will consider the effect of the more realistic increasing opportunity costs.

- **Different Costs**   The production possibilities curves of Canada and Brazil reflect different resource mixes and levels of technological progress. Specifically, the differing slopes of the two curves reflect the numbers in the figures and reveal that the opportunity costs of producing steel and soybeans differ between the two nations.

- **Canada Has Absolute Advantage in Both**   A producer (an individual, firm, or country) has an *absolute advantage* over another producer if it can produce more of a product than the other producer using the same amount of resources. Because of our convenient assumption that the Canadian and Brazilian labour forces are of equal size, the two production possibilities curves show that Canada has an absolute advantage in producing both products. If Canada and Brazil use their entire (equal-size) labour forces to produce either steel or soybeans, Canada can produce more of either than Brazil. There are greater production possibilities in Canada using the same number of workers as in Brazil. So output per worker–labour productivity–in Canada exceeds that in Brazil in producing both products.

| **FIGURE 17-3** | **Production Possibilities Curve** |

The two production possibilities curves show the amounts of soybeans and steel that (a) Canada and (b) Brazil can produce domestically. The curves for both countries are straight lines because we are assuming constant costs. (a) As reflected by the slope of *VB* in the left graph, the opportunity-cost ratio in Canada 1 steel = 1 soybean. (b) The production possibilities curve *vb* in the right graph has a steeper slope, reflecting the different opportunity-cost ratio in Brazil of 2 soybeans = 1 steel. The difference in the opportunity-cost ratios between the two countries defines their comparative advantages and is the basis for specialization and international trade.

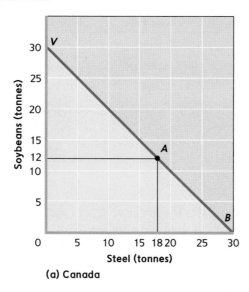

(a) Canada

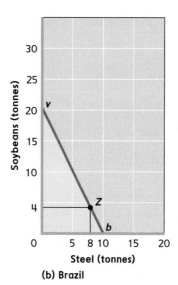

(b) Brazil

OPPORTUNITY-COST RATIO IN CANADA

In Figure 17-3a, with full employment, Canada will operate on its production possibilities curve. On that curve, it can increase its output of steel from 0 to 30 tonnes by forgoing an output of 30 tonnes of soybeans output. So, the slope of the production possibilities curve is −1 (= −30 soybeans/+30 steel), meaning 1 tonne of steel must be sacrificed for each extra tonne of soybeans. In Canada the **opportunity-cost ratio** (domestic exchange ratio) for the two products is 1 tonne of steel (S_t) for 1 tonne of soybeans (S_{oy}), or

$$1S_t = 1S_{oy}$$

(Note that the equal sign simply means "equivalent to.")

Within its borders, Canada can "exchange" a tonne of steel from itself for a tonne of soybeans from itself. Our constant-cost assumption means this exchange or opportunity-cost equation prevails for all possible moves from one point to another along Canada's production possibilities curve.

OPPORTUNITY-COST RATIO IN BRAZIL

Brazil's production possibilities curve in Figure 17-3b represents a different opportunity-cost ratio. Brazil must give up 2 tonnes of soybeans to obtain 1 tonne of steel. The slope of the production possibilities curve is therefore −2 (= −2 soybeans/+1 steel). This means that in Brazil the domestic cost ratio for the two goods is 1 tonne of steel for 2 tonnes of soybeans, or

$$1S_t = 2S_{oy}$$

SELF-SUFFICIENCY OUTPUT MIX

If Canada and Brazil are isolated and are to be self-sufficient, each must choose some output mix on its production possibilities curve. It will select the mix that provides the greatest total utility or satisfaction. Assume point *A* in Figure 17-3a is the optimal output mix in Canada. The choice of this combination of

TABLE 17-3	International Specialization According to Comparative Advantage and the Gains from Trade (in tonnes)				
Country	(1) Outputs before specialization	(2) Outputs after specialization	(3) Amounts exported (−) and imported (+)	(4) Outputs available after trade	(5) Gains from specialization and trade (4) − (1)
Canada	18 steel	30 steel	−10 steel	20 steel	2 steel
	12 soybeans	0 soybeans	+15 soybeans	15 soybeans	3 soybeans
Brazil	8 steel	0 steel	+10 steel	10 steel	2 steel
	4 soybeans	20 soybeans	−15 soybeans	5 soybeans	1 soybeans
Total output (steel and soybeans)	42	50		50	8

18 tonnes of steel and 12 tonnes of soybeans equates the marginal benefit and marginal cost of both goods. Suppose Brazil's optimal product mix is 8 tonnes of steel and 4 tonnes of soybeans, indicated by point Z in Figure 17-3b. These choices by the two countries are reflected in column 1 of Table 17-3.

Specialization Based on Comparative Advantage

A producer (an individual, firm, or nation) has a comparative advantage in producing a particular product if it can produce that product at a lower opportunity cost than other producers. Comparative advantage is the key determinant in whether or not nations can gain from specialization and trade. In fact, absolute advantage turns out to be irrelevant.

In our example, for instance, Canada has an absolute advantage over Brazil in producing both steel and soybeans. But it is still the case that Canada can gain from specialization and trade with Brazil. That is because what actually matters is whether the opportunity costs of producing the two products (steel and soybeans) differ in the two countries. If they do, then each nation will enjoy a comparative advantage in one of the products, meaning that it can produce that product at a lower opportunity cost than the other country. As a result, total output can increase if each country specializes in the production of the good in which it has the lower opportunity cost.

The idea is summarized in the **principle of comparative advantage**, which says that total output will be greatest when each good is produced by the nation that has the lowest domestic opportunity cost for that good. In our two-nation illustration, Canada has the lower domestic opportunity cost for steel; Canada need forgo only 1 tonne of soybeans to produce 1 tonne of steel, whereas Brazil must forgo 2 tonnes of soybeans for 1 tonne of steel. Canada has a comparative (cost) advantage in steel and should specialize in steel production. The "world" (that is, Canada and Brazil) is not economizing in the use of its resources if a high-cost producer (Brazil) produces a specific product (steel) when a low-cost producer (Canada) could have produced it. Having Brazil produce soybeans would mean that the world economy would have to give up more steel than is necessary to obtain 1 tonne of soybeans.

Brazil has the lower domestic opportunity cost for soybeans; it must sacrifice only ½ tonne of steel to produce 1 tonne of soybeans, while Canada must forgo 1 tonne of steel to produce 1 tonne of soybeans. Brazil has a comparative advantage in soybeans and should specialize in soybean production. Economizing requires that any particular good be produced by the nation with the lowest domestic opportunity cost, or the nation having a comparative advantage for that good. Canada should produce steel and Brazil soybeans. Note that this conclusion holds even though Canada has an absolute advantage in both steel and soybeans.

ORIGIN OF THE IDEA 17.1 Comparative Advantage

A comparison of columns 1 and 2 of Table 17-3 verifies that specialization enables the world to get more output from its fixed amounts of resources. Canada, by specializing completely in steel, produces 30 tonnes of steel and no soybeans; Brazil, by specializing completely in soybeans, produces 20 tonnes of soybeans and no steel. These figures exceed the yields generated without specialization: 26 tonnes of steel (= 18 in Canada + 8 in Brazil) and 16 tonnes of soybeans (= 12 in Canada and 4 in Brazil). As a result, the world ends up with 4 more tonnes of steel (30 tonnes, compared with 26) *and* 4 more tonnes of soybeans (20 tonnes, compared with 16) than it would if there were self-sufficiency and unspecialized production.

Terms of Trade

We have just seen that specialization in production will allow for the largest possible amounts of both steel and soybeans to be produced. But with each country specializing in the production of only one item, how will the soybeans that are all produced by Brazil and the steel that is all produced by Canada be divided between consumers in the two countries? The key turns out to be the **terms of trade**, the exchange ratio at which Canada and Brazil trade steel and soybeans. But consumers of each nation want *both* steel and soybeans. They can have both if the two nations trade or exchange the two products. But what will be the terms of trade? At what exchange ratio will Canada and Brazil trade steel and soybeans?

Crucially, the terms of trade also establish whether each country will find it in its own better interest to bother specializing at all. This is because the terms of trade determine whether each country can "get a better deal" by specializing and trading than it could if it opted instead for self-sufficiency. To see how this works, note that because $1S_t = 1S_{oy}$ in Canada, Canada must get *more than* 1 tonne of soybeans for each tonne of steel exported; otherwise it will not benefit from exporting steel in exchange for Brazilian soybeans. Canada must get a better "price" (more soybeans) for its steel in the world market than it can get domestically, or there is no gain from trade and it will not occur.

Similarly, because $1S_t = 2S_{oy}$ in Brazil, Brazil must obtain 1 tonne of steel by exporting some amount *less than* 2 tonnes of soybeans. Brazil must pay a lower "price" for steel in the world market than it must pay domestically, or it will not want to trade. The international exchange ratio or terms of trade must lie somewhere between

$$1S_t = 1S_{oy} \text{ (Canada's cost conditions)}$$

and

$$1S_t = 2S_{oy} \text{ (Brazil's cost conditions)}$$

Where between these limits will the world exchange ratio fall? Canada will prefer a ratio close to $1S_t = 2S_{oy}$, say, $1S_t = 1¾S_{oy}$. Canada wants to get the most soybeans possible for each tonne of steel it exports. Similarly, Brazil wants a rate near $1S_t = 1S_{oy}$, say $1S_t = 1¼S_{oy}$. Brazil wants to export the least amount of syobeans possible for each tonne of steel it receives in exchange.

The actual exchange ratio depends on world supply and demand for the two products. If the overall world demand for soybeans is weak relative to its supply and the demand for steel is strong relative to its supply, the exchange ratio will settle nearer the $1S_t = 2S_{oy}$, the figure Canada prefers. If the overall world demand for soybeans is great relative to its supply and if the demand for steel is weak relative to its supply, the ratio will settle nearer the $1S_t = 1S_{oy}$ level favourable to Brazil. (We will take up the topic of equilibrium world prices later in this chapter.)

Gains from Trade

Suppose the terms of trade or international exchange ratio is $1S_t = 1½S_{oy}$. The possibility of trading on these terms permits each nation to supplement its domestic production possibilities line with a **trading**

possibilities line. This can be seen in **Figure 17-4 (Key Graph)**. Just as a production possibilities line shows the amount of these products a full-employment economy can obtain by shifting resources from one to the other, a trading possibilities line shows the amounts of two products a nation can obtain by specializing in one product and trading for another. The trading possibilities lines in Figure 17-4 reflect the assumption that both nations specialize based on comparative advantage: Canada specializes completely in steel (point *B* in Figure 17-4a) and Brazil completely in soybeans (at point *v* in Figure 17-4b).

IMPROVED ALTERNATIVES

With specialization, Canada is no longer constrained by its domestic production possibilities line, which requires it to give up 1 tonne of steel for every tonne of soybeans it wants as it moves up its domestic production possibilities line, say, from point *B*. Instead, Canada, through trade with Brazil, can get 1½ tonnes of soybeans for every tonne of steel it exports to Brazil, so long as Brazil has soybeans to export. Trading possibilities line *BV′* thus represents the $1S_t = 1\frac{1}{2}S_{oy}$ trading ratio.

Similarly, Brazil, starting at, say, point *c*, no longer has to move down its domestic production possibilities curve, giving up 2 tonnes of soybeans for each tonne of steel it wants. It can now export just 1½ tonnes of soybeans for each tonne of steel it wants by moving down its trading possibilities line *vb′*.

Specialization and trade create a new exchange ratio between steel and soybeans, reflected in a nation's trading possibilities line. This exchange ratio is superior for both nations to the self-sufficiency exchange ratio embodied in the production possibilities line of each. By specializing in steel and trading for Brazil's soybeans, Canada can obtain more than 1 tonne of soybeans for 1 tonne of steel. By specializing in soybeans and trading for Canada's steel, Brazil can get 1 tonne of steel for less than 2 tonnes of soybeans. In both cases, self-sufficiency is undesirable.

GREATER OUTPUT

By specializing according to comparative advantage and trading for those goods produced in nations with greater domestic efficiency, Canada and Brazil can achieve combinations of steel and soybeans beyond their individual production possibilities curves. Specialization according to comparative advantage results in a more efficient allocation of world resources, and larger outputs of both steel and soybeans are therefore available to both nations.

Specialization according to comparative advantage results in more efficient allocation of world resources.

Suppose that at the $1S_t = 1\frac{1}{2}S_{oy}$ terms of trade, Canada exports 10 tonnes of steel to Brazil and in return Brazil exports 15 tonnes of soybeans to Canada. How do the new quantities of steel and soybeans available to the two nations compare with the optimal product mixes that existed before specialization and trade? Point *A* in Figure 17-4a reminds us that Canada chose 18 tonnes of steel and 12 tonnes of soybeans originally. But, by producing 30 tonnes of steel and no soybeans, and by trading 10 tonnes of steel for 15 tonnes of soybeans, Canada can obtain 20 tonnes of steel and 15 tonnes of soybeans. This new, superior combination of steel and soybeans is shown by point *A′* in Figure 17-4a. Compared with the non-trading figures of 18 tonnes of steel and 12 tonnes of soybeans, Canada's **gains from trade** are 2 tonnes of steel and 3 tonnes of soybeans.

Similarly, recall that Brazil's optimal product mix was 4 tonnes of soybeans and 8 tonnes of steel (point *Z*) before specialization and trade. Now, by specializing in soybeans and trading–producing 20 tonnes of

KEY GRAPH

FIGURE 17-4 Trading Possibilities Lines and the Gains from Trade

As a result of international specialization and trade, Canada and Brazil both can have levels of output higher than those attainable on their domestic production possibilities curves. (a) Canada can move from point A on its domestic production possibilities curve to, say, point A′ on its trading possibilities line. (b) Brazil can move from point Z to Z′.

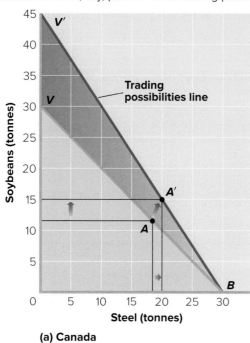

(a) Canada

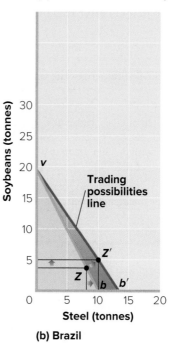

(b) Brazil

Quick Quiz

1. The production possibilities curves in graphs (a) and (b) imply
   a. Increasing domestic opportunity costs
   b. Decreasing domestic opportunity costs
   c. Constant domestic opportunity costs
   d. First decreasing, then increasing, domestic opportunity costs

2. Before specialization, the domestic opportunity cost of producing 1 unit of steel is
   a. 1 unit of soybeans in both Canada and Brazil
   b. 1 unit of soybeans in Canada and 2 units of soybeans in Brazil
   c. 2 units of soybeans in Canada and 1 unit of soybeans in Brazil
   d. 1 unit of soybeans in Canada and ½ unit of soybeans in Brazil

3. After specialization and trade, the world output of steel and soybeans is
   a. 20 tonnes of steel and 20 tonnes of soybeans
   b. 45 tonnes of steel and 15 tonnes of soybeans
   c. 30 tonnes of steel and 20 tonnes of soybeans
   d. 10 tonnes of steel and 30 tonnes of soybeans

4. After specialization and international trade
   a. Canada can obtain units of soybeans at less cost than before trade
   b. Brazil can obtain more than 20 tonnes of soybeans, if it so chooses
   c. Canada no longer has a comparative advantage in producing steel
   d. Brazil can benefit by prohibiting soybean imports from Canada

Answers: 1. c; 2. b; 3. c; 4. a

soybeans and no steel and exporting 15 tonnes of its soybeans in exchange for 10 tonnes of Canadian steel–Brazil can have 5 tonnes of soybeans and 10 tonnes of steel. This new position is indicated by point Z' in Figure 17-4b. Brazil's gains from trade are 1 tonne of soybeans and 2 tonnes of steel.

Points A' and Z' are positions superior economic positions to points A and Z. This fact is enormously important. We know that a nation can expand its production possibilities boundary by (1) expanding the quantity and improving the quality of its resources or (2) realizing technological progress. We have now established that international trade can enable a nation to get around the output constraint imposed by its production possibilities curve. The effects of international specialization and trade are the equivalent of having more and better resources or discovering improved production techniques.

WORKED PROBLEM 17.1   Gains from Trade

Table 17-3 summarizes the transactions and outcomes in our analysis. Please give it one final, careful review.

QUICK REVIEW 17.3

- The principle of comparative advantage says that total world output will be greatest when each good is produced by the nation that has the lowest domestic opportunity cost.

- The rate at which countries can trade units of one product for units of another product is referred to as the terms of trade.

- A trading possibilities line shows the amounts of two products that a nation can obtain by specializing in the production of one product and then trading for the other.

Trade with Increasing Costs

To explain the basic principles underlying international trade, we simplified our analysis in several ways. For example, we limited discussion to two products and two nations. But multiproduct/multinational analysis yields the same conclusions. We also assumed constant opportunity costs (linear production possibilities curves), which is a more substantive simplification. Let's consider the effect of allowing increasing opportunity costs (concave-from-the-origin production possibilities curves) to enter the picture.

Suppose that Canada and Brazil are initially at positions on their concave production possibilities curves where their domestic cost ratios are $1S_t = 1S_{oy}$ and $1S_t = 2S_{oy}$, as they were in our constant-cost analysis. As before, comparative advantage indicates that Canada should specialize in steel and Brazil in soybeans. But now, as Canada begins to expand steel production, its $1S_t = 1S_{oy}$ cost ratio will *fall;* Canada will have to sacrifice *more than* 1 tonne of soybeans to get 1 additional tonne of steel. Resources are no longer perfectly transferrable between alternative uses, as the constant-cost assumption implied. Resources that are less and less suited to steel production must be allocated to the Canadian steel industry in expanding steel output, and this means increasing costs–the sacrifice of larger and larger amounts of soybeans for each additional tonne of steel.

Similarly, Brazil, starting from its $1S_t = 2S_{oy}$ cost ratio position, expands soybean production. But as it does, it will find that its $1S_t = 2S_{oy}$ cost ratio begins to *rise.* Sacrificing a tonne of steel will free resources that can be used to produce something less than 2 tonnes of soybeans, because these transferred resources are less suitable to soybean production.

As the Canadian cost ratio falls from $1S_t = 1S_{oy}$ and Brazil's rises from $1S_t = 2S_{oy}$, a point will be reached at which the cost ratios are equal in the two nations, perhaps at $1S_t = 1¾\,S_{oy}$. At this point, the underlying basis for further specialization and trade–differing cost ratios–has disappeared. Most importantly, this point of equal cost ratios may be reached where Canada is still producing *some* soybeans along with its steel and Brazil is producing *some* steel along with its soybeans. *The primary effect of increasing costs is to make specialization less than complete.* For this reason we often find domestically produced products competing directly against identical or similar imported products within a particular economy.

It is a common myth that the greatest benefit to be derived from international trade is greater domestic employment in the export sector. This suggests that exports are "good" because they increase domestic employment, whereas imports are "bad" because they deprive people of jobs at home. As we have demonstrated, the true benefit created by international trade is the overall increase in output available through specialization and exchange.

A nation does not need international trade to operate *on* its production possibilities curve. It can fully employ its resources, including labour, with or without international trade. International trade, however, enables a country to reach a point of consumption beyond its domestic production possibilities curve. The gain from trade to a nation is the extra output obtained from abroad—the imports obtained for less sacrifice of other goods than if they were produced at home.

The Case for Free Trade Restated

The case for free trade reduces to one compelling argument: Through free trade based on the principle of comparative advantage, the world economy can achieve a more efficient allocation of resources and a higher level of material well-being than without free trade.

Since the resource mixes and technological knowledge of each country are somewhat different, each nation can produce particular commodities at different real costs. Each nation should produce goods for which its domestic opportunity costs are lower than the domestic opportunity costs of other nations, and exchange these specialties for products for which its domestic opportunity costs are high relative to those of other nations. If each nation does this, the world can realize the advantages of specialization. The world and each free-trading nation can obtain a larger real income from the fixed supplies of resources available to it. One side benefit of free trade is that it promotes competition and deters monopoly. The increased competition from foreign firms forces domestic firms to adopt the lowest-cost production techniques. It also compels them to be innovative with respect to both product quality and production methods, thereby contributing to economic growth. And free trade provides consumers with a wider range of product choices. The reasons to favour free trade are the same reasons to endorse competition.

A second side benefit of free trade is that it links national interests and breaks down national animosities. Confronted with political disagreements, trading partners tend to negotiate rather than make war.

17.3 / Supply and Demand Analysis of Exports and Imports

LO17.3 Describe how differences between world prices prompt exports and imports.

Supply and demand analysis reveals how equilibrium prices and quantities of exports and imports are determined. The amount of a good or service that a nation will export or import depends on differences between equilibrium world and domestic prices. The interaction of *world* supply and demand determines **world price**, the price at which the quantities supplied and demanded are equal globally. *Domestic supply* and demand determine the equilibrium **domestic price**—the price that would prevail in a closed economy. It is a price at which domestic supply and demand are equal.

In the absence of trade, domestic prices in a closed economy may or may not equal world equilibrium prices. When economies are opened for international trade, differences between world and domestic prices motivate exports or imports. To see how, let's now look at the international effects of such price differences in a simple two-nation world consisting of Canada and the United States, which are both producing aluminum. We assume there are no trade barriers, such as tariffs and quotas, and no international transportation costs.

Supply and Demand in Canada

Figure 17-5a shows the domestic supply curve S_d and domestic demand curve D_d for aluminum in Canada. The intersection of S_d and D_d determines the equilibrium domestic price of $1.25 per kilogram and the equilibrium domestic quantity is 100 million kilograms. Domestic suppliers produce 100 million kilograms and sell them at $1.25. So there are no domestic surpluses or shortages of aluminum.

FIGURE 17-5   **Canadian Export Supply and Import Demand**

(a) Domestic supply S_d and demand D_d at the domestic equilibrium price of aluminum at $1.25 per kilo. At world prices above the $1.25 domestic price create domestic surpluses of aluminum. At prices below $1.25 there are domestic shortages. (b) Surpluses are exported (top curve), and shortages are met by importing aluminum (lower curve). The export supply curve shows the direct relationship between world prices and Canadian exports; the import demand curve portrays the inverse relationship between world prices and Canadian imports.

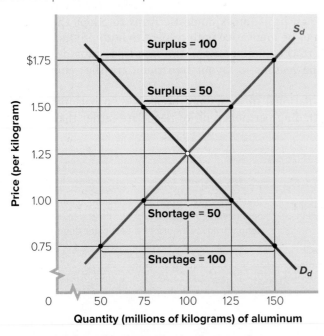

(a) Canadian domestic aluminum market

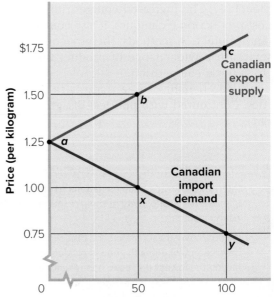

(b) Canadian export supply and import demand

But what if the Canadian economy is opened to world trade and the *world price* of aluminum is above or below this $1.25 domestic price?

CANADIAN EXPORT SUPPLY

If the world aluminum price exceeds $1.25, Canadian firms will produce more than 100 million kilograms and export the excess domestic output to the rest of the world (United States). First, consider a world price of $1.50. We see from the supply curve S_d that Canadian aluminum firms will produce 125 million kilograms of aluminum at that price. The demand curve D_d tells us that Canadians will purchase only 75 million kilograms at $1.50. The outcome is a domestic surplus of 50 million kilograms of aluminum. Canadian producers will export these 50 million kilograms at the $1.50 world price.

What if the world price is $1.75? The supply curve shows that Canadian firms will produce 150 million kilograms of aluminum, while the demand curve tells us that Canadian consumers will buy only 50 million kilograms. So Canadian producers will export the domestic surplus of 100 million kilograms.

In Figure 17-5b we assign the quantity of surplus or shortage to the horizontal scale. The domestic surpluses–the Canadian exports–occurring at world prices above the $1.25 domestic equilibrium price are plotted in red. When the world and domestic prices are equal (= $1.25), the quantity of exports supplied is zero (point *a*). There is no surplus of domestic output to export. But when the world price is $1.50, Canadian firms export 50 million kilograms of surplus aluminum (point *b*). At a $1.75 world price, the domestic surplus of 100 million kilograms is exported (point *c*).

The Canadian **export supply curve**, found by connecting points such as *a*, *b*, and *c*, shows the amount of aluminum that Canadian producers will export at each world price above $1.25. This curve *slopes upward*, revealing a direct or positive relationship between the world price and amount of Canadian exports. *As world prices increase relative to domestic prices, Canadian exports rise.*

CANADIAN IMPORT DEMAND

If the world price is below $1.25, Canada will end up importing aluminum. Consider a $1.00 world price. The supply curve in Figure 17-5a reveals that at that price Canadian firms will produce only 75 million kilograms of aluminum. But the demand curve shows that Canadians want to buy 125 million kilograms at that price. The result is a domestic shortage of 50 million kilograms. To satisfy that shortage, Canada will import 50 million kilograms of aluminum.

At an even lower $0.75 world price, Canadian producers will supply only 50 million kilograms. Because Canadian consumers want to buy 150 million kilograms, there is a domestic shortage of 100 million kilograms. Imports will flow to Canada to make up the difference. That is, at a $0.75 world price Canadian firms supply 50 million kilograms and 100 million kilograms will be imported.

In Figure 17-5b we plot the Canadian **import demand curve** from these data in blue. This *downsloping curve* shows the amounts of aluminum that will be imported at world prices below the $1.25 Canadian domestic price. The relationship between world prices and imports is inverse or negative. At a world price of $1.25, domestic output will satisfy Canadian demand; imports will be zero (point *a*). But at $1.00 Canadians will import 50 million kilograms of aluminum (point *x*); at $0.75, they will import 100 million kilograms (point *y*). Connecting points *a*, *x*, and *y* yields a *downsloping* Canadian import demand curve. *As world prices fall relative to domestic prices, Canadian imports increase.*

Supply and Demand in the United States

We repeat our analysis in Figure 17-6, this time for the United States. (We have converted U.S. dollar prices to Canadian dollar prices via an assumed exchange rate.) Note that the domestic supply curve S_d and demand curve D_d for aluminum in the United States yield a domestic price of $1.00, which is $0.25 lower than the $1.25 Canadian domestic price.

The analysis proceeds exactly as for Canada. If the world price is $1.00, Americans will neither export nor import aluminum (which gives us point *q* in Figure 17-6b). At world prices above $1.00, U.S. firms will produce more aluminum than U.S. consumers will buy. The surplus will be exported. At a $1.25 world

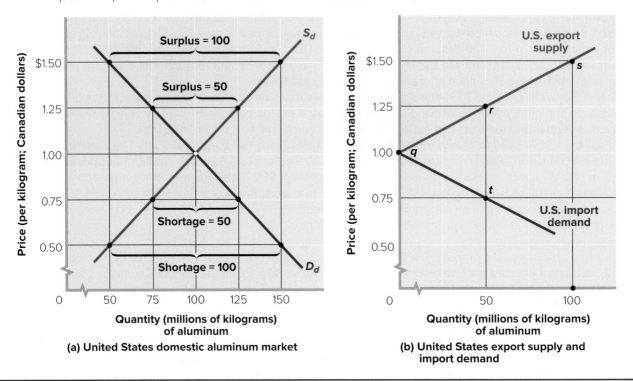

FIGURE 17-6   **U.S. Export Supply and Import Demand**

(a) At world prices above the $1.00 domestic price, production in the United States exceeds domestic consumption. At world prices below $1.00, domestic shortages occur. (b) Surpluses result in exports, and shortages result in imports. The U.S. export supply curve and import demand curve depict the relationships between world prices and exports or imports.

(a) United States domestic aluminum market

(b) United States export supply and import demand

price, Figure 17-6a tells us that the United States will export a domestic surplus of 50 million kilograms (yielding point *r*). At $1.50 it will export a domestic surplus of 100 million kilograms (point *s*). Connecting these points yields the red, upsloping U.S. export supply curve that reflects the domestic surpluses (and thus exports) occurring when the world price exceeds the $1.00 U.S. domestic price.

At world prices below $1.00, domestic shortages occur in the United States. At a $0.75 world price, Figure 17-6a shows that U.S. consumers want to buy 125 million kilograms of aluminum but U.S. firms will produce only 75 million kilograms. The shortage will bring 50 million kilograms of imports to the United States (point *t* in Figure 17-6b). The blue U.S. import demand curve in that figure shows U.S. imports at world aluminum prices below the $1.00 U.S. domestic price.

Equilibrium World Price, Exports, and Imports

We now have the tools to determine the **equilibrium world price** of aluminum and the equilibrium world levels of exports and imports. Figure 17-7 combines the Canadian export supply curve and import demand curve in Figure 17-5b and the U.S. export supply curve and import demand curve in Figure 17-6b. The two Canadian curves proceed rightward from the $1.25 domestic price; the two U.S. curves proceed rightward from the $1.00 U.S. domestic price.

International equilibrium occurs in this two-nation model where one nation's import demand curve intersects another nation's export supply curve. In this case Canada's import demand curve intersects America's export supply curve at *e*. There, the world price of aluminum is $1.125. The U.S. export supply curve indicates that the United States will export 25 million kilograms of aluminum at this price. Also at this price Canada will import

| FIGURE 17-7 | **Equilibrium World Price and Quantity of Exports and Imports** |

In a two-nation world, the equilibrium world price (= $1.125) is determined at the intersection of one nation's export supply curve and another nation's import demand curve. This intersection also decides the equilibrium volume of exports and imports. Here, the United States exports 25 million kilograms of aluminum to Canada.

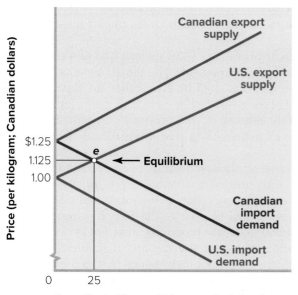

Quantity (millions of kilograms) of aluminum

25 million kilograms from the United States, indicated by the Canadian import demand curve. The $1.125 world price equates the quantity of imports demanded and the quantity of exports supplied (= 25 million kilograms). Thus there will be world trade of 25 million kilograms of aluminum at $1.125 per kilogram.

Note that after trade, the single $1.125 world price will prevail in both Canada and the United States. Only one price for a standardized commodity can persist in a competitive market. With trade, all consumers can buy a kilogram of aluminum for $1.125 and all producers can sell it for that price.

WORKED PROBLEM 17.2 Equilibrium World Price, Exports, and Imports

Why would the United States willingly send 50 million kilograms of its aluminum output to Canada for consumption? After all, producing this output uses up scarce U.S. resources and drives up the price of aluminum for Americans. Americans are willing to export aluminum to Canada because they can gain the means–the earnings of Canadian dollars–to import other goods (say, telecommunications equipment) from Canada.

QUICK REVIEW 17.5

- A nation will export a particular product if the world price exceeds the domestic price; it will import the product if the world price is less than the domestic price.

- In a two-country model, equilibrium world prices and equilibrium quantities of exports and imports occur when one nation's export supply curve intersects the other nation's import demand curve.

17.4 / Trade Barriers and Export Subsidies

LO17.4 Analyze the economic effects of tariffs and quotas.

While a nation as a whole gains from trade, trade may harm particular domestic industries and their workers. Those industries might seek to preserve their economic positions by persuading their respective governments to protect them from imports—perhaps through tariffs, import quotas, or other trade barriers.

Indeed, the public may be won over by the apparent plausibility ("Cut imports and prevent domestic unemployment") and the patriotic ring ("Buy Canadian!") of the arguments. The alleged benefits of tariffs are immediate and clear-cut to the public, but the adverse effects cited by economists are obscure and dispersed over the entire economy. When political deal making is added in—"You back tariffs for the apparel industry in my province, and I'll back tariffs for the auto industry in your province"—the outcome can be a politically robust network of trade barriers. These impediments to free international trade can take several forms.

Tariffs are excise taxes or "duties" on the dollar value or physical quantity of an imported good. They may be imposed to obtain revenue or to protect domestic firms. A **revenue tariff** is usually applied to a product that is not being produced domestically, for example, tin, coffee, or bananas in the case of Canada. Rates on revenue tariffs tend to be modest and are designed to provide the federal government with revenue. A **protective tariff** is implemented to shield domestic producers from foreign competition. These tariffs impede free trade by increasing the prices of imported goods and therefore shifting sales toward domestic producers. Although protective tariffs are usually not high enough to stop the importation of foreign goods, they put foreign producers at a competitive disadvantage. A tariff on imported auto tires, for example, would make domestically produced tires more attractive to consumers.

An **import quota** is a limit on the quantities or total values of specific items that are imported in some period. Once a quota is filled, further imports of that product are choked off. Import quotas are more effective than tariffs in impeding international trade. With a tariff, a product can go on being imported in large quantities. But with an import quota, all imports are prohibited once the quota is filled.

A **nontariff barrier (NTB)** includes onerous licensing requirements, unreasonable standards pertaining to product quality, or simply bureaucratic hurdles and delays in customs procedures. Some nations require that importers of foreign goods obtain licences and then restrict the number of licences issued in order to limit imports. Although many nations carefully inspect imported agricultural products to prevent the introduction of potentially harmful insects, some countries use lengthy inspections to impede imports. Japan and the European countries frequently require that their domestic importers of foreign goods obtain licences.

A **voluntary export restriction (VER)** is a trade barrier by which foreign firms "voluntarily" limit the amount of their exports to a particular country. VERs have the same effect as import quotas and are agreed to by exporters to avoid more stringent tariffs or quotas. In the late 1990s, for example, Canadian producers of softwood lumber (fir, spruce, cedar, and pine) agreed to a VER on exports to the United States under the threat of a permanently higher U.S. tariff.

ORIGIN OF THE IDEA 17.2   Mercantilism

An **export subsidy** consists of a government payment to a domestic producer of export goods and is designed to aid that producer. By reducing production costs, the subsidies enable the domestic firm to charge a lower price and thus to sell more exports in world markets. Here are two examples: (1) Some European governments have heavily subsidized Airbus Industries, a European firm that produces commercial aircraft. The subsidies help Airbus compete against the American firm Boeing. (2) Canada and other nations have subsidized domestic farmers to boost the domestic food supply. Such subsidies have artificially lowered export prices on agricultural produce.

Later in this chapter we will discuss some of the specific arguments and appeals that are made to justify protection.

KEY GRAPH

FIGURE 17-8 The Economic Effects of a Protective Tariff or an Import Quota

A tariff that increases the price of a good from P_w to P_t will reduce domestic consumption from d to c. Domestic producers will be able to sell more output (b rather than a) at a higher price (P_t rather than P_w). Foreign exporters are injured because they sell less output (bc rather than ad). The brown area indicates the amount of tariff paid by domestic consumers. An import quota of bc units has the same effect as the tariff, with one exception: the amount represented by the brown area will go to foreign producers rather than to the domestic government.

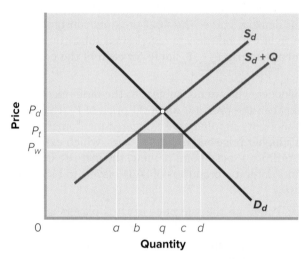

Quick Quiz

1. **At world price P_w**
   a. Domestic quantity demanded equals quantity supplied
   b. Domestic quantity demanded is less than quantity supplied
   c. Domestic quantity demanded is greater than quantity supplied
   d. Domestic quantity supplied is greater than quantity demanded

2. **At world prices above P_d Canada would**
   a. Import
   b. Export

   c. Stop producing
   d. None of the above

3. **A protective tariff**
   a. Increases domestic production
   b. Decreases domestic production
   c. Does not affect domestic production
   d. Decreases government revenue

4. **A quota**
   a. Decreases government revenue
   b. Increases government revenue
   c. Has no effect on government revenue
   d. Lowers domestic price

Answers: 1. c; 2. b; 3. a; 4. c

Economic Impact of Tariffs

Once again we use supply and demand analysis to examine the economic effects of protective tariffs. Curves D_d and S_d in **Figure 17-8 (Key Graph)** show domestic demand and supply for a product in which a nation–say, Canada–has a comparative *dis*advantage–for example, DVD players. (Disregard $S_d + Q$ for now.) Without world trade, the domestic price and output would be P_d and q respectively.

Assume now that the domestic economy is opened to world trade and that the Chinese, who have a comparative advantage in DVD players, begin to sell them in Canada. We assume that with free trade the domestic price cannot differ from the world price, which here is P_w. At P_w domestic consumption is d and domestic production is a. The horizontal distance between the domestic supply and demand curves at P_w represents imports of ad. Thus far, our analysis is similar to the analysis of world prices in Figure 17-5.

DIRECT EFFECTS

Suppose now that Canada imposes a tariff on each imported DVD player. This will raise the domestic price from P_w to P_t and has four effects.

1. **Decline in Consumption**   Consumption of DVD players in Canada declines from d to c as the higher price moves buyers up and to the left along their demand curve. The tariff prompts consumers to buy fewer DVD players and to reallocate a portion of their expenditures to less desired substitute products. Canadian consumers are injured by the tariff, since they pay $P_t - P_w$ more for each of the c units they now buy at price P_t.

2. **Increased Domestic Production**   Canadian producers—who are not subject to the tariff—receive higher price P_t per unit. Because this new price is higher than the pre-tariff or world price of P_w, the domestic DVD player industry moves up and to the right along its supply curve S_d, increasing domestic output from a to b. Domestic producers thus enjoy both a higher price and expanded sales, which explains why domestic producers lobby for protective tariffs. But from a social point of view, the increase in domestic production from b to a means that the tariff permits domestic producers of DVD players to bid resources away from other, more efficient, Canadian industries.

3. **Decline in Imports**   Chinese producers are hurt. Although the sale price of DVD players is higher by $P_t - P_w$, that amount accrues to the Canadian government, not to Chinese producers. The after-tariff world price, and thus the per-unit revenue to Chinese producers, remains at P_w, and the volume of Canadian imports (Chinese exports) falls from $d - a$ to $c - b$.

4. **Tariff Revenue**   The shaded rectangle indicates the amount of revenue that the tariff yields. Total revenue from the tariff is determined by multiplying the tariff, $P_t - P_w$ per unit, by the number of imported DVD players, $c - b$. This tariff revenue is a transfer of income from consumers to government and does not represent any net change in the nation's economic well-being. The result is that government gains a portion of what consumers lose by paying more for DVD players.

INDIRECT EFFECTS

Tariffs have a subtle effect beyond what our supply and demand diagram can show. Because China sells fewer DVD players in Canada, China will earn fewer dollars with which to buy Canadian exports. Canadian export industries must then cut production and release resources. These are highly efficient industries, as evidenced by their comparative advantage and ability to sell goods in world markets.

Tariffs directly promote the expansion of inefficient industries that do not have a comparative advantage; they also indirectly cause contraction of relatively efficient industries that do have a comparative advantage. We know that specialization and world trade lead to more efficient use of world resources and greater world output. But protective tariffs reduce world trade. Therefore, tariffs also reduce efficiency and the world's real output.

Economic Impact of Quotas

The economic impact of quotas is similar to that of a tariff with one salient difference: Although tariffs generate revenue for the Canadian government, a quota transfers that revenue to foreign producers.

Suppose in Figure 17-8 that, instead of imposing a tariff of $P_t - P_w$ per unit, Canada prohibits any Chinese imports of DVD players in excess of bc units. In other words, an import quota of bc DVD players is imposed on China. We have deliberately chosen the size of this quota to be the same amount as imports would be under a $P_t - P_w$ tariff so we are comparing "equivalent" situations. As a consequence of the quota, the supply of DVD players is $S_d + Q$ in Canada. This consists of the domestic supply plus the constant amount,

$c - b \ (= Q)$ that importers will provide at each domestic price. The $S_d + Q$ supply curve does not exist below price P_w because Chinese producers would not export DVD players to Canada at any price *below P_w*; instead, they would sell them to other countries at the world market price of P_w.

Most of the economic results are the same as with a tariff. DVD player prices are higher (P_t instead of P_w) because imports have been reduced from $d - a$ to $c - b$. Domestic consumption of DVD players is down from $d - a$ to $c - b$. Canadian producers enjoy both a higher price (P_t rather than P_w) and increased sales (b rather than a).

The difference is that the price increase of $P_t - P_w$ paid by Canadian consumers on imports of $c - b$–the shaded area–no longer goes to the Canada Revenue Agency as tariff (tax) revenue, but flows to those Chinese firms that have acquired the quota rights to sell DVD players in Canada. The economic effects of a tariff are better for Canadian taxpayers than are those of a quota, other things equal. A tariff generates government revenue, which can be used to cut other taxes or to finance public goods and services that benefit Canadian citizens. In contrast, the higher price created by quotas results in additional revenue for foreign producers.

QUICK REVIEW 17.6

- A tariff on a product increases its price, reduces its consumption, increases its domestic production, reduces its imports, and generates tariff revenue for the government; an import quota does the same, except a quota generates revenue for foreign producers rather than for the government imposing the quota.

Net Costs of Tariffs and Quotas

Figure 17-8 shows that tariffs and quotas impose costs on domestic consumers but provide gains to domestic producers and, in the case of tariffs, revenue to the federal government. The consumer costs of trade restrictions are calculated by determining the effect they have on consumer prices. Protection raises the price of a product in three ways: (1) the price of the imported product goes up, (2) the higher price of imports causes some consumers to shift their purchases to domestically produced goods, and (3) the prices of domestically produced goods rise because import competition has declined.

Study after study finds that the costs to consumers substantially exceed gains to producers, workers, and other suppliers of resources in the protected industry, and to the government. A sizable net cost or efficiency loss to society arises from trade protection. Furthermore, industries employ large amounts of economic resources to influence politicians to pass and retain protectionist laws. Because these rent-seeking efforts divert resources away from more socially desirable purposes, trade restrictions impose these additional costs on society, as well.

Out conclusion is that the gains that Canadian trade barriers create for protected industries and their workers come at the expense of much greater losses for the entire economy. The result is economic inefficiency, reduced consumption, and lower standards of living.

17.5 / The Case for Protection: A Critical Review

LO17.5 Analyze the validity of the most frequently presented arguments for protectionism.

Despite the compelling logic of specialization and trade, protectionists still exist in some union halls, corporate boardrooms, and the halls of Parliament. What arguments do protectionists make to justify trade barriers? How valid are these arguments?

Military Self-Sufficiency Argument

The argument here is not economic but political-military: Protective tariffs are needed to preserve or strengthen industries that produce the materials essential for national defence. In an uncertain world, the political-military objectives (self-sufficiency) sometimes must take precedence over economic goals (efficiency in the use of world resources).

Unfortunately, it is difficult to measure and compare the benefit of increased national security against the cost of economic inefficiency when protective tariffs are imposed. The economist can only point out that there are economic costs when a nation levies tariffs to increase military self-sufficiency.

The self-sufficiency argument is open to serious abuse. Nearly every industry can claim that it makes direct or indirect contributions to national security and hence deserves protection from imports.

Diversification for Stability Argument

Highly specialized economies such as Saudi Arabia's (based on oil) and Cuba's (based on sugar) are very dependent on international markets for their incomes. In these economies, wars, international political developments, recessions abroad, and random fluctuations in world supply and demand for one or two particular goods can cause deep declines in export revenues and therefore in domestic income. Tariff and quota protection are allegedly needed in such nations to enable greater industrial diversification. That way, these economies will not be so dependent on exporting one or two products to obtain the other goods they need. Such goods will be available domestically, thereby providing greater domestic stability.

There is some truth in this diversification-for-stability argument. There are also two serious shortcomings. First, the argument has little or no relevance to Canada and other advanced economies. Second, the economic costs of diversification may be great; for example, one-crop economies may be highly inefficient at manufacturing.

Infant Industry Argument

The infant industry argument says that protective tariffs are needed to allow new domestic industries to establish themselves. Temporarily shielding young domestic firms from the severe competition of more mature and more efficient foreign firms will give infant industries a chance to develop and become efficient producers.

This argument for protection rests on an alleged exception to the case for free trade. The exception is that young industries have not had—and, if they face mature foreign competition, will never have—the chance to make the long-run adjustments needed for larger scale and greater efficiency in production. In this view, tariff protection for such infant industries will correct a misallocation of world resources perpetuated by historically different levels of economic development between domestic and foreign industries.

There are some logical problems with this infant-industry argument. In the developing nations it is difficult to determine which industries are the infants that are capable of achieving economic maturity and therefore deserving of protection. Also, protective tariffs may persist even after industrial maturity has been realized.

Most economists believe that if infant industries are to be subsidized, there are better means than tariffs for doing it. Direct subsidies, for example, have the advantage of making explicit which industries are being aided and to what degree.

Protection Against Dumping Argument

The protection against dumping argument contends that tariffs are needed to protect domestic firms from "dumping" by foreign producers. The sale of a product in a foreign country at prices either below cost or below the prices commonly charged at home is known as **dumping**. Economists cite two plausible reasons for this behaviour.

First, with regard to below-cost dumping, firms in country A may dump goods at below cost into country B in an attempt to drive their competitors in country B out of business. If the firms in country A succeed in driving their competitors in country B out of business, they will enjoy monopoly power and monopoly prices and profits on the goods they subsequently sell in country B. Their hope is that the longer-term monopoly profits will more than offset the losses from below-cost sales that must take place while they are attempting to drive their competitors in country B out of business.

Second, dumping that involves selling abroad at a price below the price commonly charged in the home country (but still at or above production costs) may be a form of price discrimination, which is charging different prices to different customers. As an example, a foreign seller that has a monopoly in its home market may find that it can maximize its overall profit by charging a high price in its monopolized domestic market while charging a lower price in Canada, where it must compete with Canadian producers. Curiously, it may pursue this strategy even if it makes no profit at all from its sales in Canada, where it must charge the competitive price. So why bother selling in Canada? Because the increase in overall production that comes about by exporting to Canada may allow the firm to obtain the per-unit cost savings often associated with large-scale production. These cost savings imply even higher profits in the monopolized domestic market.

Because dumping is an "unfair trade practice," most nations prohibit it. For example, where dumping is shown to injure Canadian firms, the federal government imposes tariffs called *antidumping duties* on the goods in question. But relatively few documented cases of dumping occur each year, and specific instances of unfair trade do not justify widespread, permanent tariffs. Moreover, antidumping duties can be abused. Often what appears to be dumping is simply comparative advantage at work.

Increased Domestic Employment Argument

Arguing for a tariff to "save Canadian jobs" becomes fashionable when the economy encounters a recession (such as the Great Recession of 2008–2009 in Canada). In an economy that engages in international trade, exports involve spending on domestic output and imports reflect spending to obtain part of another nation's output. So, in this argument, reducing imports will divert spending on another nation's output to spending on domestic output. Thus domestic output and employment will rise. But this argument has several shortcomings.

While imports may eliminate some Canadian jobs, they create others. Imports may have eliminated the jobs of some Canadian steel and textile workers in recent years, but other workers have gained jobs unloading ships, flying imported aircraft, and selling imported electronic equipment. Import restrictions alter the composition of employment, but they may have little or no effect on the volume of employment.

The *fallacy of composition*—the false idea that what is true for the part is necessarily true for the whole—is also present in this rationale for tariffs. All nations cannot simultaneously succeed in restricting imports while maintaining their exports; what is true for one nation is not true for all nations. The exports of one nation must be the imports of another nation. To the extent that one country is able to expand its economy through an excess of exports over imports, the resulting excess of imports over exports worsens another economy's unemployment problem. It is no wonder that tariffs and import quotas meant to achieve domestic full employment are called "beggar thy neighbour" policies: they achieve short-run domestic goals by making trading partners poorer.

Finally, forcing an excess of exports over imports cannot succeed in raising domestic employment over the long run. It is through Canadian imports that foreign nations earn dollars for buying Canadian exports. In the long run, a nation must import in order to export. The long-run impact of tariffs is not an increase in domestic employment but, at best, a reallocation of workers away from export industries and to protected domestic industries. This shift implies a less efficient allocation of resources.

Cheap Foreign Labour Argument

The cheap foreign labour argument says that domestic firms and workers must be shielded from the ruinous competition of countries where wages are low. If protection is not provided, cheap imports will flood Canadian markets and the prices of Canadian goods—along with the wages of Canadian workers—will be pulled down. That is, the domestic living standards in Canada will be reduced.

This argument can be rebutted at several levels. The logic of the argument suggests that it is *not* mutually beneficial for rich and poor persons to trade with one another. However, that is not the case. A low-income farm worker may pick lettuce or tomatoes for a rich land owner, and both may benefit from the transaction. And both Canadian consumers and Chinese workers gain when they "trade" a pair of athletic shoes priced at $30 as opposed to Canadian consumers being restricted to buying a similar shoe made in Canada for $60.

Also, recall that gains from trade are based on comparative advantage, not on absolute advantage. Look back at Figure 17-3, where we supposed that Canada and Brazil had labour forces of exactly the same size. Noting the positions of the production possibilities curves, we observe that Canadian labour can produce more of *either* good. Thus, it is more productive; it has an absolute advantage in the production of both goods. Because of this greater productivity, we can expect wages and living standards to be higher for Canadian labour. Brazil's less productive labour will receive lower wages.

The cheap foreign labour argument suggests that, to maintain its standard of living, Canada should not trade with low-wage Brazil. What if it does not trade with Brazil? Will wages and living standards rise in Canada as a result? No. To obtain soybeans, Canada will have to reallocate a portion of its labour from its relatively more-efficient steel industry to its relatively less-efficient soybean industry. As a result, the average productivity of Canadian labour will fall, as will real wages and living standards. The labour forces of *both* countries will have lower standards of living because without specialization and trade they will have less output available to them. Compare column 4 with column 1 in Table 17-3 or points A′ and Z′ with A and Z in Figure 17-4 to confirm this point.

Another problem with the cheap foreign labour argument is that its proponents incorrectly focus on labour costs per hour when what really matters is labour costs per unit of output. As an example, suppose a Canadian factory pays its workers $20 per hour while a factory in a developing country pays its workers $4 per hour. The proponents of the cheap foreign labour argument look at these numbers and conclude—incorrectly—that it is impossible for the Canadian factory to compete with the factory in the developing country. But this conclusion fails to take into account two crucial facts:

- What actually matters is labour costs per *unit*, not labour costs per *hour*.

- Differences in productivity typically mean that labour costs per unit are often nearly identical despite huge differences in labour costs per hour.

To see why these points matter so much, let's take into account how productive the two factories are. Because the Canadian factory uses much more sophisticated technology, better trained workers, and a lot more capital per worker, one worker in one hour can produce 20 units of output. Since the Canadian workers get paid $20 per hour, this means the Canadian factory's labour cost *per unit of output* is $1. The factory in the developing country is much less productive since it uses less efficient technology and its relatively untrained workers have a lot less machinery and equipment to work with. A worker there produces only 4 units per hour. Given the foreign wage of $4 per hour, this means that the labour cost per unit of output at the factory in the developing country is also $1. As you can see, the lower wage rate per hour at the factory in the developing country does not translate into lower labour costs per unit—meaning that it won't be able to undersell its Canadian competitor just because its workers get paid lower wages per hour.

Proponents of the cheap foreign labour argument tend to focus exclusively on the large international differences that exist in labour costs per hour. They typically fail to mention that these differences in labour costs per hour are mostly the result of tremendously large differences in productivity and that these large differences in productivity serve to equalize labour costs per unit of output. As a result, firms in developing countries only *sometimes* have an advantage in terms of labour costs per unit of output. Whether they do in any specific situation will vary by industry and firm and will depend on differences in productivity as well as differences in labour costs per hour. For many goods, labour productivity in high-wage countries like Canada is so much higher than labour productivity in low-wage countries that it is actually cheaper *per unit of output* to manufacture those goods in high-wage countries. That is why, for instance, most automobiles are still produced in Canada, the United States, Japan, and Europe rather than in low-wage countries.

- A tariff on a product increases its price, reduces its consumption, increases its domestic production, reduces its imports, and generates tariff revenue for government; an import quota does the same, except a quota generates revenue for foreign producers rather than for the government imposing the quota.

17.6 / Multilateral Trade Agreements and Free-Trade Zones

LO17.6 Identify and explain the objectives of GATT, WTO, EU, Euro Zone, and NAFTA, and discuss offshoring and those hurt by free trade.

Aware of the detrimental effects of trade wars and the general weaknesses of arguments for trade protections, nations have worked to lower tariffs worldwide. Their pursuit of freer trade has been aided by recently emerged special-interest groups that have offset the more-established special-interest groups that have traditionally supported tariffs and quotas. Specifically, lower tariffs are now supported by exporters of goods and services, importers of foreign components used in "domestic" products, and domestic sellers of imported products.

General Agreement on Tariffs and Trade

In 1947, 23 nations including Canada signed the **General Agreement on Tariffs and Trade (GATT)**. GATT was based on three principles: (1) equal, nondiscriminatory trade treatment for all member nations; (2) the reduction of tariffs by multilateral negotiation; and (3) the elimination of import quotas. Basically, GATT provided a forum for the multilateral negotiation of reduced trade barriers.

Since World War II, member nations have completed eight rounds of GATT negotiations to reduce trade barriers. The eighth round of negotiations began in Uruguay in 1986. After seven years of complex discussions, in 1993, a new agreement was reached by the 128 nations that were by that time members of GATT. The Uruguay Round agreement took effect on January 1, 1995, and its provisions were phased in through 2005.

Under this agreement, tariffs on thousands of products were eliminated or reduced, with overall tariffs dropping by 33 percent. The agreement also liberalized government rules that in the past impeded the global market for such services as advertising, legal services, tourist services, and financial services. Quotas on imported textiles and apparel were phased out and replaced with tariffs. Other provisions reduced agricultural subsidies paid to farmers and protected intellectual property (patents, trademarks, copyrights, etc.) against piracy.

World Trade Organization

The Uruguay Round agreement established the **World Trade Organization (WTO)** as GATT's successor. Some 159 nations belonged to the WTO in 2013. The WTO oversees trade agreements reached by the member nations, and rules on trade disputes among them. It also provides forums for further rounds of trade negotiations. The ninth and latest round of negotiations–the **Doha Development Agenda**–was launched in Doha, Qatar, in late 2001. (The trade rounds occur over several years in several venues but are named after the city or country of origination.) The negotiations are aimed at further reducing tariffs and quotas, as well as agricultural subsidies that distort trade. You can get an update of the status of the complex negotiations at www.wto.org.

GATT and the WTO have been positive forces in the trend toward liberalized world trade. The trade rules agreed on by the member nations provide a strong and necessary bulwark against the protectionism called for by the special-interest groups in the various nations.

For that reason and others, the WTO is quite controversial. Critics are concerned that rules crafted to expand international trade and investment enable firms to circumvent national laws that protect workers and the environment. Critics ask, "What good are minimum-wage laws, worker safety laws, collective bargaining rights, and environmental laws if firms can easily shift their production to nations that have weaker laws or if consumers can buy goods produced in those countries?"

Proponents of the WTO respond that labour and environmental protections should be pursued directly in nations that have low standards and via international organizations other than the WTO. These issues should not be linked to the process of trade liberalization, which confers widespread economic benefits across nations. Moreover, say proponents of the WTO, many environmental and labour concerns are greatly overblown. Most world trade is among advanced industrial countries, not between them and countries that have lower environmental and labour standards. Moreover, the free flow of goods and resources raises output and income in the developing nations. Historically, such increases in living standards have eventually resulted in stronger, not weaker, protections for the environment and for workers.

The European Union (EU)

Countries have also sought to reduce tariffs by creating regional *free-trade zones*. The most dramatic example is the **European Union (EU)**, formerly called the European Economic Community. Initiated in 1958 as the Common Market, in 2003 the EU comprised fifteen European nations—Austria, Belgium, Denmark, Finland, France, Germany, Greece, Ireland, Italy, Luxembourg, the Netherlands, Portugal, Spain, Sweden, and the United Kingdom In 2004, the EU expanded by ten additional European countries: Cyprus, the Czech Republic, Estonia, Hungary, Latvia, Lithuania, Malta, Poland, Slovakia, and Slovenia. The 2007 addition of Bulgaria and Romania plus the 2013 addition of Croatia expanded the EU to twenty-eight nations.

The EU has abolished tariffs and import quotas on nearly all products traded among the participating nations and established a common system of tariffs applicable to all goods received from nations outside the EU. It has also liberalized the movement of capital and labour within the EU and has created common policies in other economic matters of joint concern, such as agriculture, transportation, and business practices.

EU integration has achieved for Europe increased regional specialization, greater productivity, greater output, and faster economic growth. The free flow of goods and services has created large markets for EU industries. The resulting economies of large-scale production have enabled them to achieve much lower costs than they could have achieved in their small, single-nation markets.

One of the most significant accomplishments of the EU was the establishment of the so-called **Euro Zone** in the early 2000s. As of 2015, nineteen members of the EU (Austria, Belgium, Cyprus, Germany, Greece, Ireland, Finland, France, Italy, Luxembourg, Malta, the Netherlands, Portugal, Slovenia, Slovakia, Spain, Latvia, Lithuania, and Estonia) were using the euro as a common currency. Notably, Great Britain, Denmark, and Sweden have opted out of the common currency, at least for now. But gone are French francs, German marks, Italian liras, and other national currencies that were once used by the Euro Zone nations.

Economists expect the adoption of the euro to raise the standard of living in the Euro Zone nations over time. By ending the inconvenience and expense of exchanging currencies, the euro has enhanced the free flow of goods, services, and resources among the Euro Zone members. Companies that previously sold products in only one or two European nations have found it easier to price and sell their products in all seventeen Euro Zone countries. The euro has also allowed consumers and businesses to comparison shop for outputs and inputs, and this capability has increased competition, reduced prices, and lowered costs.

North American Free Trade Agreement (NAFTA)

In 1993, Canada, Mexico, and the United States formed a major trade bloc. **The North American Free Trade Agreement (NAFTA)** established a free-trade zone that has about the same combined output as the

EU but encompasses a much larger geographical area. NAFTA has eliminated tariffs and other trade barriers among Canada, Mexico, and the United States for most goods and services.

Critics of NAFTA feared that it would cause a massive loss of Canadian jobs as firms moved to Mexico to take advantage of lower wages and weaker regulations on pollution and workplace safety. Also, there were concerns that Japan and South Korea would build plants in Mexico and transport goods tariff-free to Canada, further hurting Canadian firms and workers.

In retrospect, the critics were much too pessimistic. Since the passage of NAFTA in 1993, employment has increased in Canada by over 4 million workers and the unemployment rate fell from over 10 percent to under 7 percent in 2014. NAFTA has increased trade among Canada, Mexico, and the United States and has enhanced the standard of living in all three countries.

Besides NAFTA, Canada signed free trade agreements with Chile and Israel in 1997, Costa Rica in 2002, with the Euro Zone in 2009, Colombia in 2011, Jordan in 2012, Panama in 2013, and Honduras in 2014.

QUICK REVIEW 17.8

- The General Agreement on Tariffs and Trade (GATT) established multinational reductions in tariffs and import quotas. The Uruguay Round of GATT (1993) reduced tariffs worldwide, liberalized international trade in services, strengthened protections for intellectual property, and reduced agricultural subsidies.
- The World Trade Organization (WTO)—GATT's successor—rules on trade disputes and provides forums for negotiations on further rounds of trade liberalization. The current round is called the Doha Round.
- The European Union (EU) and the North American Free Trade Agreement (NAFTA) have reduced internal trade barriers among their members by establishing large free-trade zones.

Recognizing Those Hurt by Free Trade

Shifts in patterns of comparative advantage and removal of long-standing trade protection can hurt specific groups of workers. For example, the erosion of Canada's once strong comparative advantage in steel has caused production plant shutdowns and layoffs in the Canadian steel industry. The textile and apparel industries in Canada face similar difficulties. Clearly, not everyone wins from free trade (or freer trade). Some workers lose.

OFFSHORING OF JOBS

Not only are some Canadian jobs lost because of international trade, but some are lost because of globalization of factor markets. In recent years Canadian firms have found the outsourcing of work abroad to be increasingly profitable. Economists call this business activity **offshoring**–shifting work previously done by Canadian workers to workers located in other nations. Offshoring is not a new practice but traditionally has involved components for Canadian manufacturing goods. For example, recent advances in computer and communications technology have enabled Canadian firms to offshore service jobs such as data entry, book compositing, software coding, call-centre operations, medical transcription, and claims processing to countries such as India. Where offshoring occurs, some of the value added in the production process accrues to foreign countries rather than Canada. So part of the income generated from the production of Canadian goods is paid to foreigners, not to Canadian workers.

Offshoring is a wrenching experience for many who lose their jobs, but it is not necessarily bad for the overall economy. Offshoring simply reflects growing specialization and international trade in services, or, more descriptively, "tasks." That growth has been made possible by recent trade agreements and new information and communication technologies. As with trade in goods, trade in services reflects comparative advantage and is beneficial to both trading partners. Moreover, offshoring may encourage domestic investment and the expansion of firms in Canada by reducing their production costs and keeping them competitive worldwide.

In some instances, "offshoring jobs" may equate to "importing competitiveness." Entire firms that might otherwise disappear abroad may remain profitable in the Canada only because they can offshore some of their work. Moreover, Canada has a sizable trade surplus with other nations in services. Canada gains by specializing in high-valued services such as transportation services, accounting services, legal services, and advertising services, where it still has a comparative advantage. It then "trades" to obtain lower-valued services such as call-center and data-entry work, for which comparative advantage has gone abroad.

Offshoring also increases the demand for complementary jobs in Canada. Jobs that are close substitutes for existing jobs in Canada are lost, but complementary jobs in Canada are expanded. For example, the lower price of writing software code in India may mean a lower cost of software sold in Canada and abroad. That, in turn, may create more jobs for domestically-based workers such as software designers, marketers, and distributors.

QUICK REVIEW 17.9

- Increased international trade and offshoring of jobs have harmed some specific workers in Canada and have led to policies to try to help them with their transitions to new lines of work.

The LAST WORD   Petition of the Candlemakers, 1845

French economist Frédéric Bastiat (1801–1850) devastated the proponents of protectionism by satirically extending their reasoning to its logical and absurd conclusions.

Petition of the Manufacturers of Candles, Waxlights, Lamps, Candlesticks, Street Lamps, Snuffers, Extinguishers, and of the Producers of Oil Tallow, Rosin, Alcohol, and, Generally, of Everything Connected with Lighting.

TO MESSIEURS THE MEMBERS OF THE CHAMBER OF DEPUTIES.

Gentlemen—You are on the right road. You reject abstract theories, and have little consideration for cheapness and plenty. Your chief care is the interest of the producer. You desire to emancipate him from external competition, and reserve the national market for national industry.

We are about to offer you an admirable opportunity of applying your—what shall we call it? your theory? No; nothing is more deceptive than theory; your doctrine? your system? your principle? but you dislike doctrines, you abhor systems, and as for principles,

you deny that there are any in social economy: we shall say, then, your practice, your practice without theory and without principle.

We are suffering from the intolerable competition of a foreign rival, placed, it would seem, in a condition so far superior to ours for the production of light, that he absolutely inundates our national market with it at a price fabulously reduced. The moment he shows himself, our trade leaves us—all consumers apply to him; and a branch of native industry, having countless ramifications, is all at once rendered completely stagnant. This rival...is no other than the Sun.

What we pray for is, that it may please you to pass a law ordering the shutting up of all windows, skylights, dormer windows, outside and inside shutters, curtains, blinds, bull's-eyes; in a word, of all openings, holes, chinks, clefts, and fissures, by or through which the light of the sun has been in use to enter houses, to the prejudice of the meritorious manufacturers with which we flatter ourselves we have accommodated our country—a country which, in gratitude, ought not to abandon us now to a strife so unequal.

If you shut up as much as possible all access to natural light, and create a demand for artificial light, which of our French manufacturers will not be encouraged by it? If more tallow is consumed, then there must be more oxen and sheep; and, consequently, we shall behold the multiplication of artificial meadows, meat, wool, hides, and, above all, manure, which is the basis and foundation of all agricultural wealth.

The same remark applies to navigation. Thousands of vessels will proceed to the whale fishery; and, in a short time, we shall possess a navy capable of maintaining the honour of France, and gratifying the patriotic aspirations of your petitioners, the undersigned candlemakers and others.

Only have the goodness to reflect, Gentlemen, and you will be convinced that there is, perhaps, no Frenchman, from the wealthy coalmaster to the humblest vender of lucifer matches, whose lot will not be ameliorated by the success of this our petition.

Source: Frédéric Bastiat, *Economic Sophisms* (Irvington-on-Hudson, NY: The Foundation for Economic Education, Inc., 1996), abridged. Used with permission of Foundation for Economic Education, www.FEE.org.

Question

What was the central point that Bastiat was trying to make in his imaginary petition of the candlemakers?

Chapter Summary

LO17.1 LIST AND DISCUSS SEVERAL KEY FACTS ABOUT CANADA'S INTERNATIONAL TRADE.

- Goods and services flows, capital and labour flows, information and technology flows, and financial flows link Canada and other countries.

- International trade is growing in importance globally and for Canada. World trade is significant to Canada in two respects: (a) Canadian imports and exports as a percentage of domestic output are among the highest in the world, and (b) Canada is completely dependent on trade for certain commodities and materials that cannot be obtained domestically.

- Principal Canadian exports include automotive products, machinery and equipment, and grain; major Canadian imports are general machinery and equipment, automobiles, and industrial goods and machinery. Quantitatively, the United States is our most important trading partner.

- Global trade has been greatly facilitated by (a) improvements in transportation technology, (b) improvements in communications technology, and (c) general declines in tariffs. The world's major trading nations by volume of trade are China, the United States, Germany, and Japan. Other major traders include other Western European nations (France, Netherlands, Italy, and the United Kingdom), along with Canada and the Southeast Asian countries of South Korea, Taiwan, and Singapore.

LO17.2 DEFINE COMPARATIVE ADVANTAGE, AND DEMONSTRATE HOW SPECIALIZATION AND TRADE ADD TO A NATION'S OUTPUT.

- World trade is based on three considerations: (1) the uneven distribution of economic resources among nations, (2) the fact that efficient production of various goods requires particular techniques or combinations of resources, and (3) the differentiated products produced among nations.

- Mutually advantageous specialization and trade are possible between any two nations if they have different opportunity-cost ratios for any two products. By specializing based on comparative advantage, nations can obtain larger real incomes with fixed amounts of resources. The terms of trade determine how this increase in world output is shared by the trading nations. Increasing (rather than constant) costs limit specialization and trade.

LO17.3 DESCRIBE HOW DIFFERENCES BETWEEN WORLD PRICES PROMPT EXPORTS AND IMPORTS.

• A nation's export supply curve shows the quantity of product it will export at world prices that exceed the domestic price—the price in a closed, no-international-trade economy. Its import demand curve reveals the quantity of a product it will import at world prices below the domestic price.

• In a two-nation model, the equilibrium world price and the equilibrium quantities of exports and imports occur where one nation's import supply curve intersects the other nation's export demand curve.

LO17.4 ANALYZE THE ECONOMIC EFFECTS OF TARIFFS AND QUOTAS.

• Trade barriers take the form of protective tariffs, quotas, nontariff barriers, and "voluntary" export restrictions. Export subsidies also distort international trade. Supply and demand analysis demonstrates that protective tariffs and quotas increase the prices and reduce the quantities demanded of affected goods. Sales by foreign exporters diminish; domestic producers, however, enjoy higher prices and enlarged sales. Consumer losses from trade restrictions greatly exceed producer and government gains, creating an efficiency loss to society.

LO17.5 ANALYZE THE VALIDITY OF THE MOST FREQUENTLY PRESENTED ARGUMENTS FOR PROTECTIONISM

• The strongest arguments for protection are the infant industry and military self-sufficiency arguments. Most other arguments for protection are interest-group appeals or reasoning fallacies that emphasize producer interests over consumer interests or stress the immediate effects of trade barriers while ignoring long-run consequences.

• The cheap foreign labour argument for protection fails because it focuses on labour costs per hour rather than on what really matters, labour costs per unit of output. Due to higher productivity, firms in high-wage countries like Canada can have lower wage costs per unit of output than competitors in low-wage countries. Whether they do will depend on how their particular wage and productivity levels compare with those of their competitors in low-wage countries.

LO17.6 IDENTIFY AND EXPLAIN THE OBJECTIVES OF GATT, WTO, EU, EURO ZONE, AND NAFTA, AND DISCUSS OFFSHORING AND THOSE HURT BY FREE TRADE.

• In 1947 the General Agreement on Tariffs and Trade (GATT) was formed to encourage nondiscriminatory treatment for all member nations, to reduce tariffs, and to eliminate import quotas. The Uruguay Round of GATT negotiations (1993) reduced tariffs and quotas, liberalized trade in services, reduced agricultural subsidies, reduced pirating of intellectual property, and phased out quotas on textiles.

• GATT's successor, the World Trade Organization (WTO), had 159 member nations in 2013. It implements WTO agreements, rules on trade disputes between members, and provides forums for continued discussions on trade liberalization. The latest round of trade negotiations—the Doha Development Agenda—began in late 2001 and as of 2015 was still in progress.

• Free-trade zones (trade blocs) liberalize trade within regions. Two examples of free-trade agreements are the twenty-eight-member European Union (EU) and the North American Free Trade Agreement (NAFTA) comprising Canada, Mexico, and the United States. Nineteen of the EU nations have agreed to abandon their national currencies for a common currency called the euro.

• Offshoring is the practice of shifting work previously done by Canadians in Canada to workers located in other nations. Although offshoring reduces some jobs in Canada, it lowers production costs, expands sales, and therefore may create other jobs in Canada.

Terms and Concepts

labour-intensive goods
land-intensive goods
capital-intensive goods
absolute advantage
comparative advantage
opportunity-cost ratio
principle of comparative advantage
terms of trade
trading possibilities line
gains from trade
world price

domestic price
export supply curve
import demand curve
equilibrium world price
tariffs
revenue tariff
protective tariff
import quota
nontariff barrier (NTB)
voluntary export restriction (VER)
export subsidy

dumping
General Agreement on Tariffs and Trade (GATT)
World Trade Organization (WTO)
Doha Development Agenda
European Union (EU)
Euro Zone
North America Free Trade Agreement (NAFTA)
offshoring

Discussion Questions

1. Describe the four major economic flows that link Canada with other nations. Provide a specific example to illustrate each flow. Explain the relationships between the top and bottom flows in Figure 17-1. [LO17.1]

2. Quantitatively, how important is international trade to the Canadian economy? What country is Canada's most important trading partner? How can persistent trade deficits be financed? [LO17.1]

3. Distinguish among land-, labour-, and capital-intensive goods, citing an example of each without resorting to the textbook examples. How do distinctive products, unrelated to resource intensity, relate to international trade? [LO17.1, 17.2]

4. Explain the following and relate your answer to the ideas of Adam Smith and David Ricardo: Canada can make certain toys with greater productive efficiency than can China. Yet we import those toys from China. [LO17.2]

5. Suppose Big Country can produce 80 units of X by using all its resources to produce X or 60 units of Y by devoting all its resources to Y. Comparable figures for Small Nation are 60 units of X and 60 units of Y. Assuming constant costs, in which product should each nation specialize? Explain why. What are the limits of the terms of trade between these two countries? How would rising costs (rather than constant costs) impact the extent of specialization and trade between these two countries? [LO17.2]

6. What is an export demand curve? What is an import supply curve? How do such curves relate to the determination of the equilibrium world price of a tradable good? [LO17.3]

7. Why is a quota more detrimental to an economy than a tariff that results in the same level of imports as the quota? What is the net outcome of either tariffs or quota for the world economy? [LO17.4]

8. "The potentially valid arguments for tariff protection are also the most easily abused." Why are these arguments susceptible to abuse? [LO17.4]

9. Evaluate the effectiveness of artificial trade barriers, such as tariffs and import quotas, as a way to achieve and maintain full employment throughout the Canadian economy. How might such policies reduce unemployment in one Canadian industry but increase it in another Canadian industry? [LO17.4]

10. In 2014, manufacturing workers in Canada earned an average wage of $23.19 per hour. That same year, manufacturing workers in Mexico earned an average wage of $6.36 per hour. [LO17.4]

    a. How can Canadian manufacturers possibly compete?

    b. Why isn't all manufacturing done in Mexico and other low-wage countries?

11. How might protective tariffs reduce both the imports and the exports of the nation that levies tariffs? In what way do foreign firms that "dump" their products onto the Canadian market in effect provide bargains to Canadian consumers? How might the import competition lead to quality improvements and cost reductions by Canadian firms? [LO17.5]

12. Identify and state the significance of each of the following trade-related entities: (a) the WTO, (b) the EU, (c) the Euro Zone, and (d) NAFTA. [LO17.6]

13. What is offshoring of white-collar service jobs and how does that practice relate to international trade? Why has offshoring increased over the past few decades? Give an example (other than that in the textbook) of how offshoring can eliminate some Canadian jobs while creating other Canadian jobs. [LO17.6]

Review Questions

1. In Country A, a worker can make 5 bicycles per hour. In Country B, a worker can make 7 bicycles per hour. Which country has an absolute advantage in making bicycles? [LO17.2]

    a. Country A

    b. Country B

2. In Country A, the production of 1 bicycle requires using resources that could otherwise be used to produce 11 lamps. In Country B, the production of 1 bicycle requires using resources that could otherwise be used to produce 15 lamps. Which country has a comparative advantage in making bicycles? [LO17.2]

    a. Country A

    b. Country B

3. True or False? If Country B has an absolute advantage over Country A in producing bicycles, it will also have a comparative advantage over Country A in producing bicycles. [LO17.2]

4. Suppose that the opportunity-cost ratio for pears and apples is $4P:1A$ in British Columbia but $1P:2A$ in Ontario. Which province has the comparative advantage in producing apples? [LO17.2]

    a. British Columbia

    b. Ontario

    c. Neither

5. Suppose that the opportunity-cost ratio for fish and lumber is $1F:1L$ in Canada but $2F:1L$ in Iceland. Then _____ should specialize in producing fish while _____ should specialize in producing lumber. [LO17.2]

    a. Canada; Iceland

    b. Iceland; Canada

6. Suppose that the opportunity-cost ratio for watches and cheese is $1C:1W$ in Switzerland but $1C:4W$ in Japan. At which of the

following international exchange ratios (terms of trade) will Switzerland and Japan be willing to specialize and engage in trade with each other?   [LO17.2]

Select one or more answers from the choices shown.

a. 1C:3W

b. 1C:1/2W

c. 1C:5W

d. 1/2C:1W

e. 2C:1W.

7. We see quite a bit of international trade in the real world. And trade is driven by specialization. So why don't we see full specialization—for instance, all cars in the world being made in South Korea or all the mobile phones in the world being made in China? Select the best answer from among the following choices.   [LO17.2]

a. High tariffs

b. Extensive import quotas

c. Increasing opportunity costs

d. Increasing returns

8. Which of the following are benefits of international trade? [LO17.2]

Choose one or more answers from the choices shown.

a. A more efficient allocation of resources

b. A higher level of material well-being

c. Gains from specialization

d. Promoting competition

e. Deterring monopoly

f. Reducing the threat of war

9. True or False? If a country is open to international trade, the domestic price can differ from the international price.   [LO17.3]

10. Suppose that the current international price of wheat is $6 per bushel and that Canada is currently exporting 30 million bushels per year. If Canada suddenly became a closed economy with respect to wheat, would the domestic price of wheat in Canada end up higher or lower than $6?   [LO17.3]

a. Higher

b. Lower

c. The same

11. Suppose that if Iceland and Japan were both closed economies, the domestic price of fish would be $100 per tonne in Iceland and $90 per tonne in Japan. If the two countries decided to open up to international trade with each other, which of the following could be the equilibrium international price of fish once they begin trading?   [LO17.3]

a. $75

b. $85

c. $95

d. $105

12. Draw a domestic supply-and-demand diagram for a product in which Canada does not have a comparative advantage. What impact do foreign imports have on domestic price and quantity? On your diagram show a protective tariff that eliminates approximately one-half of the assumed imports. What are the price-quantity effects of this tariff on (a) domestic consumers, (b) domestic producers, and (c) foreign exporters? How would the effects of a quota that creates the same amount of imports differ?   [LO17.4]

13. Canadian apparel makers complain to Parliament about competition from China. Parliament decides to impose either a tariff or a quota on apparel imports from China. Which policy would Chinese apparel manufacturers prefer?   [LO17.4]

a. Tariff

b. Quota

Problems

1. Assume that the comparative-cost ratios of two products—baby formula and tuna fish—are as follows in the nations of Canswicki and Tunata: [LO17.2]

Canswicki: 1 can baby formula = 2 cans tuna fish

Tunata: 1 can baby formula = 4 cans tuna fish

In what product should each nation specialize? Which of the following terms of trade would be acceptable to both nations?

a. 1 can baby formula = 2½ cans tuna fish

b. 1 can baby formula = 1 can tuna fish

c. 1 can baby formula = 5 cans tuna fish

2. The following are hypothetical production possibilities tables for New Zealand and Spain. Plot the production possibilities data for each of the two countries separately. Referring to your graphs, answer the following: [LO17.2]

**New Zealand's Production Possibilities Table
(millions of bushels)**

| | | Production alternatives | | |
Product	A	B	C	D
Apples	0	20	40	60
Plums	15	10	5	0

**Spain's Production Possibilities Table
(millions of bushels)**

| | | Production alternatives | | |
Product	R	S	T	U
Apples	0	20	40	60
Plums	60	40	20	0

a. What is each country's cost ratio of producing plums and apples?

b. Which nation should specialize in which product?

c. Show the trading possibilities lines for each nation if the actual terms of trade are 1 plum for 2 apples. (Plot these lines on your graph.)

d. Suppose the optimum product mixes before specialization and trade were alternative B in New Zealand and alternative S in Spain. What are the gains from specialization and trade?

3. The following hypothetical production possibilities tables are for China and Canada. Assume that, before specialization and trade, the optimal product mix for China is alternative B and for Canada is alternative U. [LO17.2]

China production possibilities

Product	A	B	C	D	E	F
Apparel (in thousands)	30	24	18	12	6	0
Chemicals (in tons)	0	6	12	18	24	30

Canada production possibilities

Product	R	S	T	U	V	W
Apparel (in thousands)	10	8	6	4	2	0
Chemicals (in tons)	0	4	8	12	16	20

a. Are comparative-cost conditions such that the two areas should specialize? If so, what product should each produce?

b. What is the total gain in apparel and chemical output that would result from such specialization?

c. What are the limits of the terms of trade? Suppose that the actual terms of trade are 1 unit of apparel for 1½ units of chemicals and that 4 units of apparel are exchanged for 6 units of chemicals. What are the gains from specialization and trade for each nation?

4. Refer to Figure 3-6. Assume that the graph depicts the Canadian domestic market for corn. How many bushels of corn, if any, will Canada export or import at a world price of $1, $2, $3, $4, and $5? Use this information to construct the Canadian export supply curve and import demand curve for corn. Suppose that the only other corn-producing nation is France, where the domestic price is $4. Which country will export corn? Which county will import it? [LO17.3]

CHAPTER 18

Exchange Rates and the Balance of Payments

LEARNING OBJECTIVES

LO18.1 Explain how currencies of different nations are exchanged when international transactions take place.

LO18.2 Analyze the balance sheet Canada uses to account for international payments it makes and receives.

LO18.3 Discuss how exchange rates are determined in a currency market that has flexible exchange rates.

LO18.4 Describe the difference between flexible exchange rates and fixed exchange rates.

LO18.5 Explain the current system of managed floating exchange rates.

If you take a Canadian dollar to the bank and ask to exchange it for Canadian currency, you will get a puzzled look. If you persist, you may get a dollar's worth of change: one Canadian dollar can buy exactly one Canadian dollar. But in July 2015, for example, one Canadian dollar could buy 4.75 Chinese yuan, 1.05 Australian dollars, 0.49 British pounds, 0.77 American dollars, 0.70 European euros, 94 Japanese yen, or 50 Indian rupees. What explains this seemingly haphazard array of exchange rates?

In Chapter 17 we examined comparative advantage as the underlying economic basis of world trade and discussed the effects of barriers to free trade. Now we introduce the highly important monetary and financial aspects of international trade.

18.1 / Financing International Trade

LO18.1 Explain how currencies of different nations are exchanged when international transactions take place.

This chapter focuses on international financial transactions, the vast majority of which fall into two broad categories: international trade and international asset transactions. International trade involves either purchasing or selling currently produced goods or services across an international border. Examples include an Egyptian firm exporting cotton to Canada and a Canadian company hiring an Indian call centre to answer its phones. International asset transactions involve the transfer of the property rights to either real or financial assets between the citizens of one country and the citizens of another country. It includes activities like buying foreign stocks or selling your house to a foreigner.

These two categories of international financial transactions reflect the fact that whether they are from different countries or the same country, individuals and firms can exchange only two things with each other: currently produced goods and services or pre-existing assets. With regard to assets, however, money is by far the most commonly exchanged asset. Only rarely would you ever find a barter situation in which people directly exchanged other assets–such as trading a car for 500 shares of BlackBerry stock, or a cow for 30 chickens and a tank of diesel fuel.

As a result, there are two basic types of transactions:

- People trading either goods or services for money
- People trading assets for money

In either case, money flows from the buyers of the goods, services, or assets to the sellers of the goods, services, or assets.

When the people engaged in any such transactions are both from places that use the same currency, what type of money to use is not an issue. Canadians from Alberta and Newfoundland will use their common currency, the Canadian dollar. People from France and Germany will use their common currency, the euro. However, when the people involved in an exchange are from places that use different currencies, intermediate asset transactions have to take place: the buyers must convert their own currencies into the currencies that the sellers use and accept.

As an example, consider the case of a British software design company that wants to buy a supercomputer made by a Canadian company. The Canadian company sells these high-powered machines for $300,000. To pay for the machine, the British company has to convert some of the money it has (British pounds sterling) into the money that the Canadian company will accept (Canadian dollars). This process is not difficult. As we will soon explain in detail, there are many easy-to-use foreign exchange markets (or currency markets) in which those who wish to sell pounds and buy dollars can interact with others who wish to sell dollars and buy pounds. The demand and supply created by these two groups determines the equilibrium exchange rate, which in turn determines how many pounds our British company will have to convert to pay for the supercomputer. If, for instance, the exchange rate is $2 = £1$, then the British company will have to convert £150,000 to obtain the $300,000 necessary to purchase the computer.

QUICK REVIEW 18.1

- International financial transactions involve trade either in currently produced goods and services or in pre-existing assets.
- Exports of goods, services, and assets create inflows of money, while imports cause outflows of money.
- If buyers and sellers use different currencies, then foreign exchange transactions take place so that the exporter can be paid in his or her own currency.

18.2 / The Balance of International Payments

LO18.2 Analyze the balance sheet Canada uses to account for international payments it makes and receives.

A nation's **balance of payments** (also referred to as the balance of international payments) is the sum of all the financial transactions that take place between its residents and the residents of foreign nations. Most of these transactions fall into the two main categories that we have just discussed: international trade and international asset transactions. As a result, nearly all of the items included in the balance of payments are things such as exports and imports of goods, exports and imports of services, and international purchases and sales of financial and real assets. But the balance of payments also includes international transactions that fall outside these main categories—things such as tourist expenditures, interest and dividends received or paid abroad, debt forgiveness, and remittances made by immigrants to their relatives back home.

Statistics Canada compiles a balance of payments statement each year. This statement summarizes all of the millions of payments that individuals and firms in Canada receive from foreigners as well as all of the millions of payments that individuals and firms in Canada make to foreigners. It shows "flows" of inpayments of money *to* Canada and outpayments of money *from* Canada. For convenience, all of these money payments are given in terms of dollars. This is true despite the fact that some of them actually may have been made using foreign currencies—as when, for instance, a Canadian company converts dollars into euros to buy something from an Italian company.

When including this outpayment of money from Canada, the accountants who compile the balance of payments statement use the number of dollars the Canadian company converted—rather than the number of euros that were actually used to make the purchase.

Table 18-1 is a simplified balance of payments statement for Canada in 2014. Because most international financial transactions fall into only two categories—international trade and international asset exchanges—the balance of payments statement is organized into two broad categories. The *current account* given at the top of the table mostly deals with international trade. The *capital and financial account* at the bottom of the table mostly deals with international asset exchanges.

 SPECIALIZATION AND TRADE

Current Account

The top portion of Table 18-1 summarizes Canada's trade in currently produced goods and services, and is called the **current account**. Items 1 and 2 show exports and imports of goods (merchandise) in 2014. Exports have a *plus* (+) sign because they are a credit; they generate flows of money into Canada. Canadian imports have a *minus* (−) sign because they are a *debit*; they cause flows of money out of Canada.

BALANCE ON GOODS

Items 1 and 2 in Table 18-1 reveal that in 2014 Canada's goods exports of $529 billion earned enough foreign currencies to more than finance Canada's goods imports of $524 billion. A country's *balance of trade on goods* is the difference between its exports and imports of goods. If exports exceed imports, the result is a trade surplus or "favourable balance of trade." If imports exceed exports, there is a trade deficit or "unfavourable balance of trade." We note in item 3 that in 2014 Canada had a trade surplus (of goods) of $5 billion.

BALANCE ON SERVICES

Canada exports not only goods, such as airplanes and computer software, but also services, such as insurance, consulting, travel, and brokerage services, to residents of foreign nations. Item 4 in Table 18-1 shows that these service exports totalled $95 billion in 2014. Since they generate flows into Canada, they are a

TABLE 18-1	Canada's Balance of Payments, 2014 (billions of dollars)		
Current account			
(1) Merchandise exports	+529		
(2) Merchandise imports	−524		
(3) *Balance of trade*		+5	
(4) Exports of services	+95		
(5) Imports of services	−118		
(6) *Balance on goods and services*		−18	
(7) Net investment income	−20		
(8) Net transfers	−2		
(9) **Current account balance**		**−40**	
Capital and financial account			
(10) Foreign purchases of assets in Canada (capital inflow)	+178		
(11) Canadian purchases of assets abroad (capital outflow)	−141		
(12) Statistical discrepancy		+4	
(13) **Capital account balance**		**+41**	
Official settlement account			
(14) Official international reserves		−1	
Balance of payments		**0**	

Source: Statistics Canada, http://www.statcan.gc.ca/tables-tableaux/sum-som/l01/cst01/econ01a-eng.htm. Accessed July 4, 2015.

credit (thus the + sign). Item 5 indicates that Canadians import similar services from foreigners; these service imports were $118 billion in 2014 and are a debit (thus the − sign).

The **balance on goods and services**, shown as item 6, is the difference between Canadian exports of goods and services (items 1 and 4) and Canadian imports of goods and services (items 2 and 5). In 2014, Canadian imports of goods and services exceeded Canadian exports of goods and services by $18 billion. So a **trade deficit** of that amount occurred. In contrast, a **trade surplus** occurs when exports of goods and services exceed imports of goods and services. (Global Perspective 18.1 shows Canada's trade deficits and surpluses with selected nations.)

BALANCE ON CURRENT ACCOUNT

Items 7 and 8 are not items relating directly to international trade in goods and services. But they are listed as part of the current account (which is mostly about international trade in goods and services) because they are international financial flows that in some sense compensate for things that can be conceptualized as being like international trade in either goods or services. For instance, item 7, net investment income, represents the difference between interest and dividend payments people abroad have paid Canadians for the services of exported Canadian capital ("exported" capital) and what Canadians paid in interest and dividends for the use of foreign capital ("imported" capital) invested in Canada. Observe that in 2014 Canadian *net investment income* was −$20 billion; we paid more in interest and dividends to people abroad than they paid us.

Item 8 shows *net transfers*, both public and private, between Canada and the rest of the world. Included here are foreign aid, pensions paid to citizens living abroad, funds received from home by international students, and remittances by immigrants to relatives abroad. These $2 billion of transfers are net Canadian

18.1 GLOBAL PERSPECTIVE

Canada's Trade Balance with Selected Nations, 2014

Canada has a net export surplus with the United States and Japan, but a net export deficit with the European Union and other countries.

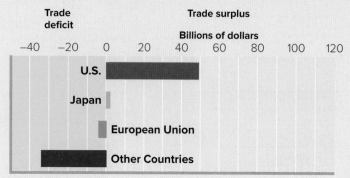

Source: Statistics Canada. http://www.statcan.gc.ca/tables-tableaux/sum-som/l01/cst01/gblec02a-eng.htm.

outpayments that decrease available supplies of foreign exchange. They are, in a sense, the exporting of goodwill and the importing of "thank-you notes."

By adding all transactions in the current account, we obtain the **current account balance** shown in item 9. In 2014 Canada had a current account deficit of $40 billion. This means that Canada's current account transactions created a greater outpayment of foreign currencies from Canada than an inpayment of foreign currencies to Canada.

Capital and Financial Account

The second account within the overall balance of payments account is the **capital and financial account**, which summarizes the flows of payments (money "capital") from the purchase or sale of real or financial assets. For example, a foreign firm may buy a *real* asset, say, an office tower in Canada, or a financial asset, for instance, a Canadian government bond. Both kinds of transactions involve the "export" of the ownership of Canadian assets from Canada in return for inpayments of foreign currency (money "capital" inflows). As indicated in line 10, these "exports" of ownership of assets are designated *foreign purchases of assets in Canada*. The amount has a plus sign, since, like exports of Canadian goods and services, it represents an inpayment of foreign currencies.

Conversely, a Canadian firm may buy, say, a hotel chain (real asset) in a foreign country or common stock (financial asset) of a foreign firm. Both transactions involve imports of the ownership of real or financial assets to Canada and are paid for by outpayments of Canadian currency (money "capital" outflows). These imports are designated *Canadian purchases of assets abroad* and, as shown in line 11, they have a minus sign; like Canadian imports of goods and services, this value represents an outpayment of foreign currencies from Canada.

Before we can arrive at the **balance on the capital and financial account** we need to include a *statistical discrepancy* (line 12), which is the unaccounted discrepancy between the balances on the current and capital accounts. Line 13 gives us the actual capital account balance, which amounted to + $41 billion in 2014. Given the current account deficit of $40 billion, this capital account surplus added $1 billion of foreign currencies to Canada.

Official Settlement Account

The third account in the overall balance of payments is the official settlement account. The central banks of nations hold quantities of foreign currencies called **official international reserves.**

These reserves can be drawn on to make up any net deficit in the combined current and capital accounts (much as you would draw on your savings to pay for a special purchase). In 2014 Canada had a $1 billion surplus in the combined current and capital accounts (line 9 plus line 13). This balance in the Canadian international payments led the Canadian government to increase its official international reserves of foreign currencies by $1 billion (item 14). The *negative* sign indicates that this increase of reserves is a debit—the inpayment to official international reserves needed to balance the overall balance of payments account.

In some years, the sum of the current and capital accounts balances may be negative, meaning that Canada paid more foreign currencies than it earned. The deficit would create an outpayment from the stock of official international reserves. As such, item 14 would have a positive sign since it is a credit.

The three components of the balance of payments—the current account, the capital and financial account, and the official settlement account—must together equal zero. Every unit of foreign exchange used (as reflected in a *minus* outpayment or debit transaction) must have a source (a *plus* inpayment or credit transaction). That's why the statement is called the *balance* of payments. It has to balance. Let's see why.

Why the Balance?

The balance on the current account and the balance on the capital and financial account must always sum to zero because any deficit or surplus in the current account automatically creates an offsetting entry in the capital and financial account. People can only trade one of two things with each other: currently produced goods and services or pre-existing assets. Therefore, if trading partners have an imbalance in their trade of currently produced goods and services, the only way to make up for that imbalance is with a net transfer of assets from one party to the other.

To see why this is true, suppose that John (a Canadian) makes shoes and Henri (a Swiss citizen) makes watches and that the pair only trade with each other. Assume that their financial assets consist entirely of money, with each beginning the year with $1000 in his bank account. Suppose that this year John exports $300 of shoes to Henri and imports $500 of watches from Henri. John therefore ends the year with a $200 goods deficit with Henri.

John and Henri's goods transactions, however, also result in asset exchanges that cause a net transfer of assets from John to Henri equal in size to John's $200 goods deficit with Henri. This is true because Henri pays John $300 for his shoes while John pays Henri $500 for his watches. The *net* result of these opposite-direction asset movements is that $200 of John's initial assets of $1000 are transferred to Henri. This is unavoidable because the $300 John receives from his exports pays for only the first $300 of his $500 of imports. The only way for John to pay for the remaining $200 of imports is for him to transfer $200 of his initial asset holdings to Henri. Consequently, John's assets decline by $200 from $1000 to $800, and Henri's assets rise from $1000 to $1200.

Consider how the transaction between John and Henri affects the Canadian balance of payments statement (Table 18-1), other things equal. John's $200 goods deficit with Henri shows up in the Canadian current account as a −$200 entry in the balance on goods account (line 3) and carries down to a −$200 entry in the balance on current account (line 10).

In the capital and financial account, this $200 is recorded as +$200 in the account for foreign purchases of assets in Canada (line 10). This +$200 then carries down to the balance on capital and financial account (line 13). Think of the transaction in this way: Henri has in essence used $200 worth of watches to purchase $200 of John's initial $1000 holding of assets. The +$200 entry in line 10 (foreign purchases of assets in Canada) recognizes this fact. This +$200 exactly offsets the −$200 in the current account.

Thus, the balance of payments always balances. Any current account deficit or surplus in the top half of the statement automatically generates an offsetting international asset transfer that shows up in the capital and financial account in the bottom half of the statement. More specifically, current account deficits simultaneously generate transfers of assets to foreigners while current account surpluses automatically generate transfers of assets from foreigners.

Official International Reserves, Payments Deficits, and Payments Surpluses

We noted above that official international reserves consist of foreign currencies owned and held by central banks. These international reserves also include certain reserves held with the International Monetary Fund, and stocks of gold. For simplicity, we will assume for now that the entire stock of Canadian official international reserves consists of foreign currency so we can speak of official reserves and foreign currency reserves interchangeably.

Although the balance of payments must always sum to zero, as in Table 18-1, in some years a net sale of official international reserves by a nation's central bank occurs in the process of bringing the capital and financial account into balance with the current account. In such years, a **balance of payments deficit** is said to occur. This deficit is in a subset of the overall balance statement and *is not a deficit in the overall account*. Remember, the overall balance of payments is always in balance. But, in this case, the balancing of the overall account includes sales of official reserves to create an inflow of dollars to Canada. In selling foreign currency in the foreign exchange market, the central bank must draw down its stock of official international reserves. This draw-down is an indicator of a balance of payments deficit.

These net sales of official reserves in the foreign exchange market show up as a *plus* (+) item on the Canadian balance of payments statement, specifically as foreign purchases of Canadian assets (line 14). They are a credit or an inflow of dollars to Canada, just as John's proceeds from the sale of $200 of his assets to Henri were in our previous example.

In other years, the capital and financial account balances the current account because of government purchases of official international reserves from foreigners. The central bank engineers this balance by selling dollars to obtain foreign currency and then adding the newly acquired foreign currency to its stock of official international reserves. In these years, a **balance of payments surplus** is said to exist. This payment surplus, therefore, can be thought of as either net purchases of official reserves in the balance of payments or, alternatively, as the resulting increase in the stock of official reserves held by the central bank.

WORKED PROBLEM 18.1   Balance of Payments

A balance-of-payments deficit is not necessarily bad, just as a balance-of-payments surplus is not necessarily good. Both simply happen. However, any nation's official reserves are limited, and persistent payment deficits must be financed by drawing down those official international reserves, which would ultimately deplete the reserves. That nation would have to adopt policies to correct its balance of payments. Such policies might require painful macroeconomic adjustments, trade barriers and similar restrictions, or a major depreciation of its currency. For this reason, nations strive for payments balance, at least over a period of several years.

QUICK REVIEW 18.2

- A nation's balance of payments statement summarizes all the international financial transactions that take place between its residents and the residents of all foreign nations. It includes the current account balance and the capital and financial account balance.

- The current account balance is a nation's exports of goods and services less its imports of goods and services plus its net investment income and net transfers.

- The capital and financial account balance includes the net amount of the nation's debt forgiveness as well as the nation's sale of real and financial assets to people living abroad less its purchases of real and financial assets from foreigners.

- The current account balance and the capital and financial account balance always sum to zero because any current account imbalance automatically generates an offsetting international asset transfer.

- A balance of payments deficit exists when net sales of official international reserves (mainly, foreign currency) occur in the balance of payments statement; in contrast, a balance of payments surplus exists when there is an increase in the stock of official reserves held by the central bank.

18.3 / Foreign Exchange Markets: Flexible Exchange Rates

LO18.3 Discuss how exchange rates are determined in a currency market that has flexible exchange rates.

Both the size and persistence of a nation's balance of payments deficits and surpluses, and the adjustments it must make to correct these imbalances, depend on the system of exchange rates being used. There are two pure types of exchange-rate systems:

- A **flexible (or floating) exchange-rate system** by which the rates that national currencies are exchanged for one another are determined by demand and supply. In such a system no government intervention occurs.

- A **fixed exchange-rate system** by which governments determine the rates at which currencies are exchanged and make necessary adjustments in their economies to ensure that these rates continue.

We begin by looking at flexible exchange rates. Let's examine the rate, or price, at which Canadian dollars might be exchanged for British pounds. **Figure 18-1 (Key Graph)** shows demand D_1 and supply S_1 of pounds in the currency market.

The *demand for pounds curve* is downsloping because if pounds become less expensive to Canadians then all British goods and services will be cheaper to Canadians. That is, at lower dollar prices for pounds, Canadians can obtain more pounds and therefore more British goods and services per dollar. To buy these cheaper British goods, Canadian consumers will increase the quantity of pounds they demand. It should also be noted that the demand curve for British pounds (or any other currency) is a derived demand in that it stems from the willingness of consumers in Canada to purchase British goods and services.

The *supply of pounds curve* is upsloping because, as the dollar price of pounds rises (that is, the pound price of dollars falls), the British will purchase more Canadian goods. When the British buy more Canadian goods, they supply a greater quantity of pounds to the foreign exchange market. In other words, they must exchange pounds for dollars to purchase Canadian goods. So, when the price of pounds rises, the quantity of pounds supplied goes up.

18.2 GLOBAL PERSPECTIVE

Exchange Rates: Foreign Currency per Canadian Dollar

The amount of foreign currency that a dollar will buy varies greatly from nation to nation. These amounts are for July 2015 and fluctuate in response to supply and demand changes in the foreign exchange market.

$1 will buy

0.49 British pounds
0.76 U.S. dollars
12.5 Mexican pesos
0.69 Euros
94 Japanese yen
4.75 Chinese yuan
49 Indian rupees

Source: Bank of Canada, http://www.bankofcanada.ca/rates/exchange/noon-rates-5-day/. Retrieved July 27, 2015.

KEY GRAPH

FIGURE 18-1 The Market for Foreign Currency (Pounds)

The intersection of the demand for pounds D_1 and the supply of pounds S_1 determines the equilibrium dollar price of pounds, here, $2. That means that the exchange rate is $2 = £1. Not shown is that an increase in the demand for pounds or a decrease in the supply of pounds will increase the dollar price of pounds and thus cause the pound to appreciate. Also not shown, a decrease in demand for pounds or an increase in the supply of pounds will reduce the dollar price of pounds, meaning that the pound has depreciated.

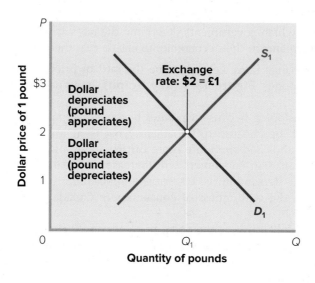

Quick Quiz

1. **Which of the following is a true statement?**
   a. The quantity of pounds demanded falls when the dollar appreciates.
   b. The quantity of pounds supplied declines as the dollar price of pounds rises.
   c. At the equilibrium exchange rate, the pound price of $1 is ½ pound.
   d. The dollar would appreciate if the demand for pounds increased.

2. **At the price of $2 for £1 in this figure**
   a. The dollar–pound exchange rate is unstable
   b. The quantity of pounds supplied equals the quantity demanded
   c. The dollar price of 1 pound equals the pound price of $1
   d. Canadian merchandise exports to Britain must equal Canadian merchandise imports from Britain

3. **All else equal, a leftward shift of the demand curve in this figure**
   a. Would depreciate the dollar
   b. Creates a shortage of pounds at the previous price of $2 for £1
   c. Might be caused by a major recession in Canada
   d. Might be caused by a significant rise of real interest rates in Britain

4. **All else equal, a rightward shift of the supply curve in this figure would**
   a. Depreciate the dollar and might be caused by a significant rise of real interest rates in Britain
   b. Depreciate the dollar and might be caused by a significant fall of real interest rates in Britain
   c. Appreciate the dollar and might be caused by a significant rise of real interest rates in Canada
   d. Appreciate the dollar and might be caused by a significant fall of real interest rates in Canada

Answers: 1. c; 2. b; 3. c; 4. c

The intersection of the supply curve and demand curve will determine the dollar price of pounds. Here, that price (exchange rate) is $2 for £1. At this exchange rate, the quantities of pounds supplied and demanded are equal; neither a shortage nor a surplus of pounds occurs. It should be noted that the demand for a currency automatically triggers the supply of another currency. In our example, the demand for British pound automatically triggers the supply of Canadian dollars to purchase the pounds.

Depreciation and Appreciation

An exchange rate determined by market forces can, and often does, change daily, just as do stock and bond prices. When the dollar price of pounds *rises*, for example, from $2 = £1 to $3 = £1, we say a **depreciation** of the dollar relative to the pound has occurred. When a currency depreciates, more units of it (dollars) are needed to buy a single unit of some other foreign currency (a pound).

When the dollar price of pounds *falls*, for example from $2 = £1 to $1 = £1, an **appreciation** of the dollar relative to the pound has occurred. When a currency appreciates, fewer units of it (dollars) are needed to buy a single unit of some foreign currency (pounds).

In our Canada-Britain illustrations, depreciation of the dollar means an appreciation of the pound and vice versa. When the dollar price of a pound jumps from $2 = £1 to $3 = £1, the pound has appreciated relative to the dollar because it takes more dollars to buy £1. But it now takes fewer pounds to buy $1. At $2 = £1, it took £1/2 to buy $1; at $3 = £1, it takes only £1/3 to buy $1.

In general, the relevant terminology and relationships between the Canadian dollar and another currency are as follows:

- Dollar price of foreign currency increases = dollar depreciates relative to the foreign currency = foreign currency price of dollar decreases = foreign currency appreciates relative to the dollar.

- Dollar price of foreign currency decreases = dollar appreciates relative to the foreign currency = foreign currency price of dollar increases = foreign currency depreciates relative to the dollar.

Determinants of Exchange-Rate Changes

What factors would cause a nation's currency to appreciate or depreciate in the market for foreign exchange? Here are three generalizations:

- If the demand for a nation's currency increases (other things equal), that currency will appreciate; if the demand decreases, that currency will depreciate.

- If the supply of a nation's currency increases, that currency will depreciate; if the supply decreases, that currency will appreciate.

- If a nation's currency appreciates, some foreign currency depreciates relative to it.

With these generalizations in mind, let's examine the determinants of exchange rates, the factors that shift the demand or supply curve for a certain currency. As we do so, keep in mind that the other-things-equal assumption is always in force. Also note that we are discussing factors *that change the exchange rate*, not things that change *as a result of* a change in the exchange rate.

Canadian exports create a foreign demand for dollars.

CHANGES IN TASTES

Any change in consumer tastes or preferences for the products of a foreign country may alter the demand for that nation's currency and change its exchange rate. If technological advances in lumber make it more attractive to British consumers and businesses, then the British will supply more pounds in the exchange market to purchase more Canadian lumber. The supply-of-pounds curve will shift rightward, the pound will depreciate, and the dollar will appreciate. In contrast, the demand curve for pounds will shift to the right if British woollen apparel becomes more fashionable in Canada. So the pound will appreciate and the Canadian dollar will depreciate.

RELATIVE INCOME CHANGES

A nation's currency is likely to depreciate if its growth of national income is more rapid than that of other countries. Here's why. A country's imports vary directly with its level of income. As total income rises in Canada, Canadians buy both more domestically produced goods and more foreign goods. If the Canadian economy is expanding rapidly and the British economy is stagnant, Canadian imports of British goods, and therefore Canadian demands for pounds, will increase. The dollar price of pounds will rise, so the Canadian dollar will depreciate.

RELATIVE INFLATION RATE CHANGES

Other things equal, changes in the relative rates of inflation of two nations change their relative price levels and alter the exchange rate between their currencies. The currency of the nation with the higher inflation rate–the more rapidly rising price level–tends to depreciate. Suppose, for example, that inflation is zero percent in Great Britain and 5 percent in Canada. Consumers in Canada will seek out more of the now relatively lower-priced British goods, increasing the demand for pounds. The British will purchase less of the now relatively higher-priced Canadian goods, reducing the supply of pounds. This combination of increased demand for pounds and reduced supply of pounds will cause the pound to appreciate and the dollar to depreciate.

According to the **purchasing power parity theory**, exchange rates should eventually adjust such that they equate the purchasing power of various currencies. If a certain market basket of identical products costs $10,000 in Canada and £5000 in Great Britain, the exchange rate should move to $2 = £1. That way, a dollar spent in Canada will buy exactly as much output as it would if it were first converted to pounds (at the $2 = £1 exchange rate) and used to buy output in Great Britain.

In terms of our example, 5 percent inflation in Canada will increase the price of the market basket from $10,000 to $10,500 while the zero percent inflation in Great Britain will leave the market basket priced at £5000. For purchasing power parity to hold, the exchange rate would have to move from $2 = £1 to $2.10 = £1. That means the dollar therefore would depreciate and the pound would appreciate. In practice, however, not all exchange rates move precisely to equate the purchasing power of various currencies and thereby achieve purchasing power parity, even over long periods.

RELATIVE INTEREST RATES

Changes in relative interest rates between two countries may alter their exchange rate. Suppose that real interest rates rise in Canada but stay constant in Great Britain. British citizens will then find Canada a more attractive place in which to loan money directly or loan money indirectly by buying bonds. To make these loans, they will have to supply pounds in the foreign exchange market to obtain dollars. The increase in the supply of pounds results in depreciation of the pound and appreciation of the Canadian dollar.

CHANGES IN RELATIVE EXPECTED RETURNS ON STOCKS, REAL ESTATE, AND PRODUCTION FACILITIES

International investing extends beyond buying foreign bonds. It includes international investments in stocks and real estate as well as foreign purchases of factories and production facilities. Other things equal, the extent of this foreign investment depends on relative expected returns. To make the investments, investors in one country must sell their currencies to purchase the foreign currencies needed for the foreign investments.

For instance, suppose that investing in England suddenly becomes more popular due to a more positive outlook regarding expected returns on stocks, real estate, and production facilities there. Canadian investors therefore will sell Canadian assets to buy more assets in England. The Canadian assets will be sold for dollars, which will then be brought to the foreign exchange market and exchanged for pounds, which will in turn be used to purchase British assets. The increased supply of dollars that is brought to the foreign exchange market will cause the dollar to depreciate relative to the pound.

SPECULATION

Currency speculators buy and sell currencies with an eye to reselling or repurchasing them at a profit. Suppose speculators expect the Canadian economy to (1) grow more rapidly than the British economy and (2) experience more rapid inflation than Britain. These expectations translate to an anticipation that the pound will appreciate and the Canadian dollar will depreciate. Speculators who are holding dollars will therefore try to convert them into pounds. This effort will increase the demand for pounds and cause the dollar price of pounds to rise (that is, the dollar to depreciate). A self-fulfilling prophecy occurs: The pound appreciates and the dollar depreciates because speculators act on the belief that these changes will in fact take place. In this way, speculation can cause changes in exchange rates. (We discuss currency speculation in more detail in this chapter's Last Word.)

Table 18-2 further illustrates the determinants of exchange rates and is worth careful study.

TABLE 18-2	Determinants of Exchange-Rate Changes: Factors That Change the Demand or the Supply of a Particular Currency and Thus Alter the Exchange Rate

Determinant	Examples
Changes in tastes	Japanese electronic equipment declines in popularity in Canada (Japanese yen depreciates, Canadian dollar appreciates).
	European tourists reduce visits to Canada (Canadian dollar depreciates, European euro appreciates).
Changes in relative incomes	England encounters a recession, reducing its imports, while Canadian real output and real income surge, increasing Canadian imports (British pound appreciates, Canadian dollar depreciates).
Changes in relative inflation rates	Switzerland experiences a 3 percent inflation rate compared to Canada's 10 percent rate (Swiss franc appreciates, Canadian dollar depreciates).
Changes in relative real interest rates	The Bank of Canada drives up interest rates in Canada while the Bank of England takes no such action (Canadian dollar appreciates, British pound depreciates).
Changes in relative expected returns on stocks, real estate, or production facilities	Corporate tax cuts in Canada raise expected after-tax investment returns in Canada rise relative to those in Europe (Canadian dollar appreciates, European euro depreciates).
Speculation	Currency traders believe South Korea will have much greater inflation than Taiwan (South Korean won depreciates, Taiwanese dollar appreciates).
	Currency traders think Finland's interest rates will plummet relative to Denmark's rates (Finland's markka depreciates, Denmark's krone appreciates).

- In a system in which exchange rates are flexible (free to float), exchange rates are determined by the demand for and supply of individual national currencies in the foreign exchange market.

- Determinants of flexible exchange rates (factors that shift currency supply and demand curves) include

(a) changes in tastes; (b) relative national incomes; (c) relative inflation rates; (d) real interest rates; (e) relative expected returns on stocks, real estate, and production facilities; and (f) speculation.

 THE EFFECTIVENESS OF MARKETS

Flexible Rates and the Balance of Payments

Flexible exchange rates have an important feature: they automatically adjust to eventually eliminate balance of payments deficits or surpluses. We can explain this idea through Figure 18.2, in which S_1 and D_1 are the supply and demand curves for pounds from Figure 18-1.

The equilibrium exchange rate of $2 = £1$ means there is no balance of payments deficit or surplus between Canada and Britain. At the $2 = £1$ exchange rate, the quantity of pounds demanded by Canadian consumers to import British goods, buy British transportation and insurance services, and pay interest and dividends on British investments in Canada equals the number of pounds supplied by the British in buying Canadian exports, purchasing services from the Canadians, and making interest and dividend payments on Canadian investments in Britain. Canada would have no need to either draw down or build up its official international reserves to balance its payments.

FIGURE 18-2 **Adjustments Under Flexible Exchange Rates**

Under flexible exchange rates, a shift in the demand for pounds from D_1 to D_2, other things equal, would cause a Canadian balance of payments deficit ab; it would be corrected by a change in the exchange rate from $2 = £1$ to $3 = £1$.

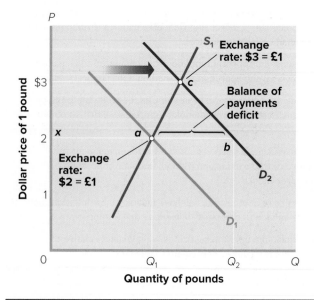

Suppose tastes change and Canadians buy more British automobiles, the Canadian inflation rate increases relative to Britain's, or interest rates fall in Canada compared to those in Britain. Any or all of these changes will cause the Canadian demand for British pounds to increase from D_1 to, say, D_2 in Figure 18-2.

If the exchange rate remains at the initial $2 = £1, a Canadian balance of payments deficit will be created in the amount of *ab*. That is, at the $2 = £1 rate, Canadians consumers will demand the quantity of pounds represented by point *b*, but Britain will supply the amount represented by *a*, there will be a shortage of pounds. But this shortage will not last, because this is a competitive foreign exchange market. Instead, the dollar price of pounds will rise (the Canadian dollar depreciates) until the balance of payments deficit is eliminated. That occurs at the new equilibrium exchange rate of $3 = £1, where the quantities of pounds demanded and supplied are equal again.

To explain why the increase in the dollar price of pounds–the dollar depreciation–eliminates the balance of payments deficit *ab* in Figure 18-2, we need to re-emphasize that the exchange rate links all domestic (Canadian) prices with all foreign (British) prices. The dollar price of a foreign good is found by multiplying the foreign price by the exchange rate (in dollars per unit of the foreign currency). At an exchange rate of $2 = £1, a British automobile priced at £15,000 will cost a Canadian consumer $30,000 (= 15,000 × $2).

A change in the exchange rate alters the prices of all British goods to Canadian consumers and all Canadian goods to British buyers. The shift in the exchange rate (here from $2 = £1 to $3 = £1) changes the relative attractiveness of Canadian imports and exports and restores equilibrium in the Canadian (and British) balance of payments. From the Canadian point of view, as the dollar price of pounds changes from $2 to $3, the British auto priced at £15,000, which formerly cost a Canadian consumer $30,000, now costs $45,000 (= 15,000 × $3). Other British goods will also cost Canadian consumers more, and Canadian imports of British goods will decline. A movement from point *b* toward point *c* in Figure 18-3 graphically illustrates this concept.

From Britain's standpoint, the exchange rate (the pound price of dollars) has fallen (from £1/2 to £1/3 for $1). The international value of the pound has appreciated. The British previously got only $2 for £1; now they get $3 for £1. Canadian goods are therefore cheaper to the British, and Canadian exports to Britain will rise. The two adjustments–a decrease in Canadian imports from Britain and an increase in Canadian exports to Britain–are just what are needed in terms of Figure 18-2 to decrease the quantity of pounds demanded from point *b* to point *c*, increase the quantity of pounds supplied from point *a* to point *c*, and thus to correct the Canadian balance of payments deficit. These changes end when, at point *c*, the quantities of British pounds demanded and supplied are equal.

Disadvantages of Flexible Exchange Rates

Even though flexible exchange rates automatically work to eliminate payment imbalances, they may cause several significant problems. These problems include (a) reduced trade because of the risks and uncertainties associated with constantly changing exchange rates, (b) worsening terms of trade if there is a sizable depreciation, and (c) the challenges to managing and designing domestic macroeconomic policies, particularly in those economies heavily dependent on trade.

QUICK REVIEW 18.4

- Flexible exchange rates automatically adjust and eventually eliminate balance of payments deficits and surpluses.

- The volatility of flexible exchange rates may have several negative consequences, including discouraging international trade, worsening a nation's terms of trade, and destabilizing a nation's domestic economy by depressing export industries.

18.4 / Fixed Exchange Rates

LO18.4 Describe the difference between flexible exchange rates and fixed exchange rates.

To circumvent the disadvantages of flexible exchange rates, nations have at times fixed or "pegged" their exchange rates. For our analysis of fixed exchange rates, we assume Canada and Britain agree to maintain a $2 = £1 exchange rate. The problem is that such a governmental agreement cannot keep the demand for and supply of pounds from changing. With the rate fixed, a shift in demand or supply will put pressure on the exchange rate system, and government (through the central bank) must intervene if the exchange rate is to be maintained.

In Figure 18-3, suppose the Canadian demand for pounds increases from D_1 to D_2 because, again, Canadians buy more British automobiles. A Canadian payment deficit *ab* arises, and if the Canadian government is committed to an exchange rate ($2 = £1), the new equilibrium rate ($3 = £1) is below the targeted rate of $2 = £1. How can the Bank of Canada prevent the shortage of pounds from driving the exchange rate up to the new equilibrium level? The answer is to alter market demand and/or market supply so that they will intersect at the $2 = £1 rate. There are several ways to do this.

Use of Official International Reserves

One way to maintain a fixed exchange rate is to engage in **currency interventions**. These are situations in which the Bank of Canada manipulates an exchange rate through the use of official international reserves. For instance, by selling part of its reserves of pounds, the Bank of Canada can increase the supply of pounds, shifting supply curve S_1 right to S_2 so that it intersects D_2 at b in Figure 18-3 and thereby maintains the exchange rate at $2 = £1.

FIGURE 18-3   Adjustments Under Fixed Exchange Rates

Under fixed exchange rates, the Bank of Canada would cover the shortage of pounds *ab* by using international monetary reserves. The central bank can also restrict trade, implement exchange controls, or enact a contractionary stabilization policy so as to reduce the demand for pounds and increase the supply of pounds.

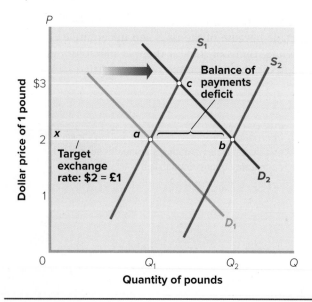

Notice that when the Bank of Canada sells some of its reserves of pounds it is transferring assets to foreigners (since they gain ownership of the pounds). In terms of the balance of payments statement shown in Table 18-1, this transfer of assets enters positively on line 14, *Official international reserves*. This positive entry, which indicates a reduction of the Bank of Canada's foreign reserves, is what offsets the balance of payments deficit caused by the fixed exchange rate and ensures that Canada's balance of payments does in fact balance.

How do official international reserves originate? Perhaps a balance of payments surplus occurred in the past. The Bank of Canada would have purchased that surplus. That is, at some earlier time, the Bank of Canada may have spent dollars to buy surplus pounds that were threatening to reduce the exchange rate to below the $2 = £1 fixed rate. Those purchases would have built up the stock of Canadian official international reserves of pounds.

Nations also have used gold as "international money" to obtain official international reserves. In our example, the Bank of Canada could sell some of the gold it owns to Britain to obtain pounds. It could then sell pounds for dollars. That would shift the supply of pounds to the right and the $2 = £1 exchange rate could be maintained.

It is essential that the amount of international reserves and gold be enough to accomplish the required increase in the supply of pounds. This is not a problem if deficits and surpluses occur more or less randomly and are about the same size. Then, last year's balance of payments surplus with Britain will increase Canada's reserve of pounds, and that reserve can be used to "finance" this year's deficit. But if Canada encounters persistent and sizable balance of payments deficits for an extended period, its international reserves can become depleted, forcing it to abandon fixed exchange rates. Or, if a nation with inadequate international reserves wishes to maintain fixed exchange rates, it must use less appealing options to maintain exchange rates. Let's consider some of those options.

Trade Policies

To maintain fixed exchange rates, a nation can try to control the flow of trade and finance directly. Canada could try to maintain the $2 = £1 exchange rate in the face of a shortage of pounds by discouraging imports of automobiles (thereby reducing the demand for pounds back to D_1 in Figure 18-3) and encouraging exports (thus increasing the supply of pounds to S_2 in Figure 18-3). Imports could be reduced with new tariffs or import quotas on automobiles; special taxes could be levied on the interest and dividends Canadian financial investors receive from foreign investments. Also, the Canadian government could subsidize certain Canadian exports to increase the supply of pounds.

The fundamental problem is that these policies reduce the volume of world trade and change its makeup from what is economically desirable. When nations impose tariffs and quotas, they lose the economic benefits of a free flow of world trade. That loss should not be underestimated: trade barriers by one nation lead to retaliatory responses from other nations, multiplying the loss.

Exchange Controls and Rationing

Another option is exchange controls and rationing. Under an **exchange control**, the Canadian government could handle the problem of a pound shortage by requiring that all pounds obtained by Canadian exporters be sold to the Bank of Canada. Then the government would allocate or ration this short supply of pounds (represented by *xa* in Figure 18-3) among various Canadian importers, who actually demand the quantity *xb*. The effect of this policy is to restrict the value of Canadian imports to the amount of foreign exchange earned by Canadian exports. Assuming balance in the capital account, there is then no balance of payments deficit. Canadian demand for British imports with the value *ab* would simply not be fulfilled. Major objections to exchange controls include the following:

- *Distorted Trade* Like *trade controls* (tariffs, quotas, and export subsidies), exchange controls distort the pattern of international trade away from that suggested by comparative advantage.

- *Favouritism* The process of rationing scarce foreign exchange can lead to government favouritism toward selected importers (big contributors to re-election campaigns, for example).

- **Restricted Choice** Controls limit freedom of consumer choice. The Canadian consumers who prefer foreign-produced Volkswagens may have to buy domestically produced Chevrolets. The business opportunities for some Canadian importers may be impaired because government limits imports.

- **Black Markets** There are likely to be enforcement problems. Canadian importers might want foreign exchange badly enough to pay more than the $2 = £1 official rate, setting the stage for black-market dealings between importers and illegal sellers of foreign exchange.

Domestic Macroeconomic Adjustments

A final way to maintain a fixed exchange rate is to use domestic stabilization policies (monetary policy and fiscal policy) to eliminate the shortage of foreign currency. Tax hikes, reductions in government spending, and a high-interest-rate policy would reduce total spending in the Canadian economy and thus domestic income. Because imports vary directly with domestic income, the demand for British goods (automobiles, in our example), and therefore for pounds, would be restrained.

If these "contractionary" policies reduce the domestic price level relative to Britain's, Canadian buyers of consumer and capital goods would divert their demands from British goods to Canadian goods, also reducing the demand for pounds. In our example of automobiles, Canadians would increase their purchases of Canadian-made cars and reduce their demand for British-made cars. Moreover, the high-interest-rate policy would lift Canadian interest rates relative to those in Britain.

Lower prices on Canadian goods and higher Canadian interest rates would increase British imports of Canadian goods and increase British financial investment in Canada. Both developments would increase the supply of pounds. The combination of a decrease in the demand for and an increase in the supply of pounds would reduce or eliminate the original Canadian balance of payments deficit. In Figure 18-3 the new supply and demand curves would intersect at some new equilibrium point on line *ab*, where the exchange rate remains at $2 = £1.

Maintaining fixed exchange rates is hardly appealing. The "price" of exchange-rate stability for Canada would be falling output, employment, and price levels–in other words, a recession. Eliminating a balance of payments deficit and realizing domestic stability are both important national economic goals, but to sacrifice macroeconomic stability simply to balance international payments is to let the tail wag the dog.

QUICK REVIEW 18.5

- To circumvent the disadvantages of flexible exchange rates, at times nations have fixed or "pegged" their exchange rates.

- Under a system of fixed exchange rates, nations set their exchange rates and then maintain them by buying or selling official international reserves of currencies, establishing trade barriers, employing exchange controls, or incurring inflation or recession.

18.5 / The Current Exchange-Rate System: The Managed Float

LO18.5 Explain the current system of managed floating exchange rates.

Over the past 130 years, the world's nations have used three different exchange-rate systems. From 1879 to 1934 most nations used a gold standard, which implicitly created fixed exchange rates. From 1944 to 1971, most countries participated in the Bretton Woods system, which was a fixed-exchange-rate system indirectly tied to gold. And since 1971, most have used managed floating exchange rates, which mix mostly flexible exchange rates with occasional currency interventions. Naturally, our focus here is on the current exchange-rate system. However, the history of the previous systems and why they broke down is highly fascinating. For that reason, we have included information about them on the book's website.

The current international exchange-rate system (1971–present) is an "almost" flexible system called **managed floating exchange rates**, or the *managed float*. Exchange rates among major currencies are free to float to their equilibrium market levels, but nations occasionally intervene in the foreign exchange market to smooth out fluctuations.

Normally, the major trading nations allow their exchange rates to float up or down to equilibrium levels based on supply and demand in the foreign exchange market. They recognize that changing economic conditions among nations require continuing changes in equilibrium exchange rates to avoid persistent payment deficits or surpluses. They rely on freely operating foreign exchange markets to accomplish the necessary adjustments. The result has been considerably more volatile exchange rates than during the Bretton Woods era.

But nations also recognize that some trends in the movement of equilibrium exchange rates may be at odds with national or international objectives. On occasion, therefore, nations intervene in the foreign exchange market by buying or selling large amounts of specific currencies. This way, they can "manage" or stabilize exchange rates by influencing currency demand and supply.

The leaders of the G8 nations (Canada, France, Germany, Russia, Italy, Japan, the United Kingdom, and the United States) meet regularly to discuss economic issues and try to coordinate economic policies. At times, they have collectively intervened to stabilize currencies. For example, in 2000 they sold dollars and bought euros in an effort to stabilize the falling value of the euro relative to the American dollar. In the previous year the euro (€) had depreciated from €1 = U.S. $1.17 to €1 = U.S. $0.87.

The current exchange-rate system is thus an *almost* flexible exchange-rate system. The "almost" mainly refers to the occasional currency interventions by central banks. It also refers to the fact that the actual system is more complicated than described. While the major currencies–dollars, pounds, yen, and the like–fluctuate in response to changing supply and demand, some of the European nations have unified their currency into one, the euro. Also, many developing nations peg their currencies to the U.S. dollar and allow their currencies to fluctuate with it against other currencies. Finally, some nations peg the value of their currencies to a "basket" or group of other currencies.

How well has the managed float worked? It has both proponents and critics. Proponents argue that the managed float has functioned far better than anticipated. For example, the global financial crisis and the severe recession of 2008–2009 greatly disrupted world trade. Flexible rates enabled the system to adjust to all these events, however, whereas the same events would have put unbearable pressures on a fixed-rate system. But skeptics say the managed float is basically a non-system: the guidelines of what a nation may or may not do are not specific enough to keep the system working in the long run.

So what are we to conclude? Flexible exchange rates have not worked perfectly, but neither have they failed miserably. On balance, most economists favour continuation of the present system of "almost" flexible exchange rates.

QUICK REVIEW 18.6

- The managed floating system of exchange rates (1971–present) relies on foreign exchange markets to establish equilibrium exchange rates.

- Under the system, nations can buy and sell official international reserves of foreign currency to stabilize short-term changes in exchange rates or to correct exchange-rate imbalances that are negatively affecting the world economy.

- Proponents point out that international trade and investment have grown tremendously under the system. Critics say that it is a non-system and argue that the exchange rate volatility allowed under the managed float discourages international trade and investment. That is, trade and investment would be even larger if exchange rates were more stable.

The LAST WORD | Speculation in Currency Markets

Are speculators a negative or a positive influence in currency markets and international trade?

Most people buy foreign currency to facilitate the purchase of goods or services produced in another country. A Canadian importer buys Japanese yen to purchase Japanese-made automobiles. A British investor purchases euros to buy shares in the German stock market. But there is another group of participants in the currency market—speculators—who buy foreign currencies solely to resell for profit, which has the following effects.

1. **Contributing to Exchange-Rate Fluctuations** Speculators were much in the news in late 1997 and 1998 when they were widely accused of driving down the values of the South Korean won, Thai baht, Malaysian ringgit, and Indonesian rupiah. The values of these currencies fell by as much as 50 percent within one month, and speculators undoubtedly contributed to the swiftness of those declines.

   The expectation of currency depreciation (or appreciation) can be self-fulfilling. If speculators, for example, expect the Indonesian rupiah to be devalued or to depreciate, they quickly sell rupiah and buy currencies that they think will increase in relative value. The sharp increase in the supply of rupiah indeed reduces the rupiah's value; this reduction then may trigger further selling of rupiah in expectation of further declines in its value. But changed economic realities, not speculation, are normally the underlying causes of changes in currency values.

   That was largely the case with the Southeast Asian countries in which actual and threatened bankruptcies in the financial and manufacturing sectors undermined confidence in the strength of the currencies. Anticipating the eventual declines in currency values, speculators simply hastened those declines. That is, the declines in value probably would have occurred with or without speculators. Moreover, on a daily basis, speculation clearly has positive effects in foreign exchange markets.

2. **Smoothing Out Short-Term Fluctuations in Currency Prices** When temporarily weak demand or strong supply reduces a currency's value, speculators quickly buy the currency, adding to its demand and strengthening its value. When temporarily strong demand or weak supply increases a currency's value, speculators sell the currency. That selling increases the supply of the currency and reduces its value. In this way speculators smooth out supply and demand, and thus exchange rates, over short time periods. This day-to-day exchange-rate stabilization aids international trade.

3. **Absorbing Risk** Speculators aid international trade in another way: *They absorb risk that others do not want to bear.* International transactions are riskier than domestic transactions because of potential adverse changes in exchange rates. Suppose AnyTime, a hypothetical Canadian retailer, signs a contract with a German manufacturer to buy 10,000 German clocks to be delivered in three months. The stipulated price is €75 per clock, which in Canadian dollars is $120 per clock at an exchange rate of $1 = €0.625. AnyTime's total bill will be $1,200,000 (= €750,000).

   But if the euro were to appreciate, say, to $1 = €0.5, the dollar price per clock would rise from $120 to $150 and AnyTime would owe $1,500,000 for the clocks (= €750,000). AnyTime may reduce the risk of such an unfavourable exchange-rate fluctuation by hedging in the futures market. Hedging is an action by a buyer or a seller to protect against a change in future prices. The futures market is a market where items are bought and sold at prices fixed now, for delivery at a specified date in the future.

   AnyTime can arrange to purchase the needed €750,000 at the current $1 = €0.625 exchange rate, but with delivery in three months when the German clocks are delivered. And here is where speculators arrive on the scene. For a price determined in the futures market, they agree to deliver the €750,000 to AnyTime in three months at the $1 = €0.625 exchange rate, regardless of the exchange rate then. The speculators need not own euros at the time the agreement is made. If the euro *depreciates* to, say, $1 = €1 in this period, the speculators make a profit. They can buy the €750,000 stipulated in the contract for $750,000, pocketing the difference between that amount and the $1,200,000 AnyTime has agreed to pay for the €750,000. If the euro *appreciates,* the speculators—but not AnyTime—suffer a loss.

   The amount AnyTime will have to pay for this futures contract will depend on how the market views the likelihood of the euro depreciating, appreciating, or staying constant over the three-month period. As in all highly competitive markets, supply and demand determine the price of the futures contract.

The futures market thus eliminates much of the exchange-rate risk associated with buying foreign goods for future delivery. Without it AnyTime might have decided against importing German clocks. But the futures market and currency speculators greatly increase the likelihood the transaction will occur. Operating through the futures market, speculation promotes international trade.

Question

Suppose Sportif de l'Hiver—a hypothetical French retailer of snowboards—wants to order 5000 snowboards made in Canada. The price per board is $200, the present exchange rate is €1 = $1, and payment is due in dollars when the boards are delivered in three months. Use a numerical example to explain why exchange-rate risk might make the French retailer hesitant to place the order. How might speculators absorb some of Sportif de l'Hiver's risk?

Chapter Summary

LO18.1 EXPLAIN HOW CURRENCIES OF DIFFERENT NATIONS ARE EXCHANGED WHEN INTERNATIONAL TRANSACTIONS TAKE PLACE.

- International financial transactions involve trade either in currently produced goods and services or in pre-existing assets. Exports of goods, services, and assets create inflows of money, while imports cause outflows of money. If buyers and sellers use different currencies, then foreign exchange transactions take place so that the exporter can be paid in his or her own currency.

LO18.2 ANALYZE THE BALANCE SHEET CANADA USES TO ACCOUNT FOR INTERNATIONAL PAYMENTS IT MAKES AND RECEIVES.

- The balance of payments records all international trade and financial transactions taking place between a given nation and the rest of the world. The trade balance compares exports and imports of goods. The balance on goods and services compares exports and imports of both goods and services. The current account balance includes not only goods and services transactions but also net investment income and net transfers.

- The capital and financial account includes (a) the net amount of the nation's debt forgiveness and (b) the nation's sale of real and financial assets to people living abroad less its purchases of real and financial assets from foreigners.

- The current account and the capital and financial account always sum to zero. A deficit in the current account is always offset by a surplus in the capital and financial account. Conversely, a surplus in the current account is always offset by a deficit in the capital and financial account.

- Official international reserves are owned by national governments and their central banks and consist of stocks of foreign currencies, certain reserves held with the International Monetary Fund, and stocks of gold.

- A balance of payments deficit occurs when the sum of the current and capital accounts is negative. Such a deficit is financed with official international reserves. A balance of payments surplus occurs when the sum of the current and capital accounts is positive. A payments surplus results in an increase in official international reserves. The desirability of a balance of payments deficit or surplus depends on its size and its persistence.

LO18.3 DISCUSS HOW EXCHANGE RATES ARE DETERMINED IN A CURRENCY MARKET THAT HAS FLEXIBLE EXCHANGE-RATES.

- Flexible or floating exchange rates between international currencies are determined by the demand for and supply of those currencies. Under floating rates a currency will depreciate or appreciate as a result of changes in tastes, relative income changes, relative changes in inflation rates, relative changes in real interest rates, and speculation.

LO18.4 DESCRIBE THE DIFFERENCE BETWEEN FLEXIBLE EXCHANGE RATES AND FIXED EXCHANGE RATES.

- The maintenance of fixed exchange rates requires adequate official international reserves to accommodate periodic payments deficits. If reserves are inadequate, nations must invoke protectionist trade policies.

LO18.5 EXPLAIN THE CURRENT SYSTEM OF MANAGED FLOATING EXCHANGE RATES.

- Since 1971, the world's major nations have used a system of managed floating exchange rates. Rates are generally set by market forces, although governments intervene with varying frequency to alter their exchange rates.

Terms and Concepts

balance of payments
current account
balance on goods and services
trade deficit
trade surplus
current account balance
capital and financial account

official international reserves
balance on the capital and financial account
balance of payments deficit
balance of payments surplus
flexible (or floating) exchange-rate system
fixed exchange-rate system
depreciation

appreciation
purchasing power parity theory
currency interventions
exchange controls
managed floating exchange rates

Discussion Questions

1. Do all international financial transactions necessarily involve exchanging one currency for another? Explain. Could a nation that neither imports nor exports goods and services still engage in international financial transactions?   [LO18.1]

2. Canadian exports earn supplies of foreign currencies that Canadians can use to finance imports. Indicate whether each of the following creates a demand for, or a supply of, European euros in foreign exchange markets: [LO18.1]

   a. A Canadian airline firm buys several Airbus planes assembled in France.

   b. A German automobile firm decides to build an assembly plant in Halifax.

   c. A Canadian university student decides to spend a year studying at the Sorbonne in Paris.

   d. An Italian manufacturer ships machinery from one Italian port to another on a Liberian freighter.

   e. The Canadian economy grows faster than the French economy.

   f. A Canadian government bond held by a Spanish citizen matures and the loan amount is paid back to that person.

   g. It is widely expected that the euro will depreciate in the near future.

3. What do the plus signs and minus signs signify in the Canadian balance of payments statement? Why must the current account and the capital and financial account sum to zero? Which of the following items appear in the current account and which appear in the capital and financial account?   [LO18.2]

   a. Canadian purchases of assets abroad

   b. Canadian services imports

   c. Foreign purchases of assets in Canada

   d. Canadian goods exports

   e. Canadian net investment income

4. What are official international reserves? How do net sales of official reserves to foreigners and net purchases of official international reserves from foreigners relate to Canadian–U.S. balance-of-payment deficits and surpluses? Explain why these deficits and surpluses are not actual deficits and surpluses in the *overall* balance of payments statement.   [LO18.2]

5. Generally speaking, how is the dollar price of euros determined? Cite a factor that might decrease the dollar price of euros. Explain this statement: A rise in the dollar price of euros necessarily means a fall in the euro price of dollars. Illustrate and elaborate on the following: The dollar–euro exchange rate provides a direct link between the price of goods and services produced in the Euro Zone and Canada. Explain the purchasing power parity theory of exchange rates, using the euro–dollar exchange rate as an illustration.   [LO18.3]

6. Suppose that a Swiss watchmaker imports watch components from Sweden and exports watches to Canada. Also suppose the Canadian dollar depreciates, and the Swedish krona appreciates, relative to the Swiss franc. Speculate as to how each currency fluctuation would hurt the Swiss watchmaker.   [LO18.3]

7. Explain why the Canadian demand for Mexican pesos is downsloping and the supply of pesos to Canadians is upsloping. Assuming a system of flexible exchange rates between Mexico and Canada, indicate whether each of the following would cause the Mexican peso to appreciate or depreciate, other things equal: [LO18.3]

   a. Canada unilaterally reduces tariffs on Mexican products.

   b. Mexico encounters severe inflation.

   c. Deteriorating political relations reduce Canadian tourism in Mexico.

   d. The Canadian economy moves into a severe recession.

   e. Canada engages in a high-interest-rate monetary policy.

   f. Mexican products become more fashionable to Canadians.

   g. The Mexican government encourages Canadian firms to invest in Mexican oil fields.

   h. The rate of productivity growth in Canada diminishes sharply.

8. Explain why you agree or disagree with the following statements. Assume other things are equal.   [LO18.3]

   a. A country that grows faster than its major trading partners can expect the international value of its currency to depreciate.

b. A nation with an interest rate that is rising more rapidly than in other nations can expect the international value of its currency to appreciate.

c. A country's currency will appreciate if its inflation rate is less than that of the rest of the world.

9. "Exports pay for imports. Yet in 2014 the nations of the world exported about $8 billion more of goods and services to Canada than they imported from Canada." Resolve the apparent inconsistency of these two statements. [LO18.2]

Review Questions

1. A Canadian company wants to buy a television from a Chinese company. The Chinese company sells its TVs for 1200 yuan each. The current exchange rate between the Canadian dollar and the Chinese yuan is $1 = 6 yuan. How many dollars will the Canadian company have to convert into yuan to pay for the television? [LO18.1]

   a. $7,200

   b. $1,200

   c. $200

   d. $100

2. Suppose that a country has a trade surplus of $50 billion, a balance on the capital account of $10 billion, and a balance on the current account of –$200 billion. The balance on the capital and financial account will be [LO18.2]

   a. $10 billion

   b. $50 billion

   c. $200 billion

   d. $200 billion

3. The exchange rate between the Canadian dollar and the British pound starts at $1 = £0.5. It then changes to $1 = £0.75. Given this change, we would say that the Canadian dollar has _____ while the British pound has_____. [LO18.3]

   a. Depreciated; appreciated

   b. Depreciated; depreciated

   c. Appreciated; depreciated

   d. Appreciated; appreciated

4. A meal at a McDonald's restaurant in Toronto costs $8. The identical meal at a McDonald's restaurant in London costs £4. According to the purchasing power parity theory of exchange rates, the exchange rate between Canadian dollars and British pounds should tend to move toward [LO18.3]

   a. $2 = £1

   b. $1 = £2

   c. $4 = £1

   d. $1 = £4

5. Suppose that a country has a flexible exchange rate. Also suppose that at the current exchange rate, the country is experiencing a balance of payments deficit. Then would it be true or false that a sufficiently large depreciation of the local currency could eliminate the balance-of-payments deficit? [LO18.3]

6. Diagram a market in which the equilibrium dollar price of 1 unit of fictitious currency zee (Z) is $5 (the exchange rate is $5 = Z_1). Then show on your diagram a decline in the demand for zee. [LO18.4]

   a. Referring to your diagram, discuss the adjustment options Canada would have in maintaining the exchange rate at $5 = Z_1 under a fixed exchange-rate system.

   b. How would the Canadian balance of payments surplus that is caused by the decline in demand be resolved under a system of flexible exchange rates?

7. Suppose that the government of China is currently fixing the exchange rate between the Canadian dollar and the Chinese yuan at a rate of $1 = 6 yuan. Also suppose that at this exchange rate, the people who want to convert dollars to yuan are asking to convert $10 billion per day of dollars into yuan, while the people who want to convert yuan into dollars are asking to convert 36 billion yuan into dollars. What will happen to the size of China's official international reserves of dollars? [LO18.4]

   a. Increase

   b. Decrease

   c. Stay the same

8. Suppose that a country follows a managed float policy but that its exchange rate is currently floating freely. In addition, suppose that it has a massive current account deficit. Does it also necessarily have a balance of payments deficit? If the country decides to engage in a currency intervention to reduce the size of its current account deficit, will it buy or sell its own currency? As it does so, will its official international reserves of foreign currencies get larger or smaller? Would that outcome indicate a balance of payments deficit or a balance of payments surplus? [LO18.5]

9. If the economy booms in Canada while going into recession in other countries, the Canadian trade deficit will tend to_____. [LO18.5]

   a. Increase

   b. Decrease

   c. Remain the same

Problems

1. Alpha's balance of payments data for 2014 are shown below. All figures are in billions of dollars. What are (a) the balance of trade, (b) the balance on goods and services, (c) the balance on current account, and (d) the balance on capital and financial account? Does Alpha have a balance of payments deficit or surplus? Suppose Alpha sold $10 billion of official reserves abroad to balance the capital and financial account with the current account.   [LO18.2]

Goods exports	+$40
Goods imports	−30
Service exports	+15
Service imports	−10
Net investment income	−5
Net transfers	+10
Balance on capital account	0
Foreign investment in Alpha	+10
Foreign investment abroad	−40
Official international reserves	+10

2. China had a $214 billion overall current account surplus in 2012. Assuming that China's net debt forgiveness was zero in 2012 (its capital account balance was zero), by how much did Chinese purchases of financial and real assets abroad exceed foreign purchases of Chinese financial and real assets? [LO18.2]

3. Refer to the following table, in which Q_d is the quantity of yen demanded, P is the dollar price of yen, Q_s is the quantity of yen supplied in year 1, and Q_s' is the quantity of yen supplied in year 2. All quantities are in billions and the dollar–yen exchange rate is fully flexible.   [LO18.3]

Q_d	P	Q_s	Q_s'
10	125	30	20
15	120	25	15
20	115	20	10
25	110	15	5

a. What is the equilibrium dollar price of the yen in year 1?

b. What is the equilibrium dollar price of the yen in year 2?

c. Did the yen appreciate or did it depreciate relative to the dollar between years 1 and 2?

d. Did the dollar appreciate or did it depreciate relative to the yen between years 1 and 2?

e. Which one of the following could have caused the change in relative values of the dollar and yen between years 1 and 2: (1) more rapid inflation in Canada than in Japan, (2) an increase in the real interest rate in Canada but not in Japan, or (3) faster income growth in Canada than in Japan?

4. Suppose that the current Canadian dollar (CAD) to U.S. dollar exchange rate is $0.85 CAD = $1 U.S. and the U.S. dollar price of an Apple iPhone is $300. What is the Canadian dollar price of an iPhone? Next, suppose that the CAD to U.S. dollar exchange rate moves to $0.96 CAD = $1 U.S. What is the new Canadian dollar price of an iPhone? Other things equal, would you expect Canada to import more or fewer iPhones at the new exchange rate?   [LO18.3]

5. Return to Problem 3 and assume that the exchange rate is fixed against the dollar at the equilibrium exchange rate that occurs in year 1. Also suppose that Japan and Canada are the only two countries in the world. In year 2, what quantity of yen would the Japanese government have to buy or sell to balance its capital and financial account with its current account? In what specific account would this purchase or sale appear in Japan's balance of payments statement—foreign purchases of assets in Japan or Japanese purchases of assets abroad? Would this transaction increase Japan's stock of official international reserves or decrease its stock?   [LO18.5]

Photo Credits

Chapter 1

p. 2, Ccfuse2003/Dreamstime.com
p. 22, Deborah Baic/*The Globe and Mail*

Chapter 2

p. 55, Mpfaff/Dreamstime.com/GetStock.com

Chapter 3

p. 62, Pricelessphotos/Dreamstime.com
p. 80, Feverpitched/Dreamstime.com
p. 82, Phartisan/Dreamstime.com

Chapter 4

p. 111, David Toase/Getty Images
p. 117, Glow Images
p. 119, Digital Vision/Getty Images

Chapter 5

p. 114, Comstock Images/Picturequest

Chapter 7

p. 178, Shusk/Dreamstime.com/
GetStock.com

Chapter 8

p. 203, © Getty Images
p. 210, Ryan McVay/Getty Images
p. 216, Caro/Alamy

Chapter 10

p. 256, Ryan McVay/Getty Images
p. 258, Digital Vision/Getty Images
p. 262, Royalty-Free/CORBIS
p. 270, © Getty Images

Chapter 12

p. 316, Glow Images
p. 324, Royalty-Free/CORBIS
p. 327 (top) © Creatas/PunchStock;
(bottom) Rumal/Alamy

Chapter 13

p. 339, © image100/PunchStock

Chapter 14

p. 366, Noodles73/Dreamstime.com
p. 369, Getty Images
p. 378, PhotoLink/Getty Images

Chapter 15

p. 411, Royalty-Free/Corbis
p. 414, Digital Vision/PunchStock
p. 422, Kyoungil Jeon/Getty Images

Chapter 17

p. 459, Getty Images/Steve Allen
p. 464, © Creatas/PunchStock
p. 467, © Bloomberg via Getty Images

Chapter 18

p. 497, Digital Vision/Getty Images
p. 506, © PhotoLink/Getty Images

Chapter 15B

p. 18, AP Photo/Mary Altaffer

Glossary

A

absolute advantage When a region or nation can produce more of a product with fewer resources compared to other regions or nations.

actively managed funds Mutual funds that constantly buy and sell assets in an attempt to generate high returns.

actual reserves The funds that a bank has as vault cash plus any deposit it may have with the Bank of Canada.

adverse selection problem A problem arising when information known to one party to a contract is not known to the other party, causing the latter to incur major costs.

aggregate A collection of specific economic units treated as if they were one unit.

aggregate demand A schedule or curve that shows the total quantity of goods and services demanded (purchased) at different price levels.

aggregate demand–aggregate supply model (AD–AS model) The macroeconomic model that uses aggregate demand and aggregate supply to explain price level and real domestic output.

aggregate expenditures The total amount spent for final goods and services in an economy.

aggregate expenditures schedule A schedule or curve that shows the total amount spent for final goods and services at different levels of GDP.

aggregate supply A schedule or curve that shows the total quantity of goods and services supplied (produced) at different price levels.

aggregate supply shocks Sudden, large changes in resource costs that shift an economy's aggregate supply curve.

allocative efficiency The distribution of resources among firms and industries to produce the goods most wanted by society.

anticipated inflation Increases in the price level that occur at the expected rate.

appreciation An increase in the value of the dollar relative to another currency, so a dollar buys a larger amount of the foreign currency and therefore of foreign goods.

arbitrage Occurs when investors try to profit from situations where two identical or nearly identical assets have different rates of return.

asset demand for money The amount of money people want to hold as a store of value; varies inversely with the rate of interest.

asymmetric information A situation in which one party to a market transaction has much more information about a product or service than the other does.

average expected rate of return The probability weighted average of an investment's possible future rates of return.

average propensity to consume (APC) The fraction (or percentage) of disposable income that households plan to spend for consumer goods and services.

B

balance of payments A summary of all the transactions that took place among the individuals, firms, and government units of one nation and those of all other nations during a year.

balance of payments deficit The amount by which the sum of the balance on the current account and the balance on the capital account is negative in a year.

balance of payments surplus The amount by which the sum of the balance on the current account and the balance on the capital account is positive in a year.

balance on goods and services The exports of goods and services of a nation less its imports of goods and services in a year.

balance on the capital and financial account The foreign purchases of assets in a nation less its purchases of assets abroad in a year.

balance sheet A statement of the assets, liabilities, and net worth of a firm or individual at a certain time.

Bank of Canada notes Paper money issued by Canada's government-owned central bank, the Bank of Canada.

bank rate The interest rate that the Bank of Canada charges on advances made to the chartered banks.

bankrupt The situation when individuals or firms are unable to make timely payments on their debts.

barter The exchange of one good or service for another good or service.

base year The year with which other years are compared when an index is constructed; for example, the base year for a price index.

beta A relative measure of non-diversifiable risk; measures the nondiversifiable risk of a given asset or portfolio.

bonds Debt contracts; most often issued by governments and corporations.

brain drain The emigration of highly educated, highly skilled workers from a country.

break-even income The level of disposable income at which households plan to consume all their income and to save none of it.

budget deficit The amount by which the expenditures of the federal government exceed its revenues in any year.

budget line A schedule or curve that shows various combinations of two products a consumer can purchase with a specific money income.

C

budget surplus The amount by which the revenues of the federal government exceed its expenditures in any year.

built-in stabilizer A mechanism that increases government's budget deficit (or reduces its surplus) during a recession and increases government's budget surplus (or reduces its deficit) during inflation without any action by policymakers.

business cycle Recurring increases and decreases in the level of economic activity over periods of years.

capital Human-made resources (buildings, machinery, and equipment) used to produce goods and services.

capital and financial account The section of a nation's international balance of payments statement that records the foreign purchases of assets in Canada and Canadian purchases of assets abroad.

capital consumption allowance Estimate of the amount of capital worn out or used up (consumed) in producing the GDP; also called *depreciation*.

capital flight The transfer of savings from developing countries to industrially advanced countries to avoid government expropriation, taxation, and high rates of inflation, or to realize better investment opportunities.

capital gains The result from selling shares in a corporation for more money than was paid for them.

capital goods Goods that satisfy human wants indirectly by aiding the production of consumer goods.

capital-intensive goods Products that require a relatively large amount of capital to produce.

capital-saving technology Technology that permits a greater quantity of a product to be produced with a specific amount of capital.

capital stock The total available capital in a nation.

capital-using technology Technology that requires the use of a greater amount of capital to produce a specific quantity of a product.

capricious universe view The fatalistic view that the future will unfold according to the will of "providence."

central bank A bank whose chief function is the control of the nation's money supply; in Canada, the Bank of Canada.

change in demand A change in the quantity demanded of a good or service at every price; a shift of the entire demand curve to the right (an increase in demand) or to the left (a decrease in demand).

change in quantity demanded A movement from one point to another on a fixed demand curve.

change in quantity supplied A movement from one point to another on a fixed supply curve.

change in supply A change in the quantity supplied of a good or service at every price; a shift of the supply curve to the left or right.

chartered bank A multi-branched, privately owned, commercial financial intermediary that has received a charter by an Act of Parliament.

circular flow diagram Depiction of the flows of resources from households to firms and of products from firms to households. These flows are accompanied by reverse flows of money from firms to households and from households to firms.

command system An economic system in which most property resources are owned by the government and economic decisions are made by a central government body.

comparative advantage When a producer can create a particular product at a lower opportunity cost than other producers.

competition The presence in a market of a large number of independent buyers and sellers competing with one another and the freedom of buyers and sellers to enter and leave the market.

complementary good A product used together with another good.

consumer goods Products and services that satisfy human wants directly.

Consumer Price Index (CPI) A measure of the prices of a fixed market basket of goods and services that is bought by a typical consumer.

consumer sovereignty Determination by consumers of the types and quantities of goods and services that will be produced with the scarce resources of the economy.

consumer surplus The difference between the maximum price consumers are willing to pay for a product and the actual price.

consumption of fixed capital Estimate of the amount of capital worn out or used up (consumed) in producing the gross domestic product; also called *depreciation*.

consumption schedule A schedule showing the amounts households plan to spend for consumer goods at different levels of disposable income.

contractionary fiscal policy A decrease in government spending, an increase in net taxes, or some combination of the two for the purpose of decreasing aggregate demand and thus controlling inflation.

coordination failures Occur when people do not reach a mutually beneficial outcome because they cannot coordinate their actions.

core inflation The underlying increases in the Consumer Price Index after volatile food and energy prices are removed.

corporation A legal entity chartered by the federal or provincial government that operates as a distinct and separate body from the individuals who own it.

corruption Using corrupt practices, such as bribery.

cost–benefit analysis Comparing the marginal costs with the marginal benefits to decide whether to employ more or less resources in that project.

cost-of-living adjustments (COLAs) An automatic increase in the income (wages) of workers when inflation occurs.

cost–push inflation Increases in the price level resulting from an increase in resource costs and hence in the per-unit production cost.

creative destruction The hypothesis that the creation of new products and production methods simultaneously destroys the market power of firms that are wedded to existing products and older ways of doing business.

crowding-out effect A rise in interest rates and a resulting decrease in planned investment caused by the federal government's increased borrowing in the money market.

currency interventions When a government buys and sells its own currency or foreign currencies to alter international exchange rates.

current account The section in a nation's balance of payments that records its exports and imports of goods and services, its net investment income, and its net transfers.

current account balance The exports of goods and services of a nation less its imports of goods and services plus its net investment income and net transfers in a year.

cyclical asymmetry The idea that monetary policy may be more successful in slowing expansions and controlling inflation than in extracting the economy from severe recession.

cyclical deficit A federal budget deficit that is caused by a recession and the consequent decline in tax revenues.

cyclically adjusted budget What the government budget balance would be if the economy were operating at full employment.

cyclical unemployment Unemployment caused by a decline in total spending (or by insufficient aggregate demand).

D

debt crisis An economic crisis in which government debt has risen so high that the government is unable to borrow any more money.

default A failure to make a bond's promised payments.

deflation A decline in the economy's price level.

demand A schedule or curve that shows the various amounts of a product that consumers are willing and able to purchase at each of a series of possible prices during a specified period of time.

demand curve A curve illustrating the inverse (negative) relationship between the quantity demanded of a good or service and its price, other things equal.

demand deposits Deposits in a chartered bank against which cheques may be written.

demand factor The increase in the level of aggregate demand that brings about the economic growth made possible by an increase in the production potential of the economy.

demand–pull inflation Increases in the price level caused by an excess of total spending beyond the economy's capacity to produce.

demand shocks Sudden, unexpected changes in demand.

demand-side market failure When demand curves do not reflect consumers' full willingness to pay for goods or services.

demographic transition view The view that rising income transforms the population dynamics of a nation by reducing birth rates.

dependent variable A variable that changes as a consequence of a change in some other (independent) variable; the effect or outcome.

depreciation A decrease in the value of the dollar relative to another currency, so a dollar buys a smaller amount of the foreign currency and therefore of foreign goods.

deregulation The removal of most or even all of the government regulation and laws designed to supervise an industry. Sometimes undertaken to combat regulatory capture.

desired reserve ratio The specified percentage of deposit liabilities a chartered bank chooses to keep as vault cash.

desired reserves The amount of vault cash each chartered bank chooses to keep on hand for daily transactions, plus its deposits at the Bank of Canada.

determinants of aggregate demand Factors (such as consumption spending, investment, government spending, and net exports) that shift the aggregate demand curve.

determinants of aggregate supply Factors such as input prices, productivity, and the legal-institutional environment that shift the aggregate supply curve.

determinants of demand Factors other than price that determine the quantities demanded of a good or service.

determinants of supply Causes other than price that determine the quantities supplied of a good or service.

developing countries (DVCs) Many countries of Africa, Asia, and Latin America that are characterized by a lack of capital goods, use of non-advanced technologies, low literacy rates, high unemployment, rapid population growth, and labour forces heavily committed to agriculture.

diminishing marginal utility As a consumer increases the consumption of a good or service, the marginal utility obtained from each additional unit of the good or service decreases.

direct relationship The (positive) relationship between two variables that change in the same direction, for example, product price and quantity supplied.

discouraged workers People who have left the labour force because they have not been able to find employment.

disinflation A reduction in the rate of inflation.

disposable income (DI) Personal income less personal taxes.

diversifiable risk The risk specific to a given investment; can be eliminated by diversification.

diversification The strategy of investing in a large number of investments to reduce the overall risk to the entire portfolio.

dividends Shares of the corporation's profits.

division of labour Dividing the work required to produce a product into a number of different tasks that are performed by different workers.

Doha Development Agenda Launched in Doha, Qatar (in late 2001), this is the ninth, and most recent, round of trade negotiations held by the World Trade Organization.

dollar votes Through their purchases in the product and resource markets, consumers and entrepreneurs determine the production of consumer and capital goods, respectively.

domestic price The price of a good or service within a country, determined by domestic demand and supply.

dumping The sale in a foreign country of products below cost or below the prices charged at home.

durable goods Products with expected lives of three years or more.

E

economic growth (1) An outward shift in the production possibilities curve that results from an increase in factor supplies or quality or an improvement in technology. (2) An increase either in real output (GDP) or in real output per capita.

economic investment Paying for new additions to the nation's capital stock, or for new replacements for capital stock that has worn out.

economic perspective A viewpoint that envisions individuals and institutions making rational decisions by comparing the marginal benefits and marginal costs associated with their actions.

economic principle A statement about economic behaviour or the economy that enables prediction of the probable effects of certain actions.

economic problem The need to make choices because society's material wants for goods and services are unlimited, but the resources available to satisfy these wants are limited (scarce).

economic resources The land, labour, capital, and entrepreneurial ability that are used in the production of goods and services.

economics The social science concerned with how individuals, institutions, and society make optimal (best) choices under conditions of scarcity.

economic system A particular set of institutional arrangements and a coordinating mechanism for producing goods and services.

economies of scale Reductions in the average total cost of producing a product as the firm expands the size of plant (its output) in the long run.

efficiency factor The capacity of an economy to combine resources effectively to achieve growth of real output that the supply factors make possible.

efficiency losses (or deadweight losses) Reduction of combined consumer and producer surplus associated with underproduction or overproduction of a product.

efficiency wages Wages that elicit maximum work effort and thus minimize labour cost per unit of output.

entrepreneurial ability The human talents that combine the other resources to produce a product, make non-routine decisions, innovate, and bear risks.

entrepreneurs Individuals who provide entrepreneurial ability *to* firms by setting strategy, advancing innovations, and bearing the financial risk if their firms do poorly.

equation of exchange $MV = PQ$, in which M is the supply of money, I is the velocity of money, P is the price level, and Q is the physical volume of final goods and services produced.

equilibrium GDP The level at which the total quantity of goods produced (GDP) equals the total quantity of goods purchased.

equilibrium price The price in a competitive market at which the quantity demanded and the quantity supplied are equal.

equilibrium price level The price level at which the aggregate demand curve intersects the aggregate supply curve.

equilibrium quantity The quantity demanded and supplied at the equilibrium price in a competitive market.

equilibrium real output The real domestic output at which the aggregate demand curve intersects the aggregate supply curve.

equilibrium world price A price determined by the intersection of exporting nations' supply of a product and importing nations' demand for the same product.

European Union (EU) An association of European nations that have eliminated tariffs among themselves, established common tariffs for goods imported from outside the member nations, and allowed the free movement of labour and capital among themselves.

Euro Zone The 17 nations of the 28 member countries (as of 2013) of the European Union that use the euro as the common currency.

excess reserves The amount by which a chartered bank's actual cash reserves exceed its desired reserves.

exchange controls The control a government may exercise over the quantity of foreign currency demanded by its citizens and firms and over the rates of exchange to limit its outpayments to its inpayments (to eliminate a payments deficit).

excludability A situation in which sellers can keep people who do not pay for a product from obtaining its benefits.

expansion The phase of the business cycle during which output and employment rise toward full employment.

expansionary fiscal policy An increase in government spending, a decrease in net taxes, or some combination of the two, for the purpose of increasing aggregate demand and expanding real output.

expansionary monetary policy Bank of Canada actions that increase the money supply to lower interest rates and expand real GDP.

expectations The anticipations of consumers, firms, and others about future economic conditions.

expected rate of return The increase in profit a firm anticipates it will obtain by purchasing capital.

expenditures approach The method to measure GDP that adds up all the expenditures made for final goods and services.

export subsidy A government payment to a domestic producer of export goods, designed to aid that producer.

export supply curve An upsloping curve that shows the amount of a product domestic firms will export at each world price that is above the domestic price.

externality Benefit or cost from production or consumption accruing without compensation to nonbuyers and nonsellers of the product.

external public debt Public debt owed to foreign citizens, firms, and institutions.

F

factor market A market in which households sell and firms buy factors of production.

factors of production Economic resources: land, labour, capital, and entrepreneurial ability.

final goods Goods and services purchased for final use and not for resale or further processing or manufacturing.

financial investment Purchasing financial assets (stocks, bonds, mutual funds) or real assets (houses, land, factories), or constructing such assets, in the expectation of financial gain.

fiscal policy Changes in government spending and tax collections designed to achieve a full-employment and noninflationary domestic output.

fixed exchange-rate system A rate of exchange that is prevented from rising or falling with changes in currency supply and demand.

flexible (or floating) exchange rate system A rate of exchange determined by the international demand for and supply of a nation's currency.

flexible prices Product prices that react within seconds to changes in supply and demand.

follower countries As it relates to economic growth, countries that adopt advanced technologies that previously were developed and used by leader countries.

foreign direct investment The building of new factories (or the purchase of existing capital) in a particular nation by corporations of other nations.

foreign-trade effect The inverse relationship between the net exports of an economy and its price level relative to price levels in the economies of trading partners.

45° (degree) line A reference line that bisects the 90° angle formed by the two axes, and along which consumption equals disposable income.

fractional reserve banking system A banking system with a reserve ratio that is less than 100 percent of the deposit liabilities of a chartered bank.

freedom of choice The freedom of owners of property resources to employ or dispose of them as they see fit, and of consumers to spend their incomes in a manner that they think is appropriate.

freedom of enterprise The freedom of firms to obtain economic resources, to use these resources to produce products of the firm's own choosing, and to sell their products in markets of their choice.

free-rider problem The inability of potential providers of an economically desirable but indivisible good or service to obtain payment from those who benefit, because the exclusion principle is not applicable.

frictional unemployment A type of unemployment caused by workers voluntarily changing jobs and by temporary layoffs; unemployed workers between jobs.

full employment Use of all available resources to produce want-satisfying goods and services.

G

gains from trade The extra output that trading partners obtain through specialization of production and exchange of goods and services.

GDP deflator An implicit price index calculated by dividing nominal GDP by real GDP and multiplying by 100.

GDP gap The amount by which actual GDP falls below potential GDP.

General Agreement on Tariffs and Trade (GATT) The international agreement reached in 1947 in which 23 nations agreed to give equal and nondiscriminatory treatment to one another, to reduce tariff rates by multinational negotiations, and to eliminate export quotas.

government failure Inefficiencies in resource allocation caused by problems in the operation of the public sector (government).

government purchases The expenditures of all governments in the economy for final goods and services.

gross domestic product (GDP) The total market value of all final goods and services produced annually within the boundaries of Canada.

gross investment Expenditures for newly produced capital goods (such as machinery, equipment, tools, and buildings) and for additions to inventories.

H

horizontal axis The left-right or west-east axis on a graph or grid.

households One or more persons occupying a housing unit, who buy businesses' goods and services in the product market using income derived from selling resources in the factor market.

human capital The accumulation of prior investments in education, training, health, and other factors that increase productivity.

hyperinflation A very rapid rise in the general price level.

I

immediate-short-run aggregate supply curve An aggregate supply curve for which real output, but not the price level, changes when the aggregate demand curve shifts.

import demand curve A downsloping curve that shows the amount of a product an economy will import at each world price below the domestic price.

import quota A limit imposed by a nation on the quantity (or total value) of a good that may be imported during some period of time.

income approach The method to measure GDP that adds up all the income generated by the production of final goods and services.

income effect A change in the price of a product changes a consumer's real income (purchasing power) and thus the quantity of the product purchased.

increasing returns An increase in a firm's output by a larger percentage than the percentage increase in its inputs.

independent variable The variable causing a change in some other (dependent) variable.

index funds Mutual funds that choose their portfolios to exactly match a stock or bond index.

industrially advanced countries (IACs) High-income countries such as Canada, the United States, Japan, and the nations of Western Europe that have highly developed market economies based on large stocks of technologically advanced capital goods and skilled labour forces.

inferior goods Goods or services whose consumption falls when income increases and rises when income decreases, price remaining constant.

inflation (1) An increase in the overall price level. (2) A continual rise in the general level of prices in an economy.

inflationary expenditure gap The amount by which aggregate expenditures exceed those required to achieve full-employment GDP.

inflationary gap The amount by which equilibrium GDP exceeds potential GDP.

inflation targeting A Bank of Canada policy of maintaining the inflation rate within a specific range, currently 1–3 percent.

inflexible prices Product prices that remain in place (at least for a while) even though supply or demand has changed; also called *sticky prices*.

information technology New and more efficient methods of delivering and receiving information using computers, fax machines, wireless phones, and the Internet.

infrastructure The capital goods usually provided by the public sector for the use of its citizens and firms; the stock of public capital goods.

injection An addition of spending to the income-expenditures stream.

insider–outsider theory The hypothesis that nominal wages are inflexible downward because firms are aware that workers (insiders) who retain employment during recession may refuse to work cooperatively with previously unemployed workers (outsiders) who offer to work for less than the current wage.

interest The payment made for the use of money.

interest-rate effect The direct relationship between price level and the demand for money, which affects interest rates, and as a result, total spending in the economy.

intermediate goods Products purchased for resale or further processing or manufacturing.

inventory Goods that have been produced but remain unsold.

inverse relationship The (negative) relationship between two variables that change in opposite directions, for example, product price and quantity demanded.

investment Spending for the production and accumulation of capital.

investment demand curve A curve that shows the amount of investment demanded by an economy at a series of real interest rates.

investment schedule A curve or schedule that shows the amounts firms plan to invest at various possible values of real GDP.

invisible hand The tendency of firms and resource suppliers seeking to further their own self-interest in competitive markets to also promote the interest of society as a whole.

L

labour The physical and mental talents of individuals used in producing goods and services.

labour force Persons 15 years of age and older who are not in institutions and who are employed, or are unemployed and seeking work.

labour force participation rate The percentage of the working-age population that is actually in the labour force.

labour-intensive goods Products that require a relatively large amount of labour to produce.

labour productivity The average product of labour; output per worker per hour.

Laffer Curve A curve relating government tax rates and tax revenues.

laissez-faire capitalism A hypothetical economic system in which the government's economic role is limited to protecting private property and establishing a legal environment appropriate to the operation of markets in which only mutually agreeable transactions take place between buyers and sellers.

land Natural resources used to produce goods and services.

land-intensive goods Products that require a relatively large amount of land to produce.

land reform Redistribution of land ownership to give farmers incentive to produce more.

law of demand Other things equal, as price falls the quantity demanded rises, and vice versa.

law of increasing opportunity costs As the production of a good increases, the opportunity cost of producing an additional unit rises.

law of supply The principle that, other things equal, an increase in the price of a product will increase the quantity of it supplied, and a decrease in the price of a product will decrease the quantity of it supplied.

leader countries As it relates to economic growth, countries that develop and use advanced technologies, which then become available to follower countries.

leakage A withdrawal of potential spending from the income-expenditures stream via saving, tax payments, or imports.

learning-by-doing Achieving greater productivity and lower average total cost through gains in knowledge and skill that accompany repetition of a task; a source of economies of scale.

legal tender Anything that government says must be accepted in payment of a debt.

limited liability rule Rule that limits the risks involved in investing in corporations by capping their potential losses at the amount they paid for their shares.

liquidity The ease with which an asset can be converted quickly into cash with little or no loss of purchasing power.

liquidity trap A situation in which adding more liquidity to banks has little or no additional positive effect on lending.

loan guarantees A type of investment subsidy in which the government agrees to guarantee the money borrowed by a private company to fund investment projects if the private company itself fails to repay the loan.

logrolling The trading of votes by legislators to secure favourable outcomes on decisions concerning the provision of public goods and quasi-public goods.

long-run aggregate supply curve The aggregate supply curve associated with a time period in which input prices (especially nominal wages) are fully responsive to changes in the price level.

long-run vertical Phillips Curve A Phillips Curve that shows that in the long run there is no trade-off between the unemployment rate and the annual rate of increase in the price level.

lump-sum tax A tax that yields the same amount of tax revenue at all levels of GDP.

M

M1+ Currency (coins and paper money) and demand deposits in chartered banks.

M2 A broad definition of money that includes M1+ plus personal and business savings deposits that require notice before withdrawal.

M2+ A broader definition of money that includes M2 plus deposits at credit unions, *caisses populaires*, trust companies, other nonbank deposit-taking institutions, and money market mutual funds.

M2++ The broadest definition of the Canadian money supply; consists of M2+ plus Canada Savings Bonds and non-money-market mutual funds.

macroeconomics The part of economics concerned with the economy as a whole.

managed floating exchange rates Exchange rates that are allowed to change (float) as a result of changes in currency supply and demand but at times are altered (managed) by governments via their buying and selling of particular currencies.

marginal analysis The comparison of marginal (extra or additional) benefits and marginal costs, usually for decision-making.

marginal cost = marginal benefit rule For a government project, marginal benefit should equal marginal cost to produce maximum benefit to society.

marginal propensity to consume (MPC) The fraction (or percentage) of any change in disposable income spent for consumer goods.

marginal propensity to import (MPM) The fraction (or percentage) of any change in GDP spent for imported goods and services.

marginal propensity to save (MPS) The fraction (or percentage) of any change in disposable income that households save.

market Any institution or mechanism that brings together buyers and sellers of particular goods, services, or resources for the purpose of exchange.

market failures When markets do not function properly, whether by overproducing, underproducing, or failing to produce economically desirable goods.

market portfolio Contains every asset available in a financial market.

market system An economic system in which property resources are privately owned and markets and prices are used to direct and coordinate economic activities.

median-voter model The theory that under majority rule the median (middle) voter will be in the dominant position to determine the outcome of an election.

medium of exchange Items sellers generally accept and buyers generally use to pay for a good or service.

menu costs Costs associated with changing the prices of goods and services.

microeconomics The part of economics concerned with such individual units as industries, firms, and households.

microfinance When groups of people pool their money and make small loans to budding entrepreneurs and owners of small businesses.

modern economic growth The historically recent phenomenon in which nations for the first time have experienced sustained increases in real GDP per capita.

monetarism The macroeconomic view that the main cause of changes in aggregate output and the price level are fluctuations in the money supply; advocates a monetary rule.

monetary multiplier The multiple of excess cash reserves by which the banking system can expand demand deposits and thus the money supply by making new loans.

monetary policy A central bank's changing of the money supply to influence interest rates and assist the economy in achieving price-level stability, full employment, and economic growth.

monetary rule The rule suggested by monetarism; the money supply should be expanded each year at the same annual rate as the potential rate of growth of the real gross domestic product.

money Any item that is generally acceptable to sellers in exchange for goods and services.

moral hazard problem The possibility that individuals will change their behaviour as the result of a contract or agreement.

mortgage-backed securities Bonds backed by mortgage payments.

multiple counting Wrongly including the value of intermediate goods in the GDP.

multiplier The ratio of a change in GDP to the change in investment or in any other component of aggregate expenditures.

mutual fund A company that maintains a professionally managed portfolio, or collection, of stocks or bonds.

N

national income Total income earned by resource suppliers for their contributions to gross national product; equal to the gross domestic product minus nonincome charges, minus net foreign factor income.

national income accounting The techniques used to measure the overall production of the economy and other related variables for the nation as a whole.

natural rate of unemployment (NRU) The unemployment rate that occurs when no cyclical unemployment exists and the economy is achieving its potential output.

near-monies Financial assets (such as savings and term deposits in banks and savings institutions) that are not a medium of exchange but can readily be converted into money.

net export effect The idea that the impact of a change in monetary or fiscal policy will be strengthened or weakened by the consequent change in net exports.

net exports Exports minus imports of goods and services.

net investment Gross investment less consumption of fixed capital.

network effects Increases in the value of a product to each user, including existing users, as the total number of users rises.

new classical economics The theory that when the economy occasionally diverges from its full-employment output, internal mechanisms within the economy will automatically move it back to full employment.

nominal GDP The dollar value of all goods and services produced within the borders of a given country using the country's current prices during the year the goods and services were produced.

nominal income The number of current dollars received as wages, rent, interest, or profits.

nominal interest rate The interest rate expressed in terms of annual amounts currently charged for interest and not adjusted for inflation.

non-diversifiable risk Risk that pushes all investments in the same direction at the same time; eliminates the possibility of using good effects to offset bad effects.

nondurable goods Products with expected lives of less than three years.

nonexcludability When there is no effective way to prevent individuals from enjoying the benefit of a good once it has been created.

nonrivalry When the consumption of a good by one person does not preclude consumption of the good by others.

nontariff barrier (NTB) All restrictions other than tariffs that nations erect to impede international trade.

normal good A good or service whose consumption rises when income increases and falls when income decreases, price remaining constant.

normative economics The part of economics involving value judgments about what the economy should be like.

North American Free Trade Agreement (NAFTA) A 1993 agreement establishing a free-trade zone composed of Canada, Mexico, and the United States.

O

official international reserves Foreign currencies owned by the central bank of a nation.

offshoring Shifting work previously done by Canadian workers to workers located in other nations.

Okun's law The generalization that any one-percentage-point rise in the unemployment rate above the natural rate of unemployment will decrease GDP by 2 percent of the economy's potential GDP.

open-market operations The buying and selling of Canadian government bonds by the Bank of Canada to carry out monetary policy.

operating band The Bank of Canada's 50-basis-point range (one-half of one percentage point) for the overnight lending rate.

opportunity costs The amounts of other products that must be forgone or sacrificed to produce a unit of a product.

opportunity-cost ratio An equality showing the number of units of two products that can be produced with the same resources.

optimal reduction of an externality The point at which society's marginal cost and marginal benefit of reducing that externality are equal.

other-things-equal assumption The assumption that factors other than those being considered are held constant.

overnight lending rate The interest rate that the Bank of Canada charges on advances made to the chartered banks; the interest rate at which major participants in the money market borrow and lend one-day funds to each other.

P

paradox of thrift Refers to the possibility that a recession can be made worse when households become more thrifty and save in response to the downturn.

paradox of voting A situation in which paired-choice majority voting fails to provide a consistent ranking of society's preferences for public goods or services.

partnership An unincorporated firm owned and operated by two or more people.

passively managed funds Mutual funds that exactly match the assets contained in their respective underlying indexes.

peak A phase in the business cycle during which the economy is at full employment and the level of real output is at or very close to the economy's capacity.

percentage rate of return The percentage gain or loss (relative to the buying price) on stocks or bonds over a given time period, typically a year.

personal consumption expenditures The expenditures of households for durable and nondurable consumer goods and services.

personal income (PI) The earned and unearned income available to resource suppliers and others before the payment of personal income taxes.

per-unit production cost The average production cost of a particular level of output; total input cost divided by units of output.

Phillips Curve A curve showing the relationship between the unemployment rate and the annual rate of increase in the price level.

planned investment The amount that firms plan or intend to invest.

political corruption When government officials abuse their power for personal gain.

portfolio A collection of investments.

positive economics The analysis of facts to establish cause-and-effect relationships.

positive relationship Direct relationship between two variables.

post hoc fallacy Incorrectly reasoning that when one event precedes another the first event must have caused the second event.

potential GDP The real output an economy can produce when it fully employs its available resources.

present value The present-day value, or worth, of returns or costs that are expected to arrive in the future.

price ceiling A legally established maximum price for a good or service.

price floor A legally established price above an equilibrium price.

price-level surprises Unanticipated changes in the price level.

price index A number that shows how the weighted average price of a "market basket" of goods and services changes through time.

prime interest rate The interest rate banks charge their most creditworthy borrowers; the benchmark interest rate used by chartered banks as a reference point for a wide range of interest rates charged on loans to businesses and individuals.

principal–agent problems Conflicts that arise when tasks are delegated by one group of people (principals) to another group of people (agents).

principle of comparative advantage When a region or nation can produce a good at a lower domestic opportunity cost compared to a potential trading partner.

private goods Products or services that are individually consumed and that can be profitably provided by privately owned firms because they can exclude nonpayers from receiving the benefits.

private property The right of private persons and firms to obtain, own, control, employ, dispose of, and bequeath land, capital, and other property.

probability-weighted average When the possible future rate of return is multiplied by its probability expressed as a decimal (e.g., a 50 percent probability is 0.5 and a 23 percent probability is 0.23).

producer surplus The difference between the actual price producers receive for a product and the minimum acceptable price.

product market A market in which products are sold by firms and bought by households.

production possibilities curve A curve showing the different combinations of goods or services that can be produced in a full-employment, full-production economy where the available supplies of resources and technology are fixed.

productive efficiency The production of a good in the least costly way.

productivity A measure of average output or real output per unit of input.

productivity growth The percentage change in productivity from one period to another.

progressive tax system An average tax rate that increases as the taxpayer's income increases and decreases as the taxpayer's income decreases.

proportional tax system An average tax rate that remains constant as the taxpayer's income increases or decreases.

protective tariff A tariff designed to shield domestic producers of a good or service from the competition of foreign producers.

public choice theory The economic analysis of government decision-making, politics, and elections.

public debt The total amount owed by the federal government to the owners of government securities.

public goods Goods or services that can be simultaneously consumed by everyone, and from which no one can be excluded, even if they don't pay for them.

public investments Government expenditures on public capital (such as roads and highways) and on human capital (such as education and health).

public sector The part of the economy that contains all government entities; government.

purchasing power The amount of goods and services that a monetary unit of income can buy.

purchasing power parity theory The idea that exchange rates between any two nations adjust to reflect the price level differences between the countries.

Q

quasi-public goods Goods provided by the government that fit the economist's definition of a public good but can be produced in such a way that exclusion would be possible.

R

rational expectations theory The hypothesis that firms and households expect monetary and fiscal policies to have certain effects on the economy and (in pursuit of their own self-interest) take actions that make these policies ineffective.

real-balances effect The inverse relationship between the price level and the real value (or purchasing power) of financial assets with fixed money value.

real-business-cycle theory The theory that business cycles result from changes in technology and resource availability, which affect productivity and thus increase or decrease long-run aggregate supply.

real GDP (real gross domestic product) (1) The value of final goods and services produced within the borders of a given country during a given time period, typically a year. (2) Nominal GDP adjusted for inflation.

real GDP per capita The real GDP per person, found by dividing real GDP by a country's population.

real income The amount of goods and services nominal income can buy.

real interest rate The interest rate expressed in dollars of constant value (adjusted for inflation).

real wage The amount of goods and services a worker can purchase with his or her nominal wage; the purchasing power of the nominal wage.

recession A period of decline in total output, income, and employment.

recessionary expenditure gap The amount by which aggregate expenditures fall short of those required to achieve full-employment GDP.

regressive tax system An average tax rate that decreases as the taxpayer's income increases and increases as the taxpayer's income decreases.

regulatory capture The situation that occurs when a governmental regulatory agency ends up being controlled by the industry that it is supposed to be regulating.

rent seeking The actions by persons, firms, or unions to gain special benefits from government at the taxpayers' or someone else's expense.

restrictive monetary policy Bank of Canada actions that contract, or restrict, the growth of the nation's money supply for the purpose of reducing or eliminating inflation.

revenue tariff A tariff designed to produce income for the federal government.

risk Refers to the fact that investors never know with certainty what future payments on an asset will be.

risk-free interest rate A rate of return that does not compensate for risk.

risk premium The rate of interest that compensates for risk; depends on the size of the investment's beta.

rivalry A situation in which when one person buys and consumes a product, it is not available for another person to buy and consume.

Rule of 70 A method for determining the number of years it will take for some measure to double, given its annual percentage increase, by dividing that percentage increase into 70.

S

saving The accumulation of funds that results when people in an economy spend (consume) less than their incomes during a given time period.

saving schedule A schedule that shows the amounts households plan to save at different levels of disposable income.

Say's law The largely discredited macroeconomic generalization that the production of goods and services (supply) creates an equal demand for these goods and service.

scarce resources The limited quantities of land, capital, labour, and entrepreneurial ability that are never sufficient to satisfy the virtually unlimited material wants of humans.

scarcity The limits placed on the amounts and types of goods and services available for consumption because there are limited economic resources from which to produce output.

scientific method The systematic pursuit of knowledge through formulating a problem, collecting data, and formulating and testing hypotheses to obtain theories, principles, and laws.

seasonal unemployment Unemployment caused by seasonal factors.

securitization The process of slicing up and bundling groups of loans, mortgages, corporate bonds, or other financial debts into distinct new securities.

Security Market Line The relationship between average expected rates of return and risk levels that must hold for every asset or portfolio trading in a financial market.

self-interest That which each firm, property owner, worker, and consumer believes is best for itself.

services The work done by service providers.

shocks Situations in which one thing is expected to occur, but in reality, something different occurs.

short-run (1) In macroeconomics, a period in which nominal wages and other input prices do not change in response to a change in the price level. (2) In microeconomics, a period of time in which producers are able to change the quantity of some but not all of the resources they employ; a period in which some resources (usually plant) are fixed and some are variable.

short-run aggregate supply curve An aggregate supply curve for which real output, but not the price level, changes when the aggregate demand curve shifts.

shortage The amount by which the quantity demanded of a product exceeds the quantity supplied at a specific (below-equilibrium) price.

slope of a straight line The ratio of the vertical change (the rise or fall) to the horizontal change (the run) between any two points on a line. The slope of an upsloping line is positive, reflecting a direct relationship between two variables; the slope of a downsloping line is negative, reflecting an inverse relationship between two variables.

sole proprietorship An unincorporated firm owned and operated by one person.

special-interest effect Any result of government promotion of the interests (goals) of a small group at the expense of a much larger group.

specialization The use of the resources of an individual, a firm, a region, or a nation to produce one or a few goods and services.

stagflation Simultaneous increases in the price level and the unemployment rate.

start-up firm A new firm focused on creating and introducing a particular new product or employing a specific new production or distribution method.

sticky prices Product prices that remain in place (at least for a while) even though supply or demand has changed; also called *inflexible prices*.

stocks Ownership shares in a corporation.

store of value An asset set aside for future use.

structural unemployment Unemployment of workers whose skills are not demanded by employers, who lack sufficient skills to obtain employment, or who cannot easily move to locations where jobs are available.

subprime mortgage loans High-interest-rate loans by financial institutions to home buyers with higher-than-average credit risk.

substitute goods Products or services that can be used in place of each other.

substitution effect A change in the price of a product changes the relative expensiveness of that good and hence changes the willingness to buy it rather than other goods.

supply A schedule or curve that shows the amounts of a product that producers are willing and able to make available for sale at each of a series of possible prices during a specific period.

supply curve A curve illustrating the positive (direct) relationship between the quantity supplied of a good or service and its price, other things equal.

supply factors An increase in the availability of a resource, an improvement in its quality, or an expansion of technological knowledge that makes it possible for an economy to produce a greater output of goods and services.

supply shocks Sudden, unexpected changes in aggregate supply.

supply-side economics A view of macroeconomics that emphasizes the role of costs and aggregate supply in explaining inflation, unemployment, and economic growth.

supply-side market failure When supply curves do not reflect the full cost of producing a good or service.

surplus The amount by which the quantity supplied of a product exceeds the quantity demanded at a specific (above-equilibrium) price.

T

tariffs Taxes imposed by a nation on imported goods.

Taylor Rule A modern monetary rule proposed by economist John Taylor that stipulates exactly how much a central bank should change interest rates in response to divergences of real GDP from potential GDP and divergences of actual rates of inflation from a target rate of inflation.

terms of trade The rate at which units of one product can be exchanged for units of another product.

time preference The fact that people typically prefer to consume things in the present than in the future.

token money Coins that have a face value greater than their intrinsic value.

total demand for money The sum of the transactions demand for money and the asset demand for money.

trade deficit The amount by which a nation's imports of goods (or goods and services) exceed its exports of goods (or goods and services).

trade surplus The amount by which a nation's exports of goods (or goods and services) exceed its imports of goods (or goods and services).

trading possibilities line Shows the different combinations of two products an economy is able to obtain when it specializes in the production of one product and exports it to obtain the other product.

transactions demand for money The amount of money people want to hold for use as a medium of exchange, and which varies directly with the nominal GDP.

trough The point during a recession or depression when output and employment reach their lowest levels.

U

unanticipated inflation Increases in the price level that occur at a rate greater than expected.

underemployment A situation in which workers are employed in positions requiring less than the amount of education and skill that they have.

unemployment A failure of the economy to employ its labour force fully.

unemployment rate The percentage of the labour force that is unemployed at any time.

unfunded liability A future government spending commitment (liability) for which the government has not legislated an offsetting revenue source.

unit of account A standard unit in which prices can be stated and the value of goods and services can be compared.

unplanned changes in inventory Changes in inventory that firms did not anticipate.

utility The satisfaction a person gets from consuming a good or service.

V

value added The value of the product sold by a firm, less the value of the products purchased and used by the firm to produce the product.

vault cash The currency a bank has in its vault and cash drawers.

velocity The average number of times per year a dollar is spent on final goods and services.

vertical axis The up–down or north–south axis on a graph or grid.

vertical intercept The point at which a line meets the vertical axis of a graph.

vicious circle of poverty A problem common in some developing countries in which low per capita incomes are an obstacle to realizing the levels of savings and investment requisite to acceptable rates of economic growth.

voluntary export restriction (VER) Voluntary limitation by countries or firms of their exports to a particular foreign nation.

W

wealth effect A downward shift of the saving schedule and an upward shift of the consumption schedule due to higher asset wealth.

will to develop Wanting economic growth strongly enough to change from old to new ways of doing things.

world price The international market price of a good or service, determined by world demand and supply.

World Bank A bank that lends (and guarantees loans) to developing nations to assist them in increasing their capital stock and thus to achieve economic growth.

World Trade Organization (WTO) An organization of 159 nations (as of 2013) that oversees the provisions of the current world trade agreement, resolves trade disputes stemming from it, and holds forums for further rounds of trade negotiations.

Index